AF342704

INTRODUCTION TO
URBAN SCIENCE

INTRODUCTION TO URBAN SCIENCE

EVIDENCE AND THEORY OF CITIES AS COMPLEX SYSTEMS

LUÍS M. A. BETTENCOURT

THE MIT PRESS   CAMBRIDGE, MASSACHUSETTS   LONDON, ENGLAND

The MIT Press would like to thank the anonymous peer reviewers who provided comments on drafts of this book. The generous work of academic experts is essential for establishing the authority and quality of our publications. We acknowledge with gratitude the contributions of these otherwise uncredited readers.

This book was set in Stone Serif and Avenir by Westchester Publishing Services. Printed and bound in the United States of America.

Library of Congress Cataloging-in-Publication Data is available.

Names: Bettencourt, Luís M. A., author.
Title: Introduction to urban science : evidence and theory of cities as complex systems / Luís M. A. Bettencourt.
Description: Cambridge, Massachusetts : The MIT Press, [2021] | Includes bibliographical references and index.
Identifiers: LCCN 2020045141 | ISBN 9780262046008 (hardcover)
Subjects: LCSH: Urbanization. | Cities and towns—Growth. | Urban policy. | System theory.
Classification: LCC HT361 .B485 2021 | DDC 307.76—dc23
LC record available at https://lccn.loc.gov/2020045141

10 9 8 7 6 5 4 3 2 1

To my family

To Aline, whose hope for the world and boundless energy set me on this path;

To Laura, whose love and challenge make everything possible;

To Stella and Phillip, who will be citizens of a big urban world,

let it be all that it is meant to be.

CONTENTS

LIST OF FIGURES

PREFACE

The best way to know a thing is in the context of another discipline.
—Leonard Bernstein, *Norton Lectures*

This is a book about *urban science*, about what we can know about cities that is *generalizable*. By generalizable, I mean observable processes or signals that we can experience or measure across history and throughout the world despite different geographies, cultures, levels of development, and so on.

This is also a book about bringing together different ways of thinking. This is always a clarifying exercise that can guide us through complex and multifaceted phenomena. The objective is to create a comprehensive approach to discovering the general processes by which cities form and grow and to explain why they are such singular sources of change in human societies. I hope to show that different ways of thinking across traditional disciplines can fit together well to form a new body of theory and a set of mathematical models that can generate the mesmerizing complexity and open-endedness of cities.

This approach and objectives may appear controversial and even a little heretical. I have experienced three types of objections that I would like to get out of the way or at least ask the reader for their patience and to hold their judgment until later.

The first is that cities are such complex systems—the products of so many decisions and accidents and so rich in history—that any attempt at a synthetic mathematical description is futile and therefore misguided. To that argument, I would note that the same can be said, perhaps with more substance, of biology, where we have a more advanced scientific understanding of the phenomena involved. Such an understanding brings together structural aspects dictated by physics and biochemistry with a theory of natural history and learning in the form of evolution by natural selection. Such a theoretical synthesis has matured only relatively recently, thanks to a profusion of evidence, experiments, and theory development across scales of organization. There will be a number of parallels, but also some innovations, in this comparison.

Second, scholars trained in the humanities and sometimes in the social sciences often treat references to *science* and *data* in their realms of expertise with suspicion. They have good reason, as appeals to science have too often been used in policy (and politics) to justify control, normalization, standardization, and associated social injustice and oppression. I want to acknowledge this concern as absolutely valid, something that we must always keep in mind in urban science.

However, such appeals to the putative authority of science refer to it only in name, not in spirit. Science is a body of contingent and collaborative knowledge that nevertheless improves over time. Science is plural, a deeply humanizing experience based on curiosity, collaboration, creativity, and humility in the face of the facts that shape our experience—it stands in opposition to dogma. Thus, good science is never a technocratic exercise in the service of oppressive bureaucracies but rather an act of imagination following the human instinct to discover how the world works and how it could be better. This certainly includes engaging with the richest depths of the human experience, many of which are associated with cities.

Third, from a philosophical perspective, many see any incursion of science, and especially of mathematical methods, into the realm of human societies as entailing a tragic loss of freedom and humanity. This is a terrible misunderstanding that I hope some of the material in this book can help repair. The things that we will use as constraints to build mathematical theories of people in cities are very few and absolutely mundane. They include simple facts, such as that we all live in space and time and that we must balance our energy budgets and/or bank accounts over some period of time. Almost everything else is left free: all our detailed behavior, our thoughts and desires, our successes and failures.

This growing comfort with uncertainty has not been typical of classical approaches in the social sciences, where individual "rationality" or structural determinism has often been taken as absolute. Studying real lives in real cities forces us to dispel such simple assumptions. In this sense, we will be able to understand—even mathematically— why each city, each place, each life course is indeed unique. What may be surprising is that some of the statistical averages over time and over the behavior of groups of people still bear a trace of the environments we build and the shared costs and benefits underlying our diverse living experiences. This will give us a background of aggregated predictive statistics that form a methodological basis for urban science.

In this light, being special is always a relative state: any sense of uniqueness requires a background pattern of general mechanisms and facts against which it can be appreciated. Such a pattern is not a description of—or a model for—individual behavior! It represents instead aggregated social statistical tendencies that are very familiar to us all, long exploited by successful businesses such as insurance companies or casinos.

We will use this analytical device in different ways throughout the book to show how each city and every one of its people is the result of the aggregation of many choices, accidents, and influences from their compounded joint history. Interestingly, the resulting statistical properties of cities will be more than the sum of these parts.

The most important thing we can do with science is to "see the world from a different point of view," to borrow physicist Richard Feynman's words. There is nothing more critical or more exciting intellectually than sneaking up to an old and difficult problem from a different perspective that renders it clearer and simpler. Finding new perspectives and insights, and discovering new ways in which the world comes together to reveal its mysteries, is the greatest joy of any curious mind. I hope the reader sees, as I do, the enormous power of looking at cities from a different point of view and the many insights that follow.

Why invoke science and not concentrate on other forms of inquiry to understand cities? Science is the only collective human process I know that can learn extraordinary new things from the accumulated experience of myriads of people. Science as a process is uniquely good at creating insights that vastly transcend our daily experience and intuitions.

This allows us ultimately to escape the mental and institutional traps we live in today and helps us imagine—but does not determine!—how we may build a better tomorrow. These general features of science are what make it such a critical and powerful human endeavor on any subject, but I feel that these features are even more important in the context of urban science, because cities feel so familiar to us all. Science is not a substitute for other practices of scholarship, especially in the humanities, but it does have its unique and powerful role to play.

This book has been the work of a lifetime, as I joyfully experienced many different cities, and almost six years of dedicated learning, research, and teaching. Writing it feels to me like assembling a colossal puzzle that, as it comes together, reveals to me a new picture, where old ideas make sense alongside new ones, emerging data and methods acquire surprising new uses, and a long view of what cities have been and what they could become starts to come into focus. I hope that this book settles some old questions but also that many new ones arise.

The ideas of this book are the result of discussions and collaborations with a large number of people across many disciplines, each of them important to the final result. It is difficult to single out some without naming them all. However, a small number of people have been key. José Lobo has been a dear friend, intellectual partner, and kind collaborator from the beginning, when we met at the Santa Fe Institute in 2003. We started out in a common position, asking cheeky questions from the back of the room in a series of seminars. We asked primarily why speakers manifesting interesting but sometimes (to us) fanciful ideas about cities had not used more data to test them. Doing so ourselves opened up the floodgates of urban scaling analysis. Geoffrey West motivated us to use scaling as an analytical framework, which ultimately created a new cornerstone for urban science while also exposing some of the similarities and differences between cities and other complex systems. Deborah Strumsky opened my eyes to phenomena of innovation in cities and the riches of patent data. Scott Ortman walked into my office one day and asked me to explain urban scaling theory, only to tell me afterward that what I was saying was not really about cities. He noted that it should apply equally well to any other settlement, including the ones he studies in archeology. This opened up the doors to a new quantitative comparative analysis of settlements throughout history and also shed light on the origins of settlements themselves. Michael Smith amplified these ideas, pointing out that common assumptions of industrialization or modern political organization had to be overcome to truly understand the origins of settlements and early cities and opening up new lines of continuity on issues of socioeconomic organization throughout history. Celine D'Cruz and Anni Beukes became friends and collaborators during a challenging project on informal settlements, which exposed me to the difficult but hopeful realities of contemporary African and South Asian cities. Christa Brelsford became a wonderful, brave collaborator formalizing some of these rich observations toward a better understanding, and new methods, of human development in neighborhoods.

Many others contributed to shaping the ideas of this book through collaboration, discussions, encouragement, or criticism. They include Clio Andris, Elsa Arcaute, Michael Batty, Marc Berman, Elizabeth Bruch, Kate Cagney, Charlie Catlett, Rudy Cesaretti, Andres Gomez-Lievano, John German, Marcus Hamilton, Joe Hand, Jack Hanson, Colin Harrison, Dirk Helbing, Christian Kühnert, David Lane, Sander van der Leeuw, Taylor Martin, Nicholas de Monchaux, Daniel O'Brien, Juval Portugali, Denise Pumain, Carlo Ratti, Celine Rozenblat, Diego Rybski, Horacio Samaniego, Robert Sampson, Markus Schläpfer, Karen Seto, Devin White, Vicky Yang, HeyJin Youn, and Daniel Zünd.

I am immensely grateful to my brilliant students at the University of Chicago taking Introduction to Urban Science during the 2018–2019 and 2019–2020 academic years, where some of the material in the book was ironed out. A last and very special huge thanks is owed to everyone at the Mansueto Institute for Urban Innovation—especially Anne Dodge, Heidi Lee, Diana Petty, Grace Cheung, and Nico Marchio—who work so hard every day and with so much passion to make urban science a reality in Chicago and around the world.

This book was started at the Santa Fe Institute. Its beautiful environment of radical interdisciplinary scholarship and its encouragement of adventurous and fun collaborations were key in sowing the seeds for a new systemic perspective on cities and urbanization and providing contrasts and connections to many other complex systems. This book was finished at the University of Chicago, whose rich history of urban scholarship propitiated another set of encounters at the interface between critical concepts and practice from the social sciences and new methods and data. I owe an enormous debt of gratitude to both these institutions for nurturing the origins and development of this work and to the Mansueto Institute for Urban Innovation for the challenge of putting it into practice.

As I finish this book, I hear more and more frequently of the advent of urban science or of a "science of cities" and learn with great pleasure of new publications or discoveries big and small. I also hear of new institutes and centers dedicated to the field, developing in many different places and in many different ways. To me, this is a state of grace when urban science feels young and open, fast and full of vitality, perhaps much like so many of the cities it studies. Any discipline requires a common framework, without which knowledge cannot be tested and accumulate. I hope this book contributes to that effort.

Chicago, Illinois
September 2020

1

WHY CITIES? WHAT IS URBAN SCIENCE?

Give me your tired, your poor,
Your huddled masses yearning to breathe free,
The wretched refuse of your teeming shore.
Send these, the homeless, tempest-tost to me,
I lift my lamp beside the golden door!
—Emma Lazarus

Where else to start? This poem, engraved at the feet of the Statue of Liberty, is possibly the single most compelling vision for human hope and reinvention in a new world. This new world is both metaphorical and real. It is no accident—but it is a fact often overlooked—that the "golden door" to that new world was New York City, then a furiously growing urban area, which would soon become the world's largest city and define urbanism for much of the twentieth century.

Urban environments, created less than ten thousand years ago, have unleashed one of the greatest transformations in earth's history. They have catapulted humans from being a relatively inconspicuous species to becoming the greatest creative force on the planet, the apprentice masters of our natural environment, capable of changing its condition in a seemingly limitless—and often destructive—number of ways. The need to harness this transformative power is ultimately why a scientific understanding of cities is so important.

As the ideas of this book are being developed, we are living through the fastest stage of this global transformation (figure 1.1).[1] Over the next few decades, the vast majority of humans still leading a traditional subsistence existence today will likely come to live in urban environments. Although definitions vary, it has become standard to identify 2007 as the year when more than half the world's population became urban (figure 1.1A). The next major landmark year will be 2021 (figure 1.1B), when we are estimated to reach *peak rural population*. After that, each net new human on the planet will be urban! Because of

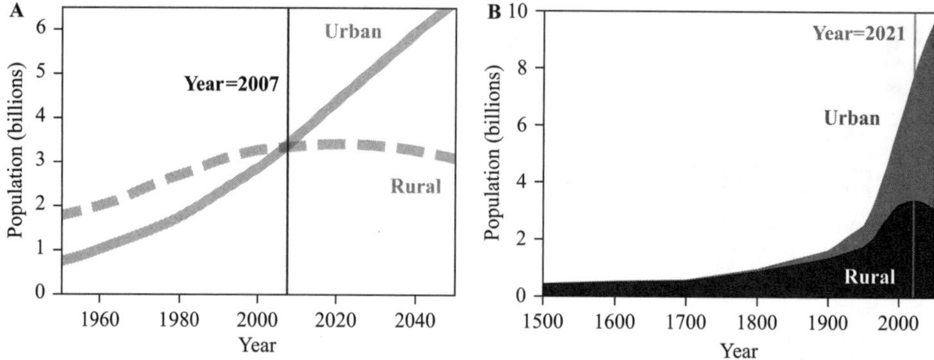

1.1 The world has become urban. (A) The world's total urban (solid line) and rural populations (dashed line), with urban surpassing rural in 2007. (B) World population estimates going back to 1500 and projected forward until 2050. Total rural world population (black) is expected to peak in 2021, with the consequence that any additional net human thereafter will be an urban dweller (gray). *Source*: Figures created by the author, data compiled by Our World in Data, https://ourworldindata.org.

these transformations, the typical daily experience for most people around the world will change and become familiar to most of us already living in urbanized countries. Through this process, we will become more connected to each other and, surprisingly perhaps, to all earth's natural environments.

The nature of these connections is also changing, from strong local relations with a few people to weaker global ties, characterized by rapidly shifting exchanges with many strangers. In these circumstances, the consequences of our actions can quickly resonate over large distances, including remote natural environments from the thickness of the Amazon forest to the wilderness of Antarctica.

In an urban world, the power of human imagination can be greatly magnified and becomes capable of affecting greater change faster than at any other time in history. Perhaps even more critically, our capacity for collective action—our "Politics," in the etymological meaning of the word as "the stuff of cities"—will be tested in unprecedented ways that may save or doom the earth within the next few decades. While many people lament these transformations of the human condition, especially a loss of intimacy with nature and with other people, and the feeling of breathlessness in the face of fast change, billions of people around the world are voting with their feet to make them happen as fast as possible in their own lives.

This transformative power of cities is on full display in thousands of places today all over the world, especially in Asia and Africa, the world's most rapidly urbanizing continents. At its most spectacular (figure 1.2), some places have grown from almost nothing to become world-leading cities in just a few decades—less than a human lifetime! This has been especially true in Asia, where in a single generation the cities of Japan, South Korea, Taiwan, Hong Kong, Singapore, and now mainland China produced economic growth and access to new opportunities for over a billion people and pushed their

1.2 Radical urban transformations. Tokyo, Japan, was almost completely destroyed by bombing during the Second World War (bottom panel). Within just a few decades, it was reconstructed and grew explosively to become the largest urban area in the world, with a current population of nearly 40 million people (top panel).

Sources: Terence Starkey, @terences via unsplash (top panel); US National Archives, Washington, DC, RG-342-FH-289973 (bottom panel).

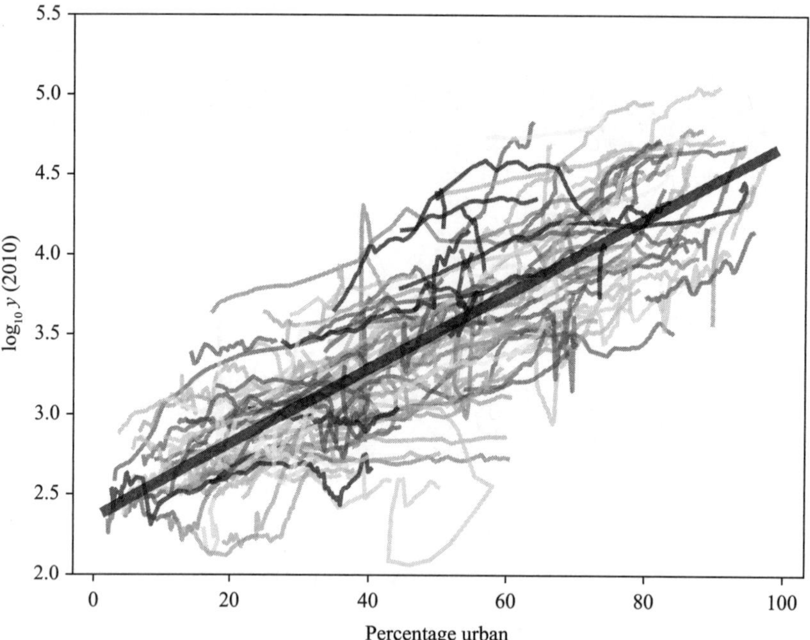

1.3 Correlation between extent of national urbanization and per capita GDP. Each thin line in different shades of gray shows the trajectory of a different nation in terms of its percentage of people living in cities (percentage urban) and its real GDP per capita, $\log_{10} y$ (in 2010 real US dollars). This association is well described, on average, by a linear relation (solid line) and is usually interpreted as evidence for the general fact that urbanization is necessary for national economic development. This relation is explained in chapter 9.

Source: Created by the author with data from World Bank Development Indicators, https://datacata log.worldbank.org/dataset/world-development-indicators, and Our World in Data, https://ourworld indata.org.

societies to the forefront of wealth, human development, and well-being worldwide. During a recent visit to Japan, I met Masahisa Fujita, a leading economic geographer, whose ideas we will encounter in chapter 2. I asked him what he thought was the greatest challenge for urban science. He looked out the window slowly, thoughtfully, and I followed his gaze to see a spectacular view of Tokyo much like the one in the upper panel of figure 1.2. He told me his age and that he had grown up in poverty in a city that had been totally destroyed by war, where people were forced to live in slum-like conditions. "The biggest mystery," he said, "is how we went from *that* to *this* so quickly." Such transformations are now taking place in thousands of cities worldwide. We just do not know how to create fast and sustained growth and human development without cities.

But although cities are necessary for fast human development, they are certainly not sufficient. There are a number of well-known statistical associations between urbanization and human development. The most famous is the relation between national economic income per capita GDP and the percentage of people who live

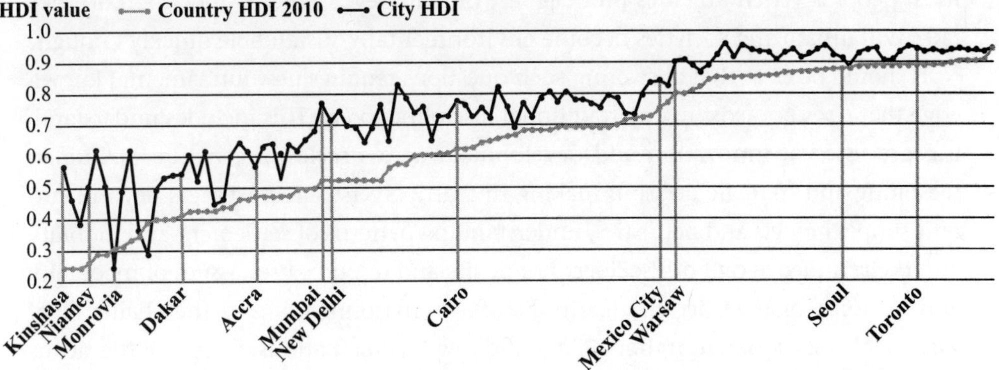

1.4 Human development: Comparing large cities to their nations. The human development index (HDI) measures broad progress toward improving human capabilities and includes three main components: real income, life expectancy, and education. In almost every case, we see that large cities in each nation display higher levels of human development than their corresponding nations, implying a general tendency for the HDI to increase with city population size. The few exceptions are low-income nations recently torn apart by civil war, such as Liberia and its capital, Monrovia.
Source: Adapted from UN-Habitat, *State of the World's Cities 2012/2013, Prosperity of Cities* (Nairobi: UN-Habitat, 2012), http://mirror.unhabitat.org/pmss/listItemDetails.aspx?publicationID=3387.

in cities (urbanization). Figure 1.3 shows the trajectories of different nations on the plane defined by these two variables. It is striking that out of such a noisy set of trajectories there is a clear average trend (solid black line), which we will analyze and explain in chapter 9.

But it is also true that if you follow any of the national trajectories in detail you will find many exceptions. There are times when urbanization increases without corresponding growth in GDP per capita (*urbanization without growth*) and vice versa (*growth without urbanization*).

Fitting a line is not enough; we must understand the fundamental processes at work. We all know of times when cities become stuck and mired in conflict, displaying crushing segregation, inequality, and poverty, failing to deliver basic services or working institutions to most people. To some extent, for reasons we will better understand in the course of this book, these challenges are always an important part of urban environments. The difference between success and failure, between miraculous development and tragic paralysis, is the realization that cities are not zero-sum games and that knowledge, human cooperation, and collective action can build a future that is better—in material terms but also in many other ways (figure 1.4)—than the past and present. This realization is neither obvious nor robust; the unique transformative power of cities lies in its improbable realization.

These general considerations lead us to some of the great questions of our time, most involving cities and urbanization more or less directly: Why is urbanization now proceeding so relentlessly and globally? How can its consequences be good for most people? When do cities produce fast human development, and when do they fail? Will urbanizing societies become environmentally sustainable quickly enough?

It should be clear that answering such questions requires new fundamental knowledge that does not exist in any traditional discipline today. This includes understanding processes of innovation and development across scales, the nature of human reasoning and strategic decision making in many diverse circumstances beyond current simple models and heuristics, understanding patterns of settlement and mobility and their influence on both socioeconomic life and resource uses, issues of inequality and inequity, biodiversity change in disturbed environments, and the challenge of sustainable development in both high- and low-income nations. Cities are the nexus for *all* these issues, providing many examples of systemic phenomena that we do not yet understand. They also generate copious empirical evidence and the necessity for action that can lead to new insights and discoveries.

1.1 WHY URBAN SCIENCE?

Answers to these challenges must take ethical and political dimensions that go far beyond science. However, I will argue that until recently our understanding of urban processes all around us was very limited and that a much deeper and systematic scientific engagement with cities and urbanization is a necessary precondition for us to fulfill the enormous positive potential of these transformations.[2]

The key, in my view, is a more fundamental understanding of the *processes* facilitated and, in many cases, unleashed for the first time by urban life.[3] All great scientific theory relies on the understanding and formalization of fundamental *processes of change*. Interesting states, which are recognizable when change is slow, are often conceived as *equilibria*, but they are merely situations where opposing "forces" are balanced in specific ways. We will see in chapters 2–4 that to understand cities we will need an analogous framework but that its ingredients require assembling together a set of very diverse phenomena, studied traditionally by distinct disciplines and at different scales.

This emphasis on the *connections* between many different aspects of cities[4]—their built spaces and land uses, their infrastructure and services, their social life and its outcomes—is the business of *complex systems* as a relatively new field of scientific inquiry. It is this integrative approach that is novel and makes this book worth reading (and writing). The integration of ideas and concepts from many disciplines also forces each piece to shift and change as it is constrained and enabled by others into new frameworks. Additionally, new pieces become necessary and must be created.

This process of creative synthesis requires much closer connections with empirical evidence than has been possible in the past. Evidence must reflect the actual reality of cities, stemming from many diverse environments and at many different scales, from individual behavior to entire nations as networks of cities and towns. Thus, building a more comprehensive empirical basis for urban science is necessarily predicated on harnessing new and better data as well as embracing more powerful technologies and methods.[5] It also requires seeking a diversity of knowledge across geographic and cultural contexts and throughout history, and engaging with people whose experience of cities spans a wider variety of different perspectives, reflecting their own history, socioeconomic status, gender, race and ethnicity, citizenship, and other qualities.[6]

These three main ingredients, specifically interdisciplinary integration and synthesis, a rich and expanding empirical basis and methods across scales, and honoring diverse human experiences create a culture for *urban science* that holds a special new place among traditional disciplines. The integration of these ingredients also enables urban science as a unique platform that welcomes diverse knowledge and is uniquely situated for scientific coproduction with people, civic organizations, governments, and businesses, as well as with other researchers.[7]

1.2 CHALLENGES OF URBAN POLICY

Urbanization is proceeding in most of the world without the guiding hand of architects or planners, let alone of any other scientists.[8] To a large extent, urbanization is a universal spontaneous phenomenon. Planners and engineers deal with its consequences, but most often they come late and must act in adaptive ways. Much of what is happening in the fastest-growing cities of the world today is *informal*,[9] both in terms of the settlement of space and associated economic activity. While this condition tends to change gradually over time and along with socioeconomic development, such transformations historically have *not* hinged on great insights from economics, political science, or complex systems.

Besides challenges of development in fast-growing urban areas, it is hard to find any city, big or small, that does not have several of a long list of challenges, from pollution and congestion to crime, poverty, inequality, unaffordable housing, and inadequate infrastructure. The list goes on and most often frames any study of cities, even at universities, in terms of a long list of familiar *wicked problems*.[10] On the face of such obvious and pervasive challenges, how useful can any general scientific knowledge really be? One often gets the impression, especially when listening to policymakers, that with a better mayor and a larger budget all problems in our city would be solved—yet they persist.

The power of scientific knowledge is *not* in its ability to solve specific problems but rather in that it forces us to change our intuitive frameworks and adopt new perspectives from which new transformative solutions become not only possible but often relatively easy. We can illustrate the power of knowledge through many examples from some of the most challenging applied projects in history. Consider, for example, the moonshot. Could we have gone to the moon without knowledge of the physical laws of motion and gravity? The answer, in principle, is *yes, of course*!

Given a large budget and a powerful enough rocket, we could point it at the moon, blast off, adjust the trajectory as we go, and get there from here, so to speak. All we need is a good pilot and a big rocket.

But this is *not at all* how we did it! To understand that, we must do the math. Going to the moon the intuitive way would require such a powerful and maneuverable spaceship that the enterprise would have been impossible in 1969, or today for that matter. The way we actually did it was by being smart—*scientifically* smart: We did it with a small rocket and great science. Through science, we learned how to use the motion created by gravity—our opponent in the game of escaping the earth—to our own advantage: to accelerate our spacecraft by whirling it backward around the earth and indirectly toward the moon. It is this "judo move" that makes the moonshot possible. Attempting such a counterintuitive strategy only makes sense because we understand how to create complicated trajectories so precisely that they can land us in the right spot on the moon with relatively modest rocket technology.

The practical power of science is that it makes seemingly impossible things possible. It also makes certain solutions to difficult problems much easier, cheaper, and more likely to succeed. It reduces the space of possible engineering designs and political interventions substantially, making convergence on good solutions a much easier process, a point made to me by master engineer Colin Harrison, who for a while headed the Smarter Cities program at IBM. This is well understood in fields where we have predictive scientific theory, say in physics and chemistry and even in population biology, where we run complicated machines such as airplanes, computers, and massive power and chemical plants in ways that defy any simple and intuitive management plan.

But in regard to cities and many related problems that involve people and their socioeconomic lives, we do not yet have comparable knowledge that can tell us simultaneously, for example, how to create jobs and make the economy sustainable. One often hears calls to make cities "smarter" through the use of information and communications technologies so some of these problems can be better tackled. But what are the scientific "judo moves" that allow our always limited choices and technologies to be truly revolutionary so that cities can become truly green, prosperous, and fair?

1.3 A BRIEF HISTORY OF IDEAS ABOUT CITIES AS COMPLEX SYSTEMS

Cities have always been conceptualized—philosophically at least—as complex systems either in their own right or through analogies to organisms, beehives, ecosystems, nervous systems, and other things. However, a couple of seconds' reflection immediately manifests the insufficiency of any of these metaphors. For example, cities are much larger, achieve much higher power densities, and create new information much more quickly than any of these other complex systems. Cities, in fact, are made by connecting all these different complex systems together in specific ways, generating a new "metadynamics" that appears more complex and open-ended than any of its parts.

Describing the complexity of urban processes has been a major goal for the social sciences especially in sociology, anthropology, and economics. In sociology, the idea of "human ecology" developed by researchers at the Chicago School of Urban Sociology,[11] but also by some early urbanists and planners such as Patrick Geddes,[12] became a foundational concept for understanding cities and for developing appropriate interventions and policies. According to this view, the properties of cities are systemic ("ecological") and do not pertain to individuals in isolation.[13] As a result, new cognitive processes, new behaviors, new social organizations, and new ways to build and manage spaces emerge in cities out of the *interactions* between people, creating both challenges and opportunities. This approach emphasizes the empirical characterization of urban environments in terms of collective social properties, or "ecometrics,"[14] and the importance of collective-action problems in human well-being and socioeconomic development. In architecture and planning, many of the formal ideas about the importance of ecological and evolutionary thinking with respect to cities and human development have lived on through successive generations of influential urbanists, such as Lewis Mumford,[15] Christopher Alexander,[16] William H. Whyte,[17] Jane Jacobs,[18] Kevin Lynch,[19] Manuel Castells,[20] and John F. C. Turner,[21] among many others.[22] The recognition that cities are complex adaptive systems[23] and not arbitrary human artifacts to be reconfigured at will is now mainstream and inspires much contemporary architecture and planning, especially toward sustainable cities and people-oriented planning and design. These are also the foundational concepts for worldwide international policy agreements such as the New Urban Agenda and the United Nations' Sustainable Development Goals.[24]

The clearest idea that cities are complex systems was first articulated in a very practical context in New York City in 1961. At this point in space and time, Jane Jacobs, a young writer[25] and keen observer of the nature of cities, pitted her wits against one of the most powerful men in America—master builder Robert Moses—and eventually won. Her ideas saved the soul of American cities and set the intellectual agenda for the next 50 years of urbanism, at least in the US. As she thought about the nature of cities, inspired by observing life in her own neighborhood of the West Village, Jacobs experienced the serendipity of an urban encounter with a mathematician—Warren Weaver—who encouraged her in her task and told her about new ideas of information[26] and specifically about systems that expressed what he called organized complexity. Jacobs finished her landmark book *Death and Life of Great American Cities*[27] with this idea in a curiously tentative (for her!) chapter titled "The Kind of Problem the City Is." This chapter looked forward to the way we should conceptualize the city and, in many ways, still defines the challenges for urban science today.[28]

Jane Jacobs's main point was that cities are problems in *organized complexity* because they "present situations in which several dozen quantities are all varying simultaneously and in subtly connected ways." This implies that many factors in cities affect each other and that causality is almost always circular, organized as *vicious* and *virtuous* cycles of change. Jacobs contrasted this kind of problem with simpler situations, such as the stuff of dynamic systems in physics (such as the solar system) and problems in "disorganized complexity," such as gases or liquids, in which statistical averages over anonymous entities give good descriptions of how a system works.

This structure of connections and interdependencies of cities as problems of organized complexity is not an abstraction. It is very real in your own life or that of any other person in a city (figure 1.5). In a city, we are all interdependent, necessarily relying on each other through social, political, economic, and other connections to obtain all the basic necessities that make life possible and indeed other functions and support that can lead to opportunities and development. This obvious insight has become a pivotal point in the social sciences, requiring the understanding of new forms of agreement and cooperation between very different people, a condition that Émile Durkheim famously described as *organic solidarity*.[29]

But this is not the way city agencies work. They deal with transportation, housing, education, and all other urban services *separately*, often in uncoordinated ways. Severing connections between the basic interdependent realities of life in the city—even if sometimes necessary for manageable city operations—is a recipe for policies that underserve people and in many cases create insurmountable coordination problems that perpetuate acute urban challenges, such as persistent poverty and segregation, as we will see later in this book.

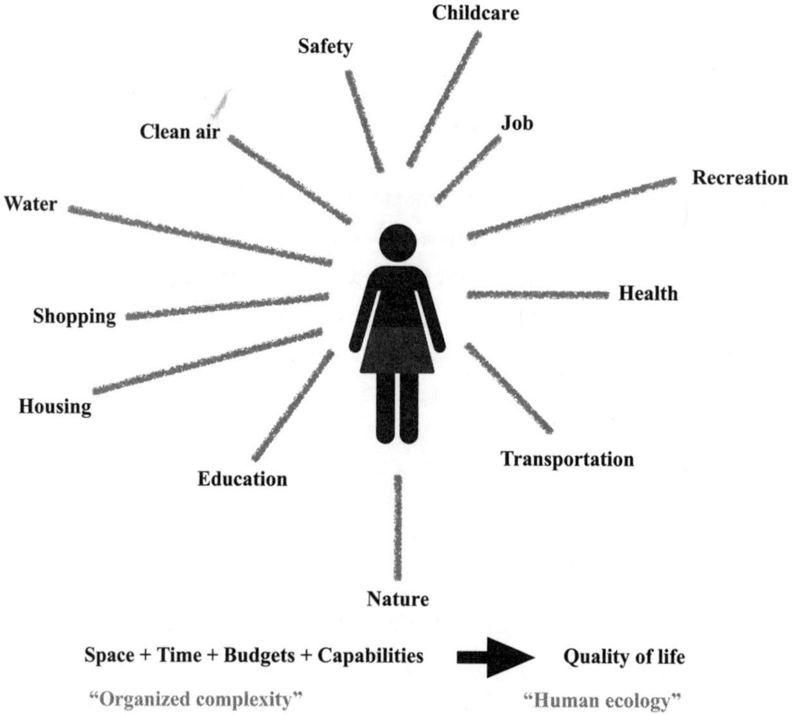

1.5 Complexity, interdependence, and the human ecology of urban environments.

As figure 1.5 shows, in urban environments, individuals become connected to each other in terms of many of their daily needs, contributions, and exchanges. This necessarily creates a dynamic web of interdependencies over built space and time, mediated by socioeconomic exchanges. These complex networks create the need to describe cities as complex adaptive systems and gave rise to their conceptualization as "human ecologies"[30] and problems in "organized complexity."[31]

Jacobs also proposed a strategy for discovering how cities actually work. She encouraged a focus on *processes* rather than structures; *inductive reasoning*, which discovers general features from particular ones; and *a search for unaveraged clues*, as many salient agents of change in cities are unique and local. We will use and make sense of her strategies throughout this book and will pay attention to what we may be sacrificing whenever we violate her recommendations.

Ideas about organized complexity have become, in due course, what we call today *complex adaptive systems*.[32] It is a tribute to urbanists and to the importance of cities as complex systems that this was one of the earliest articulations of what complex systems are and that to the end of her life Jane Jacobs persisted in writing about the need to understand cities in light of the dynamics of other natural systems, such as ecosystems, especially in terms of the diversity and sustainability of their "economies."[33]

Complex systems are hard to define precisely, and there are certainly many different types. Living systems and human social systems are certainly complex systems, but it is possible to think of the weather, certain materials (such as a grainy magnet), or nonlinear dynamic mathematical models as also expressing some characteristics of complex systems. A more productive perspective on complex adaptive systems emphasizes the kinds of processes they embody (figure 1.6). From this perspective, cities as complex adaptive systems exhibit to various degrees the following properties: heterogeneity, interconnectivity, scaling, circular causality, and evolution.

The remainder of the book will deal with these issues in greater detail, but for now let me sketch the meaning of each of these properties. The reader is encouraged to think about what these properties mean in other complex systems.

Cities as complex systems

Heterogeneity	Differences in information, profession, culture, race, ethnicity, and economic status
Interconnectivity	Interdependence between people, organizations, and infrastructure in networks
Scaling	Self-similar economies of scale per capita in material infrastructure and increasing returns to socioeconomic activity
Circular causality	Interdependence dynamics between socioeconomic activities, institutions, and services
Evolution	Open-ended change supported by new information, investment, and collective action

1.6 Five general properties of cities as complex systems.

First, *heterogeneity* refers to the fact that large cities are very diverse. There is a positive and a negative side to this. Heterogeneity may refer to types of professions or businesses in a city, to wealth disparities, to race and ethnicity, and other things. It should be clear that all these properties vary immensely among individuals in a city but also across urban space, such as from one neighborhood to another. This makes "averaged" urban planning and policy very problematic and potentially wasteful (see chapters 5 and 6). Is the heterogeneity of cities a "bug" or a "feature"? Does it have a purpose? Should it be sustained or discouraged?

Second, everything in a city is subtly *interconnected* in networks. For example, issues of economic development or public health are connected to physical places and to urban services, and these in turn are connected to economic budgets at the individual and municipal levels. How may we disentangle some of these issues so we can develop practical solutions? Chapter 3 gives us an overview of these networks, while later chapters derive more of their consequences.

Third, the character of cities changes with their *scale*, usually measured by population size. Larger cities within the same nation are usually denser and make more intense use of their infrastructure, with both associated benefits and costs. Larger cities are also more productive economically but also more expensive. Thus, dealing with issues of cities is generally a scale-dependent problem, as we show explicitly in chapters 2 and 3. In particular, larger cities have some advantages and disadvantages in terms of social and spatial freedoms relative to smaller towns, which exactly compensate each other across an urban size hierarchy. This leads to a number of curious properties of cities and helps explain why they exist at many different scales.

Fourth, virtually all important issues of cities show *circular causality*. For example, is a city rich because it has good infrastructure or does it have good infrastructure because it is rich? This is obviously an important question: should we try to make a city richer by investing in better infrastructure or wait and build it once we are richer? This circular causality is characteristic of cities as systems in approximate spatial equilibrium, a concept we will explore in chapters 2 and 3.

Finally, people, businesses, and the city itself change over time to adapt and to explore new circumstances. This typically leads to processes of economic growth and development that are gradual (but often fast!) and history dependent: cities *evolve*. The use of words such as *development* or *evolution* is loaded with different meanings. For good or bad, they provide connections with similar ideas in biology. As we will see, the meaning of these terms in human societies is certainly different in many respects but at present still less clear and less well formalized than in biology. Nevertheless, all evolutionary dynamics involve mechanisms by which individuals and organizations carry information and use it (strategically) in uncertain environments to derive some relative advantage. In cities, knowledge and collective agency are critical for economic expansion to emerge and for improving public services, such as those supporting health, infrastructure, and much more. The main difficulty in improving testable theories of these processes results from the need to articulate noisy dynamics and information at many different scales,[34] from the diverse and idiosyncratic behavior of people and organizations to the macroscopic interdependencies between cities and emergent aggregate national growth rates. Chapters 4 and 9 will show how.

OBJECTIVES AND THE STRUCTURE OF THIS BOOK

These properties of cities as complex systems will force us to frame urban science in a way that goes beyond existing theory in any particular discipline, be it sociology, geography, economics, or complex systems. The challenge requires identifying and formalizing essential *phenomena at different scales* and articulating their consequences in both the "macroscopic" aggregate (entire cities and nations), where these effects are typically first measured, and their "microscopic" origins and influences on people and places (see figure 1.7). To this end, we close this chapter with a brief overview of the themes of each upcoming chapter to summarize their main subjects and interconnections.

Chapter 2 provides an overview of classical models of cities, especially from geography, sociology, and economics. In these approaches, cities are conceived functionally, as places of (economic) interaction and exchange. Spatial structure and urban extent follow from associated socioeconomic cost-benefit analysis. Aspects of human mobility from geography and transport studies are also introduced, as they play a critical part in defining functional urban areas. These definitions and their practical implementations are reviewed and illustrated.

Chapter 3 distills, connects, and expands the underlying ideas of classical models and confronts many of their consequences with empirical data on cities from around the world. We introduce the concept of *urban scaling*, first as a unifying method to study the macroscopic properties of any complex system and then as the basis for the development of a theory of cities as self-consistent social and spatial complex networks. This theory builds a general picture of human behavior and interactions over urban built spaces and allows the derivation of many different "scaling laws" describing the nonlinear self-similar properties of urban indicators according to city size. A diverse and interconnected set of quantitative predictions for the properties of cities are derived and discussed, which will allow us to identify both formal similarities and differences from other complex systems.

Chapter 4 develops a statistical approach to urban quantities. It shows how deviations from scaling relations become natural benchmarks for evaluating the relative performance of cities in scale-independent ways. It also shows the consequences of this type of analysis for different quantities in different national urban systems to identify what are unique and historically contingent aspects of each city and region. We then develop a statistical theory of cities that expands the ideas of chapter 3.

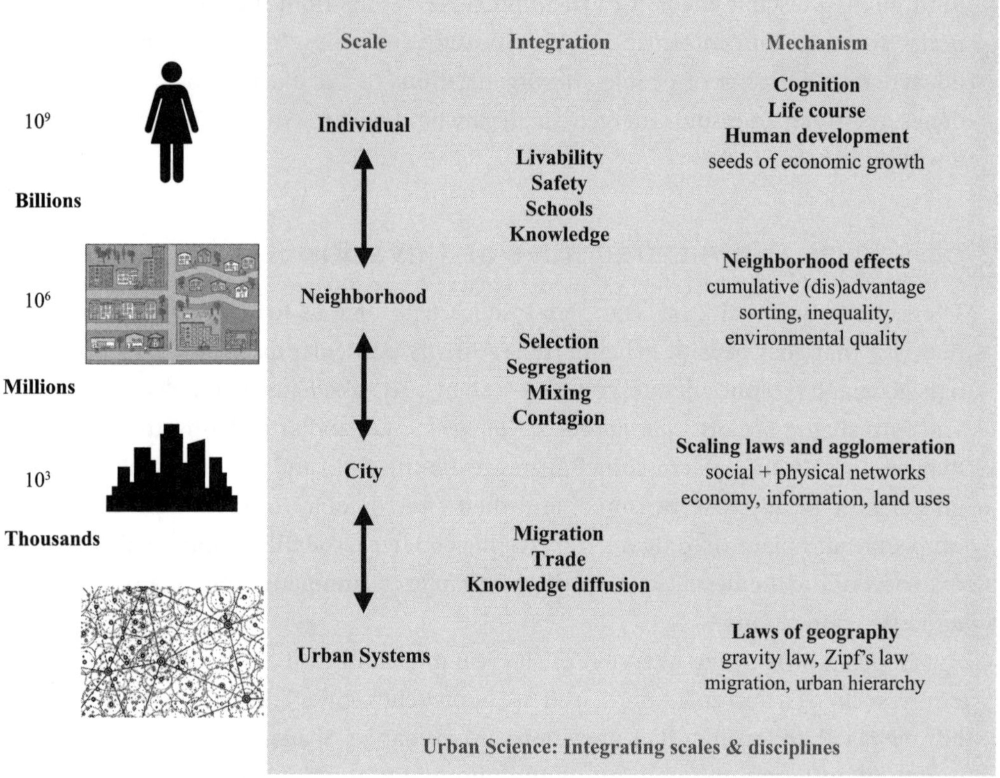

1.7 Urban science deals with diverse interconnected phenomena across different scales and traditional disciplines. Providing an articulation between billions of people living in millions of neighborhoods in thousands of cities worldwide is key, as is identifying phenomena that occur primarily at specific scales but have impact on the system as a whole. For example, economic growth and human development have their origins in people's opportunities and decisions over time, at home and at work, and on their capabilities in neighborhoods, but these outcomes are also facilitated by network effects in cities (scaling), which amplify local decisions into national economic growth processes and other broad aspects of change.

Such a theory allows us to understand how inequality develops across population scales, from individuals to entire cities, points to the mechanisms at its origins, and derives corrections to scaling exponents when these variations become scale dependent. As a whole, the microscopic dynamic theory developed in this chapter allows us to understand how scaling becomes a natural emergent property of cities and when it may also fail, in regimes dominated by strong statistical variations.

Chapter 5 deals with issues of diversity in cities and their relationship to economic productivity. It first discusses classical theories in sociology and economics for the heterogeneity of urban populations, the deep division of labor and knowledge in urban societies, and the self-organization and origins of diversity in both economic markets and ecosystems. It then shows how the diversity of professional occupations and business types in each urban area is expressed across city sizes and how observed results can be accounted for by the properties of socioeconomic networks derived under urban scaling theory. This connection also establishes a formal link and set of quantitative predictions between socioeconomic network structure, informational diversity, and economic productivity. We discuss the consequences of these connections in cities in light of processes of economic development. As some of the same mechanisms are also mediated by other information networks, we can also understand how the internet becomes mostly a complement for cities rather than a substitute, expressing its own strong network effects.

Chapter 6 deals with the spatial sorting of people in cities and associated "neighborhood effects." It starts out by describing a large body of work, mostly from sociology, on the importance of place within cities and on both its advantages and pitfalls for sustaining sociocultural diversity but also creating economically and racially segregated populations. We will spend some time understanding how patterns of spatial diversity are best measured in terms of information and how human development in cities is predicated on multiple types of connectivity, from urban services to socioeconomic opportunities and entrepreneurship. These challenges will be illustrated by approaches to community organization and emergent data and maps of informal urban settlements (slums), especially in Africa and South Asia.

Chapter 7 takes us deep in time to a variety of historical contexts to appreciate the generality of human settlement patterns in history and provide a series of unique, independent tests on urban scaling theory. The result is an extension of the theory of chapter 3 to all sorts of human settlements, which we will refer to as *settlement scaling theory*. These ideas are tested in many different contexts from pre-Columbian settlements that must have developed independently from Old World cities to the metropolises of the Roman Empire and to medieval European cities and towns. We will also show how the ideas of settlement scaling theory break down for temporary camps of mobile *hunter-gatherers* for reasons that are both energetic and institutional. Such insights will allow us to hypothesize necessary and sufficient conditions for the origins of permanent settlements in human history and consequently for the advent of the first cities.

Chapter 8 addresses the structure of urban systems as interconnected networks of cities and associated "laws of geography," a set of empirical regularities at these larger scales. We start by reviewing the status of these laws and assessing how well they describe empirical evidence. We then show how they arise in specific limits starting out from fundamental demographic dynamics of births, deaths, and migration. This approach reveals that many of the laws of geography are "neutral" in the sense of describing an urban system in relative demographic equilibrium. This insight leads to a natural description of observed deviations from such idealized situations in terms of information.

Chapter 9 deals with the origins of human development in cities and more specifically with mechanisms of endogenous economic growth. This remains in many ways the greatest mystery for economics and indeed for the social sciences and complex systems. We will show that well-known positive correlations between urbanization and GDP (figure 1.2) per capita are the result of a statistical population dynamics involving both sorting and growth. We then focus on theories of endogenous economic growth, their basis on knowledge production, and their current difficulties in formalizing such insights mathematically. This problem is addressed by developing a theory of strategic investments under uncertainty that shows that the economic growth rate is ultimately the mutual information between local knowledge and the outside stochastic environment, which must be learned by individuals and organizations. The chapter finishes by discussing how such mechanisms are embodied in institutions, both economic and civic, which exposes challenges of collective production and distribution. Cities are discussed as social environments where such challenges can naturally be met but only when there is suitable institutional and infrastructural support. When these dynamics can be implemented and supported across scales—from individuals to firms, governments, and infrastructure—a virtuous cycle of interdependent learning, economic growth, and human development is predicted to emerge.

Chapter 10 summarizes the properties of cities and points to their main purpose as environments where complex new knowledge can be generated and applied through emergent socioeconomic collectives. It also discusses several key challenges ahead for urban science in a fast-changing world in search of more sustainable forms of development.

An important aim of this book is to show that many well-known phenomena and empirical regularities of cities are intrinsically interconnected and can be made sense of from a common body of theory. This includes the concepts of functional cities as central markets, agglomeration effects, economies of scale in material infrastructure, urban scaling laws, persistent diverse performance of different cities, path dependency and historical contingency, the division of knowledge and labor, economic complexity, neighborhood effects, spatial fractal dimensions, Zipf's law and lognormal statistics, the gravity law of mobility and migration, central place theory and other laws of geography, the basis for diversity and economic growth in information, and the importance of emergent institutions in development processes.

The overarching goal of the book is to create a comprehensive theoretical framework for understanding cities and urbanization and for generating useful and falsifiable predictions and confronting them with a growing body of empirical evidence so urban science can continue to improve and grow.

2

CLASSICAL MODELS OF CITIES AND URBAN FUNCTIONAL DEFINITIONS

The world is full of self-organizing systems, systems that form structures not merely in response to inputs from outside but also, indeed primarily, in response to their own internal logic.
—Paul Krugman, *The Self-Organizing Economy*

Let us now start thinking more specifically about how cities work. The ideas of this chapter have long roots in economics, geography, sociology, urban planning, and a range of other disciplines, where they were pioneering in demonstrating how space acquires structure via the self-organization of agents in interaction with each other. This is a fundamental concept of urban science that will recur with elaboration throughout this book.

Though there has been an enormous amount of scholarship about the key characteristics of cities, here we will limit our discussion to models that are analytical and mathematical, illustrating how cities may work, at least along some of their facets. As we will see, most of these models are not models of cities at all! Rather, several of the more developed ones describe a central market: a point in space where goods are exchanged at a distance from their surrounding production locations. This situation is interesting because it can lead to a self-organized differentiation of space by land uses and emphasizes transportation costs as the limiting factor determining the extent of cities (and markets). A fertile twist on this idea is to consider the city as a central *labor* market, where everyone works in the central business district and lives somewhere else. The assumptions introduced in these models are typically unrealistic and are limited in their scope to processes of city formation that emphasize economic exchange. By identifying some of these limitations as well as some of their achievements, we will be able to elaborate and improve on models for cities in later chapters, both conceptually and mathematically.

CHAPTER OUTLINE

This chapter is organized in three main sections. Section 2.1 deals with models of economic geography for why central markets and spatially concentrated production may emerge through the self-organizing dynamics of consumers and producers in interaction. We will introduce and discuss two famous models: Johann Heinrich von Thünen's *isolated-state* model and Krugman's *core-periphery* model, which accounts for spatial agglomeration at the regional scale. Section 2.2 deals with models of city structure, especially those developed in urban economics. This starts with the conceptual flip from goods to labor markets, mapping the von Thünen model into the spatial structure of cities. Section 2.3 discusses the importance of *time*, especially through the lens of *time geography*. This approach emphasizes the trajectories of people over urban built space-time, which will prove to be the foundation for all models and theory in later chapters. We finish with some examples of how these ideas are used to make sense of data about land uses and urban expansion and define functional urban areas.

2.1 MODELS OF SPATIAL AGGLOMERATION

The term *agglomeration* is often used by economists to signal the formation of spatially bound clusters of people and firms. Although we will use the word throughout the book, I do not particularly like it, because—as we have already seen in the words of Jane Jacobs[1] or Louis Wirth[2]—it may be interpreted as denoting an undifferentiated clump of people interacting mostly via economic exchange, which cities are not. We will use the term here mostly with reference to models from economic geography.

The simplest mathematical models of spatial agglomeration go back almost 200 years. They are very simple and intuitive. Their basic ideas permeate all subsequent theories of spatial concentration of socioeconomic activity and cities, so they are an ideal place to start.

2.1.1 THE VON THÜNEN MODEL OF A CENTRAL MARKET

Johann Heinrich von Thünen was a landowner in northern Germany in the nineteenth century. He was born in 1783 in Canarienhausen, Wangerland, now in the state of Mecklenburg-Vorpommern, in the countryside near the great Hanseatic trade cities of Bremen, Hamburg, and Rostock, where he died 67 years later. It is hard to imagine a less likely place for the birth of urban science (see figure 2.1).

Von Thünen wanted to know what sets the value of (his) land. He understood that this was not about the land itself but instead about the value it created as an input to production for goods that could be sold at a market. Happily, he had a knack for simple and fiercely analytical thinking that made his answers the basis for much of modern spatial economics, inspiring not only later models of cities but also models of international trade and price formation.[3]

2.1   Modern countryside around the town where von Thünen was born in 1783. The setting is agricultural, punctuated by small towns.
Sources: Google Earth and Wikipedia.

Von Thünen's model for land value is not a model of a city at all. It is a model of a closed rural economy, also known as the *isolated state*, but with a critical ingredient: a central market. It is at this market that all products of agricultural activity are exchanged. The market is central relative to all its surrounding land, which means that each land parcel on the landscape is characterized by its distance to market, with some near and some far. Thus, transportation costs to market must necessarily enter any calculation of the net incomes of farmers choosing to produce different goods.

Von Thünen's insight was that each farmer's income (net of transportation and production costs, including living necessities) would equal the land rent to be paid. The key observation is that different products, i, say tomatoes, apples, and potatoes, have different given prices as well as typical production expenses and transportation costs per unit of distance traveled, R. Let us call these transportation costs c_T and take $c_{T_1} > c_{T_2} > c_{T_3}$, so transportation costs for tomatoes are higher than for apples and these higher than potatoes, because of the relative perishability of each. The key question is *how much income per year, y* (or *rent income*, in the language of economics), *can one expect to obtain by growing each crop* i *in each parcel of land*? We can write the answer mathematically as

$$y_i(R) = q_i[(p_i - c_{p_i}) - c_{T_i}R].$$
(2.1)

Here, q_i is the yield for crop i (in units of weight per year), p_i is the market price per unit of weight (considered as given), and c_{p_i} are the corresponding production costs. The distance to market R is usually measured as a radius in the simplest case of a featureless landscape, so the last term accounts for total transportation costs.

When plotted versus the distance to market (figure 2.2), we observe that the rent for each crop, y_i, is highest closest to market (as this minimizes transportation costs) but that it decays with distance with different slopes, set by each c_{T_i}. This now gives us a basis to choose what to produce where: goods with high net value and the highest transportation costs should be produced closest to the market, whereas

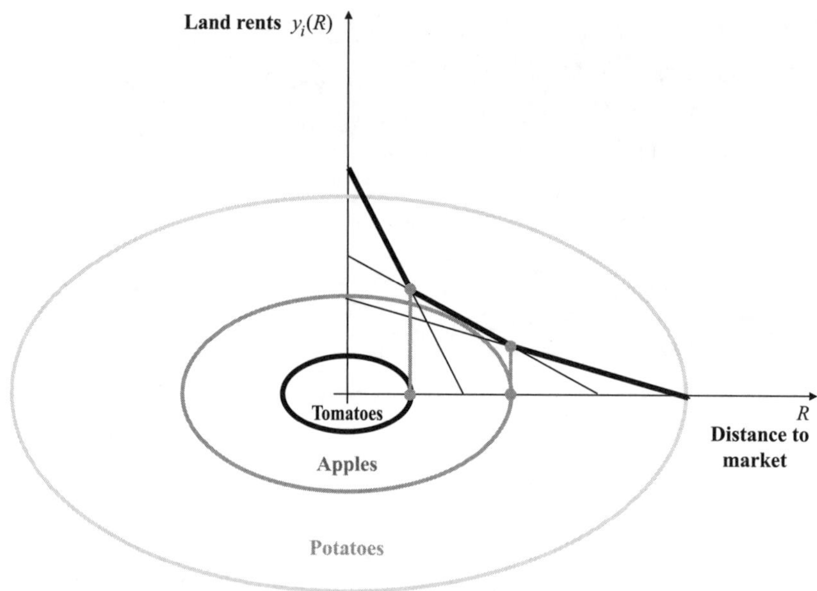

2.2 Land rents as a function of market prices and transportation costs for different agricultural produce sold at the central market. The dotted lines show the rents as a function of distance to market; the rough line shows which crop fetches the highest rent at different distances to market, R. As a consequence of the self-organization for highest profits and rents, agricultural land becomes heterogeneous in terms of its uses, an example of a market's "invisible hand."

lower-priced items with low transportation costs should be produced farthest away. The self-organization of production toward profit (rent) maximization around the central market results in a heterogeneous pattern of land uses! This is a nice example of the "invisible hand" of markets at work: markets are an important means for self-organization of production, and of cities more generally.

The von Thünen model is the first instance of an economic model that explicitly includes the effects of space. Given market prices, it shows how *land uses* are determined by their distance to a market and produces the first spatially heterogeneous equilibrium solution. Economists really like the von Thünen model; Paul Samuelson, in a landmark textbook on economics,[4] credited it as the origin of formal thinking in models of comparative advantage, theories of rent, factors-and-goods pricing, and input-output models. The von Thünen model also provides a basis for models of international trade and is, of course, at the heart of modern theories of cities, as we will see.

However, despite its bare simplicity, the model makes unnecessary assumptions and leaves a number of critical quantities to be specified externally ("exogenously"). The model is not dynamic and does not reflect the innovation characteristic of modern cities. It is really about tomatoes and potatoes. It assumes prices, yields, costs of production, and transportation; none of these quantities can be derived within the model.

But von Thünen's formulation does give us the first hints of what can happen as an urban economy grows, produces more goods and services, and improves its transportation technologies. Imagine such a scenario: What would happen to the production of potatoes as new products of higher value and with lower transportation costs become part of the economy? What sets the ultimate extent of the market and the diversity of goods sold? Can such factors be changed, for example by technology?

2.1.2 THE CORE-PERIPHERY MODEL

Paul Krugman is famous to many noneconomists for his fiercely insightful columns in the *New York Times*. He was the first to propose a simple model that shows why economies may *spontaneously* concentrate in different regions of space.[5] This is Nobel Prize stuff, so hold on to your hats! This subsection is more mathematical than most. More details of the derivations are given in appendix A.

Krugman's theory and its extensions have become known as the *core-periphery model*, though it is more precisely about the concentration in space of certain industries (manufacturing) and consumer/worker populations. This concentration—when it happens—breaks the spatial homogeneity of population and economic activity distributions set by the productivity of land. It does so in a different way than in the von Thünen model, as we now show.

There are two main ideas to the argument. The first is that manufacturing is subject to *economies of scale*, while agricultural production is (assumed) not to be.[6] This means that producing more to serve a larger market may reduce the costs of manufacturing each additional unit. Second, any products must travel to market and in doing so incur *transportation costs*. So, locating production close to consumers is best. If the vast majority of such consumers are farmers distributed all over the landscape, transportation costs work against concentrating production and dampen spatial agglomeration. But, as cities grow, they create their own demand and enlarge a set of new consumers. Once most consumers are urban, economies of scale and reduced transportation costs work together to produce the spatial concentration of population, production, and consumption, creating an instability toward urbanization: a spontaneous *urban implosion*.[7] This argument then creates the conditions for a process of urbanization and industrialization to emerge and to come to dominate an economy, introducing us to the important concept of *positive feedback*[8] or *circular causation* in urban economies.[9] This theme will recur in later chapters, as virtuous cycles of economic growth and population sorting are common in urban systems.

Now let us see how these ideas are implemented in a model of economics. If you are not an economist, it will likely appear a little abstract to you, so please hang in there. The point is that the model brings together a minimal set of common economic modeling assumptions that until the advent of the core-periphery model were not known to produce spatial agglomeration.

Model Setup   Krugman's model has two spatial regions (figure 2.3). In each region, there are two types of individuals: *farmers*, who are assumed to be tied to the land

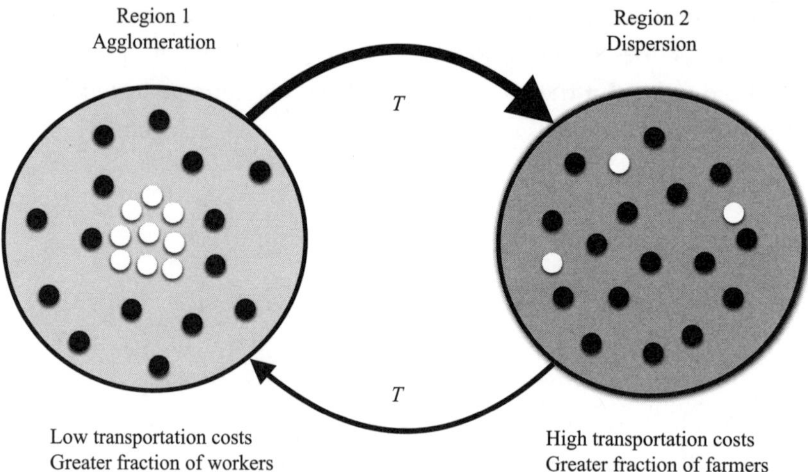

2.3 Schematic two-region core-periphery model. The two regions shown in lighter and darker background gray, have the same number of farmers (black dots) but a different number of manufacturing workers (white dots), who are also consumers. Manufactured goods shipped to the other region incur transportation costs, which reduce the amount of good that arrives by a fraction $1/T$. The model tells us when an imbalance between the manufacturing populations of the two regions is unstable: low enough transportation costs and/or a high enough ratio of workers to farmers breaks spatial symmetry and leads to agglomeration of manufacturing in a single region.

and cannot leave, and manufacturing *workers*, who will move between regions if their economic conditions improve. They are assumed to move to the region where their *real* wage is highest, thus potentially concentrating together in the same place.

Let y_{ω_1}, y_{ω_2} be the real income from wages (the buying power) of workers in regions 1 and 2, respectively. Let $0 \leq f_1 \leq 1$ be the fraction of these workers in region 1. Then the model assumes that f_1 will change in response to real wage differentials:

$$\Delta f_1 = (y_{\omega_1} - y_{\omega_2})f_1. \tag{2.2}$$

If $y_{\omega_1} > y_{\omega_2}$, f_1 will grow, and vice versa. We now need to compute the real wages in the two regions.

To do this, the model assumes two kinds of economic agents: *individuals* and *firms*. Individuals are *consumers*, who are assumed to want to maximize their utility[10] U, parameterized as

$$U = U_0 c_M^{n_{MF}} c_F^{1-n_{MF}}, \tag{2.3}$$

where c_M is the individual consumption of manufactured goods (made by workers) and c_F is the consumption of agricultural products (made by farmers). (We use the symbol c for both costs and consumption, because consumption is most often measured as an expenditure.) This form of utility function is very common in economic modeling. It is known as Cobb-Douglas, and we will encounter it again later (chapters 3 and 9) in other contexts. This mathematical form means that the consumption of both types of goods is necessary for the individual to experience high utility and that the relative fractions of the two types are n_{MF} and $1-n_{MF}$, respectively.[11]

In addition, Krugman assumes a kind of consumer preference for manufactured goods, c_M, of the form

$$c_M = \left[\sum_{i=1}^{n_M} q_i^{(\sigma_S-1)/\sigma_S}\right]^{\sigma_S/(\sigma_S-1)}, \tag{2.4}$$

where n_M is the total number of manufactured *product types* and q_i is the quantity of each consumed type, i. The parameter $\sigma_S > 1$ is known as the *elasticity of substitution* (see appendix A). It accounts for the change in the amounts of two products consumed as a function of their relative price changes. For large σ_S, there is strong substitution, so people are relatively indifferent to swaps between product types. For small $\sigma_S \to 1$, each different product matters more in achieving high utility.

This form of utility function takes some getting used to for anyone not steeped in economic theory. Mathematically, it is related to an index of monopoly (lack of *diversity*; see chapter 5). This utility function has two important properties that will prove critical for generating spatial agglomeration. First, it allows *incomplete competition* between firms because there are a number n_M of products that are not identical (this is called *monopolistic competition*). Second, it sneaks in a fundamental property of cities, namely a specific form of *increasing returns to scale*. To get a glimpse of this effect, consider the simplified situation where all products have the same price, p, and are consumed in the same amount, q. Then

$$U \propto c_M = n_M^{\frac{\sigma_S}{\sigma_S-1}} q. \tag{2.5}$$

Writing the total consumer expenditure (which equals total income) as $Y = pqn_M$ results in a utility that behaves as $U \propto n_M^{\frac{1}{\sigma_S-1}} \frac{Y}{p}$. With $\sigma_S > 1$, this shows that the utility is a growing function of the total number of different products, n_M (or product *richness*; see chapter 5). This means that the system shows increasing returns in utility on a *diversity scale*. (In chapter 3, we will see that cities show many different kinds of increasing returns on a *population* scale.) This arises from the fact that people will feel greater utility by consuming a larger number of product types, a property that is often referred to as a *taste for variety*. Note that this property is *assumed* through the form chosen for the utility function; it is not derived. Remember also that the closer σ_S gets to 1, the stronger this effect becomes; in fact, the effect disappears when $\sigma_S \to \infty$, because then products are interchangeable and there is no local monopoly at all.

Next, the model parameterizes populations and wages in the two regions as follows. There are a total of N_F farmers, *equally divided between the two regions*, and N_M manufacturing workers, for a total population of $N = N_F + N_M$ individuals. The parameter $n_{MF} = N_M/N$ measures the *given* fraction of people who are manufacturing workers across the two regions (figure 2.3). We will call y_{w_F} the average nominal wage of farmers and y_w the average nominal wage of workers, so $Y_w = N_M y_w$ is the total wage of workers. The use of the same parameter n_{MF} to measure the fraction of workers and the fraction of manufactured good consumption in the utility function (2.3) ensures that the *total* wages of farmers and workers are the same, because

$$y_{w_F} = \frac{Y_{w_F}}{N_F} = \frac{c_F N}{N_F} = \frac{(1-n_{MF})N}{(1-n_{MF})N} U = U,$$
(2.6)

$$y_w = \frac{Y_w}{N_M} = \frac{c_M N}{N_M} = \frac{n_{MF} N}{n_{MF} N} U = U,$$
(2.7)

so $y_{w_F} = y_w = U \equiv 1$. This justifies maintaining the ratio of farmers to workers constant in the model; by assumption, no one has an incentive to switch professions, just places. The only thing that can differ between the two regions is the real wage of workers.

Firms, Prices, and Transport Costs The last ingredient in the model setup concerns accounting for *transportation costs*. In general, we should set up a physical model for transportation flows, but Krugman assumes a simple prescription called *iceberg costs*, also originally due to Samuelson.[12] This means that only a fraction $0 \leq \tau \leq 1$ of goods moved across regions arrives at their destination. In general, this is product specific (as in the von Thünen model) and depends on distance and the mode of transportation. Here, however, the only point about transportation costs is that they increase the consumer price of products imported from the other region (products from the same region do not incur transportation costs), so in such cases the price becomes $\frac{p_i}{\tau} > p_i$.

Now let us see how this affects consumption and thereby real wages in each region. To relate prices to quantities of goods consumed, we need the relationship between the q_i and the corresponding price, p_i. This is standard marginal utility theory in economics, $p_i = \frac{dc_M}{dq_i}$ (see appendix A), which leads to the relationship

$$q_i = \frac{y_w N}{\bar{p}^{-\sigma_s}} p_i^{-\sigma_s},$$
(2.8)

where $\bar{p} = \left(\sum_{i=1}^{n_M} p_i^{1-\sigma_s}\right)^{\frac{1}{1-\sigma_s}}$. The quantity $\bar{p}$ is a consumer price index. This will become region specific because prices between imported and *home market* products will vary. Consequently, the consumption of region 1 goods within the region is $q_{11} \propto p_1^{-\sigma_s}$, and the consumption of region 2 goods in region 1 is $q_{12} \propto (p_2/\tau)^{-\sigma_s}$. The important quantity is the ratio

$$\frac{q_{11}}{q_{12}} = \left(\frac{p_1 \tau}{p_2}\right)^{-\sigma_s}.$$
(2.9)

Real Wages for Manufacturing Workers We now want to compute how these variations in price by region impact *real wages*. This means that we have to determine how much the wages of a region 1 worker buys in terms of manufactured products versus those in region 2. All we need to compute is the equivalent of equations (2.6) and (2.7) for the two regions. For the total wages Y_{W_i} in the two regions, this now looks like

$$Y_{W_1} = y_{w_1} n_{MF} f_1 N = n_{MF} \left[\frac{e_{11}^Y}{e_{11}^Y + e_{21}^Y} Y_1 + \frac{e_{21}^Y}{e_{21}^Y + e_{22}^Y} Y_2 \right];$$

$$Y_{W_2} = y_{w_2} n_{MF} (1 - f_1) N = n_{MF} \left[\frac{e_{12}^Y}{e_{11}^Y + e_{21}^Y} Y_1 + \frac{e_{22}^Y}{e_{21}^Y + e_{22}^Y} Y_2 \right], \tag{2.10}$$

where e_{ij}^Y is the fraction of income from region i, Y_i, spent in region j. Given the ratios of workers to farmers, n_{MF}, and those in each region, f_1, we can write

$$y_1 = \frac{Y_1}{N} = n_{MF} f_1 y_{w_1} + \frac{1 - n_{MF}}{2}, \quad y_2 = \frac{Y_2}{N} = n_{MF} (1 - f_1) y_{w_2} + \frac{1 - n_{MF}}{2}, \tag{2.11}$$

as the total income—workers plus farmers—in regions 1 and 2, respectively (recall that farmers have their wage set to unity). Now it is easier to compute the fractions $\frac{e_{11}^Y}{e_{12}^Y}$ and $\frac{e_{21}^Y}{e_{22}^Y}$, which are

$$\frac{e_{11}^Y}{e_{12}^Y} = \frac{n_{M_1}}{n_{M_2}} \cdot \frac{p_1}{p_2/\tau} \frac{q_{11}}{q_{12}}, \frac{e_{21}^Y}{e_{22}^Y} = \frac{n_{M_1}}{n_{M_2}} \frac{p_1/\tau}{p_2} \frac{q_{21}}{q_{22}}, \tag{2.12}$$

where q_{ij} is the quantity of a product from j consumed in region i. We can now use the relationships between q, p, and y_w (see appendix A) to write

$$\frac{e_{11}^Y}{e_{12}^Y} = \frac{n_{MF}}{1 - n_{MF}} \left(\frac{y_{w_1}}{y_{w_2}} \right)^{1 - \sigma_S} \tau^{1 - \sigma_S}, \quad \frac{e_{21}^Y}{e_{22}^Y} = \frac{n_{MF}}{1 - n_{MF}} \left(\frac{y_{w_1}}{y_{w_2}} \right)^{1 - \sigma_S} \tau^{\sigma_S - 1}. \tag{2.13}$$

Introducing equations (2.13) in equation (2.10) and simplifying, one obtains a self-consistent equation for the nominal wages:

$$y_{w_1} = [y_1 \, \bar{p}_1^{\sigma_S - 1} + y_2 \, \bar{p}_2^{\sigma_S - 1} \tau^{\sigma_S - 1}]^{\frac{1}{\sigma_S}}, \quad y_{w_2} = [y_1 \, \bar{p}_1^{\sigma_S - 1} \tau^{\sigma_S - 1} + y_2 \, \bar{p}_2^{\sigma_S - 1}]^{\frac{1}{\sigma_S}}. \tag{2.14}$$

We have to take one final step before obtaining our answer. We need to consider *real wages* instead of their nominal value.[13] To do this, we need to account for the cost of living in each region, computed by dividing the nominal wages by the *cost of one unit of utility in each region*, i, $\bar{p}_i$. This can also be computed from the utility function, equation (2.5) (see appendix A), and leads to the expressions

$$\bar{p}_1 = \left[f_1 \, y_{w_1}^{1 - \sigma_S} + (1 - f_1) \left(\frac{y_{w_2}}{\tau} \right)^{1 - \sigma_S} \right]^{\frac{1}{1 - \sigma_S}}, \quad \bar{p}_2 = \left[f_1 \left(\frac{y_{w_1}}{\tau} \right)^{1 - \sigma_S} + (1 - f_1) y_{w_2}^{1 - \sigma_S} \right]^{\frac{1}{1 - \sigma_S}}. \tag{2.15}$$

Putting these expressions together allows the real wages in one region to be compared to those of the other, defined as

$$y_{\omega_1} = y_{w_1} \bar{p}_1^{-n_{MF}}, \quad y_{\omega_2} = y_{w_2} \bar{p}_2^{-n_{MF}}, \tag{2.16}$$

where the exponent of the price index accounts for the fact that manufactured products only receive a share n_{MF} of the expenditure. Computing the solutions for y_{ω_1}, y_{ω_2}

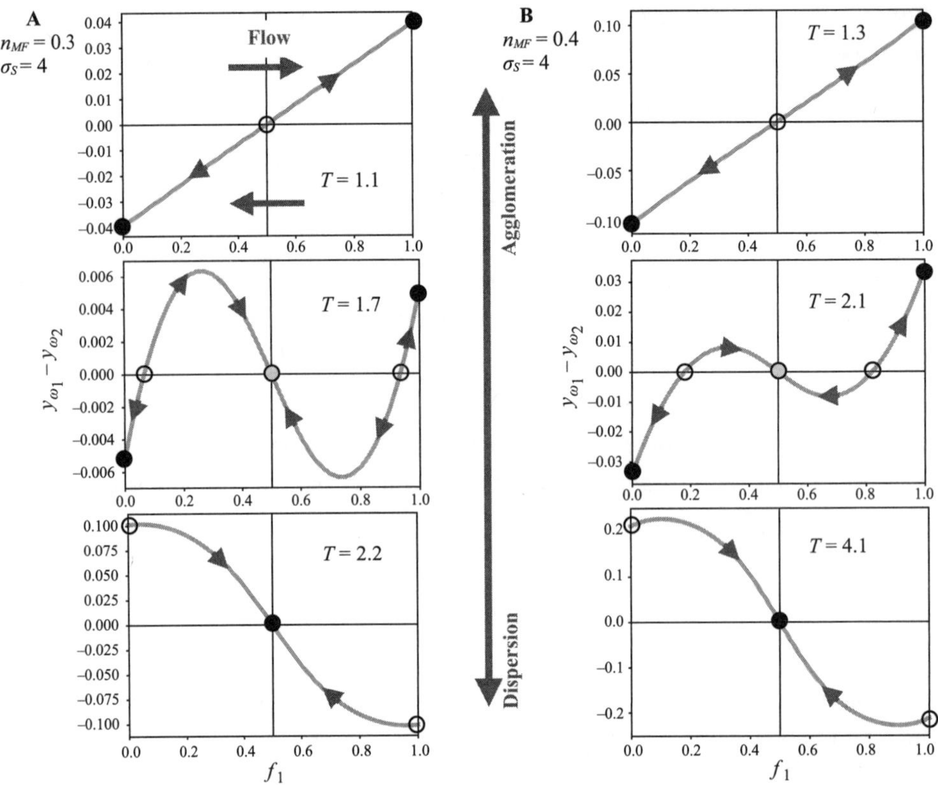

2.4 Workers' agglomeration and dispersal in the core-periphery model. (A) and (B) show two cases with different ratios of workers to farmers, with $n_{MF} = 0.3$ (lower) and $n_{MF} = 0.4$ (higher). The black dots show stable points, the open dots show unstable points, and the gray represents metastability. The trajectories flow to the right for $y_{\omega_1} - y_{\omega_2} > 0$ and vice versa, as indicated by the arrows in the upper panel of (A). We observe that decreasing transportation costs facilitate workers' spatial agglomeration in one zone or the other. What constitutes high or low transportation costs depends on the values of the ratio of workers to farmers and the substitutability parameters n_{MF} and σ_S, respectively.

as functions of the four variables, f_1, τ, n_{MF}, and σ_S, can now be done by solving the problem numerically (see appendix A and figures 2.4 and 2.5).

Spontaneous Transition between Dispersion and Agglomeration   Figure 2.4 shows the solutions of the core-periphery model obtained for several sets of input parameters. The gray lines show the value of the difference in real wages between the two regions, plotted as a function of the fraction of workers in region 1. Solutions will flow to the right (increasing the fraction of workers in region 1) when $y_{\omega_1} - y_{\omega_2} > 0$, which corresponds to the upper half of the diagram. Conversely, they flow to the left in the lower half of the diagram. This means that stable solutions (known as attractors) vary depending on the slope of the solution lines, terminating in the states shown as filled circles. For low transportation costs, $T = 1/\tau$, the system will evolve toward having all workers in either zone 1 or zone 2, depending on the initial conditions. However, when transportation costs are high, workers will remain dispersed between the two zones. At intermediate costs (middle panel), the state of dispersal may remain meta-stable (gray circle). When perturbed sufficiently, however, the dynamics will lead to full agglomeration in either of the two regions.

This general tendency toward agglomeration of manufacturing workers in a single region is facilitated by a larger ratio of workers to farmers, n_{MF}, and greater monopoly, $\sigma_S \to 1$. The metastability of the dispersed state at intermediate transportation costs can be shown in a different way by plotting the endpoint solutions versus transportation costs (figure 2.5). Here the curved gray line shows the region of the solution's coexistence between the agglomerate and dispersed states. In this region of parameter space, an unstable solution may persist temporarily because it is separated from the stable solution by a barrier, leading to the phenomenon called *hysteresis*. This means that the jumping-off point between types of solutions occurs at different T, depending on the direction from which one approaches it. The critical transportation

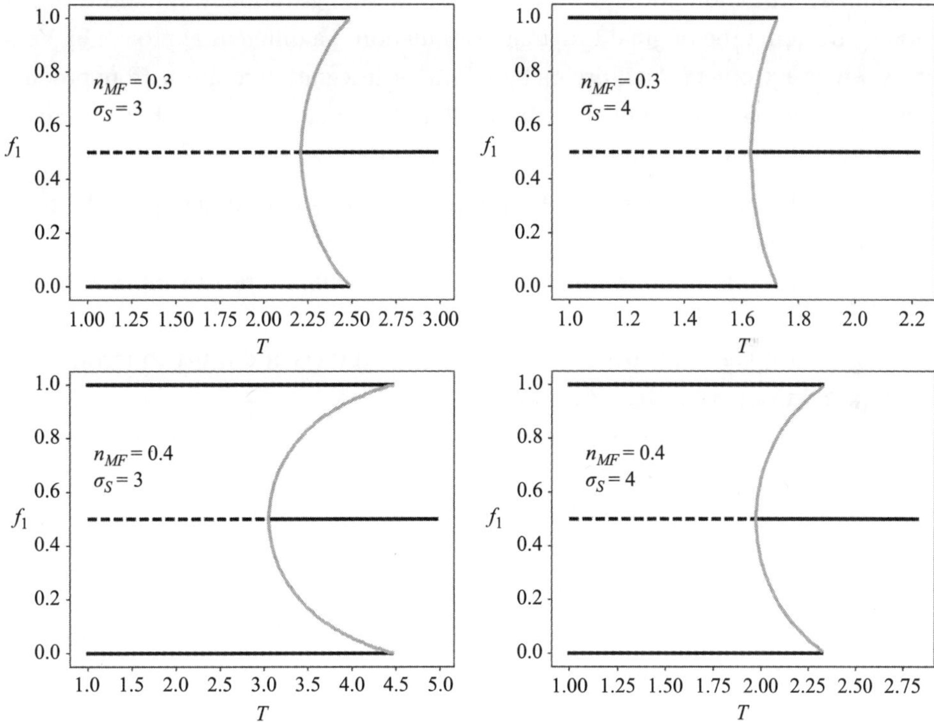

2.5 Tomahawk diagrams characterizing the solutions of the core-periphery model with two regions. Thick solid lines indicate stable solutions, and dashed lines show unstable points. We see across parameter space that for large transportation costs, agglomeration ceases and workers remain dispersed between the two regions. Below a parameter-dependent critical point, agglomeration emerges as the stable solution in one of the two regions. In between, there is a region where the dispersed state is metastable so agglomeration would only emerge as a result of a large perturbation of the population distribution. The location of the unstable bifurcation points is shown as the curved gray line. Note how a larger ratio of workers to farmers, n_{MF}, and greater monopoly, lower σ_S, promote agglomeration for a wider range of lower transport costs.

costs at which the thick black line intersects the $f_1 = \frac{1}{2}$ line can be calculated as $T^* = \left[\frac{\sigma_S(1 + n_{MF}) - 1}{\sigma_S(1 - n_{MF}) - 1} \frac{1 + n_{MF}}{1 - n_{MF}} \right]^{\frac{1}{\sigma_S - 1}}$, which implies the condition $\sigma_S > \frac{1}{1 - n_{MF}}$.

Discussion The core-periphery model is a big deal in economic geography because it demonstrates a point of principle: that the spatial agglomeration of industries (a proxy for a city) can form under general conditions when the advantages of socio-economic interaction can overcome dispersion because of transportation costs. The model, with variations and elaboration, became the basis for a field known as *new economic geography*.[14] Research in new economic geography developed a variety of themes related to spatial agglomeration at different scales, from industry and innovation clusters to cities and international trade.

As we have seen, the main appeal of the core-periphery model and its extensions is its generality and relative simplicity. This synthetic quality is inevitably a source of both strength and criticism. On the subject of strengths, many variations of the model, including the original Krugman formulation,[15] a different approach by Venables, where agglomeration is driven by economic integration resulting from production with intermediate inputs,[16] or by capital accumulation[17] and other variants,[18] come up with the same common emergent properties, specifically:[19]

- *Home-market effects*, where the disproportional location of industry results from demand change;
- *Circular causality*, whereby larger industries beget higher real incomes and vice versa;
- *Emerging asymmetries* between regions, in that workers and firms concentrate in one region versus another;
- *Discontinuous agglomeration*, where small changes in parameters result in sudden agglomeration in a single region;
- *Degenerate equilibria*, where which region ends up agglomerating depends on choices and history—this is connected to *path dependence*;
- *Hysteresis*, where dispersion can persist temporarily even as transportation costs fall below the critical point, and the same is true starting with agglomeration as transportation costs rise.

This means that the nature of the relationship between agglomeration and transportation costs discussed earlier holds in many different situations, implemented by a variety of models.

Nevertheless, many of the assumptions of most models of new economic geography are too simplistic if one wants to describe real problems of agglomerations and of cities. These issues have led to different kinds of criticism, some superficial in my opinion, others deeper. The main difficulties have to do with the unrealistic and homogeneous representation of space, time, and human preferences: *iceberg costs* in a discrete space of regions have very little to do with real geography or actual transportation.

Spatial equilibrium does not account for exponentially growing historic processes of human development and economic expansion over time, and homogeneous utility functions are not real "microfoundations" for human decision making. Other criticisms, having to do with the nature of monopolistic competition and the absence of forward-looking decisions in terms of migration, were addressed by later models.[20]

In my view, the shortcomings of new economic geography models go beyond these issues. The approach makes almost no predictions about the processes going on in cities or their gradual evolution. It also only makes mostly qualitative predictions out of quantitative modeling. It is also fair to note that model assumptions based on the properties of (nineteenth-century) manufacturing describe neither present-day cities—dominated by services—nor preindustrial urban centers (chapter 7), where nonexplicitly economic functions, such as defense and religion, were important. Thus, other factors creating forces for spatial concentration must be at work to explain cities of the past and present.

2.2   CLASSICAL MODELS OF THE CITY'S INTERNAL STRUCTURE

The models of section 2.1 gave us some formal ways of thinking about how cities may form as central markets. However, they do not tell us much about what happens inside cities. It turns out that the same logic can be used to develop models of how a city is put together by trading central markets for *goods* for markets for *labor*. Such models constitute the core of urban economics and are also foundational for other social sciences.

2.2.1   THE BURGESS MODEL OF CHICAGO

Von Thünen's isolated-state model for a central market immediately suggests a city in terms of its center as the main locus of economic exchange and its land dedicated to different economic and social activities, each with a different value. The first recognizable model expressing these ideas was not quantitative at all but ethnographic. It was proposed by Ernest W. Burgess to describe the growth of cities, the city of Chicago in particular (see figure 2.6).

In the 1920s, when *The City*[21]—the central document of the Chicago School of Sociology—was written, Chicago's population was growing very quickly, at about 2%–3% a year, following a couple of decades of sustained growth that was even faster. Data from the 1920 census shows that the US had just become an urban nation, crossing the watermark of 50% of its population living in cities in the preceding years (recall that the world population passed this mark in 2007 and China passed it in 2010, almost a century later than the US). Through observations of their city, both quantitative[22] and ethnographic, Burgess and his colleagues could glimpse patterns of mixing and spatial segregation that roughly depended on the socioeconomic status of various populations, some newer and more dynamic and others wealthier and more established. The pattern of concentric rings is clearly an idealization, but it carries

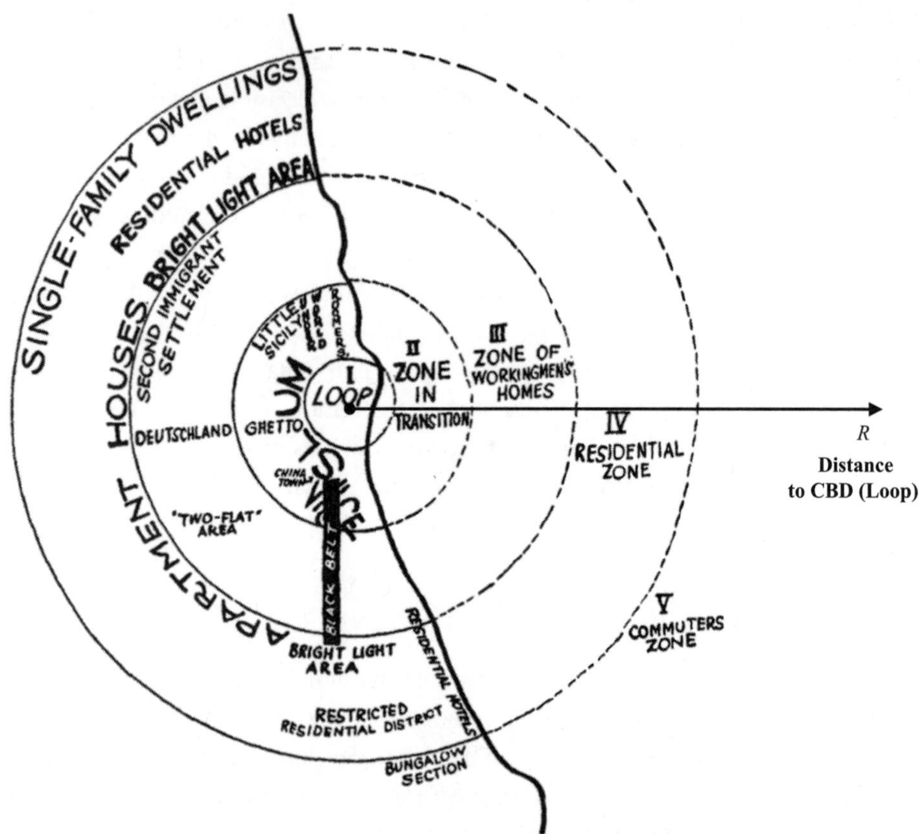

2.6 Burgess's conceptual map of the city of Chicago. The Chicago School of Sociology performed many studies of its city to try to understand processes of urban growth and spatial expansion. In a famous paper, part of Park, Burgess, and McKenzie's book *The City*, Burgess created a concentric ring model for Chicago as a function of distance to the central business district (known as *the Loop*). The focus is on a sociological identification of groups of people by their ethnic and economic status. For example, zone 2, next to the Loop, was characterized by the settlement of poor immigrants and described as a zone of transition and "disorder." Progressively richer residential areas went out from the Loop, so long as commuting was possible, defining the city in terms of socioeconomic ties made possible by transportation.
Source: Adapted by the author from the original illustration in Robert E. Park, Ernest W. Burgess, and Roderick Duncan McKenzie, *The City* (Chicago: University of Chicago Press, 1984).

forward von Thünen's essential ideas toward the problem of urban structure. The next step, which would take urban science almost another three decades, would require a more careful examination of the relation between land rents and transportation costs.

2.2.2 ALFRED MARSHALL: EXTERNAL ECONOMIES OF SPATIAL AGGLOMERATION

We now turn to some of the economic reasons why spatial agglomeration is typically advantageous. The classic framework is due to Alfred Marshall in his *Principles of*

Economics[23] (published in 1890), where he introduces the concept of *industrial districts* and proceeds to describe why firms and workers concentrate spatially. Marshall was one of the great economists of the late nineteenth century and lived and worked until the early decades of the twentieth century, strongly influencing the course of his field, partly in the form of what would later become known as the Cambridge school of economics.

Marshall's observations of industrial districts, specifically the locations where firms (nineteenth-century manufacturers in his case) colocated, required an explanation for their strong spatial concentration. Marshall identified three types of advantages that are *not* part of the direct functioning of economic markets. For this reason, they are referred to as *external economies*. External economies are, in this sense, serendipitous consequences of a set of economic exchange systems; they are part of life but not part of most economic models. Marshall singled out *specialization, better labor pooling*, and *information sharing* as the critical advantages of firm and labor spatial agglomeration. The first effect is a spatialized version of Adam Smith's famous dictum that "the division of labor is limited by the extent of the market."[24] We will return to some of these arguments in greater depth in chapter 5. If the extent of the market is set by transportation costs, then a spatially more concentrated population indeed provides a larger market and thus greater specialization. The second effect is perhaps the most intuitive; there is both a hedging advantage and positive selection for both workers and firms to exist together in space in order to find better matches between jobs and labor. The last point is best explained in Marshall's own famous words: "The mysteries of the trade become no mysteries; but *are as it were in the air*, and children learn many of them unconsciously" (my emphasis). It is not as simple as that, of course, since there is some intentionality to learning. But this is Marshall's shrewdest insight because it is about *information*, which we will see later (chapter 9) is the basis for economic growth and human development. In the modern literature, these *learning effects* facilitated by spatial proximity in cities are often called *information spillovers*.[25]

All three of these effects (and others) have been discussed and elaborated in the urban economics literature and are largely confirmed empirically via correlation studies as a general property of firm colocation.[26] The last of Marshall's propositions, on the importance of knowledge spillovers, has proven hard to measure and characterize,[27] because the effects of knowledge are qualitatively different from other quantities.

Marshall's observations are very important in characterizing the emergence and maintenance of spatial structure in economic production and consumption. They can, however, also be understood in a much larger context, as they connect to issues of diversity, division of labor, and knowledge, on the one hand, and information, innovation, and economic growth on the other. For these reasons, we will revisit these concepts throughout the book, but for now we will simply describe their general consequences for urban economics.

2.2.3 AGGLOMERATION DISECONOMIES AND POPULATION SIZE EQUILIBRIUM

If the advantages of the spatial concentration (in cities) of economic activity with group size were unlimited, then we should expect that the entire population would concentrate in a single giant and dense city. This is clearly wrong, so we also need to be able to account for disadvantages (*diseconomies*, in the language of economics) of agglomeration and search for the conditions where they may become dominant and arrest or reverse urban development.

This theme will also be developed throughout the book, but we start here with important work in the 1970s by Henderson, who tried to pose the problem of the city as an economy in light of these concepts. In chapter 7, we will return to the idea of diseconomies of scale through a concept from anthropology and organization theory known as *scalar stress*. Figure 2.7 shows a scheme for how external agglomeration economies and diseconomies may hypothetically pan out. The critical assumption here is in positing a common quantity that can account at once for the role of Marshall's effects, such as employment matching, specialization, and access to information—along with many other social and political advantages of cities—against many disadvantages, including congestion, high costs of living, crime, environmental challenges, and others. Henderson invokes the workhorse quantity in economic modeling: *utility.*

Henderson's assumption is that, in a city, utility is dependent on population size. Qualitatively, it works as follows. At first, when cities are small, one collects the benefits of living in a larger group that result from external agglomeration economies. But, as the group gets larger, diseconomies from population size set in and utility eventually starts to decrease (see figure 2.7). The result is a prediction for an *ideal city*

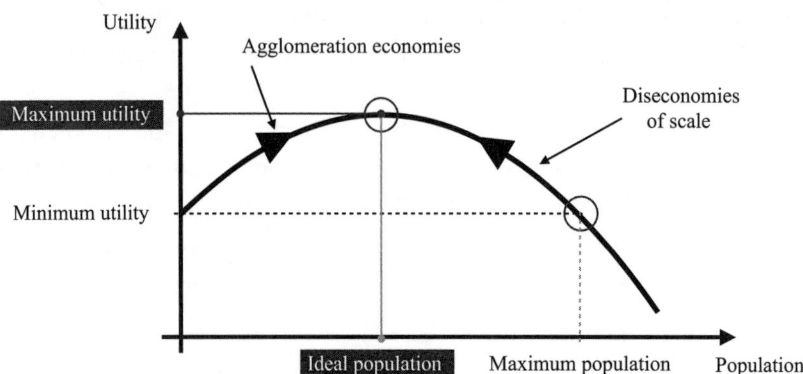

2.7 Possible utility variation scheme with city size as a result of external agglomeration economies and diseconomies. By assuming a concave curve for the utility, growing at first because of agglomeration economies and later declining for larger populations because of diseconomies, Henderson suggested a means for deriving an ideal population size for a city as well as the maximum size at which it can no longer be maintained.

population size, given a utility curve of this (assumed!) type. Presumably, people and firms would adjust their behavior by joining or leaving cities so that maximum utility can be achieved for those who stay, resulting in the city taking this scale.

It is immediately clear that this is a very artificial model of a city. In particular, cities occur over a continuum of population sizes from very small to megacities (chapter 8) and with diverse (not fully specialized) economic and social makeups (chapters 5 and 6). To deal with this issue, Henderson proposed that there should be different *types of cities* in terms of their dominant economic sector—at least in terms of exports.[28] The idea then is that different industries may have different external agglomeration economies, leading to different utility curves, as shown in figure 2.8. For example, a city dominated by the financial industry may be larger than a city dominated by textile manufacturing, possibly because finance creates less pollution. These ideas have been very inspiring to urban economists, who have discussed whether this picture can be true in light of firm location data. But cities are not generally so specialized, of course, so one argument is that the sectors that matter for city size are related to exports (to other cities and internationally). We will see in chapter 5 that there is a general logic to cities' economic diversity and specialization that is at once more complex and less specialized at the city level than proposed here.

The other issue is the assumed *different* population size dependencies of economies and diseconomies of agglomeration. While the picture here contains some grains of empirical truth, we must calculate the city size dependence of various costs and benefits of living in cities and compare them to empirical data. This will be done primarily in chapter 3, where we will show that in fact these two effects typically have the *same population size dependence*, allowing cities of many sizes to exist and thrive and changing the nature of the city as a spatial equilibrium away from what was proposed here.

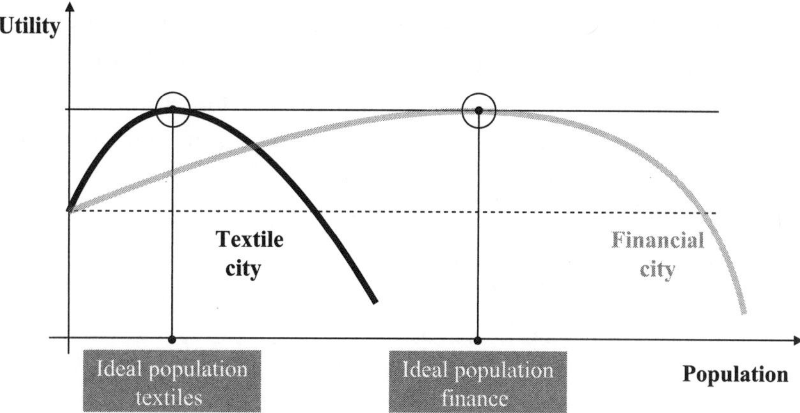

2.8 Henderson's scheme for variable urban agglomeration externalities for different dominant industries. Because, by assumption, the utility curve is different for cities dominated by different (export) industries, such cities would have different optimal population sizes. Note, however, that their relative maximum utility must be the same, so as not to attract all the population to the type of city with maximum utility.

In conclusion, we see that although utility curves for cities can provide schematic models of external agglomeration economies and diseconomies, much needs to be assumed if we are to make sense of why diverse cities provide alternative places to live and work and to determine their size. A deeper, more microscopic foundation for understanding, measuring, and calculating these effects is therefore necessary. We now take a different tack and try to understand, still based on economic modeling, under what conditions agglomeration economies create differentiated land uses within the city.

2.2.4 THE ALONSO MODEL

The next significant step in urban modeling and theory was taken by William Alonso, who adapted von Thünen's mathematics and Burgess's idea of socially and economically differentiated spaces to the general characteristics of modern cities. Alonso was born in Argentina and was a polymath in the social sciences: a leading scholar in demography, sociology, political science, *and* economics. Motivated by his diverse upbringing, living experiences, and interests, he wanted to understand why different cities show different spatial patterns of land rents. Specifically, why in US cities richer people tend to live away from the city center (as in Chicago's map; see figure 2.6), while in many European and South American cities the opposite is true.

Alonso's best-known work, *Location and Land Rents*,[29] was published in 1964 at a historic turning point in the study of cities and urban planning, coinciding with other transformative thinking by Lewis Mumford,[30] Jane Jacobs,[31] Christopher Alexander,[32] and others. Alonso contributed particularly to a synthesis of ideas and methods from the social sciences and geography to describe cities. His work was probably the first clear mathematical synthesis of economic principles over urban space. His setup became the basis for most subsequent urban economics models all the way up to today.

To develop a mathematical model for the city, Alonso dissociated land rents from agricultural production and focused on urban real estate. Like von Thünen and Burgess, he assumed for simplicity that the city is radially symmetric and that all work (and income generation) takes place at the central location, known as the *central business district* (CBD; see figure 2.9).

The critical assumption of the model is the so-called *budget condition*, equation (2.17). Each individual has a given budget, y, net of other living expenses, which they can allocate to pay for (real estate) rents, c_R, and transportation, c_T, both dependent on the distance from the CBD, R, as

$$y = c_R(R) + c_T(R). \tag{2.17}$$

It is often assumed that commuting costs are proportional to distance, so $c_T(R) = c_{T_0}R$. We can now solve for rents as a function of distance to the CBD as

$$c_R(R) = y - c_{T_0}R. \tag{2.18}$$

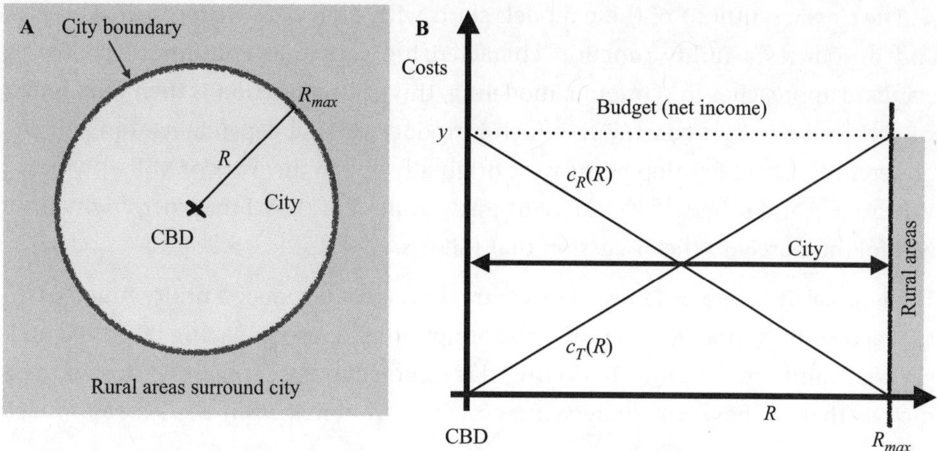

2.9 Alonso's model for land rents in the city. The model is a version of the von Thünen model for a central market, except now incomes accruing to each individual are the result of urban employment at the CBD (panel A). Each individual then apportions their budget net of other consumption, y, between land rents and transportation costs. The farther away from the CBD, the lower the former and the higher the latter. The edge of the city, $R = R_{max}$, is defined by equating $y = c_{R_r} + c_T(R_{max})$, where c_{R_r} are rent costs from agriculture (not urban).

Thus, rents are predicted to be highest, and commensurate with net incomes, next to the CBD and to go to zero (effectively become the same as agricultural land rents, c_{R_r}) at the edge of the city. This allows us to predict the spatial extent of the city as

$$R_{max} = \frac{(y - c_{R_r})}{c_{T_0}} \approx \frac{y}{c_{T_0}}, \tag{2.19}$$

since urban incomes, y, are generally much higher than agricultural land rent costs, c_{R_r}. Thus, richer (larger y) cities, with better transportation (lower c_{T_0}; i.e., lower cost of transportation per unit distance traveled), are predicted to be larger spatially, everything else being equal. This is an interesting prediction in that it says that with economic growth and technological improvements in transportation, cities are expected to be more spatially extended and presumably less dense, not the opposite as is sometimes hoped by city planners. We will revisit this issue later in light of more sophisticated models and data.

The Alonso model produces a *spatial equilibrium* for real estate rents and establishes the spatial size of the city given its incomes and transportation costs. Much work in geography and in regional and urban economics soon followed and elaborated on these ideas.

2.2.5   MODELS OF URBAN ECONOMICS

We now turn to models of urban economics specific to a single city that elaborate on the Alonso model of land rents. These models are able to make a number of predictions for the structure of cities, so we will also discuss how well they fare empirically.

The classic synthesis of these models starts with Alonso, as we have already seen, and introduces a utility function characterizing people as consumers. Following standard approaches in economic modeling, this utility function is then maximized subject to the budget constraint, which introduces spatial dependencies in people's preferences. These developments were originally due to the work of Mills,[33] Muth,[34] Wheaton,[35] and others.[36] A clear synthesis was produced by Brueckner,[37] which we will follow closely in the discussion that follows.

The Internal Structure of Cities   The central idea is to introduce a utility function, U, that accounts for preferences in the consumption of housing, having taken the budget constraint into account. To do this, it is assumed in the simplest version of these models that we have a radially symmetric city, as described in the Alonso model, with distance to the CBD, R.

Everyone works at the CBD and must commute there from their residence. As before, the cost of commuting per unit distance is c_{T_0}, so the total cost is (proportional to) $c_{T_0}R$. All "consumers" are assumed to have the *same* income, y, and identical "tastes," meaning the *same utility function*, written $U(c, a_f)$, where a_f is the floor area of housing used by our agent and c accounts for their consumption of everything else (goods and services). The standard assumption is that the utility function grows with both c and a_f, which means that people will try to get more stuff and to live in bigger houses. For simplicity, we measure prices in units of consumption—the aggregate price of c. In economic modeling, this reference price is called the *numeraire*. The critical ingredient is that the price of housing (land rents), $p_f(R)$, depends on the distance from the CBD. This means that the budget constraint can now be written as

$$y - c_{T_0}R = c + p_f(R)a_f. \tag{2.20}$$

The problem is solved by maximizing utility, using the constraint and assuming that, as a result, at every location in the city, consumers derive the *same* maximum utility, U_{max}. Mathematically, this means that we want to adjust the consumption of housing, a_f, so that we maximize the utility; that is,

$$\max_{a_f} U(y - c_{T_0}R - p_f\, a_f, a_f) \equiv U_{max}. \tag{2.21}$$

This can be achieved by taking derivatives of both arguments of the utility relative to each variable, which tells us what the land rent price (relative to the price of consumption) should be:

$$\frac{dU}{dc}\frac{dc}{da_f} + \frac{dU}{da_f} = 0 \;\rightarrow\; p_f^* = \frac{dU/da_f}{dU/dc}. \tag{2.22}$$

This is the usual expression for prices as marginal (derivatives of) utilities. The solution is evaluated with this price set at the optimal $a_f = a_f^*$ to give

$$U(y - c_{T_0}\, R - p_f^*\, a_f^*, a_f^*) = U_{max}. \tag{2.23}$$

This solution relates the given net income for someone living at a distance, R, from the CBD, $y - c_{T_0} R$, to their amount of housing consumption, a_f^*, such that their utility is maximized.

From the assumed general analytical properties of the utility functions, a number of expectations arise. First, by taking a total derivative of equation (2.23) with relation to distance, we obtain the behavior of land prices,

$$\frac{dU}{dc}\left(-c_{T_0} - \frac{dp_f^*}{dR}a_f^* - p_f^*\frac{da_f^*}{dR}\right) + \frac{dU}{da_f^*}\frac{da_f^*}{dR} = 0, \tag{2.24}$$

which, introducing the expression for p_f^*, leads to

$$a_f^*\frac{dp_f^*}{dR} = -c_{T_0} \;\rightarrow\; \frac{dp_f^*}{dR} = -\frac{c_{T_0}}{a_f^*} < 0. \tag{2.25}$$

Thus, we conclude that housing prices per unit area, p_f^*, decrease monotonically from the CBD to the city's periphery. In the following equations, we simplify the notation and do not explicitly signal that variables are evaluated at the utility maxima (by dropping the asterisks).

We can also compute the amount of space used per person, because

$$\frac{da_f}{dR} = \frac{da_f}{dp_f}\frac{dp_f}{dR} > 0. \tag{2.26}$$

The sign follows from the assumed concave shape of the utility function (utility increases more slowly than proportionally with greater consumption), which leads to the typical consequence that $\frac{da_f}{dp_f} < 0$, meaning that people use less floor space when prices are higher (remember that everyone has the same fixed income). Taking these two results at face value means that, going from the CBD to the suburbs, people pay less per area of housing and consume proportionally more—big houses in the suburbs, small apartments close to the CBD—which is often a reasonable description.

We can proceed in the same way to see how floor area and its price change with the other parameters in the budget constraint. Taking derivatives as before, we get

$$\frac{dp_f}{dy} = \frac{1}{a_f} > 0, \quad \frac{dp_f}{dc_{T_0}} = -\frac{R}{a_f} < 0, \quad \frac{dU}{dp_f} = -a_f\frac{dU}{dc} < 0, \tag{2.27}$$

$$\frac{da_f}{dy} = \frac{da_f}{dp_f}\frac{1}{a_f} < 0, \quad \frac{da_f}{dc_{T_0}} = -\frac{da_f}{dp_f}\frac{R}{a_f} > 0, \quad \frac{dU}{da_f} = -a_f\frac{dU}{dc}\frac{dp_f}{da_f} > 0, \tag{2.28}$$

where, to obtain the signs, we relied on the assumptions that utility increases with consumption, $\frac{dU}{dc} > 0$, and that the utility is concave, $\frac{da_f}{dp_f} < 0$. These results say simply that utility increases with bigger dwellings and decreases with larger rents per area, given fixed incomes. They also say that rents increase with incomes and decrease with higher transportation costs. This last effect is a consequence of a fixed budget: if you have to spend more on transportation, you will have less to spend on housing. The amount of floor space one consumes varies in the opposite direction to its price. Consequently, it decreases with higher income citywide and increases with transportation costs. These conclusions may seem counterintuitive and even counterfactual. They are simply the consequence of the assumption in the model that one has a fixed budget and that housing prices are higher because of higher incomes for everybody, so one needs to consume less area in response. The effect of transportation costs is similar, since paying for higher transportation expenditures leaves the price of housing lower so one can afford more, which is assumed to provide greater utility.

Economic models almost always rely on a market equilibrium between *consumers* and *producers*. We have so far only considered the consumers' point of view. Let us now turn to the perspective of producers of housing (land developers). To derive their behavior, analogous with the utility function for consumers, we need to specify a *production function*. This is written by Brueckner[38] as $A_H (a_l, K_P)$, where the inputs are land (area), a_l, and capital, K_P. The subject of production measured by $A_H (a_l, K_P)$ is the habitable area of floor space in a building, given the two inputs in the argument: a land parcel and resources invested. This function is assumed to be concave in the sense that $\frac{d^2 A_H}{dK_P^2} < 0$, which means that there are decreasing returns in building usable floor space relative to capital invested. For example, as buildings get taller, because of structural challenges and the cost of equipment such as elevators, costs eventually rise quickly, increasing the cost per unit of area added.

The reasoning follows from computing the profit (net income) for the developer of the building after they pay for land and the costs of capital invested. Let a_l be land and p_l its cost per unit area (rent), and similarly let capital be K_P and p_k its price (cost due to interest charged). Recall that housing produced is rented to consumers, so the developer's profit is $p_f A_H - a_l p_l - K_P p_k$. It is typical to work with intensive variables, so we factor out the amount of land involved and write this expression as $a_l(p_f a_H(K_{P_l}) - p_l - K_{P_l} p_k)$, where $a_H(K_{P_l}) = \dfrac{A_H(a_l, K_{P_l})}{a_l}$ and $K_{P_l} = \dfrac{K_P}{a_l}$. The quantity $a_H(K_{P_l})$ is the building density (the amount of usable floor space built per unit of land), while K_{P_l} is the capital spatial density (the amount of capital per unit of land). It was *assumed* that the building density is only a function of the capital density; in particular, that it is a growing concave function of this variable. The building density can be more intuitively expressed as building height, since it represents the amount of housing floor area produced in each area of land.

We require one last assumption: that there is perfect competition, so the maximum profit (net income) is actually zero! With these assumptions, we can now compute the consequences for the behavior of a_H and K_{P_l} analogous with the rent paid by consumers and the amount of floor space used. The price of capital, p_k, is assumed given; for example, in terms of a loan's interest rate. The conditions of maximum and zero profit translate into

$$K_{P_l} = \frac{p_f}{p_k} a_H - \frac{p_l}{p_k}, \quad \frac{da_H}{dK_{P_l}} = \frac{p_k}{p_f}, \tag{2.29}$$

which generally gives the optimal amounts of capital invested and rents per unit area charged. These variables will in turn depend on income, transportation costs, distance from the CBD, and level of consumer utility. To evaluate those dependencies, we can take derivatives of (2.29) and use the zero-profit condition to obtain

$$\frac{dp_l}{d\phi_e} = a_H \frac{dp_f}{d\phi_e}, \quad \frac{dK_{P_l}}{d\phi_e} = -\frac{\dfrac{da_H}{dK_{P_l}}}{\dfrac{d^2 a_H}{dK_{Pl}^2}} \frac{1}{p_f} \frac{dp_f}{d\phi_e}, \tag{2.30}$$

$$\frac{da_H}{d\phi_e} = \frac{da_H}{dK_{P_l}} \frac{dK_{P_l}}{d\phi_e} = \frac{p_k}{p_f} \frac{dK_{P_l}}{d\phi_e}, \quad \phi_e = y, c_{T_0}, R, U.$$

Because $\dfrac{d^2 a_H}{dK_{P_l}^2} < 0$, the variations in both land prices and capital density increase in the same direction as rent prices per floor area paid by consumers. This should not be a shock but shows consistency.

Finally, we can evaluate the population density, $n_A = \dfrac{N}{A} \sim \dfrac{a_H}{a_f}$, as the habitable built area divided by the floor space consumed per individual. We can also take derivatives relative to our variables of interest to get

$$\frac{dn_A}{d\phi_e} = \frac{1}{a_f} \frac{da_H}{dK_{P_l}} \frac{dK_{P_l}}{d\phi_e} - \frac{a_H}{a_f^2} \frac{da_f}{d\phi_e} = \left[-\frac{1}{a_f\, p_f} \frac{\left(\dfrac{da_H}{dK_{P_l}}\right)^2}{\dfrac{d^2 a_H}{dK_{P_l}^2}} - \frac{a_H}{a_f^2} \frac{da_f}{dp_f} \right] \frac{dp_f}{d\phi_e} \sim \frac{dp_f}{d\phi_e}. \tag{2.31}$$

This shows that the variation of the spatial population density with our parameters has the same sign as the variations in consumer rents. So, for example, as consumer rents decrease with distance to the CBD, so does density, or as rents increase with incomes, so do densities! This latter prediction may feel counterintuitive, but again it is just the result of everyone's identical income and of a fixed budget constraint: as prices per square foot go up, everyone consumes less, resulting in higher densities.

Global Constraints and Population Size We can now reflect on the results so far and extract their global consequences for the properties of cities. This brings us back to considering what happens at the spatial edge of the city and introduces population size more explicitly.

As we have seen, beyond the spatial edge of the city, defined by $R = R_{max}$, we expect to encounter nonurban land uses, which produce value (land rents) denoted by p_{l_r}. This land is dedicated to housing not for commuters but rather for other (rural, or nonurban) uses. Thus, at the edge of the city, we have the boundary condition

$$p_l(R_{max}, y, c_{T_0}, U) = p_{l_r}. \tag{2.32}$$

Because we expect land rents to decrease monotonically with distance from their highest values at the CBD, this implicitly defines the spatial scale of the city, $R_{max}(y, c_{T_0}, U, p_{l_r})$ (see appendix B).

The second global constraint deals with summing up the population in every building and land parcel up to its given total in the city, N. Because we assumed that the city is radial and monocentric, there are $R dR\, n_A(R)$ people per unit length of radius, dR. We can perform the integral over the disk that constitutes the total area of the city to obtain

$$N = 2\pi \int_0^{R_{max}} R\, dR\, n_A(R) = 2\pi \int_0^{R_{max}} R\, dR \frac{a_H(R)}{a_f}. \tag{2.33}$$

Migration and City-Size Relationships   The last two relationships introduce two measures of city size: total area, $A = \pi R_{max}^2$, and population, N. Having looked at their internal structure, we can now ask how properties of the city depend on these measures of size. These questions preview the urban scaling analysis in chapter 3.

These relationships depend on one last factor, which is a characteristic of the urban system as a set of cities: whether the city is *open* or *closed* to migration. The latter case is typically artificial, though it may apply to certain city-states. Opening the city to migration means that we must consider the relative attraction of various places within an urban system, defined as a set of cities between which people (as well as goods and capital) can move freely. (We will consider the structure of urban systems in chapter 8.) To proceed with the analysis in this section, we will need to assume that the urban system in the open city case is in *equilibrium*, meaning that all cities share the same level of utility and therefore are equally attractive to migrants. Urban systems in this sort of steady state express certain "laws of geography," which we will derive later in this book.

Closed city In the case where migration is not allowed, we take the total population N to be given and compute the residents' utility along with other variables. Then, the exogenous parameters to the model are N, p_{l_r}, y, and c_{T_0}. Our task is to calculate the effects of these putative external parameters on the spatial size of the city R, housing prices p_f, land rents p_l, dwelling sizes a_f, and building heights, proxied by capital investment spatial density, Kp_l. Through these quantities, we can also derive how the area of the city changes with population.

One can work out these relationships by taking various derivatives and using the earlier results to find[39] (see appendix B)

$$\frac{dA}{dN} > 0, \ \frac{dU}{dN} < 0, \ \frac{dp_f}{dN} > 0, \ \frac{da_f}{dN} < 0, \ \frac{dp_l}{dN} > 0, \ \frac{dK_{Pl}}{dN} > 0, \ \frac{dn_A}{dN} > 0. \tag{2.34}$$

This means that city size gets to be larger spatially as it gets larger in population. All other quantities are local in the city: utility and area of housing decrease with population, while housing costs, price of land, capital density, and population density all increase. Note that important variables, such as income, are assumed to be exogenous, so there are no increasing returns in incomes from population size, for example, nor are there scale efficiencies in transportation.

For spatial area, and the city radius in particular, we obtain

$$\frac{dR_{max}}{dN} = \frac{a_f}{c_{T_0} a_H} \left(\frac{dp_l}{dU} \frac{dU}{dN} \right)\Bigg|_{R=R_{max}} = -\frac{1}{\pi \frac{dU}{dc} \int_0^{R_{max}} dR \frac{dp_l}{dU}} > 0.$$

(2.35)

We see that the variation of the city radius—while keeping other exogenous variables fixed—depends on the changes in the utility function chosen. For other exogenous parameters, we obtain

$$\frac{dR_{max}}{dp_{l_r}} < 0, \quad \frac{dR_{max}}{dy} > 0, \quad \frac{dR_{max}}{dc_{T_0}} < 0,$$

(2.36)

which are all intuitive, since the city will be spatially smaller if it can afford less land because it is more expensive or because transportation is. When incomes are higher, more land can be afforded and the city can sprawl.

Open city When the city is open and migration between places is allowed, we require that the *utility of residents in all cities becomes the same*. This means that the utility becomes a fixed number for all cities, set by urban system dynamics, while the city's population is now a variable. This means that the exogenous parameters are now $\phi_e = U, p_{l_r}, y$, and c_{T_0}. This calculation is a particular case of that for the closed city when the utility is fixed and leads to (see appendix B)

$$\frac{dR}{d\phi_e}\Bigg|_{R=R_{max}} = \frac{\frac{dp_{l_r}}{d\phi_e} - \frac{dp_l}{d\phi_e}}{\frac{dp_l}{dR}} = -\frac{a_f}{c_{T_0} a_H} \left(\frac{dp_{l_r}}{d\phi_e} - \frac{dp_l}{d\phi_e} \right)\Bigg|_{R=R_{max}}.$$

(2.37)

Thus,

$$\frac{dR_{max}}{dp_{l_r}} = -\frac{a_f}{c_{T_0} a_H} < 0, \quad \frac{dR_{max}}{dN} = \frac{a_f}{c_{T_0} a_H} \frac{dp_l}{dN} = 0,$$

$$\frac{dR_{max}}{dy} = \frac{a_f}{c_{T_0} a_H} \frac{dp_l}{dy} = \frac{1}{c_{T_0}} > 0, \quad \frac{dR_{max}}{dc_{T_0}} = \frac{a_f}{c_{T_0} a_H} \frac{dp_l}{dc_{T_0}} = -\frac{R}{c_{T_0}} < 0,$$

(2.38)

where all expressions are evaluated at the city boundary, $R \to R_{max}$. These equations can actually be integrated to give

$$R_{max} = \frac{\left(y - \frac{p_{l_r} a_f}{a_H} \right)}{c_{T_0}} \simeq y/c_{T_0}.$$

(2.39)

Though we had to work much harder, this is just the same as equation (2.19) obtained in a much more straightforward way from the Alonso model, except that we now account more explicitly for the price of housing at the city boundary. This is because $\left.\dfrac{a_f}{a_H}\right|_{R=R_{max}} = \dfrac{1}{n_A(R_{max})}$, so the second term in the brackets is the cost of housing per person at $R=R_{max}$. The last approximate equality applies when housing costs at the city's boundary are very cheap compared to urban incomes and commuting costs are correspondingly high, as may happen in large, sprawling urban areas.

The independence of the spatial size of the city on population, $\dfrac{dR_{max}}{dN}=0$, may come as a surprise. This is the result of the fact that, in this type of model, direct variations are mediated through the inhabitant's utility, as we have seen in the closed city case, where people had no chance to leave. Once the city is open, the model's would-be negative variation of utility with population size leads to population size regulation. Thus, covariations of population and the physical size of cities in the open city case *can only co-occur indirectly*, if other variables treated here as exogenous are also changing.

For example, the increase in the maximum radius, R_{max}, with larger incomes, y, is also accompanied by increases in housing costs per unit area, p_f, land prices, p_l, and building heights, $h_b \sim K_{P_l}$, leading to larger population densities everywhere. Larger population density in a spatially larger city results in a larger population, N, by equation (2.33). Thus, there can be linkages between a larger city—spatially and demographically—in this model, but the effect is indirect, mediated via other exogenous variables, such as income. Clearly, transportation costs have a similar effect, but in the opposite direction. This means that *decreasing* transportation costs also leads to a larger city, both spatially and demographically.

Finally, we note that without specifying the consumer utility and housing production functions, the best we can do is predict the *sign* of correlations between observed variables in data. However, observing specific relationships empirically would constrain the utility function and possibly also indicate that the theory is incomplete or wrong; for example, in that some of the assumed exogenous variables—such as incomes and transportation costs—should actually be endogenous. We will address these issues motivated by data in chapter 3.

Discussion: Tests and Generalizations of Urban Economics Models The greatest strength of the urban economics approach to modeling cities is that it makes a number of quantitative predictions. These are typically testable empirically only in the weak sense of qualitative agreement with the various dependencies of observable quantities on various state variables (the derivative signs). This means that one can perform econometric tests on data and assess whether key variables are positively or negatively correlated at some level of statistical significance.

However, these are not generally strong quantitative predictions about specific numbers, such as the magnitude of derivatives. There have been many comparisons with empirical evidence of this type, but I will single out recent work by Angel and his collaborators,[40] who created the *Atlas of Urban Expansion*,[41] mapping and tracking all large cities worldwide (those having more than 100,000 people, of which there are presently about 4,000).

Because the main strength of their dataset is the spatial extent of cities, they tested most often the expectations of equations (2.34) and (2.36). To test these hypotheses, they aggregated variables at the national level (e.g., total urban land cover in a nation) and correlated them with carefully chosen proxies, such as amount of arable land, to judge possible (inverse) land prices.[42] They indeed find general qualitative agreement for the increase in land area of cities with population and with rising incomes, and some evidence for its negative covariation with transportation costs (measured as the cost of gasoline) and more valuable agricultural rents. They also found that cities had a smaller area if they had a higher share of their population estimated to live in informal settlements. This empirical finding stands in contrast to expectations from extensions of the model discussed here for situations where high and low incomes are present and the assumption that inequality diminishes competition for the same land.[43]

But Angel et al.[44] tested not only general qualitative expectations but also the quantitative form for the average functional relationship between these variables. They found a number of strong empirical regularities; for example, for the elasticity of population density with city population size. We will return to their findings and derive these specific numbers at the end of chapter 3.

The models described in this section are only a gateway into the world of urban economics, which elaborates and extends them to include different socioeconomic groups, firms, housing types, and many other effects.[45]

One particular issue, which was on Alonso's mind, that we have not yet resolved is why the centers of many cities are actually occupied by poorer populations (in US cities and perhaps also Indian cities), while in other cases we observe the opposite pattern (in most European and East Asian cities). To resolve this conundrum, one clearly has to introduce different income groups and specify whether they compete or become segregated relative to the same urban land (see chapter 6). But this is not enough; one needs to align the preferences of different income groups with specific parts of the city, central or peripheral. One way to do this is to posit a given spatial distribution of desirable amenities. These can then become the anchors for where the population with the highest bidding power (highest income) will choose to be. Brueckner, Thisse, and Zenou[46] proposed just such a model, based on the idea that space-bound amenities create peaks of utility in specific places, especially near city centers. Maximizing consumer utility then leads to the sorting of population by income, either attracted by, repelled by, or outbidden for these spatial amenities. Of course, this only shifts the nature of the problem to the specification of spatial distribution of amenities and preferences, but that question may suggest a closer relationship to measurement and policy.

The Many Uses of Urban Economics Models and Their Policy Implications   Modeling cities through the lens of urban economics is a very versatile general approach. Economists have applied their framework to almost any issue (of cities) you can think of, including housing, transportation and congestion, industrial and professional composition and location, urban services, government expenditures and taxes, crime, pollution, quality of life, amenities, and more. Several excellent books provide an introduction to these themes and present an overview of relevant literature.[47]

Whether one is happy or unhappy with the framework of urban economics, including its assumptions and modeling devices, remains at present a bit in the eye of the beholder. Even though these models are mathematically precise, they suffer from the fact that their basic quantities—especially utility and production functions—are highly stylized and not easily observable, implying that resulting predictions are essentially qualitative, involving the sign of correlations between variables but not typically strong universal forms of quantitative behavior. While we will carry the concept of cost-benefit analysis (the budget constraint) along with us throughout this book, we will also show that other assumptions, such as utility and production functions and the emphasis on maximization based on consumption or profits, are not fundamental or even necessary for theory development in urban science. On the other hand, endogenizing incomes and transportation costs will be critical.

Arguably, the biggest problem with urban economics is its widespread use for deriving public policy outside its realm of plausible assumptions. It often results in prescriptions that are disturbing and that may lead to downright harmful social consequences. Critical thinking from a broader interdisciplinary perspective is essential in such cases.

As an illustration, consider a well-known approach to modeling crime,[48] originally due to Nobel laureate Gary Becker, who became famous for his use of economic thinking to address social issues. The model assumes a heterogeneous city population of size N, ranked by a given income structure (see figure 2.10). Crime is conceptualized as an occupational choice, *crime pays* (horizontal lines), where there is an assumed stable income associated with criminal behavior. It follows that when criminal incomes are higher than the lowest "legitimate" income in the population, a life of crime should be adopted on economic grounds. Specifically, the fraction of the population with "legitimate" incomes below that afforded by crime should "rationally" opt for becoming criminals.

From the point of view of the city, there is a cost-benefit relation characterizing law enforcement, which can be analyzed given a response curve between crime reduction and its economic costs. Because total crime eradication is typically too costly, the result is the calculation of a "socially optimal" level of crime. A similar line of reasoning may be applied to other social challenges, such as life expectancy, sanitation, or homelessness. Try explaining this line of thinking to your friends and colleagues, and I am sure you will find some who will be horrified, while others may think that it is just the way to go! How do we decide? Can we test this kind of model scientifically? Can we improve on it? When should we be satisfied with it, and when should we reject it altogether?

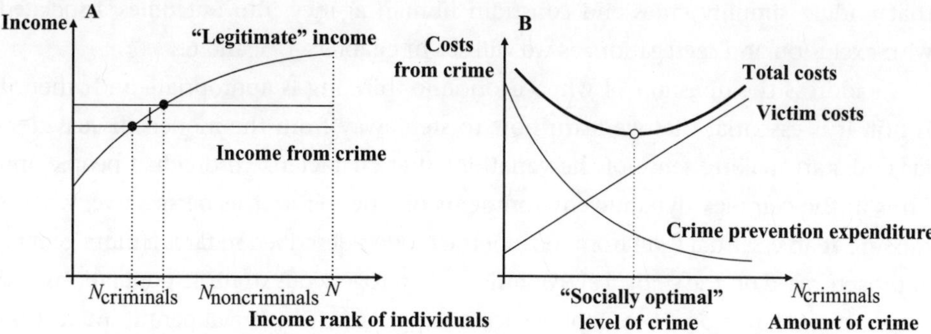

2.10 A simple economic model for crime in cities. (A) Crime is conceptualized as an occupational decision related to income alternatives. In a city with a range of ranked incomes (convex curve), some individuals have low incomes in their "legitimate" occupations. If crime generates an income larger than the smallest "legitimate" income (horizontal line), then all individuals with incomes below this threshold should rationally become criminals, leading to $N_{criminals}$. As the relative income level for criminals drops (two horizontal lines), for example because of law enforcement, so does the fraction of criminals in the population. If the city gets richer and criminals rob the rich, in this scheme it is possible to have a positive association between increasing crime and wealth. (B) A "socially optimal" level of crime can be computed by equating the total cost of fighting crime with its benefits, according to some given response curve.

Thinking about crime in this way exposes some of the failures of the framework of urban economics for not embracing the concept of "organized complexity." No one should argue against the fact that not all low-income individuals are criminals! If you accept that, you may be led to conclude that noncriminal poor people are irrational. . . . But this contradicts the propositions of the model, so something is broken.

Crime is a complex, historically and socially contingent phenomenon. It is well known to be statistically associated with gender (males) and age (younger people) and to be very different in distinct societies with a different history of violence, trust, and institutional capacity. Criminologists and sociologists would argue vigorously against crime being an individual rational decision based on an economic trade-off. They would propose instead that it is primarily a *human ecological* effect, resulting from a complex life-course accumulation of opportunities, accidents, and choices for adaptive individuals in complex environments. In my view, the strong spatial concentration of crime in any city, as well as its strong temporal predictability, support such a contention.

This does not mean that crime is unpredictable in a statistical sense, but these two frameworks have completely different implications in terms of causal mechanisms and associated recommendations for public policies (chapter 6). The central challenge is whether the ahistorical and socially homogeneous economic choices posited by economic models are the causal drivers of human decisions in cities. The even more consequential question, from a practical perspective, is whether such a line of reasoning should drive public policy at all. Conceptualizations of housing policy, public health, crime and conflict, education, and other social *wicked problems* on a homogeneous individual economic basis may indeed box individual choice into harmful situations that unduly simplify cities and constrain human agency into outcomes associated with exclusion and segregation, as we will see in chapters 4, 5, and 6.

To address the question of when economic thinking is appropriate and when it is not, it is essential that we learn how to step away from the models discussed so far and start making sense of the variations that characterize individual people and firms in the complex dynamic environments of cities. From this perspective, what is missing at an essential level from most of the models described so far is a more general approach based on the statistical dynamics of heterogeneous strategic populations and their social interactions. Developing such an approach, which will permit interaction with many other disciplines, is the objective of the rest of this book.

2.3 TIME, DISTANCE, AND THE DEFINITION OF FUNCTIONAL CITIES

Time has a critical importance when it comes to fitting people and things together for functioning in socio-economic systems, whether these undergo long-term changes, or rest in something which could be defined as a steady state.
—Torsten Hägerstrand, "What about People in Regional Science?"

To conclude this chapter, we now emphasize the importance of *time*. We saw already in the context of the von Thünen and Alonso models and their elaborations that time is tightly associated with space through transportation costs. However, we did not really deal with time as a primary factor. Instead, we worked with variables that were only implicitly defined as temporal and with population averages through the concept of spatial equilibrium. It is therefore important to start to zoom in to learn how to unpack questions of detailed individual behavior and derive implications for how we define cities in empirical studies of their properties and dynamics.

2.3.1 TIME GEOGRAPHY
Economic geography emphasizes space and associated transportation costs in shaping cities as spatial equilibria.[49] Most of the arguments involve homogeneous agents and choices, which is roughly equivalent to considering only population averages.

Another tradition, called *time geography*, emphasizes time.[50] Embracing time means that we must follow individuals as they develop their trajectories in space-time in the city. These trajectories are what Torsten Hägerstrand described as *life paths* (see figure 2.11 for an illustration). I also like Alan Pred's take on these ideas as summarizing a "choreography of existence," echoing Jane Jacobs's own observations of the urban life of individuals and neighborhoods.[51]

There are two main points[52] of novelty emphasized by time geography in relation to the remaining approaches in this chapter. The first is that it establishes the primacy of "microscopic" individual behavior as the starting point. Each person has their own *life path*, and any aggregate results will follow from the interactions of these diverse structures into social organizations over space and time.

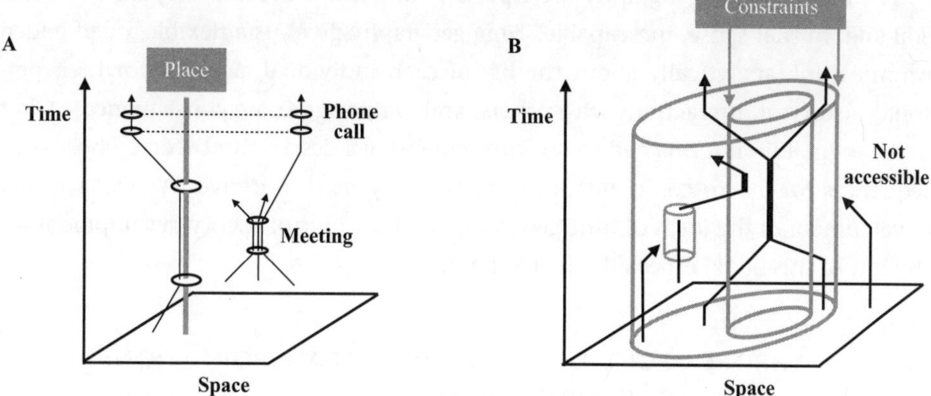

2.11 Principles of time geography. Individuals are represented in space-time diagrams (two-dimensional space on the plane and time on the vertical axis) as *life paths*. These are continuous lines flowing on the plane and simultaneously from bottom to top. When individuals coincide with fixed objects (solid bold line in panel A), such as staying at their home or place of work for a while, their life path temporarily flows vertically. As individuals meet in space, they form temporary bundles. They can also have contact at a distance, via a phone call or the internet, indicated by dashed lines. Panel B shows life paths that are constrained and bounded by tubes that express domains of interactions tied to institutions, such as firms or universities, at particular spaces and times. Such institutions may be arranged hierarchically and structure both opportunities and exclusions, thus shaping life paths of individuals differently.
Source: Adapted by the author from Torsten Hägerstrand, "What about People in Regional Science?," *Papers of the Regional Science Association* 24, no. 1 (December 1970): 6–21, https://doi.org/10.1007/BF01936872.

Second, the structure of life paths is *constrained* in a number of different ways that are brought into the theory explicitly.[53] This is what Hägerstrand means by the role of time in "fitting people and things together." Space-time diagrams identify physical constraints as limitations of transportation and mobility. One can only go so far given a technology and cost of movement. This is related to the steepness of life paths in time versus space. Such slopes can be changed by technology, expanding the amount of space that can be covered in the same time, for example. These *capability constraints* are expressed as a causal diagram, similar to the trajectories of particles in physics, and form a *prism* (a spatial extent over a certain time: a space-time volume) that is the maximum space available to the agent.

Then, there are also *coupling constraints*, which refer to obstacles to realizing social and economic interactions, including access to means of production if the interaction is economic. Finally, there are *authority constraints*, mediated by institutions, including firms, universities, and others, where specific interactions between people must occur at specific fixed spaces and times. Institutions have purposeful spaces (buildings and rooms) as well as times (schedules) in order to promote collective social behavior, and these combine to regulate and coordinate the life paths of individuals. These institutions may have the power to include or exclude people in their functions, thereby shaping life paths over the longer term.

The ideas of time geography are especially important because they are very general and, in that sense, inescapable. Time geography gives us a flexible, open-ended way to think analytically about the life of each individual, account for their personal history of interactions with others, and derive aggregate consequences.[54] Part of its original limitations had to do with remaining a descriptive theory, whose consequences for macroscopic outcomes are typically hard to derive. We will see that development of the ideas of time geography is at the core of theory development for the rest of this book, especially in chapter 3.

2.3.2 ANTHROPOLOGICAL INVARIANTS IN TRANSPORTATION: SPACE AND TIME INTERTWINED

Another tradition concerned with modeling cities in space and time deals with travel behavior in cities, or urban *mobility*. Transportation studies have been arguably the most empirically rich parts of urban planning.[55] The analysis of data on travel behavior has therefore generated a number of insights and empirical regularities. The most famous is a set of empirical results pointing to an approximately universal maximum amount of travel time people are willing to commute to work. This has been most clearly expressed by Zahavi,[56] in terms of a constant "travel-time budget" (see figure 2.12), but has become known in some of the literature as *Marchetti's constant* because of Marchetti's contention of the generality of the phenomenon[57]

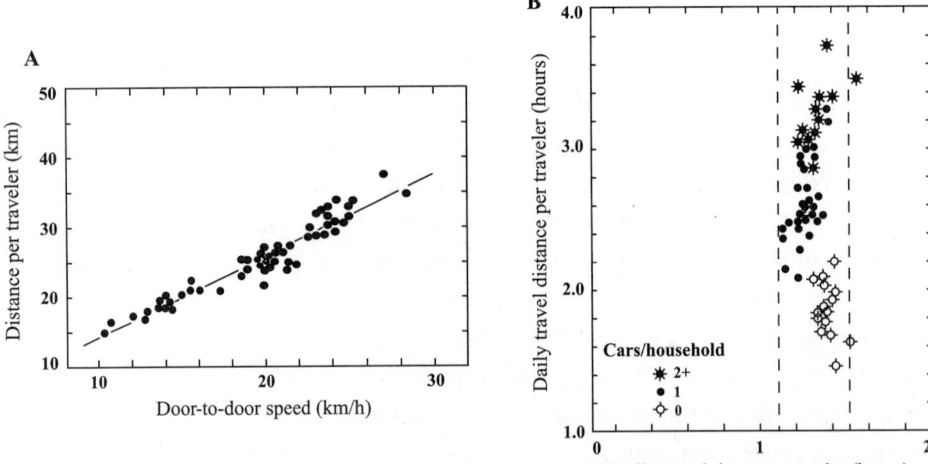

2.12 Concept of the constant travel-time budget. (A) Data show that passengers who travel longer distances also travel at faster average speeds, so travel time is approximately constant (slope). (B) Daily travel time per traveler is approximately constant, at a little over one hour per day, even as faster transportation modes (cars) are used and longer distances can be covered.
Source: Adapted by the author from Y. Zahavi, M. J. Beckmann, and T. F. Golob, *The "UMOT"/Urban Interactions* (Washington, DC: U.S. Department of Transportation, Research and Special Programs Administration, Systems Analysis Division, 1981), https://trid.trb.org/view/206233.

(figure 2.13). These authors arrived at this conclusion by studying data on travel behavior across different modes, finding that as speed increases so does distance, but that total time is much more conserved.

In practice, this means that time is much more important than spatial distance when considering the *transportation costs* that shape cities. The approximate constancy of travel time has important consequences for transportation technologies and associated energy consumption and for infrastructure investments. From the point of view of investments—for example, in new roads and highways—greater and faster access will tend to lead to the phenomenon of *induced travel demand*, since people can travel longer distances over the same time. This may in turn also lead to *induced congestion*, where infrastructure investments to improve traffic flows—and reduce travel times—end up generating new choke points that regulate that time. Finally, if one can travel longer distances on the same time budget, say by using a

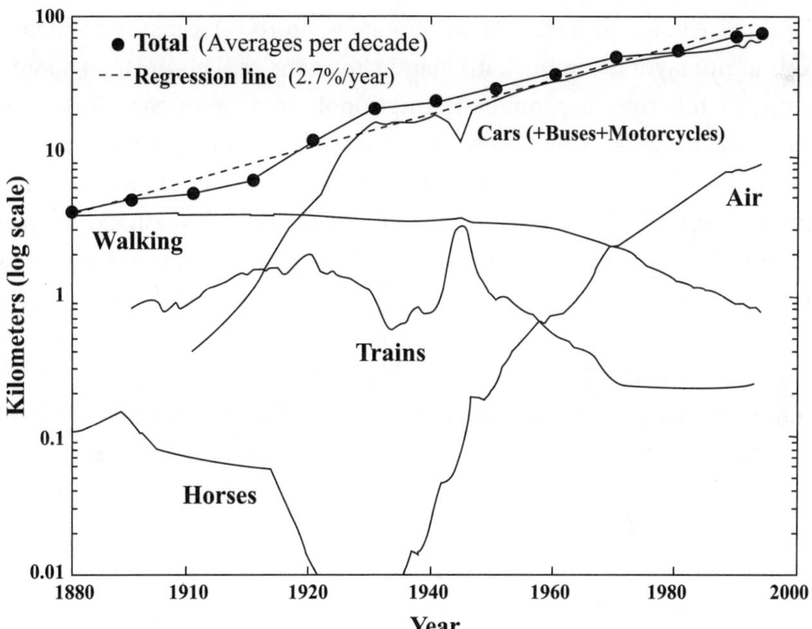

2.13 Marchetti's constant. US passenger distance traveled per capita and per day. The approximately straight line shows an exponential increase (2.7% a year) in distance traveled per person over the same amount of time as a result of the introduction of wave after wave of faster transportation technologies. In the aggregate, this translates into Zahavi's constant travel-time budget, even as longer distances are covered at greater speeds because of technological change and infrastructure investments.

Source: Adapted by the author from C. Marchetti, "Anthropological Invariants in Travel Behavior," *Technological Forecasting and Social Change* 47, no. 1 (September 1994): 75–88, https://doi.org/10 .1016/0040-1625(94)90041-8; Jesse H. Ausubel, Cesare Marchetti, and Perrin S. Meyer, "Toward Green Mobility: The Evolution of Transport," *European Review* 6, no. 2 (May 1998): 137–156, https://doi.org /10.1017/S1062798700003185.

car or a bus, one is contributing to urban spatial expansion and to higher energy consumption in transportation, which with current technologies also means higher greenhouse gas emissions.

Thus, as cities develop economically and technologically and invest in their infrastructure, it is often the case that their space effectively expands and energy consumption goes up, while travel times remain approximately constant. This implies faster speeds of movement. These are some of the dimensions whereby larger and richer cities seem to accelerate human social behavior, as we will see in the next chapter.

2.3.3 THE DEFINITION OF FUNCTIONAL CITIES

We conclude this chapter with the implications that thinking about cities as interacting populations over space and time have for how we *define urban areas* empirically. The term *city*—at least in American English—when strictly used, refers only to the *political* unit and often just to its government. New York City, for example, means specifically the five boroughs (Manhattan, Brooklyn, Bronx, Queens, and Staten Island) and their joint mayoral administration and city agencies. This unit has about 8 million people, while the functional city (metropolitan area) of New York has about 20 million people and encompasses a much vaster area and many distinct political units. Thinking about cities in urban science in terms of political units is generally a red herring: all the classical models described in this chapter have made *no reference* to such units at all! What needs to be done then is to define cities in terms of how they function. Not surprisingly, these units are known as *functional urban areas* or, in less technical language, *metropolitan areas*.

Defining the extent and scope of any complex system is always problematic. Attempting definitions, such as spatial delineations, without a theory of what the system does is plain foolhardy and leads to endless confusion. Put in a different way, any definition of a city requires an underlying scientific theory of what a city is and what it does.

In geography, the main issue is how to create a *spatial* boundary—a contour in space—that defines the functional city as the space within. But we have already seen that the essence of cities is not space itself but rather the interplay between socioeconomic interactions, incomes, and transportation. This socioeconomic construction of space (and time) requires, from a principled point of view, that we start with the city's networks of socioeconomic activity, construct them as a whole, including people's places of work, residence, civic activity, commerce, and so on, and thereby construct a spatial entity that encloses all of them together within a given time budget. Using the framework of time geography, we want to build spatial boundaries that contain the life paths of all people in concentrated daily interaction.

This is easier said than done, of course. People occasionally travel outside urban areas for many reasons, so the construction must allow some statistical flexibility.

Travel is also differentiated by age and occupation, so, for example, adults may commute from an outlying region to the CBD to work, while children and the elderly may stay local. This would mean that the place of residence is generally considered part of the urban area even if the majority of people living there do not commute! The household economic tie here is critical and must be emphasized in the definition.

Empirically, constructing functional urban areas requires that we know a lot about individuals' daily behaviors, particularly commuting flows and the spatial distribution of employment. This is still lacking in terms of available data in many contexts, especially for rapidly developing cities. To fill this methodological gap, geographers, urban planners, and economists attempt to build algorithmic city delineations based on a number of direct and proxy quantities.

The crux of the problem is changes in transportation technologies, which, as we have seen, can make cities spatially huge. For cities that predated modern transportation systems, it was relatively easier to estimate that they could only have a spatial extent of a few kilometers.[58] Classical Rome, for example, had a population of about 1 million people at its height, residing in about 20 km^2. This gives it a radius of ~2.5 km. By contrast, Tokyo's metropolitan area (the largest in population in the world) has a total land area of about 13,500 km^2, while New York's metropolitan area is even bigger, at 17,405 km^2. This gives Tokyo and New York much larger radii, of 66 and 74 km, respectively, which require an elaborate transportation infrastructure, such as fast rail and a highway system, to function.

These vast areas require a systematic approach to defining functional cities that engages with the introduction of modern means of transportation. This need has been recognized in the US since at least the 1950s, when the mass adoption of cars and highways was radically transforming American cities in space.[59] In the spirit of the theoretical models of this chapter, the key to new functional definitions was the measurement of commuting flows over space, which started to be performed by the US Census Bureau across the entire national territory in the 1960s. The result has been the systematic construction of *Metropolitan Statistical Areas* (MSAs) ever since. These will be the main "cities" used throughout this book to develop and test theory. They are *unified labor markets*, in the sense that they integrate in the same spatial territory places of employment and residence for most of their households. The main drawback of the definition of US MSAs is that they rely on counties as the geographic building blocks. This means that every MSA is defined as a set of counties, which belong to it based on the evaluation of commuting flows between them.

Counties are political and administrative units and as such are not themselves functionally defined. They can be very large or very small in terms of both population and land area. For example, Los Angeles County has over 10 million people, while Kalatkao County in Hawaii had 89 people in 2015. As a result, US MSA definitions often include massive amounts of land that is not settled and may also fail to include some peripheral populations at their edges if they are only a small portion of the population of a large county.

To deal with some of these shortcomings, a more recent joint effort from the European Union (EU) and Organisation for Economic Co-operation and Development (OECD) statistics has attempted a similar construction starting with smaller building blocks. This is described in figure 2.14.

The EU/OECD algorithm is worth mentioning as a good example of how functional urban areas are defined in practice. First, the procedure requires the following data resources:

1. A spatialized residential population map, in this case a given number of people per 1 km² cell. Over the same scale, one usually has a share of built surfaces obtained from multispectral satellite data.

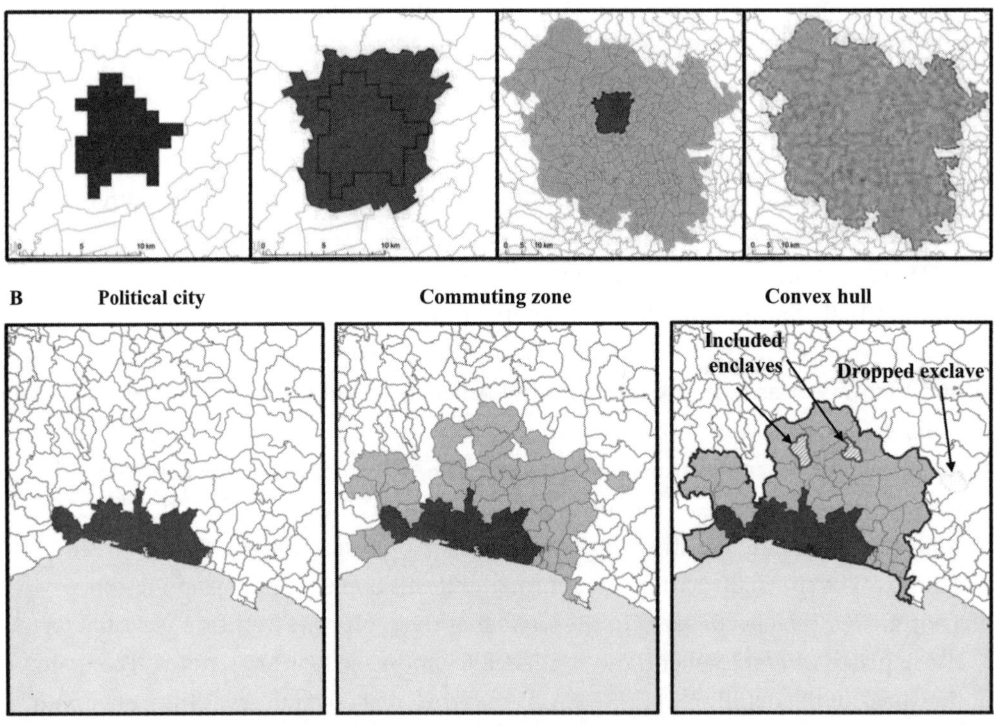

2.14 Definition of functional metropolitan areas. (A) The EU/OECD identification of the functional city of Graz, Austria. From left to right, an urban core is identified by high population density, starting with world population maps at 1 km spatial resolution. This is then mapped to political units and their boundaries. Next, one identifies commuting flows to adjacent spatial units. The union of these units is the final functional urban area definition. (B) An example where commuting areas can be spatially disconnected or absent, even when surrounded by other included commuting areas. In such cases, the EU/OECD definition makes a spatial convex hull of the resulting geography.
Source: Adapted by the author from Lewis Dijkstra, Hugo Poelman, and Paolo Veneri, "The EU-OECD Definition of a Functional Urban Area" (Paris: OECD, 2019); OECD, ed., *Redefining "Urban": A New Way to Measure Metropolitan Areas* (Paris: OECD, 2012).

2. Digital shape boundaries for local political or administrative units (these typically vary by nation).

3. Data on commuting flows between these local units and employment in each unit.

Using this information leads to the maps constructed in figure 2.14. The subtlest step has to do with using commuting ties. The EU/OECD procedure is as follows:

3.1. Include the unit in the set representing the functional urban area if 15% of employed persons living in one unit work in another unit. This includes commuting between suburbs and the CBD (in both directions) as well as between suburbs and other peripheral units, so the city need not be monocentric.

3.2. Some exceptional units, such as *enclaves*—disconnected units entirely surrounded by other local units that belong to a commuting zone—are included to form a convex hull, while noncontiguous local units are dropped from the set. This is not necessary as part of the definition but has the virtue of creating a single compact boundary line.

We analyze these data on functional cities in the US, Europe, and in other nations in the chapters that follow and will show that by and large they share consistent—"universal"—quantitative properties, while other definitions of cities, such as those based on political units or only on population density thresholds, typically do not.

One word of caution relates to using residential population density (or density of built fabric) above some given threshold as the driver of city definitions. This is convenient as a procedure because it is available from remote sensing data and a number of worldwide demographic maps. But in places without high residential density contrasts, such as smaller cities, this means that the population density is approximately constant, $n_A = const$, leading to a trivial relationship between city size and population, $A(N) = n_A^{-1} N$, at least over a range of smaller city scales. Conversely, in cases of high "rural" population density, such as in northern India, the same definitions can lead us to conclude that places where the population is primarily dedicated to subsistence activities are functional cities. There is a real debate between two of the gurus of global urban definitions—Angel[60] and Dijkstra[61]—that requires further analysis and better-integrated data, as it has an impact on the numbers of chapter 1, about how urbanized the world really is.[62] These definition-based disputes fundamentally highlight that considerations of density—Angel emphasizes built-area density, while Dijkstra emphasizes population density—alone are not sufficient to define functional cities. Unfortunately, in the context of India, for example, at this point we do not have data on commuting flows that may help resolve the issue. The dependence of urban properties on definitions of cities is known as *the modifiable areal unit problem*,[63] but because space is not primary to city definitions, we should in fact expect such differences and embrace them as a means of testing theoretical hypotheses. None of this, in my view, should be confusing. The key is to always keep in mind function above and beyond spatial form.

EPILOGUE: FOUNDATIONAL CONCEPTS, DESCRIPTION, AND QUANTIFICATION

Many features of classical models of cities have survived the test of time and have been incorporated in wave after wave of improved urban modeling and theory. These concepts include the idea that the foundation of what a city is rests on its self-organizing processes of socioeconomic interactions, that these interactions constitute networks that are shaped and in turn shape urban space and time, and that occupation and movement through space incur costs that must be paid out of incomes derived from the city. This, in turn, allows space to become differentiated, which is expressed in terms of distinct costs and land uses between locations. All these foundational ideas will be carried forward in this book and, I believe, are central to any future scientific theory of cities. Because of this backbone of basic concepts and empirical regularities, we can talk of an emergent science of cities.

The approaches discussed in this chapter suffer, however, from some fundamental shortcomings. These are expressed not so much in terms of the quantities involved or their articulations but by their lack of true "microscopic" foundations. They lack a consistent description of cities as stochastic population dynamics of interacting, strategic, heterogeneous agents. These statistical foundations are the lingua franca for many different intellectual traditions, providing a common pool of methods and concepts across disciplines such as statistical physics, ecology and evolution, population health and epidemiology, neuroscience and cognition, and financial mathematics. A dialogue between urban science and these disciplines is just beginning. Manifesting such connections more clearly is critical for making urban science the hub for the many traditional disciplines it touches and through their recombination and synthesis to create something new. Above all, considering the statistical dynamics of heterogeneous populations will allow us to describe cities in terms of *information*. This connection will prove to be the most fertile of all for understanding how cities operate and ultimately what they are for.

3

COMPLEX NETWORKS
AND URBAN SCALING

We are in the epoch of simultaneity: we are in the epoch of juxtaposition, the epoch of the near and far, of the side-by-side, of the dispersed. We are at a moment, I believe, when our experience of the world is less that of a long life developing through time than that of a network that connects points and intersects with its own skin.
—Michel Foucault, "Of Other Spaces: Utopias and Heterotopias"

The networked quality of the contemporary human experience described so vividly by Foucault likely originated with life in the first cities, but it has recently accelerated to become the norm for most people. It has been this process of transformation of how we live, how we relate to each other and to the earth's natural environments, that motivates the creation of a scientific understanding of cities and urbanization. As Foucault suggests, these processes are best understood in terms of complex networks. Social and infrastructural networks in cities are universal in the mundane sense that they are common to all human settlements. They transform the basic nature of space and time experienced by people, resulting in the spatial concentration and temporal acceleration of social interactions that promote interdependence, specialization, and knowledge creation. Developing a theory of cities based on networks that at once includes and extends the classical models introduced in chapter 2 and that expresses the quality of the living experience described by Foucault is the main goal of this chapter.

More specifically, we will set ourselves two tasks. The first is to find a set of empirical characteristics of cities that are sufficiently general to justify the development of urban scientific theory. We will find many nontrivial and fascinating relations between a city's population size, its structure, and the magnitude of its socioeconomic outputs. Because urban quantities vary in predictable but nonlinear ways with city population size, this empirical exercise has become known as *urban scaling*. These relationships will point to network structures as the fundamental starting points for understanding cities, above and beyond economic markets, political organizations, transportation technologies, or typologies of built spaces, which are much more contingent on geography, history, and levels of development. We will see that some of these patterns and modes of organization emerge instead from general scaling properties of urban quantities and from local histories.

Second, we will want to explain these scaling relationships in a way that is systemic and falsifiable by predicting both interlocking mechanisms and specific quantities that can be measured and assessed in practice. This will lead us, in the chapters ahead, to develop *urban scaling theory*, which not only predicts scaling quantities but will also provide a stepping-stone for more elaborate theoretical developments involving statistics, socioeconomic diversity, and growth. This theory conceptualizes cities as interdependent socioeconomic and spatial (infrastructural) networks that coevolve to support each other. According to the theory, the necessary self-consistency between social structure and urban built spaces becomes the key element for understanding how cities work, because it sets cost-benefit relationships experienced by all urban agents, including people, households, and socioeconomic organizations.

CHAPTER OUTLINE

This chapter is divided into three main sections. Section 3.1 provides a number of empirical examples of the dependence of many different urban indicators on city size. Because we observe a general set of quantitative regularities, which take the form of scale-invariant relations (power laws), the resulting body of evidence is known as *urban scaling*. Section 3.2 develops a network theory of cities to explain these patterns, known as urban scaling theory. We will clarify its assumptions, derive its consequences, and discuss its relations to other urban theories, past and present. In section 3.3, we discuss several important observable consequences of urban scaling theory, including predictions about quantities as varied as the structure of social networks in cities, the physical features of infrastructure networks, building sizes and heights, land uses and associated spatial geometries, economic productivity, and the temporal rhythms of social life. We end with a discussion of cities as complex systems, specifically how they compare to organisms, ecosystems, and other metaphors often invoked to understand them. We will conclude that cities manifest new, unique dynamics compared to other complex systems and specifically that they are fundamentally *social reactors*, enabling the production of innovation out of the dynamic juxtaposition of socially distributed knowledge and learning.

3.1   URBAN SCALING: GENERAL EMPIRICAL PROPERTIES OF CITIES

One has to look for different ways. One has to look for scaling structures—how do big details relate to little details. The process doesn't care where it is, and moreover it doesn't care how long it's been going. The only things that can be universal, in a sense, are scaling things.
—Mitchell Feigenbaum, quoted in James Gleick, *Chaos: Making a New Science*

We now show how the analysis of the quantitative variation of urban quantities with population size can reveal a number of general properties of cities. It is important to keep in mind that this kind of approach is not new to cities. It is the basic analytical path that scientists always take to investigate the population-averaged properties of any system, be it in physics, biology, or society. For this reason, urban scaling analysis is more than just another strategy for studying the quantitative properties of cities. It is a means of placing cities on a par with many other complex systems and of identifying their own (specific) scaling relations. In order to set up the framework, we start with some of these general connections to scaling in other disciplines.

3.1.1 THE MOTIVATION FOR SCALING ANALYSIS

Scaling analysis is the most basic strategy one can pursue to investigate the properties of any system beyond single-variable statistics (such as the relative size distribution of cities; see chapter 8). It asks how *extensive* properties vary on average with measures of the *system's size*. This variation is a population average because each instance of the system—for example, each city—will display its own variations from a general statistical trend. By *extensive* property we mean a variable that captures the system's behavior as a whole, not that of each agent or particle. The latter are known as *intensive* variables and are sometimes referred to as densities or rates. This idea of systemic properties in turn reflects the emphasis on "ecological" properties of cities introduced in chapters 1 and 2.

Scaling analysis describes an extensive system property such as total energy or GDP or the surface area of roads, written as $Y_i(t) > 0$, in a system of size N_i and at time, made up of many instances (cities) $i = 1, \ldots, N_c$

$$Y_i(t) = Y(N_i(t), t) = Y_0(t) N_i(t)^\beta e^{\xi_i(t)}. \tag{3.1}$$

Let us focus on the meaning of each of the quantities on the right-hand side of equation (3.1) and introduce the general terms describing scaling. The *prefactor*, $Y_0(t)$, is independent of scale, $N(t)$ (taken as a continuous variable), but may depend on time and on other system-level variables. The scaling *exponent* β measures changes in the magnitude of our quantity of interest, on average over instances, relative to system size. It can be written in several different ways, such as

$$\beta = \frac{d \ln Y(N, t)}{d \ln N(t)} = \frac{\frac{dY}{Y}}{\frac{dN}{N}}. \tag{3.2}$$

These logarithmic derivatives (or finite variations, denoted by Δ) are the key quantities in a *comparative analysis*[1] of the system across different sizes. Economists refer to them as *elasticities*. As the second inequality shows, they express the average relative (percentage) change in Y, given a percentage variation in size N at fixed time t. In general, β is also a function of time, but we will see empirically in this chapter and in terms of statistical theory in chapter 4 that it is often time independent, a fact that when true carries great significance. The fact that $\beta \neq 1$ is particularly interesting. For $\beta = 1$, variations in Y are proportional to size, which signals a system with no effective ("ecological") interactions. Each element has the same properties regardless of population: the per capita Y, which is $y = \dfrac{Y}{N}$, is independent of system size. In such cases, we will say that Y is *linear* in N. An example is an ideal gas in physics (a good approximation to the gas in the room you are in while reading this book), which has a total average energy $E = Y_0\, N$, where, $Y_0 = \dfrac{3}{2} k_B T_E$ is the energy per molecule of air (where k_B is Boltzmann's constant and T_E is temperature). This makes $\beta = 1$, $\xi_i = 0$ in equation (3.1). The situation is more interesting when there is a nonlinearity, because this signals interactions between the elements that make up the system. We will speak of *sublinearity* when $\beta < 1$ and *superlinearity* when $\beta > 1$. Sometimes these two situations are also known as *decreasing returns to scale (or economies of scale)* and *increasing returns to scale*, respectively. Cities present specific and interrelated patterns of sublinearity and superlinearity, as we will see soon.

Finally, the *residuals*, $\xi_i(t)$, account for the statistical deviation of city i from the average scaling pattern for all cities. The relationship between Y and N, as written in equation (3.1), is *exact* because any deviation from the power law can be accounted for by changes in the magnitude of the residuals, ξ_i. We will investigate the properties of these deviations in detail in chapter 4 to understand the specificity of each city and create a *statistical theory* of urban areas. For now, note that these deviations are also scale independent by construction and that their ensemble average in any population of cases, $i = 1, \ldots, N_c$, such as a set of cities, is zero: $\sum_{i=1}^{N_c} \xi_i = 0$. Therefore, the first nontrivial statistical quantity characterizing the deviations is the population variance, $\sigma^2 = \dfrac{1}{N_c} \sum_{i=1}^{N_c} \xi_i^2$. When this variance is scale independent, a property with the scary name of *homoscedasticity*, we can say that the quantity Y obeys a *scaling law*, because on average over fluctuations it is true that $Y(N) = Y_0\, N^\beta$. If instead the fluctuations (residuals) are very large, the pattern becomes very noisy and the scaling relation effectively disappears; it is no longer a good characterization of the data. The term *scaling law* is a bit aspirational, but it does convey that there is a set with many entities—such as cities, ecosystems, or organisms—that share a common property such that their collective behavior is scale invariant, meaning that, on average, $\dfrac{\Delta Y}{Y} = \beta \dfrac{\Delta N}{N}$ regardless of any particular values of the quantity or scale. In plain language, we can say that gases, cities, or organisms are general entities that can be large or small, with common properties for each entity varying on a continuous sliding scale, set by their own scaling laws. This is why we can talk about a city of a few thousand people at the beginning of history (chapter 7) or one of 10 million people today, or predict the properties of an urban area with 75 million people by the end of the century, and know—in a precise way, because of scale invariance—that they are "the same kind of thing." As Feigenbaum tells us, "The only things that can be universal are scaling things."

Later in this chapter, we will even see how scaling allows us to calculate properties of cities that have never even existed before, say with 100 million people, or in outer space in three spatial dimensions instead of two. We will be able to tell how dense such cities would be, their amount of infrastructure, the heights of their skylines, how congested their transportation systems would be, how quickly an epidemic will spread, how often people meet, and how quickly they move! The ability to make such predictions and extrapolations from current and past evidence to entirely new situations is what distinguishes urban science from more contextually bound knowledge.

3.1.2 EXAMPLES OF SCALING LAWS

Let us now illustrate a few cases of the best-known scaling laws across a variety of fields so we can better appreciate the generality of the strategy. Scaling itself can be used as a general method of analysis[2] and as a precursor to more sophisticated theories of how statistical quantities vary (physicists say "run") with scales[3] (see chapter 4).

Ideal Gas Law While we may not often think of the equation of state for a gas as a scaling law, it is just that. You will likely have learned this in introductory physics or thermodynamics.[4] It is the basis for understanding (and building!) thermal engines, including the internal combustion motors that have powered the Industrial Revolution and still move most of our cars today.

The conservation of energy in a gas can be written in a variety of ways, such as

$$P_r V = N k_B T_E, \quad E = E_0 N, \quad E_0 = \frac{3}{2} k_B T_E, \tag{3.3}$$

where P_r is the pressure exerted by the gas on the walls of a container with volume V, N is the number of gas molecules, E is the gas's total energy, k_B is Boltzmann's constant (a universal number), and T_E is the temperature. We see that the gas's internal energy scales *linearly* ($\beta = 1$) with the number of molecules multiplied by the energy per molecule, which is its degrees of freedom (3 in three dimensions, the directions of motion) multiplied by the thermal energy of $\frac{1}{2} k_B T_E$ per direction. Note that $P_r V$ has physical dimensions of energy. The relationship between energy and number of molecules is linear because the molecules in a gas are assumed (and observed, on average, to an excellent approximation) to be noninteracting. Introducing interactions, such as in the van der Waals gas,[5] can break scale invariance and lead to a phase transition where the gas changes state to become a liquid or a solid. The ideal gas example is instructive in one additional respect, having to do with *causality*: Which variables predict which events? In physics, one refers to an equation of this type as an *equation of state*. It provides a set of relations between observable (manipulatable) properties of the gas, such as its pressure, volume, energy, temperature, and, implicitly, its entropy. The relationships expressed by an equation of state are *causal* in a generalized sense. For example, by increasing the number of particles (everything else being equal), we will increase the pressure proportionally. But this is *not* what social scientists typically mean by *causality*, which requires specifying a directional mechanism for the constituent parts. Finding tight and clear causal mechanisms in social systems is generally very difficult, so asking for very strict unentangled causality often leads to endless debates (see chapter 6). For this reason, it is good to have a generalized macroscopic sense of causality resulting from some state of approximate equilibrium, which is what scaling laws as equations of state do.

A Star's Mass-Luminosity Relation A very different example from physics comes from understanding the basic way in which a star works. Stars are nuclear fusion reactors, which concentrate large amounts of matter to extremely high densities through gravitational forces. If the mass is large enough, critically high densities are reached at which hydrogen nuclei will spontaneously combine into helium. This releases a prodigious amount of energy in the form of light and neutrinos because a little bit of mass, M, creates incredibly large amounts of energy, $E = M\, c_{light}^2$, because the speed of light, c_{light}, is such a large number.

In a star, these interactions are held in a dynamic state of self-consistent spatial equilibrium where the centripetal forces of gravity, which crunch matter together, are balanced by the centrifugal pressure of outgoing radiation to make up the shape of the star. This state of equilibrium changes very slowly, lasting billions of years, as hydrogen and progressively heavier elements undergo reactions with different energy outputs. This *spatial equilibrium* allows us to relate two complex quantities, the star's gravity and the forces exerted by the products of nuclear interactions at its core, and make sense of both. This is because they must be balanced in order for the star to keep its general shape. This leads to another famous scaling relation, which tells us how big a star is by observing how bright it is. Conversely, we can know how bright a star will be if we know the mass of the cloud of gas imploding to form it.

The total energy of light emitted by a star per unit time, known as the star's *luminosity*, L_S, obeys a scaling relationship to its total mass, M, which is the best measure of a star's size. This can be written as

$$L_S(M) = L_{S_0} M^{a_S},\tag{3.4}$$

where $L_{S_0} = L_\circ / M_\circ^{a_S}$ and $L_\circ$ and $M_\circ$ are the luminosity and mass of the sun, respectively. The relationship is *superlinear*, with $1 \le a_S \le 6$. Specifically, $a_S \simeq 3.5$ for main-sequence stars, which are the most common "sunlike" stars. (Though expressing general features, scaling relations are ideal for placing the things we care most about—such as our sun—in context.) Relationship (3.4) shows that a star's luminosity increases *superlinearly* with its mass. This is because nuclear reactions at the star's core are proportional to products of densities (there is a similar effect in chemical reactions and social interactions), which results in their products being related more than proportionately to mass. In turn, this is associated with faster reaction rates and higher energy released per unit of mass and per unit time the larger the star. Because of this, larger stars are also faster and brighter per unit of mass and live shorter lives. A little more theory allows astrophysicists to compute the volume (or radius) of the star, its spectrum, and many other properties related to its behavior in space and time.

Kleiber's Law of Biological Metabolism   What about life? In biology, energy management is also key. This is known as *metabolism*. Analogies between organisms and cities lead to the concept of urban metabolism,[6] a field of industrial ecology[7] and civil engineering. Kleiber's law is an extraordinary law of biology relating the metabolism of a biological organism at rest, E_M, to its mass, M. On average, this is also well expressed by a power law,

$$E_M(M) = E_0 M^{b_M},\tag{3.5}$$

where the scaling exponent b_M varies with taxa but is remarkably constant for multicellular animals, with $b_M \simeq \frac{3}{4} < 1$, indicating that the organism's total power consumption (energy per unit time) is *sublinear* with its mass. Proposed explanations for this number rely on the internal network geometry of biological organisms, including their surface-to-volume ratios and especially the fractal networked structure of their vascular systems,[8] which is assumed to be optimal in terms of its space-filling properties and energy efficiency. Because biological metabolism tends to be sublinear with mass, biological rhythms slow down with body size, making whales and elephants slower than mice or rabbits. Such behaviors are also affected by ecology and evolution, but are still to an extraordinary degree the result of general strategies for energy management in all biological organisms.

Species-Area Law in Ecology   Another remarkable scaling law relates biodiversity, measured by the number of different species in an ecosystem, D_s, to the ecosystem's spatial area, A, as

$$D_s = D_{S_0} A^{b_S}.\tag{3.6}$$

The prefactor, D_{S_0}, varies with latitude and other conditions, indicating baseline biodiversity for small systems, which tends to be higher in the tropics and in wet regions. D_S is also known as the *species richness* of an ecosystem. The observed exponent b_s varies somewhat but tends to be about $b_S \simeq 0.15 - 0.3$. Because the exponent is small, the data can sometimes be well fit by a logarithmic function instead of a power law. For small b_S these functions are analytically indistinguishable because

$$A^{b_S} = e^{b_S \ln A} \simeq 1 + b_S \ln A + \cdots = b_S \ln \frac{A}{A_0} + \cdots.$$

This "species-area law" indicates that larger ecosystems are more diverse and thus support more biological information (new species). This is critical to ecological resilience and adaptation, including in situations where humans create disturbances and split up larger ecosystems into smaller patches. It also suggests strategies for ecological conservation that preserve large wild areas rather than a collection of smaller patches with the same area.

These four examples of scaling laws share something fundamental. They all refer to energy management in a state of approximate equilibrium. The ideal gas law accounts for the actual energy content of the gas—its internal energy—but this is conceptualized as being permanently exchanged (lost and reacquired) by contact with a "heat bath" at the same temperature. For a star, gravitational potential energy accelerates matter to collide in the star's core. The star becomes a nuclear fusion reactor, keeping its shape approximately constant by dynamically balancing its gravitational potential with the forces exerted by the outgoing products of these reactions, including the centrifugal pressure exerted by light and neutrinos. For organisms, Kleiber's law with $b_M \sim \frac{3}{4} < 1$ reflects the steady state at which a set of cells sharing a common distribution infrastructure transforms incoming energy from food into all necessary biological processes, supporting the organization of their mass and releasing heat and waste as by-products. Finally, remember that the area of the ecosystem is proportional to the incoming solar power that ultimately allows it to exist and grow. How much of this energy influx becomes available for life depends on its primary producers, such as trees, grasses, or phytoplankton, and other limiting resources, such as water and nutrients. We should think of the species-area law as a relation between biodiversity (biological information) and power (energy per unit time) input into an ecosystem. It tells us that the buildup of information with input energy in ecosystems is actually quite slow and sublinear ($b_S < 1$).

Energy shows up—directly or indirectly—in many scaling relations because scaling is closely associated with conservation laws. The most fundamental of these conservation laws—the one we can always count on being there—is the first law of thermodynamics. It states that total energy is conserved, but particular forms of energy may be transformed into each other. Although systems as complex as cities evade the strictest consequences of energy conservation by very intentionally importing resources from the outside, these conservation laws enforce inevitable *constraints*—such as the budget conditions in the economic models of chapter 2. These constraints leave a strong fingerprint on the system's average properties. Around states of equilibrium, these constraints allow us to mathematically equate unexpected quantities, such as gravity and light, or mass and life span. We will see that the same kind of "magic" works for cities, allowing us to read off patterns of human behavior from amounts of infrastructure or the wealth of cities from their skylines. We will keep an eye on these constraints throughout the book. Accounting for resource inputs, outputs, and accumulations will be the key.

Urban Scaling Laws Before we get too deeply into questions of explanation and interpretation, let us explore some urban quantities and their scaling properties. This will allow us to contemplate the task ahead of us.

Throughout the book, we will see many examples of scaling relations for diverse urban quantities in different contexts; for example, for cities in history (chapter 7) or in contemporary settings. There were a number of early studies, especially in geography,[9] that dealt with the relationship between the land area and the population of urban areas (for a review, see the supplement in my paper "The Origins of Scaling in Cities"[10]). Many of these early studies use the term *allometry* instead of scaling, which is inspired by the study of biological organisms and refers to the relative morphological aspects of their bodies.[11] These studies do not generally recognize that there are different ways to measure the spatial extent of urban areas or that there is an emergent generality to the sublinear values of exponents found. Around the same time, economists also started measuring economic productivity in urban areas,[12] finding instead typically superlinear exponents; for example, relating value added (firms' profits) to urban population size in US metropolitan areas.

As data on urban areas became more available and researchers pressed some of the hypothesized analogies between cities and other complex systems,[13] it was realized that there is an emergent general logic to urban scaling relations.[14] This logic is illustrated by the examples of scaling relations shown in figures 3.1–3.3 and tables 3.1 and 3.2.

First, very roughly, there is a general tendency for scaling exponents to fall into three distinct categories. Socioeconomic rates, which include total socioeconomic activity (GDP, wages, income) but also violent crime, patents, and jobs reflecting economic specialization, all scale with population size in a superlinear way with exponent values $\beta \simeq 1 + \frac{1}{6} = \frac{7}{6}$. Second, measures of urban infrastructure and the spatial extent of cities scale sublinearly with population size. Initially, a number of different quantities were lumped together in this category, but it was eventually understood that the volume of infrastructure networks and built spaces is special and, in terms of scaling exponents, differs from the spatial extent (radius, as in chapter 2) of cities or the length of their roads. Measures of the volume of infrastructure and built spaces are observed to scale with population size of urban areas with an exponent $\beta \simeq 1 - \frac{1}{6} = \frac{5}{6}$.

Finally, a number of quantities that pertain to individuals and households scale essentially linearly with city size, $\beta \simeq 1$, including number of jobs, number of housing units, and household consumption of basic services such as water or electrical power. Such quantities are typically associated with basic individual needs that cannot be easily accumulated. This means that many aspects of life at home do not change between large and small urban areas. It is outside the home, in socioeconomic settings and through the experience and use of built spaces, that urban life becomes transformative. Scaling relations tell us that such transformations are scale invariant across cities, at least to a very good approximation, so observations at one scale (say small towns) contain in themselves quantitative predictions as to what a large city will look like and vice versa.

What is most interesting and suggestive is the quantitative generality of these results, applying to urban areas across many sizes, different geographies, levels of socioeconomic development, and times (see figures 3.1–3.3 and chapter 7). Note that

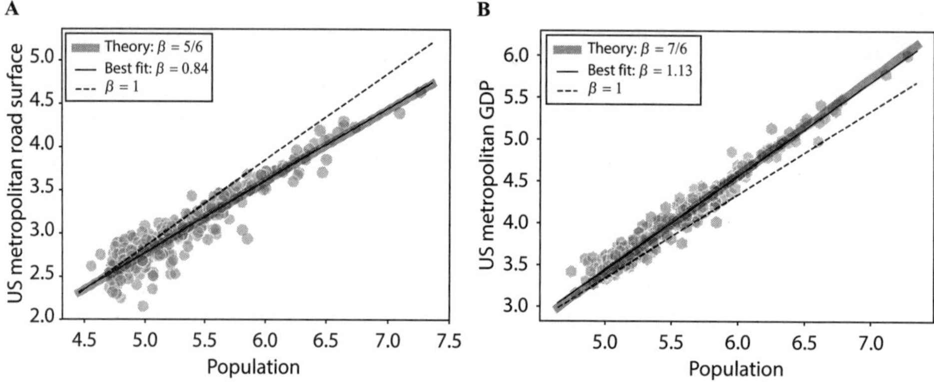

3.1   Urban scaling in the US. Scaling of urban infrastructure and socioeconomic output with city population size. (A) Total lane miles (volume in log_10 scale) of roads in US Metropolitan Statistical Areas (MSAs) in 2006 (circles). Data for 415 urban areas, obtained from the Office of Highway Policy Information of the Federal Highway Administration. Lines show the best fit to a scaling relation (solid black), with $\beta = 0.84 \pm 0.04$ [95% confidence interval (CI), $R^2 = 0.65$]; the theoretical prediction, $\beta = 5/6$ (gray); and linear scaling, $\beta = 1$ (dashed black). (B) Gross metropolitan product of MSAs in 2006 (hexagons). Data obtained for 363 MSAs from US Bureau of Economic Analysis. Lines describe best fit (black) to data, $\beta = 1.13 \pm 0.02$ [95% CI, $R^2 = 0.96$]; the theoretical prediction, $\beta = 7/6$ (gray); and proportional scaling, $\beta = 1$ (dashed).

many of the differences between cities in different urban systems—rich and poor, old and new—are in this sense accounted for by the baseline prefactor, Y_0. For example, today urban areas in the US are about six times richer (on average, per capita) than those in China, so $Y_0^{\mathrm{US}} = 6Y_0^{\mathrm{China}}$. However, once we account for this difference in prefactors, looking at a city in China and another twice its size typically shows that the latter's economy is about 17% bigger per capita; the same applies for two cities in the US and elsewhere. The same reasoning applies for spatial quantities, where baseline areas are larger for US cities than for European cities, for example, but where doubling the size of cities begets the same relative increase in density from their respective (different) baseline prefactors. How these prefactors get to change in time so that one day China may catch up with the US economically is the result of systemic processes of change and development, which we will study in chapters 5 and 9. We will see that endogenous processes of economic growth based on learning and new information, distributed across the urban system, are key.

The main point of the empirical exercise on urban scaling so far is that it suggests an emergent logic where socioeconomic outputs of cities tend to scale in their own consistent *superlinear* way, while the volumes and extent of spatial infrastructure scale consistently *sublinearly*. A few other quantities having to do with basic living needs are linear on the population (tables 3.1 and 3.2). Consequently, the deviation in exponents for socioeconomic products above unity, $\beta = 1 + \delta$, is of roughly the same magnitude as the deviations in the exponents of infrastructure volumes below 1, $\beta = 1 - \delta, \delta \approx \dfrac{1}{6}$. This is the clue on which we can now start to build theory based on the integrated modeling of self-consistent socioeconomic and infrastructural networks.

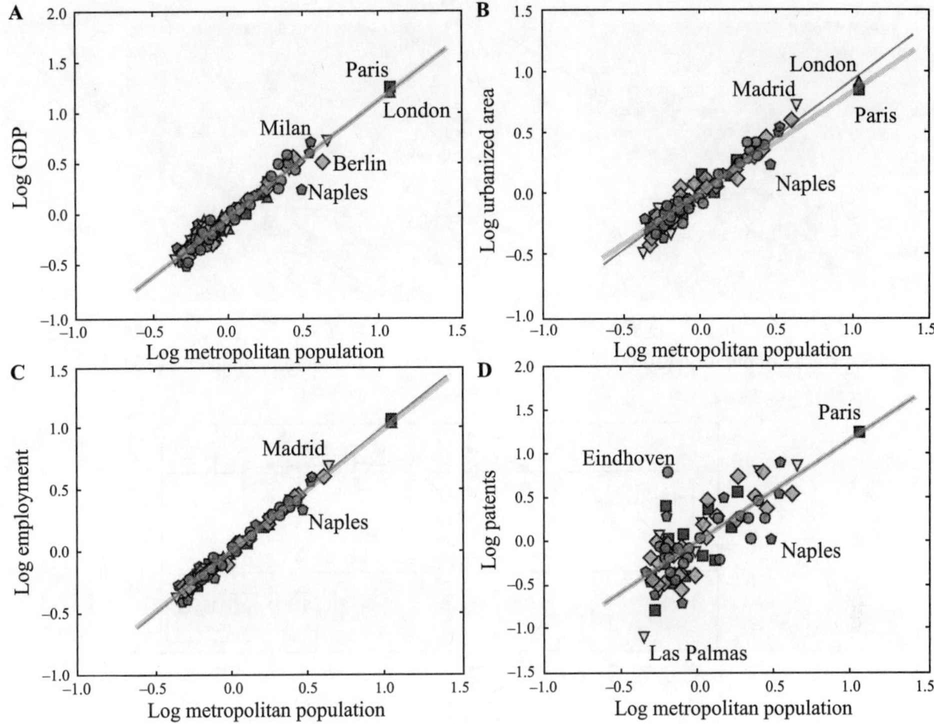

3.2 Urban scaling in Europe. Scaling of various urban quantities with population size for metropolitan areas in Europe (OECD/EU definition). These data include all urban systems in the EU and Switzerland with more than two cities having at least 500,000 people (102 functional cities in 12 nations: Austria, Belgium, the Czech Republic, France, Germany, Italy, the Netherlands, Poland, Spain, Sweden, Switzerland, and the UK). The data have been centered to a common prefactor, $Y_0 = 1$, in each nation (see the text) so the scaling relation has intercept zero in a logarithmic plot. (A) Results for GDP, with nearly exact agreement between best fit (black line, $R^2 = 0.90$) and theory (gray line); see table 3.1. (B) Results for urbanized area. The best fit gives a slightly larger β (black line, $R^2 = 0.88$) than predicted by theory (gray) but fails to describe the largest cities. (C) Employment is linear ($R^2 = 0.97$). (D) Patents are more variable, but the best fit (black line, $R^2 = 0.30$) and prediction from urban scaling theory (gray line) are statistically consistent and predict innovation rates for the largest city, Paris.

3.2 CITIES AS SELF-CONSISTENT SPATIAL AND SOCIAL NETWORKS

The empirical results so far suggest that, despite their apparent complexity, cities on the whole may actually be quite simple. Their average global properties may be set by just a few key parameters involved in determining the values of exponents and prefactors of scaling relations. What we mean by this is not that each real city is simple or devoid of unique character or history but rather that the essence common to all cities—captured by scaling—may be.

In our exploration of urban data so far, we have found a strong clue that the total volumes of built spaces of cities, A_n, and urban socioeconomic outputs, Y, such as GDP, are in a type of reciprocal scaling relationship such that

$$A_n = A_0 N^{1-\delta} \sim N^{1-\delta}, \; Y = G \frac{N^2}{A_n} \sim N^{1+\delta} \rightarrow \left(\frac{A_n}{N}\right)\left(\frac{Y}{N}\right) \equiv G = const, \tag{3.7}$$

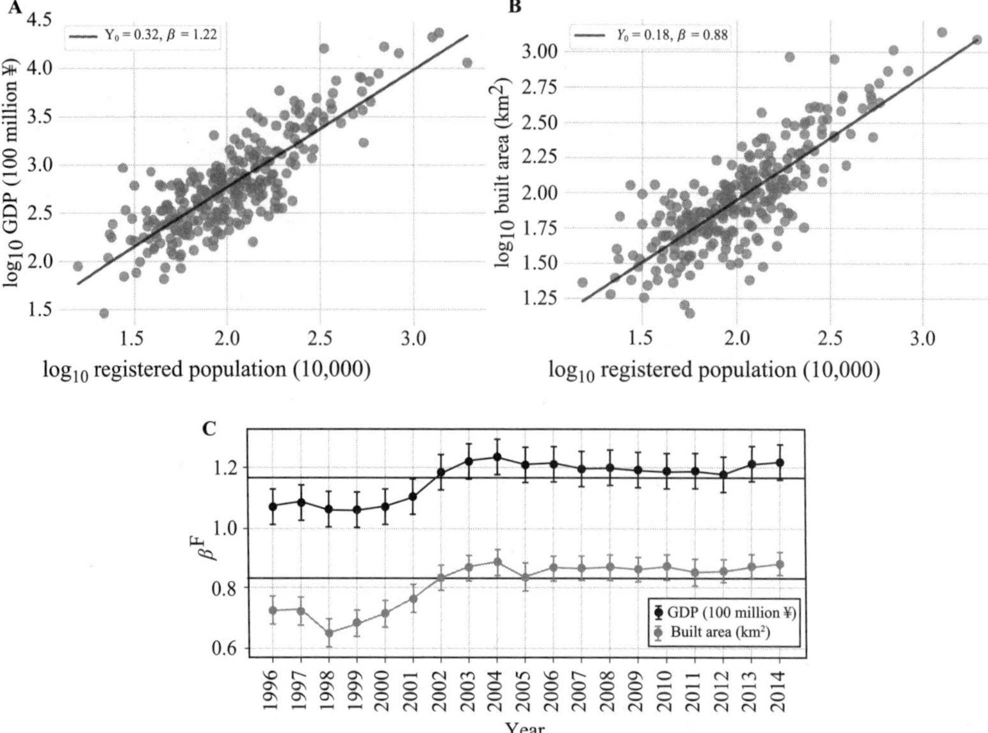

3.3 Urban scaling in China. (A) Superlinear scaling of urban GDP in 2014, with an estimated exponent $\beta = 1.22$ (black line, 95% CI [1.17, 1.23]). (B) Sublinear scaling of built-up area with an estimated exponent $\beta = 0.88$ (black line, 95% CI [0.84, 0.92]). (C) Variation of exponents over time. Error bars show the 95% confidence interval on the exponent estimate. Horizontal gray lines show the expectation from urban scaling theory.

where $\delta \simeq \frac{1}{6}$ is the same number and *const* is a constant of population size, N. The quantity G will prove important. Its constancy relative to city size means that built space volumes per capita multiplied by socioeconomic outputs per capita are conserved across city sizes, from small towns to megacities. Note that G is generally *not a constant in time*; for example, it will tend to increase as a result of economic growth.

At a more abstract level, the constancy of G across city sizes means that any freedoms (in the sense of choices) urbanites may gain in social interactions in larger cities will be lost in terms of available physical space. Conversely, people can clearly have more space for themselves in smaller towns, but they will then pay a price in terms of having fewer different people to interact with, resulting in less socioeconomic choice. This trade-off expresses an important mathematical duality between physical and social spaces in cities, which we can all experience intuitively. To me, it has all the right echoes in the qualitative observations made by Jane Jacobs, Louis Wirth, and many others in chapter 1 on the nature of cities and *urbanism as a way of life*.[15] We will now develop these hints into a mathematical theory that can include and extend some of these classical ideas. Before we do so, we need to take one last

Table 3.1 Observed scaling exponents for urban systems around the world

Quantity	Exponent	Error	Nation	Observations	Year	Unit of analysis	Reference
Land area							
Built area	0.87	NR	Canada	51	1966	Urban areas	Coffey
Built area	0.93	[0.88, 0.98]	EU	102	2010	MAs	Bettencourt and Lobo (2016)
Built area	0.82	$R^2 = 0.84$	China	660	2005	Urban areas	Chen (2010)
Built area	0.85	0.84–0.86	World	3,629	2000	Urban areas >100,000	Angel et al. (2011)
Road surface	0.85	[0.81, 0.89]	US	451	2006	MSA	Bettencourt (2013)
Road surface	0.83	[0.74, 0.92]	Germany	29	2002	Larger urban zones	Bettencourt (2013)
Road length	0.83	[0.55, 0.78]	Japan	12	2005	MA	Bettencourt (2013)
Household needs							
Total housing	1.00	[0.99, 1.01]	US	316	1990	MSA	Bettencourt et al. (2007)
Total employment	1.01	[0.99, 1.02]	US	331	2001	MSA	Bettencourt et al. (2007)
Total employment	1.02	[1.00, 1.05]	EU	102	2010	MA	Bettencourt and Lobo (2016)
Electricity consumption	1.00	[0.94, 1.06]	Germany	377	2002	Cities	Bettencourt et al. (2007)
Water consumption	1.01	[0.89, 1.11]	China	295	2002	Prefectural	Bettencourt et al. (2007)
Social rates							
GDP	1.13	[1.11, 1.15]	US	363	2006	MSA	Bettencourt (2013)
GDP	1.17	[1.11, 1.22]	EU	102	2010	MA	Bettencourt and Lobo (2016)
GDP	1.22	[1.17, 1.27]	China	293	1996–2014	Prefectural	Zünd and Bettencourt (2019)
GDP	1.14	[0.98, 1.30]	India	22	2011	UAs	Sahasranaman and Bettencourt (October 2019)
Personal income	1.11	[1.03, 1.20]	Brazil	39	2010	MAs	Brelsford et al. (May 2017)
Personal income	1.35	[1.19, 1.53]	South Africa	8	2001	MMs	Brelsford et al. (May 2017)

(*continued*)

Table 3.1 (continued)

Quantity	Exponent	Error	Nation	Observations	Year	Unit of analysis	Reference
New patents	1.27	[1.22. 1.32]	US	337	1980–2000	MSA	Bettencourt, Lobo, and Strumsky
New patents	1.13	[0.91, 1.34]	EU	102	2010	MA	Bettencourt and Lobo (2016)
Supercreatives	1.15	[1.13, 1.17]	US	331	1999–2001	MSA	Bettencourt, Lobo, and Strumsky
R&D jobs	1.19	[1.12, 1.26]	US	278	1987–2001	MSA	Bettencourt, Lobo, and Strumsky
Violent crime	1.16	[1.11, 1.19]	US	287	2003	MSA	Bettencourt et al. (2007)
Violent crime	1.12	[1.07, 1.33]	Japan	12	2008	MA	Bettencourt (2013)
Violent crime	1.20	[1.15, 1.25]	Brazil	275,570	2003–2007	MA, municipal	Bettencourt (2013); Alves et al. (2015)
AIDS cases	1.23	[1.17, 1.29]	US	93	2002–2003	MSA	Bettencourt et al. (2007)
Social interactions							
Contacts	1.12	[1.00, 1.25]	Portugal	415	2006–2007	Cities, municipalities	Schläpfer et al.
Contacts	1.26	[1.19, 1.34]	Côte d'Ivoire	215	2011–2012	Prefecture	Andris and Bettencourt
Power dissipation							
Electrical	1.11	[1.05, 1.17]	Germany	380	2002	Cities	Bettencourt et al. (2007)
Traffic congestion	1.15	[1.09, 1.21]	US	360	2005–2014	MSAs	Depersin and Barthélemy; Bettencourt et al. (2019)
Land rents							
Home value	1.35	[1.13, 1.57]	US	40	2010	MSAs	Glaeser and Gottleib; Schläpfer, Lee, and Bettencourt
Building height	0.167	[0.03, 0.29]	US	50	2015	MSAs	Schläpfer, Lee, and Bettencourt

Sources: See the bibliography at the back of the book for full references for the works cited in the last column. The year and month appear only if the list contains multiple works by the same author or by multiple authors with the same last name.

Table 3.2 Summary of scaling regimes—sublinear, superlinear, and linear—and their associated effects, forms of system organization, and consequences for systemic growth

Scaling exponent	Driving effect	Organization	Growth
$\beta < 1$	Economies of scale	Structural (spatial)	Subexponential, logistic (stable)
$\beta > 1$	Network effects	Social, informational	Superexponential (open-ended)
$\beta = 1$	Individual needs	Individual, household	Exponential

preparatory step and understand under what circumstances networks generate superlinear scaling effects.

3.2.1 NETWORK EFFECTS AND METCALFE'S LAW

It is useful to have a basic understanding of what we mean by a network, specifically how to describe networks in mathematical terms. There has been a recent surge of enthusiasm for this subject, with many emergent uses of networks as models for different complex systems. The interested reader is referred to a number of recent textbooks on the subject.[16]

Figure 3.4 shows a basic representation of a network (with just six nodes) as a mathematical *graph*. A graph is a mathematical object made up of N nodes (numbered points) and links (the lines connecting them), represented as an $N \times N$ *matrix*, F_{ij}. We can immediately imagine many different types of networks, such as those with nodes being people and links being relationships. These links may be of different types, such as friendship or being employed in the same firm. We will denote different types of interactions by another index, m, so we can write a set of these networks as F_{ij}^{m}.

These first examples already highlight the critical fact that generally *networks aren't real*. What we mean by this is that friendship, for example, is not a directly measurable physical quantity. This simple but fundamental point will be consequential later. Networks, represented as graphs, are schematic models for exchanges and interactions that involve more basic physical quantities, which are the things we can actually measure. Many of these quantities represent flows such as the movement of people, goods, or information. In other cases, nodes and links may be objects or things, such as places and the streets connecting them in an infrastructure network.

The advantage of representing interactions or relationships as networks is that their structure becomes immediately apparent and pretty simple to describe and manipulate mathematically. We can model any network represented as a graph by changing its matrix, F_{ij}. We can also measure any network property by performing various operations on F_{ij}. Depending on how sophisticated we want to be, this matrix may also become more complicated; for example, when the links have weights so

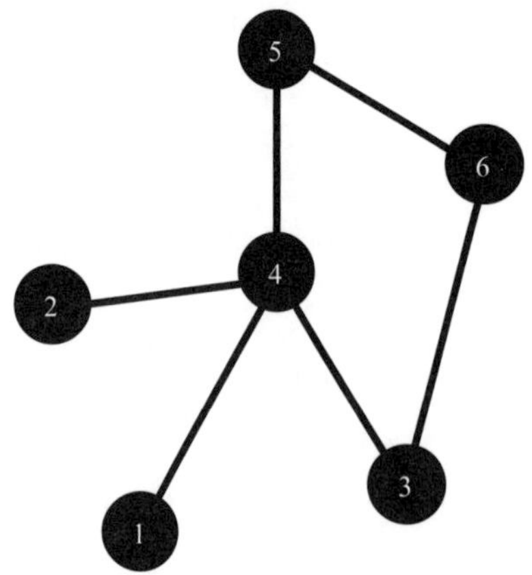

$$F_{ij} = \begin{pmatrix} 0 & 0 & 0 & 1 & 0 & 0 \\ 0 & 0 & 0 & 1 & 0 & 0 \\ 0 & 0 & 0 & 1 & 0 & 1 \\ 1 & 1 & 1 & 0 & 1 & 0 \\ 0 & 0 & 0 & 1 & 0 & 1 \\ 0 & 0 & 1 & 0 & 1 & 0 \end{pmatrix}$$

3.4 Example of a network. The graph has $N=6$ nodes (numbered circles), illustrating node degree and the network representation as a graph, F_{ij}. The degree (number of connections, shown as lines) of each node i is $k_i=(1, 1, 2, 4, 2, 2)$.

that some relationships can be stronger than others, or when they are directed so that love or an economic transaction, for example, may not be reciprocated.

For our purposes, we will only need a few basic network quantities. The most important is the *degree*, $k_i = \sum_{j=1}^{N} F_{ij}$, which is simply the number of connections that a node i has (and could be their total weight). For example, this could count all the people you know. In the example of figure 3.4, we have that $k_1=1$, $k_4=4$, $k_6=2$. We can average this number in the population of nodes and obtain the mean degree, k ($k=2$ for the graph of figure 3.4), as well as other statistics, such as the degree variance, $\sigma_k^2 = \frac{1}{N} \sum_{i=1}^{N} (k_i - k)^2$ ($\sigma_k^2 = 1$ in figure 3.4), or its statistical distribution in the population, $P(k)$, the fraction of people with zero, one, or two connections, and so on.

The most important general property of networks is so-called *network effects*, often expressed in terms of a statistical regularity known as *Metcalfe's law*. Network effects say that the *value of a network* is proportional to its number of links, not its number of nodes. Curiously, the concept was invented to describe the growth of the internet (actually its early precursors, involving phone lines and modems). The connection between cities and modern information networks is not accidental (see chapter 5): it is based on the fact that both express network effects. I find it fascinating that we needed to see this phenomenon really explode in a new form before we could understand it playing out in our own daily experience.

Network effects are general in that they apply to any kind of graph. They are not specific to economic exchange, for example, or crime or innovation. They generally lead to the expectation of a *superlinear* relationship between total network value, measured proportionally to total connections, and population size, measured as the number of nodes. At its simplest, this phenomenon is illustrated by the connectivity pattern of a fully connected graph (every node connected to every other node) with N nodes, which has total connectivity $K(N)=Nk(N)$,

$$K(N) = \frac{N(N-1)}{2} \sim N^2, \tag{3.8}$$

where the simplifying approximation denoted by $\sim$ applies when $N \gg 1$. We can obtain a similar average scaling result if each of the $K(N)$ connections is realized only with a nonzero probability. Thus, connectivity and, by extension, *value* scale superlinearly with population, with an exponent $\beta_M = 2$. We will refer to this special value as Metcalfe's exponent. It is the upper bound (largest possible value) of the connectivity exponent exhibited by any real network, so $\beta \leq \beta_M$, including in cities. This is because in practice not everyone can interact with everyone else in an increasingly larger population. Understanding the source of these limitations will provide the answer for computing actually observed values of urban scaling exponents.

3.2.2 URBAN SCALING THEORY

To develop a theory that derives urban scaling relations, we will have to take several steps, each building on the previous one; see figure 3.5 for a road map and objectives involved at each stage. The setup also requires that we think self-consistently, so that some types of networks, such as social interactions, derive their properties from spatial networks of infrastructure and associated flows *and vice versa*. In this sense, we need to build a theory of dynamic interdependencies between these different types of quantities leading to a logic that is not linear in terms of causality. We already encountered this kind of approach when we introduced the idea of spatial equilibria in chapter 2, and we generalized these ideas to other scaling relations earlier in this chapter. Describing cities mathematically in these ways is a bit more complex than any of these examples, so we need to develop the argument in parts and then bring everything together at the end of this section.

In part 1, we will show why social interactions constrained by mobility costs generally lead to interdependent superlinear social outputs *and* sublinear infrastructure volumes as functions of population size. This effect is very general and independent of the detailed form of how the spaces of cities are structured. We will find, however, that such structures do change with settlement sizes and affect the specific values of the exponents we want to predict. Consequently, in part 2, we will propose four basic principles that are sufficient to predict typical exponents observed for cities, based on a few basic features of human behavior and infrastructure networks. Part 3 formalizes these principles in terms of more detailed, multiscale models of infrastructure networks and derives associated movement flows and transportation costs, which allow us to recover, in part 4, the idea of a city as a (short-term) spatial equilibrium.

Part 1: The Amorphous Settlement Model Let us see why combining social interactions and mobility costs over space leads naturally to sublinear infrastructure volumes and superlinear socioeconomic products. The simplest model starts from some of the classical assumptions introduced in chapter 2 and is known as the *amorphous settlement*.

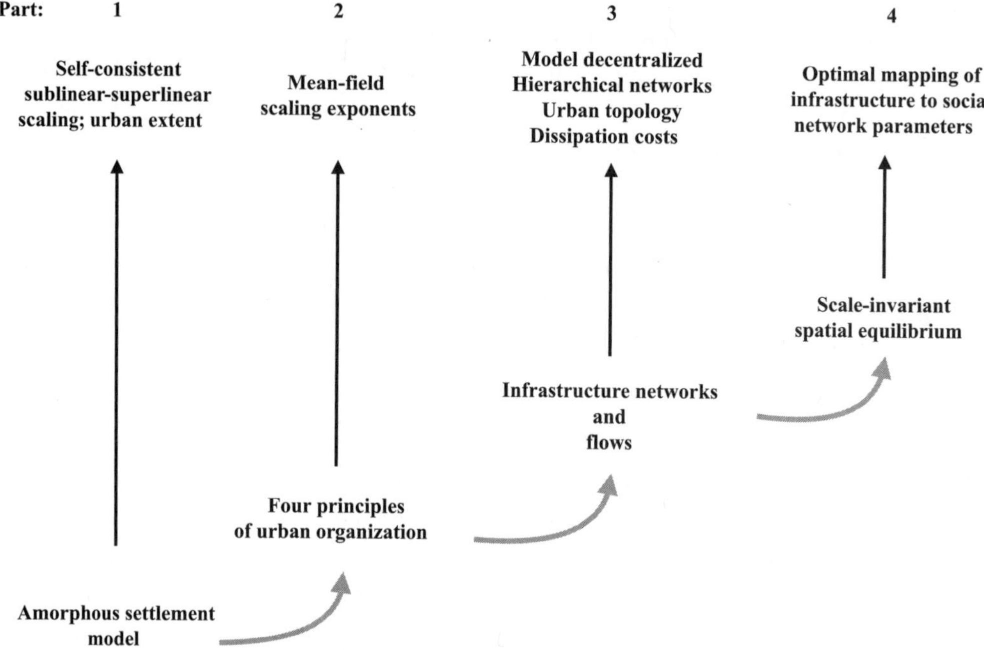

3.5 Urban scaling theory development in four parts. Each part provides a necessary step for setting up a self-consistent spatial equilibrium between socioeconomic interactions and movement costs that derives quantitative predictions for urban scaling exponents and prefactors.

By amorphous, we mean that the settlement is spatially unstructured in the sense that it has no streets or other explicit infrastructure. There are, however, dwellings distributed in space, but these may appear scattered randomly. See figure 3.6 for a real example of Capilco, a small Aztec town with these features. There are also human interactions, whose rate in this context becomes easy to compute on average.

The pattern of settlement of figure 3.6 is amorphous in terms of its shape, but it still describes the spatial concentration of people and dwellings. As such, it can be characterized by a characteristic length scale, R, that accounts for its overall size (a "radius";[17] note that the settlement is no longer radially symmetric!). The other scale in the problem is the number of dwellings, or correspondingly the number of people, N, as we may reasonably assume that each dwelling contains on average a given number of people (say a household, which historically is about four people). We should not expect that either of these scales—R or N—by itself takes any specific value. After all, settlements can and do have different populations and spatial sizes (see figure 3.7), but, as in the Alonso and von Thünen models, we may expect that the two scales are interrelated so that by changing one we must also change the other. This is the essence of scaling.

In other words, why do the dwellings in figure 3.6 appear at the scale that they do? Why aren't they closer, as in figure 3.7A, or farther apart, as in figure 3.7C? To answer

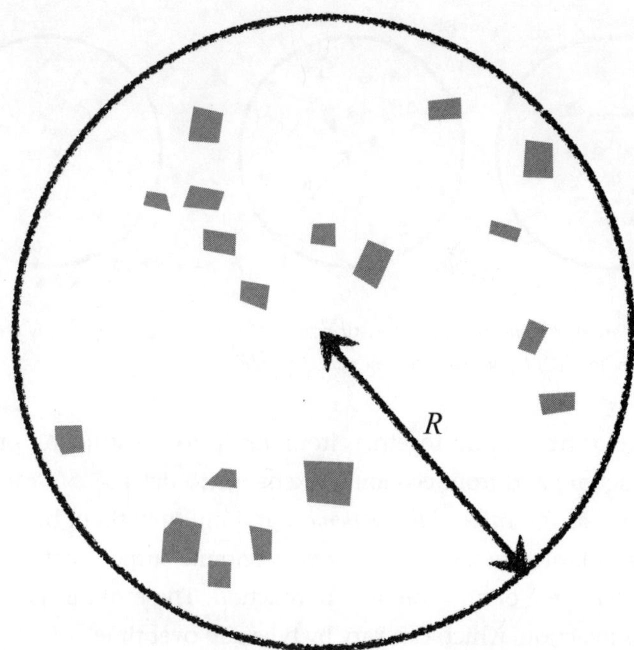

3.6 Spatial scheme of the small town of Capilco. This is a rural settlement consisting of buildings (gray polygons) dispersed over the landscape. The circle shows the approximate spatial extent of the settlement, which in turn defines a radius, R, as its characteristic length scale.

this question, we may posit that people organize themselves over space so that they can visit each other or meet in public spaces by walking around. In other words, they want to settle neither too close to their neighbors nor too far away. In such circumstances, "transportation costs" are set by the energetics and time involved in walking around. We can then say, as in the Alonso and von Thünen models, that the cost of movement over some period of time, t, is proportional to the total length of travel in units of the spatial size of the city, R. We will write this in units of resources (which could be energy or money) as a cost per unit time as

$$c_T(R; t) = c_{T_0} R, \tag{3.9}$$

where c_{T_0} is the cost of travel per unit time and unit length. We could have introduced a dimensionless proportionality number to account for the amount of travel in units of R, but we will omit it for simplicity. The quantity c_{T_0} may vary because of terrain or the availability of different modes of transportation, but for now we consider it as given.

What can we say about the income, y? In the models of chapter 2, incomes are given (economists say "exogenous"), or are the result of selling produce or labor. This is a good place to start walking away from economic assumptions and find more general reasons for human social interactions. The basic point of a settlement is that people can interact more frequently with each other. In real life, this facilitates all kinds of things

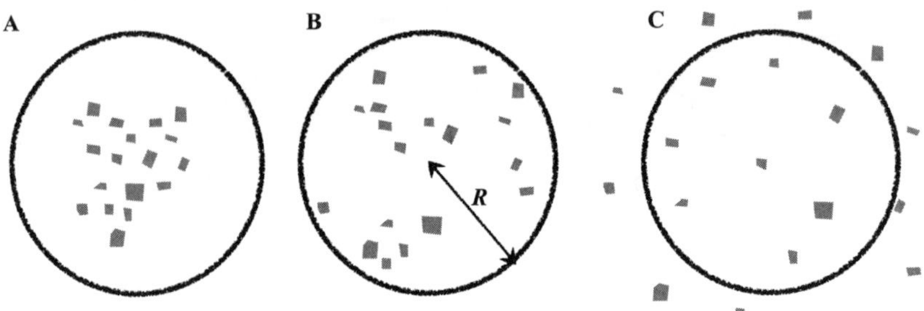

3.7 Why do settlements have the characteristic size (radius) that they have? Why are they not more concentrated (A) or less (C) compared to their actual size (B)?

that people like or need to do together, from gossip to construction of temples and shared infrastructure, and from economic exchange to defense. So, we simply count these interactions as the *value of the settlement* and multiply them by parameters that translate each encounter into a potential socioeconomic output, such as gaining information or the outcome of an economic transaction. These numbers also attribute a value to each interaction, which can vary by type and over time.

How many interactions may we expect someone to have over some period of time, such as a day? Let us do the math. Imagine moving around the settlement a distance ℓ, along which we are available for interaction with a probability a_0. It is important that this distance not be confused with the commuting distance, as you do not typically interact much while in your car or on public transit. The product $a_0\ell$ has the meaning of a social interaction area (analogous to a *cross section* in physics). We will take this quantity as an intrinsic property of individuals, independent of the size of the settlement, at least on average (we will later consider more general situations). Now the expected number of contacts with others depends on the total number of other people, $N-1$, multiplied by the total volume spanned by my path over that time t, divided by the total area. This gives an estimate of the probability for each encounter, which we then must multiply by the number of people one could encounter in each situation. Then, we can write the expected total number of interactions, k, per capita as

$$k = \frac{a_0\ell}{A}(N-1). \tag{3.10}$$

Now let us also assume that the (net!) social benefit of these interactions is the definition of "income," y (the value produced by the settlement per unit time), which is proportional to k, multiplied by a number g, which converts interactions into a common "currency" of social outputs such as energy or money. Then we obtain our average expectation for y as

$$y = \frac{g a_0 \ell}{A}(N-1) \equiv G\frac{N-1}{A}, \tag{3.11}$$

where we defined $G \equiv g a_0 \ell$ as a coupling (analogous to a *conductivity*) that transforms population density $\dfrac{N}{A}$ into average social outputs per capita, y. We will see later that this quantity plays a very special role in urban scaling theory and can be maximized in the sense of creating cities and settlements that are more efficient (better social outputs per interaction).

We can finally bring interactions and transportation costs together to determine the scaling of the settlement's area with population. We note that we can write these relations in terms of physical dimensions, $R \sim A^{1/2}$, so

$$G\frac{N-1}{A} = c_{T_0} A^{1/2} \;\rightarrow\; A(N) = \left[\frac{G}{c_{T_0}} (N-1) \right]^{2/3}. \tag{3.12}$$

This is the *area-population scaling relation* for an amorphous settlement, whose spatial extent is set by the balance of interactions and transportation costs, leading to $A \sim N^{2/3}$ for $N \gg 1$. The prefactor is defined up to a numerical factor that accounts for the shape of the settlement (including factors of 2 and π) and distance traveled. This result implies that average socioeconomic outputs scale as

$$Y = G\,\frac{N-1}{A} = G^{\frac{1}{3}} c_{T_0}^{\frac{2}{3}} (N-1)^{\frac{4}{3}} \simeq Y_0 N^{\frac{4}{3}}, \tag{3.13}$$

where $Y_0 = G^{\frac{1}{3}} c_{T_0}^{\frac{2}{3}}$. This shows how settlement areas are naturally *sublinear* and socioeconomic outputs *superlinear* by the same amount, specifically

$$A \sim N^{1-\delta}, \quad Y \sim N^{1+\delta}, \tag{3.14}$$

which is what we have been looking for.

However, the number $\delta = \frac{1}{3}$ is too big, at least in relation to the scaling relations observed in most cities today (table 3.1), which are also clearly *not* amorphous settlements! This gives us our next clue: to do better, we need to consider more of the structure of built spaces in cities and think of them also as interaction spaces. In chapter 7, we will also see why increasing the density of settlements does not increase their socioeconomic outputs indefinitely, because the nature of interactions changes at short distances and all kinds of problems ensue. Before we turn to the nature of built spaces in cities, we will spend a little bit more effort making the calculation of socioeconomic interactions more general and precise and showing their origins in the reasoning introduced by *time geography*.

Part 2: Four Principles of Urban Organization and Scaling We have now seen how combining social interactions in settlements as encounters in space-time together with associated movement costs leads to the right kind of model for scaling in cities. However, we also saw that this overestimates the exponent's magnitude away from unity because, as cities grow, space becomes occupied and transportation of people, goods, and information must be channeled into networks. The space created by these networks gives the correct average measure of the social interactions that can occur in cities. Let us then propose a more realistic model of cities by generalizing these ideas in terms of four simple general assumptions.

Urban areas are mixing populations The concept is that cities develop so that citizens can explore cities in full, given the resources at their disposal. The concept of *mixing* arises in epidemiology, where it refers to populations where all individuals can—in principle—come into contact with each other with some finite (but possibly unequal) probability. In the city, individuals ultimately need to acquire resources and information from each other, so the concept is generalized to all kinds of socioeconomic contacts, not just those that mediate contagion.

We can formalize this principle as an *entry condition* (a minimum "income") by requiring that the minimum resources accessible to each urbanite, $y_{min} = GN/A$, match the cost of reaching anywhere in the city. Thus, the reasoning associated with the amorphous settlement here no longer defines typical (mean) costs of movement. It is used instead to define the maximum extent of the city (radius) but not its internal structure and, as we will see, not its average rate of interactions. Note that this "income" is not necessarily monetary: it could be manifested in terms of energy and time. This entry condition plays a role analogous to the boundary condition setting land rents at the edge of the city in models of urban economics.

At this point, we can introduce one more generalization of these ideas, which will also provide a *control parameter* for the network effects that make up our functional cities and will allow us to appreciate the geometric origin of urban scaling exponents. Because travel paths need not be linear, we generalize their geometry via a fractal dimension, H_m, so distance traveled becomes $A^{H_m/D}$ (see figure 3.8). To exercise this concept, let us consider a city that exists in D spatial dimensions. Usually, we would take $D = 2$, where the volume taken up by a city is a land area, but this is not essential. We can imagine more general kinds of cities. Then we consider the

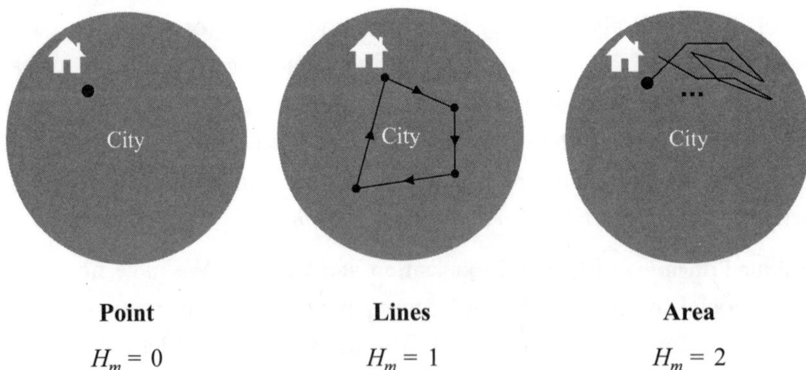

3.8 The geometry of human mobility in cities. The paths taken by people in cities can span spatial volumes with fundamentally different geometries, as single places (points), lines, or whole volumes parameterized by a quantity H_m, a fractal dimension. This quantity is measurable from observing people's trajectories over space and time. The panels exemplify three different situations: a point or set of points (left, $H_m = 0$), a line (middle, $H_m = 1$) where we perform a trajectory spanning the city but sample only a few points along the way, which in turn defines the agents' worldline, or an area (right, $H_m = 2$) that fills the entire areal extent of the city. Urban scaling relations reflect the interplay between this geometry of mobility and the spaces of the city shaped by its infrastructure networks.

generalized cost of travel that would follow from trajectories like those in figure 3.8. The (maximum) cost of mobility across the city will now read

$$c_T = c_{T_0} \, A^{\frac{H_m}{D}}, \tag{3.15}$$

where A is now a D-dimensional volume, so $A^{\frac{1}{D}}$ is a length. Thus, if $H_m = 1$, our agent threads a line through this volume—as in time geography—but, in general, other situations are imaginable by varying the geometry of mobility spaces and their corresponding embedding physical spaces.

The consequence of this generalization is that the scaling of the city volume with its population will now look like

$$A(N) = \left(\frac{G}{c_{T_0}} \right)^{\frac{D}{D+H_m}} N^{\frac{D}{D+H_m}}. \tag{3.16}$$

This expression teaches us a few things. If we want strong nonlinear effects, then small D is better because encounters between people become easier (in a sense, there is less "space," meaning fewer dimensions, to get lost in). Compensating for the increase in D would require an increase in our mobility volumes in the form of a bigger H_m. The limit $H_m \to 1$ allows individuals to fully sample the city within the smallest distance traveled, implying that the population size, N, scales as $N \sim R^{D+H_m}$, which for $H_m = 1$ means that it scales like a physical volume, $N \sim R^{D+1}$, as noted long ago by Nordbeck[18] in the context of Swedish cities. We will see later that cities work well in $D = 2$ and that making H_m and D very different from what they typically are either creates tremendous congestion and associated high costs of movement or a space where meeting becomes almost impossible so the fruits of society become increasingly improbable.

Incremental network growth Despite a few well-known examples of cities planned from the start, the infrastructure of the vast majority of urban areas develops gradually and is built as needed, indeed often after it is needed! In most cases, this forces streets and roads and other infrastructure to be coadapted to patterns of settlement and not take up more space than needed functionally. Urban networks provide local connectivity so people can visit their neighbors by traveling only a short distance, unlike what happens in other complex systems, such as river networks or the vascular system of organisms, which are hierarchically configured as tree graphs. By contrast, urban networks become so-called *decentralized networks*, as first shown empirically by Samaniego and Moses.[19] Specifically, the scaling of figures 3.1, 3.2, and 3.3 and table 3.1 is obtained when the average distance between individuals is $d_A = n_A^{-\frac{1}{2}} = \left(\frac{A}{N} \right)^{1/2}$ and so equals the average length of infrastructure network per capita so the total *network area* is $A_n(N) \sim N d_A = N \left(\frac{A}{N} \right)^{\frac{1}{2}} = N^{\frac{1}{2}} A^{\frac{1}{2}}$.[20] Together with the condition of mixing, this implies that $A_n \sim a^{\frac{1}{2}} N^{1-\delta}$, with $\delta = \frac{1}{6}$ (or $\delta = \frac{H_m}{D(D+H_m)}$

for general D, H_m). This is the observed scaling exponent in US and German road networks (table 3.1) and tracks the average built area of more than 3,600 large cities worldwide,[21] measured using remote sensing. As we have seen, the infrastructure networks of cities connect places of residence and work, so these spaces all become isomorphic to the infrastructure network, a property we return to in subsection 3.3.8.

Human effort is bounded This principle reflects something quite obvious and inescapable, that the total effort per person placed on movement and interactions is limited by time and by basic human capabilities. The increasing mental and physical effort that growing cities can demand from their inhabitants has been a pervasive concern to social scientists, especially psychologists,[22] as we saw in chapter 1. The assumption here is that the scaling of productivity and contacts per capita is primarily the result of socioeconomic network effects (which express human "ecological effects" in the sense of chapter 1). This means that allocating finite time and effort to social activities poses severe fundamental trade-offs at the individual level, which we will explore more fully in chapters 4 and 5. In terms of modeling, this limitation means that the factors that make up the coupling G are such that, on average, this quantity tends to become independent of city size, $\frac{dG}{dN} = 0$ (because $G > 0$, this is equivalent to $\frac{d\ln G}{dN} = 0$). This assumption is necessary to lift an important objection to any conceptualization of cities as scale-invariant systems: any open-ended increase in socioeconomic outputs is a network effect, not an individual effort effect. Bounded effort is observed in urban cell phone communication networks[23] and is generally a function of human constraints and urban services and structure. We will derive how G depends on these factors later.

Socioeconomic outputs are proportional to local social interactions We already made this assumption when we introduced the amorphous settlement model. From this perspective, the social outputs for individual i of type m are given by $y_i^m = g_m k_i^m$, and total output for the city results from summing over all individuals, $Y^m = g_m \sum_i k_i^m = g_m K^m$. On the whole, over types of interactions, such as when we consider the total size of a city's economy (its GDP), we may write $Y = \sum_{i;m} g_m k_i^m$, with the general expectation that it is the number of interactions and not so much the prefactors that scale superlinearly with population size. Note, however, that there can be a certain amount of substitution between these two effects, especially as we measure interaction modes very finely, as in chapter 5.

From this perspective, cities are concentrations not just of people but of social interactions. This point was emphasized by Jacobs[24] but has been difficult to quantify until recently. Before we proceed to consider a more detailed model of decentralized infrastructure networks, let us consider how a given behavior channeled by these network interactions can be calculated.

The Time Geography of Interactions: Entangled Life Paths and Worldlines   We have just started to see how important it is to consider a person's trajectory over space and time in cities. Each person's trajectory maps their socioeconomic interactions, including the choices and accidents that create resulting observable products. We introduced these ideas in the context of time geography. It is now time to show how to flesh them out mathematically.

Let us define the trajectory of individual i in space-time as $x_i[t]$. Specifically, $x_i[t]$ is the position in space of our agent i at time t, typically a two-dimensional vector such as latitude and longitude: the kind of thing you see in your cell phone mapping app. We can change t and unfold this trajectory, generating the agent's *worldline* or *life path*. (I like both terms and will use them interchangeably.) As a schematic picture, these trajectories look like figure 3.9. It may be interesting for the reader to try to draw their own worldline (or download it from their mapping app), at least for a typical working day, over the map of the region you live in. If you do so, I'll bet that you will have something close to the middle pattern of figure 3.8.

For people to meet in person, their worldlines must coincide in space-time; they must become *entangled* in this sense. This allows us to consider the $x_i[t]$ over all agents in a population and compute the city as a set of colocations at which socioeconomic interactions likely occur. We will use this procedure as a way to derive theory, but it is also a perfectly adequate way to measure behavior; for example, if we know people's life paths based on their mobile device location data.[25]

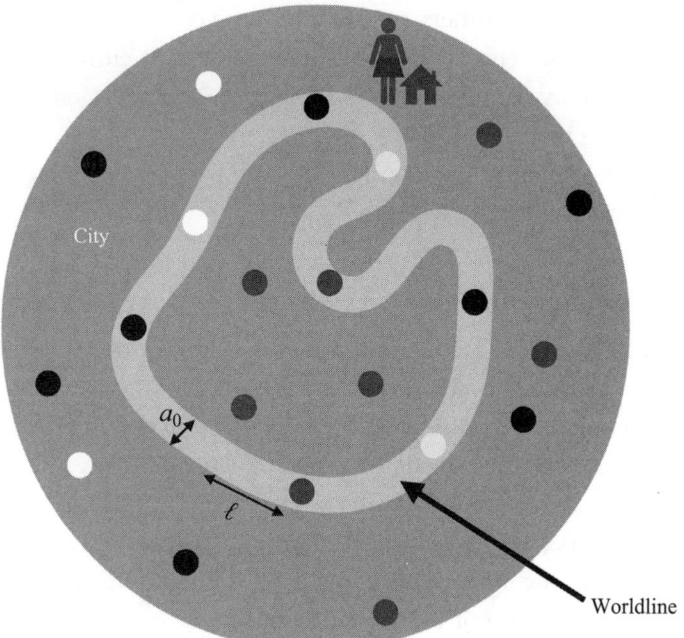

3.9   Scheme of an individual's trajectory. The individual's worldline (or life path) over some time period is shown as the thick gray line with linear extent ℓ and interaction area a_0. The average number of interactions of each type, m (circles with different tones), is proportional to $a_0\ell/A_n\, P(m)$.

Let us now see how to compute the socioeconomic outputs of cities in terms of the social network $F_{ij}^{m}(t)$ between agents (persons) i and j, mediated by a set of different interaction types—friendship, employment, acquaintance, and others—indexed by m. This network only exists over some long period of time, t (days, months, years), that includes a large number of interactions, each playing out instantaneously. Over longer time periods, say from year to year, $F_{ij}^{m}(t)$ will be dynamic and we will have to account for phenomena such as changes of residence and work and for aggregate economic growth. The sum over all the products of these interactions is

$$Y(t) = \sum_{i,j;m} g_m F_{ij}^{m}(t), \tag{3.17}$$

where g_m is the strength per link of the interaction of type m to generate the total output of the city, Y. Note that the couplings, g_m, can be either positive (attractive, expressing a social benefit, such as mutually beneficial economic relations) or negative (repulsive, expressing a social cost, such as crime), though for the city to exist the balance must be positive. The couplings g_m have dimensions of Y per interaction; for example, units of money or energy per unit time. In a city, there are many forms of interactions. For example, economic transactions contribute to economic output in terms of wages, profits, and many other quantities. Crime, in contrast, may be the output of noneconomic interactions such as those between the perpetrator and the victim as well as those mediated by law enforcement and by citizens themselves. Likewise, the interactions that lead to the spread of a contagious disease will be mediated by their specific types of encounters. Some of these modes of interaction may naturally coincide with others, such as catching a cold while shopping, or learning gossip while at work. The urban environment affects its citizens across all these dimensions, so a theory of cities must take them into account *together*, as we heard from Jane Jacobs in chapters 1 and 2.

To see this more explicitly, first consider the number of interactions (degree), k_i^{m}, of a specific individual i and mode m,

$$k_i^{m} = \sum_{j} F_{ij}^{m}. \tag{3.18}$$

Then, the socioeconomic products of type m for agent i are $y_i^{m} = g_m k_i^{m}$, with the expectation that, on average over individuals, the product of the value and the number of interactions should be superlinear on the population of the city. This should now start to sound plausible in light of our discussion of network effects and Metcalfe's law.

To do this, we need to consider how to calculate the likelihood of interactions and their population averages. This procedure requires two types of averaging, one over interaction types and the other over people. If we are interested only in these averages (as in this chapter but not further in the book), we can consider the situation where the probability of the interaction type m is statistically independent from the specific pair i, j so we can write the interactions as $F_{ij}^{m} = P(m|i,j)F_{ij} = P(m)F_{ij}$, where $P(m)$ is the probability of different interaction types, m, per link in the population and F_{ij} is the social network across all interaction types, without distinction, as is often measured, say, using cell phones or spatial colocation. This type of simplification, where we cease to pay attention to particular individuals and care only about population-level probabilities, is known as a *mean-field approximation*. With this approximation, we can now easily write the average over interaction modes in equation (3.17) as $\bar{g} = \int dm\, g_m P(m)$.

Now consider the second type of averaging, where these interactions take place over space and time as emphasized by time geography. Let us imagine the spaces involved. We characterize each individual by an interaction area, a_0, and by a length traveled in the network, ℓ. This spans a *worldsheet* (a thick line with width a_0 in figure 3.9) that is a fraction of the total public space area, A_n, of the city. Because both a_0 and ℓ cannot vary very much, we may think of them as intrinsic properties of individuals (the hypothesis of bounded human effort). Thus, in what follows in this chapter, we will take these two parameters as independent of the type of interaction m.

Let us now compute the average interactions in equation (3.18),

$$k_i^m(t) = \int dt' \sum_j P(m|ij)\, \Gamma^m\, (x_j[t'] - x_i[\,t']),$$

$$\simeq \frac{P(m)}{A_n} \int dt'\, d^D x\, \Gamma(x - x_i[t']) \simeq P(m)\, \frac{a_0 \ell}{A_n}\, (N - 1). \tag{3.19}$$

Here, $\Gamma^m\, (x_j[t'] - x_i[t'])$ is an interaction kernel, which accounts for the probability ("strength") of interactions of type m between agents, i and j, whenever they become close spatially. It is a sort of a "coincidence detector" between the two worldlines in space and time. An example is a delta function, which equals 1 whenever $x_j[t'] = x_i[t']$ (i.e., the agents coincide in space and time), but we can imagine a softer kernel where this probability is nonzero if they are in sight of or in earshot of each other (at a distance $\sim a_0$). The first line is exact and depends only on defining an appropriate kernel and conditional interaction type probability. This expression can generally be used and defines a socioeconomic network of exchange over space and time.

The second line shows the *mean-field approximation*. We see explicitly two parts to this approximation. The first relies on dropping the dependence of the probability on the specific agents, allowing us to take it out of the sum/integral. The second expresses the volume spanned by the worldsheets (worldline multiplied by length of interaction) of everybody in a city as its total networked volume, A_n, which we integrate over. Then, the integration over the interaction kernel gives us back the volume of our particular agent's worldsheet and the simple geometric result that the average probability of interaction over some time is proportional to the individual's worldsheet divided by the interaction volume of the city over that time, multiplied by the number of other agents, $N - 1$. Note that the temporal dependence becomes implicit in the length traveled, so $\ell = v_d t = \ell_d \left(\dfrac{t}{t_d} \right)$, where $v_d = \ell_d / t_d$ is the average speed of motion and the second equality denotes the length traveled per macroscopic unit of time t_d (say a day) so t/t_d becomes the number of days over which $Y(t)$ is measured (e.g., a year). Overall, equation (3.19) gives us both an exact expression to compute socioeconomic interactions of particular agents and types in cities and their mean-field approximation, which is sufficient for deriving scaling relations. When in doubt, and for more statistical quantities, we can return to the first expression before we take the mean-field approximation.

Returning to the products of interaction, we obtain the mean-field result for the total socioeconomic interactions,

$$Y = \sum_{i,m} g_m \, k_i^m = \bar{g} \, \frac{a_0 \ell}{A_n} (N-1)N \simeq G \frac{N^2}{A_n}, \tag{3.20}$$

where the parameter $G \equiv \bar{g} \, a_0 \ell$. This in turn means that the products of socioeconomic interactions *per capita* are, on average,

$$y = \frac{Y}{N} = \bar{g} \left(\frac{a_0 \ell}{A_n} \right) N = G \frac{N}{A_n}. \tag{3.21}$$

It is important to stress that although social interactions are local and take place at the most microscopic level between two individuals, equations (3.18)–(3.20) nevertheless lead to *effective* interactions between individuals who are not directly connected, through chains of people between them, and between individuals and institutions (firms, public administration) as well as between institutions themselves. This makes cities searchable networks within a few interaction steps, as we will see (figure 3.10). These effective interactions are obtained via the appropriate groupings of individuals in social or economic organizations and by considering the resulting coarse-grained interactions between such entities (which are always ultimately mediated by people). Institutions and industries that benefit from strong mutual interactions may aggregate in space and time within the city in order to maximize their interactions minus associated movement costs, a point first made by Marshall[26] (see chapter 2).

We are now finally ready for part 3, where we develop a detailed model of how the area of cities relevant for interactions, A_n, depends on population.

Part 3: Decentralized Networks and Mobility Costs Thus far, we have obtained expressions for scaling exponents without the need for a detailed model of infrastructure. Next, we show how network models of infrastructure can help to illuminate these questions and, as a bonus, also inform some classical dilemmas of urban planning and policy.

A feature of modern cities that is qualitatively different from amorphous settlements is the development of infrastructure networks that themselves add new levels of organization with city size. For example, larger roads and highways in large cities allow faster movement across a metropolis than local roads that may have been present in a smaller village. This is illustrated in figure 3.12.

To make this sort of structure mathematical, consider dividing the infrastructure networks of a city in terms of h hierarchical levels (figure 3.12). This number is a parameter, and we can choose to define these levels more or less coarsely; it is not a fundamental rigid typology. Between any two consecutive levels, we also define a

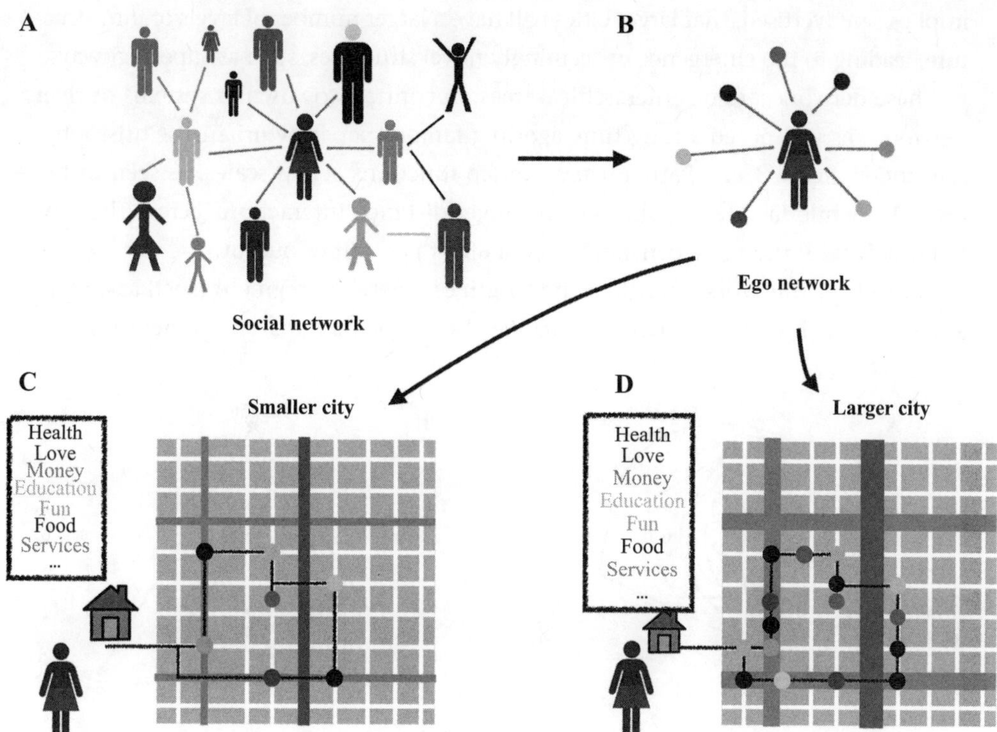

3.10 Interplay between social and infrastructural networks in cities. (A) Social networks of diverse individuals, usually with functional complementarities, can be represented as ego networks, centered in each person (B), which are a set of embedded social interactions in the city's infrastructure network (C and D). In a smaller city, population densities are lower, so the rate of diverse social interactions is smaller for the same time and effort. In larger cities, infrastructure networks present higher levels of complexity, and larger population densities during active times lead to socioeconomic networks with higher degree, resulting in larger network effects.

parameter that accounts for the change in these scales. Thus, the network branching, b_h, measures the average ratio of the number of units of i infrastructure at successive levels $N_i = b_h^i$; for example, the number of paths to small roads or from larger roads to highways. This may seem artificial at first, but in modern cities it is common to have a discrete category of streets and roads; for example, from local neighborhood lanes, to streets and major thoroughfares, to highways. These are shown on any city map in different colors and with different widths. Other infrastructure networks arguably also share some of this discrete categorical distinction, with different levels holding larger or smaller capacities in terms of the fluxes they mediate, such as water flow, electrical current, or information bandwidth.

Next, we will assume that the number of infrastructure units at the lowest level, $i = h$, equals the number of people, so $N_h = N$ and $h = \ln N / \ln b_h$. This means that, at the lowest levels, there is a typical amount of network (and flows) per person, commensurate with the linear scaling of household quantities in table 3.1. This parameterization also implies, as advertised, that larger cities will have a larger number of levels of infrastructure, leading to the emergence of seemingly novel structures, such as superhighways.

These networks are not hierarchical trees, in contrast to vascular systems or river networks, as was noted a long time ago in a famous paper by urbanist Christopher Alexander (figure 3.11). Rather, they overlap functions across scales, as seen in figure 3.12, while facilitating shorter- or longer-distance interactions across the city, essentially with the same constant level of effort per unit of output.

To see how this works, consider the length of a network segment (such as a road) at level i to be l_i, crossing a land area a_i. We also define its transverse dimension (i.e.,

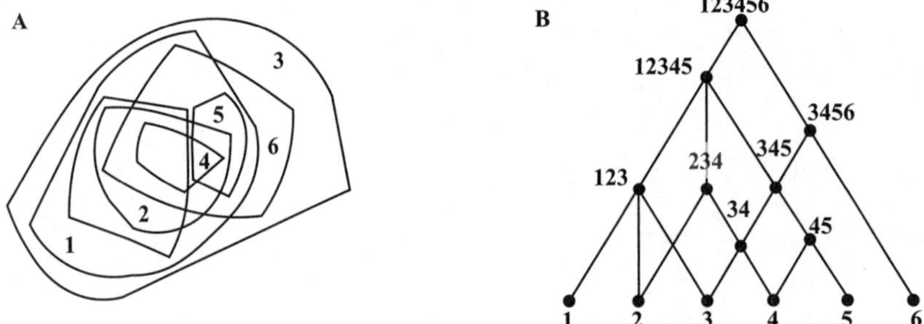

3.11   The city is not a tree. This famous diagram from a 1965 paper by Christopher Alexander emphasizes that the spaces of cities overlap in uses, people, and timescales and should not be understood as a simple hierarchy (a tree, in the sense of a tree graph). These overlaps are best understood as complex networks with structures that do not repeat in simple ways but that can be characterized statistically. *Source*: Adapted by the author from Christopher Alexander, "A City Is Not a Tree," *Architectural Forum* 122, no. 1 (1965): 58–62.

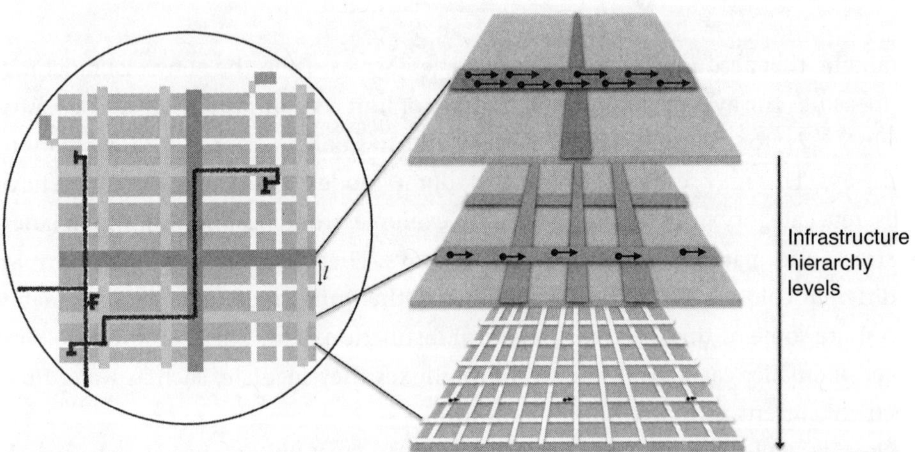

3.12   Scheme of infrastructure networks in the city and corresponding flows. The complete network can be understood as the overlap of a number of different levels, all of which are area filling but each characterized by different densities, widths, and flows. Small streets (white) are dense, narrow, and mediate slow flows, while highways (darker gray) are sparse, broad, and mediate faster flows (black arrows).

its width), a_s, which is an area in $D=3$ networks (such as for pipes) and a length in $D=2$ (such as surface roads).

To make these local quantities consistent with overall scaling relations and the four principles enunciated earlier, we need to specify how l_i, a_i, and a_{s_i} change across levels of the infrastructure network.

Because infrastructure must reach everyone in the city,[27] total network length is area filling (in the sense of the urbanized area) at all scales, so $l_i = \dfrac{a_i}{l}$, with $a_i = a\, b_h^{(\alpha-1)i}$, which reproduces the scaling of total area with population. To see this, note that this relation implies that the land area per person is $a_h = aN^{\alpha-1}$ (so $A = a_h N = aN^\alpha$) and the shortest distance over the network, $l_h = \left(\dfrac{a}{l}\right)N^{\alpha-1}$, which defines l, decreases with city size, thus "compressing" people together over the structure of urban built spaces. We will also assume that the transverse dimension of the smallest network units, a_{s*}, is independent of city size, N, consistent with the linear scaling of individual needs. Finally, this implies the scaling of network width as $a_{si} = a_{s*}\, b_h^{(\delta-1)(i-h)}$, which says simply that highways or water mains are much wider than building corridors or household pipes, $a_{s_0} = b_h^{h(1-\delta)} \gg a_{s_h} = a_{s*}$. The total network length, L_n, and area, A_n, can now be calculated. They are given by the sum of these quantities over levels as a standard sum of a geometric series,

$$L_n(N) = \sum_{i=0}^{h} l_i N_i = \frac{a}{l}\sum_{i=0}^{h} b_h^{\alpha i} = \frac{a}{l}\,\frac{b_h^{\alpha(h+1)}-1}{b_h^\alpha - 1} \simeq L_0 N^\alpha, \quad L_0 = \frac{a}{l},$$

$$A_n(N) = \sum_{i=0}^{h} a_{s_i} l_i N_i = a_{s*}\frac{a}{l}\,b_h^{(1-\delta)h}\sum_{i=0}^{h} b_h^{(\alpha+\delta-1)i} \simeq A_0 N^{1-\delta}, \quad A_0 = \frac{a_{s*}\, a}{l(1-b_h^{\alpha+\delta-1})},$$

$$(3.22)$$

where, for the series to converge, we need to assume that $\alpha + \delta < 1$, which always holds for $D > 1$ (see table 3.3 in section 3.3).

Besides these calculations, we can develop an intuition for how infrastructure networks fill the total spatial area of the city, A. This assumption is implicit in the principle that infrastructure networks grow in a decentralized way in order to connect each addition of a new inhabitant in an additional dwelling. This assumption means more explicitly that any occupied land area (as a residence, business, or any other use) can be reached by people, goods, and information traveling over the city's infrastructure networks. The technology involved in these networks varies enormously with the level of urban development, but we will assume that the geometry of the networks does not. Figure 3.12 illustrates this situation for a regular grid. In this simple case, the total length of the network can be calculated easily as

$$A = L^2 = (n_b l)^2, \quad L_n = 2(n_b + 1)n_b l = \frac{2}{l}A + 2\sqrt{A} \xrightarrow[n_b \gg 1]{} A, \qquad (3.23)$$

where l is the average block length (the minimum separation along the network, which is independent of city size), n_b is the (linear) number of blocks across the city, and $L = n_b l$. The factor of 2 in the first term of L_n accounts for vertical plus horizontal network segments, and the factor of $n_b + 1$ counts the number of segments across the city, including one at the edge, each with length $L = n_b l$. The factor of n_b^2 that results is then identified with the area, A, up to a multiplicative constant. For networks that are not, on average, square grids, the constants multiplying the factors of area A will differ but not the space-filling character of the network, expressed as $L_n \sim \frac{A}{l}$. In cities where settlement precedes the development of infrastructure networks, such as when slums develop in fast-growing cities (discussed in subsection 3.3.8), the length of the network will not be area filling and can be used as a diagnostic for missing infrastructure. In other situations, where all space is built up, as in the city centers of larger urban areas, we may also observe $L_n \sim A \sim A_n$, which would show that our urban definition is too strict and does not include peripheral commuting zones.

Mobility Costs over Networks So far, we have considered only a very crude sense of urban mobility, where costs were proportional to distance or even simpler, as in the discrete iceberg costs of the core-periphery model in chapter 2. Now that we have a handle on models of infrastructure that change their structure with scale, we can calculate these costs in more realistic circumstances.

From an aggregate perspective, these are the costs of keeping the city connected, measured as the total energy per unit time necessary for moving people, goods, and information across its infrastructure networks. These movements form a set of *currents* transporting various quantities across the city, which can be quantified by means of the general language of circuits in physics. The most important concepts we will need are current conservation and resistive dissipation costs. Current conservation here means that quantities being transported across the city—people, cars, information, and so on—can generally be assumed to be conserved across levels of the infrastructure network: a car does not vanish when it enters a highway; it will reappear again on a local street somewhere else in the city (we are neglecting movement in and out of the city here, or assuming that they are balanced). Basic physics tells us also that there is a dissipative cost to moving *anything*. This cost will give us a general microscopic model for the origin of transportation costs.

To do this, consider the scaling of the width a_{s_i} together with total current, J, conservation across levels meaning that

$$J_i = a_{s_i} \rho_i v_i N_i = a_{s_{i-1}} \rho_{i-1} v_{i-1} N_{i-1} = J_{i-1}, \tag{3.24}$$

for all levels i. This current conservation sets the necessary scaling of the flow density $\rho_i v_i$ across levels, where ρ_i is the density of carriers on the network and v_i is their velocity (e.g., cars per area of road and their speed). This quantity is especially interesting because it controls the dissipation mechanisms in any network. Using the preceding conservation condition and the scaling of N_i and a_{s_i} leads to

$$\rho_i v_i = b_h^{-\delta} \rho_{i-1} v_{i-1}, \tag{3.25}$$

which implies that the current density *decreases* with increasing i, so highways are faster and/or more densely packed than smaller roads.[28] (Next time you are on an airplane flying over a city, look down and I bet that you'll see that this is true! I often do this, and it never fails to bring a big smile to my face!) To end the calculation, we need to set a boundary condition on these flows. This in itself raises a rather profound question: how much stuff will a city move around, and why? As already mentioned, we use the fact that individual needs per capita do not vary on average, so $\rho_h v_h = \rho_* v_*$, independent of city size. This results in $\rho_i v_i = b_h^{\delta(h-i)} \rho_* v_*$, and the total current is $J = J_0 N$, with $J_0 = a_{s_*} \rho_* v_*$ an inevitable but elegant result: the sum of individual needs at each terminal point of the network where people live and work. We could have started with this condition, of course, but it is satisfying to derive it from a set of nonlinear scaling relations for socioeconomic products and infrastructure networks.

To calculate the energy dissipation associated with these currents, we need to have a sense of the city's *conductivity*, or equivalently the total *resistance* of infrastructure networks. To compute this, we can make the standard assumption that the resistance per unit length per transverse network area, r_J, is constant,[29] leading to the resistance per network segment, $r_{J_i} = r_J \dfrac{l_i}{a_{s_i}}$. This means, for example, that all roads are made of the same materials. For the N_i parallel resistors in our network, this becomes a standard calculation, which leads to the *total* resistance per level, $R_{J_i} = \dfrac{r_{J_i}}{N_i} = \dfrac{a r_J}{l a_{s_*}} b_h^{-(1-\alpha+\delta)i-(1-\delta)h}$. Then the total power dissipated, $W(N)$, by all these currents operating across the city follows from summing the power dissipations at each level, $W_i = R_{J_i} J_i^2$, so

$$W(N) = J^2 \sum_{i=1}^{h} R_{J_i} = J^2 \frac{a r_J}{l a_{s_*}} b_h^{-(1-\delta)h} \frac{1 - b_h^{-(1-\alpha+\delta)(h+1)}}{1 - b_h^{-1+\alpha-\delta}} = W_0 N^{1+\delta}, \tag{3.26}$$

with $W_0 = \dfrac{a r_J J_0^2}{l a_{s_*}(1 - b_h^{-1+\alpha-\delta})}$. This shows that the total costs of mobility (not just for people but for *everything*, including packages, water, electrical power, and information) over the city's infrastructure networks scale superlinearly with the same exponent as socioeconomic outputs! Observe carefully where this comes from because it is *not a network effect* in the sense of Metcalfe's law. It is the result of the basic physics of energy flow. The power dissipation can also be written as $W = E_{V_C} J$, where $E_{V_C} = R_{J_c} J \sim N^\delta$ is the (energy) potential across the city, with $R_{J_c} = \sum_{i=1}^{h} R_{J_i} \sim N^{\delta-1}$ the effective total resistance across all levels of infrastructure. Thus, we see that the decentralized (parallel) nature of the urban infrastructure networks greatly reduces dissipation with city size. This is because, unlike in hierarchical networks, flows in decentralized networks can take many different paths (you can reroute your commute if some roads are jammed). The "problem" of superlinear costs is simply the result of power dissipation being quadratic on the currents, proportional to kinetic energy, not velocity or distance. Without reducing the provision for individual needs, power dissipation in cities will inevitably increase superlinearly with population size, even with infrastructure networks that are rather efficient, at least in terms of their structural design. By comparison, biological organisms increase efficiency by reducing the power delivery to their cells (i.e., reduce currents), resulting in a slowdown of individual metabolism with scale (Kleiber's law), as we have seen. This is the *opposite* of what happens energetically in cities, where instead individual consumption is maintained across scales and social interactions are intensified. Needless to say, in cities where people vote or can move away, it would be very difficult to elect a mayor on a platform of making the city more *organic* in the sense of reducing power provision to people, in order to mirror the strategies of biological organisms.

This also means that the ratio of socioeconomic output value to power dissipation, $\frac{Y}{W}$, is independent of population size. This ratio is a measure of the efficiency of a city. Its conservation across city sizes is immensely consequential. This means specifically that cities are *not limited in size* by their (movement) costs as long as they are sufficiently productive in their socioeconomic dynamics. This is essentially what one observes in practice, leading to an expectation completely different from those of some of the urban economics models in chapter 2. Thanks to the constancy of this ratio on urban population magnitudes, cities can remain open-ended relative to size. This means that we can have cities big and small today and that we can, in principle, create cities that are much larger in the future.

Part 4: The Budget Condition and Scale-Invariant Equilibria Finally, let us show that these results can be derived by maximizing *net urban output*, $\mathcal{L}$, defined as the difference between social interaction outcomes, Y, and infrastructure energy dissipation, W, under settlement and network constraints,

$$\mathcal{L} = Y - W + \lambda_1\left(c_{T_0} A^{\frac{H_m}{D}} - G\frac{N}{A}\right) + \lambda_2(A_n - A_0' N n_A) \xrightarrow[\frac{d\mathcal{L}}{dG}=0]{} \frac{2\alpha - 1}{\alpha} G^* \frac{N^2}{A_n(N)}, \tag{3.27}$$

where $A_0' = A_0 a^{-\frac{1}{D}}$ and λ_1 and λ_2 are Lagrange multipliers enforcing the decentralized networks and entry condition constraints. The novelty of this equation is that it gives us a basis for predicting an optimal value of the coupling $G=G^*$ through the optimization condition, $\frac{d\mathcal{L}}{dG} = 0$. Values of G for each city should then cluster around this special value. To see this, consider that social outputs and mobility costs have different dependencies on G. Keeping c_{T_0} fixed, both Y and W increase with G, but $Y_0 \sim G^{1-\alpha}$, while $W_0 \sim G^\alpha$. The tension between seeking increases in the value of social interactions and the consequent faster rise in transportation costs is at the root of most problems of urban planning.

The calculation shows that the two quantities are connected in a very specific way and can be balanced to generate the best possible outcome for the city as a whole. First, consider the limiting outcomes when costs of transportation equal advantages of interaction and the city presumably becomes unstable for the average agent (person). There are two solutions,

$$G \equiv G_{min} = 0 \;\; or \;\; G \equiv G_{max} = \left[\frac{(c_{T_0} l)^{2\alpha}}{r_J' J_0^2} l^{2(1-\alpha)}\right]^{\frac{1}{2\alpha-1}}, \tag{3.28}$$

with $r_j' = \dfrac{r_j}{\left(1 - b_h^{\alpha-\delta-1}\right)\left(1 - b_h^{\alpha+\delta-1}\right)}$. Then the value of G that maximizes social benefits minus transportation costs can be computed as

$$G^* = \left[\frac{1-\alpha}{\alpha}\right]^{\frac{1}{2\alpha-1}} G_{max} \leq G_{max}, \tag{3.29}$$

where the prefactor is a pure geometric factor (depending on the scaling exponents!). This expression shows that the optimum, G^*, lies between the minimum and maximum limiting values of G. In fact, for our simplest value of $\alpha = \dfrac{2}{3}$, this leads to the very simple result that $G^* = \dfrac{G_{max}}{8}$.

Thus, cities will form if the balance of social interactions is positive, $\bar{g} > 0$. However, there is always an upper value of $G = G_{max}$ (figure 3.13B) beyond which transportation costs overcome social benefits and a city disintegrates spatially and splits into smaller regions. For $G < G^*$, the social interaction potential of a city is underdeveloped and can grow. Such places tend to be poorer and have less advanced infrastructure, such as in developing cities. Conversely, cities with $G > G^*$ become victims of their own socioeconomic success by sprawling too much and thus incurring unnecessary mobility costs that lead to an inefficient use of their productivity, which is simply dissipated away in the form of waste heat.

This shows that cities may be inefficient either because they do not realize their full social potential or because they do so in a manner that renders transportation costs too high. In either case, urban scaling theory shows how urban planning must take into account the delicate net balance between density, mobility, and social connectivity and how it provides a general framework for the iterative development and assessment of urban policies. This would imply measuring and improving the input parameters to equations (3.28) and (3.29) in a system of cities and attempting to affect parameters such as productivity, infrastructure efficiency, or travel patterns so as to make cities better at realizing more valuable social interactions for more people at lower transportation costs.

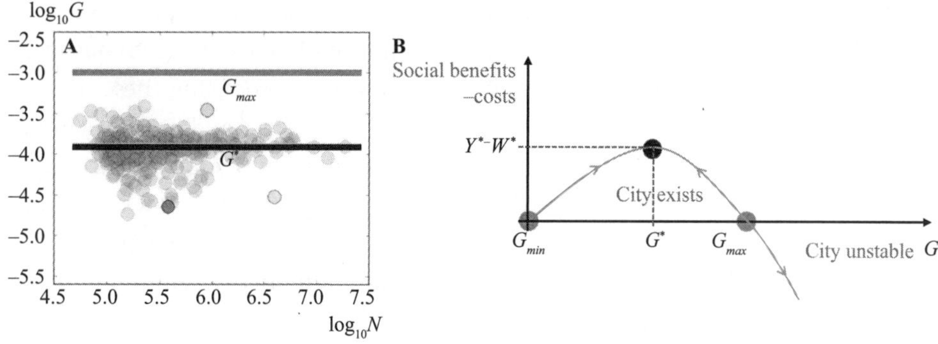

3.13 Scale independence of the coupling G and its range for city stability. (A) Data for US metropolitan areas show the constancy of G, and its limiting maximum value. (B) Schematic of phase diagram for a city showing the interval in the value of the couplings that renders a city possible and stable, and the value that maximizes net social benefits minus mobility costs.

Discussion: Caveats and Other Approaches to Urban Scaling We have now developed a general framework to describe cities systematically in quantitative terms as interconnected social and infrastructural complex networks. This framework connects new data and emerging concepts of cities as complex adaptive systems to classical models across a wide range of disciplines. It also extends and sharpens general concepts such as the generality of an agent's life course as a space-time trajectory, its resulting socioeconomic interactions and associated products exchanged, and the networked nature of built spaces. We have also shown in this chapter how these phenomena can be averaged over entire cities and over time to calculate specific scaling relations in terms of numerical expectations for exponents and prefactors.

We emphasize, however, that the general picture developed so far also provides us with a basis for a statistical theory of cities beyond the "mean-field" predictions for scaling laws. Such a theory will allow us in later chapters to unpack the averages expressed by scaling relations in terms of the properties of individuals and places within urban areas at the additional cost of calculating higher-order statistical quantities. Ultimately, when dynamic fluctuations dominate these means, we will be able to predict when scaling fails altogether.

In addition to the theory developed in this chapter, there have been a number of other efforts to derive scaling relations, some of them old and some more recent. As early as some of the first observations of scaling relations, Nordbeck[30] noted that the exponent of 2/3 characteristic of total area scaling implied that population scales as a conventional volume, $N \sim R^3$. He tried to provide several qualitative arguments to support this observation but did not tie the result to interactions mediated by social encounters. It is interesting to return to equation (3.16) and figure 3.8 and realize that two of these dimensions are simply ordinary two-dimensional space but that the third, associated with the fractal dimension H_m, unfolds as the result of the mobility of agents over *time*.

We have also recognized that economists were the first to identify agglomeration effects in cities, though rarely in the form of simple scaling relations of economic quantities with population size. Nevertheless, some economic concepts, from Adam Smith, to Alfred Marshall, to more mathematical formulations by recent authors,[31] do imply the role of social and economic interactions in producing these network effects. More recently, after the logic of systemic superlinear and sublinear urban scaling effects became appreciated,[32] Arbesman, Kleinberg, and Strogatz[33] developed a network model that shows that superlinear effects arise naturally from social interactions. Pan et al.[34] proposed another way to derive a superlinear relationship for social outcomes. They used a gravity law (chapter 8) to model human mobility and interactions within cities to derive a scale-dependent form of the type $Y \sim N \log \frac{N}{N_0}$. Although this form can fit weakly superlinear data, the necessary introduction of the scale N_0 (logarithms are *not* scale-invariant functions) predicts the breakdown of urban scaling for small enough cities, $N < N_0$, which is possible but not plausible or actually observed.[35]

Another approach considers a differential structure of occupations or "functions" in different cities and proposes that superlinear scaling is the result of complementarities between them that can naturally be stronger in larger cities. In this spirit, Pumain and her collaborators[36] proposed that the observed superlinear relations for some professions in France and the US could be interpreted as the result of an evolutionary dynamics at the urban system level. We will revisit this idea in chapter 5, which deals with professional diversity and productivity. Gomez-Lievano and his collaborators[37] developed the same idea of occupational complementarities, but now playing out within the city, to predict some observed correlations between superlinear scaling exponents, prefactors, and the variance of deviations. We will examine these ideas in chapters 4 and 5. Yang, Papachristos, and Abrams[38] used a similar idea of propitiating encounters necessary for certain socioeconomic outcomes to build a statistical model that predicts non-power-law "scaling" relations and apply their approach to an interesting new dataset on different types of crime.

In my view, all these models contain true elements of urban dynamics, but none makes a comprehensive connection with classical theory or predicts specific values for scaling exponents. They are also arguably too specific to provide us with a general theory of cities that together describes built spaces, mobility, dissipation costs, and socioeconomic life in a self-consistent way. We will see in the chapters to follow that the emphasis of all these other interesting approaches is contained in the theory developed throughout the book but often necessitates considerations beyond mean-field averages.

Besides some of these technical considerations, it is important to briefly comment on some of the limitations of scaling relations and their meaning relative to worldwide urbanization. That many cities are becoming more global in their economic relations and political and cultural influence[39] does not alter the basic premises of the theory. The internal dynamics and organization of cities (as social networks of people and institutions) produces new socioeconomic functions that allow cities to exchange goods, services, people, and information within and across national borders.[40] Thus, even if some singular places such as Hong Kong, Singapore, or Dubai are primarily part of international economies, the majority of the world's most global cities, such as Tokyo, New York, Los Angeles, Beijing, Shanghai, Berlin, or Frankfurt, show clear scaling effects in line with their own national urban systems, as seen in figures 3.1–3.3, table 3.1, and elsewhere in this book.

Scaling relations predict only population-averaged quantities such as personal incomes across entire urban areas. But all cities have spatial and social pockets of greater and lower mobility, social integration and segregation, better or worse access to services, justice, and opportunity. Addressing these fundamental issues of inequality will require that we go beyond scaling—that is, beyond averages in each city—which will be the purpose of the chapters ahead.

3.3 OTHER OBSERVABLE PREDICTIONS FROM URBAN SCALING THEORY

Urban scaling theory makes a wide range of interconnected, quantitative predictions about social life, socioeconomic production, infrastructure networks, city form, transportation costs, and more. We will return to these predictions several times in the book, but this section illustrates some of the most important ones. Table 3.3 summarizes some of the scaling relations derived earlier.

3.3.1 SOCIAL NETWORK STRUCTURE AND CONTAGION PROCESSES

An important prediction of urban scaling theory is that the advantages (and some disadvantages) of cities are realized through their socioeconomic networks, not so much via properties intrinsic to individuals.

This entails a tricky distinction because individuals who are better connected in cities will likely acquire certain properties—such as higher income or better information—that can be measured at the individual level. Individuals with a propensity to be more connected and to take greater advantage of urban environments

Table 3.3 Summary of urban scaling relations and exponent predictions for various important quantities.

Urban scaling relation	Exponent prediction $D=2$, $H_m=1$	Exponent prediction general D, H_m
Land area $A = aN^{\alpha}$	$\alpha = 2/3$	$\alpha = \dfrac{D}{D + H_m}$
Network volume $A_n = A_0 N^{\nu}$	$\nu = 5/6$	$\nu = 1 - \delta$
Network length $L_n = L_0 N^{\lambda}$	$\lambda = 2/3$	$\lambda = \alpha$
Interactions per capita $k = k_0 N^{\delta}$	$\delta = 1/6$	$\delta = \dfrac{H_m}{D(D + H_m)}$
Social outputs $Y = Y_0 N^{\beta}$	$\beta = 7/6$	$\beta = 1 + \delta$
Power dissipation $W = W_0 N^{\omega}$	$\omega = 7/6$	$\omega = 1 + \delta$
Land rents (\$ per sq. meter) $P_L = P_0 N^{\beta_L}$	$\beta_L = 4/3$	$\beta_L = 1 + 2\delta$

Note: Note that agglomeration effects vanish when $H_m \to 0$, because then people remain spatially separated (everyone stays home) and social networks fail to emerge.

may also sort themselves into larger cities or places where network effects are stronger and have greater scope. This is not a contradiction, just another reminder of the argument that there are many forms of circular causality that create and sustain the processes of social interaction and densification characteristic of cities.

It is nevertheless important to measure urban social networks as completely and directly as possible. At present, there are essentially two methodological approaches for doing this, one driven by traditional survey methods and another using mobile communications technologies, such as cell phones. In both cases, the prediction is that the average degree of people's contact networks and, more specifically, measures of value mediated by such links should be superlinear on their population size with exponents $\beta \simeq 1 + \frac{1}{6} = \frac{7}{6}$ in the simplest scenario and with more elaborate exponents, as in table 3.3, if additional considerations become appropriate.

Cell phone networks can be readily measured because their operating data are usually recorded. The predictions of the theory are indeed observed in a number of nations and cities, including in Portugal, the UK,[41] and Côte d'Ivoire.[42] See figure 3.14 for an illustration.

Despite clear average results, these measures are observed to be very variable among people. For example, a good general description of the distribution of degree in cell phone networks is that it is approximately lognormal,[43] which is a broad distribution that will become familiar as we probe urban statistics more closely (see figure 3.15). This kind of probability distribution, as well as power-law distributions of degree, follows from processes in which degree grows multiplicatively as the result of new connections introduced with a probability proportional to the number of connections a person already has.[44] (We will develop and analyze some of these models in chapters 4 and 8.) A simple mechanism for this to happen is that we meet most new people through someone we already know[45] and make a link with some finite probability. Another way in which the same effect can arise is when we meet groups of people mediated by common contexts and institutions, as emphasized by time geography; for example, at work or school. This type of insight is sometimes expressed in simple algorithms of so-called *preferential attachment*[46] but is also a much more general property of exponential growth processes where the growth rate itself is a stochastic quantity[47] (see chapter 4).

The data also show a suggestive universal feature of clustering in that observed contact networks retain a certain invariant amount of multiple contacts (my friends are mutual friends) regardless of the size of the city (see figure 3.16A). Though cell phones constitute only a slice of a much larger urban social network, the balance between exploration of new people and opportunities in complex social environments and maintaining a close-knit community made up of households and close friends is interesting and likely reflects some of the different functions of social networks in achieving that balance,[48] a classical theme in sociology.

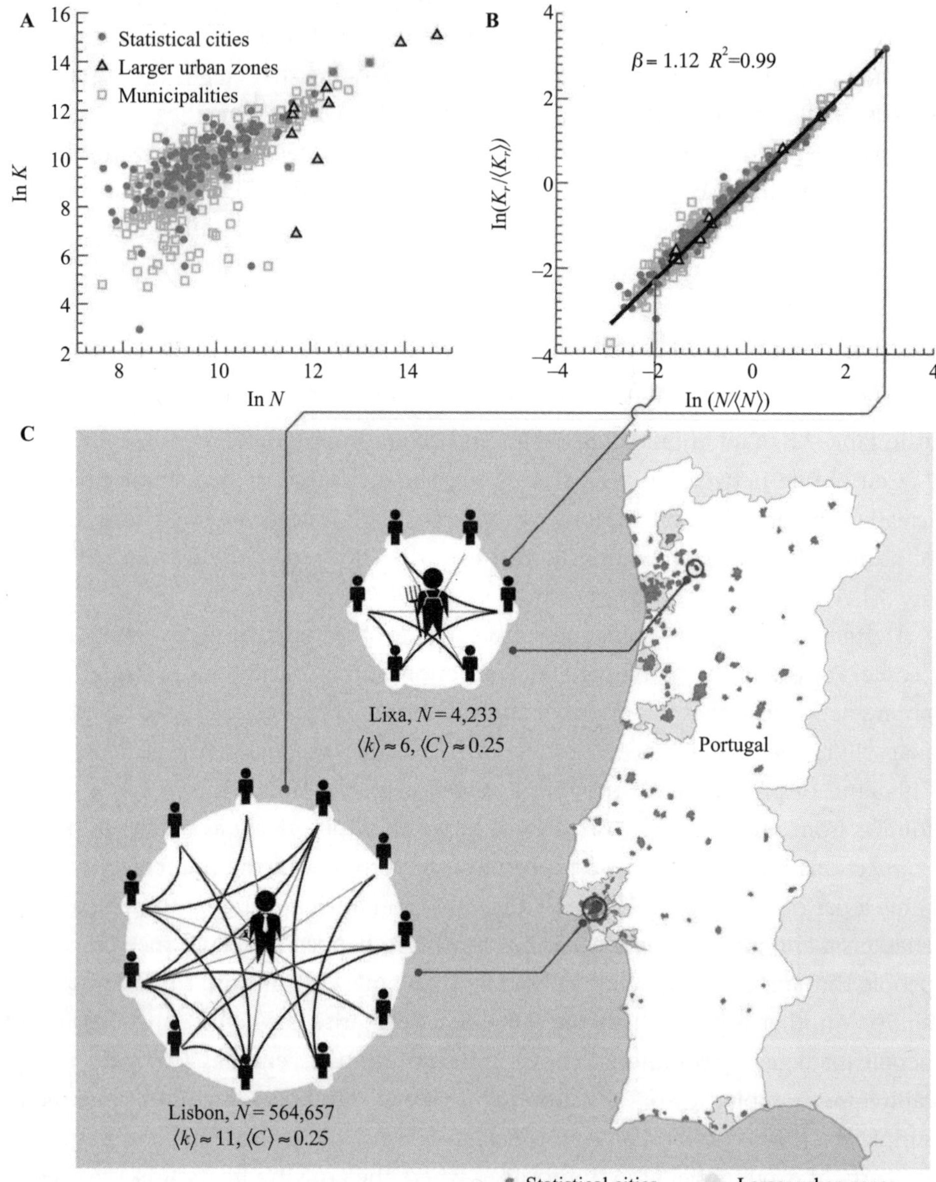

3.14 Human interactions scale superlinearly with city size. (A) Cumulative degree, K, measured from cell phone networks versus city population size, N, for three different city definitions in Portugal. (B) Data collapse of the cumulative degree onto a single curve after rescaling by service coverage (market share) in each place, K_r. (C) An average urban dweller in the capital, Lisbon, has approximately twice as many reciprocated mobile phone contacts, k, as an average individual in the rural town of Lixa. The fraction of mutually interconnected contacts (black lines) remains constant, as indicated by the invariance of the average clustering coefficient, C. The map shows the location of statistical cities and larger urban zones in Portugal, with the exception of the Azores and Madeira.

Source: Adapted by the author from M. Schläpfer, L. M. A. Bettencourt, S. Grauwin, M. Raschke, R. Claxton, Z. Smoreda, G. B. West, and C. Ratti, "The Scaling of Human Interactions with City Size," *Journal of the Royal Society Interface* 11, no. 98 (July 2, 2014): 20130789, https://doi.org/10.1098/rsif .2013.0789.

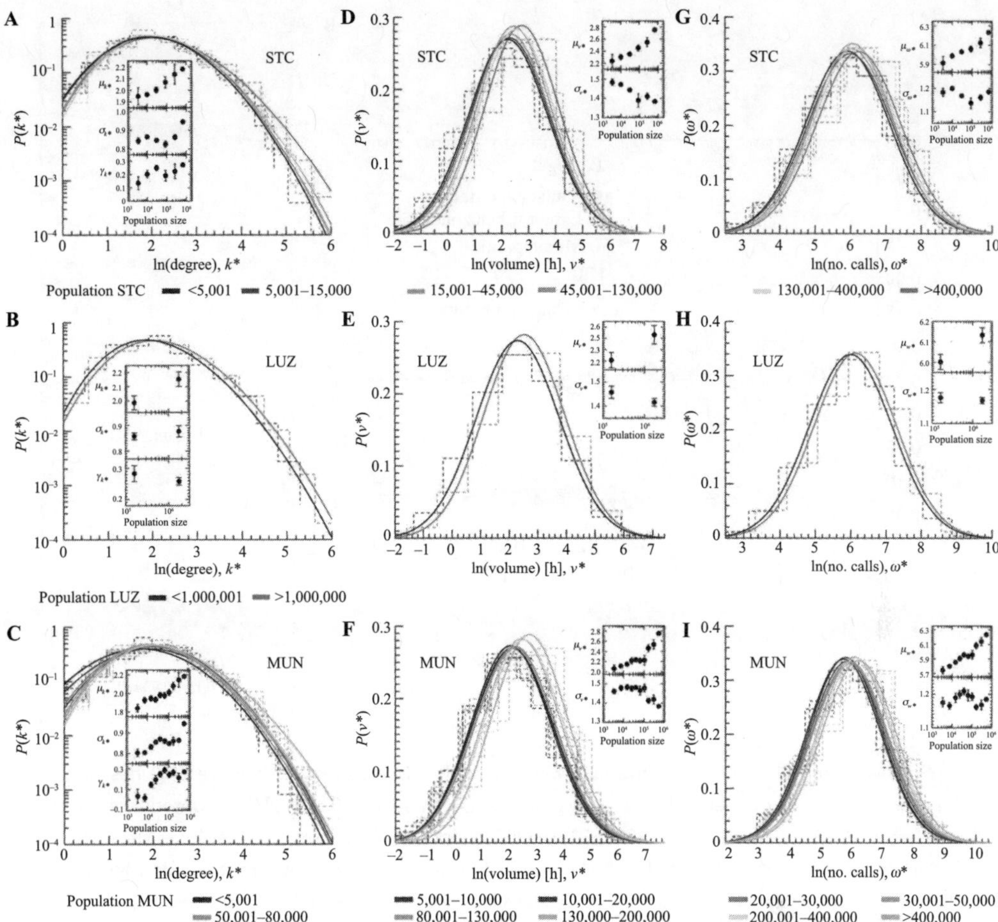

3.15 Statistical distributions of degree for different measures of connectivity and city definitions. (A–C) Degree distributions, $P(k^*)$, for statistical cities (STC), larger urban zones (LUZ), and municipalities (MUN) in Portugal; the individual urban units are log binned according to their population size. The dashed lines indicate the underlying histograms, and the continuous lines are best fits of the skew-normal distribution with mean μ, standard deviation σ (and skewness γ) (insets). (D–F) Distribution of the call volume, $P(v^*)$. (G–I) Distribution of the number of calls, $P(w^*)$. In (D–I), the continuous lines are best fits of the normal distribution with mean values μ_{v*} and μ_{w*} and standard deviations σ_{v*} and σ_{w*}, respectively (insets).

Source: Adapted from M. Schläpfer, L. M. A. Bettencourt, S. Grauwin, M. Raschke, R. Claxton, Z. Smoreda, G. B. West, and C. Ratti, "The Scaling of Human Interactions with City Size," *Journal of the Royal Society Interface* 11, no. 98 (July 2, 2014): 20130789, https://doi.org/10.1098/rsif.2013.0789.

The superlinear scaling of the connectivity of urban social networks has another interesting and important consequence for spreading processes, such as contagious diseases or information. In epidemic models, an infected state (e.g., having a cold) spreads in a population through network contacts, crossing each link with a certain probability. The most important quantity characterizing this process is the reproductive number, $\mathcal{R}$, which measures the number of secondary cases induced by a

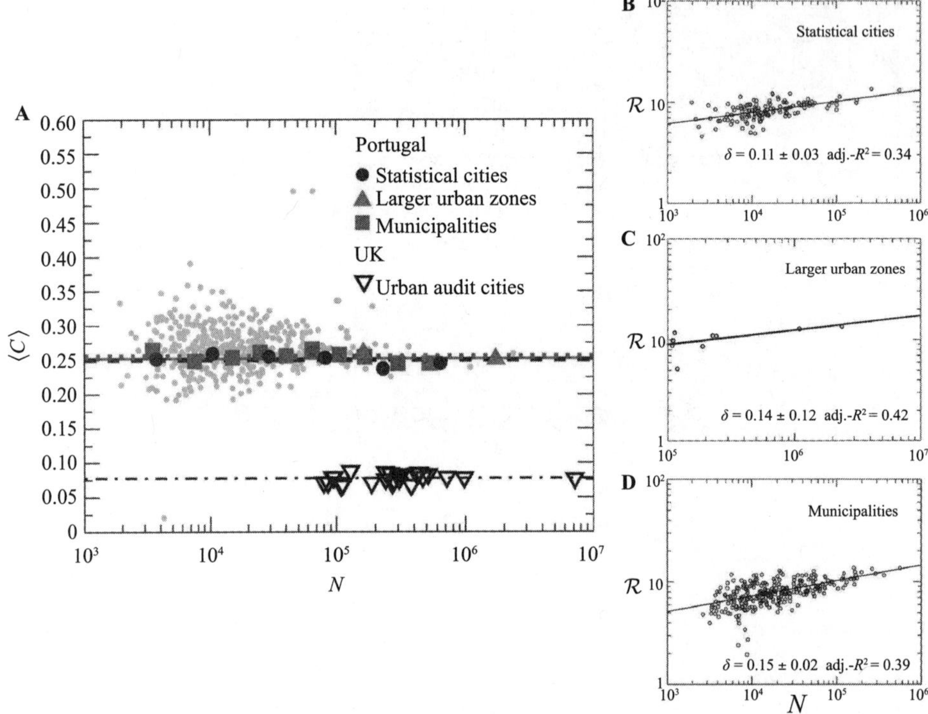

3.16 The clustering coefficient is invariant, while contagion accelerates with city size. (A) Lines indicate the average values of the network clustering coefficient, with 0.25±0.02 for STC (weighted average and standard deviation, dashed line), 0.25±0.01 for LUZ (continuous line), and 0.26±0.02 for MUN (dotted line) in Portugal and 0.078±0.004 for the UK (dash-dotted line). Gray points are the underlying scatter plot for all urban units. (B–D) Larger cities facilitate interaction-based contagion processes. The panels show the average "spreading speed" (reproductive number, $\mathcal{R}$) versus city size, broken down into the different city definitions. For each urban unit, the values of $\mathcal{R}$ result from averaging over 100 simulation trials performed on the reciprocal network in Portugal ($\Delta t = 409$ days), weighted by the accumulated call volume between each pair of nodes. The solid lines are the best fit of a power-law scaling relation $\mathcal{R} \propto N$.

Source: Adapted from M. Schläpfer, L. M. A. Bettencourt, S. Grauwin, M. Raschke, R. Claxton, Z. Smoreda, G. B. West, and C. Ratti, "The Scaling of Human Interactions with City Size," *Journal of the Royal Society Interface* 11, no. 98 (July 2, 2014): 20130789, https://doi.org/10.1098/rsif.2013.0789.

contagious process starting in a given node.[49] For a contagion network, the reproductive number is related to the statistics of degree, $k(N)$, as

$$\mathcal{R} = P_I \frac{\langle k^2 \rangle}{\langle k \rangle} = P_I \, k \left(1 + \frac{\sigma_k^2}{\langle k \rangle^2} \right), \tag{3.30}$$

where P_I is the infection probability per contact, $\langle \cdots \rangle$ denotes expectation values over the population, and σ_k^2 is the degree variance. For a lognormal degree distribution, the degree average and variance are given by

$$k = \langle k \rangle = e^{\mu + \frac{\sigma^2}{2}}, \quad \sigma_k^2 = (e^{\sigma^2} - 1)e^{2\mu + \sigma^2}, \tag{3.31}$$

with the parameters $\mu=\langle\ln\ k\rangle$, $\sigma^2=\langle(\ln\ k-\langle\ln\ k\rangle)^2\rangle$. This results in a simple and elegant expression for the reproductive number,

$$\mathcal{R}(N) = P_I\ e^{\sigma^2}\ k(N) \simeq P_I\ k_0\ e^{\sigma^2}N^\delta, \tag{3.32}$$

where, in the last equality, we introduced the scaling relation for degree with city population size. We therefore see that generally the reproductive number is expected to be a function of city size N and to be larger in bigger cities.[50] How much larger depends on the behavior of the log-variance, σ^2, and whether this parameter is dependent on city size (as discussed in chapter 4).

A larger reproductive rate for spreading processes in larger cities has two important consequences.[51] First, the most important meaning of the reproductive rate, $\mathcal{R}$, is as a threshold for an epidemic to propagate through a population.[52] For $\mathcal{R}<1$, an introduction will die off because it is damped in transmission, while for $\mathcal{R}>1$, the process will be amplified (it becomes a "chain reaction") and results in an epidemic in the sense that it can be transmitted quickly to almost everyone in the population. Because we expect $\mathcal{R}$ to increase with city size, we should at once expect large cities to be more susceptible to both contagious diseases and the spread of information, both formally and in terms of culture, fashion, and behavior (see figure 3.17). This is anecdotally true, of course. The fact that $\mathcal{R}$ may be locally larger in more densely interacting communities *within* cities may make such communities the natural reservoirs of certain contagious diseases.

Second, the reproductive number sets the growth rate, and thus "speed of diffusion," of a signal in a population. Thus, we expect that superlinear scaling of degree makes these processes *faster* in larger cities, with epidemics and information rippling through urban communities at a higher pace than in smaller towns. This makes

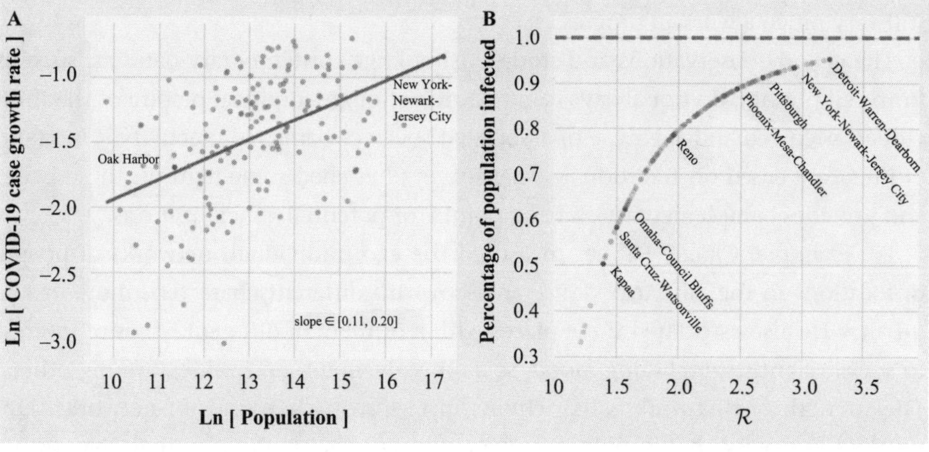

3.17 COVID-19 reported cases grow superlinearly with city size. (A) Estimated exponential daily growth rates of COVID-19 in US MSAs. (B) In the absence of effective controls, larger cities are expected to have more extensive epidemics than smaller cities.

efforts to contain epidemics harder in larger cities but may facilitate certain processes for the spread of information and innovations, possibly including interventions to stop disease spread. The best way to fight an exponential is with a faster exponential!

Finally, the size of an epidemic outbreak is also related to the reproductive number. In complex epidemic models, this needs to be computed numerically, but for a simple susceptible-infected-recovered (SIR) model,[53] we can integrate the dynamics and write the explicit expression

$$S_\infty = S_0 \, e^{-\mathcal{R}\left(1-\frac{S_\infty}{N}\right)}, \tag{3.33}$$

where S_0 is the initial population size of susceptibles (before the outbreak) and S_∞ is its (smaller) final value. We see that a larger $\mathcal{R} \sim N^\delta$ leads to more extensive epidemics (smaller S_∞/S_0) in the sense that a larger fraction of the susceptible population is affected. Thus, with an $\mathcal{R} > 1$ that is larger in larger cities, we should expect epidemics to be more extensive, which on the one hand involves larger fractions of the population but on the other hand may also create crowd immunity to future outbreaks if exposure triggers long-lasting defenses (figure 3.17). A final interesting point deals with the vaccination rate, $P_\mathcal{R}$, the fraction of the population that needs to be immunized to avoid a disease outbreak when $\mathcal{R} > 1$. In the SIR model, this is simply $P_\mathcal{R} = 1 - 1/\mathcal{R}$, showing that as cities get larger the vaccination rate must also increase.

These effects quantify the importance of large cities in promoting processes of contagion and specifically characterize their extraordinary capacity as natural *endemic reservoirs* of both diseases and information ("memes"). The dynamics of epidemic processes in populations highlight the importance of connectivity in general and its dependence on city characteristics in particular. However, much more complicated dynamics of human development or economic growth require knowledge of the detailed dynamics of these quantities and their connections to networks, which is still very much a work in progress.

The general observations and studies using large contemporary datasets, such as from cell phones, do not always lead to a rich enough empirical picture of the individuals involved and their use of associated socioeconomic connectivity.[54] A strand of literature based on traditional social surveys has shed some light on these issues and provides complementary starting points for potential generalizations.

For example, Claude Fischer measured the ego (individual) networks of people in locations in the Bay Area (San Francisco) with different characters, more or less urban.[55] He also associated these places with a number of different issues of interest to social scientists, including mood, social involvement, and values, among others. The strength of this work is its richness in terms of what kinds of networks (kin, neighbors, professional) people form depending on the character of their lives (more or less urban) but also their own personal status in terms of employment, age, education, and other characteristics.

In general, Fischer's and other similar studies[56] find qualitatively different personal networks in rural and urban areas, with the former involving more kin and neighbors and the latter involving more work relations and (non-kin-related) friends. This structural transformation does not seem to be associated with a degradation of psychological condition in larger cities (quite the contrary) or less social and civic involvement, but it does express qualitative changes in the condition of living in cities and the fact that urban environments tend to be more attractive to younger professionals, for example. Other large sociological surveys have focused on issues of collective action and efficacy related not so much to the rural-urban divide but to how well local neighborhood communities can handle challenges and cultivate trust and agency.[57] This research is intimately connected to the idea of *neighborhood effects* (chapter 6) and the realization that local environments in cities are important in shaping people's behaviors and opportunities, especially for children and young adults.[58] Thus, better-connected neighborhoods, both in terms of the personalities of residents and their linkages to civic and political organizations, tend to do better in terms of their socioeconomic indicators and ability to create broad positive change. A similar association between the connectivity of places and socioeconomic status has also been observed at the national level, using telephone networks.[59] It is also related to the observed connection between the economic complexity of cities and nations,[60] their larger and more diverse trade flows, and their higher levels of economic wealth[61] (chapter 5).

Thus, we see that there is a general expectation—which plays out at different scales—between larger connectivity and the socioeconomic status of individuals, communities, and cities. Connectivity in these contexts is both the cause and effect of an expanded set of opportunities, ideas, and influences[62] that dynamically integrates agents with networked processes of knowledge and resource flows. These ideas transcend time, space, and forms of political and economic organization. There is a need, however, for a better understanding of the dynamic mechanisms by which the extent and kinds of connectivity mediate learning processes and resource flows that, in the aggregate over time and populations, result in human development and economic growth. We will return to these important questions in future chapters.

3.3.2   FINITE SOCIAL HORIZONS AND NETWORK SEARCHABILITY

A critical property of social networks that was uncovered by the analysis in this chapter but that we have not yet commented on is that their structure creates finite *social horizons*. What we mean by this is that in larger cities one can know more people (our social horizon) but they are a smaller sample of the total urban population. Other people remain accessible but only indirectly, through searching below this horizon, as it were. This means that urban social networks have two interesting properties: they are *modular* and *searchable*.

To see this, consider that the average connectivity per person was derived to scale as $k(N) = k_0 N^\delta$ with $\delta \simeq \frac{1}{6}$. This means that, in larger cities, individuals on average are in contact with more people but also that their contacts are a smaller and smaller fraction of the population of the city, $\frac{k(N)}{N} \sim 1/N^{1-\delta}$. Taken together, these two effects entail that one can simultaneously know more people in absolute terms but a smaller number relative to all that is going on in total in a larger city. Note that this effect is independent of the specific value of $\delta < 1$ and vanishes only in the Metcalfe limit $\delta \to 1$, when an agent becomes connected to the entire network.

At a more qualitative level, the psychological experience of this effect may feel like expanding one's horizon in absolute terms, especially compared to smaller cities and towns, but also—simultaneously—a sense of isolation and disempowerment relative to the dynamics of the big metropolis. This tension is connected to issues of information overload and the resulting adaptive behaviors, which are of great interest to social psychologists.[63] In a famous paper titled "The Experience of Living in Cities," Stanley Milgram discussed several general behavior adaptations resulting from the information overload of large city environments. These include (1) the allocation of less time to each social "input," resulting in the speedup of certain behaviors; (2) disregard for certain "low-priority" inputs, such that principles of selectivity are developed to ensure that investments of time and energy are reserved for carefully defined social relations, which can make people in larger cities behave in more callous ways; (3) the redrawing of boundaries in social transactions so the burden of overload falls on the other party (for example, more brisk service); (4) reception being blocked off prior to entrance to a system, such as measures to establish privacy and control over unsolicited interactions; (5) diminishing of the intensity of contact by filtering devices and demeanor, resulting in weak and/or superficial contacts with others; and (6) creation of special institutions to absorb social inputs that would overwhelm individuals (social assistance agencies dealing with poverty, for example). These behavioral adaptations and institutional developments have a mixed effect on people. They simultaneously protect and estrange individuals from their surrounding expanding social environments. They present barriers to social life that typically require effort, capabilities, hustle, and intelligence to unlock, so the potential of cities becomes accessible for each individual. Sociologists often invoke similar issues of *anomie* and *alienation* as features of urban environments,[64] though there is little empirical evidence to support that these issues have, on balance, negative consequences on individual social life or mental health.[65]

Besides the personal experience of individuals, this effect has another critical consequence for the city as a whole, influencing the quality of decisions that people can make. Because most contacts and associated information remain below the social horizon, people necessarily make choices without complete information. This fundamental uncertainty leads to the impossibility of "global optimization," at least for decisions that are local in time. These limitations of decision making may appear to be a bug of cities, anathema to both models of rational choice in economics and global optimization strategies in engineering or technology, but they are also a feature, allowing cities to remain fluid environments where change and improvement remain open-ended, allowing cities to contain more subcultures,[66] more "moral regions,"[67] and more specializations than smaller and more unified communities.[68] This is also why evolutionary dynamics are relevant for cities and why cities remain complex systems.

The issue of how to operate in such complex networks relates to the concept of *searchability*[69] or *navigability* in networks, which is more general than in cities but is interesting to invoke in the present discussion. Searchability in a network measures the difficulty of sending or receiving a signal between two (not directly connected) nodes without disturbing the remaining network. In other words, it asks how, despite the lack of a direct connection, resources or signals far from someone can be summoned or accessed over a network.

The difficulty of this search is typically quantified by the amount of information involved in the choice between alternatives at each node of a network along the path between the origin and destination. This can be written as a Shannon entropy, H_x, for a path x, which is typically taken to be the shortest path between the two nodes.[70] This can be written as

$$H_x \sim \sum_{i \in x} \log_2 k(i-1, i), \tag{3.34}$$

where the sum is over nodes along the path and $k(i-1, i)$ is the network's connectivity along the way, with node $i=1$ being the origin. We can take this formula to be well approximated by the average of the logarithm over degree multiplied by the average length of the path. We saw earlier, when computing the reproductive number, that $\mu = \langle \ln k \rangle \sim \delta \ln N$. The length of the path depends on the structure of the network, but if we ask for an estimate based on the number of links that cross a network of size N, we will also obtain the length as $\ln_k N \sim \dfrac{\ln N}{\ln k} = const.$ Then we would estimate the searchability of an urban social network, $H_x = H_0 \ln N$. Numerical calculations over a number of model networks[71] (not necessarily urban) suggest that $H_0 \simeq 1$. We conclude that, even by this very general estimate, urban social networks are searchable with a relatively small cost. This information "choice cost" is also smaller in large cities than those associated with transportation costs, which as we have seen are expected to be superlinear with population. In practice, the information cost of navigating urban networks—physical and social—is likely much smaller, as people go to great lengths to produce signals and navigational technology that reduce the uncertainty costs of searching; for example, through maps or identities embedded in various technologies and through signs, markets, advertising, and public services. We can therefore reasonably conclude that cities are indeed modular, searchable networks. This is a functional quality that was suggested by the principle of mixing but that must be verified through human behavioral patterns. The searchability of human social networks is also expressed by another famous experiment associated with Milgram, namely the fact that generally any person can be found within six degrees of separation in a social network, making human societies—and cities!—"small worlds."[72]

3.3.3 URBAN LAND AREA SCALING AND GLOBAL URBAN EXPANSION

We have already seen how the densification of urban built-up spaces, recently measured via remote sensing mapping of impervious surfaces,[73] generally confirms the expectations from urban scaling theory for a networked area,

$$A_n(N_i(t),t) = A_0(t) \, N_i(t)^\nu \, e^{\xi_i(t)}, \tag{3.35}$$

measuring the exponent $\nu \simeq \dfrac{5}{6} = 0.83$.

However, the main empirical finding from this line of research was a general tendency for worldwide per capita urban land expansion over time. This means specifically that if we observe any given city over time, we will tend to see that the total area of its impervious built surfaces has increased faster than its population. This implies, in turn, that the population density in most cities in the world has been *decreasing* over time, even as most of these same cities increase in population and even as larger cities remain denser than smaller towns.

How are these findings consistent with urban scaling? The key to answering this question is the observation that expression (3.35) is exact since any deviations from the scaling relation are accounted for by the residuals, ξ_i. Consequently, it must account for urban scaling effects along with temporal urban expansion over time. There are two possible ways in which land expansion can occur, one general to all cities and another specific to a particular place. The first deals with the time dependencies of the prefactor, $A_0(t)$, the second with the scaling residuals, $\xi_i(t)$. We will discuss the behavior of the residuals in much greater detail in chapter 4, but note that on average over cities they must equal zero, meaning that if some cities experience land expansion by having $\xi_i(t)$ increase over time, others must necessarily be getting denser.

On the other hand, the prefactor, $A_0(t)$, expresses a change in baseline area per capita common to all cities in the urban system, since it can be interpreted as the average over cities of $A_n(N_i = 1, t)$. This is the right quantity to look at when we want to identify land expansion as a general effect common to all cities, big and small.

Note that we can isolate this factor by averaging the logarithm of the scaling relation (3.35), leading to $\ln A_0(t) = \langle \ln A_n(t) \rangle - \nu \langle \ln N(t) \rangle$, because the average of the residuals over cities is zero by definition. The time derivative, $\gamma_A = \dfrac{d}{dt} \ln A_0(t)$, is the temporal growth rate of the baseline area, the measure of urban land expansion across the urban system. Note that if this rate is approximately constant in time, we expect $\ln A_0(t) \simeq \ln A_0(0) + \gamma_A t$, which results in a linear relationship for this quantity in time, implying the global land expansion exponential dynamics, $A_0(t) = A_0(0) e^{\gamma_A t}$.

Figure 3.18 shows an example of this behavior for the built areas of Chinese prefectural cities (limited to their urban districts) for the period between 2002 and 2015. We see that by using the theoretical exponent $v = 5/6$ we obtain a very regular time dependence of A_0 with a growth rate of $\gamma_A = 1.8\%$ per year. Fitting the exponents also results in a noisier set of points with a smaller $\gamma_A = 0.8\%$ per year but a much larger error. This noisiness is the result of recent land expansion, which is more concentrated in larger cities in China. We will revisit some of these data and statistics in figures 4.14–4.16; see also Zünd and Bettencourt.[74]

Why does urban land expansion recently appear to be such a common effect across cities and nations? Urban scaling theory provides a possible answer. Recall that the prefactor $A_0 \sim \left(\dfrac{G}{c_{T_0}} \right)^{\frac{1}{3}}$, so it is predicted to increase as the value of interactions, parameterized by the prefactor G, increases over time and the cost of mobility per unit length traveled per unit time, parameterized by c_{T_0}, decreases. There can be very little doubt that in an environment with economic growth, infrastructure development, and technological change, the ratio G/c_{T_0} will increase over time. Thus, similarly to models of urban economics in chapter 2, urban scaling theory predicts general urban land expansion mediated through *other structural factors*, especially economic growth and progress in transportation technologies. These transformations are therefore likely to be at work everywhere, regardless of specific local urban

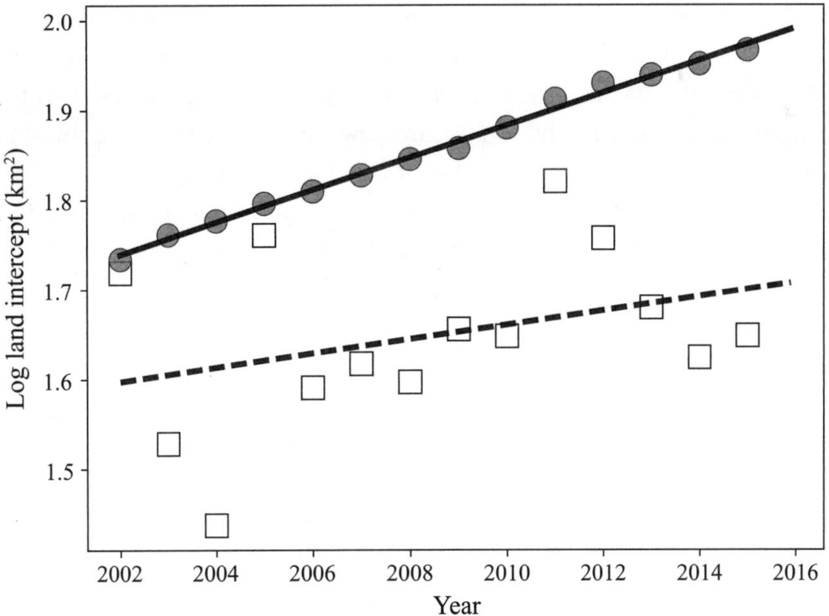

3.18 Urban land expansion of Chinese prefectural cities. Adopting the predicted scaling exponent $v = 5/6$ (gray circles) results in an estimate of the scaling prefactor, $\ln A_0(t) = \ln A_0(0) + \gamma_A t$, with $\gamma_A = 0.018 \pm 0.001$ (black line). Also estimated annual exponents (squares) result in a noisier fit with $\gamma_A = 0.008 \pm 0.012$ (dashed line).

planning approaches. Urban scaling also suggests a general mechanism for reducing urban land expansion by creating urban environments that have high value per connection but where this value is *not* invested proportionally in relatively cheaper transportation, such as cars. This will typically require mobility alternatives that are actually better than cars (that save time and money) and that have to keep improving in their appeal as societies get richer and more advanced technologically. This sort of public transit system is still to be invented.

3.3.4 INFRASTRUCTURE NETWORKS AND THE FRACTAL DIMENSION OF URBAN LAND USE

Related to spatial densities are the morphologies of how these spaces are occupied and shaped. For example, when we look at a map of a city, do buildings fill most of the land surface homogeneously or with variable densities? What about roads, streets, and other infrastructure networks? Answers to these questions are, of course, rather variable in different cities with different formal and informal land uses, traditions of building, and technological and urban planning policy levels. However, in laying down urban scaling theory, we have posited a number of general principles about how land uses should be naturally organized to reproduce observed scaling behavior. It turns out that these principles also predict some of the characteristics of the fractal dimension of built-up spaces in cities.

In the quantitative geography literature of the 1980s and 1990s (especially the work of Batty and Longley), there was great enthusiasm for conceptualizing urban land uses as spatial fractals[75] and measuring their specific geometries in terms of a single number, the fractal dimension, D_f. A fractal dimension can be used to characterize any spatial pattern and to measure how close it may be to canonical Euclidean dimensions, such as $D_f = 1$ for a line or $D_f = 2$ for a two-dimensional surface. We introduced such considerations when characterizing patterns of individual mobility in figure 3.8. Note that D_f is different from H_m, defined earlier, because the former measures how built spaces (buildings, infrastructure networks, and other impervious surfaces) occupy two-dimensional land, while the latter describes how these built spaces are used by individual agents over time. In particular, we came to the expectation that $H_m \simeq 1$, while for a city that occupies land consistently at a homogeneous density, we would generally have $D_f \simeq 2$. We will find that, as usually defined, D_f is not a general scale-invariance quantity.

There is an important difference between measuring a fractal dimension of urban built spaces, which can always be done in practice, and hypothesizing that urban land uses are fractal, which is a much stronger assumption.[76] A fractal, in terms of its mathematical definition, is a pattern in which any part has the same geometry as the whole. The canonical example is a Mandelbrot set. The repetition of a pattern at different scales is a strong form of spatial self-similarity; it is much more specific than the existence of power-law statistics, though it also leads to scaling relations.[77] Thus, fractal geometries imply scaling, but scaling is much more general and does not imply fractal geometry.[78] Indeed, as we have shown in this chapter, the most important urban scaling relations are the result of social network effects, where physical space plays a role but spatial geometry is only a secondary consideration.

The absence of *strictly* fractal structures in cities is the norm, not the exception. Clearly, there is some communality of structure across scales in cities, including in terms of infrastructure and buildings, but these structures are not repeating at different spatial scales. Despite these limitations, the fractal dimension D_f of land uses in cities was measured in many instances, yielding a number of insights. The most interesting implication of these ideas for cities is associated with densities of built areas and how well they fill in existing land. To see this, consider how the fractal dimension is typically measured.

As figure 3.19 suggests, larger cities fill more of the same space than smaller ones. This means that the fractal dimension D_f measured over the patterns of figure 3.19 increases with city size. To see this, consider the "mass," M, of any quantity distributed over two-dimensional space as a function of the radius, R, away from the CBD,[79] much as we did in models of urban economic geography in chapter 2,

$$M(R) = M_0 \, R^{D_f}, \tag{3.36}$$

where M_0 is a prefactor. The fractal dimension characterizes this quantity's spatial distribution in terms of its accumulation as we increase the circular area starting out at the city center by increasing the radius R. Note that this is an average over all directions and distances up to R, as can be seen in figure 3.19. This definition of the fractal dimension exposes why it is not a universal quantity. Inverting equation (3.36) leads to

$$D_f = \log \frac{M(R)}{M_0} \bigg/ \log R, \tag{3.37}$$

which depends on the value of the radius R and implicitly also on its discretization and the choice of origin (i.e., the choice of the city center).[80] We can set a minimal radius, R_m (corresponding to 1 pixel in figure 3.19), and check that, if the mass is homogeneous, we have $M = M_0 \left(\dfrac{R}{R_m} \right)^2$, to obtain the simple limit

$$D_f = \log \left(M_0 \left(\frac{R}{R_m} \right)^2 \bigg/ M_0 \right) \bigg/ \log \frac{R}{R_m} = 2, \tag{3.38}$$

which also defines the normalization, M_0. For distributions that do not fill in all space, we therefore expect $D_f < 2$.

We can apply these expressions to urban scaling. Consider the mass of land occupied by infrastructure networks as

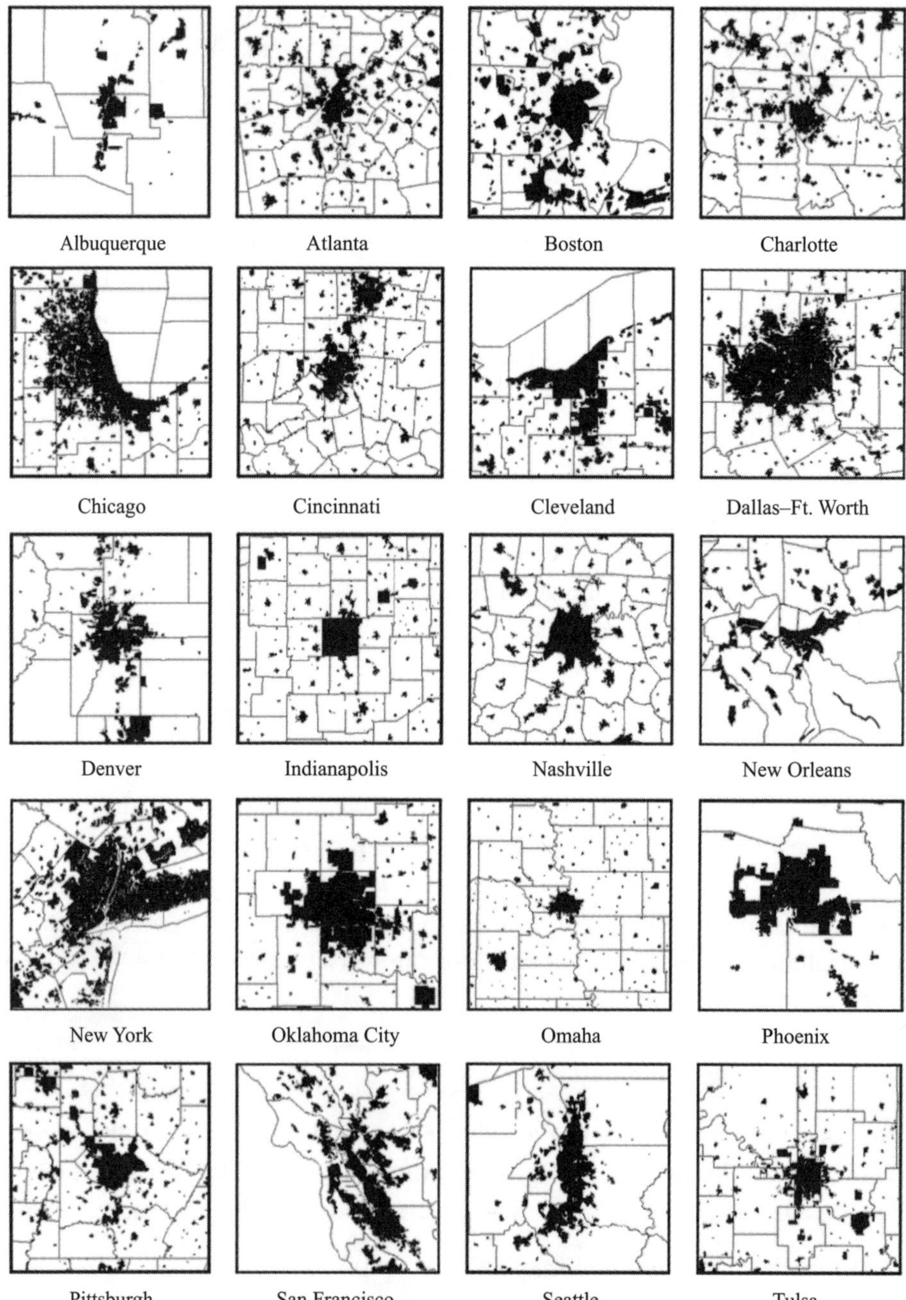

3.19 Built-up area (black) of 20 US urban areas in 1992. Each tile has a fixed spatial resolution (1,000×1,000 pixels) and the same total linear size of 0.8 degrees of latitude and longitude from the city center. The fractal dimension of the built-up area is computed using a conventional box counting technique. Note that for New York City the overall box does not cover the metropolitan area and that while all cities have a compact central area, many smaller peripheral clusters also contribute to land use patterns. *Source*: Adapted from Guoqiang Shen, "Fractal Dimension and Fractal Growth of Urbanized Areas," *International Journal of Geographical Information Science* 16, no. 5 (July 2002): 419–437, https://doi .org/10.1080/13658810210137013.

$$D_f^A = \log \frac{A_n}{A_0} \Big/ \log R_m = v \log N / \log R / R_m, \tag{3.39}$$

which now depends on how R varies with N. In figure 3.19, R is a fixed number (0.8 degrees = 89 km), independent of city size. Figure 3.20 shows the correlation between the fractal dimension and both population and the built-up area across the cities in figure 3.19. The slopes of the relationship are roughly consistent with the scaling relation for the built-up area, given a value of $\log R \approx 5 - 6$.[81]

However, these two relationships between the fractal dimension and both population and built-up area, when taken *together*, allow us a more direct relationship to scaling. To see this, consider the fractal dimension associated with *population* (mass = population) to be

$$D_f^N = \log \frac{N}{N_0} \Big/ \log \frac{R}{R_m}, \tag{3.40}$$

where we can then immediately see that the *ratio* of the two fractal dimensions for built spaces and population is free from the choice of R, and

$$\frac{D_f^A}{D_f^N} = \frac{\log A_n - \log A_0}{\log N - \log N_0} = \frac{\Delta \log A_n}{\Delta \log N} = v, \tag{3.41}$$

which is, of course, the *definition* of the scaling exponent as the elasticity of built area to population. Thus, while individual fractal dimensions are generally nonuniversal, measurement-dependent quantities, ratios of fractal dimensions to those of the population result in direct estimates for scaling exponents. This strategy was recently

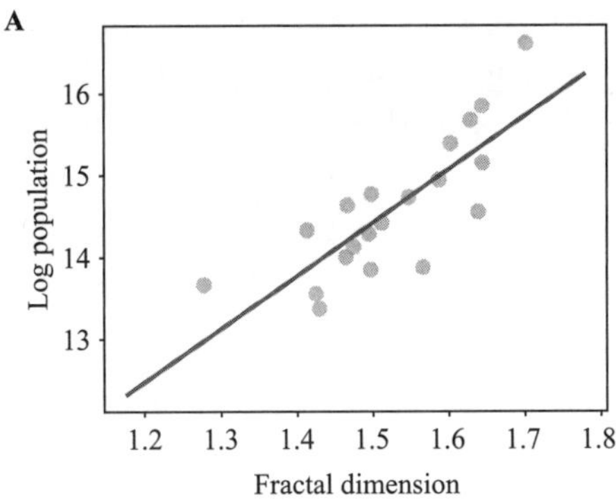

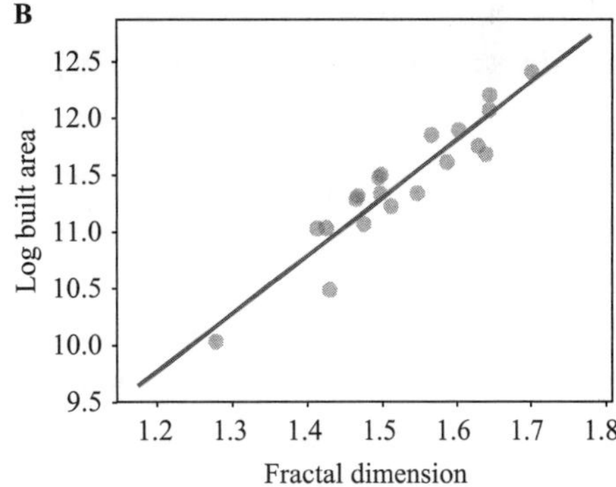

3.20 Relationship between population, built area, and the fractal dimension for 20 metropolitan areas in the US in 1992. (A) The relationship between population and fractal dimension, $\log \frac{N}{N_0} = a_N D_f$, $a_N = 6.496 \pm 2.29$, $R^2 = 0.64$. (B) The relationship between built area and fractal dimension, $\log \frac{A_n}{A_0} = a_A D_f$, $a_A = 5.097 \pm 0.90$, $R^2 = 0.88$, provides a better fit. Note that these two fits are consistent with the scaling relationship for urban built-up area, $A_n(N) = A_0 N^v$, $v = 5/6$.
Source: Created by the author with data from Guoqiang Shen, "Fractal Dimension and Fractal Growth of Urbanized Areas," *International Journal of Geographical Information Science* 16, no. 5 (July 2002): 419–437, https://doi.org/10.1080/13658810210137013.

used by Molinero and Thurner[82] to measure the exponent $v \simeq 5/6$ in several European urban systems, where creating self-consistent urban definitions has remained difficult, especially for small cities and towns.[83]

3.3.5 LAND RENTS, BUILDING HEIGHTS, AND ENERGY EFFICIENCY

We saw in chapter 2 that models of urban economics make predictions for the variation of land rents on various variables, including the intensification of capital invested per unit land area, which is interpreted as increasing building height. These general predictions can be made more quantitative if we specify a particular utility function, which is rarely done in practice. In the absence of such specification, models of urban economics make only qualitative predictions for the sign of the covariation of capital intensification per unit area with a variety of factors, including city size.

Urban scaling theory arguably gives us a more direct quantitative route to predicting the dependence of both land rents and building heights with city size, including specific exponent values. These predictions can be tested thanks to the growing availability of detailed information on the built environment from a variety of sources, including digital property records, LiDAR measurements, and 3D maps of cities built through the combination of this information with remote and aerial sensing, photogrammetry, and shape and texture reconstruction using artificial intelligence. Sources for this type of information for 50 cities in North America have recently been summarized by Schläpfer, Lee, and Bettencourt.[84] Better data of this kind are certain to become available in more parts of the world in the coming years and will eventually be standard in every human settlement.

Building heights So how can we make predictions about something as unique as a city's skyline? We start with the derivation of the scaling of building heights based on the built-up area, A_n. For US urbanized areas, which are defined by the US Census Bureau and constitute the urban built-up cores of MSAs, area is observed to scale with population size as $A_n \sim N^{1-\delta}$, with $\delta \simeq 0.15$ and the resulting scaling exponent $1 - \delta \simeq 0.85$,[85] as predicted by urban scaling theory. This is further supported by the observation that the total road surface within MSAs exhibits the same scaling exponent[86] as we saw earlier and that the built-up area is generally isomorphic with the road infrastructure,[87] since each building requires street access. The sublinear scaling of the built-up area ($1 - \delta < 1$) implies that population density (over built spaces) increases with population size ($N/A_n \sim N^\delta$), forcing cities to develop a systematic change in their land uses as they grow larger.

In practice, this adaptation can happen in two ways. First, individuals may adjust by consuming less land (i.e., less built-up area per capita). We can provide a simple argument for what this choice alone implies by returning to a_f, the average floor space per capita. Dividing the built-up area among all inhabitants leads to $a_f = \dfrac{A_n}{N} \sim N^{-\delta}$, which corresponds to a reduction of $\approx 16\%$ in floor space per person with every doubling of the population size. The ultimate expression of this logic is to be found in informal settlements and urban slums.[88] It is estimated, for example, that the population density of the Lower East Side of Manhattan in the nineteenth century reached almost 150,000 people/km^2, the highest density ever registered in the US.[89] Data from today's MSAs show that, while smaller floor spaces per person are indeed a feature of larger cities, this reduction is much less pronounced than predicted by this simple argument. For a scaling relation of the form $a_f \sim N^{\delta_{a_f}}$, we find an empirical exponent of $\delta_{a_f} \approx -0.04$. Second, to avoid having to use substantially less space per capita, cities must produce more floor space per unit of built-up area, which primarily requires taller buildings. To account for this effect, we now introduce the third spatial dimension of cities through the average number of building floors, h_b/h_f, where h_b is the average building height of a given city and h_f denotes a typical floor height (usually mandated by building codes, in the US this is around 4.3 m, or 14 ft). Thus, the available floor space per person becomes $a_f = \dfrac{h_b}{h_f}\dfrac{A_n}{N}$. Combined with the scaling of a_f and solving for average building height, we obtain

$$h_b(N) = a_f\, h_f\, \frac{N}{A_n} \sim N^{\delta_h} \quad \text{with} \quad \delta_h = \delta + \delta_{a_f} \approx 0.11, \tag{3.42}$$

in excellent agreement with the data (see figure 3.21). Hence, the scaling of average building height is driven by the scaling of population density (δ) and, to a lesser extent in today's US cities, by crowding; that is, by the consumption of less individual floor space (δ_{a_f}).

To further characterize urban skylines, defined as the height of buildings in city centers, we need to place an emphasis on urban cores and not so much on entire metropolitan areas, which also include residential suburbs. As we discussed, urban cores concentrate employment at a metropolitan level and fill the central areas of urban areas almost entirely, leaving very little land vacant. In that sense—for these centers only—we may expect that the radial density $A \sim A_n \sim N^\alpha$, $\alpha \approx 2/3$. Introducing these scaling dependencies of area in equation (3.42) leads to $h_b \sim N^{1/3}$, in good agreement with the measurements of figure 3.21A. Another argument in this direction appeals to recent attempts to characterize average population density profiles of urban areas as a function of distance to the CBD,[90] R, which proposed a "homothetic" scaling relation of the form $n_A(R, N) = N^{\frac{1}{3}}\phi_b(R/N^{1/3})$, with $\phi_b(\ldots)$ a characteristic function. Inside dense urban cores, we can assume that average building height is approximately proportional to this population density, so $\phi_b(d/N^{1/3}) \approx const$ for small R.[91] This also leads to $h_b(N) \sim N^{1/3}$ for the average height of buildings in the city center, which is consistent with the data, as shown in figure 3.21A. In the remaining panels, we see other characteristics of the data, specifically that the distributions of building heights are broad and dominated by relatively short buildings with one or two floors (figure 3.21B). We also see how average height varies with distance from the city center (figure 3.21C). The scaling of average building height with population for entire cities is shown in figure 3.21D, with an exponent $\delta \approx \dfrac{1}{6}$, in agreement with

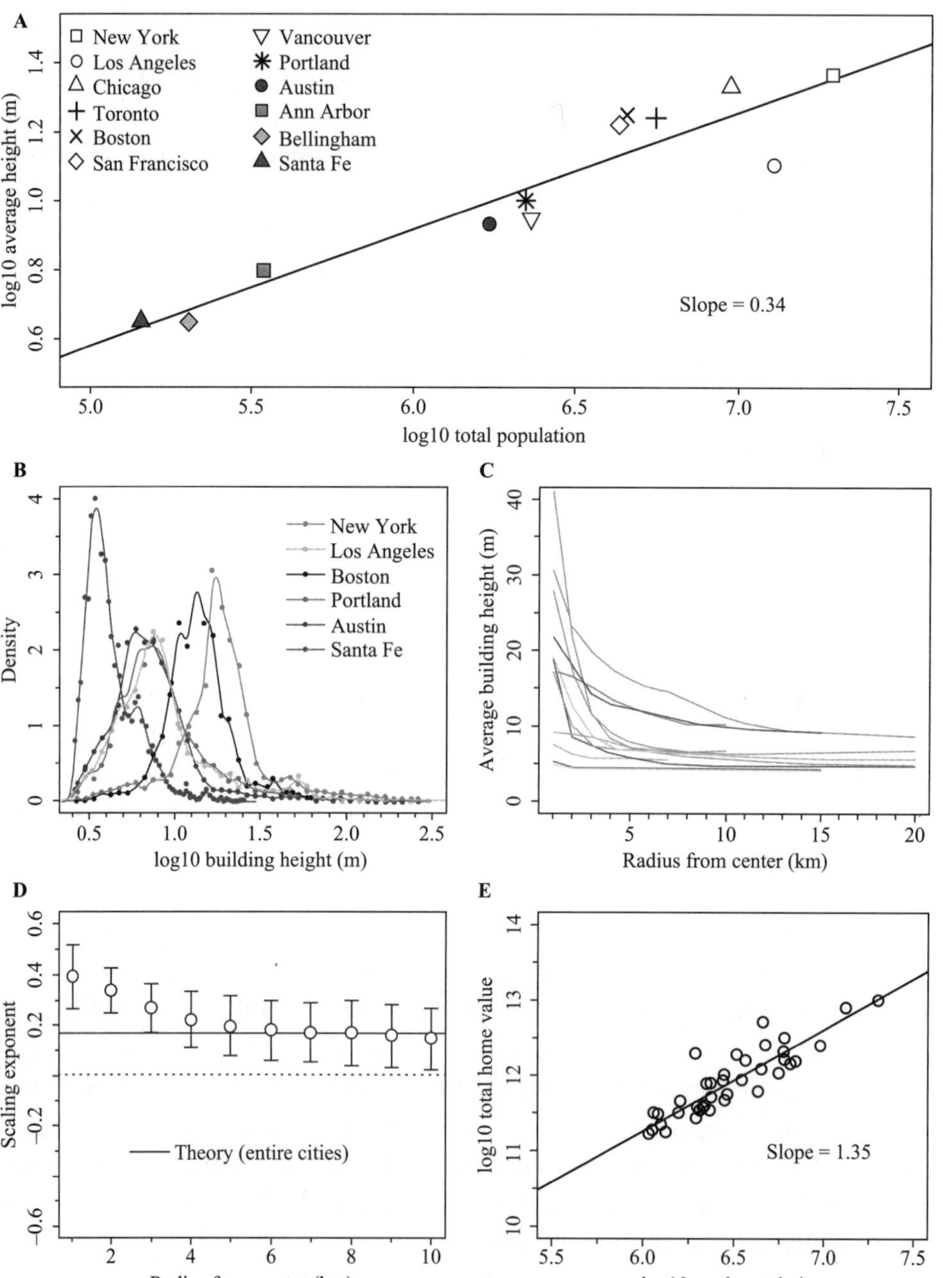

3.21 Building heights, height distributions, and land rents in US MSAs. The variation of building height with city population size. (A) Scaling relation between average building height, h_b, and city population size, N, within $R=2$ km distance from the city center (measured as the location of city hall). The best-fit line has slope 0.34, with 95% CI [0.25, 0.42], $R^2=0.87$. (B) Statistical distributions of individual building heights. The continuous lines are kernel density estimations. (C) Average building heights within radius R from the city center that defines the perimeter of the analyzed area. (D) Scaling exponent for height versus R; error bars indicate the 95% confidence interval. The continuous line is the theoretical prediction $\delta \approx 1/6$. (E) The scaling of the value of single-family homes with population size in major US MSAs. The best-fit line has slope 1.35, with 95% CI [1.13, 1.57], $R^2=0.79$, statistically indistinguishable from the theoretical prediction, with exponent $1+2\delta \approx 1+1/3=1.33$.

theory. Finally, figure 3.21E shows the consistency of these results with the scaling of land rents (see table 3.3), measured as the value of single-family homes in US MSAs, which scale as $\sim N^{2\delta}$ because of the compounding effect of allocating higher incomes per capita with smaller built area per capita, so land rents $\sim \dfrac{Y}{A_n} \sim \dfrac{N^\delta}{N^{-\delta}} = N^{2\delta}$. From an economic perspective and in the absence of crowding within buildings, it is

this strongly superlinear rise in land values, which is faster than the rise in incomes, that always creates extreme pressure on the cost of housing in large cities. To my knowledge, there is no large city in the world where people find housing "afford-able." The resulting adaptations to this general scaling effect are twofold: either we build more floor space per unit of land, increasing building height in such a way that $h_b(N) \sim N^\delta$, or we trade off lower housing costs far away, at the periphery of cit-ies, for transportation costs, if commuting longer distances is possible. The second solution is often easier and tends to dominate in the absence of intentional policy, but it leads to sprawl (fast urban land expansion as we have seen above) and gener-ally entails higher energy dissipation, which with current technologies implies larger carbon emissions and pollution. It also results in huge amounts of time allocated to commuting, which tends to be economically unproductive and unpleasant. Making cities taller, however, requires a number of innovations, such as more sophisticated building technologies, financing, and supporting urban services, including transit, not to mention land planning and policies that can promote and evaluate such proj-ects on a timely basis. The development of these capabilities, which requires growing local government capacity, business know-how, vision, and cultural change, is often hard to implement in fast-growing cities but tends to take place eventually, as urban areas grow demographically and economically.

Building shape and energy use We can also characterize the *shape* of buildings, namely how other dimensions, specifically their footprints, relate to variations in height. This is the closest we will come to "allometric scaling" in cities. Because the term *allometric* refers to proportions in the body of a biological organism, it is naturally applicable to the covariations of different building dimensions. Gains in building height typically involve changes in building shapes because structural demands, space limitations, land rents, natural lighting, and other factors constrain individual footprints.

The analysis of the allometric scaling of buildings requires that we consider differ-ent scales affecting their shape, not just height. The most important first consider-ation on a 3D shape is its *surface-to-volume ratio*, which is defined as $a_{A/V} = A_b / V_b$, with A_b the building's surface and V_b its volume. The surface-to-volume ratio is a critical performance parameter for built environments because it quantifies the building's skin—its exposure to the outside—and therefore mediates its energy use for climate control and lighting.

To model the shape of buildings more systematically, we first consider a reference shape. We adopt the cube with side length $l_c = V_b^{1/3}$, which is the closest analogue to a sphere—the simplest shape in 3D—but also closer to what most buildings look like. Then, $A_b = 6\,l_c^2$ (including the floor surface), and the surface-to-volume ratio is $a_{A/V} = 6/l_c$. Now consider a square cuboid with footprint area l_b^2 and building height h_b. Then, the building volume is $V_b = l_b^2\,h_b$ and its surface $A_b = 2l_b^2 + 4\,h_b l_b$, so the surface-to-volume ratio becomes

$$a_{A/V} = \frac{6}{l_c}\left(\frac{x_b^{-2/3} + 2\,x_b^{1/3}}{3}\right),\tag{3.43}$$

where $l_c = (l_b^2 h_b)^{1/3}$ and $x_b = h_b/l_b$ is a dimensionless shape parameter. We can make sense of this expression by noting that by minimizing the surface-to-volume ratio relative to x_b (shape), one obtains $x_b = 1$ (or $h_b = l_b$), which is the shape with the smallest ratio, recovering the cube.

It follows from equation (3.43) that the shape of any building can be characterized by two numbers, an extensive quantity l_c (a length), measuring the average linear size of the building, and a quantity x_b, characterizing how far this shape deviates from a cube. We can now easily derive the allometric relation between A_b and V_b, by using the expressions for $a_{A/V}(l_c, x_b)$ and the fact that $l_c = V^{1/3}$, as

$$A_b(V_b, x_b) = 6V_b^{2/3}\left(\frac{x_b^{-2/3} + 2\,x_b^{1/3}}{3}\right).\tag{3.44}$$

We see that the simplest allometric relation between surface and volume, $A_b \sim V_b^{2/3}$, requires that the shape parameter be independent of l_c. To the extent that such parameters are correlated—for example, because taller buildings may require a larger base—such a relation will receive a correction. For $x_b \ll 1$, the building is "flatter" and looks more like a planar sheet, and for $x_b \gg 1$, it is thinner, more like a needle (figure 3.22).

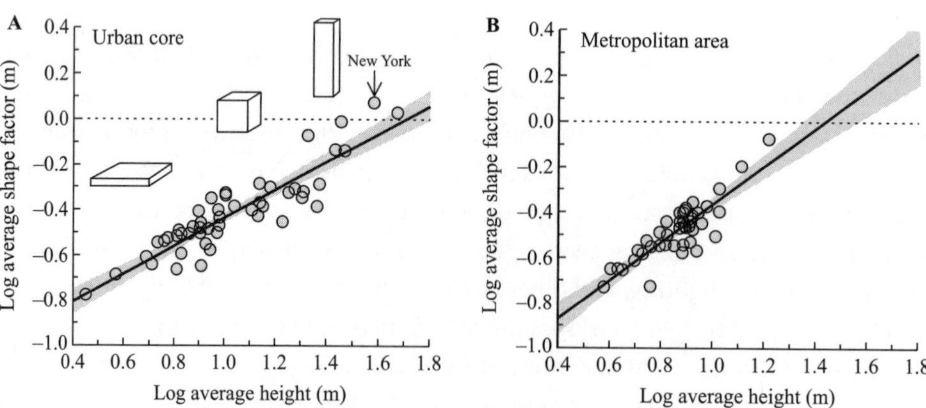

3.22 Relation between average building height and building shape. (A) Shape parameter averaged over all buildings within the urban cores, x_b, versus h_b. The best-fit line has slope 0.620 ± 0.085 (95% CI, $R^2 = 0.82$). In the center of New York City, the value of x_b becomes slightly larger than 1 because of the proliferation of tall, needle-like buildings. (B) Average shape parameter x_b for metropolitan areas versus h_b with best-fit slope 0.838 ± 0.152 (95% CI, $R^2 = 0.74$).

The point at which $x_b = 1$ is the most *cubic* shape and the specific place for which one obtains the simplest allometric relation $A_b \sim V_b^{2/3}$.

In terms of its influence on energy use, we now show that the cube (and the sphere!) is also the shape for which buildings are most efficient in terms of climate control (Buckminster Fuller, a visionary inventor concerned with sustainability, loved spherical buildings). To see this, consider the power (energy per unit time) necessary to maintain a temperature (and possibly a light intensity) gradient, ΔT_E, between the interior of the building and its exterior as

$$\frac{\Delta E_c}{\Delta t} = \mu_b A_b \Delta T_E. \tag{3.45}$$

The parameter μ_b accounts for both the efficiency of converting energy into an ambient temperature and the average thermal diffusion across the walls (related to insulation). We define building efficiency as energy use *per capita*. To estimate the number of people who can use the building, N_b, we write this quantity as

$$N_b = C_b(h_b) \frac{l_b^2}{a_f} \frac{h_b}{h_0} = \frac{V_b}{v_b}. \tag{3.46}$$

Here, $C_b(h_b)$ is a dimensionless function accounting for the fractional amount of usable space in a building as a function of its height[92] (in taller buildings, some space must be used for access and structural support). These factors define an effective volume of the building per person, v_b, so the total occupancy is the natural ratio of the total volume to this quantity. With these definitions in hand, we can finally write the energy use per unit time (power) per capita in a building with a given shape as

$$\frac{1}{N_b} \frac{\Delta E_c}{\Delta t} = \mu_b \, v_b \, a_{A/V} \, \Delta T_E, \tag{3.47}$$

which shows that energy efficiency is proportional to how much space individuals use, v_b, and the surface-to-volume ratio of the building, $a_{A/V}$, besides the materials of the building and its temperature variation due to weather. Figure 3.23 shows that US urban areas with taller buildings are also more efficient in terms of energy expenditures in buildings and for transportation, once we account for the weather via ΔT_E.

3.3.6   THE PRODUCTION FUNCTION OF CITIES

We already saw in chapter 2 that both production and utility functions characterizing the behavior of firms, nations, cities, and consumers often have the form

$$Y = A_P \, L_P^{a_Y} \, K_P^{1-a_Y}. \tag{3.48}$$

Here we wrote a *Cobb-Douglas production function*, which is often taken to characterize the total economy of a nation (chapter 9) but can also characterize the economy of a metropolitan area with total economic production (GDP), Y, given in terms of factors of production, labor, L_P, and capital, K_P. A_P is the overall amplitude, known as the *total factor productivity*. This is an important quantity that expresses how much

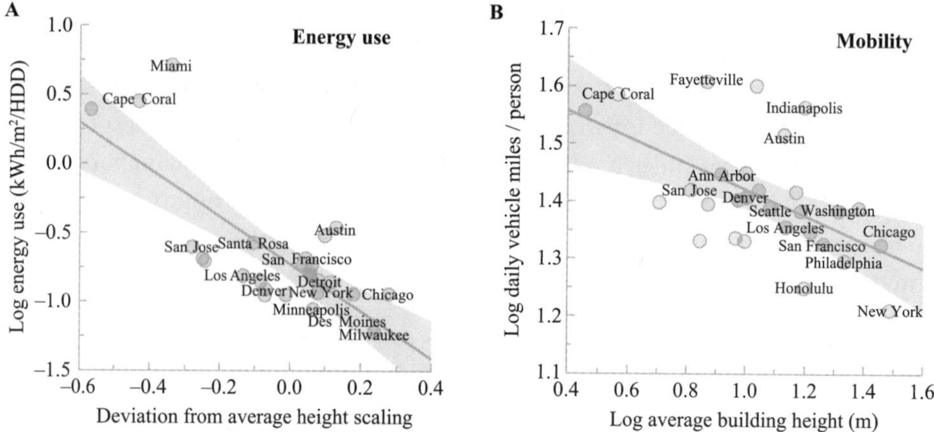

3.23 Impact of building height on energy use and mobility. (A) Building energy use, normalized by the number of heating degree-days, versus the residuals from the log-log regression of average building height on city population size (figure 3.21). The slope of the best-fit line is -1.71 ± 0.58 [95% CI, $R^2 = 0.58$]. (B) Daily per capita vehicle-miles traveled, averaged over a five-year period (2012–2016), versus average building height. The slope of the best-fit line is -0.23 ± 0.13 [95% CI, $R^2 = 0.31$]. The correlation for building energy use is substantially stronger and more direct than that for mobility.

total output value can be created with some given labor and capital inputs. It is critical in theories of economic productivity and growth, which attempt to derive the creation of greater value (via bigger A_P) using the same inputs to production. The quantity a_Y measures the fraction of labor and capital for each unit of output, as we will see. The Cobb-Douglas production function is very common in economics. We used a similar function to characterize individual consumption in the core-periphery model in chapter 2, where the output was utility (individual satisfaction) and the inputs were the consumption of agricultural and manufactured goods, or of housing versus other products, in models of urban economics.

We now want to show that this form of aggregate economic output for a city follows under certain conditions from urban scaling and that the derived value of $A_P(N)$ will express the rise in economic productivity with city size as well as city-specific deviations. First, let us write economic output as the sum of income from wages and rents (capital gains),

$$Y(t) = Y_W(t) + Y_K(t). \tag{3.49}$$

The fractional shares are

$$a_Y = \frac{Y_W(t)}{Y(t)}, \quad 1 - a_Y = \frac{Y_K(t)}{Y(t)}. \tag{3.50}$$

This makes the fractional share parameter, a_Y, generally dependent on both time and city size, $N(t)$. We will see later that this dependence tends to be very slow, and we will derive its implications. To proceed, we now differentiate equation (3.49) and divide by the total product Y to obtain

$$\frac{1}{Y(t)}\frac{dY(t)}{dt} = \frac{Y_W(t)}{Y(t)}\frac{1}{Y_W(t)}\frac{dY_W(t)}{dt} + \frac{Y_K(t)}{Y(t)}\frac{1}{Y_K(t)}\frac{dY_K(t)}{dt}, \tag{3.51}$$

which is equivalent to

$$\frac{d\ln Y(t)}{dt} = a_Y \frac{d\ln Y_W(t)}{dt} + (1 - a_Y)\frac{d\ln Y_K(t)}{dt}. \tag{3.52}$$

This can now be integrated[93] to give something that starts to resemble a production function,

$$Y = c_0(1 - a_Y)^{a_Y - 1} a_Y^{-a_Y} Y_W{}^{a_Y} Y_K^{1-a_Y}, \tag{3.53}$$

where c_0 is an integration constant. To turn this expression into equation (3.42), we need to introduce labor and capital, which are the inputs to wages and capital rents, so we can write

$$Y = c_0(1 - a_Y)^{a_Y - 1} a_Y^{-a_Y} \left(\frac{Y_W}{L_P}\right)^{a_Y} L^{a_Y} \left(\frac{Y_K}{K_P}\right)^{1-a_Y} K_P^{1-a_Y} = A_P\, L_P^{a_Y} K_P^{1-a_Y}. \tag{3.54}$$

This defines the total factor productivity, A_P, as

$$A_P(N_i, t) = A_{P_0}(t)N_i^{\beta_A}e^{\xi_i^A(t)}, \tag{3.55}$$

with

$$A_{P_0}(t) = C(a_Y)\frac{Y_{W_0}(t)^{1-a_Y}}{L_{P_0}(t)}\frac{Y_{K_0}(t)^{a_Y}}{K_{P_0}(t)}, \quad C(a_Y) = (1 - \alpha_Y)^{a_Y - 1}\alpha_Y^{-a_Y}, \tag{3.56}$$

$$\begin{aligned} \xi_i^A(t) &= a_Y\big(\xi_i^{Y_W} - \xi_i^{L_P}\big) + (1 - a_Y)\big(\xi_i^{Y_K} - \xi_i^{K_P}\big), \\ \beta_A &= a_Y\big(\beta_{Y_W} - \beta_{L_P}\big) + (1 - a_Y)\big(\beta_{Y_K} - \beta_{K_P}\big), \end{aligned} \tag{3.57}$$

where we used scaling relations for each of the quantities, Y_W, L_P, Y_K, K_P, of the form

$$Y_W(N_i(t),t) = Y_{W_0}(t)\, N_i^{\beta_{Y_W}}e^{\xi_i^{Y_W}(t)}. \tag{3.58}$$

This shows how a production function for cities is not a fundamental microscopic quantity but instead may emerge from the structure of social and infrastructural networks and their averages in the sense of the scaling relations derived earlier in this chapter. The exponent β_A is generally larger than zero because we expect $\beta_{Y_W} \simeq 1 + \delta$, $\beta_{L_P} \simeq 1$. I am not currently aware of direct ways to measure β_{Y_K}, β_{K_P} in cities except possibly through the fraction of capital derived from real estate rents and prices. As we have seen, profits in the form of value added in the activity of firms are also generally superlinear, while the price of capital (loan interest rate) may be the same everywhere. In such cases, $\beta_{Y_K} - \beta_{K_P} > 0$, adding a positive contribution to the total factor productivity. Another set of issues is related to city-specific performance and deviations from the simple form of the Cobb-Douglas production function in each place resulting from the magnitude of $\xi_i^{Y_W} - \xi_i^{L_P}$ and $\xi_i^{Y_K} - \xi_i^{K_P}$. We will analyze these quantities in the next chapter, including their origins, typical magnitude, and temporal dynamics. In closing, it is interesting that for A_P to grow (exponentially) in time (see chapter 9) we need exponential growth in per capita wages (labor productivity) and/or capital rents (capital productivity) as well as, in cities, some population growth. In this sense, uses of labor and of capital should really be seen as investments that require good information to be successful.

3.3.7 THE SPEED OF LIFE IN CITIES

Among the behavioral adaptations that result from urban scaling, none is quite so striking as the speedup of the pace of life with city size. This *need for speed* demonstrates a human ecological effect of how the city becomes part of people's behaviors and not just the other way around. Figure 3.24 shows that the speed of walking increases with city size. This has been measured by setting up observations in an unimpeded section of sidewalk in various cities and towns, so it also reflects the demographics of walking downtown. In parallel experiments in some American "car" cities, the results were so biased by disadvantaged populations who had no choice but to walk (especially the homeless and poor) that a blind analysis of this quantity would be very different.[94] Thus, these data are far from perfect. It will continue to be interesting to observe typical human behaviors across different cities, especially throughout the world.

There are two ways in which we derive quantitative expectations for the effect of the speedup of various human behaviors with city population size. The first equates time with money in a way that is characteristic of economic thinking.[95] In our context, we can recognize that all socioeconomic quantities are rates: money per unit time for wages, crimes per unit time for violence, and so on. It follows that since the speed of walking is also a temporal rate, we may expect that it scales in ways similar to all other socially mediated incomes and costs and that the individual speed of walking would scale as $v_w = v_{w_0} N^\delta$.

A different hypothesis follows from considering the energetic effort involved in walking. Given v_w, we may expect that a fraction of the kinetic energy involved, $E_w = \frac{1}{2} M v_w^2$, is dissipated per unit time. Equating this dissipated energy to social incomes per capita, y, leads to $v_w \sim \sqrt{\frac{y}{M}} \sim N^{\frac{\delta}{2}}$. The data shown in figure 3.24 are not sufficiently precise to distinguish between these two scenarios, but the observed exponent is closer to $\frac{\delta}{2} \sim 0.083$ versus $\delta = \frac{1}{6} \sim 0.166$, suggesting that the energetic hypothesis is perhaps more plausible.

3.3.8 SLUMS AND INCIPIENT URBAN NETWORKS

When setting up the theory developed in this chapter, we proposed the hypothesis that infrastructure networks connect all spaces in the city, including all buildings where people live and work, public facilities, and other spaces. This is a reasonable expectation in developed cities, which can be easily verified (figure 3.25). However, this basic expectation often fails in cities that are still forming and that are characterized by informal settlement and other unplanned and uncoordinated land uses.

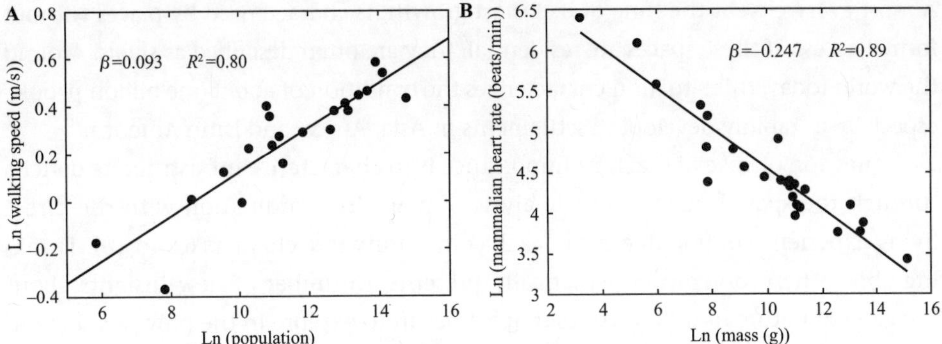

3.24 Scaling of walking speed in cities versus population size and of the heart rate of organisms versus their mass. The pace of urban life increases with city size, in contrast to the pace of biological life, which decreases with organism size. (A) Scaling of walking speed versus population for cities around the world. (B) Heart rate versus the size (mass) of organisms.

Source: Created by the author, adapted from Luís Bettencourt et al., "Growth, Innovation, Scaling, and the Pace of Life in Cities," *Proceedings of the National Academy of Sciences* 104, no. 17 (April 24, 2007): 7301–7306, https://doi.org/10.1073/pnas.0610172104.

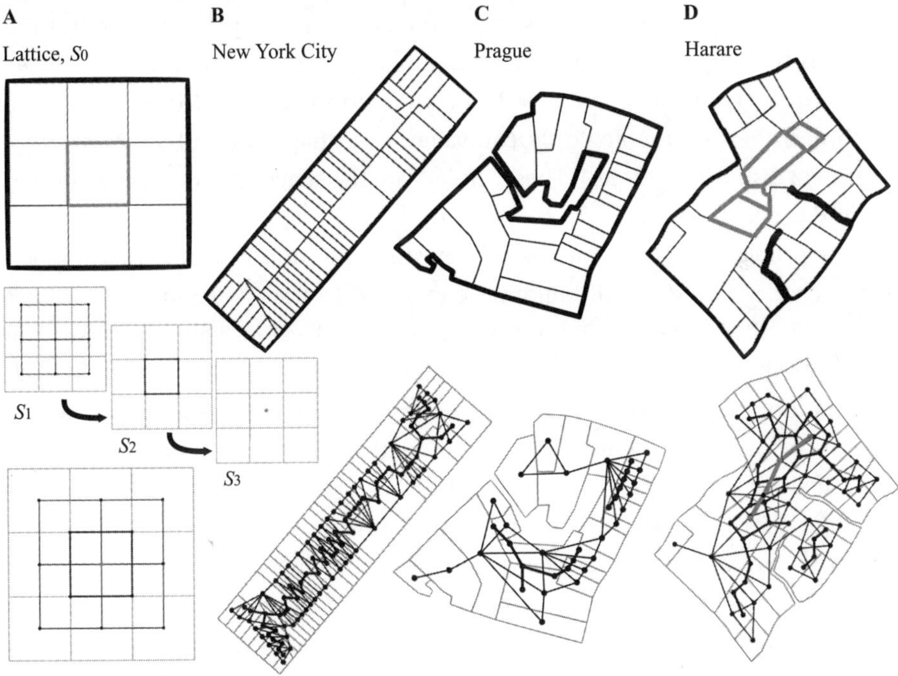

3.25 Topology of places and city block complexity. (A) Schematic city block (top) with one internal place (thick gray outline) and its characterization in terms of a hierarchy of weak dual graphs, S_1, S_2, and S_3 (bottom). (B) New York City. (C) Prague. (D) Construction of nested dual graphs (shown as thinner darker to lighter thicker lines) for a block in Epworth in Harare, Zimbabwe, with block complexity $k^*_{max}=3$. In this case, internal parcels are only one layer deep relative to existing accesses.

Source: Created by the author, adapted from Christa Brelsford, Taylor Martin, Joe Hand, and Luís M. A. Bettencourt, "Toward Cities without Slums: Topology and the Spatial Evolution of Neighborhoods," *Science Advances* 4, no. 8 (August 2018): eaar4644, https://doi.org/10.1126/sciadv.aar4644.

Almost every city, at the time of its fastest growth, is characterized by places without formal access. If these spaces are residential, they are often described as *slums*. Around the world today, this situation characterizes the condition of about one billion people, especially in rapidly developing settlements in Asia, Africa, and Latin America.[96]

A question of special practical importance is to characterize infrastructure deficits through the spatial quantitative analysis of maps in coordination with the direct living experience of populations in each community (see chapters 6 and 10). Thinking about the problem mathematically presents a number of new insights about the general nature of urban spaces that we began to explore in the previous section. Once we have cities that fill in self-consistent fractions of two-dimensional space, their networks organize all interior space. Inside each city, places exist as city blocks, which are portions of land surrounded by streets and other boundaries. This means that, independently of any specific geometry of street networks—whether they are grids or curvy mazes—we can build a well-defined modular spatial decomposition of a city as a set of city blocks. Several theorems can be proven about the nature of the spaces of cities,[97] including the fact that the size of each city can be measured in terms of a topological invariant, the Euler characteristic $\chi_c = 1 - n_b$, where n_b is the number of city blocks, regardless of geometry.[98] This has the curious effect that it allows us to compare the kind of shape (topology) of a city to any other object, such as a disk ($\chi_c = 1$), a sphere ($\chi_c = 2$), or a doughnut ($\chi_c = 0$)! Cities are none of these things; they are topologically equivalent to a shape with a boundary and n_b punctures (a disk with n_b holes). These "holes" are the spaces dedicated to buildings, parks, and other *places*.

For the problem at hand, the more interesting question is about what happens within each city block: are all buildings connected to the city's infrastructure networks? If not, they—and the city in general—cannot develop. This is because, from the perspective of daily experience, people cannot get urban services such as water and sanitation, they do not have an address, and cannot obtain emergency services in case of fire or illness. Figure 3.25 shows how this situation can be diagnosed. To do this, the land in each block is divided into parcels (as is done in property records). A network (graph) can now be constructed by connecting all the centers of adjacent parcels. This is called an S_1 *weak dual graph*. The centers of the parcels created by this graph can be taken to generate a second graph S_2 and so on to S_k until one obtains a point (see examples in figure 3.25). Just before we get a point, we obtain a graph with no faces, a *tree graph*. We call k^*_{max} the index of the graph at which this construction creates a tree graph. It turns out that if $k^*_{max} \leq 2$, we are dealing with a city block where all parcels have direct street access.[99]

The advantage of this procedure is that it is very simple and can be implemented iteratively on a computer to deal with any street block anywhere, even those with very high complexity; see the real-life example in figure 3.26 from an informal settlement outside Cape Town, South Africa.

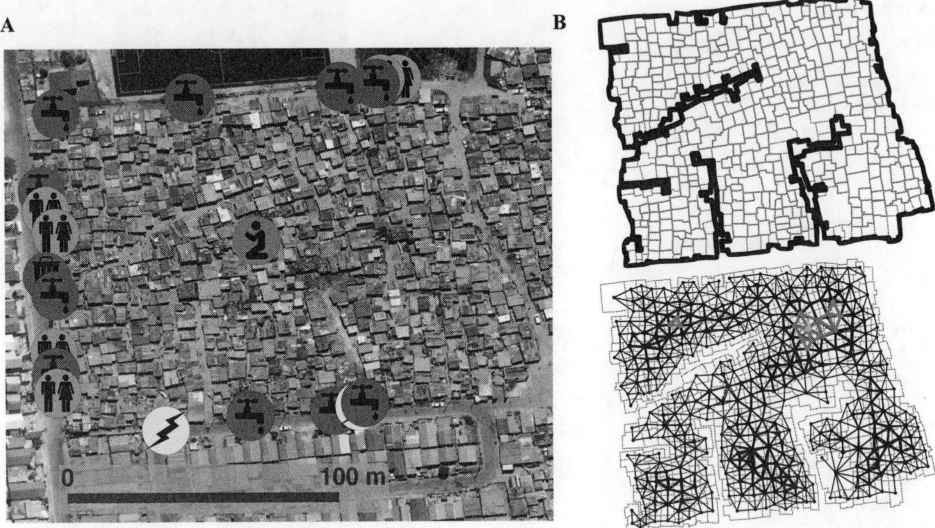

3.26 Neighborhood topology and the access networks of informal settlements. (A) An informal settlement in Khayelitsha, a township of Cape Town, South Africa. As is typical of most informal settlements, services provided by the city, including power, water, toilets, and trash collection (symbols), are located exclusively along the roads defining the periphery of the block. In contrast, public spaces created by the community, such as a religious and community center (kneeling figure), are located near the block's center. (B) Parcel layout for (A) showing many internal places on the block, outlined in thin gray lines (top). The corresponding odd-numbered weak dual graphs S_k (figure 3.25) are shown in different shades of gray, from darker to lighter. $k^*_{max} = 9$, defines the complexity of this particular block.

Finally, having an index of lack of universal access to all buildings in each street block is halfway to also having a mathematical construction of the minimum set of accesses that need to be added to solve the problem. This is shown in figure 3.27, which demonstrates how street networks can be grown into city blocks with infrastructure deficits by solving a constrained optimization problem of reducing the block complexity subject to the minimum amount of new street length added. The requirement of creating a minimal street network tends to produce a lot of dead ends. If this is an issue because not enough thoroughfares exist at the block level, we can strategically connect these dead ends using just a little bit more street length, as shown in figure 3.27C.

The strength of these procedures is the demonstration that city networks, including infrastructure and associated land uses, can evolve gradually without the wholesale destruction (and often associated social injustice) of evictions and demolitions and the homogenization of spaces. More "organic" spatial evolution typically produces interesting—historically and culturally—urban built spaces, of the type revered by urbanists, characteristic of old cities in Europe and Asia[100] but that have been anathema to twentieth-century urban planning practices, which were often driven by ill-defined concepts of efficiency and geometry.

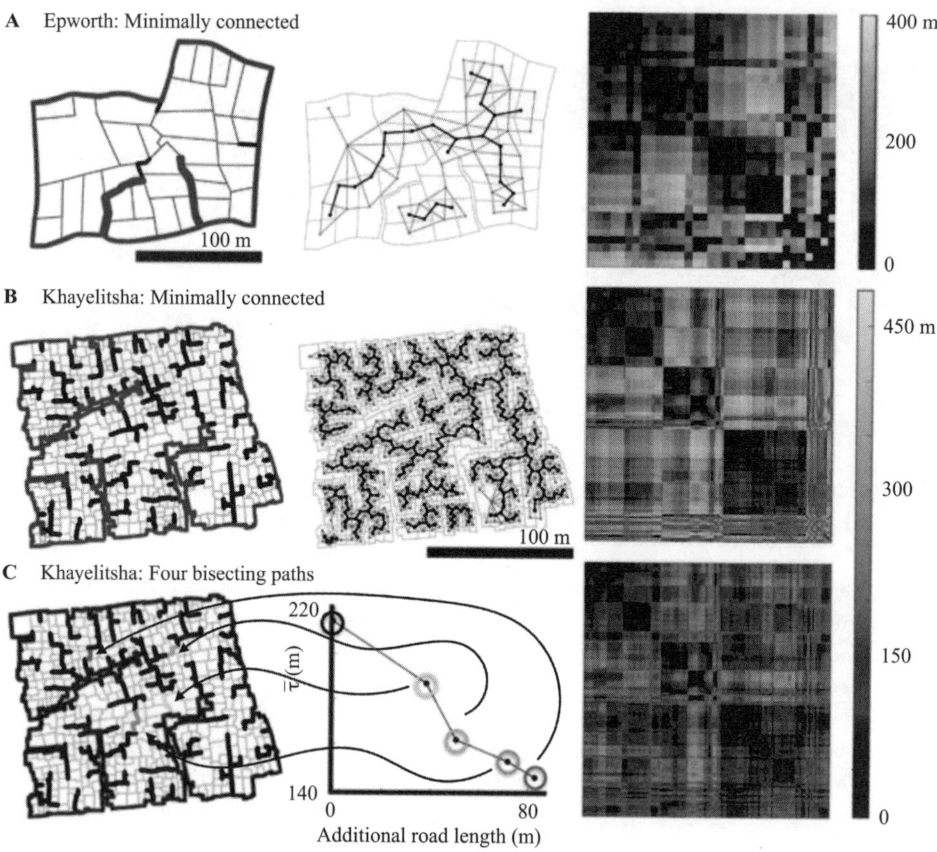

3.27 Expanding street networks in underserviced city blocks. (A) The topologically optimal solution for the Epworth block of figure 3.25D, with additional street segments shown by arrows. The resulting dual graph shows that the S_2 dual graph (blue) is now a tree (middle). The parcel-to-parcel travel-cost matrix $\mathfrak{I}$ (right) shows that all parcels are connected but that some remain distant from each other over the network. Each entry of $\mathfrak{I}$, T_{ij}, shows the minimum on-network travel distance from i to j, where darker entries are shorter distances and lighter entries are longer distances. The matrix has been reordered using a hierarchical clustering algorithm to reveal parcel clusters with short distances over the network. (B) The topological solution for the Khayelitsha neighborhood of figure 3.26, the resulting weak dual graphs (middle), and the corresponding minimum travel-cost matrix, $\mathfrak{I}$ (right). (C) The result of the geometric optimization for (B), where four new bisecting paths were added (left), resulting in substantial decreases in $\bar{\mathfrak{I}}$ (middle) by introducing 81 m of new roads and reducing the average parcel-to-parcel travel distance, $\bar{\mathfrak{I}}$, from 214 to 145 m (right).

Source: Adapted from Christa Brelsford, Taylor Martin, Joe Hand, and Luís M. A. Bettencourt, "Toward Cities without Slums: Topology and the Spatial Evolution of Neighborhoods," *Science Advances* 4, no. 8 (August 2018): eaar4644, https://doi.org/10.1126/sciadv.aar4644.

3.28 Section of Nairobi, Kenya, showing how deficits in local infrastructure can be diagnosed in every city block and minimal extensions of the street network proposed (thin white lines) that create universal access. This procedure provides initial proposals to grow infrastructure networks anywhere; see millionneiborhoods.org. It estimates the quantity and placement of new accesses and encourages local communities and governments to engage with detailed challenges of urban planning.
Source: Christa Brelsford, Taylor Martin, Joe Hand, and Luís M. A. Bettencourt, "Toward Cities without Slums: Topology and the Spatial Evolution of Neighborhoods," *Science Advances* 4, no. 8 (August 2018): eaar4644, https://doi.org/10.1126/sciadv.aar4644.

As this book is being written, it is becoming possible to apply these techniques to every city block in the world (see example in figure 3.28) and use the kind of urban science developed here in close interaction with community needs and local governments to support an evolutionary model of urban growth, at least at the level of neighborhoods. This approach should help create more inspiring urban environments that bridge existing situations and human needs with new science-based models of urban sustainable development.

EPILOGUE: CITIES ARE A DIFFERENT KIND OF COMPLEX SYSTEM

Cities are not organisms, any more than they are machines, and perhaps even less so. They do not grow or change of themselves, or reproduce or repair themselves. They are not autonomous entities, nor do they run through life cycles, or become infected. . . . But it is more difficult, and more important, to see the fundamental ineptness of the metaphor and how it leads us unthinkingly to cut out slums to prevent their "infectious" spread, to search for an optimum size, to block continuous growth, to separate uses, to struggle to maintain greenbelts, to suppress competing centers, to prevent "shapeless sprawl," and so on.

—Kevin A. Lynch, *Good City Form*

This quotation from influential and inspiring urbanist Kevin Lynch on the nature of cities and on the danger of easy metaphors can now guide us through some final considerations of *what kind of system a city is*.[101] Before we return to this question at the end of the book, it is instructive to see what urban scaling can tell us already.

We have seen that scaling relations define statistical phenomena that apply to different kinds of systems from gases to stars and from ecosystems to cities. We have also seen that even though scaling relations often reflect basic energy management, these relations are quantitatively different for distinct system types. This should show beyond any reasonable doubt that cities are not like biological organisms or like any of the other systems described in this chapter for that matter, vindicating Lynch. Such metaphors can only really apply in the loosest sense. By the same token, cities are not just massive engineered systems either, "machines" to be optimized by better algorithms, as they are sometimes conceptualized in engineering and technology. The combinatorial possibilities from the actions of all urban agents, which build what the city is and vastly transcend the data necessary for describing the city in any particular situation,[102] create enormous *computational complexity* so detailed future scenarios are too numerous to generate and evaluate. In this sense, cities are impossible to plan in detail.[103]

As we have seen, cities can be conceptualized as networked systems. But different types of networks—physical and social—are necessary to describe cities. In this sense, cities as spatial networks share some similarities to river basins or vascular systems, but we showed that such networks in cities are more decentralized and operate in a regime driven not by maximum energy efficiency but rather by the needs of realizing network effects in socioeconomic productivity. Cities also share some of their properties with stars, even though their superlinear scaling relations with size are quantitatively different. This allows us to conceptualize cities as places that facilitate the quantity, scope, and diversity of human social encounters and interactions, mediated by specific kinds of networked built spaces.

This is—mechanically, at least—what cities are for: they are *social reactors* that provide an open-ended solution to the central problem of a creative social species capable of immense innovation only when working together in large and diverse groups. I believe this perspective shines some new light on the "triumph of the city"[104] as the constructed general-purpose "ecological niche"[105] that has created and still supports fast cultural evolution as the "secret of our success."[106] To more fully appreciate how these mechanics of accelerating social encounters with city size can become the basis for innovation and growth in human societies will require development of several other ingredients, which will be done in the chapters that follow.

4

THE STATISTICS OF URBAN QUANTITIES: PREDICTABILITY, IDENTITY, AND UNIVERSALITY

Nothing happens quite by chance.
  It's a question of accretion of information and experience.
—Jonas Salk, quoted in Richard Carter, *Breakthrough: The Saga of Jonas Salk*

This chapter deals with urban statistics, quantifying and attempting to explain the origins of deviations from averages given city sizes and, by extension, identifying what is special and unique about each place. The main consideration in dealing with variations from averages in complex systems is that they carry *information*. This is unlike fluctuations in simpler physical systems, which are typically signs of disorder (e.g., induced by thermal fluctuations). Complex systems exploit both sources of disorder and mechanisms of selection to generate their temporal evolution and to structure populations. We will characterize these empirical variations for urban processes and interpret their meaning in terms of the unique character and history of each city. We will also develop a statistical theory of urban quantities that not only allows us to make sense of these variations as the result of the aggregation of an agent's accidents and choices at more microscopic levels but also calculate how such variations contribute to the values of scaling quantities, including corrections to exponents. This approach will generalize urban scaling theory (chapter 3) and introduce ideas of renormalization group flows to the stochastic dynamics of finite populations in cities.

CHAPTER OUTLINE

This chapter is divided as follows. Section 4.1 shows how scaling analysis leads naturally to the systematic identification of quantities that are both dynamic and stochastic, including the statistical behavior of deviations from scaling relations. The statistical and dynamic behaviors of these deviations are illustrated through several empirical studies of cities in the US, Europe, Brazil, India, and China, and a number of different indicators. Section 4.2 develops mathematical models and a general theoretical framework to predict this statistical and dynamic behavior using models of multiplicative random growth and their aggregation across population and temporal scales. The chapter ends with a brief discussion of universality in urban systems (and its breakdown), quantified in terms of the statistical behavior of deviations from scaling.

4.1 GROWTH PROCESSES AND EMERGENT STATISTICS OF URBAN INDICATORS

As we saw in chapters 2 and 3, classical approaches to urban theory—in economic geography[1] and more recently in complex systems[2]—treat cities as spatial equilibria where a balance of benefits and costs is achieved out of a set of social and economic exchanges, land rents, transportation, and other costs..[3] While these approaches have proven powerful for predicting many observed average scaling properties of cities,[4] they leave unresolved two fundamental issues: the *problem of statistics* and the *problem of growth.*

Both growth and statistics denote a broad set of issues. We must unpack these terms so we can fully appreciate what is at stake. By statistics, we mean that in dealing with real cities we must appreciate the wide variation observed between individuals and places[5] (see also chapters 5 and 6). This may be positive in that cities are extremely diverse in terms of the types of people and lifestyles they support, including a broad set of coexisting cultures, professions, languages, races, and ethnicities.[6] Negative expressions of these same heterogeneities are also familiar, such as ethnic, racial, and economic segregation,[7] inequality,[8] and deficits in the access to justice and opportunity for some segments of the population[9] (chapter 6). Sociologists have shown that these differences between places and people within each city are very persistent in time[10] and do not typically have the fleeting character of fluctuations in, say, statistical physics. Instead, they can add up over time, leading to patterns of cumulative advantage and disadvantage.[11] Thus, the problem of statistics in cities deals not only with the existence of structural differences regarding how the same quantity (e.g., income) is expressed for different people but also with the temporal persistence and amplification of these effects.

By growth we will mean that (modern) cities are typically characterized by fast change across many variables.[12] From this perspective, it may seem that basing urban theory on ideas of equilibrium, as we did in chapters 2 and 3, is a nonstarter. Growth means several different phenomena at different scales: On the one hand, modern cities tend to experience annual population growth rates between about a fraction of 1% and about 4%. Exceptions exist at either end, at least over some periods of time, as specific places experience contextual factors, as we will see. The most important change in contemporary cities has to do with the pace of their economic growth and technological change. Across the world today, we observe rates of urban economic growth that are typically larger than the growth in their corresponding populations, in some cases reaching 10% a year, with 2%–4% being typical. These growth rates mean that the size of a city's economy doubles every few decades (recall that a 1% growth rate means a doubling every 70 years), making it possible to transition from poverty to wealth in a single generation, as has happened in several nations over the past century (chapter 1). With such fast growth rates at work, how is it tenable to model cities as spatial equilibria? Even more importantly, how do different growth rates, experienced by different individuals, neighborhoods, or cities, shape the heterogeneity (inequality) of outcomes for different people? Why aren't cities inevitably blown apart by unequal growth?

To answer this type of question in new ways, we must do the math! It turns out that these two issues—the problems of *statistics* and *growth*—are intimately connected and must be tackled together. It will be by understanding the essence of growth processes in the presence of variations that we can start to establish a more complete and predictive theory of cities and, from this point of view, come to appreciate how urban growth, short-term spatial equilibrium, and the heterogeneity of agents and places are all features of an integrated emergent statistical dynamics of cities and urban systems.

4.1.1 SCALING RELATIONS AND STATISTICAL DEVIATIONS

We now take on the statistical and dynamic content of scaling relations. This section also shows that scaling provides a parameterization of growth for urban economies that differs from growth accounting in economics,[13] which is typically applied at the level of nations (see chapter 9). Recall the general form of the scaling relation in equation (3.1). What is usually meant by the *scaling relation* is the statistical mean over cities, given their size; that is,

$$\langle Y_i(N_i, t)\rangle_{N_i} = Y_0(t)N_i(t)^\beta \langle e^{\xi_i(t)}\rangle_{N_i}, \tag{4.1}$$

where $\langle \cdots \rangle_{N_i}$ denotes an average over cities, here limited to a range of population sizes around N_i. Consequently, we may say that there are *scaling laws* that describe cities and urban systems only to the extent that the deviations are well behaved and that their average, $\langle e^{\xi_i(t)}\rangle_{N_i}$, is small and independent of city size. We will make sense of these conditions later in this chapter.

In the particular case where the deviations ξ_i are normally distributed, with mean zero and variance σ_ξ^2, the expectation value of the exponential in equation (4.1) is simply $e^{\frac{\sigma_\xi^2}{2}}$. We will see that if σ_ξ^2 is small but a function of city size, N, a situation called *heteroscedasticity*, the fluctuations will contribute a correction to the scaling exponent, β, and that the size of such correction is controlled by the magnitude of the variance. If large, these deviations can destroy scaling as a power-law relation. However, if σ_ξ^2 is not a function of city size, then the mean-field results of chapter 3 will still stand and the scaling prefactor, Y_0, is simply multiplied by a number, which is close to 1 for small variances. The rest of this chapter will give a number of empirical examples of the behavior of the deviations from scaling for various quantities in urban systems throughout the world and discuss their practical meaning. We will then construct a statistical theory for explaining the origins, dynamics, and magnitude of these deviations.

4.1.2 CENTERED SCALING RELATIONS AND DYNAMIC QUANTITIES

We now use the average over cities to isolate a few quantities of interest, which will allow us to zero in on the general properties of *growth and statistics* in cities. To do this, let us first take the logarithm of the scaling relation to obtain

$$\ln Y_i(N_i, t) = \ln Y_0(t) + \beta \ln N_i(t) + \xi_i(t), \tag{4.2}$$

followed by averaging over all cities,

$$\langle \ln Y(t) \rangle = \ln Y_0(t) + \beta \langle \ln N(t) \rangle. \tag{4.3}$$

The average over cities is defined by the ensemble mean

$$\langle \ln Y(t) \rangle = \frac{1}{N_c} \sum_{i=1}^{N_c} \ln Y_i(N_i(t), t), \quad \langle \ln N(t) \rangle = \frac{1}{N_c} \sum_{i=1}^{N_c} \ln N_i(t), \tag{4.4}$$

where N_c is the total number of cities in the urban system, such as the US.

We will refer to the quantities $\langle \ln Y \rangle$ and $\langle \ln N \rangle$ as the *centers*.[14] These are the collective coordinates that track the temporal motion of the urban system as a whole (square symbols in figures 4.1A and B) and are analogous to *center-of-mass* coordinates in many-body physics.

By the definition of the scaling relation as a mean in logarithmic variables, the ensemble average of the deviations is always zero, $\langle \xi(t) \rangle = 0$. From the preceding expressions, we can write two expressions for these deviations as

$$\xi_i(t) = \ln \frac{Y_i(N_i, t)}{Y_0(t)N_i^\beta(t)} = [\ln Y_i(N_i, t) - \langle \ln Y(t) \rangle] - \beta[\ln N_i(t) - \langle \ln N(t) \rangle]. \tag{4.5}$$

The first expression gives the most common interpretation of the $\xi_i(t)$ as (multiplicative, percentage) deviations from the scaling relation, whereas the second makes their status as deviations from the collective coordinates (centers) fully explicit. Characterizing these three dynamic quantities,

1. $\langle \ln Y(t) \rangle$, which will be the main topic of chapter 9;
2. $\langle \ln N(t) \rangle$, which will be the subject of chapter 8; and
3. the time dependence of the scaling residuals, $\xi_i(t)$,

which will be done in the present chapter, gives a complete description of the statistics of growth and deviations in a system of cities. We will also see how all these quantities are associated with stochastic growth processes and specifically with exponential growth rates.

Figure 4.1 illustrates the meaning of these quantities and their usefulness in parameterizing growth and statistics. Figure 4.1A shows the total wages, $Y_{W_i}(N_i(t), t)$, for US Metropolitan Statistical Areas (MSAs) between 1969 and 2016 (47 years) year by year. The growth trajectory of some specific places, such as New York City, Los Angeles, Chicago, and Silicon Valley (San Jose–Santa Clara MSA), are easily visualized in this way. The solid lines show the scaling relation for each year (see the figure 4.1 caption for details). Scaling is a good fit to the data each year, reproducing a slowly shifting spatial equilibrium in each instance (figure 4.1 inset; see also

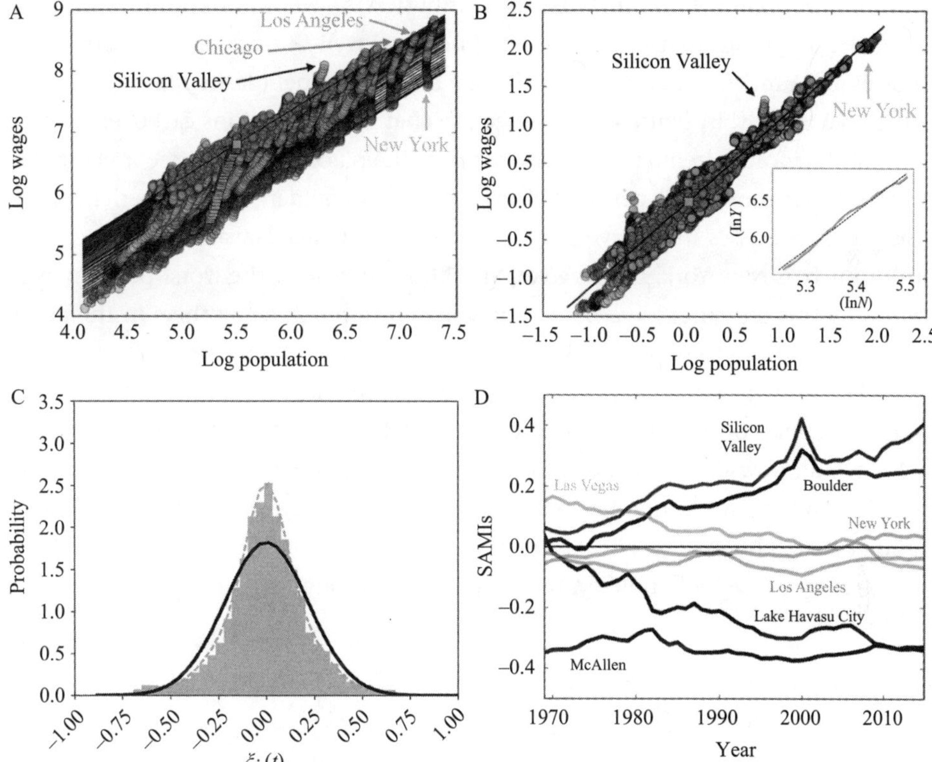

4.1 Urban scaling and the dynamics of growth and deviations. (A) Total wages for US MSAs, 1969–2016. Circles show each city in a given year from 1969 to 2016 (bottom to top). Squares show the location of the urban system's center ($\langle \ln N \rangle$, $\langle \ln Y_W \rangle$). Urban scaling relations for each year (straight lines) change intercept at a very slow timescale. (B) Centered data, obtained from figure 4.1A by removing the center's motion (inset). This allows the decomposition of temporal change into two separate processes: collective growth (center's motion) and deviations from scaling, ξ_i. We see that scaling with a common exponent (global fit $\beta = 1.11$, 95% confidence interval [1.11, 1.12], $R^2 = 0.94$) is preserved over time and that net growth is a property of the urban system and not of individual cities (inset). (C) The statistics of deviations. While the ξ distribution is well localized and symmetrical, it is not very well fit by a Gaussian (solid line). Instead, the dashed line produces a much better account of the data. (D) ξ_i for a few selected places: Silicon Valley (San Jose–Santa Clara MSA) and Boulder, Colorado, show exceptional trajectories in wage gains for their city sizes, whereas Las Vegas, Nevada, and Lake Havasu City, Arizona, illustrate wage losses. New York City, Los Angeles, and the exceptionally poor McAllen, Texas, show no change in their relative positions over nearly 50 years.

chapter 3). We also see how the positions of the centers (squares) move from year to year, reflecting the overall growth in population (shifts to the right) and especially in the magnitude of wages (movement upward). The dynamics of these centers are very simple and smooth.

Figure 4.1B shows the result of removing collective growth by moving all data clouds so their centers coincide at the origin (0,0). Removing the center's temporal motion (inset) reproduces the same essential scaling pattern with small and slow-moving deviations changing only slightly from year to year. Figure 4.1C shows the histogram of these deviations (gray) about the overall best-fit scaling relation (figure 4.1B). We observe that the statistical distribution is well localized and symmetrical about the origin but that in this case it is not very well fit by a normal distribution (solid line). A much better fit is provided by another model (dashed line), which we will derive. Finally, in figure 4.1D, we see the change in deviations $\xi_i(t)$ over time for some of the most extreme trajectories. Some of the places have become much richer in relative terms over this period (Silicon Valley and Boulder), some experienced the most dramatic losses in relative status (Las Vegas and Lake Havasu City), and a few others, such as New York, Los Angeles, and McAllen (one of the worst performers in the US by this measure) have not changed much in relation to others in the urban system. These trajectories also show how *very slow* relative change is most of the time. We can identify the effects of particular events in different cities at specific times, such as the dot.com economic boom and bust around 2000 for Silicon Valley and Boulder.

We would now like to account for the behavior of collective growth in a system of cities and the pattern of relative fluctuations. Specifically, we would like to understand at a fundamental level the slowness and persistence of these deviations from scaling as well as get a handle on their typical magnitudes.

4.1.3 DEVIATIONS AS MEASUREMENTS OF SIZE-INDEPENDENT URBAN PERFORMANCE

As we have just seen, the residuals from scaling account for what is different about a city once scaling or agglomeration effects have been identified and removed. This makes the $\xi_i(t)$ for each city and at each time a measure of performance relative to other cities that is independent of population size. For this reason, the ξ's are sometimes known as *scale-adjusted metropolitan indicators* (SAMIs).[15] SAMIs are more appropriate indicators of the performance of cities than more common *per capita* quantities (crime rates, GDP per capita) because they account for the general fact that, because of nonlinear scaling, some quantities will be larger and others smaller per person in larger cities. Moreover, the time dependence of the $\xi_i(t)$ gives us a sense of the development trajectory for each place independent of city size. This feature can be used to identify *kindred* cities as those types that share common histories in terms of their SAMI temporal trajectories. We now illustrate these properties and uses of the SAMIs in some examples from around the world.

Example 1: The US Urban System—Crime, Patents, and Incomes   The first and most common use of the SAMIs is in the production of city performance rankings.[16] Figure 4.2 shows the rankings of US MSAs according to the magnitude of their ξ_i for income and number of patents generated per year. Because this measure accounts for the superlinear effects in both quantities, several smaller cities can now be rightfully recognized as exceptionally successful. For income, these include Bridgeport, Connecticut; Napa, California; and some beach towns in Florida. For patents, Corvallis, Oregon; Burlington, Vermont; Silicon Valley; and Boise, Idaho, appear in the top four. We see immediately that there are various reasons for success (and failure). Some cities (Bridgeport) do well because they thrive in the shadow of a very large city and concentrate related finance and insurance. Others may be extraordinarily pleasant places to live or retire to (beach, mountains, wine country, climate), attracting wealthy populations. In terms of patents, some of the most successful places simply concentrate firms to an extraordinary degree for their size. For example, Corvallis was at this point in time the headquarters for Hewlett-Packard Labs and Boise was the headquarters of Micron Technologies. All of them, along with Burlington, are university towns. An analysis of cities that underperform also reveals various reasons for the observed trends, from cities on the border with Mexico to postindustrial cities and urban areas in some of the poorest parts of the country.

The temporal change of the $\xi_i(t)$ shown in figure 4.3, as we also started to see in figure 4.1D, is very slow. It also displays strong memory effects (deviates in time very slowly), which make urban dynamics *path dependent*. This means that if a city was poor or rich (high or low in whatever property) in the past relative to others, it is very likely to remain so for *decades*. Figures 4.3B and C make these observations clearer by showing the temporal autocorrelation of the $\xi_i(t)$, and the power spectrum of their time series. Typical timescales for substantial change in the SAMIs are decades, specifically about 20 years for income and 35 years for patents.

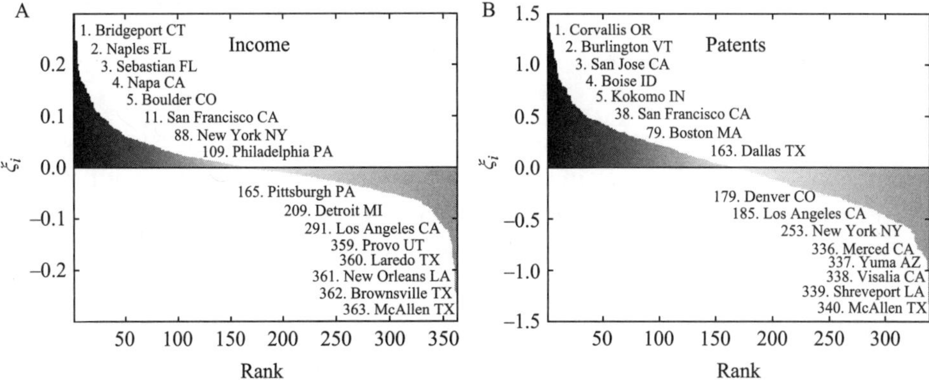

4.2 Rank-ordered distribution of scaling residuals. Subtracting nonlinear scaling effects produces a local measure of urban dynamics independent of city size and a reference frame for ranking cities. Scale-independent rankings (SAMIs) for US MSAs by (A) personal income and (B) patenting (darker denotes more positive deviations).

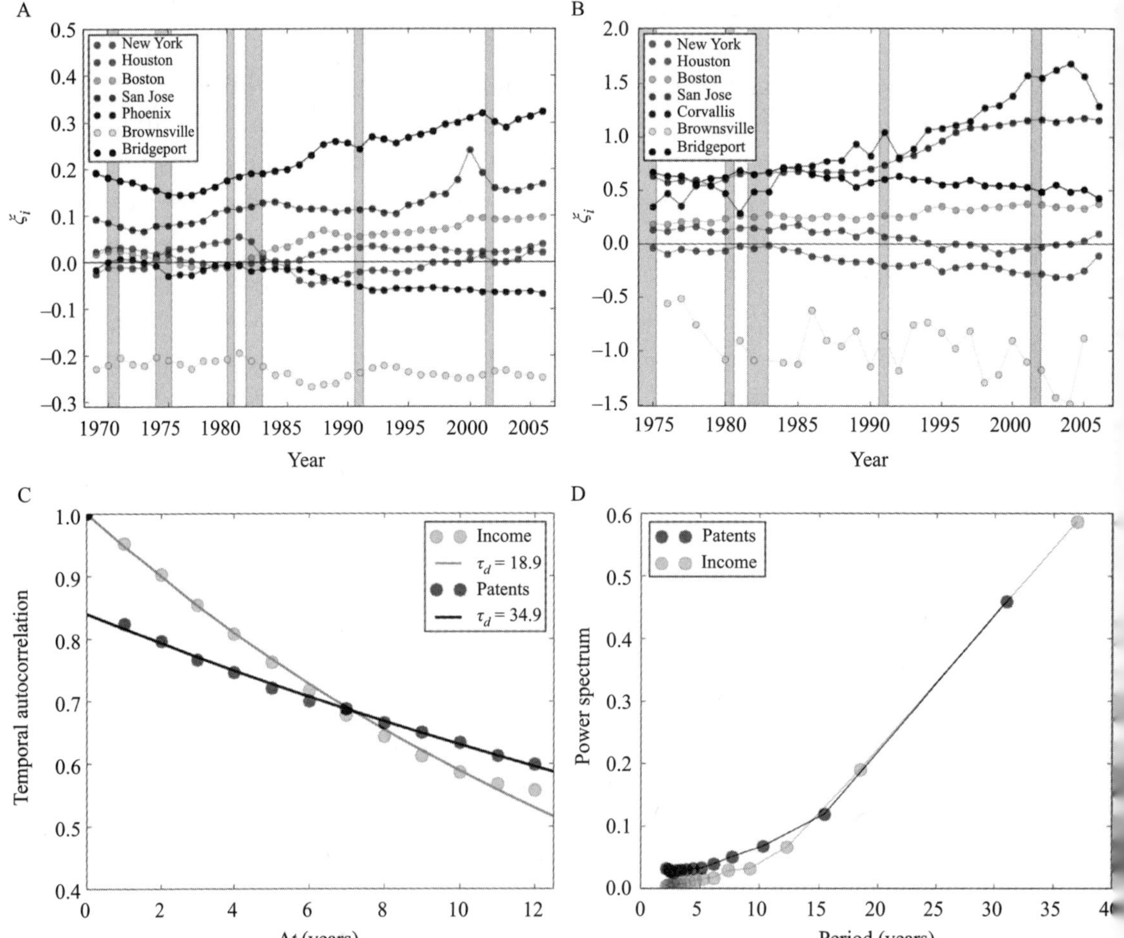

4.3 Temporal evolution of scale deviations displays long-term memory. The value of SAMIs as functions of time for (A) income (1969–2006) and (B) patents (1975–2006) for selected metropolitan areas in the US. Vertical gray bands indicate periods of national economic recession. (C) The temporal autocorrelation for patents and personal income and exponential fits, e^{-t/τ_d}, with characteristic decay times of $\tau_d = 18.9$ and 34.9 years, respectively. (D) Temporal Fourier power spectrum for the same quantities shows their dynamics are dominated by long timescales.

We can also use the correlations of the SAMIs across quantities to see how much the exceptionality of one place, say in terms of income, is related to other quantities, such as crime or invention (patents) (figures 4.4A–C). In general, the remaining correlations are small, explaining at most about 10%–20% of the variation in each set of ξ.

There are also some spatial correlations, so nearby cities perform in somewhat similar ways. In the US, urban system correlations decay over about 200 km, or a little over 100 mi. Thus, spatial effects of similarity between SAMIs are relatively local (figures 4.4D and E).

Finally, we can get a little more inventive and ask for the similarity of SAMI trajectories according to some metric of (normalized) distance, such as their inner product or autocorrelation function,

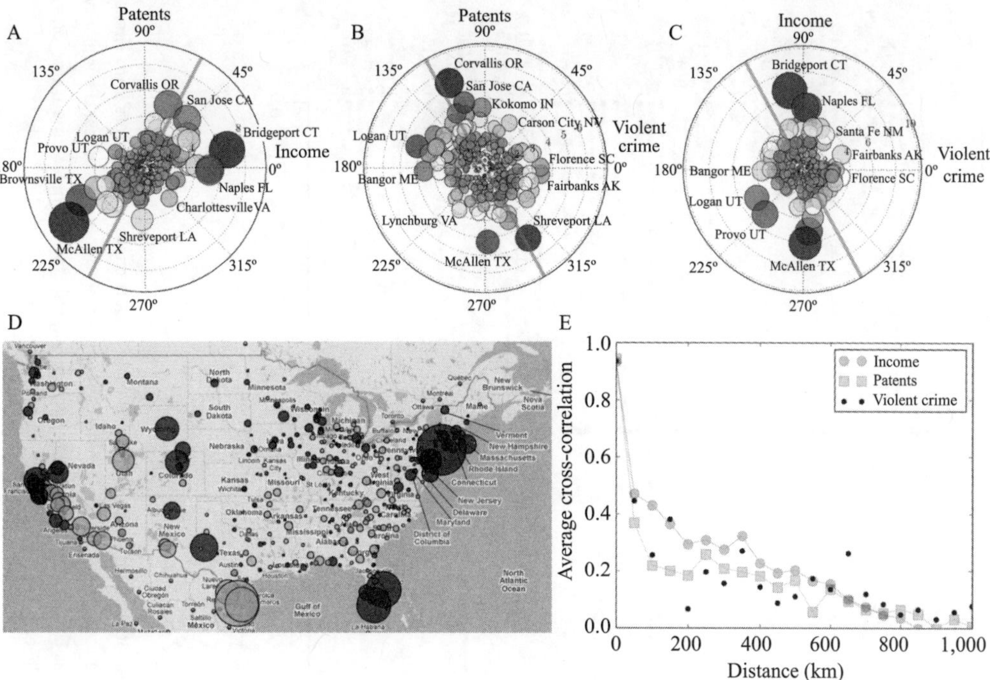

4.4 Relationships between local urban performance and their spatial distribution. (A) Normalized SAMIs for income versus patents are shown in polar coordinates together with the best-fit linear relation capturing overall average correlation (solid line, gradient$=0.38\pm0.04$, $R^2=0.20$). The shade and size of circles denote the magnitude of the combined SAMIs for each city. (B) Similar representation for income versus violent crime with the best-fit linear relation (gradient$=-0.19\pm0.07$, $R^2=0.05$), and (C) for patents versus violent crime with the best-fit linear relation (gradient$=-0.34\pm0.05$, $R^2=0.12$). Note that (B) and (C) show a small amount of anticorrelation between SAMIs, contrasting with the positive correlations for the per capita quantities because of their size dependence. (D) Spatial distribution of income residuals (SAMIs) in 2006. Darker circles show deviations above expectation for city size and lighter circles show deviations below expectation. The size of the circle denotes the magnitude of the SAMI. (E) Average cross-correlation between SAMIs versus spatial separation distance, showing short-range spatial correlation. Averages shown are subject to large variation for distances >200 km (124 mi), with standard deviation ≥ 0.6.

$$d_{ij}^{\xi} = \frac{1}{2}\left(1 - \frac{\vec{\xi}_i \cdot \vec{\xi}_j}{\|\xi_i\|\|\xi_j\|}\right) = \frac{1}{2}\left(1 - \frac{1}{\|\xi_i\|\|\xi_j\|}\sum_{t'=1}^{t}\xi_i(t')\xi_j(t')\right), \tag{4.6}$$

where $\|\xi_i\|$ is the vector's norm. This measure of distance can then be used to cluster *kindred* cities by the similarity of their trajectories (figure 4.5). This allows us to create a "recommendation system" for each city in terms of potential collaborators sharing similar developmental paths.

Example 2: Congestion Costs in US Urban Areas   We can apply the same reasoning and methods to a very different kind of quantity related to extra traffic congestion costs in US urban areas. Existing data (see figure 4.6) deal only with extraordinary road (automobile) costs resulting from congestion, defined as above and beyond costs of transportation under normal conditions. Urban scaling theory does not have a prediction

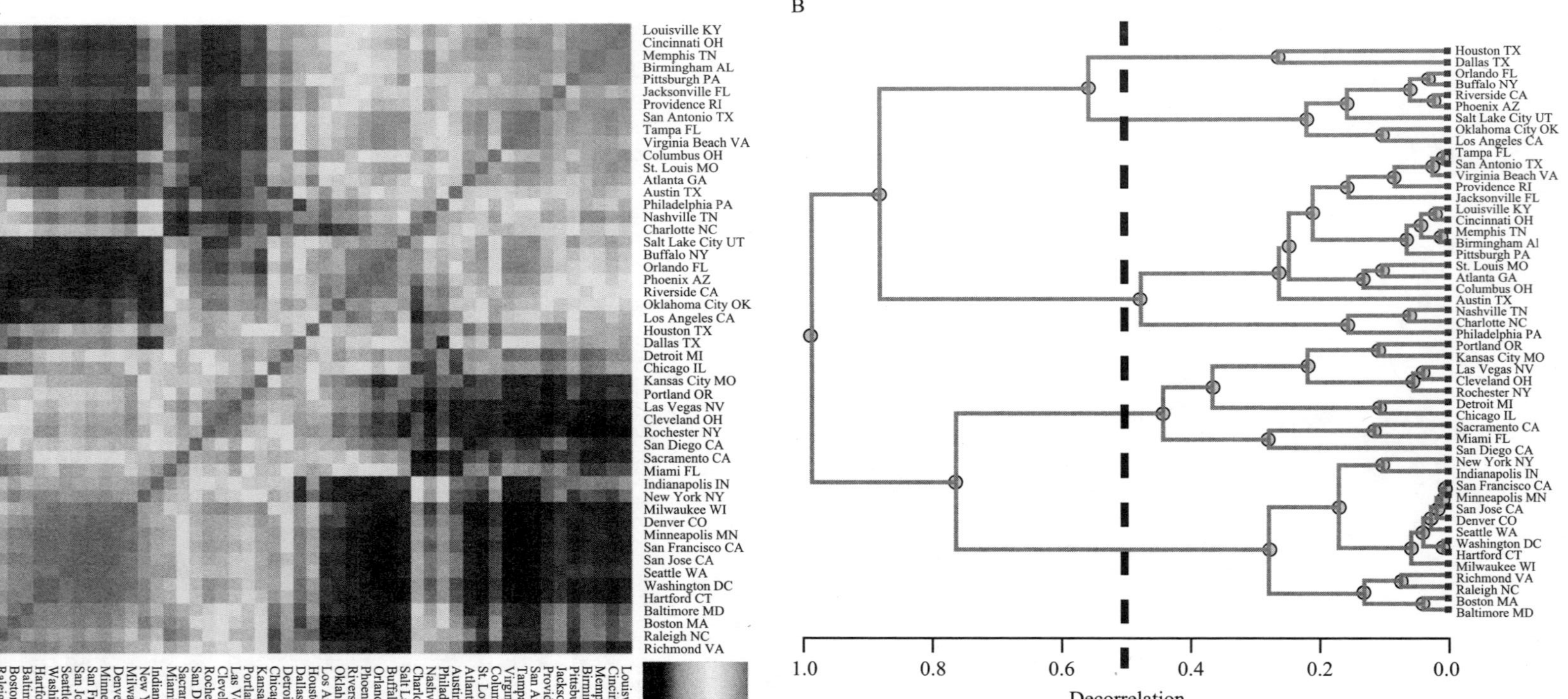

4.5 Families of kindred cities. The cross-correlation between SAMI time series gives a measure of similarity that can be used to group cities into clusters with similar characteristics. (A) Sorted correlation matrix (heat map) for personal income in US MSAs with populations over 1 million, where darker shading denotes greatest dissimilarity. (B) Dendrogram showing detailed urban taxonomy of US MSAs according to personal income. This clearly manifests clustering among cities with similar time trajectories. When the decorrelation $d_{ij} = d_{ij}^{\xi} = 0.5$, indicating no correlation (dashed line), we obtain five families of kindred cities.

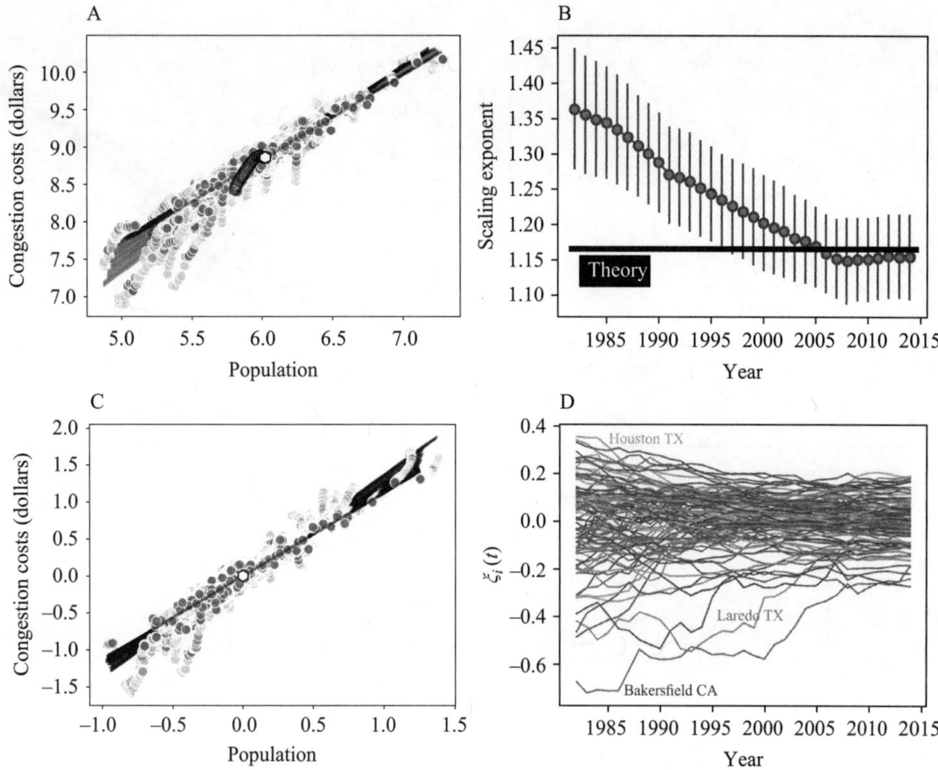

4.6 Scaling of excess traffic congestion costs in a subsample of 100 US cities. (A) Scaling plots year by year over the period 1982–2014; centers are shown as hexagons. The scaling best fit for each year is shown as a solid line. (B) Convergence of estimated scaling exponent (circles with 95% confidence error bars) to the value predicted by theory (horizontal solid line). (C) Centered scaling plot showing convergence to the theoretical expectation. (D) Individual city SAMI trajectories over time are convergent and are well behaved statistically.

for this quantity, but one may hypothesize that it is proportional to dissipative costs of regular transportation, since it is also proportional to fluxes and their matching and spatial density in a manner analogous to the analysis of chapter 3 but perhaps with more severe resistance behavior. This expectation is borne out by the data, at least for recent years, as congestion has increased in many smaller cities and in some cases also decreased in some of the most congested cities (see figures 4.6B–D).

We can also see that congestion costs have become better described over time by the simplest superlinear exponent, $\beta = 7/6$, and that these costs are now on average a fixed fraction (about 1%) of metropolitan GDP (figures 4.7A and B). We can use the idea of SAMI trajectories to produce a clustering of kindred cities for congestion costs. For example, once their SAMIs are normalized by their respective norms, Chicago and New York City are very similar in terms of the change in their SAMIs over time (figure 4.8). This example also shows that typologies of kindred cities are *not universal* and depend explicitly on the measure of similarity employed.

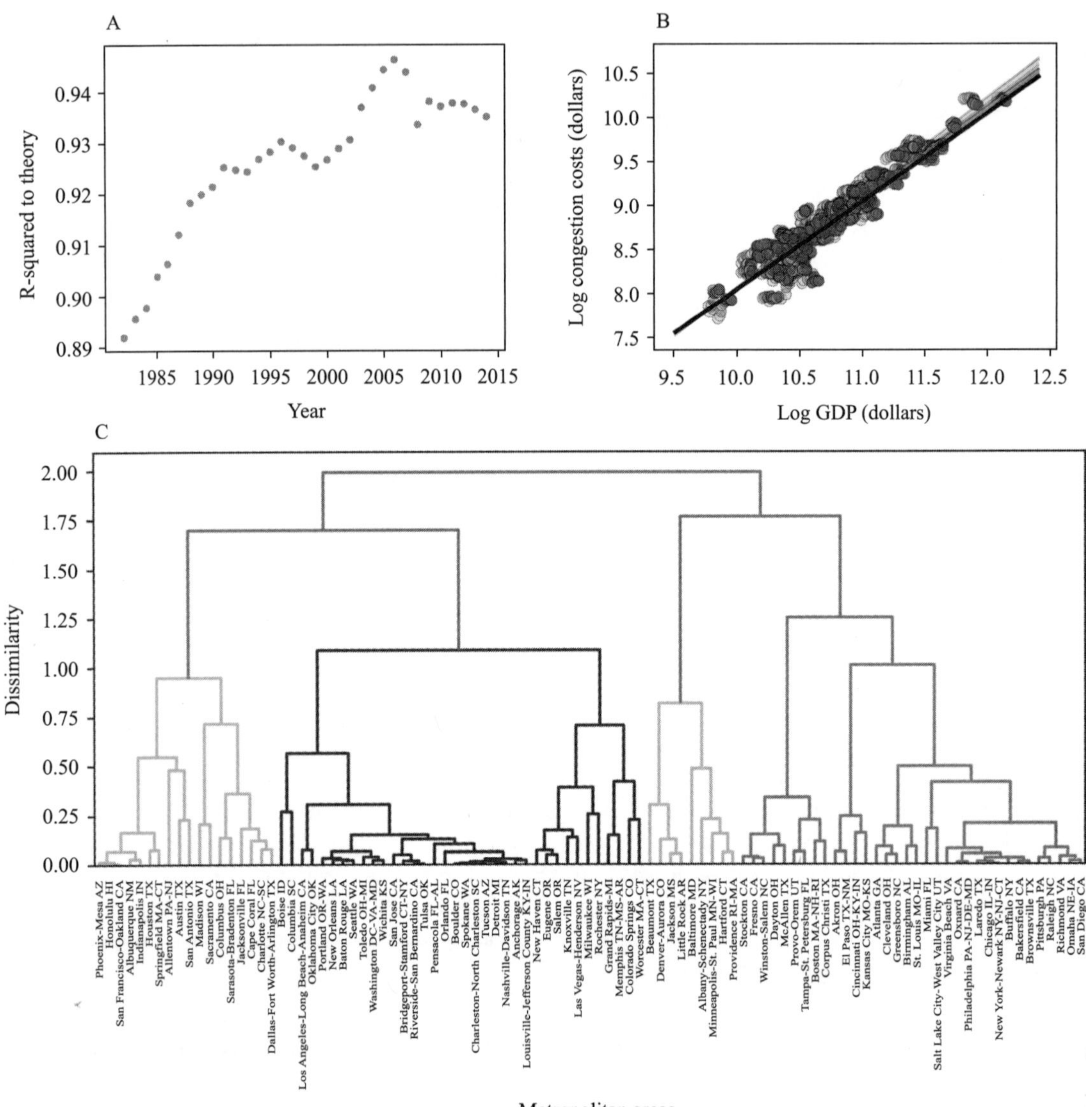

4.7 Convergence, spatial equilibrium, and individual city trajectory typology. (A) The variation of the R^2 of excess traffic congestion data relative to theory over time shows another way to assess convergence. (B) Excess congestion costs have converged over time to be proportional (slope = 1, black line) to GDP. (C) The normalized inner product of the SAMI trajectories (figure 4.6D) provides a natural—scale and growth independent—measure of the similarities and differences between cities, generating a hierarchical city typology relative to the temporal evolution of their traffic congestion costs.

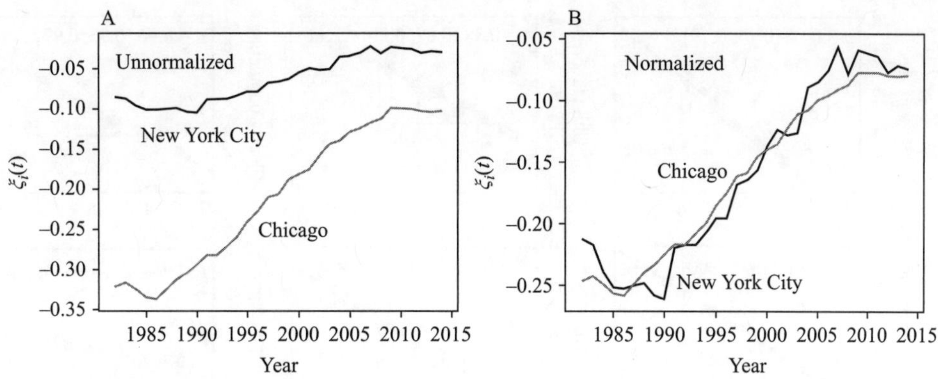

4.8 Typologies are not universal. The way measures of distance between SAMIs (and other urban indicators) are computed matters for how cities are associated together in clusters. (A) The raw (unnormalized) SAMI trajectory for New York City and Chicago in terms of additional congestion costs in figure 4.6D. (B) The same vectors normalized by dividing by their norm. In this second guise, the two trajectories are very similar and their internal product leads to a very small distance, and thus a strong kindred association in figure 4.7C. Note, however, that if we had clustered the data based, for example, on the similarity of the SAMI magnitudes, the two cities would have been judged to be quite different.

Example 3: Urban Scaling and Homicides in Brazil   In a series of studies, Alves and his colleagues[17] used the SAMIs for characterizing various quantities in Brazilian cities in interesting and original ways. In particular, they found certain nonlinear relationships between residuals from scaling for different urban indicators, especially related to homicide, a stark challenge for Brazilian urban areas.

Alves et al. characterized many scaling relations for Brazilian municipalities (figure 4.9), in broad agreement with expectations from theory. Critically, they analyzed the population size dependence of the standard deviation of residuals for different population size intervals and tested the hypothesis that residuals from scaling are approximately distributed as a normal probability density (figure 4.10). Except for homicides and perhaps unemployment, standard deviations are roughly independent of city size (homoscedasticity), and the normal distribution does a reasonable job of fitting the cumulative SAMI distribution, implying the approximate lognormality of urban indicators.

Finally, Alves et al. studied the relationship between the SAMIs as a "distance from the scaling law" for various urban indicators and their relationship to the SAMIs for homicides in each city (figure 4.11). This analysis shows several interesting nonlinear and bimodal relationships and may provide important new interpretations of the factors that influence violence in Brazilian cities.

Example 4: Crime and Innovation in India's Urban Agglomerations   India, as a huge, ancient, and now fast-growing system of cities, is perhaps the most critical test of ideas of urban scaling and agglomeration, including what is general and what is

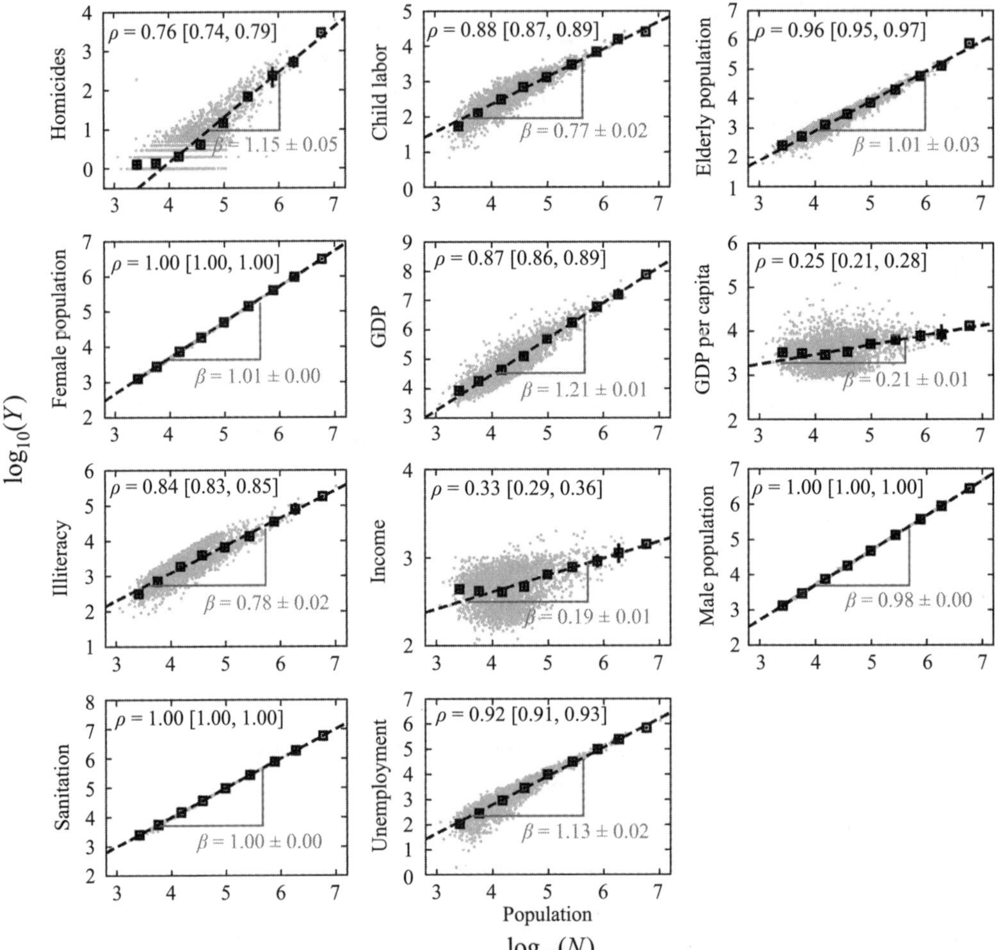

4.9 Scaling relations for various urban indicators in Brazilian cities. Data have been binned (squares) in 10 logarithmic intervals. ρ is the Pearson correlation coefficients, with the 95% confidence interval (CI) shown for each panel. Straight dashed lines are linear fits obtained by the least-squares method with slope (scaling exponent β) shown for each case together with its 95% CI.
Source: Adapted from Luiz G. A. Alves et al., "Distance to the Scaling Law: A Useful Approach for Unveiling Relationships between Crime and Urban Metrics," *PLoS One* 8, no. 8 (August 5, 2013): e69580, https://doi.org/10.1371/journal.pone.0069580.

particular to each place. There is still a great lack of good data that are explicitly urban in India, though the Census 2011 produced a consistent definition of so-called *urban agglomerations* as an approximation (without considering commuting flows) to metropolitan urban areas. By these definitions, India was judged to be only 31% urbanized in 2011, a number that has been disputed by other studies that consider the density of population agglomerations obtained via remote sensing data or night lights (chapter 2). In order to designate a place as urban, the Indian census requires that more than 75% of the male population be involved in nonagricultural occupations. This is considered a stringent definition by some authors.

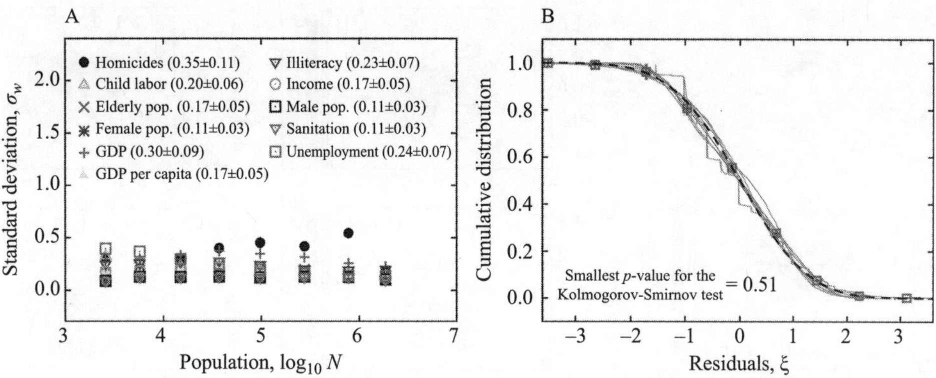

4.10 Distribution of SAMIs and their standard deviations. Panel A shows the standard deviation of the ξ's for the quantities indicated by the various symbols, while panel B shows the cumulative distribution of these quantities, which is reasonably well described by a normal distribution, implying that urban indicators, Y, are approximately lognormal. We also see no clear signs of scale dependence for σ_ξ. *Source*: Adapted from Luiz G. A. Alves et al., "Distance to the Scaling Law: A Useful Approach for Unveiling Relationships between Crime and Urban Metrics," *PLoS One* 8, no. 8 (August 5, 2013): e69580, https://doi.org/10.1371/journal.pone.0069580.

At any rate, quantities associated with urban agglomerations, especially those tied to service provision and population, are also given by the Indian Census and other government agencies. These quantities have been used to characterize the properties of Indian cities in terms of scaling analysis,[18] together with estimates of the size and variation in their economies, by adapting district-level measures of GDP. Although there are many areas of agreement with other urban systems,[19] two quantities— crime and patents—show interesting deviations, which we characterize here in terms of their SAMI statistics.

As earlier, we try to confirm this intuition by clustering cities based on the correlation distance between their crime and innovation SAMIs. Figures 4.12 and 4.13 show the ranking of SAMIs, their comparison to per capita indicators, and their spatial distribution across the country. Additional analysis shows that there are two main clusters comprised largely of southern and western cities and two clusters of northern, central, and eastern cities. There are also two significantly large, geographically mixed clusters of cities. This north-northeast/south-southwest divide in India is even more stark for crime than for patents. A few interesting cases of smaller cities with exceptional inventiveness are also easily identified in this way. Clearly, these patterns are connected to many factors, including different cultural traditions in different parts of this huge country, as well as a federal system of national governance that for good or bad provides states with strong autonomy and results in many divergent policy approaches. As India continues to urbanize, it is likely that some of these extant regional differences may be superseded by a common urban system network dynamics, as discussed in chapter 8.

Example 5: Wealth, Built Area, and the True Population Size of Chinese Cities   Finally, in this set of examples taking us around the world, it is interesting to consider cities

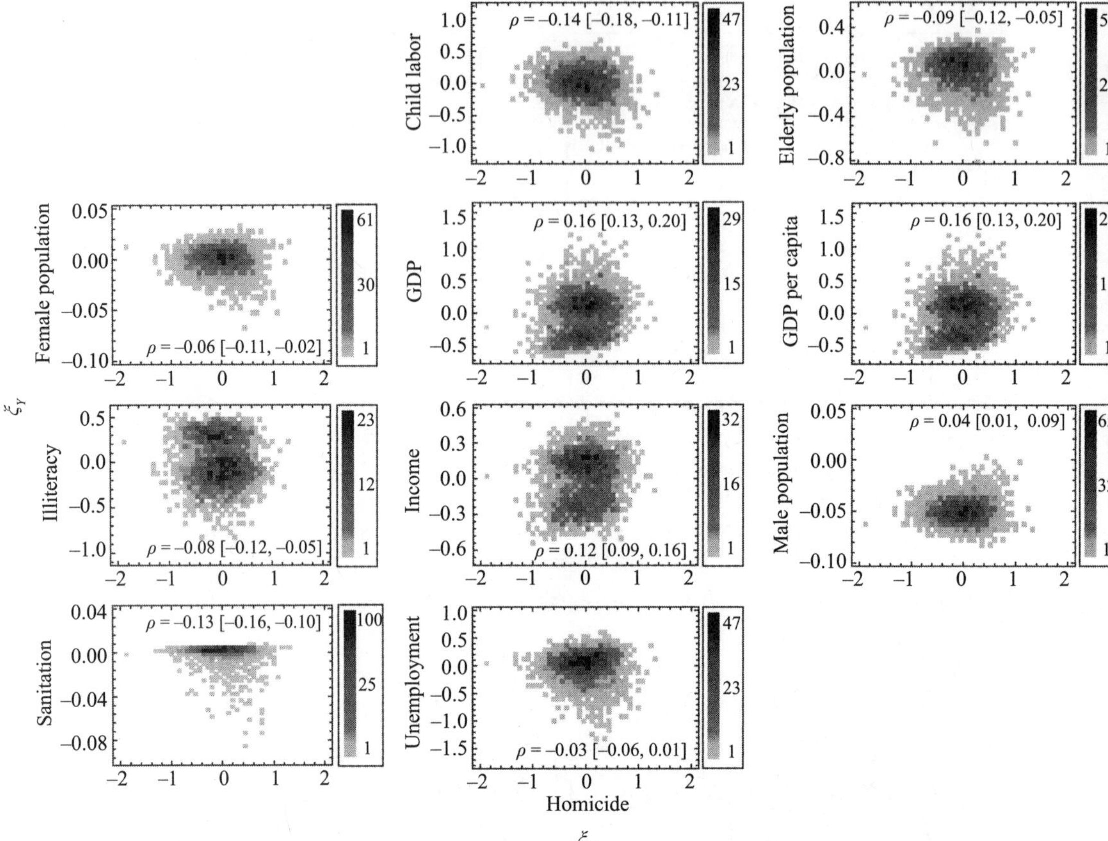

4.11 SAMIs for several urban indicators versus those for homicides in Brazilian cities ξ_H. Note that while in general there is no simple, clean relationship (such as the points aligning along a straight line), there are some nonsymmetric, and in some cases bipolar, correlations; for example, for male population, illiteracy, and GDP or income. Gray tones denote the density of points, quantified by the vertical tone bar for each subplot.
Source: Adapted from Luiz G. A. Alves et al., "Distance to the Scaling Law: A Useful Approach for Unveiling Relationships between Crime and Urban Metrics," *PLoS One* 8, no. 8 (August 5, 2013): e69580, https://doi.org/10.1371/journal.pone.0069580.

in China. Again, the concept of a metropolitan area or of a functional city more generally is only just emerging and being worked out in China. China does have, however, a system of territorial administration based on so-called *prefectural cities*. These include a classification of constituent subunits as predominantly urban or rural districts and counties. An approximation to a functional city can therefore be constructed using the *urban* districts and counties of each prefectural city,[20] for which the National Bureau of Statistics of China produces a number of interesting consistent indicators. These urban units show, on average, the expected scaling relations for quantities such as urban GDP and built-up areas, as in other nations (see figure 4.14), albeit perhaps with greater intercity variation (measured as SAMI

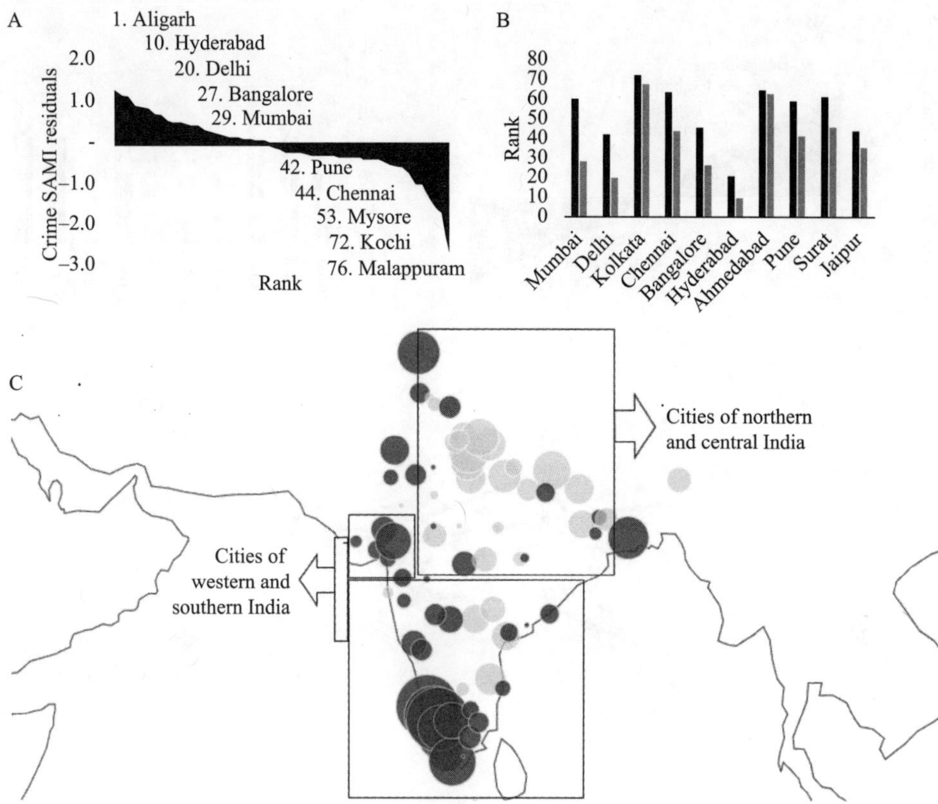

4.12 Residuals and per capita metrics for crime in Indian urban agglomerations. Crime is actually sublinear on city size in India, with smaller cities, especially in the north, showing higher levels of violence, associated with issues of caste and gender. (A) Ranking of cities by SAMIs. (B) Comparing city rankings by SAMIs (darker gray) to per capita rankings (lighter gray). This emphasizes that, for example, Mumbai and Bangalore have less crime than perceived on a per capita basis. (C) Spatial distribution of crime SAMIs in 2011. Dark circles correspond to deviations below expectation for city size, and light circles correspond to deviations above expectation. The size of the circle denotes the magnitude of crime SAMIs. We see that southern Indian cities are generally very safe, while northern ones are typically unsafe. The boxes show clustering associations reflecting these regional trends.

variance). This variation (figure 4.15) is at present not very well understood and may be the result of fundamental factors in a rapidly changing urban system but also the result of data issues and inconsistent definitions of urban areas.

As in other urban systems, we can use the SAMIs to rank and map the performance of Chinese cities (figure 4.16). This shows, as is well known, that many of the richest cities in China are coastal, with Shenzhen being by far the most exceptional large city in China in terms of GDP. The analysis shows that some of these southern cities (Shenzhen, Dongguan, Guangzhou) are also much more compact than is typical of contemporary Chinese cities in general. Finally, the analysis also flags some interesting exceptions among smaller cities, such as Ordos, with very high GDP performance resulting from a wealth of natural resources, including coal and related extractive industries.

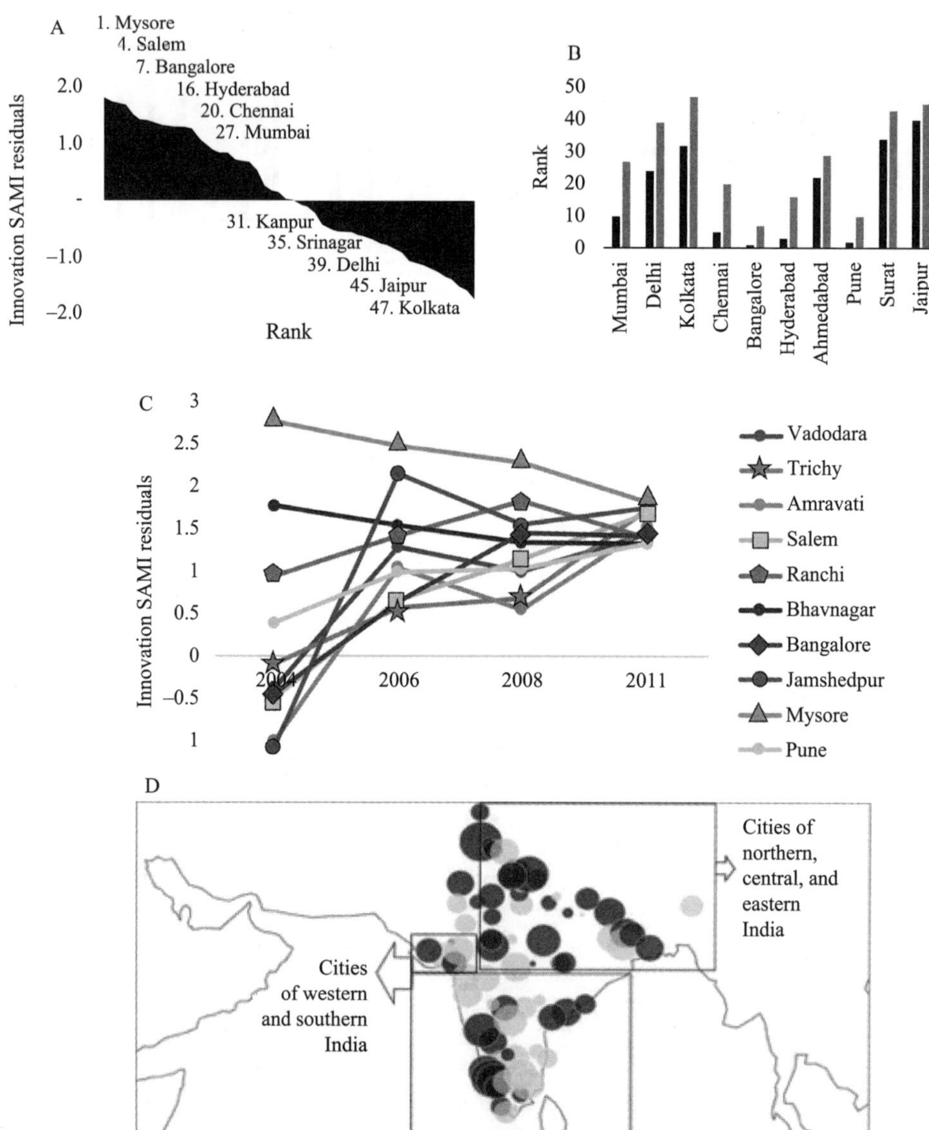

4.13 Residuals and per capita metrics for technological innovation in Indian urban agglomerations. (A) Rank order of innovation SAMIs in 2011. (B) Technological innovation rank in 2011 by SAMIs (dark gray) versus per capita rank (light gray). (C) Temporal change in innovation SAMIs for select Indian urban agglomerations, suggests some convergence across the nation. (D) As for crime, the spatial distribution of SAMIs shows strong regional signatures. Dark gray circles correspond to deviations below expectation for city size, and light gray circles indicate deviations above expectation. The size of the circle denotes the magnitude of the corresponding innovation SAMI. The SAMI ranking emphasizes some smaller regional technology centers, such as Mysore (information technologies) and Salem (steel, electronics), both in southern India.

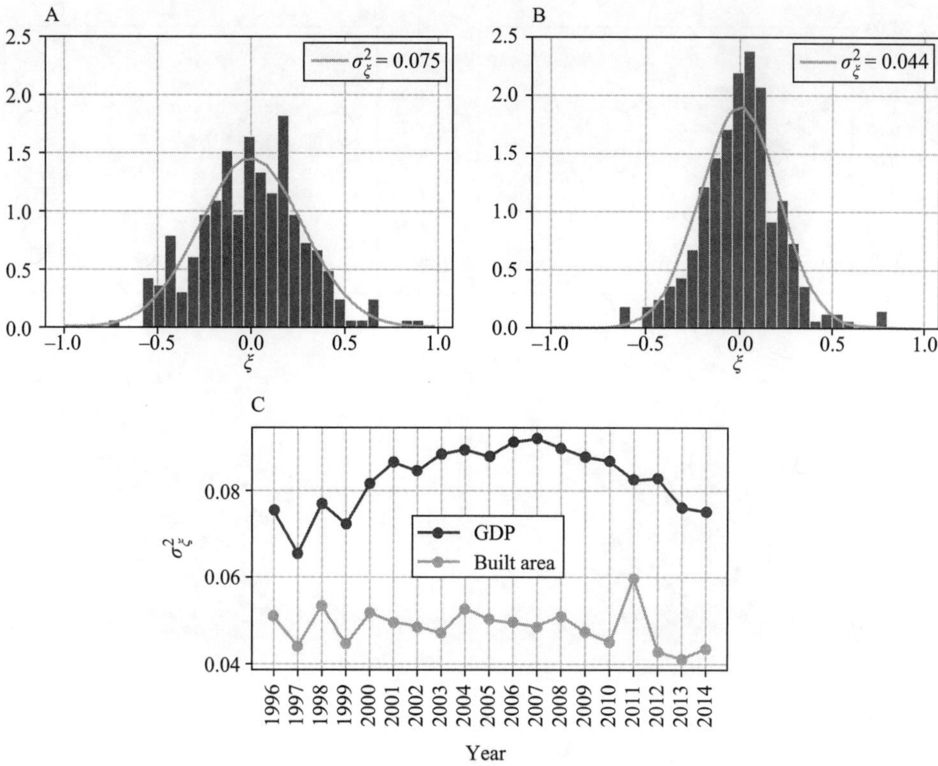

4.14 Distribution of SAMIs for Chinese prefectural cities. Histograms showing the frequency distribution of the residuals for (A) GDP and (B) built-up surface area, both in 2014. The histograms can be roughly described by a normal distribution (gray line). (C) Temporal variation in the SAMI variance.

One major issue for any quantitative study of Chinese cities, and for scaling analysis in particular, is being able to estimate their true population sizes. China has a system of residential registration (*hukou*) that strongly controls migration and leads at present to vast underreporting of actual resident and working populations in some places. This is especially true in larger cities:[21] keen observation of the GDP of the largest cities in China (figure 3.3A) shows that with the exception of Chongqing (the largest prefectural city), all others have larger GDPs than predicted by scaling based on their *hukou* population.

This is unlikely to be true. We can imagine moving each point in the plot toward the right (thereby increasing its actual population) so the SAMI for each of these cities would be reduced or made to vanish. Mathematically, we can express this transformation as estimating a new ("true") population for a city, $\hat{N}_i$, by a multiplicative factor δ_i^{ξ}, $\hat{N}_i = N_i e^{\delta_i^{\xi}}$. Introducing this expression into the scaling relation (equation 3.1) and asking that this factor cancel out the residual, ξ_i, leads to the estimate, $\delta_i^{\xi} = \dfrac{\xi_i}{\beta}$. We can produce δ_i^{ξ} using the estimated exponent, β^F, or the theoretical prediction, β^T

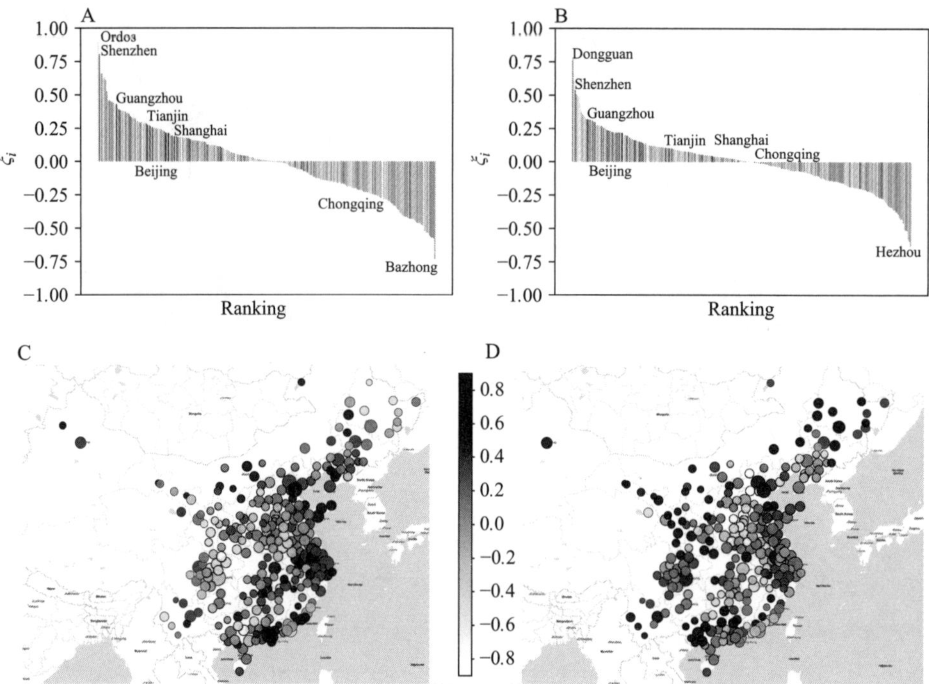

4.15 Rankings and spatial distribution of SAMIs for Chinese prefectural cities. (A) GDP. (B) Built area. (C) Spatial distribution of the scores from the scale-independent measure for GDP and built-up surface area. (D) Many coastal cities tend to outperform (darker gray) in terms of wealth and also are often more spatially compact.

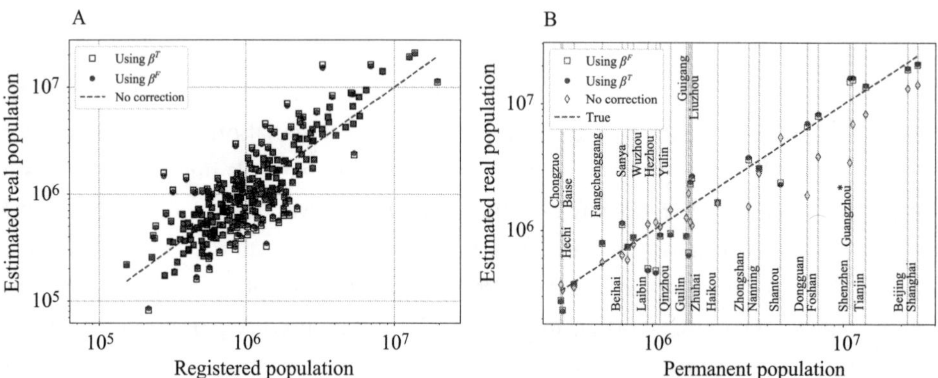

4.16 Using SAMI behavior to estimate working populations in Chinese cities. Correction of city population sizes relative to given registered population numbers using the prefecture-level GDP of each city as the estimator. β^F is the scaling exponent derived from fitting the data and β^T that from theory. (A) Comparison of the method with existing counts for prefecture-level cities. (B) Corrected city sizes for all prefecture-level cities.

(see figure 4.16). Estimated populations agree well with actual counts where they exist (from the decennial census or total local population counts performed in select cities) and can be extrapolated to places where they do not. This procedure illustrates another use of scaling expectations to produce generative models of city characteristics in the case of absent or biased data.

4.2 STOCHASTIC GROWTH: VOLATILITY CONTROL AND EMERGING UNIVERSAL STATISTICS OF CITIES

Every man bears the whole stamp of the human condition.
—Michel de Montaigne, *Essays*, Book 3

We now link the macroscopic empirical studies of urban statistics characterized in section 4.1 to a general microscopic model of an agent's behavior. To do this, we will be searching for a stochastic (noisy) model of urban growth that is as simple as possible while being consistent with urban scaling theory and generating observed aggregate statistics over time and populations, such as those observed in the previous section. We will see that all these objectives can be achieved starting from a very general model of multiplicative stochastic growth and studying how its dynamics aggregate from individuals to entire cities. This model is the common starting point of several complex systems adjacent to cities, including demography, financial mathematics, and population biology. What will be critical in our analysis is how this model behaves across scales, specifically how to relate agent-level behavior in the short term with population averages at the city level over longer times. A road map of this section is given in figure 4.17.

Let us start by introducing a variable, $r(t)$, which denotes the accumulation of the net quantity of $y(t)$ over time t. For example, if $y(t)$ stands for wages, then $r(t)$ becomes monetary wealth, but we should think of $r(t)$ more generally as *resources* that can be grown in time and used in turn ("reinvested") to generate more $y(t)$. We mean this in both a mundane sense (that everyone needs some resources to pay bills and expenses, which allow them to have an income) and as more formal investments, whether they are financial or toward an education. An important noneconomic example is when $r(t)$ is stored energy and $y(t)$ takes the role of an energy income per unit time, which is relevant across biology and must have been the principal logic of early human settlements (see chapter 7). We write the dynamics of $r(t)$, given $y(t)$, as

$$\frac{dr(t)}{dt} = y(t) - c(t) = \eta_r(t)r(t),\tag{4.7}$$

where $\eta_r(t)$ is the resources' stochastic growth rate. The first equality in equation (4.7) is basic accounting. It states that resources grow by the accumulation of the difference between income and costs, c (i.e., net income), over some time interval,

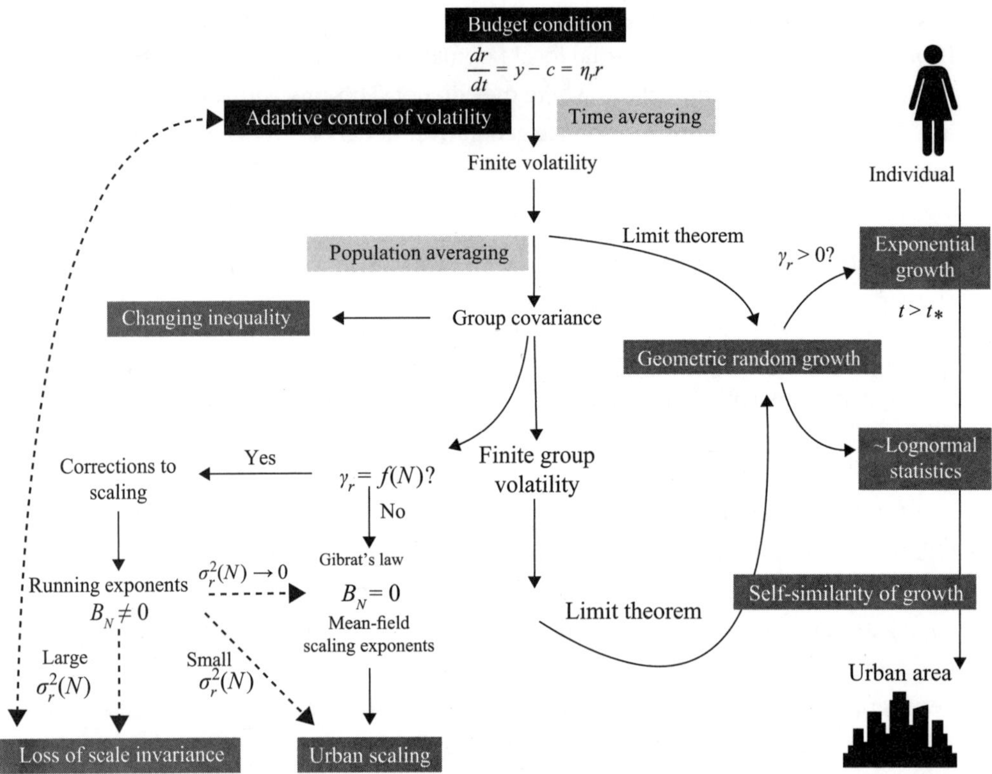

4.17 Statistical theory of growth and scaling in cities. Scheme of assumptions and derived consequences are shown as boxes, following the direction of the arrows. Dashed arrows indicate alternative scenarios. Dark boxes show basic assumptions, and light gray boxes show methods. Dark gray boxes show derived results.

dt. The centerpiece of this equation is the difference between income and costs, $y(t) - c(t)$, which must be balanced by all agents in their specific environments. Recall from chapter 3 that this quantity was *maximized* (via a choice of G) in order to reason about the relationship between the value of socioeconomic interactions and the costs of transportation and infrastructure.

As such, this relation is an old friend. For urban agents, this is the *budget condition* for the spatial equilibrium that defines a city according to the Alonso model of economic geography (chapter 2), urban economics models, and urban scaling theory[22] (chapter 3). In the original Alonso model of spatial equilibrium, this difference is typically set to zero, though the meaning of incomes and costs is rather generic and can include savings. In constructing urban scaling theory in chapter 3, we saw that this difference may be nonzero and obtained conditions on the balance between the productivity of socioeconomic interactions and the mobility and infrastructural costs that maximize its value. This implies that a positive difference between incomes and transportation costs is necessary for cities to exist (figure 4.1A, inset) and, as we show next, to generate exponential (resource) growth. It also implies that the scaling of resources, incomes, and costs has the same population size dependence, characterized by a single common exponent for all these quantities, $\beta > 1$.

The second equality in equation (4.7) is a *definition* of the growth rate $\eta_r(t)$, implying that

$$\eta_r(t) \equiv \frac{y(t)}{r(t)} - \frac{c(t)}{r(t)}. \tag{4.8}$$

We see that this becomes simple when the two ratios are independent of population size and are slow or constant quantities in time, possibly up to small fluctuations. Specifically, agents may naturally seek to obtain a maximum positive $\eta_r(t)$, not only on average but also in terms of its variability over time. We will show that this can be achieved via a process of feedback control (such as cash-flow management) necessary for the agent to remain alive and/or solvent, which requires that $\eta_r(t)$ be nonnegative on average over long times. Thus, we see how a generalized spatial equilibrium already contained in urban scaling theory, especially one generating a small but stable $\eta_r(t)$, is not only compatible with but is indeed the basis for an agent's survival and growth in the city.

Let us see how this works in practice. The stochastic equation (4.7) must be made sense of through temporal integration. Because the equation is nonlinear (the stochastic term is multiplicative), we have to be careful and use the rules of stochastic Itō calculus to obtain

$$\ln\frac{r(t)}{r(0)} = \left[\bar{\eta}_r - \frac{\sigma_r^2}{2}\right]t + \Theta(t), \tag{4.9}$$

where $\bar{\eta}_r$ and σ_r^2 are the mean and variance of the growth rate, respectively, in the usual sense of those obtained over the probability density of a stochastic variable. Now let us define the average *effective* growth rate, $\gamma_r = \bar{\eta}_r - \frac{\sigma_r^2}{2}$. This quantity is fundamental in geometric random growth models and will recur in our discussion. Keeping track of physical dimensions tells us that $\bar{\eta}_r$ and σ_r^2 are temporal rates and have dimensions of 1/time. Thus, the standard deviation, σ_r (known in finance as the *volatility*), has dimensions of $1/\sqrt{t}$.

The stochastic noise $\Theta(t)$ is the sum over the integration time, t, or, more explicitly,

$$\Theta(t) = \sum_{i=1}^{t} \epsilon_r(i), \tag{4.10}$$

with $\epsilon_r(i) = \eta_r(i) - \bar{\eta}_r$, which is a random variable with zero mean. Because it is the sum of stochastic variables, we expect that $\Theta(t)$ approaches a limiting case as a consequence of the *central limit theorem*. In the simplest case, where η_r is statistically independent across time with finite variance, we obtain that $\Theta \to \sigma_r \Theta_W(t)$ becomes a *Wiener process* (unitary random walk), which is a Gaussian random variable with zero mean and variance $\sigma_\Theta^2 = \sigma_r^2 t$. This will later define the key property of *ergodicity* for stochastic growth of populations.

A number of standard results follow from this simple model and its nonlinear integral. First, the central limit of Θ implies that $\ln\dfrac{r(t)}{r(0)}$ approaches, in the same limit of long times, a Gaussian variable, with t-dependent mean $\gamma_r t$ and variance $\sigma_r^2 t$. This implies that $r(t)$ is asymptotically distributed as a lognormal variable. In turn, the temporal mean,

$$\frac{1}{t}\ln\frac{r(t)}{r(0)} = \gamma_r + \frac{\Theta(t)}{t} \to \gamma_r, \tag{4.11}$$

is time independent for long times. Finally, the characteristic time

$$t_* = \frac{\sigma_r^2}{\left(\bar{\eta}_r - \dfrac{\sigma_r^2}{2}\right)^2} \tag{4.12}$$

marks the temporal interval necessary for net exponential growth to become apparent over the shorter-term effect of fluctuations.

These properties are illustrated in figures 4.18A–C, obtained using numerical simulations of equation (4.7), with η_r taken as Gaussian white noise. The asymptotic behavior of all quantities depends critically on whether the effective growth rate is positive, $\gamma_r > 0$, or equivalently $\bar{\eta}_r > \dfrac{\sigma_r^2}{2}$ (figures 4.18A and C). When this condition holds, there is net growth (figure 4.17A, regular and noisy growing trajectories). Growth of resources becomes apparent on a timescale larger than t_* (figure 4.18A), which becomes quite short when the volatility is small. In this regime, the distribution narrows on the scale of the mean as time horizons become longer, and predictable growth with vanishing variance becomes apparent. However, when $\bar{\eta}_r < \dfrac{\sigma_r^2}{2}$, the mean effective growth rate is *negative* and $r(t)$ decays toward zero while experiencing large fluctuations (figure 4.18A) (noisy, decaying trajectories). When $\bar{\eta}_r \approx \dfrac{\sigma_r^2}{2}$, there is very little growth or decay and the dynamics appears purely random (figure 4.18A, middle noisy trajectory). Then the resources display large (asymptotically lognormal; figure 4.18B inset) fluctuations, which appear increasingly wider for larger times (figure 4.18B). This is a dynamic regime transition between growth and collapse, made possible by reducing (or increasing) volatilities in the presence of a positive average growth rate. It is analogous to a phase transition in statistical physics (but technically it is a dynamic bifurcation), which can occur at different scales from individual lives to collectives, such as cities and urban systems.

Multiplicative growth processes thus have the curious property that because drift is asymmetric (we will encounter this again in chapter 8 for demography), it follows that a positive mean growth rate, $\bar{\eta}_r > 0$, is *not sufficient* to guarantee long-term

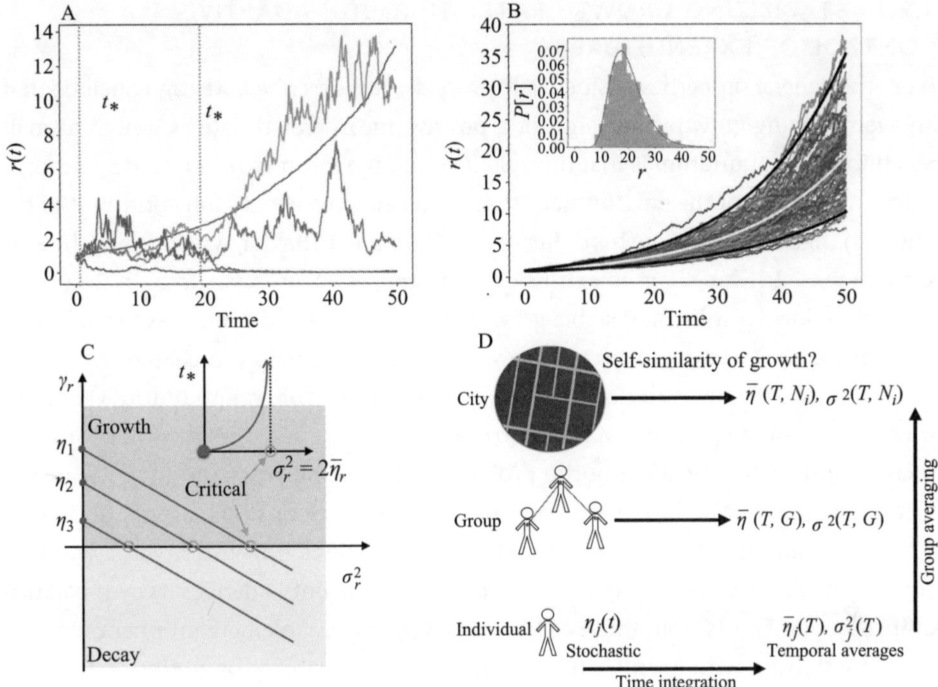

4.18 General properties of stochastic growth and their consequences for cities. (A) Growth trajectories for a process of geometric Brownian motion, equation (4.7). The regular trajectory shows typical growth with small fluctuations and positive effective growth rate, the upper jagged line shows a similar situation with larger fluctuations, and the next line up shows a trajectory with critical $\gamma_r \approx 0$. Other lines illustrate stochastic negative effective growth rate trajectories. The critical growth time, t_*, is shown for growing trajectories. (B) An ensemble of trajectories with stochastic growth rates similar to those of US MSAs, starting with the same initial conditions. The solid white line in the middle shows the temporal trajectory of the ensemble average, and the black lines show the 95% confidence interval. Note that both the mean and the standard deviation are time dependent. The inset shows the resource distribution at a later time, which becomes asymptotically lognormal (solid line). (C) The general properties of stochastic growth imply that a positive growth rate is necessary to overcome temporal decay caused by fluctuations. The critical point, $\bar{\eta}_r = \dfrac{\sigma_r^2}{2}$, is characterized by large fluctuations with a diverging t_*, so agents will not be able to tell whether they are experiencing growth and may be unable to exert effective control. (D) Under general conditions, multiplicative random growth can be self-similar across group sizes, providing a simple theory that applies at all scales, from individual agents to populations and cities. The key parameters of the theory characterizing the statistics of growth "run" across scales and are sensitive to population size, temporal averaging, and inequality.

growth. Instead, a finite threshold in growth rates, $\bar{\eta}_r > \dfrac{\sigma_r^2}{2}$, must be overcome. Approaching this threshold from a regime with net positive growth, an agent will experience wild fluctuations as t_* goes to infinity (figure 4.18C inset) and will struggle to tell whether growth persists and to estimate its timescale in order to plan. As a consequence, low volatility *and* positive average rates are necessary for sustained growth (figure 4.18C).

4.2.1 STABILIZING GROWTH RATES THROUGH ADAPTIVE CONTROL OF EXPENDITURES

From the general properties of stochastic processes just described, we can conclude that an agent seeking growth must aim for a positive mean growth rate as well as a small volatility. The conundrum is that the volatility and the mean growth rate are, to a large extent, properties of the environment that are outside the agent's full control. What is under the agent's control are his or her own actions and behavior, which, as we show in subsections 4.2.1, can adapt to extrinsic circumstances via processes local in time so as to produce low volatility and stable growth. The meaning and choices associated with maximizing the average growth rate, $\bar{\eta}_r$, will be treated separately in chapter 9.

Our objective now is to derive the statistics not only of compounding variables, such as $r(t)$, but also of *flow variables* $y(t)$ and $c(t)$, such as wages or other forms of income and costs. Considering the problem of balancing costs and incomes as the primary objective also brings us closer to the experience of single agents (individuals, households, firms, governments). In turn, we will see how the city as a whole—conceived as a social and economic network of these agents—derives its own balance of incomes and costs from those of its primary agents as an emergent phenomenon. Thus, by starting with agents' choices, we gain the possibility of getting to the root of the short-term equilibria that determine many of the properties of cities without having to start from a macroscopic average or make the unrealistic assumption of homogeneous representative agents.

Besides levels of population aggregation, there is also a hierarchy of timescales involved in the process of balancing costs and benefits and observing growth (see figure 4.17D). In the very short term, there will be many moments when the agent's resource flow is negative (when at home, not working, and spending money). However, judicious choices over time should result in more even, positive net flow over the longer term. This process of balancing costs and benefits over time (over the *life path*) creates strong correlations between y, c, and r and results in ratios that can become independent of the level of wealth.

To see this, consider the basic accounting equation (4.7) for a single agent. As we have seen, dividing by $r > 0$ gives us the definition of the growth rate, η_r. Defining the two resulting ratios as $b_c(t) \equiv \dfrac{y(t)}{r(t)}$, $a_c(t) \equiv \dfrac{c(t)}{r(t)}$ and averaging over time leads to

$$\frac{1}{t}\int_0^t dt'[b_c(t') - a_c(t')] = \bar{b}_c - \bar{a}_c + \frac{1}{t}\int_0^t dt'[\eta_r(t) - \bar{\eta}_r] \to \bar{\eta}_r. \tag{4.13}$$

This means that we can also define $\eta_r(t) = \bar{\eta}_r + \epsilon_r(t)$, where again $\epsilon_r(t)$ is the *error* (or "fluctuations") away from the growth rate's temporal mean, $\bar{\eta}_r$.

What kind of process sets the statistical properties of these fluctuations? What can we say about the statistics of $\epsilon_r(t)$ that renders the statistics of $\eta_r(t)$ sufficiently well behaved to enable net growth over the long term?

On a short-term basis, fluctuations will be large if a_c and b_c fluctuate strongly and independently of each other. Then, the amplitude of $\epsilon_r(t)$ may be large over some period of time and, if negative, may completely deplete stored resources ($r \to 0$) and lead to the demise of the agent by death or bankruptcy. It is in the vital interest of the agent to act to minimize, or at least control, fluctuations.

How is this achieved? The point is that $a_c(t)$ can be seen not simply as passive costs but rather as the source of strategic dynamic investments of resources under the agent's control (figure 4.19). Conversely, the returns on this investment, $b_c(t)$, are stochastic and will always fluctuate, because of environmental dynamics. Thus, $a_c(t)$ should be chosen to generate a target growth rate (chapter 9) and reduce fluctuations; in other words, to achieve stable and predictable growth.

To demonstrate how this can be achieved, let us write the returns as $b_c(t) = \bar{b}_c + v_c(t)$ and the investment as $a_c(t) = \bar{a}_c + u_c(t)$. Here, $v_c(t)$ are (stochastic) variations in returns, whereas $u_c(t)$ will play the role of a *control variable* adjusted by the agent over time in an adaptive way.

This leads to

$$\bar{b}_c - \bar{a}_C + v_c(t) - u_c(t) = \bar{\eta}_r + \epsilon_r(t) \to \epsilon_r(t) = v_c(t) - u_c(t). \tag{4.14}$$

We must now specify how managing expenditures adaptively (i.e., *feedback control* in the language of engineering, as in a thermostat) is implemented to tame the errors. To give an explicit example, most practical controllers are in the *proportional-integral-derivative* (PID) class,[23] which specifies $u_c(t)$ as a function of the dynamic error as

$$u_c(t) = u_c[\epsilon_r(t)] = k_P \epsilon_r(t) + k_I \int_0^t dt' \epsilon_r(t') + k_D \frac{d\epsilon_r(t)}{dt}, \tag{4.15}$$

where k_P, k_I, k_D are constants in time, to be chosen by the agent; they express the *quality of the controller*. The variations in expenditures, $u_c(t)$, written in this way, can be updated locally in time via the current observed error and its addition and subtraction from the integral and difference, which require remembering only two numbers across time. The stochastic dynamics of the errors is best captured via the derivative of equation (4.15),

$$\frac{du_c(t)}{dt} = k_P \frac{d\epsilon_r(t)}{dt} + k_I \epsilon_r(t) + k_D \frac{d^2\epsilon_r(t)}{dt^2}, \tag{4.16}$$

leading to a dynamic equation for the error,

$$k_D \frac{d^2\epsilon_r}{dt^2} = (k_P + 1)\frac{d\epsilon_r}{dt} + k_I \epsilon_r = \frac{dv_c}{dt} \tag{4.17}$$

This is a familiar equation for a *damped harmonic oscillator* driven by the force $F_S \equiv \frac{dv_c}{dt}$. By comparison, for the canonical equation for a harmonic oscillator with $\epsilon_r(t)$ taken as the displacement coordinate, we would find

$$\frac{d^2\epsilon_r}{dt^2} + 2\,\zeta_o\omega_o\,\frac{d\epsilon_r}{dt} + \omega_o^2 \epsilon_r = F_S/m_o, \tag{4.18}$$

where we made the correspondences $m_o = k_D$, $\omega_o^2 = k_I/k_D$, and $\zeta_o = \dfrac{k_P + 1}{2\sqrt{k_D k_I}}$, where m_o is the mass, ω_o is the oscillator's natural frequency, and ζ_o is the (dimensionless) damping ratio.

Because this is a linear differential equation, it can be integrated *exactly*. Therefore, we can obtain a general solution for $\epsilon_r(t)$, given the statistical dynamics of the external field, $v_c(t)$. In particular, we can make a general statement that if $v_c(t)$ and $\epsilon_r(t)$ are constants in time, then they must be zero. Note that this only follows when k_I is nonzero (i.e., when *integral control* is implemented). In particular, the derivative component of the PID controller is not essential. Setting it to zero ($k_D = 0$) makes the dynamics of the error simpler, corresponding to a well-known overdamped driven oscillator.

We are particularly interested in the situation where the force resulting from income fluctuations is stochastic and cannot be known in advance, only statistically. Other cases are straightforward and are treated at length in several excellent textbooks,[24] but they are less general and are left as an exercise to the reader. Suppose then that $\dfrac{dv_c(t)}{dt}$ is Gaussian white noise (no time correlations) with variance Ω_ϵ^2. Then equation (4.19) describes an overdamped driven oscillator (known as an *Ornstein-Uhlenbeck process*),[25] which is

$$d\epsilon_r = -\frac{M_o}{2}\epsilon_r\, dt + \Omega_\epsilon\, d\Theta_W(t), \tag{4.19}$$

with $M_o = \dfrac{\omega_o}{\zeta_o}$, and $d\Theta_W(t)$ is Gaussian white noise with unit variance. It is well known that the solution for the probability of $\epsilon_r(t)$ at time t, given $\epsilon_r(0)$ at $t=0$, is

$$P[\epsilon_r(t), t, \epsilon_r(0), 0] = \sqrt{\frac{M_o}{2\pi\Omega_\epsilon^2(1 - e^{-M_o t})}}\; e^{-\frac{M_o}{2\Omega_\epsilon^2}\left[\frac{\left(\epsilon_r(t) - \epsilon_r(0)e^{-\frac{M_o t}{2}}\right)^2}{1 - e^{-M_o t}}\right]} \tag{4.20}$$

$$\rightarrow \sqrt{\frac{M_o}{2\pi\Omega_\epsilon^2}}\; e^{-\frac{M_o}{2\Omega_\epsilon^2}\epsilon_r^2(t)},$$

where the arrow indicates the limiting behavior for times $t \gg \dfrac{1}{M_o} = \dfrac{\zeta_o}{\omega_o} = 2\dfrac{k_P + 1}{k_I}$. This emphasizes the essential role of integral control, set by k_I. In general, we want to make $k_I > 0$ and can let the other control parameters be small or zero.

The stochastic dynamics of the error generally leads to a Gaussian distribution for $\epsilon_r(t)$ with variance $\sigma_r^2 = \dfrac{\Omega_\epsilon^2}{M_o} = 2\,\Omega_\epsilon^2\dfrac{k_P + 1}{k_I}$. Thus, making k_I larger has the doubly happy effect of accelerating the temporal convergence to a time-independent distribution and narrowing the error variance; the *quality* of control improves. The effect of the *environmental variance* Ω_ϵ^2 is, as might have been expected, to increase the error variance proportionally. Thus, as we see in figure 4.19, the process of adaptive control effectively filters out environmental noise and makes its variance smaller as a function of parameters under the agent's control!

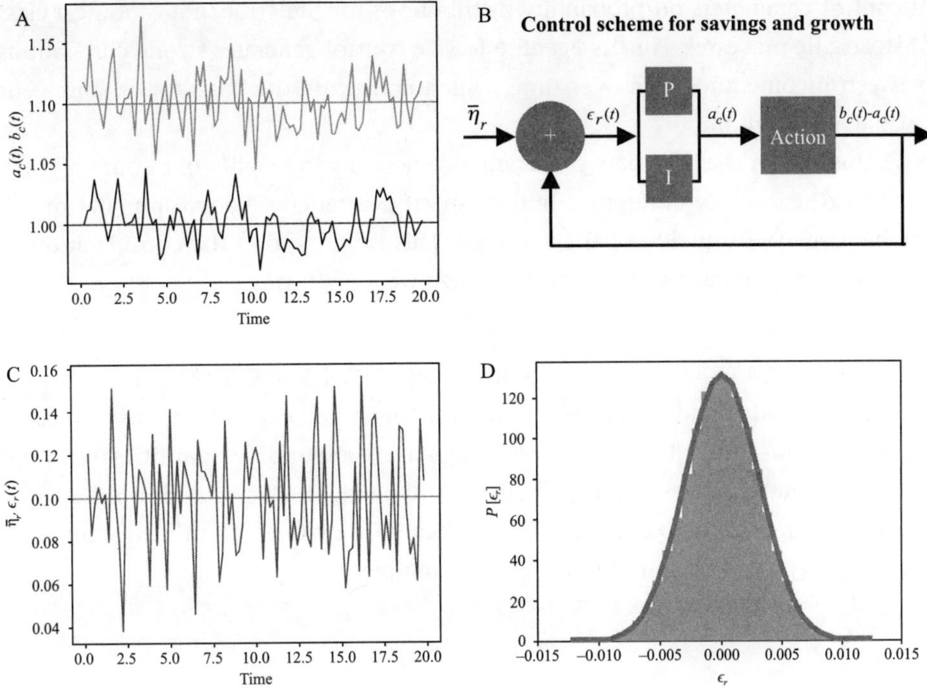

4.19 Dynamically balancing income and costs via feedback control leads to simple statistics for resource growth rates. (A) Example trajectories for the income-to-resources and costs-to-resources ratios, $b_c(t)$ and $a_c(t)$, respectively. Note that when income is larger than costs there can be growth, but fluctuations need to be controlled. (B) Control scheme to deliver average growth rate and tame fluctuations. By adjusting expenditures dynamically, costs $a_c(t)$ become in part a control variable that adapts to environmental fluctuations to generate errors with small, known variance. (C) The dynamics of the resulting error ϵ_r is now centered around zero. (D) A Gaussian distribution (solid line) with variance given by the ratio of the environmental variance in income and control parameters describes the errors very well. In this way, an adaptive agent's behavior can lead to predictable growth with a small and knowable volatility, starting from arbitrary stochastic environments.

This is a very simple but also very general mechanism that allows agents to cope with environmental uncertainty and generate growth. Much more sophisticated strategic behavior is possible that can maximize growth rates if more of the structure of returns, b_c, is known (chapter 9). Many more complicated control strategies can also be implemented, especially if the forces are time dependent in nonpurely random ways. All these possibilities open up many interesting problems for the application of control theory methods and investment strategies for problems of growth and statistics of human groups, and of cities in particular.

We have now deduced a simple but general mechanism whereby agents can make their average resource growth rate take on a target value up to stochastic fluctuations with variances given by the balance between the unpredictability of the environment and what we may call the "quality" of their control. While the implementation of control can take many other forms, we showed how the time averaging of fluctuations in returns and expenditures (integral control) is key and computed the effects of control parameters on probability distributions for the error in a canonical class of stochastic processes. For the agent, effective control generates strong correlations between income and costs over time, which constitute the basis for an emergent (spatial) equilibrium.

In this light, variations between agents—generating inequality of resources—may persist as the result of differences in their specific experienced environments and/or the heterogeneous quality of their control. This issue requires the consideration of averages over populations of agents, to which we now turn.

4.2.2 POPULATION DYNAMICS AND EMERGING INEQUALITY

We are now ready to address how balancing incomes and expenditures dynamically, at the individual agent level, leads to changes in corresponding quantities over populations, including cities. Computing growth dynamics for a population will give us the basis for returning to the statistics of urban indicators. To do this, we define the averages over a population of size N as, for example,

$$r_N = \frac{1}{N}\sum_{j=1}^{N} r_j, \tag{4.21}$$

where r_j is individual j's resources, and so on for growth rates, incomes, and costs. To derive the corresponding dynamics, we take these averages over equation (4.7), which results in

$$\frac{dr_N}{dt} = y_N - c_N = (\eta r)_N, \tag{4.22}$$

where for simplicity of notation we will drop the r subscripts so $\eta_r \rightarrow \eta$. The average of the product is the only nontrivial part. It can be written as

$$(\eta r)_N = \eta_N\, r_N + \mathrm{covar}_N(\eta, r) = \left[\eta_N + \mathrm{covar}_N\left(\eta, \frac{r}{r_N}\right)\right] r_N. \tag{4.23}$$

Thus, the quantity $\eta'_N = \eta_N + \mathrm{covar}_N\left(\eta, \frac{r}{r_N}\right)$ is the *effective* stochastic growth rate for the group average resources, r_N. This quantity equals the simple arithmetic group average plus a correction because growth rate variations may not be statistically independent from variations in levels of resources across individuals in the group. The covariance term is familiar from evolutionary theory and signals *selection* effects. For example, if richer individuals experience higher growth rates across the group, then the average growth rate will be higher, and vice versa. This flags the important issue that pursuing the *highest possible group-level growth* rates in a heterogeneous population will actually increase inequality, and conversely, pursuing growth where poorer individuals enjoy on average higher rates leads to a more equal outcome in distribution but subtracts from the average, η_N, because the covariance is negative! This conundrum is a mathematical identity built into the fabric of growth in populations.

It can only be resolved if there is an additional feedback mechanism such that the average growth rate, η_N, increases with decreasing inequality. This can happen, for example, if more people in a more equal population are in a position to develop their knowledge and/or entrepreneurship (chapter 9), but it should not be taken for granted as the result of reducing the inequality of growth rates.

To revisit the previous subsections in 4.2, we now need to characterize the mean versus the stochastic contributions to η'_N. To do this, we express the individual growth rate as in the previous section, as $\eta_j = \bar{\eta}_j + \epsilon_j$. Introducing it in the group averages results in

$$\eta_N = \frac{1}{N} \sum_{j=1}^{N} \eta_j = \frac{1}{N} \sum_{j=1}^{N} (\bar{\eta}_j + \epsilon_j) = \bar{\eta}_N + \epsilon_N, \tag{4.24}$$

where $\bar{\eta}_N$ is the group mean of individual temporal means and ϵ_N is a stochastic noise term resulting from the group average of the errors for each individual.

The properties of ϵ_N are inherited from those for each agent and their statistical correlations. The mean remains zero, while the variance in general is given by

$$\sigma_N^2 = \frac{1}{N} \sum_{j,k=1}^{N} \sigma_j \sigma_k \rho_{jk}^c, \tag{4.25}$$

where σ_j and σ_k are the volatilities for agents j and k, and ρ_{jk}^c is the correlation matrix between them. The correlation matrix is symmetric, with $-1 \le \rho_{jk}^c \le 1$ and with ones in the diagonal, corresponding to each agent's squared volatilities (variances of growth rates).

In the simplest case, when errors are statistically independent across agents, $\rho_{jk}^c = 0$ for $j \neq k$, and if all standard deviations are the same, we have $\sigma_N^2 = \frac{1}{N} \sigma_r^2$, and therefore the magnitude of fluctuations is reduced by group size and vanishes in the infinite N limit. Thus, if errors are independent across individuals in the group, both long times and large population pooling lead to a convergence to the behavior set by the simple temporal means. This, curiously, implies that because of smaller fluctuations the group average grows faster than the agent's temporal average in general and provides a strong quantitative argument for pooling resources together either via government action or risk-management instruments, such as insurance. In such cases, Peters and Adamou[26] emphasize that there is a business model for the insurance aggregator because the growth rate on their capital is generally larger (higher returns) than for individual agents.

The case of nonindependent variables is interesting because the treatment of the previous subsection suggests that it would follow either from experiencing correlated fluctuations to their income returns (e.g., from working in the same firm) and/or generating coordinated control responses (e.g., via city services and social assistance), which is plausible in many circumstances. In the extreme case when all variables are fully correlated, $\rho_{jk}^c = 1$ and $\sigma_N^2 = \sigma_r^2$ (assuming the same variance σ_r^2 across all agents), so the volatility associated with r_N becomes independent of group size. In more realistic cases in urban settings, we may expect some correlation between agents as they experience the common spatial and socioeconomic environment of the city. We will see that in US MSAs, σ_N^2 is approximately constant (see figures 4.10 and 4.14).

The covariance term between individual growth rates and resources adds additional corrections,

$$\text{covar}_N\left(\eta, \frac{r}{r_N}\right) = \left[\frac{1}{N}\sum_{j=1}^{N}\left(\frac{\bar{\eta}_j}{\bar{\eta}_N}-1\right)\left(\frac{r_j}{r_N}-1\right)\right]\bar{\eta}_N + \left[\frac{1}{N}\sum_{j=1}^{N}\left(\frac{\epsilon_j}{\epsilon_N}-1\right)\left(\frac{r_j}{r_N}-1\right)\right]\epsilon_N$$

$$= \text{covar}_N\left(\frac{\bar{\eta}}{\bar{\eta}_N},\frac{r}{r_N}\right)\bar{\eta}_N + \text{covar}_N\left(\frac{\epsilon}{\epsilon_N},\frac{r}{r_N}\right)\epsilon_N.$$

(4.26)

With these results, we can now write the time evolution of average resources in the group as

$$\frac{dr_N}{dt} = \eta'_N r_N, \text{ with } \eta'_N = \bar{\eta}'_N + \epsilon'_N,$$

with

$$\bar{\eta}'_N = \left[1+\text{covar}\left(\frac{\bar{\eta}}{\bar{\eta}_N},\frac{r}{r_N}\right)\right]\bar{\eta}_N, \epsilon'_N = \left[1+\text{covar}\left(\frac{\epsilon}{\epsilon_N},\frac{r}{r_N}\right)\right]\epsilon_N.$$

(4.27)

As long as these aggregate rates and errors are approximately constant in time, we may conclude that the population average resources, r_N, will generally follow a multiplicative random growth process, with well-defined mean and finite variance inherited from the microscopic behavior of agents in the population. Then, this process, like equation (4.12), integrates to give us the evolution of $\ln r_N(t)$,

$$\ln\frac{r_N(t)}{r_N(0)} = \left(\bar{\eta}'_N - \frac{\sigma'^2_N}{2}\right)t + \sigma'_N \, d\Theta_W(t),$$

(4.28)

showing that, as $d\Theta_W(t)$ converges to a Gaussian variable as a result of the central limit theorem, the statistics of r_N become lognormal.

It is important to stress that growth rates and volatilities generally *run* (i.e., change with scale), with group sizes, N, and time, t, depending on the correlations captured by the several covariance terms (see figure 4.17D). Some of these variations must be forbidden if scaling invariance is to be preserved by the system dynamics, an issue to which we now return.

4.2.3 CITIES AS POPULATION AVERAGES

Let us now bring the results of the previous subsections together to show how to predict the statistical properties of the ξ for resources and income. We return to the notation of subsection 4.2.1, with the index i denoting cities (not individual agents) and the values in brackets averaging over cities within an urban system such as the US, China, or Brazil. We can then take each city to be a group with $N = N_i$ in the sense of subsection 4.2.2, and write the simplified notation $\gamma_i = \gamma'_{N_i}$, $\sigma_i = \sigma'_{N_i}$, and so on. We will also write the averages of these quantities over the ensemble of cities as $\gamma = \gamma_i$, by dropping the indices.

Stochastic Dynamics of Scale-Invariant Urban Indicators   What are the dynamics of the fluctuations? Let us start by deriving the equation of motion for the fluctuations, ξ_i^r, for resources, r. We take total resources in the city, written as a scaling relation, $R_i(N_i, t) = R_0(t) N_i^\beta e^{\xi_i^r(t)}$. Combined with equations (4.2)–(4.4), this leads to

$$\frac{d\xi_i^r}{dt} = \frac{d \ln R_i}{dt} - \frac{d \ln R_0 N_i^\beta}{dt} = \frac{d \ln R_i}{dt} - \frac{d\langle \ln R \rangle}{dt} - \beta \frac{d \ln N_i}{dt} + \beta \frac{d\langle \ln N \rangle}{dt}. \tag{4.29}$$

The intensive resource growth rate (net of growth because of agglomeration effects) is

$$\frac{d \ln R_0}{dt} = \frac{d\langle \ln R \rangle}{dt} - \beta \frac{d\langle \ln N \rangle}{dt}, \tag{4.30}$$

which is a function only of the scaling center's dynamics. This quantity is the fundamental measure of endogenous change in an urban system; for example, in terms of intensive economic growth. Next, we introduce explicit growth dynamics,

$$\frac{d \ln R_i}{dt} = \gamma_i + \epsilon_i, \tag{4.31}$$

so

$$\frac{d\xi_i^r}{dt} = \gamma_i + \epsilon_i + \frac{d \ln R_0 N_i^\beta}{dt}. \tag{4.32}$$

Note that the presence of γ_i recognizes that we are dealing with stochastic calculus. This expression applies to a quantity such as resources, $R_i(t)$, but not for flows such as income or costs, to which we will return. Now take the average over cities to get $\gamma = \dfrac{d\langle \ln R \rangle}{dt} - \epsilon$. Bringing these expressions together leads to

$$\frac{d\xi_i^r}{dt} = (\gamma_i - \gamma) + (\epsilon_i - \epsilon) - \beta(\gamma_{N_i} - \gamma_N), \tag{4.33}$$

where $\gamma_{N_i} = \dfrac{d}{dt} \ln N_i$, $\gamma_N = \dfrac{d}{dt}\langle \ln N \rangle$. This is the main result of this subsection. First, check that the ensemble averages over both sides of this equation vanish. The most important part of the dynamics is that it is essentially Brownian motion, because of the ϵ terms, which set the variance. The two other terms enforce the convergence to the ensemble averages in terms of growth rates of resources and population; they would vanish if these average growth rates were the same across cities, as in a typical ensemble in statistical mechanics. However, for cities this is the most general result, as even average rates may vary across places.

Ergodicity and Scaling Invariance   Let us now see under which circumstances urban scaling is a conserved quantity of the stochastic dynamics of growth. We start with the integral trajectory for total resources, $R_i(t)$,

$$\ln\frac{R_i(t)}{R_i(0)} = \gamma_i t + \sigma_i d\Theta_W(t). \tag{4.34}$$

This equation is *ergodic* in the sense that long time averages coincide with ensemble averages,[27] because

$$\left(\frac{1}{t}\ln\frac{R_i(t)}{R_i(0)} - \gamma_i\right)^2 = \frac{\sigma_i^2 W^2(t)}{t^2} \to \frac{\sigma_i^2}{t} \to 0. \tag{4.35}$$

Note that this meaning of ergodicity—typical of population dynamics experiencing exponential growth[28]—is more general than the more familiar concept in statistical physics, which applies for systems in the absence of growth.[29]

Ergodicity is at the root of the invariance of scaling relations over time, and specifically associated necessary conditions. Consider the quantity

$$B_N(\ln N_i) = \frac{d\gamma_i}{d\ln N} \to \gamma_i = \gamma^{(0)} + \int B_N d\ln N_i \simeq \gamma^{(0)} + \bar{B}_N \ln N_i + \cdots, \tag{4.36}$$

where $\gamma^{(0)}$ is independent of time and scale, and we assume that B_N varies only slowly with $\ln N_i$, where $\bar{B}_N$ is a nonzero constant. The quantity B_N so defined is analogous to a beta function, expressing the running of a *coupling* with scale in statistical physics and field theory.[30] Using the last term and replacing it in the ergodic condition gives

$$R_i(t) \to R_i(0)e^{\gamma_i t} = R_0(0)N_i(0)^{\beta+\bar{B}_N t}\, e^{\gamma^{(0)}t}, \tag{4.37}$$

which shows that if $\bar{B}_i$ is nonzero, the scaling exponent $\beta = \beta + \bar{B}_N t$ becomes time dependent—and is *not* conserved by the dynamics of growth. In such cases, scaling relations will vary over time, becoming steeper (larger exponent) if $\bar{B}_N > 0$ or shallower if $\bar{B}_N < 0$. It is also possible, of course, that the integral (4.36) yields a more complicated function of $\ln N_i$ that not only makes the exponent time dependent but also changes the dependence on size to become different from power-law scaling.

The most interesting consequence of this result is that the term proportional to the volatility $\sim\dfrac{\sigma_i^2}{2}$ in the effective growth rate, γ_i, can be expected to be dependent on both time and population scales, while the mean $\bar{\eta}_i$ is typically independent of both scales. This means that in most circumstances $B_N(\ln N) = -\dfrac{1}{2}\dfrac{d\sigma_i^2}{d\ln N}$, which should be expected to be small because of the agent's control over fluctuations. To illustrate the consequences of this dependence, consider the specific example where

$$\sigma_i^2(N) = \frac{\sigma_r^2}{tN^\alpha} \to B_N = \alpha\sigma_i^2(N), \tag{4.38}$$

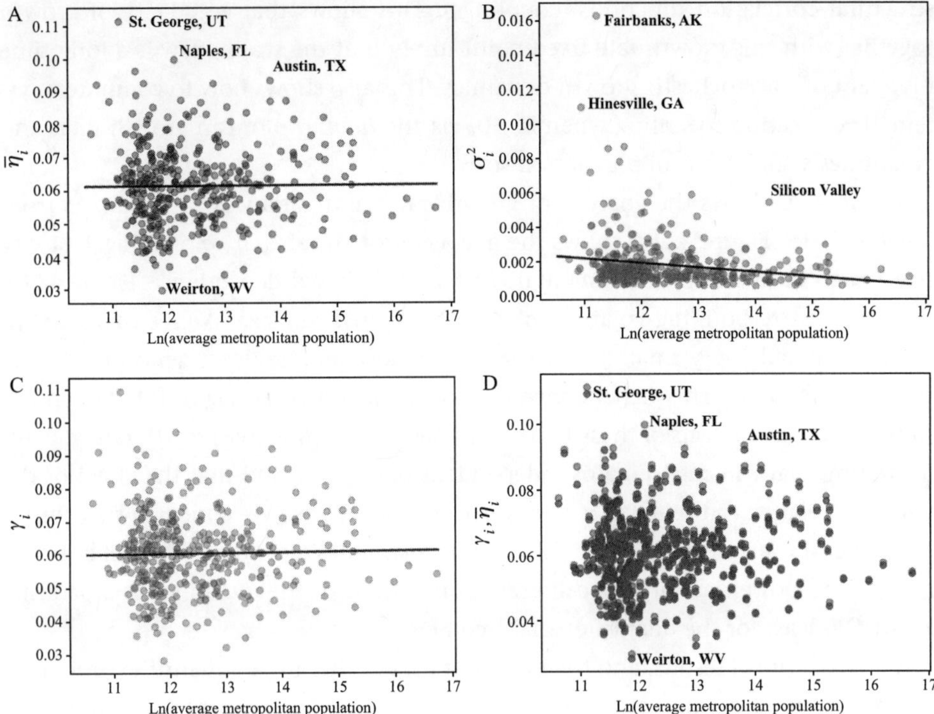

4.20 Measured growth parameters for US MSAs in the period 1969–2015. (A) The average growth rate $\bar{\eta}_i$ is statistically independent of city size (gradient=0.00008, 95% confidence interval (CI)=[−0.0011, 0.0013]; intercept=0.0606, 95% CI [0.0459, 0.0752]). (B) The growth rate squared volatilities σ_i^2 display a very small negative dependence on city size (gradient=−0.00026, 95% CI [−0.00040, −0.00013], intercept=0.00512, 95% CI=[0.00341, 0.00683]), primarily the result of a few high-volatility small cities. (C) The effective growth rate γ_i shows no significant dependence on population size (gradient=0.00021, 95% CI=[−0.00093, 0.00136], intercept=0.05799, 95% CI=[0.04365, 0.07233]). (D) The effective growth rate and mean growth rate for each city (lighter and darker dots, respectively). The contribution of the volatilities to the total effective growth rates is very small, as seen from this difference, with a few outstanding examples noted.

which in turn implies the exact result $\beta \to \beta - \dfrac{\sigma_r^2}{2\ln N N^\alpha}$. This shows in this example that β, while remaining time independent, is no longer a constant across population scales but increases with N. In this case, only at sufficiently large N and small σ_r^2 should we expect the value of the scaling exponent to coincide with that predicted by mean-field urban scaling theory (chapter 3). In particular, for smaller cities, β may become measurably smaller than for larger ones. Because the magnitude of variations away from scaling is dependent on the urban system and type of urban variable, this may help account for some reported variations of observed scaling exponents.[31]

These considerations allow us to conclude that true scaling invariance is predicated on $B_N = 0$, which is analogous to a renormalization group fixed point in statistical mechanics, except now applied to the population growth rate rather than to structural correlation functions (couplings). This shows that ergodicity of growth together with this growth rate fixed point imply that the scaling law is a long time invariant of the stochastic growth dynamics. This also shows how to compute a systematic correction to scaling when $B_N \neq 0$, via the *running* of mean growth rates and volatilities as functions of population size.

Figure 4.20 shows the analysis of growth rates and variances for US MSAs from 1969 to 2015. Figure 4.20A shows the average growth rates, $\bar{\eta}_i$, plotted against city size, which show some variation but no systematic city size dependence. Figure 4.20B shows the corresponding volatility σ_i^2 plotted against city size. We see that volatilities are generally very small and perhaps show a small size dependence, becoming smaller with $\ln N$. This dependence is very noisy, however. Figures 4.20C and D show the relative effects of these two parameters on the effective growth rate γ_i, demonstrating that this rate remains independent of city size and that the effect of the volatility relative to the mean is very small for most cities. We conclude that for US cities over the last nearly 50 years, effective growth rates are independent of city size, $B_N \simeq 0$, and power-law urban scaling is an invariant of the dynamics of stochastic growth, at least for the quantities analyzed here.

These empirical results, and their application to other urban quantities, underpin the generality of urban scaling as a statistical regularity preserved by multiplicative growth dynamics, even under extreme conditions where the system grows exponentially. To express this conservation at the level of the ξ_i, we now express the integral of their dynamics as

$$\xi_i^r(t) = [(\gamma_i - \gamma) - \beta(\gamma_{N_i} - \gamma_N)]t + (\sigma_i - \sigma)d\Theta_E(t), \tag{4.39}$$

which is Brownian motion with drift. Finally, the quantity

$$\Delta_i^r = \frac{1}{t}[\xi_i^r(t) - \xi_i^r(0)] - [(\gamma_i - \gamma) - \beta(\gamma_{N_i} - \gamma_N)] \tag{4.40}$$

is ergodic in the sense discussed earlier, since the stochastic expectation value of

$$(\Delta_i^r)^2 \to \frac{(\sigma_i - \sigma)^2}{t} \to 0, \tag{4.41}$$

for long times. Note, however, that the ensemble deviations ξ_i^r are not necessarily ergodic in the same strict sense of the ϵ_i and that the difference depends on the rates of resource and population growth conforming with their ensemble averages over a given time period (i.e., on the dynamics of inequality between cities).

It is interesting to recall that well-known models of urban population growth, built with the main objective of deriving Zipf's law for the rank-size relation for cities, *assume* that growth rates and volatilities are independent of city size, becoming parameters common to all cities in an urban system, a hypothesis known as Gibrat's law (chapter 8). In such cases, we see that the ensemble deviations ξ_i^r become ergodic. Figure 4.21 shows the growth rates of US metropolitan areas year by year as well as their averages over the urban system. Figure 4.21A shows the effective growth rates γ_i

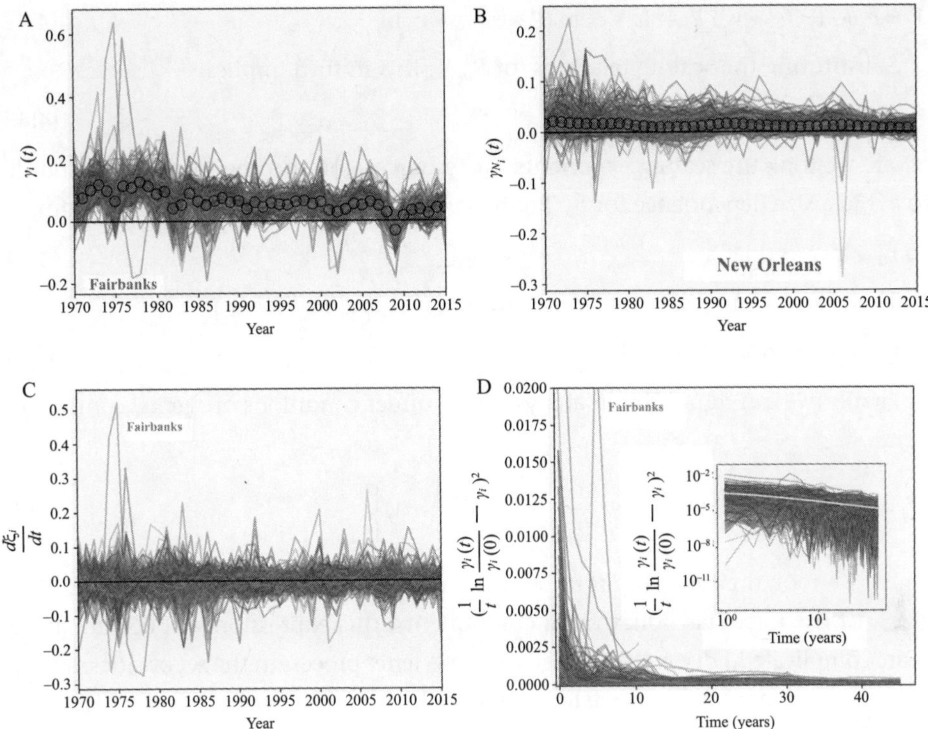

4.21 Measured growth rates for US MSAs and the dynamics of deviations. (A) Effective growth rate $\gamma_i(t)$ for wages measured each year, for every US MSA (different lines). Open circles show the averages over all cities, $\gamma(t)$. (B) Effective growth rate $\gamma_{N_i}(t)$ for population measured each year for every city (different lines). Open circles show the averages over all cities, $\gamma_N(t)$. The salient negative growth of New Orleans shows the temporary effects of Hurricane Katrina. (C) Dynamics of deviations ξ_i, according to equation (4.39). Observe how there is now no mean growth rate, so the dynamics become purely diffusive. (D) Measured ergodicity of wages' growth. At long times, the effect of fluctuations averages out and growth in $\gamma_i(t)$ is as expected from the pure effect of exponential growth under a constant, γ_i. The inset shows that the decay of the fluctuations is given on average by the pure Brownian diffusive expectation $\sim t^{-1}$, though in detail different cities show specific dynamics, often driven by nonrandom events.

for wages, and figure 4.21B the effective growth rates for population, γ_{N_i}. Figure 4.21C shows the derivative of the fluctuations $\dfrac{d\xi_i}{dt}$, demonstrating that, on average over cities and time, they are zero. Finally, figure 4.21D shows the ergodic property of wages, where fluctuations away from the mean trajectory of growth fall over time (roughly as $1/t$, inset) to become negligible. In this long-term regime, growth is clearly manifest and urban scaling emerges as a symmetry of the dynamics as long as $B_N = 0$.

4.2.4 THE STATISTICS OF INCOME AND COSTS

We have just characterized the statistics of the fluctuations for resources. Income and costs are often more accessible variables empirically. The statistics of these flow quantities follow from the analysis of subsections 4.2.2–4.2.3, where we wrote

$$Y_i = b_{c_i} R_i = (\bar{b}_{c_i} + v_{c_i}) R_i \rightarrow \ln Y_i = \ln R_i + \ln(\bar{b}_{c_i} + v_{c_i}). \tag{4.42}$$

Substituting the scaling relations for R_i, Y_i, this in turn implies

$$\xi_i(t) = \xi_i^r(t) + \ln R_0 - \ln Y_0 + \ln b_{c_i}, \tag{4.43}$$

where we took the scaling exponents for resources and income to coincide in order to avoid a size dependence for b_c. Taking averages over cities gives the constraint

$$\ln Y_0 - \ln R_0 = \langle \ln b_c \rangle. \tag{4.44}$$

This allows us to relate the SAMIs for incomes and resources as

$$\xi_i(t) = \xi_i^r(t) + \ln b_{c_i} - \langle \ln b_c \rangle. \tag{4.45}$$

Finally, we can return to our analysis of b_{ci} under conditions of agents' control and write

$$d\xi_i = d\xi_i^r + (\ln \bar{b}_{ci} - \langle \ln \bar{b}_c \rangle) dt + \left[\frac{\Omega_{\epsilon i}}{\bar{b}_{ci}} dW_i - \left\langle \frac{\Omega_\epsilon}{\bar{b}_c} \right\rangle dW \right], \tag{4.46}$$

where we took the force dv_{ci}/dt to be white noise with variance $\Omega_{\epsilon_i}^2$ as in subsection 4.2.3. (If the force has nonrandom components, this expression will be similar but more complicated.) dW is the average for the Wiener process in the set of cities, and we took fluctuations to be uncorrelated with population variations in Ω_ϵ and $\bar{b}_c$. This then implies that the quantity $\Delta_i^y = \Delta_i^r - (\ln \bar{b}_{c_i} - \langle \ln \bar{b}_c \rangle)$ inherits the property of ergodicity from Δ_i^r. Thus, we expect the quantity $t^2 \langle \Delta^y \rangle \sim \sigma^2 t$ to behave like a displacement of a one-dimensional random walk, as demonstrated in figure 4.22A. Note, however, that even though the general behavior is well described by a straight line in time with slope given by the variance, there are periods of acceleration or deceleration of the trend toward dispersion among cities, and that some light can be shed on the nature of these periods via the analyses of periods of economic recession (gray) or economic expansion in between. Figure 4.22B shows an analogous picture by more directly depicting each SAMI trajectory, having started all cities at $\xi_i = 0$ in 1969. This demonstrates the spread of the SAMIs over time according to what one would expect from a random walk (solid line, same as the straight line in figure 4.22A). Figure 4.22C shows the volatility and mean growth rates for all cities over the 47 years and the estimates for the former from measurements of dispersion over time (figures 4.22A and B) and over the ensemble of cities. The statistical agreement (within errors) of these two measurement strategies is another demonstration of the ergodicity of the SAMIs once drift has been removed.

We have now come full circle from the beginning of this chapter and are ready to discuss the statistics of ξ. We note from equations (4.39) and (4.45) that the dynamics of the SAMIs for wages is the same kind of stochastic process as for resources, with the addition of a drift component (when $\ln \bar{b}_{c_i} \neq \langle \ln \bar{b}_c \rangle$) and a (narrow) noise source resulting from the variations in the external force $\frac{1}{\bar{b}_{c_i}} \frac{dv_{c_i}}{dt}$. The first term simply says that a city with higher-income returns to their resources (perhaps like Silicon Valley

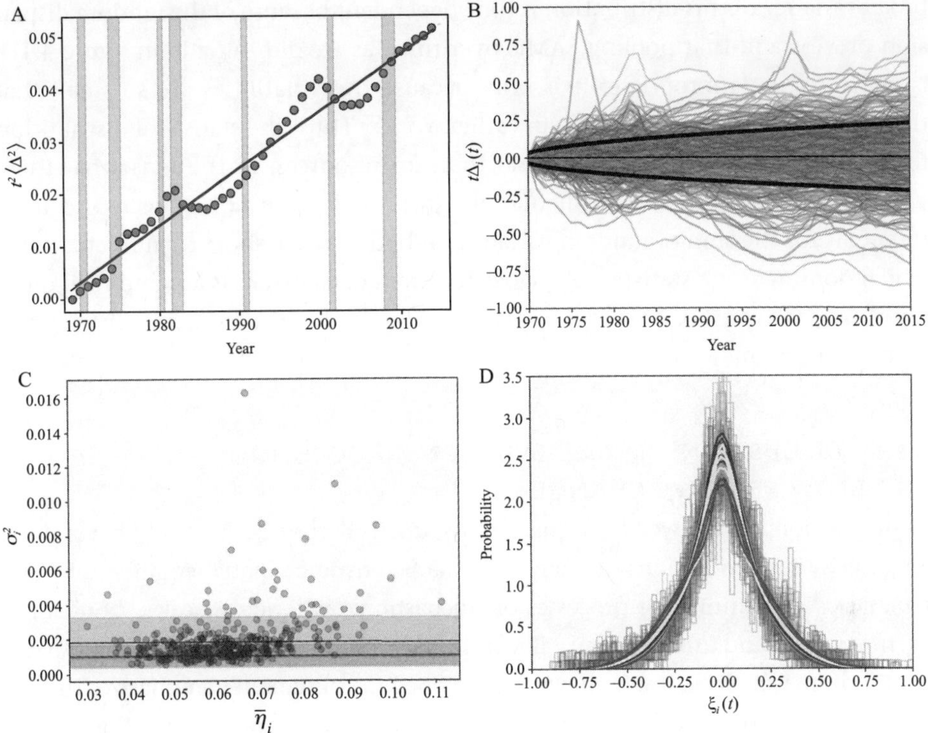

4.22 Effective diffusive growth of deviations and the emerging statistics of cities. (A) On average over cities, the displacement from their initial deviations in 1969 grows linearly (solid line, gradient=0.00108, 95% CI=[0.00102, 0.00115], intercept=−2.13279, 95% CI=[−2.25885, −2.00672], R^2=0.93), as expected from pure random diffusion of the growth rates. This is a mean temporal behavior, and there are periods when deviations grow faster (superdiffusively) and slower (subdiffusively). Periods of economic recession are shown as shaded vertical bands. (B) Trajectory of deviations for all cities (different lines, similar to figure 4.1D) but having set all deviations in 1969 to zero, so all trajectories depart from a common origin. The solid line indicates the diffusive behavior (panel A) showing that deviations tend to increase in magnitude over time. (C) Prediction of the wage growth volatility for US MSAs by three methods: the fit of A−B, and the averages over time and sets of cities, demonstrating the ergodic character of the dynamics. Shaded areas show the overlapping 95% confidence intervals in these estimates. (D) Distribution of deviations year by year using the same shades as in figures 4.1A and B. We see that, unlike our first approach in figure 4.1C, the width of the distributions is increasing slowly over time (wider distributions are most recent) and the data for wages (a flow) should be fit by a distribution that is well described as the sum of two Gaussians, a universal broad distribution resulting from long-term resource compounding and a contingent short-term narrow distribution, which depends on the most recent environmental shocks.

in the last few decades) will grow its SAMIs faster, and vice versa (perhaps like Las Vegas). The additional noise term arises from short-term income volatility, not smoothened in Y_i (a flow) by control. Because the sum of normal variables is also normal, we should expect ξ to approach a normal distribution in the same limiting sense as ξ'. However, the addition of the much narrower noise on a short time basis makes the statistics of ξ better described approximately by the sum of two Gaussians, one broad and one narrow, as in figures 4.1D and 4.22D. Note also that the broad variance of this distribution is time dependent because of the random dispersion process and that pooling SAMIs over time, as we did initially in figure 4.1D, is generally *not* appropriate. It is only because the volatilities are so small that this pooling appeared reasonable in earlier work.[32] Thus, the statistical distribution for income (or costs) is less universal than for resources, in the sense that these variables contain short-term fluctuations in growth rates not subjected to limit theorems for the sum of random variables. Whether these short-term fluctuations, which dominate the statistics of ξ close to zero, are Gaussian is an empirical question that deserves further study. In general, they could arise from any distribution with finite variance.

4.2.5 DISCUSSION: SMALL DEVIATIONS, ACCRETION, AND SLOW RELATIVE CHANGE

In this section, we showed how quantitative urban theory can be taken beyond the mean-field approximations of chapter 3, characteristic of spatial equilibria, by systematically accounting for processes of stochastic growth across scales, from single agents to cities and urban systems. Beyond preserving a generalized version of spatial equilibrium at its core, the framework developed in this chapter emphasizes the primacy of stochastic growth processes and an agent's strategic behavior as the basis for a dynamic statistical theory from which more particular results follow. This framework points to the critical role played by growth rate variations in a number of important urban phenomena.

Specifically, the properties of the growth rate volatility are implicated in the (lack of) preservation of urban scaling invariance and set the nature of growth, including the timescale for exponential growth to become manifest. We have also seen how variations in growth rates within a population are a basis for emerging inequality, especially if these variations are correlated with an agent's resources. Finally, we saw how regime changes in growth (versus collapse) and scaling are mediated by the behavior of these fluctuations.

The material in this chapter only starts to explore many possibilities for critical phenomena, scale (in)variance, selection, and a more quantitative statistical account of growth and development in cities.

Empirically, the US urban system, at least in terms of changes in total wages in its MSAs, turns out to be very well behaved. Its growth volatilities are almost always very small, fluctuations quickly converge to limiting statistics, and scaling relations are conserved over time. However, our theoretical results show that these properties pertain only to quantities and systems of cities with small growth rate volatilities independent of population size. In the US over the last nearly 50 years, despite a number of dramatic events, average squared volatilities associated with wages and population growth are about one order of magnitude smaller than average growth rates, making their effects almost negligible. It will be interesting in the future to investigate other urban systems and quantities characterized by greater volatility—such as crime or innovation[33]—for which the present framework makes a number of predictions.

The flip side of the observed constancy and stability of growth rates in American cities is that extant wage disparities between urban areas become extremely slow to reverse. The typical squared displacement in ξ_i over nearly five decades (figure 4.22A) is just 0.054. Assuming a similar rate of change in the past means that the observed variance in deviations from scaling at the beginning of our dataset (in 1969, about 0.043) would have been the product of the previous 40 years, taking us back to the time of the roaring 1920s and the subsequent Great Depression. Thus, the answer to the question at the beginning of this chapter about predicting the magnitude of deviations from scaling in any given year is now recast not so much in terms of parameters of stationary statistics. Rather, this variance is the result of accounting for the accumulation of much smaller accidents and variations that make up the stochastic history of cities, which compound short-term noisy growth under partial control of heterogeneous agents over entire urban areas and periods of many decades.[34] This is the precise quantitative sense in which history matters for cities, and their development is path dependent.[35]

EPILOGUE: PREDICTABILITY, IDENTITY, AND UNIVERSALITY OF URBAN INDICATORS

We have identified in this chapter the limits of predictability of urban scaling relations and the meaning and origins of associated deviations from scaling for each city. The most important feature of deviations is that they provide a quantification of the accumulating unique identity and history of each place, and by extension of the particular accidents and decisions made by their agents and organizations. Embracing this problem in terms of growth and statistics, away from simpler spatial equilibrium models, sent us down a path that requires us to unpack every urban quantity in terms of its growth rate statistics, from urban systems all the way down to individuals.

So far, we have learned that—depending on the quantity and urban system under consideration—what is general and what is unique certainly varies. Nevertheless, it is perhaps surprising how small the deviations from scaling can be, given all that is going on in cities. In such cases, we can model cities as slowly changing spatial equilibria in the sense of the structural theories of the previous chapters. This is the simplest sense of universality for the properties of cities.

As growth rates and associated fluctuations become larger, however, we find correspondingly more special behaviors and a stronger sense of uniqueness and specific identity. This tends to characterize different cities but is sometimes also characteristic of entire regions, as we have seen in China and India. This chapter has shown how a dynamic statistical theory can be developed to describe cities. It shows that we must pay close attention to how growth rates "run" with both population size and time. We have seen how such a theory can be developed, and indeed how it can predict statistical corrections to scaling and incorporate individual agents' dynamics of maximization of growth and control of volatilities, necessary for survival. There is then a second, weaker but more interesting, sense of universality: statistical predictions for urban indicators receive calculable corrections from fluctuations that may preserve scale invariance (power-law scaling) under specific conditions. These conditions identify necessary fixed points of scale transformations analogous to renormalization group ideas in other statistical theories.

Strongly stochastic regimes have hardly been explored at all in cities, so the reader is encouraged to attempt to break some of the models and situations described in this chapter and, especially, find situations where a statistical theory of cities is truly necessary and can be confronted with data. Steps in this direction can be taken by analyzing urban phenomena at smaller scales, such as in neighborhoods (chapter 6) and eventually pertaining to small organizations and individuals (chapter 9), where some of the loose ends of the present chapter will be tied. Before we do that, we need to better understand why cities promote and nurture so much variation and diversity, which is the subject of chapter 5.

5

DIVERSITY AND THE PRODUCTIVITY OF CITIES

The fundamental law of human beings is interdependence.
A person is a person through other persons.
—Desmond Tutu, "Who We Are: Human Uniqueness and the African Spirit of Ubuntu"

One of the most fascinating and important features of cities is their mesmerizing diversity. Diversity is a difficult issue in science. It is *not* a feature of simple systems, as in physics, where every elementary particle is exactly the same (all electrons are *identical*). As we ascend in scale through the sciences away from physics to chemistry, biology, ecology, and the social sciences, the subject of diversity acquires increasingly greater importance, culminating with all the distinct features that make each of us a unique and creative person. Diversity then is a feature of complex systems and complex systems *only*; it is arguably their telling and most beautiful property. In Darwin's words, "If everything were cast in the same mold, there would not be such thing as beauty."[1]

By Darwin's own measure, large cities create and nurture some of the most beautiful things on earth, in the sense that cities sustain a density of diversity that is unlike anything else in nature, including the richest biological ecosystems. Diversity always arises at the threshold between accident and function. This makes it especially difficult to measure and predict. It is this ability to occasionally amplify ceaseless "noise" into invention that makes evolutionary processes so vital and cities so important. There are many aspects of the diversity of cities that remain, to my knowledge, hard to foresee in any scientific terms. For example, in New York City, more than 800 languages are supposedly spoken, making it the most linguistically diverse place on earth. Many of these languages are extinct in their places of origin but can persist—for a while at least—in a great metropolis! How can that be? In turn, this points to the great variety of speakers of these languages, making large cities the crucible of all kinds of people: racially, ethnically, culturally, professionally, and in other ways. Presumably, if we could study the genetic diversity—human and nonhuman—of cities, as we are starting to do, I am sure that we would also find a greater and more peculiar density of biodiversity in larger cities.[2]

This chapter is dedicated to the analysis of some of the diversity patterns of cities, especially those that are *functional* and therefore become stable and observable. Such patterns are expressed not so much in terms of people's race, ethnicity, language, or place of birth but in what they *do* for a living. A fundamental process at work in all urban environments is a deep *division of labor and knowledge* among people and organizations. This goes hand in hand with the many network connections that put this specialized knowledge back together again, which at once explore the efficiencies of close colocation and the possibilities for new combinations as valuable novel inventions.

CHAPTER OUTLINE

This chapter is organized in three main sections. Section 5.1 provides a general context for the functional emergence of diversity in terms of ideas from classical sociology and economics on unconventionality and heterogeneity and the division of knowledge and labor in cities. This discussion motivates the connections between diversity and (economic) productivity and other processes of cultural and social matching in large, collocated human societies. Section 5.2 shows how to measure the diversity of occupations and business types using US metropolitan areas as an example. This exposes the contingencies of deriving general patterns of diversity from taxonomies. Section 5.3 makes sense of these patterns by linking the rise of connectivity in socioeconomic networks characteristic of cities (chapter 3) to specialization, information, and productivity. This will also allow us to consider the analogies and differences between cities and other forms of social networking mediated by technology—including those underpinned by the internet—and discuss when distinct networks may compete or cooperate.

5.1 MULTIDISCIPLINARY CONCEPTS FOR THE ORIGINS OF DIVERSITY

Because the idea of diversity is central to so many different complex systems, it has been studied separately by different traditional disciplines, from ecology, to sociology, to economics. Although not sufficient, each of these perspectives is useful in framing how we may approach and understand the diversity of cities. There are many approximate synonyms for *diversity* across these contexts, including *heterogeneity*, *unconventionality*, *variety*, and *specialization*, which we will use almost interchangeably in the next few subsections. The reader is warned that these terms are loaded with distinct meanings in specific contexts.

5.1.1 SUBCULTURE THEORY AND URBANISM AS A WAY OF LIFE

The broadest historical perspective on the diversity of cities comes from classical sociology. The heterogeneity of cities has been a feature of critical interest from the beginning of the discipline in Western Europe at the turn of the nineteenth century up to the twentieth century, which marked the continent's fastest period of urbanization and industrialization. The work of classical sociologists, such as Durkheim,[3] Simmel,[4] and others, was mostly concerned with the changes in social life that happen between rural settings and urban environments. To these sociologists such changes included the dissolution of traditional social structures, the deep division of labor in cities that makes urbanites at once more unique and more interdependent, and the accompanying changes in their "mental life" and behavior, including "deviance" and "unconventionality." These themes continued to be developed in the US, contemporaneously with its own fastest period of urbanization and industrialization, especially in the context of the Chicago School of Urban Sociology and its themes of human ecology, the psychological adaptations of urbanites, and the nature of social relations in the city, often from the perspective of segregation and race.[5]

Culminating in most of this classical work, as we saw in chapter 1, the heterogeneity of people in cities was one of the three pillars used by Louis Wirth,[6] working in Chicago, to define *urbanism*. You may get the two other pillars—population size and density—together occasionally in different organizations, such as an army, a refugee camp, or a festival, but to Wirth, *heterogeneity* of the population along many different dimensions was key to defining a city. He conceived heterogeneity mostly as a qualitative change in social relations, which in the city become less rigid and acquire a greater gradation of norms and behaviors than in more traditional settings, where they are bounded by historical social constructs such as caste or class.[7] This tends to make social interactions more fluid, "contradictory," and dynamic. It allows, and sometimes forces, individuals to acquire multiple identities across different spheres of life only tangentially connected to each other.[8] This segmentation and "depersonalization" of social relationships was often seen as a social *pathology* of cities relative to smaller agrarian societies.[9] This problem is often expressed in terms of psychological concepts, such as *anomie*[10]—the situation in which a society provides little moral or normative guidance to individuals—and *alienation*, which will recur later when we discuss the division of labor.

The primary question that will concern us here is the nature of the association between city size and the emergence of heterogeneity and diversity. While the correlation is clear to see, in what sense is the relationship causal? What socioeconomic mechanisms underlie the creation and maintenance of greater diversity of people and behavior in larger cities?

Given the theoretical context developed in the previous chapters, this question can be posed in a more specific form: how do socioeconomic networks that realize more connections as a function of city size relate to greater heterogeneity and diversity at the individual level? What we are looking for is a more specific link between the shifting social structure of cities as a function of their population size and the superlinear costs and benefits that allow larger cities to exist and thrive.

In this section, we will explore how, starting with Wirth's framework, diversity and heterogeneity may be the result of the dissolution ("breakdown") of social networks or instead the result of increased social opportunities and larger connectivity. A compelling answer is given in terms of the so-called *subcultural theory of urbanism*, proposed by Claude Fischer. Fischer posits that the concentration of people in cities is a causal driver of differentiation and the emergence of "unconventionality" (figure 5.1). Larger cities, according to his argument, create the necessary and sufficient conditions for a diversity of subcultures (group identities) to nucleate and coexist. A larger city population also contributes to strengthening these subcultures and to diffusion between them in terms of individual identities and affiliations. The causal diagram for how subcultural theory works is shown in figure 5.1, adapted from Fischer's original papers.[11]

In Fischer's original formulation, the theory is a bit complicated, structured in terms of ten propositions and four exogenous factors. Essentially, it describes a virtuous cycle (feedback loop) whereby a larger urban population ("urbanism") draws in, accommodates, and sustains more varieties of cultural forms. These varieties compete ("culture clash") for individual affiliations, sometimes acquiring "critical mass" (i.e., sufficient size) to persist and intensify in contact with each other. This dynamic process of many identities competing for individuals presents statistically as the frequent emergence of social novelty and "unconventionality" in larger cities. The presence of these various types ("varieties") also creates diffusion and accumulation between them, allowing channels for "conventional" individuals to become part of more unconventional groups.

The idea that more social interactions fail to produce a more mixed population and consequent dilution of differences but instead lead to the creation and maintenance of many different subcultures, each with potentially novel identities, is very interesting because it is a uniquely *ecological* concept. For example, in physical systems, if we increase the strength of interactions, we expect systems to "freeze," with each element becoming less free, making the system as a whole typically more homogeneous. But in rich ecosystems and among people in cities, it works the other way around: we often obtain greater social freedom (more choice) from being more (selectively and dynamically) connected! Fischer's ideas constitute an important contribution, in my view, toward countering the common misconception that larger cities are primarily places where human societies disintegrate and become depersonalized. Perhaps more importantly, it gives us a causal nexus between the expanding nature and structure of social networks at the individual level, with their consequences for how individuals change internally and how cities emerge as more creative and productive. Let us explore further how this may come about. The challenge ahead is how to turn these very general qualitative considerations into predictions about diversity in cities that can be tested against evidence.

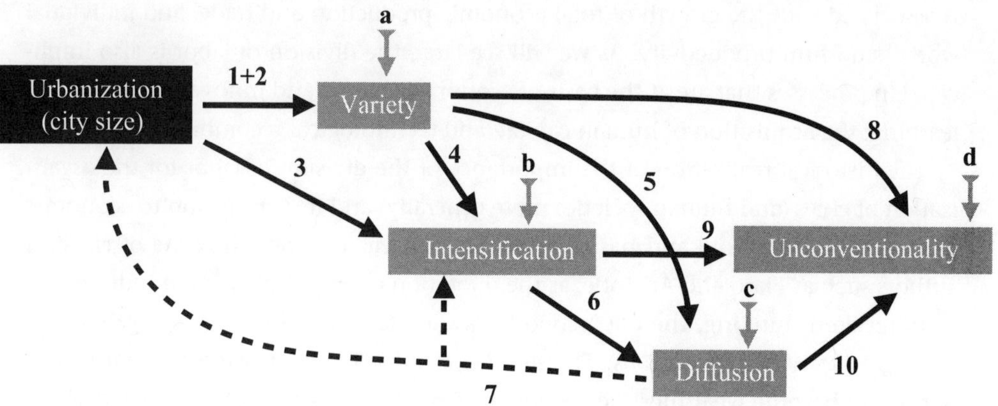

Processes

1. Structural differentiation
2. Size of migration catchment area
3. Critical mass
4. Culture clash
5. Variety of sources
6. Social strength of sources
7. Assimilation (conventional to unconventional)
8. Compositional effect
9. In-group socialization and influence
10. Unconventional to conventional diffusion

Exogenous influences

a. Economic structure of city; migration; degree of interaction (dynamic density)
b. Degree of distinctiveness; demographic structure; power and status of groups
c. Relative sizes, power, prestige of groups, degree of contact, utility of diffused item
d. Political structure; material resources for protection; climate of tolerance

5.1 Causal diagram describing Fischer's subcultural theory of urbanism. This theory explains the emergence of greater "unconventionality" in larger cities via a feedback loop of causality consisting of ten propositions and four exogenous factors. In a nutshell, larger cities can attract and accommodate a larger number of different cultures, placing them in competition in terms of their character and their recruitment of individuals. These two processes can lead to qualitative changes in these cultures themselves and to the more frequent emergence of rare types. As these changes occur, more variety is sustained, increasing the likelihood of the emergence of novelty. The subcultural theory of urbanism is an ecological ("evolutionary") theory that shows how a socially larger and more connected human society can also become more diverse in terms of group types. This is in opposition to earlier ecological theories that posited that diversity arises primarily from disconnection and social disintegration.

5.1.2 THE DIVISION OF KNOWLEDGE AND LABOR

Of necessity, he who pursues a very specialized task will do it best.
—Xenophon, *Cyropaedia*

One of the most important concepts across the social sciences is the phenomenon of the *division of labor*. The division of labor means that the production of a single good or service can be decomposed into a number of different individual tasks, which can be assigned to different agents (usually people, but also machines). Typically, the division of labor allows the *parallel production* of a final output. This process naturally leads to increased knowledge being dedicated to each component and to gains in productivity (in time and costs) on the whole. For these reasons, an increasing division of labor is associated with the growth of total economic production and trade, and individual worker and firm productivity. As we will see later, the division of labor is also implicated in processes that are at the basis of economic growth and innovation, including learning, the acquisition of human capital, and technological recombination.

The historical realization of the importance of the division of labor for the organization of cities (and human societies more generally) and its connection to economic productivity is very old and has certainly been discussed since the time of classical authors such as Plato and Aristotle, as the quotation opening this section indicates.

In modern thinking, the big "reboot" was due to Adam Smith, in his celebrated book *On the Wealth of Nations*. The *division of labor* is his answer for what causes nations to become wealthier. He spends the first three chapters of the book discussing the ways in which the division of labor is a feature of rich societies, how it is organized, and in estimating the spectacular economic productivity improvements it creates. Smith illustrated this point through the increases in productivity per capita of workers at a pin factory. Smith estimated that by specializing in different small tasks and coordinating their labor as a whole to produce the final product, each worker was able to produce about 480 pins a day, while a person working alone may produce just a few. Thus, we obtain an increase in average productivity of about 50!

Why then are we not "dividing" labor as much as possible? Smith notes, in what is sometimes called Smith's "theorem," that "the division of labor is limited by the extent of the market." What he meant by this statement was tied mostly to transportation costs and the fact that, for example, navigable waterways facilitate trade, and trade is predicated on complementarities of production and hence requires the division of labor. But the general implication for forms of social organization that lower transportation costs and that more generally extend the extent of the market, such as trust, institutions, financial instruments, or fair markets, is clear: Cities, of course, do all this and more.

Although the division of labor happens in many settings and at diverse scales, it was conceptualized in modern terms not so much at the scale of cities and nations but as a process managed by firms, especially in manufacturing. In this context, it has attracted persistent criticism, most famously by Karl Marx, as a dehumanizing process that is often predicated on rigid power structures that reduce human creative work to the repetitive routine of a machine. Marx argued that in such contexts the division of labor produces workers with less skill and less personal freedom, a condition he described as *alienation*, whereby labor becomes a mechanical device in the structure of production, detached from its own objectives and its economic gains.

This is certainly true to some extent. So, depending on the point of view one adopts, we may conclude that the division of labor—and situations of functional interdependence more generally—may be positive or negative for the various people involved. While it may often be one or the other extreme, the key for discussion here is to find a way of balancing costs and benefits from specialization and production. This tends to happen not so much in firms but across urban areas.

The Self-Organization of Diversity: Networks and Markets   From the perspective of the preceding discussion, it may not be clear what drives the division of labor and *who benefits* from its mode of production. The classical answer is that it is the firm as the unit of economic production, but this is manifestly incomplete, since the phenomenon is broader and applies to any collective-action problem. A critical issue also has to do with *who divides* labor and whether such an arrangement is fair and efficient.

The deepest early thinker about these issues, in my view, was Émile Durkheim. He saw the division of labor as a "universal law," applying not only to human industrialized societies but also to other human societies, as well as to biological organisms and ecosystems.[12] From this broader perspective, the division of labor calls for self-organizing and regulating mechanisms, such as evolutionary processes in biology and markets and social institutions in human societies. More generally, in human societies, Durkheim thought that the division of labor would arise from what he called "organic solidarity," which means ways in which reciprocity relations between specialized individuals would produce exchange and interdependence arrangements for mutual benefit.

Echoing these ideas, combined with those of Adam Smith and other classical economists, von Mises and especially Friedrich Hayek from the Austrian School of Economics proposed that economic markets would be the main means for the self-organization of production and consumption. Hayek, in particular, elucidated how economic prices should be interpreted as signals that allow economic agents to behave in self-interested ways in order to make the best possible decisions in terms of their consumption and production.[13] These ideas were pursued further and mathematized in the period after World War II to create what is known today as neoclassical economics. This perspective, at least in common policy, often overreaches in the sense that it proposes that economic markets free from social or environmental considerations[14] are efficient at solving most problems of human collective action, an issue we will revisit in chapter 9 in light of ideas connecting economic growth to information and selection.

The moral of the story of the *division of labor and knowledge* for the rest of this chapter is that it provides arguably the best illustration of a functional process whereby increased network interconnectivity between agents creates diversity in the form of occupational specialization and associated deeper knowledge, which in turn becomes self-sustaining in terms of the consequences of this network arrangement for novel and more valuable production. We have also seen that these processes can naturally be self-organized by political, social, and market dynamics, which may be more or less intentional or efficient. On the whole, however, we start to see clearly the mechanisms by which greater network connectivity (in cities) can produce simultaneously greater diversity and productivity in human societies.

Jane Jacobs, Diversity, and the Nature of Economies   Before we proceed to illustrate these ideas, we would be remiss not to check in with Jane Jacobs, who after her indictment of classical urban planning practices[15] spent a large part of her later career elucidating the nature of innovation and development in human societies and their links to economic growth.[16] Her inspirations were natural complex systems capable of evolution. Echoing Durkheim, she wrote, "I'm convinced that economic life is ruled by processes and principles we didn't invent and can't transcend, whether we like that or not, and that the more we learn of these processes and the better we respect them, the better our economies will get along."[17]

In this light, Jacobs saw cities and their socioeconomic networks through the lens of ecosystems, and she took economic growth and human development to be evolutionary processes. It would be wrong to take this perspective as being fundamentally different from the arguments in sociology about subcultures or the emphasis in classical economics on the division of labor and consequent specialization and interdependence. Jacobs recognizes economic and social diversity as both a cause and consequence of networks of exchange. Where she differs is in her emphasis that each of these insights is part of a larger common evolutionary framework, in which cities differ from ecosystems in details but share the same essential processes connecting diversity to prosperity.

More specifically, Jacobs sees the essence of *economic expansion* as a process of successive *differentiations* and *generalizations*, in which specific activities become successful in a human society and spread to become common, which she calls "generalities." These *generalities* then provide a new basis for new *differentiations* among a few people and places: these can then spread. This hierarchical cycling dynamics can give rise to an open-ended process of development, complexification, and economic expansion that is supported by an ever more intricate, complex network of codependencies and codevelopment relationships. The implication is that these processes and their telltale diverse networks arise *naturally* in cities, especially in larger ones.

For Jacobs, diversity is the basis of all processes of development and growth. Diversity in this context is a rather abstract and polyphonic quantity that speaks mostly to ideas and specifically to what different people know and do. This supports Hayek's insight[18] that information in human societies is *heterogeneous* and *local*, as well as his stance that central planners therefore cannot access all this information in order to make good decisions. Diversity then is functional and, much as in biological evolution, provides the seeds for new activities to grow via recombination, transfer, repurposing, and other processes, an idea that is common in studies of technological innovation.[19] As some of these activities succeed, they attract more energy and resources (the material base of the economy in terms of energy is primary to money in Jacobs's approach) and become more abundant in the sense that they expand production. The ubiquity of some products and activities, such as the cell phone, car, internet, calculus, or programming languages, becomes a set of generalities that in turn supports processes of new diversification, leading to the growth of complex ecologies; for example, of apps, services, or commerce.

Thus, for Jacobs, the absence of diversity in economic activity, such as in very specialized sector manufacturing cities such as Detroit in the 1950s (cars) or Manchester in the 1920s (textiles) and possibly Shenzhen today (electronics), is a sign of failure and impending doom. This comes about because she describes the processes of development as dynamic and open-ended, so a city that lacks diversity cannot sow the seeds of its own future. From this perspective, she sees the primary role of government as keeping the process of development open-ended by preventing violence, fraud, monopolies, and monocultures, and by stimulating—but not prescribing—various forms of knowledge and practice. For example, she laments the decline of manufacturing in US cities not so much as the loss of employment or production but more fundamentally as the loss of a rich ecosystem of tacit knowledge no longer available to generate future economic expansions.

Jacobs's arguments, though purely qualitative, provide several bridges between classical ideas in economics and sociology and present research on the nexus between cities, innovation, and economic growth. Her framework allows us to integrate fundamental ideas such as Smith's depiction of the division of labor, Marshall's observations of knowledge "spillovers," or Marx's concern for labor alienation into a multidisciplinary framework from which we can understand economies that are very different from those based on manufacturing.

Jacobs's critics find that her analogies between economic networks, cities, and ecosystems run too close to biology and that she falls short of emphasizing the important role of human agency, intentionality, or the social institutions that support innovation. We will return to some of these issues when we address economic growth in chapter 9.

5.1.3 MEASURING DIVERSITY

Taking a hint from Jacobs, Durkheim, and ideas of human ecology, let us now make a brief digression and discuss how diversity is most commonly *measured*. The experts at measuring diversity in populations are ecologists. The problem of accounting for and explaining biodiversity is the central question of theoretical biology, and methods have been worked out for several centuries now.

Needless to say, this connection is mostly metaphorical, but it suggests many useful methods for measuring diversity and forming expectations about how it may scale with the size of the ecosystem. Consider a specific ecosystem, such as a forest or a coral reef, defined as a spatial area that includes all its constituent biological organisms, organized in terms of distinct groupings such as taxa or species.

There are actually many measures of diversity in ecosystems, so we will limit ourselves to a few that are both more common and more related to socioeconomic phenomena discussed elsewhere in the book. The simplest measure is called the *species richness*. It is simply the count of the number of different species present in the ecosystem, D_S, as we already saw in equation 3.6. This has a simple expression for cities; for example, how many different types of businesses or occupations should there be in a city with a given population size? (We will find out in the next section.) Most other measures of diversity depend on the fraction of individuals in each type, which we call simply $P_i = \dfrac{N_i}{\sum_{i=1}^{D_s} N_i}$, where N_i is the number of individuals counted in species i.

One of the most common indices of diversity that uses the distribution of types is the Shannon entropy (see appendix C), which is written as

$$H = -\sum_{i=1}^{D_s} P_i \ln P_i. \tag{5.1}$$

The Shannon entropy is one of the most important quantities in statistical theories of physics and information.[20] It counts the number of yes/no questions (also known as *bits*) necessary to describe the distribution of types in the ecosystem. (You may know from the game of 20 questions that you can describe *anything*—guess what it is—in less than 20 bits!) In the special case where the species abundances are distributed as lognormal distributions (chapter 4), the Shannon entropy takes the value

$$H = \eta + \frac{1}{2} \ln 2\pi e_E \sigma^2, \tag{5.2}$$

where e_E is Euler's constant. This is insensitive to the richness, D_S, but depends on both parameters of the distribution: the log mean, η, and the log variance, σ^2.

For future reference, related to the Shannon entropy is the so-called *Theil index* of inequality, which is not about abundances of types per se but rather about inequality: how some additional characteristic, such as income, y_i, pertains to those types. It is written as

$$T_I = \sum_{i=1}^{D_s} \frac{y_i}{\langle y \rangle} \ln \frac{y_i}{\langle y \rangle}, \tag{5.3}$$

where $\langle y \rangle = \dfrac{1}{D_s} \sum_{i=1}^{D_s} y_i$ is the sample mean.

Another common measure used to characterize diversity starts out with a measure of concentration, written as

$$\lambda_{HH} = \sum_{i=1}^{D_s} P_i^2. \tag{5.4}$$

This quantity has been named many times by people in different disciplines. It is known as the *Simpson index* in ecology and is perhaps even better known as the *Herfindahl-Hirschman (HH) index* in economics and other social sciences. This index measures the probability that, taking two samples at random in a population, they correspond to the same type. It is easy to see that $1 \geq \lambda_{HH} \geq 1/D_S$. The first equality is obtained for the most *unequal* distribution, where $P_i = 1$ and $P_j = 0$ for all $j \neq i$, while the second is obtained for the most *equal* (uniform) distribution of types, $P_i = \dfrac{1}{D_s}$. In economics, λ_{HH} is a measure of *monopoly*. In that context, the proportion, P_i, is the market share of each firm. It is used as a heuristic to judge how competitive a market sector is, often by taking the 50 largest firms and computing λ_{HH}. Using percentages (out of 100) instead of fractions, we get that $\lambda_{HH} \leq 10,000$; a market with $\lambda_{HH} \geq 2,500$ is conventionally considered highly concentrated, "quasimonopolistic." Firm mergers that increase the index in such situations are typically scrutinized and could be blocked by government.

Because λ_{HH} measures concentration, we can get an index of *diversity* by inverting it, obtaining $^2D_s = \dfrac{1}{\lambda_{HH}}$, which is naturally known as the *inverse Simpson index*. The quantity ^2D_s is one of a family of diversity indices known as *Hill numbers*, ^iD_s,

$$^iD_s = \left[\sum_{j=1}^{D_s} P_j^i \right]^{\frac{1}{1-i}}. \tag{5.5}$$

We recognize an old friend: the Dixit-Stiglitz consumer preferences function in chapter 2 (equation 2.4). We can now better understand why Krugman described its maximization in terms of a "taste for diversity." We can also better appreciate where that quantity came from, as an *i*-family of weighted averages. When $i=0$, $^0D_s=D_s$; and when $i=1$, $^1D_s=e^H$ (with H the Shannon entropy! This may not be obvious, as it relies on the tricky properties of the limit as $i \to 1$ in equation 5.5), and, as we have just seen, $i=2$, $^2D_s = \dfrac{1}{\lambda_{HH}}$. In the limit of large i, only the largest fractions survive in the sum, and the index becomes approximately the largest P_j, the population share of the most abundant type. In this limit, the index ceases to discriminate types, whereas in the limit when i is small, many types contribute to the index and diversity is more important.

Limits to Diversity   There is a final consideration that we would like to carry along with us when considering the diversity of cities. It is called the *error catastrophe* in population genetics, and it is a relation written as

$$N_I \epsilon_I < I_T. \tag{5.6}$$

Usually, N_I is the number of information-encoding elements (the size of a memory), ϵ_I is the error per element, and I_T is a number, known as the *information threshold*. The idea is that one can only increase the number of informational elements in a population to the extent that the variations in these types have a lower error rate, or information loss, that in total stays below the threshold needed for the system to continue to function. This inequality therefore asks us to consider that the functioning of a system depends on most of its diverse elements performing their function reliably; diversity is good as long as it does not introduce too much disorder or undermine resilience.

This issue in biology is often described in terms of *Eigen's paradox*, which says that biological complexity, for example in terms of a larger genome (larger N_I), requires mechanisms to control errors or mutations (keeping ϵ_I small) but that these mechanisms require an increase in N_I, as they themselves must be encoded as information. The point is that increasing diversity is subject to benefits *and costs*. There may be a special boundary case where increases in N_I are compensated by decreases in ϵ_I precisely so that the product $N_I \epsilon_I$ stays constant or at least remains below a threshold necessary for the system as a whole to function.

How may these ideas translate to cities? To function and prosper, cities require the integration of an enormous number of diverse elements. These are expressed to a large extent as diverse identities, professions, and roles. In this sense, cities typically welcome difference because they can often integrate it to everyone's advantage, but if too many of these diverse elements (people, groups) become unreliable or cease to contribute to the whole, they will create systemic impacts, negatively affecting everyone else, which cannot be tolerated. To function, cities typically must develop mechanisms that discourage and control antisocial behavior and free riding, which include the development of law and justice systems as well as policing.[21] These institutions are costly and do not contribute directly to the creativity and diversity of cities. They often overreach, quashing diversity, but if they work well, they promote the kind of prosocial differences that do not harm cities and indeed help them to thrive.

We will also see that this criterion for the limits to diversity has an interesting translation in terms of the maximum amounts of specialization that we can achieve as we concentrate our own activities and externalize more and more functions to others. Thus, it is by incurring greater risks that we obtain new vital functions in cities.

5.2   THE DIVERSITY OF BUSINESSES AND OCCUPATIONS IN US CITIES

It is now time to see how these ideas work empirically in the context of actual cities.

5.2.1   BUSINESS DIVERSITY

As we have already seen, processes of specialization are often measured through the characteristics of firms, which are the basic units of economic production and entrepreneurship in modern human societies. While most firms are small, and many are simply self-employed individuals, the most famous are large and employ many thousands and sometimes even millions of individuals. In the context of cities, we also often think of specialization in terms of the prevalence of certain business types: think of Silicon Valley, Motown Detroit, coal in Newcastle, electronics in Shenzhen, Hollywood in Los Angeles, Bollywood in Mumbai, and many others. So, is that the way it works? Are most cities specialized in specific industries (recall Henderson's model in chapter 2)? What is the general pattern of economic diversity for businesses in cities?

This type of data is becoming increasingly available, both from official statistics and from new sources, such as technology companies scraping online information and creating their own directories. To illustrate how we can answer this question, we will use in most of this section a unique dataset in the US called the *National Establishment Time Series (NETS)*. This is a proprietary (but widely available) longitudinal database built by Walls & Associates to capture the economic dynamics of establishments in the US over space and time.[22] Establishments are workplaces, not companies, so, for example, if you consider a supermarket chain, we are counting each individual store, not the company as a whole.

At the time of the present study, NETS included records of nearly the entire set of establishments in US urban areas (over 32 million), each of which is classified according to the North American Industry Classification System (NAICS). This is a hierarchical taxonomy of business types. We will discuss this type of data organization later when dealing with professions, where it is a bit more intuitive. For the moment, you can consider a hierarchical scheme like that illustrated in figure 5.2, which has a resolution $r_s = 2, 3, 4, 5,$ or 6 "digits," where $r_s = 2$ indicates broad sectors and $r_s = 6$ indicates the finest extant classifications.

We can aggregate these data into the standard definition of functional cities, which here consists of 366 Metropolitan Statistical Areas (MSAs). To start, we can simply count total establishments, N_f, and see how this number depends on the

Sector 71 – Arts, Entertainment, and Recreation $\cdots\cdots\ r_S = 2$

711 Performing Arts, Spectator Sports, and Related Industries $\cdots\cdots\cdots\ r_S = 3$

7111 Performing Arts Companies $\cdots\cdots\cdots\cdots\cdots\cdots\cdots\cdots\cdots\cdots\ r_S = 4$

71111 Theater Companies and Dinner Theaters $\cdots\cdots\cdots\cdots\cdots\ r_S = 5$

711110 Theater Companies and Dinner Theaters $\cdots\cdots\cdots\cdots\ r_S = 6$

71112 Dance Companies

711120 Dance Companies

71113 Musical Groups and Artists

711130 Musical Groups and Artists

71119 Other Performing Arts Companies

711190 Other Performing Arts Companies

7112 Spectator Sports

71121 Spectator Sports

711211 Sports Teams and Clubs
711212 Racetracks
711219 Other Spectator Sports

5.2 Example of North American Industry Classification System (NAICS) for a subsection of sector 71, Arts, Entertainment, and Recreation (resolution $r_s = 2$). Note how sectors are successively subdivided, down to six-digit codes ($r_s = 6$), such as Racetracks, 711212, which corresponds to a successively higher resolution view of business activity.

population size of cities. We find linear scaling; that is, $N_f = N_0 N$, with the proportionality constant $N_0 = 1/21.6$ (see figure 5.3A for details). This means that on average there are about 22 people in the general population "served" per establishment in any US urban area, regardless of its size. Total employment (total number of jobs) also scales linearly with population (recall that it is a "basic individual need"; see chapter 3) and number of establishments, so $\frac{N_e}{N_f} = 11.9$, which is then the average size of each establishment (average number of people employed) in any city. This means that the population density of establishments and employment is on average a common property of all US urban areas regardless of size! This is a very simple property that speaks to the idea in chapter 3 that individual needs should scale linearly.

Next, let us look at business richness, $D_S(N)$, the total number of different types in a given city. Figure 5.3B shows that $D_S(N)$ increases logarithmically with population size but starts saturating for large cities and eventually levels off. To understand the implications of these results, we now use a trick that follows from observing that in any city with size N, its business richness is also the *rank*, of its rarest business, which naturally is the probability of a single establishment (since establishments are counted in units of one, two, etc.). This means that the relative frequency, $P(Rank)$, of $rank = D_S(N)$, the number of establishments of a type divided by the total, is $P(rank = D_S(N)) = \frac{1}{N}$, or equivalently $D_S(N) = P^{-1}\left(\frac{1}{N}\right)$. We can solve for P numerically and find the business type rank distribution. The resulting shape is shown in figure 5.4. The result is universal in the sense that it is the same for all cities in the US. It has a somewhat complicated shape, however, characterized approximately by

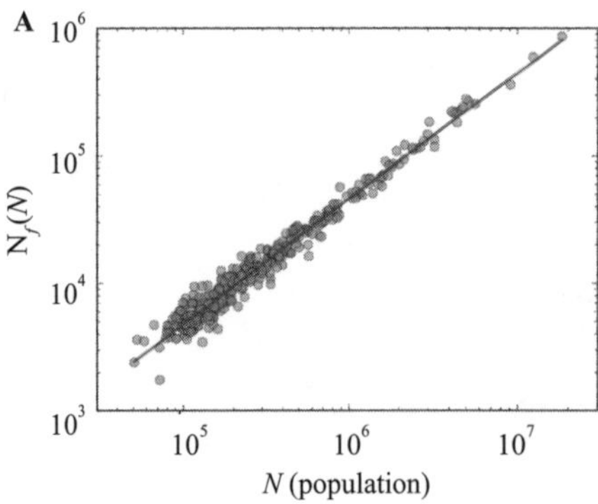

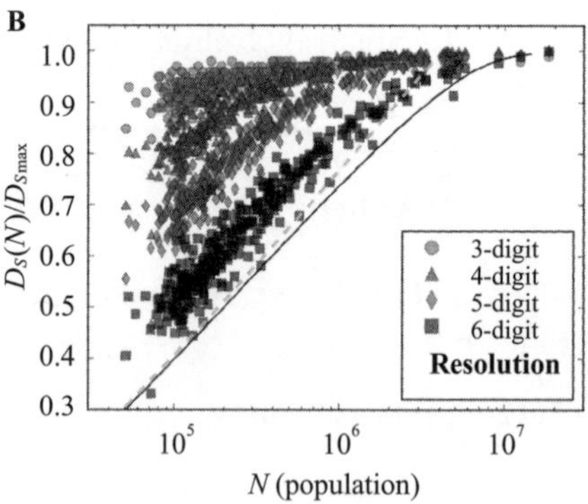

5.3 Total number of establishments and business richness. (A) The total number of firms N_f scales linearly with city size: $N_f \sim N^{\alpha_f}$, where $\alpha_f = 0.98 \pm 0.02$, with $R^2 = 0.97$. (B) Business richness (number of distinct business types in a city), $D_S(N)$, normalized by its maximum, D_{Smax}, at various classification resolutions, r_S, based on the NAICS scheme, from the lowest resolution (three-digit) to the highest (six-digit) (corresponding values of $D_{Smax} = 17{,}722$ and $1{,}160$). All values are scaled by the corresponding size of the classification scheme at that resolution, D_{Smax}, such that all values fall between 0 and 1. The black solid line and gray dashes are the predictions from equation (5.7) with and without ϕ_r, respectively.

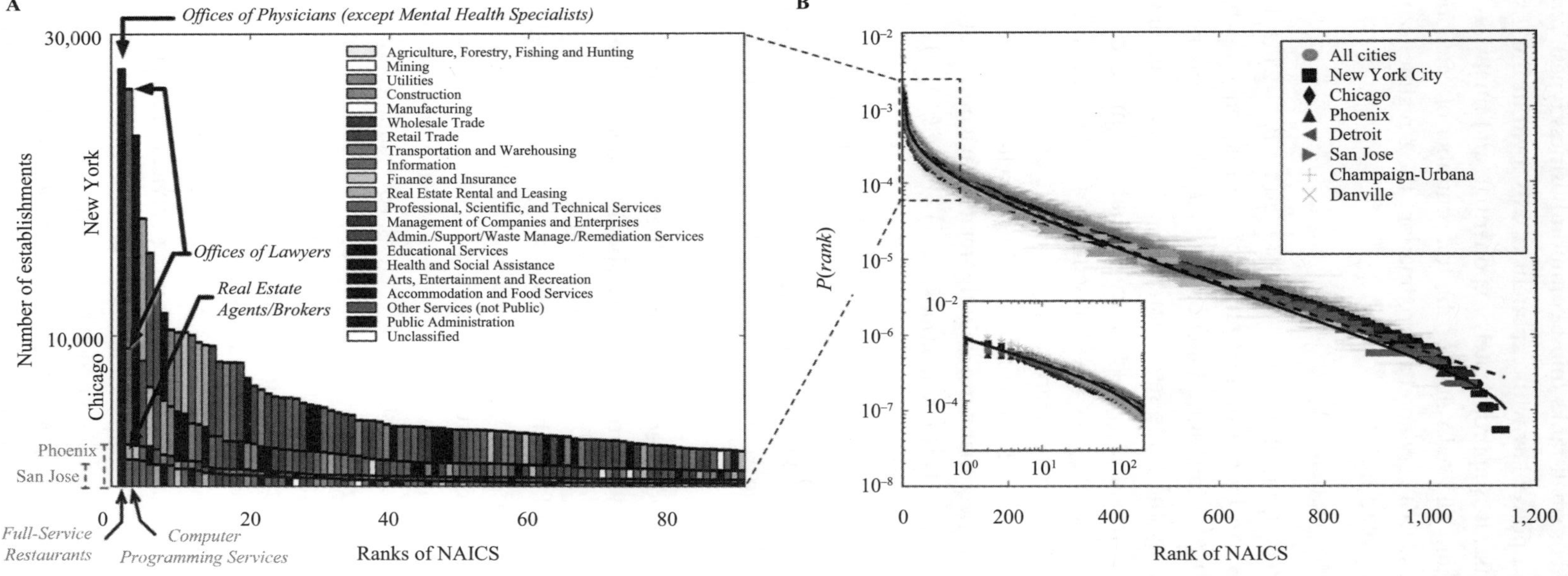

5.4 Rank abundance of establishment types. (A) Number of establishments at rank x, ranging from 1 to 90 in descending order of their frequencies (from common to rare) for New York City, Chicago, Phoenix, and San Jose. Establishment types are shaded by their classification at the two-digit level. (B) Universal rank-abundance shape of the establishment type obtained by dividing by the population size of the city in semilog for all ranges. All MSAs are denoted by gray circles. Seven selected cities are denoted by various shades and shapes: New York City, Chicago, Phoenix, Detroit, San Jose, Champaign-Urbana, and Danville, Virginia. The black dashed line and the black solid line are fits predicted from equation (5.7) with and without the saturation function φ_r, respectively. The inset shows the first 200 types on a log-log plot showing an approximate power-law behavior.

three distinct regimes. For small ranks (most common business types), $rank < rank_0$, it is well described by a power law with exponent α_r as shown in the inset of figure 5.4B; for larger ranks, it is approximately exponential; and finally, as the rank approaches the maximum allowed value for the total number of categories, D_{Smax}, $P(rank)$ drops off quickly. To a very good approximation, these regimes can be combined into a single analytic form:

$$P(rank) = P_0 \, rank^{-\alpha_r} \, e^{-rank/rank_0} \, \phi_r(rank, D_{S_{max}}). \tag{5.7}$$

Estimating parameters from data gives $\alpha_r \approx 0.49$ and $rank_0 \approx 211$. The overall factor, P_0, is determined by the normalization of the frequencies, which gives $P_0 \simeq P(rank = 1) = 0.0019$. The saturating function, $\phi_r\,(rank,\, D_{Smax})$, parameterizes the cutoff that is enforced by the finite resolution, $D_{S\,max}$. This function must satisfy three conditions: (1) $\phi_r(rank \ll D_{Smax}) \to 1$, since saturation only occurs close to maximum ranks; (2) $\phi_r(rank,\, D_{Smax} \to \infty) \to 1$, essentially for the same reasons; and (3) $\phi_r(rank \to D_{S_{max}},\, D_{S_{max}}) \to 0$, which enforces the cutoff and decay as the rank approaches its maximum value. These conditions do not determine the functional form per se, but we can expect that since only the relative magnitude of $rank/D_{Smax}$ matters when the $\phi_r\,(rank,\, D_{Smax})$ are equal $\phi_r(rank, D_{S_{max}}) = \phi_r(rank/D_{S_{max}})$.

A function that satisfies all these conditions is $\phi_r(rank, D_{S_{max}}) = e^{\,1 - \frac{1}{1 - rank/D_{S_{max}}}}$. For comparison, to illustrate the effect of this cutoff, see fits to the data both with and without ϕ_r in figures 5.3B and 5.4A. It also follows that the analytic solution for infinite resolution—a limit that we can now take on the taxonomy—reduces to

$$D_S(N) \to rank_0 \ln N. \tag{5.8}$$

This represents open-ended, ever-expanding business diversity, increasing with population size. It is not a very fast increase with N, but it is approximately commensurate with what one may see in ecosystems relative to area.

The universality of the rank distribution of business types has a number of important consequences that we can see in figures 5.3–5.6. Each city has a core of functions or services, which includes physicians, restaurants, lawyers, real estate agents, and other basic services. However, some business types become more abundant and others less, in relative terms, as we look at increasingly larger cities. For example, lawyers' offices scale superlinearly with city size (like social interactions, $k(N)$; is this a coincidence?). Primary activities, such as agriculture, fisheries, and mining, scale sublinearly, as might have been expected, but are often nevertheless present in large cities. In this sense, we do not see any citywide specialization of businesses in different cities. We see merely that in some urban areas some business types can have a relatively higher (and unusual) rank, such as Computer Programming Services in Silicon Valley, but this is embedded in a typical ("universal") urban ecology of types common to all cities (figure 5.4A). Figure 5.6 summarizes which types increase, stay approximately the same, or decrease in relative terms with city population size, computed in terms of their scaling exponent, analogously to lawyers' offices in figure 5.6A. We see that it is

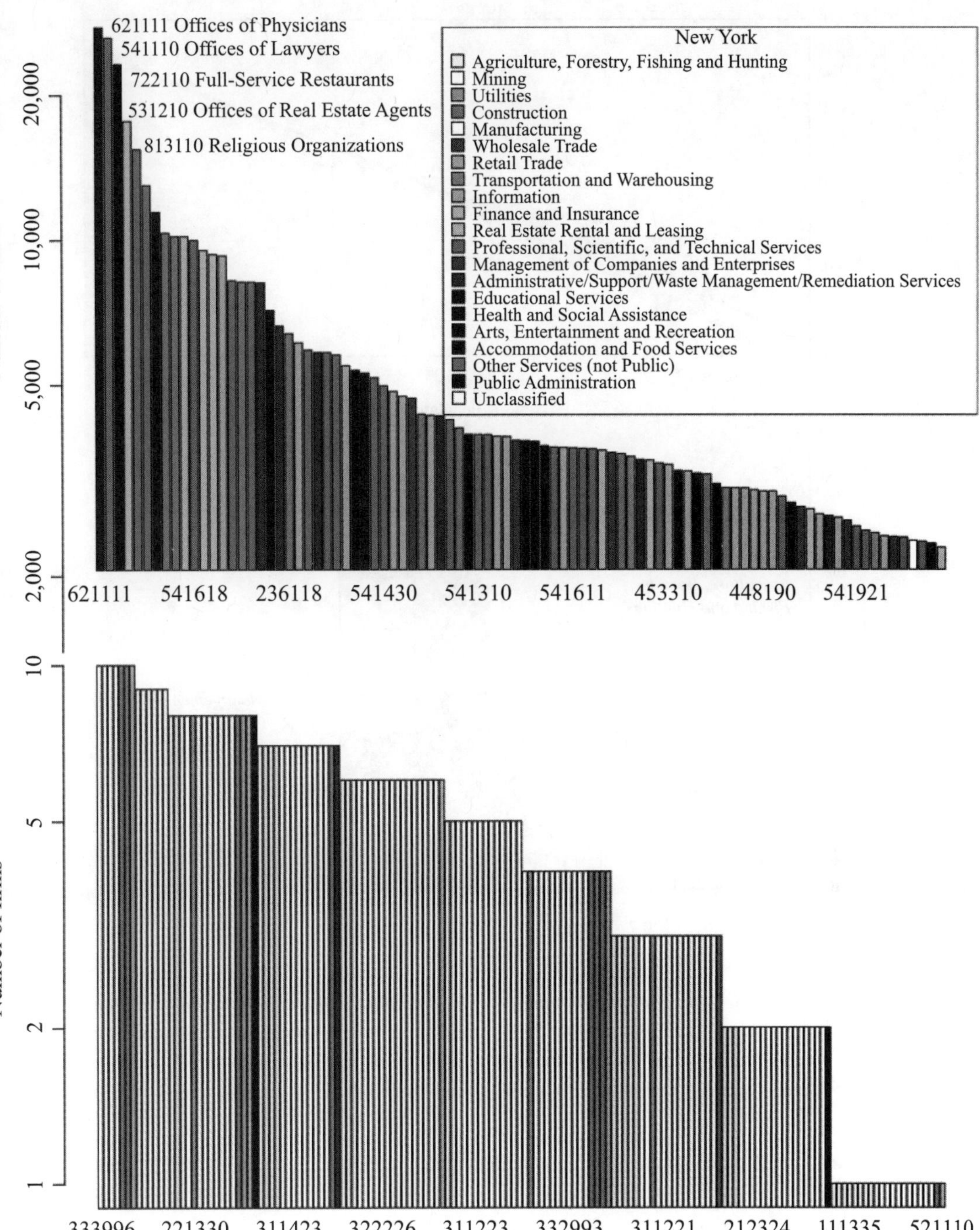

5.5 Rank size distribution of business types in New York City. Note the variety of sectors at low ranks (high abundance, upper panel) and the presence of most common services, including physicians, lawyers, restaurants, real estate agents, and religious institutions. These business types are a sort of start-up kit for all US cities. As cities grow, they add more business types but also reduce their relative abundance, such as primary sector activities (agriculture, fisheries, mining; lower panel). These changes structure the nature of the urban system and an urban hierarchy of functions across city size. Large cities tend to contain nearly all business types in a nation and consequently its full business diversity.

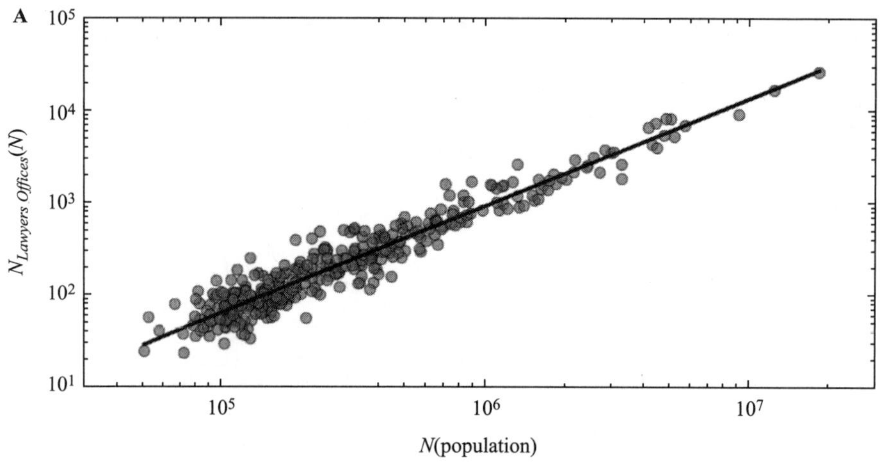

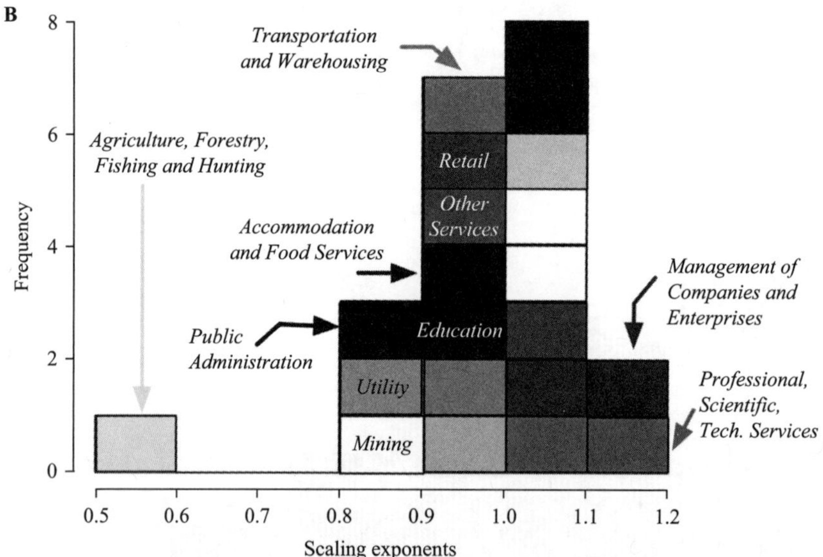

5.6 Multidimensional scaling of industry types. (A) The number of lawyers' offices scales superlinearly with population size $\sim N^{1.17 \pm 0.04}$, with $R^2 = 0.92$. (B) Histogram of scaling exponents for all establishment types at the two-digit level. While primary sectors gradually disappear in larger cities, managerial, professional, technical, and scientific firms increase in relative abundance.

managerial, professional, scientific, and technical services that gain most in relative prevalence with city size and are thus most concentrated in larger cities. Economists have characterized these patterns of relative abundance of business types in terms of other metrics, such as location coefficients, and have sometimes emphasized that export sectors of the economy may in specific cities be more specialized than average businesses, echoing Adam Smith's idea that a more extensive market servicing the urban system and international clients can indeed generate stronger specialization. All this can be true of course in specific situations, but the reality of the business ecology of cities tends to be more complex than when taken narrowly, yet simpler and more universal when we look at it on the whole. It will be interesting to continue this type of study as data continue to improve and become available in other nations.

5.2.2 PROFESSIONAL DIVERSITY AND LABOR PRODUCTIVITY

Now that we have characterized the business diversity of US urban areas, let us turn to job types and ask a similar set of questions. To start, let's ask how many different professions there are in a large city like New York.

In general, there is no objective answer to this question: It depends on how finely one differentiates similar functions. This introduces us to fundamental questions about the issue of building taxonomies that we must contend with in order to meaningfully discuss the diversity of cities.

Occupational Taxonomies Statistical agencies are great at organizing data, but sometimes they do it in peculiar ways. When we think of different jobs (occupations), there are two aspects to how we may organize different types. The first is to create an exhaustive account of all occupations. Figure 5.7 shows the most common professions in the US according to the *Standard Occupational Classification (SOC)* scheme, developed and updated regularly by the US Bureau of Labor Statistics.

The second aspect has to do with how to *organize* these types relative to each other. Clearly, a chef is closer to a waiter than to a farmer. This leads to the idea of categories of employment, which naturally can be described at different levels of coarseness or detail. For example, it may make sense to group all service professions together and all agricultural occupations separately. This leads to the concept

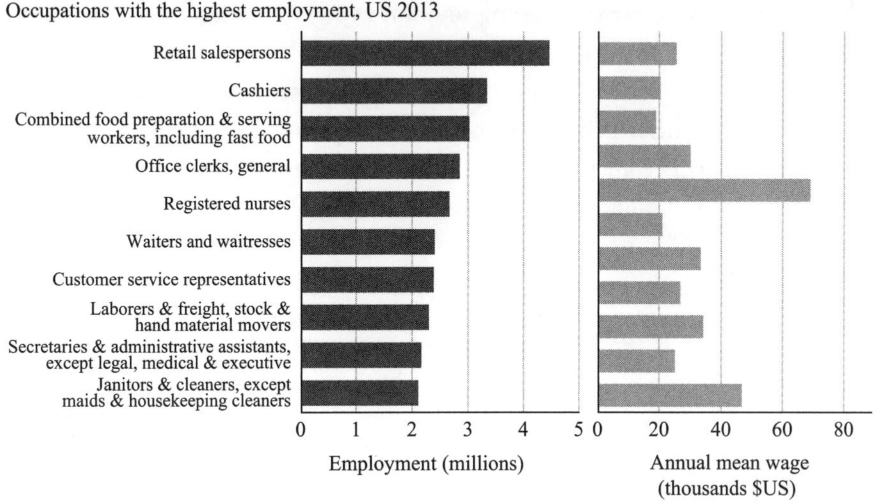

5.7 The most common occupations in the US and their annual wages according to the Standard Occupational Classification scheme.

of occupational hierarchies (table 5.1), which we have already encountered in the establishment classification scheme used in subsection 5.2.1.

Taxonomies are hierarchical classification schemes for types and can be represented as a tree (i.e., as a branching structure from a few branches to many leaves), successively splitting each type into finer varieties. Among other issues, there is a curious category in the SOC called "All Other," which includes occupations that did not fit anywhere in the earlier scheme. Table 5.2 shows some of these "new occupations" introduced in the 2018 classification scheme relative to the 2010 scheme.

Since we have been frequently mentioning ecology, it is interesting to invoke the parallel concept in biology and briefly explore its conceptual implications. There is only one figure in Darwin's famous work *On the Origin of Species*,[23] and it is the *tree of life* shown in figure 5.8.

In ecology, in light of evolutionary theory, the tree of life is more than a classification scheme: it is a *map of natural history*. This history is one of *lineages*, essentially of changing types, which beget their present differentiated form as leaves on the tree from their ancestors via descent, with modification subject to natural selection. This allows us a wonderful thought experiment: we can run history backward and converge on the root of the tree. This root is the common ancestor of all types, the original seed for all subsequent diversity. Thus, we can, in principle, understand present diversity, starting with a simpler and less diverse population together with dynamic processes of evolution, describing how various biological populations adapt to changing environments.

The processes by which diversity emerges in human societies are clearly different, but it will be interesting to run a similar thought experiment at the end of this section. We will try to imagine a sliding scale as follows: imagine a number of different essential jobs done by the same person, leading to a less expressed variety of occupations in a population. This would be a less specialized—jack-of-all-trades—situation and possibly an ancestor of a number of "future" specialized functions and jobs. Then imagine a situation where, because of changing environmental conditions, externalizing some of these jobs to others becomes possible as long as the same functions remain available in the network. We should now observe a diverse population in terms of professional

Table 5.1 Hierarchical classification of occupations according to the Standard Occupational Classification scheme developed by the US Bureau of Labor Statistics

Occupation	Resolution	Group type
29–0000 Healthcare Practitioners and Technical Occupations	$r_s = 3$	Major group
29–1000 Health Diagnosing or Treating Practitioners	$r_s = 4$	Minor group
29–1020 Dentists	$r_s = 5$	Broad occupation
29–1022 Oral and Maxillofacial Surgeons	$r_s = 6$	Detailed occupation

Table 5.2 New occupations introduced in the 2018 SOC scheme out of the "All Others" category in 2010

2018 SOC code	2018 SOC title
11–9072	Entertainment and Recreation Managers, Except Gambling
11–9179	Personal Service Managers, All Other
13–1082	Project Management Specialists
14–2051	Data Scientists
17–3028	Calibration Technologists and Technicians
19–4044	Hydrologic Technicians
25–3031	Substitute Teachers, Short-Term
25–3041	Tutors
27–2091	Disc Jockeys, Except Radio
27–4015	Lighting Technicians
29–1212	Cardiologists
29–1213	Dermatologists
29–1214	Emergency Medicine Physicians
29–1217	Neurologists
29–1222	Physicians, Pathologists
29–1224	Radiologists
29–1229	Physicians, All Other
29–1241	Ophthalmologists, Except Pediatric
29–1291	Acupuncturists
29–2036	Medical Dosimetrists
29–9021	Health Information Technologists and Medical Registrars
29–9093	Surgical Assistants
33–1091	First-Line Supervisors of Security Workers
33–9094	School Bus Monitors
39–4012	Crematory Operators

Note: Such updates show the emergence of more full-fledged occupations (such as data scientists!) out of more generic categories.

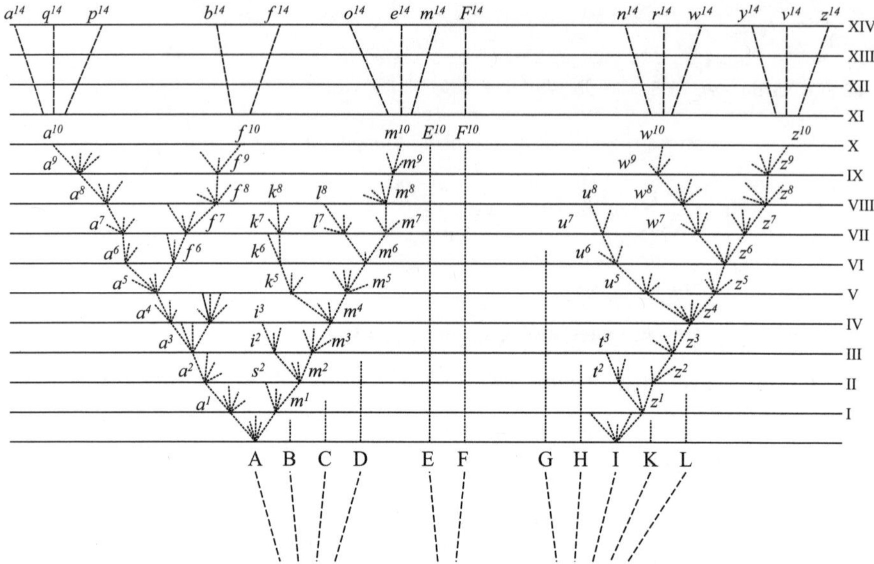

5.8 Tree of life in Darwin's *On the Origin of Species*. In ecology and evolution, trees of life have the implication that existing types (labeled by letters) are the result of changed ancestors, so lineages of change can be traced back in time (numbers) to their origins in terms of common ancestors, which were typically less specialized.

types. Can we associate this general transformation with what happens to the complex networks of cities? What advantages and costs does it bring for agents?

But before we can answer these questions, let us first learn how to deal with taxonomies in a more enlightened and quantitative way so we can extrapolate what may happen to diversity without being hampered by specific classification choices.

5.2.3 MEASURING DIVERSITY IN THE LIMIT OF TAXONOMIC INDEPENDENCE

We now return to the question of how many types of jobs exist in a given city. How do we proceed in practice? For example, we could count *chefs*. But if we start distinguishing by cuisine—French, Chinese, Thai, and so on—we end up with more professional types in the same city. Any professional occupation can typically be disaggregated or aggregated into finer or coarser types. However, under specific conditions, a limit of infinite resolution can be obtained. In such a limit, scheme-independent measures of diversity can emerge. Let us see how this works.

The Occupational Richness of Cities   First, let us see how the simplest measure of functional diversity in a city with population N, the count of the number of distinct professions (richness), $D_S(N)$, can be made independent of the classification scheme.[24]

Figure 5.9A shows $D_S(N)$ for US metropolitan areas as a function of their total employment, N_e. Because N_e is, on average, proportional to population, N, we use

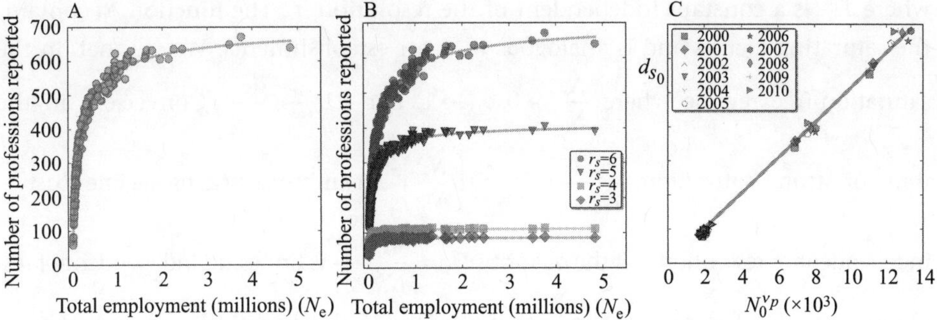

5.9 Scaling occupational richness of US Metropolitan Statistical Areas (MSAs) versus total employment. (A) The relationship between the number of professions, $D_s(N_e)$, in each city (dots) and city size, N_e, is well described by equation (5.9) with $d_{s_0} = 686$ and $v_p = 0.84$, $N_0 = 1.48 \times 10^5$ (solid line). (B) $D(N_e)$ at different levels of resolution of the occupational classification scheme, r_s, with $r_s = 6$ the finest and $r_s = 3$ the coarsest. (C) d_{s_0} is proportional to N_0 across levels of classification scheme resolution and time, suggesting that there is an r_s-independent limit to the form of the occupational diversity of cities and that D is open-ended. In this limit, $D_s(N_e) = D_{s_0} N_e^{v_p}$, and larger cities are always more diverse as a whole but more specialized per capita.

the two measures of scale interchangeably. We observe that $D_s(N_e)$ increases with N_e initially and then saturates for large cities. This behavior is well fit by

$$D_s(N_e) = d_{s_0} \frac{\left(\dfrac{N_e}{N_0}\right)^{v_p}}{1 + \left(\dfrac{N_e}{N_0}\right)^{v_p}}, \tag{5.9}$$

where d_{s_0}, N_0, and v_p are parameters independent of scale, N_e. For our data, this equation holds over time and for the various levels of hierarchical resolution, r_s, at which the data are given. However, the parameters in equation (5.9) are functions of r_s, which is the same as saying that they are functions of the taxonomy chosen. This includes the overall asymptotic value of the richness, $d_{s_0}(r_s)$, and the city size at which the saturation starts, $N_0(r_s)$. Importantly, for reasons we will see more clearly, the exponent v_p is empirically found to be independent of resolution.

The two other parameters change with scale in specific ways: d_{s_0} naturally increases with resolution as more professions become available, and N_0 also increases with r_s, leading to a saturation effect that starts to set in at increasingly larger populations. Do you see where this is going? We can ask what happens as we continue to increase resolution beyond what the data actually give us. The number of occupations would continue to grow with each refinement in resolution and, at some point, we may cease to have any saturation. Mathematically, this corresponds to writing the occupational richness as

$$D_s(N_e) = d_{s_0} \left(\frac{N_e}{N_0}\right)^{v_p} \phi_D\left(\frac{N_e}{N_0}\right) \to \begin{cases} D_{s_0} N_e^{v_p}, & N_e \ll N_0 \\ d_{s_0}(r_s), & N_e \gg N_0 \end{cases}, \tag{5.10}$$

where D_{s_0} is a constant independent of the resolution, r_s. The function ϕ_D contains the saturating factors and is analogous to ϕ_r for establishments. We see that, in the saturation-free regime where $\frac{N_e}{N_0} \to 0, \phi_D \to 1$, and $D_{s_0} \to \frac{d_{s_0}}{N_0^{v_p}}$. Conversely, in the limit of strong saturation, $\frac{N_e}{N_0} \to \infty, \phi_D \to \left(\frac{N_e}{N_0}\right)^{v_p}$. A universal scaling regime exists—independent of resolution!—if the quantity $D_{s_0} = \frac{d_{s_0}(r_s)}{N_0^{v_p}(r_s)}$ is finite and independent of resolution as $r_s \to \infty$. Figure 5.9C shows that this is indeed the case. We conclude that, as far as data allow us to tell, there is an infinite resolution limit at which we can calculate the occupational diversity (richness) of cities as a simple scale-invariant power-law function: $D_S(N) = D_{s_0} N^{v_p}$. Measuring the exponent yields $v_p \simeq 0.84 \simeq v = 1 - \delta$, which is therefore compatible with the scaling exponents computed in chapter 3.

A Universal Distribution of Occupations in Cities? As we have already seen for business types, the scaling pattern of unsaturated diversity actually contains in itself information on the full distribution of professions. To see this, consider the abundance of a type i, $f(i|N)$, in a city with population N. Let the types in $f(i|N)$ be ordered from most common to least common, expressing their abundance *rank*, as we did for business types. Then, the rarest type should have only one person, so we can write $f(D_s|N) = \frac{1}{N}$. Inverting this relationship and generalizing to all ranks i gives

$$f(i|N) = \frac{1}{N_0}\left(\frac{d_{s_0} - i}{i}\right)^{\frac{1}{v}} \to \left(\frac{D_{s_0}}{i}\right)^{\frac{1}{v}}. \tag{5.11}$$

Here the arrow corresponds to the high-resolution limit, which is independent of r_s. We can then write the probability of each profession in a city of size N as

$$P(i|N) = \frac{f(i|N)}{\sum_{i=1}^{D_s} f(i|N)} = \frac{1 - v}{v} \frac{i^{-\frac{1}{v}}}{1 - D_S(N)^{-\frac{1-v}{v}}}. \tag{5.12}$$

As for establishments but with a simpler form, what is most interesting is that this says that the distribution of occupations for different cities is *universal*. When adjusted for scale, N, the frequency curves for every city collapse onto a single line (see figure 5.10)!

This universality shows that there is an expected *nested sequence* of occupations predicted by city size, as expected by the hierarchy principle of central places (chapter 8) and its extensions in regional economics.[25] This sequence of professions arising with growing city size is also analogous to the hierarchy of products versus level of economic development observed at the national level[26] and shows how large cities play a fundamental role in embodying the economic diversity of entire nations.

What may be most surprising about this concept is that many functions that we associated with larger cities, from more specialized restaurants, to advanced medical services, to art and fashion, are therefore in a sense already *latent* in smaller places

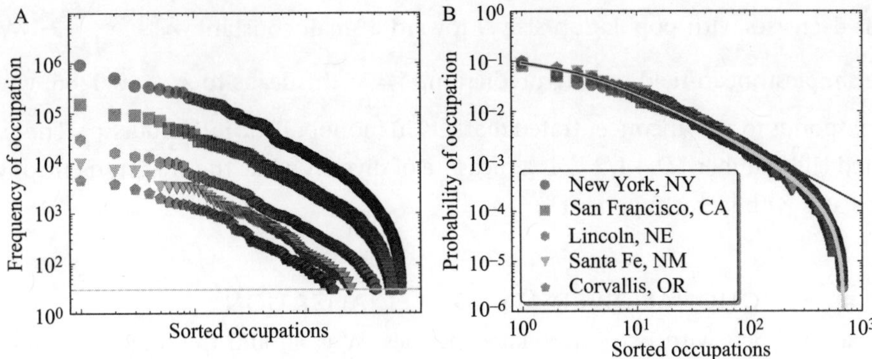

5.10   The distribution of occupations in US metropolitan areas is universal. (A) Frequency distributions for several cities with different population sizes only differ in their amplitude, which is set by city size and the extent to which they probe rare occupations. The horizontal gray line shows the minimum number of professions (30) reported. (B) The rank probability distributions for different cities collapse on each other when adjusted for city size (total employment). The solid light gray line shows the fit of the universal form to $P(i|N_e) = \frac{1}{N_0}\left(\frac{d_{S0} - (i + i_0)}{i + i_0}\right)^{\frac{1}{v}}$, where a scale $i_0 \simeq 3$ at small ranks was introduced. The black line shows $P(i|N_e) = \left(\frac{D_{S0}}{i}\right)^{\frac{1}{v}}$ in the absence of saturation.

(see figure 5.11). Recent work shows that the process of population growth in cities is also one of recapitulation of this hierarchical ecology of sectors.[27]

Distributional Indices of Occupational Diversity   Finally, the point of having a probability distribution of types such as equation (5.12) is that we can compute other measures of diversity besides the occupational richness, D_S. For example, the Shannon entropy corresponding to this distribution,[28] with $\delta = 1 - v$, is

$$H(N) = -\sum_{i=1}^{D_S(N)} P(i|N)\ln P(i|N) = \frac{1}{\delta} - D_{S_0}^{-\frac{\delta}{(1-\delta)}}N^{-\delta}\ln\left(D_{S_0}^{\frac{1}{1-\delta}}N\right). \tag{5.13}$$

This means that the diversity of a city of population size N increases with its population size as the second (negative) term decreases. Note that the $H \to \frac{1}{\delta}$ for infinite city size makes the maximum diversity smaller the larger the superlinear scaling of cities, a point to which we will return later. It is curious that in this limit the information content of this distribution predicted by the arguments of chapter 3 is precisely six bits ($H = 6$). This suggests an urban *game of six questions*: on average, you should be able to guess anyone's occupation by asking six or fewer independent yes/no questions! In smaller cities, this will be easier, whereas in larger cities you may need more questions.

The HH index is

$$\lambda_{HH} = \sum_{i=1}^{D_S(N)} P(i|N)^2 = \frac{\delta^2}{1-\delta^2}\frac{1 - D_{S_0}^{\frac{1+\delta}{1-\delta}}N^{-1-\delta}}{1 - D_{S_0}^{\frac{\delta}{1-\delta}}N^{-\delta}} \simeq \frac{\delta^2}{1-\delta^2}\left(1 + \frac{2}{D_{S_0}^{\frac{\delta}{1-\delta}}N^{\delta}}\right). \tag{5.14}$$

This decreases with population size N toward a small constant, $\lambda_{HH} \to \dfrac{\delta^2}{1-\delta^2}$. With the simplest mean-field scaling prediction, $\delta = \dfrac{1}{6}$, this leads to $\lambda_{HH} \to 0.0286$, which corresponds to an "unconcentrated market" in monopolistic jurisprudence. The associated Hill number, $^2D_S = 1/\lambda_{HH}$, is a measure of diversity; like the Shannon entropy, it decreases with larger exponent δ.

5.2.4   FUNCTIONAL DIVERSITY AS SPECIALIZATION

We are now left with two interrelated puzzles: Why should the total occupational richness of a city with population N scale sublinearly, and specifically with exponent $\nu = 1 - \delta$, relative to other urban scaling quantities? Why does the diversity of cities measured by distributional quantities decrease as these exponents become more nonlinear? Above all, we would like to understand why there would be a *specific* form for the expected division of labor with city population size.

To get us started, consider the average wages in a city of population size N. We argued in chapters 3 and 4 that increases in productivity (and consumption) were the result of higher connectivity per person (network degree), $k(N) = k_0 N^\delta$, which on average increases with population size since $\delta \simeq \dfrac{1}{6}$. However, in section 5.1, we noted the general argument from classical economics that the division of labor is *the* primary reason (according to Adam Smith) for increases in productivity. The division of labor means that each worker is more specialized, in the sense that he or she

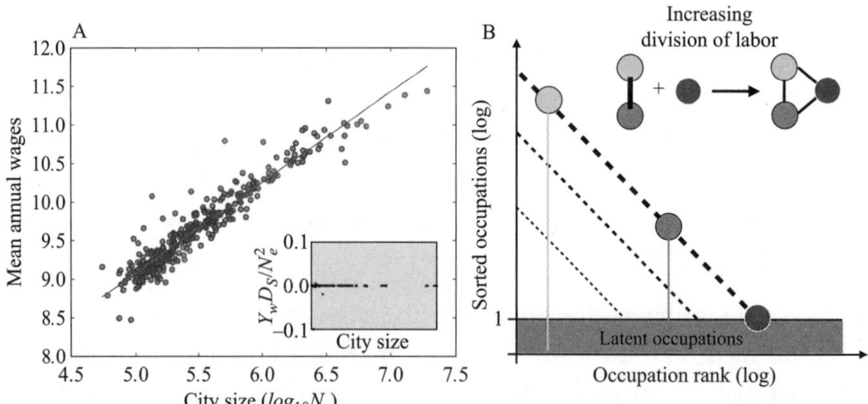

5.11 Scaling of economic productivity with city size and the generation of professional diversity. (A) Superlinear scaling relation between total wages in US metropolitan areas ($Y_W(N_e) = Y_{W_0} N_e^{1+\delta}$ with $\delta = 0.18 \pm 0.03$. Inset shows the product $l_T = y_w d_s$, demonstrating that l_T is, on average, independent of city size. (B) The process of generating new occupations as a function of city size. As the self-similar frequency distribution of occupations is pushed up by city size, latent occupations cross the lowest probability threshold and appear explicitly in D_S. The schematic shows how such a new explicit function (darker circle) allows other occupations (lighter gray circles) to specialize further while remaining available to each other through network ties.

performs *fewer* occupations. We have also seen that the average number of occupations per capita is $d_S = \dfrac{D_S}{N} = D_{S_0} N^{v-1} \simeq D_{S_0} N^{-\delta}$, which supports this contention.

This argument would lead us to conclude that increases in labor productivity (paid as wages) may be the result of this concentration in fewer tasks; that is, $y_w \sim \dfrac{1}{d_S} = \dfrac{1}{D_{S_0}} N^\delta$ (see figure 5.11). We have also seen that specialization is only possible when individuals become interdependent in the sense that as they narrow and deepen the scope of their own labor and knowledge, they can trade it for the goods and services produced by others. Consider a gradual process by which individuals go from a state of self-sufficiency (known as *autarky*) in terms of a total number of basic functions (e.g., obtaining food, shelter, clothing, energy, entertainment). There will be $d_S(N \to 1) = D_{S_0}$ such functions that the individual (or household) will have to execute over some time, and a number of nuclear connections, $k(N \to 1) = k_0$. We could take this number to zero, but it is likely that some connections are preserved, such as at the level of the household, where the division of labor by age and gender is common in traditional small-scale societies. Now imagine that households can externalize a certain fraction of these functions and therefore concentrate their time and effort on others. Because they still require the goods and services associated with externalized functions (such as getting food!), such households will have to establish a number of connections in order to obtain them via exchange with others. Consequently, their connectivity k will go up, while their d_S will go down. If they do this in the most efficient manner possible—they do not give up more functions than they can obtain through exchange and do not establish more connections than they need—the *rate* of change in these two quantities must be equal,

$$\frac{\Delta k}{k} = -\frac{\Delta d_S}{d_S} \to \Delta \ln k\, d_S = 0 \to k d_S = I_T, \tag{5.15}$$

with I_T constant. For the expected urban scaling discussed earlier, $I_T = D_{S_0} k_0$, which is independent of city size but may depend on time as more basic functions become part of a society and as the means of connectivity can be increased or decreased (e.g., via new technologies). If we take this condition as a constraint, we can now ask for the dependence of wages on the division of labor. We do this by setting up a very simple constrained optimization problem, where we maximize wages, written as $y_w(N) = \dfrac{\phi_w(k d_S)}{d_S}$, subject to equation (5.15), which is

$$\mathcal{L}(d_N; \lambda_0) = \frac{\phi_w(k d_S)}{d_S} + \lambda_0(k d_S - I_T). \tag{5.16}$$

The parameter λ_0 is a Lagrange multiplier. Taking derivatives relative to d_S, λ_0, we derive the conditions

$$d_S(N) = \frac{I_T}{k(N)} = \frac{I_T}{k_0} N^{-\delta}, \quad y_w(N) = \frac{\phi_w(I_T)}{I_T} k_0 N^\delta, \text{ and } \frac{d\phi_w}{dI_T} - \frac{\phi_w}{I_T} - \lambda_0' I_T = 0, \tag{5.17}$$

where $\lambda_0' = \dfrac{\lambda_0}{k}$ is in general also dependent on I_T. The solution of the last equation is

$$\phi_w(I_T) = \left(C_\phi + \int\limits^{I_T} dI' \lambda'_0(I') \right) \Big| I_T = y_{w_0} D_{S_0}. \tag{5.18}$$

Here, the constant of integration C_ϕ and the value of the Lagrange multiplier are set by the observation of the prefactor for wages, $y_{w_0}(t)$, which may vary over time. The constraint in equation (5.15) is analogous to the condition of maximum diversity in equation (5.6) associated with the *error catastrophe* limit in other complex systems. The quantity I_T—the number of essential functions at the household level—plays the role of the *information threshold*, the information necessary for each household to function. This is an "individual need" and as such is independent of city size. It is because diversity as specialization is statistically associated with greater productivity and more overall information that we are driven to this limit, no more and no less.

As we will see in later chapters, it is this freedom to create new functions, to organize them in networks, and to allocate different amounts of effort across an urban system that will lead to economic growth and the typically exponential growth of incomes in time. Having seen how connectivity is related to productivity, diversity, and city size, we now discuss some of their implications in terms of limits and processes of growth and structural change.

5.3   MORE GENERAL CONNECTIVITY: THE CITY AND TECHNOLOGICAL NETWORKS

We have now developed several arguments and even some mechanisms for why productivity should increase systematically with occupational specialization, and how on average this process must be associated with greater connectivity in cities.

We now focus on some general aspects of the *costs of connectivity*, which will allow us to generalize the theme of this chapter to other situations, where the trade-offs of living in cities become clearer. We will also discuss how other forms of connectivity, especially those mediated by technological networks, can perform functions similar to personal encounters. This leads to common questions such as whether the internet is like a city and whether technological networks will replace face-to-face contact and render physical cities irrelevant in the future.

5.3.1   THE GENERAL ADVANTAGES OF CONNECTIVITY
We can now attempt to create a framework for how connectivity gradually develops in networks of certain types and how it can become increasingly pervasive under certain conditions that rely on infrastructure, technology, and institutional change.

Let us return to the basic ingredients of the spectacular gain in labor productivity that can result from the division of labor. Adam Smith originally identified three contributions by which the division of labor increases productivity. Each of these remains important in modern complex networks, though they may not be sufficient. First, there is the effect of *learning* to perform a task better; that is, the process of acquiring knowledge and expertise through accumulated experience.[29] This sort of effect has since been extensively studied in manufacturing at the organizational level and in cognitive sciences at the individual level.[30] Clearly, the more time someone spends on a task or problem, the more expertise and knowledge we should expect them to acquire.

Second, there are sources of productivity gains arising from the *time savings* gained from avoiding frequent switches between tasks. This was one basis for the value of the hierarchical (modular) organization of tasks, advocated by Herbert Simon, when considering the "architecture of complexity."[31] He emphasized the importance of creating modules of stable tasks and their hierarchical assembly. Finally, the third source of gains relies on the possibility that a task that has been rendered sufficiently simple through the successive division of labor can be made automatic and in that sense be performed by a machine, thus saving human labor. Many technologies started this way, as a specialized worker observed a solution that could save them labor and time. Of course, such gains may not ultimately accrue to the laborer being replaced by the machine.

These different sources of productivity gains are very general and clearly transcend the context of economic production in manufacturing. Thus, we should think of the process of the division of labor not in terms of vertical integration of minutely specialized jobs in manufacturing firms (though it is that, too) but rather in terms of the distribution of tasks in networks that are generally not hierarchies and the necessary creation of knowledge entailed by the specialized task and its integration (recombination) in many products and services.[32] In this form, the ancient concept of the division and coordination of labor gains new life as a modern process, at work everywhere around us. In its modern form, it emphasizes information and communication in evolving complex networks. Many of the most modern socioeconomic phenomena, from online collective intelligence to the sharing economy, depend on these processes in fundamental ways.

In this brighter light, the creation and interdependence of knowledge imply complex and dynamic network structures as an evolving process, which is sketched in figure 5.12. For simplicity, let us start by imagining a situation where each member of a set of agents (usually people) replicates the same functions (different shades of gray in figure 5.12). One example of this is a subsistence human society[33] (chapter 7) where as we have already mentioned, despite some typical specialization of labor by age and gender, all households perform essentially the same tasks of hunting, gathering, or small-scale farming. The information content of such societies may be high in each family, whose members must know a lot about their environment to survive mostly on their own, but this knowledge is replicated in each nuclear unit (figure 5.12A) and therefore does not add up to new information across many households for these societies as a whole.

Thus, the total information content in the society (what it knows how to do *collectively*) in this situation is that of the typical family unit, because each is redundant

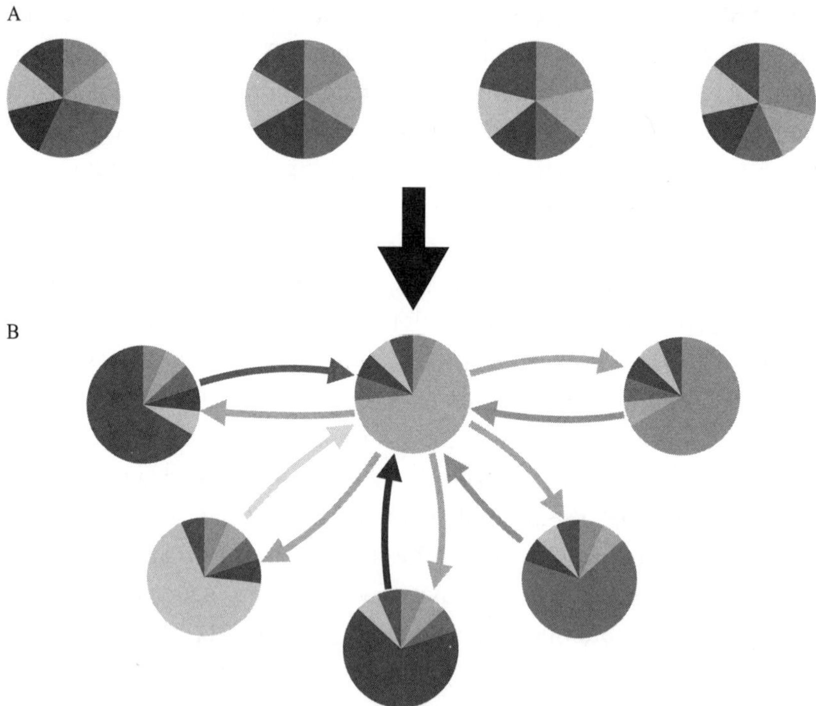

5.12 Structural transformation in occupational networks resulting from interconnection and special-ization. The disconnected phase (A) is characterized by low levels of connectivity, functional redun-dancy (different shades), low productivity, and slow learning (see the text). As connectivity becomes less costly, a transition to a new phase (B) is possible, characterized by increasing connectivity with scale, accompanied by increasing complementarity of functions, growing productivity, and fast overall learning at the individual and network levels. In this phase, nodes (circles) become more specialized (pie charts more dominated by single activity type, shown in different shades) so that they must become functionally interdependent and exchange complementary information, goods, and services (curved arrows). (For simplicity, only the arrows in which the central node participates are shown.)

with (not differentiated from) all the others. This is why, in this type of *disconnected phase*, information content does not accumulate with increases in population size.

The situation can change radically as large-scale connectivity becomes possible (figure 5.12B). As we have already seen, it is then possible for nodes to differentiate and specialize in different problems and tasks, relying on their functional comple-mentarities to preserve overall function at the network level and make it available to each agent. So, for example, in modern urban societies, most of us do not grow our own food or harvest energy. Instead, we devote our time to extremely specialized tasks, often in services and in learning and organization. We rely on a vast number of people (mostly complete strangers) to provide the most critical products and ser-vices we need daily for our survival. In this situation, the information content of a network can scale up with the size of the society, N, as individual differentiation becomes the norm: Everyone has something new to contribute. Thus, even if the size of a network, N, were to remain constant, its information content would now be much larger, roughly proportional to the number of its nodes, which naturally confers economic and technological advantages to large, connected systems. We will see in chapter 9 that the information content of a society is key for its development and for setting its economic growth rate.

As we have also seen, in real human societies, differentiation and specialization are typically not fully extensive, as many people perform the same professions, for example.

5.3.2   QUANTIFYING THE GENERAL BENEFITS OF CONNECTIVITY

Having stated the general benefits of increasing network connectivity in terms of gains in information and productivity, let us now quantify these effects in general terms, as functions of network size (see table 5.3 for a summary).

First, the situation of figure 5.12A—the *disconnected phase*—is very simple and can be characterized by a constant small connectivity per node (degree), $k = k_D \simeq k_0$, approximately constant information content $i = i_D$, and small productivity per person, $y_w = y_{w_D}$ (see table 5.3). Two related quantities are also worth specifying: the number of functions per person, $d_S = \dfrac{D_S(N)}{N} = d_{S_D}$, which is a measure of individual specialization, as we saw in the section 5.2 and the average time spent on each task, $t_T = t_{T_D} = \dfrac{t_{T_0}}{d_S}$, where t_{T_0} is the total activity time for an individual, which we will assume is a physiological constant. Thus, in the disconnected phase, the average fraction of time spent on each task is very small: each person needs to be a jack-of-all-trades. Consequently, because of low connectivity, individual functional differentiation is impossible and learning (information acquisition) is very slow as a result of the very small amount of time spent on each problem. Because of a lack of connectivity and interdependence, all individuals on average replicate this process around similar tasks linked to survival. Learning and productivity per capita remain approximately constant in such a network, even as it grows in size, N. Figure 5.13 summarizes this situation by the horizontal line.

When connectivity and interdependence become possible, a network can then follow an entirely different trajectory as it grows. Let us for a moment ignore the costs of creating and maintaining connectivity, which are discussed in the subsection 5.3.3. Then, let us suppose further that connectivity per capita increases according to a scale-invariant function (a power law) of the form $k = k_C N^\delta$, where the amplitude, k_C, depends on technology and time (and cost). This is a form we derived for cities in chapter 3, but for the purpose of the present discussion, we can consider the exponent $\delta > 0$ a property of any given network, taking different values.

Let us assume that the number of functions accessible to each individual remains constant but becomes increasingly available through network connections (figure 5.12B), such that $k(N)d_S(N) = I_T$, which is independent of N, as we have seen in patterns of professional specialization and social connectivity in US cities[34] and

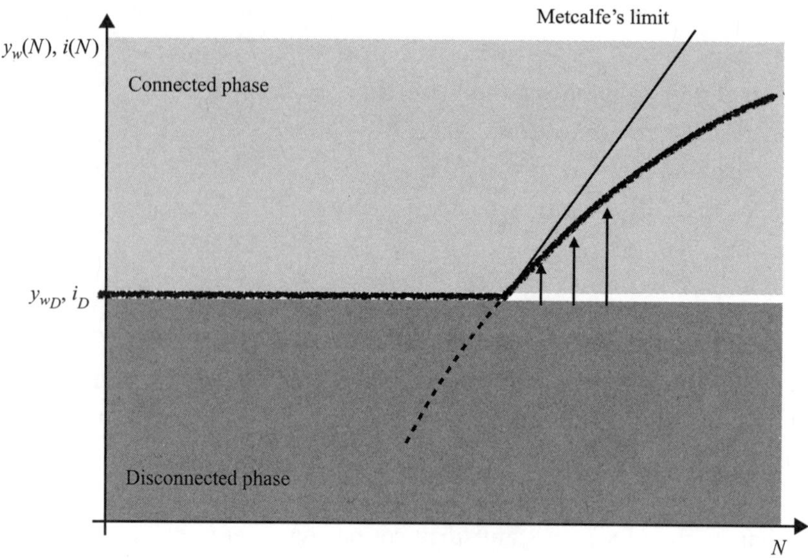

5.13 Schematic nature of the transition between subsistence (disconnected phase) and urbanism (connected phase). Small systems where communication and exchange are costly will tend to be in the disconnected phase, while larger systems with relatively inexpensive connectivity will tend to be in the connected phase and under continuous growth of information and productivity. Thus, as size or technological circumstances change, disconnected systems become susceptible to entering the connected phase. As this happens, the transition may be gradual (along the thick, rough line) or sudden (arrows) if the conditions that make the connected phase advantageous are latent but the state of the system has not yet realized them. Reversals are also possible if connectivity becomes more expensive. Some of the current explosive trends in urbanization and online network growth may be the result of this type of sudden dynamic shift (chapter 9). Metcalfe's limit refers to the situation where productivity and information increase linearly with system size.

may already be present in smaller-scale human societies,[35] though the discussion in these contexts is ongoing.[36]

Then we conclude that $d_S(N) = d_{S_0} N^{-\delta}$, so each individual on average specializes in a smaller number of tasks and spends on average an amount of time on each task $t_T(N) = \dfrac{t_{T_0}}{d_S(N)} = \dfrac{t_{T_0}}{d_{S_0}} N^{\delta}$, which increases proportionally to connectivity. Finally, we should expect that the total new information acquired is, on average, proportional to the time on a task, $i(N) \propto t_T(N) = i_C N^{\delta}$, and that productivity is proportional to such information, $y_w(N) \propto i(N) = y_{w_0} N^{\delta}$, and thus, ultimately, to connectivity and specialization. These patterns are summarized in figure 5.13 as the rising line and in table 5.3. They hold for any dependence of connectivity on size, not just the assumed power law, and express how a dynamic phase of network growth can take hold and lead to associated increases in overall information content, functional diversity, and individual productivity.

Table 5.3 Relationship between different urban scaling properties and the diversity, productivity, connectivity, and information in cities. Metcalfe's limit is obtained when the exponent $\delta \to 1$.

Symbol	Agent property	Disconnected phase	Connected phase (general)	Connected phase (cities)
k	Connectivity	k_D (small)	$k(N)$ (increasing)	$k(N) = k_0 N^\delta$
d_S	Number of functions	d_{S_D} (large)	$d_S(N) = I_T/k(N)$ (decreasing)	$d_S(N) = d_{S_0} N^{-\delta}$
i	Information	i_D (small)	$i(N) \sim t(N)$ (increasing)	$i(N) = i_0 N^\delta$
y_w	Productivity	y_{w_D} (low)	$y_w(N) \sim k(N)$ (increasing)	$y_w(N) = y_{w_0} N^\delta$
t_T	Time/function	t_{T_D} (small)	$t_T(N) \sim k(N)$ (increasing)	$t_T(N) = t_0 N^\delta$
c	Cost/node	c_D (large)	$c(N) = R_J j^2 k(N)$ (increasing)	$c(N) = c_0 N^\delta$

5.3.3   THE COSTS OF CONNECTIVITY

Connectivity is generally *very costly*. We will discuss in chapter 7 why traditional human societies have remained *disconnected* for most of our history as a species, mostly because of conflict and the lack of general trust, institutions, and infrastructure that can promote predictably mutual beneficial exchanges (recall Eigen's paradox).

In chapter 3, we approached the problem of connectivity mostly via the costs of moving people, goods, and information through the networks of the city. We can generalize these arguments by considering *connectivity as a physical act of exchange*. Thus, each process of connectivity is mediated by a current, J. In all macroscopic networks, there are dissipative energy losses associated with such exchanges that lead to costs that depend on the current as $\sim R_J J^2$, where, recall from chapter 3, R_J is the resistance, set by whatever dissipative processes are relevant for the given exchange (e.g., friction in transportation, conductivity losses for electricity, etc.).[37] This reasoning also shows that energy costs are inevitable in irreversible exchanges (as a consequence of the second law of thermodynamics), whereas the translation of these costs into other units, such as money, may vary more widely; for example, as a result of the price of energy and choices of technology.

We should expect a dissipative cost associated with each connection (as an independent current) proportional to the square of the intensity of the exchange and to the relevant source of energy loss. The result is the cost per node, $c_C(N) = R_J J^2 k(N) = c_0 N^\delta$. This becomes $c_0(N) = c_D N$ in Metcalfe's limit, which is more like the idea of scalar stress in interpersonal relations discussed in chapter 7.

5.3.4   COST-BENEFIT ANALYSIS AND PHASE TRANSITIONS

Finally, we can assemble the general picture of benefits and costs of connectivity in networks to derive general expectations about when the connected network phase and its associated dynamics of learning and increasing productivity may take place.

First, let us consider the net gain, $\Delta r = y_W - c_C$, from connectivity (recall chapter 4). This is

$$\Delta r = y_w - c_C = (y_{w_0} - c_0)N^\delta = \left(\frac{y_{w_0}}{k_0} - \frac{c_0}{k_0} \right) k(N). \tag{5.19}$$

From this expression, we immediately see that the *connected network phase does not always pay off* (see figure 5.13). In particular, if the costs exceed the average productivity per connection, $c_0 > y_{w_0}$, the behavior typical of the connected phase cannot develop at all. Only in the opposite regime, where connectivity becomes inexpensive in units of productivity, does the network become able to probe its dynamic learning regime and explore the advantages of the division and interdependence of labor and information. To see the nature of the transition more clearly, note that, starting in the disconnected phase, the transition to the connected state occurs when

$$\Delta r \geq y_{w_D} \rightarrow k(N) \geq \frac{y_{w_D} k_0}{y_{w_0} - c_0} \leftrightarrow N \geq \left(\frac{y_{w_D}}{y_{w_0} - c_0} \right)^{\frac{1}{\delta}}. \tag{5.20}$$

This condition shows that *there is a minimum population size threshold* necessary for the advantages of population connectivity to tell. This result resonates with Claude Fischer's proposition of critical mass for a subculture, and the greater likelihood of achieving it in a larger city and getting something new rolling. This also says that, everything else being equal, the transition to the connected phase is inexorable as *network* size, N, increases! Although this phenomenon may be connected to ideas of development through population pressure and circumscription,[38] the key to these structural changes in complex networks is more general and the underlying necessary conditions likely more subtle. However, this transition can also be produced at fixed size, N, as the trade-off between advantages and costs of connectivity in the connected phase shift. This transition may be smooth or sudden (as in a *tipping point*), depending on whether the system is able to immediately capitalize on the new available dynamics of connectivity or remains temporarily stuck in the disconnected phase even as favorable circumstances for the shift develop.

The role of technology in complex information networks now starts to come into focus: by creating a more positive benefit-cost trade-off for connectivity across the largest possible realm of interaction, technological change can place networked systems on a path of collective learning and of gains in terms of diversity and productivity. Here, technologies should be understood in the broadest possible sense, from cultural and political institutions that reduce conflict and help realize the benefits of social interdependence to fast computing or inexpensive transportation. Most often, transformative technologies must operate both in the purely technological realm and in extant social conditions.

5.3.5 BEYOND THE CITY: GLOBAL ONLINE NETWORKS

The general reasoning of subsection 5.3.4 naturally applies to cities, where spatial transportation costs make $\delta \simeq \frac{1}{6}$, as we saw in chapter 3. They also flesh out the ideas of disaggregated cost-benefit analysis for different agents introduced in chapter 4. In this subsection, we also show that these properties are *not exclusive to cities*. They are also observable in other networks, especially in technology, which like cities can help people realize general network effects in socioeconomic and cultural production.

Better Networks? The Internet and the World Wide Web The internet is supposed to be the ultimate "city killer," precisely by replacing the messy, costly interactions typical of urban life with safe and efficient connections at a distance, potentially reaching more and "better" contacts.

By any measure, progress in computing and telecommunications technologies has enabled unprecedented growth in connectivity between people. We will see in chapter 6, for example, how slum dwellers in West Africa today can express their development priorities in ways that make sense to community organizers in India and international organizations and researchers at universities worldwide. These technologies are also creating networks of knowledge that are, in specific senses, external to individual humans and their social networks and where information is instead encoded in webs of interlinked documents, without an explicit spatial location. Increasingly, this type of informational superstructure is being generated automatically as a product of the latest generative algorithms of artificial intelligence. The internet and the World Wide Web (the web for short) enable and embody these global changes and continue to evolve from more specific and smaller networks into new and more pervasive realms.

It is therefore interesting to study the evolution of these networks in light of the general concepts developed earlier. To what extent are the internet and the web examples of *connected phase* dynamics? What sort of productivity and learning do they enable? Are they a substitute for cities?

Perhaps surprisingly, the actual size and connectivity of these networks remain largely unknown both because they have become immensely large and because of their decentralized and bottom-up dynamics. In practice, this requires that the entire network be visited, node by node, in order to map its global structure, which has become effectively impossible. Nevertheless, surveys give us a sense of their structural dynamics as their user base has increased over time.

Figure 5.14 shows the number of *domain name system* (DNS) hosts and two estimates of the number of web pages as functions of the total worldwide online population. These two quantities give measures for the sizes of the internet and the web, respectively. The first interesting feature of figure 5.14 is that, in both cases, we observe clear superlinear scaling. While this sort of behavior for DNS hosts suggests an increase in task load (cost) on servers with each additional person online, the growth in the number of web pages is especially interesting, as it suggests a more

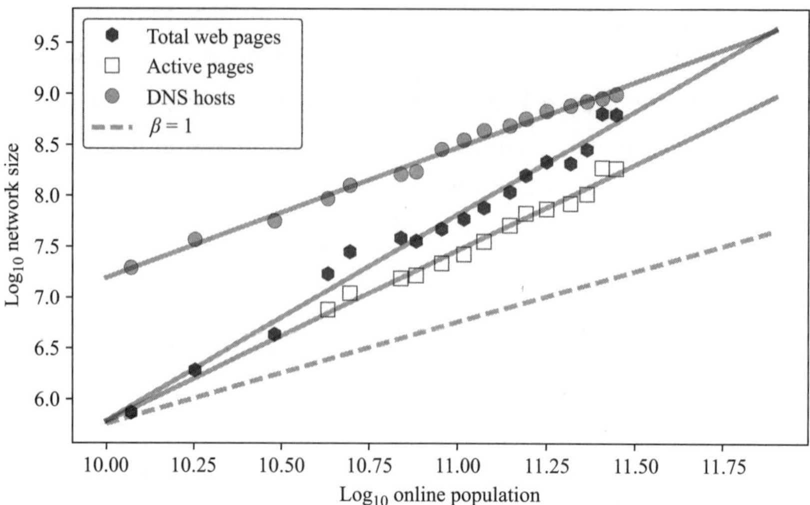

5.14 Scaling of global computer networks with online population size. The size of the internet, measured in terms of DNS hosts, is characterized by the exponent 1.28 (95% CI=[1.22, 1.34], R^2=0.99), while the growth of the web in terms of an estimate of total web pages is characterized by the exponent 2.03 (95% CI=[1.88, 2.17], R^2=0.98) and that of active pages by the exponent 1.68 (95% CI=[1.55, 1.82], R^2=0.98). In all cases, the size of online networks has been growing superlinearly with the number of internet users, indicating that more pages and more computation per capita is effectively used as the network grows, much as in other open-ended social systems (e.g., cities). Exponents are manifestly different (more superlinear) from those observed for cities.

strongly superlinear increase in content and thus, in some sense, in the productivity of the system. The number of total web pages (which we should think of as links between users), in particular, exhibits scaling with an exponent consistent with Metcalfe's law. However, this web page count is plagued by spurious effects related to incentives to create pages artificially. Thus, the number of *active pages*, which scales with a smaller superlinear exponent, may be a more accurate measure of these links.

In any case, it is interesting that we infer from these results that the number of web pages has grown with online population size at a rate much faster than social connections do with the population size of urban agglomerations. In this sense, each individual may typically have access to more pieces of information online and be able to specialize in his or her own production to a larger extent.

To my knowledge, when this work was done,[39] it was the first demonstration of pervasive superlinear scaling of the internet and the web with online population size. However, these measures remain very rough estimates of the growth of these networks, and it would be very interesting to revisit the present results with better data. In addition, it would be desirable to obtain other measures more directly related to online connectivity, information, and individual attention and their evolution over time.

Collective Knowledge Production in Cyberspace: Wikipedia Another, more particular online network example, where more thorough measures of network properties are readily available, is the online encyclopedia Wikipedia. Wikipedia started in January 2001 and has grown spectacularly ever since, currently comprising over 40 million articles in 293 languages (that *is* impressive, but it is still fewer languages than in New York City!).

Wikipedia is not a general-purpose network aimed at increasing general productivity or connectivity. Its goal is to create encyclopedia articles collaboratively through the contributions of anyone who wishes to participate. In this sense, nodes treated as articles increase their information content over time through the intervention of human contributors. Thus, even though nodes do not learn per se, we can treat them as analogous to the scheme developed earlier, with humans being part of the connectivity structure (and bearing some of the costs) of creating and growing the network.

The growth of the body of cross-referenced articles hence created then provides us with a picture of how information as a whole increases and how its productivity in terms of impact may change in tandem. This happens in two ways: (1) through the successive process of improvement of each entry, which is a form of collective learning encoded as the article, and (2) through the linkages (connectivity) that an entry establishes to others, both internal and external to Wikipedia. Thus, it is this network of documents that encodes information, and its change represents the process of learning. Although readers of Wikipedia may also benefit (and learn) from this encoding of knowledge, contributors to Wikipedia may not individually possess all the knowledge that a single page reflects. This turns the process of learning in cities (and the parallel suggestive structure of scaling on the web) upside down and suggests that the best measure for the size of Wikipedia is articles and that their connectivity is supplied by human contributors as well as document links, not vice versa.

If we adopt this perspective, we find scaling results that broadly agree with those we invoked for cities and the web. Figure 5.15A shows how the connectivity of articles, in terms of human contributors as well as internal and external links, grows superlinearly with the number of articles. Figure 5.15A further justifies the identification of Wikipedia contributors with page links by showing that these scale linearly (proportionally) to each other. Figure 5.15B also shows that the number of edits in Wikipedia is proportional to the number of contributors, supporting the assertion that the cost of connectivity per link is fixed, as is human effort approximately in cities. Finally, figure 5.15C shows that the productivity of an average article (and of each contributor) increases superlinearly, at least in terms of audience reach. This also establishes that the benefit of creating a connection (the effort of a contributor) is outpaced by its benefits in terms of audience reach, suggesting indeed that Wikipedia is an information network expressing *connected phase* dynamics.

These examples supply evidence that *information networks* typically enable payoffs that are superlinear on the number of learner elements and that they are limited in their growth primarily by the cost of establishing and maintaining this connectivity. Whenever benefits outstrip costs, these networks grow and connect explosively. Eventually, they may equilibrate to a scale-invariant regime where costs and benefits scale up in the same (superlinear) way.

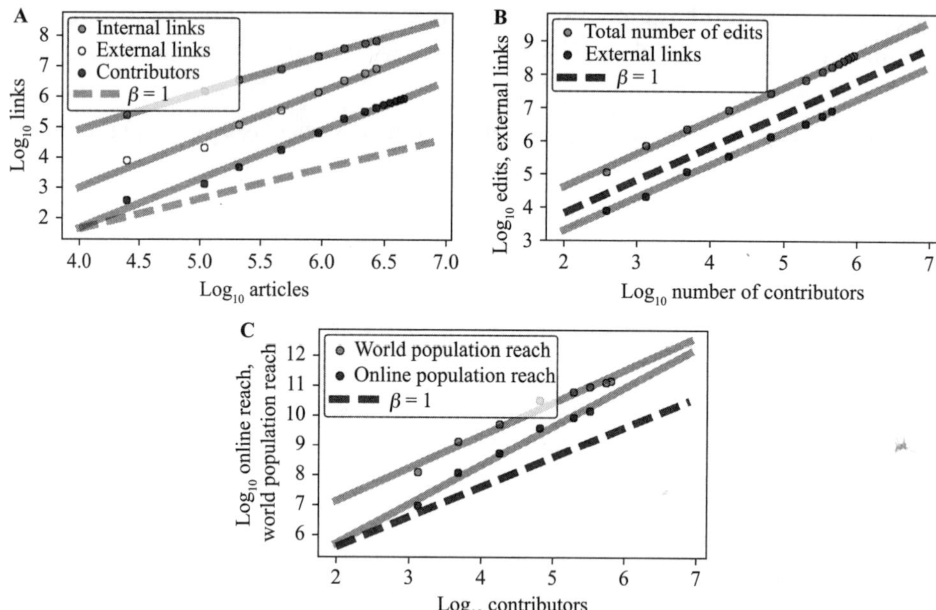

5.15 Contributors and external and internal links to Wikipedia articles scale superlinearly. (A) The number of contributors scales with the number of Wikipedia articles with exponent 1.61 (95% CI=[1.51, 1.72], R^2=0.99). The number of external links scales approximately in the same way with exponent 1.59 (95% CI=[1.40, 1.79], R^2=0.98). The larger number of internal links scales more slowly, with exponent 1.21 (95% CI=[1.18, 1.24], R^2=0.99). If we interpret these quantities as different measures of connectivity between articles, we see that they all scale with exponents larger than those observed for social connectivity in cities. (B) The total number of edits and external links to Wikipedia articles is proportional to the number of individual contributors. The gray line shows the best fit to the number of edits versus contributors with exponent 1.00 (95% CI=[0.97, 1.03], R^2=0.99). The darker gray line shows the best fit to the number of external links versus contributors with exponent 0.99 (95% CI=[0.95, 1.03], R^2=0.99). The dashed line shows the exact proportionality $b=1$ for comparison. (C) The audience reach of contributors to Wikipedia increases superlinearly. Lines show the best fit to Alexa online reach surveys, which estimate the number of internet users who use Wikipedia, as 1.10 (95% CI=[0.95, 1.25], R^2=0.97) and the best fit to the reach in terms of total worldwide population as 1.31 (95% CI=[1.13, 1.38], R^2=0.98). The second gray line is steeper because it accounts for the growth of the online population, which in 2013 was estimated at 39%, versus the total world population.

5.3.6 BACK IN TOWN: WHERE IS THE INTERNET?

The results so far treat internet infrastructure in the absence of space, but the *internet is physical*, so where are the computer servers? It might surprise you that they form a *city of their own*, coinciding with the networked city of humans.

At any rate, we can map internet device identities (IP addresses) to geography. In this way, we can also analyze the abundance of the computers that make up the internet against city size (figure 5.16).

Scaling analysis of number of IPs versus human population in urban areas, in the US and internationally, shows that they scale like economic production (GDP) and presumably like socioeconomic connections more generally (and lawyers). The

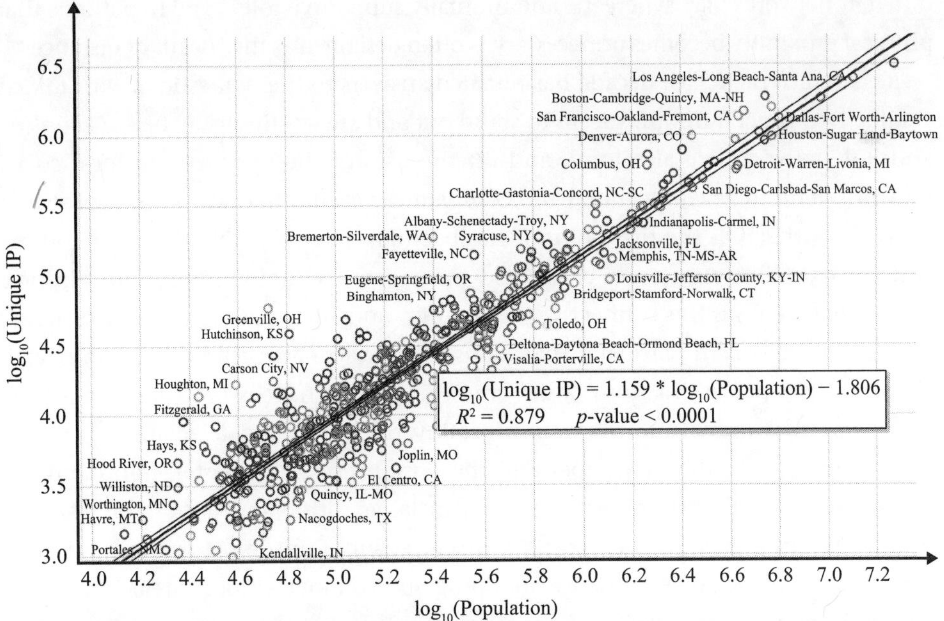

5.16 Scaling of number of IP addresses with city size in US metropolitan areas. IP addresses scale superlinearly (black line with gray lines shows statistical uncertainty) with an exponent statistically indistinguishable from social network connectivity or urban GDP. They are a good proxy for total metropolitan GDP in the US and internationally.

proximate reasons for this coincidence are not very clear at present but are likely connected to the fact that mimicking the interactions between people in an urbanized population reduces latency and increases the value of these technologically mediated connections. Consequently, the structure of the internet manifests the same network effects and the same general agglomeration patterns as human populations in cities! A fascinating question is to what extent are these effects fundamental to the technological network itself: Will they persist even if human populations one day deurbanize or vanish? In a world of intelligent, cooperative robots, will there be robot cities?

5.3.7 DISCUSSION: NETWORKS AND TECHNOLOGICAL CHANGE, THE INTERNET VERSUS CITIES

We argued earlier that the dynamics characteristic of the connected network phase are primary to its specific underlying infrastructure or spatial embedding. This means that whether these dynamics can be realized in cities, where physical space and infrastructure play an essential role, or online, where attention and time appear to be more relevant, is a secondary consideration, except of course to the extent that one of these modes overcomes disadvantages of another and may substitute for it altogether. In this light, a common question is whether the internet and information and communication technologies (ICTs) can eliminate the need for cities?[40] Or, instead, do these very different networks play synergetic and mutually supportive roles? The hypothesis that physical proximity becomes unnecessary is often described as the "death of distance."[41]

Research over the last decade has pursued answers to these questions with mixed results. Two general findings seem to stand out and are worth noting here: (1) online and ICT networks are also local, and (2) the uses of the internet and local social networks tend to be cointegrated and complement each other rather than substitute for one another. On the first point, it has been found empirically that more online content is available in larger cities,[42] so these new technologies tend to reinforce rather than replace the connectivity dynamics and information content of larger places. This means in particular that maps and services are disproportionally available online if they stem from larger cities. In this vein, it is probably interesting to remark that previous introductions of informational and telecommunications technologies, from the newspaper and the postal service to the telegraph and the telephone, have almost always originated in larger cities, and not simply for economic reasons related to their cost.[43] On the second point, most findings are both intuitive and obvious. Whether for shopping and commerce[44] or for telecommuting and routing deliveries,[45] new ICTs are extremely useful in helping organize the complex life patterns typical of larger cities, including the fine temporal coordination of encounters that is necessary for the exchange of goods, services, and information. In this sense, new informational technologies are most useful in the most intensely connected networked places, which typically are found in larger cities (this is a kind of digital-to-urban *Matthew's effect*). This does not mean that these technologies are not transformative elsewhere, such as in rural settings with low population density. What it says is that these technologies do not seem to contribute to making larger cities less attractive in relative terms than before. On the contrary, one could argue that very large emergent cities, such as Mumbai or Lagos, could not function at their present scale without modern ICTs, especially mobile phones.

Despite these findings, the question remains as to whether future vastly improved telecommunications technologies, capable of reproducing the nuances of sharing space and meeting face-to-face, can one day replace personal travel.[46] While there is no reason to exclude such a possibility in principle, my guess is that all connected networks will tend to mesh together and reinforce one another and that substitution is only possible when new modes fully include and transcend the advantages of previous modes of interaction and learning.

The Resilience of Connected Information Networks   In real circumstances in human societies, extreme labor and knowledge specialization is sometimes only possible inside vertically integrated organizations (hierarchies), such as those of governments, large firms, and universities. Such environments can promote the stability and continuity necessary for the pursuit of more speculative research and development or for extreme specialization, say in an assembly line, in ways that economic markets cannot support. The danger of this *internal* specialization is that knowledge hence created remains tied to a very specific context and cannot be used in new generative ways in larger networks. In science and technology, publication of scientific manuscripts and patents helps bridge this gap, but much knowledge still remains tacit and local. This difficulty may prove more severe in large-scale manufacturing, where workers on the factory floor are typically at once very specifically matched to their tasks and redundant with each other and with automated solutions. In these circumstances, labor is not free to specialize further or to learn in ways that may benefit the individual over the long term as well as the networked system as a whole, outside the worker's immediate organization.

This creates an apparent contradiction. While the creation and full use of specialized knowledge often requires protective environments inside organizations, its value depends on broad openness and exchange at the network level. These two processes, taken together, suggest that dynamics of formation and dissolution of organizations are likely necessary for new information to be created and for it to acquire its full value. This can be achieved through open and dynamic labor markets, entrepreneurship, and through processes by which knowledge can be accumulated in stable but open ways; for example, through open platforms such as online wikis and open-source repositories.

A second issue relates to the resilience of the connected network phase. It should be clear that the disconnected phase, though it is characterized by low productivity and information content, is generally very robust to the loss of nodes. This is a direct result of its functional redundancy at the node level, a mechanism that is often employed in engineering solutions to hedge against random local failures.[47]

The source of resilience of the connected state emerges not so much from its structure but from its dynamics. In this phase, the loss of nodes implies some loss of information, and the loss of connections may reverse the process of learning. This was in dramatic evidence during the pervasive lockdowns necessary to slow down the COVID-19 pandemic. These processes are to some extent reversible, however. The idea is that, being ultimately dynamic, the system can adjust to a loss in size by tracing its evolution backward. This implies some loss in knowledge, as well as some degradation of productivity, but still maintains the system in a state ready to bounce back and evolve again.

Thus, the question is whether, upon a shock, the connected system can degrade gracefully and bounce back quickly. Anecdotal evidence from recent disasters in cities suggests that people can take up many of the functions that are usually performed by infrastructure and services. Examples are walking or bicycling as a substitute for disrupted mass transit, but, as on the upside, the possibility remains that fast and reversible adaptation may not always be possible. Transitions that are hard to reverse may occur, accompanied by the destruction of network connectivity and critical information.

EPILOGUE: THE VALUE OF DIVERSITY

Cities are some of the most diverse environments on earth. Among all these variations in people and organizations, what is accident and what is necessity? Necessity can be identified where diversity is the result of functional specialization, associated with the use of resources and time and with socioeconomic production. The link between connectivity, productivity, and the division of knowledge and labor is one of the most important avenues for understanding how diversity becomes functional and why larger cities play such important roles in this process. In this context, we saw how the diversity of cities may be "universal" and be tied to the underlying general structure of their socioeconomic and infrastructural networks (chapter 3).

But there is certainly much more to the diversity of cities. Before differences between individuals become "useful," a certain amount of accident, unconventionality, and experimentation is certainly tolerated or even encouraged. If you had a skill or an idea that did not fit anywhere, where would you go? If you want to hear about the next thing, where might it happen? If you are looking to assemble your own network that may define your career, where might this quest lead you? These searches for social matches, for new information, and for new value take many people—especially younger people, specialized workers, and foreigners—to larger cities, as we will see in chapter 8. When the costs of connecting to a diversity of strangers are low and opportunities abundant, cities become magnets for hosting and reassembling diversity. They become crucibles of new possibilities that, through interactions with others, may indeed allow us to become more ourselves.

But who benefits from this diversity? Who was right, Smith or Marx? Or maybe Jacobs or Durkheim? Do cities emancipate excluded people or fool them into new traps? Do they destroy or create culture? Do they promote social capacity or alienate individuals? The most wonderful thing about the diversity of cities is that it is a very dynamic phenomenon. Its downsides constantly need to be balanced against its advantages. Such balancing is sometimes a frustrating feature of *urbanism as a way of life*, but it cannot be avoided or taken for granted. When such struggles succeed and the generative powers of diversity stay open-ended and connected, everyone—present and future—benefits from the promise of cities.

6

NEIGHBORHOODS AND HUMAN DEVELOPMENT

A bad neighbor is a misfortune, as much as a good one is a great blessing.
—Hesiod, *Works and Days*

Why are there neighborhoods in cities? How do people adapt to different urban spaces? And how do urban spaces adapt to different people?

We saw in chapter 5 that cities promote extreme diversity, expressed as different types of people, their knowledge, and their activities. It turns out that this diversity can have very different spatial arrangements within cities, often generating local patterns of clustering and segregation. Among other things, this creates *neighborhoods* as places within the city with different populations, socioeconomic characteristics, cultures, services, and so on. It has been argued that the existence of neighborhoods is an urban universal, being present in ancient cities as well as contemporary ones.[1] Why?

At the most fundamental level, we have seen that our touchstone relationship, $y-c$, for balancing benefits and costs is not to be evaluated in the same way for everyone. It is plural; it applies to each urban agent differently, from households to firms and other organizations.

This relationship involves both short-term tactical behavior about balancing costs and incomes (chapter 4) and longer-term strategic choices expressing investments in people's own knowledge and wealth and, critically, that of their children (chapter 9). Urban space, being one of the greatest constraints in the city, can benefit agents by becoming structured, creating niches that can support different human ecologies at lower connectivity cost, whether they are made of clusters of poor migrants arriving in the city, fearful tycoons, kindred businesses, or people with shared lifestyles.

There are many ways in which a diversity of people and organizations can benefit from being at once clustered and protected and also challenged and connected to other elements in the city. Correspondingly, the phenomenon of neighborhood formation and persistence has many dimensions, including the different locations of employment, services, and, of course, people's residences. The causes and effects of these heterogeneous spatial distributions of types within cities are complex and can have both generally positive (economic agglomeration) and negative consequences (racial segregation) over the short and long terms.

In this chapter, we introduce a background of expectations and methods to study processes of human development in neighborhoods. Specifically, we will develop mathematical methods to classify differences in type frequency in terms of *information*. We will also show that heterogeneities in neighborhood services are typically associated with dynamic conditions of human development that can generate more or less inequality depending on various bottom-up socioeconomic dynamics and top-down policy choices. These analyses will be concurrent with the discussion of the life course effects of spatial inequality on individuals and the phenomenon of spatially concentrated (dis)advantage in the context of ideas of *neighborhood effects*.

CHAPTER OUTLINE

This chapter consists of three main sections. Section 6.1 introduces the concept of *neighborhood effects*, developed mostly in urban sociology to characterize racial and economic segregation in US cities and its consequences for human development. Section 6.2 analyzes patterns of neighborhood organization and service delivery in developing cities, especially in South Africa and Brazil, to find, as in the US, strong patterns of place-based inequality and connect these heterogeneities to processes of human development. Section 6.3 introduces a methodological framework to measure these effects in units of information and thus quantify residential choice and the strength of local selection one neighborhood at a time. We conclude the chapter with a discussion of what we know about spatial selection, the prospect of measuring it consistently in cities throughout the world, and the need for better knowledge on the consequences of exposure to diverse urban environments, especially during childhood.

6.1 HUMAN ECOLOGY AND NEIGHBORHOODS

The most developed literature at the neighborhood scale arose in the US in the context of "ecological" approaches to the city, especially those started by the Chicago School of Urban Sociology. We have already heard from Park and Burgess, the school's most famous members. Roderick McKenzie, in the third essay of *The City*, tells us about "the ecological approach to the study of the human community." He defines it as "the study of the spatial and temporal relations of human beings as affected by the selective, distributive and accommodative forces of the environment. . . . Society is made up of individuals socially separated, territorially distributed, and capable of independent locomotion. These spatial relationships of human beings are the product of competition and selection, and are continuously in the process of change as new factors enter to disturb the competitive relations or to facilitate mobility. Human institutions and human nature itself become accommodated to certain spatial relationships of human beings."[2]

All this is apparent to any keen observer of cities. Over the last century, there has been a lot of progress toward making these general observations clearer and the development of methods to study communities and neighborhoods within cities.

McKenzie makes two important conceptual points that apply to both general urban theory and many particular situations. The first deals with the nature of human ecology in cities. This is translated into the general expectation that socioeconomic outcomes pertaining to individuals are *not* the result of individual-level traits alone but depend instead on the opportunities, relationships, benefits, and costs experienced in their local (urban) environment. (We will develop a model of how this happens in chapter 9, but the stage was already set in chapter 4.) This has important implications for theory, modeling, and policy. It says that individual-level outcomes in cities cannot be solely attributed to individual virtues or pathologies. In other words, *good people can go bad* and, more hopefully, sometimes vice versa, *bad people can go good* depending on the environment. This situation is sometimes known as the *Lucifer effect*[3] in social psychology. The opposite of the Lucifer effect (sometimes described as *heroism*) requires that people be able to organize and act for the collective good, an idea sometimes referred to in sociology as *collective efficacy*. This concept is also related to *altruistic behavior*, a major theme in evolutionary theory of culture and society (chapters 7 and 9) and of *custodianship*.[4] Many of these concepts play important roles in neighborhoods.

The second point, connected to collective efficacy, is subtler and often leads to some controversy. It deals with the idea that apparent structural determinants of social problems such as racism, power, a "culture of violence," or a "culture of poverty" are not in themselves leading causal variables but instead are coemergent in certain contexts given systemic dynamics. This point is best illustrated by an argument from sociologist William Julius Wilson, whose landmark work *The Truly Disadvantaged* revived interest in *neighborhood effects* in order to discuss the rise of African American poverty ghettos in the 1970s and 1980s in US cities.[5]

6.1.1 NEIGHBORHOOD EFFECTS

The idea that neighborhoods influence their residents in many systemic fundamental ways has deep roots in the social sciences and has been discussed historically by many authors.[6] The revival of interest in modern studies of *neighborhood effects*, however, is often credited to William Julius Wilson's publication in 1987 of *The Truly Disadvantaged: The Inner City, the Underclass, and Public Policy*. The book performs a detailed empirical analysis of the changing economy of US cities, especially Chicago, in the 1970s and 1980s and of parallel transformations in neighborhood structure and the spatial concentration of African American poverty in inner-city neighborhoods (figures 6.1 and 6.2). Wilson's main point is that the resulting observed pattern—associating spatially concentrated poverty with African Americans—should not be primarily attributed to racism or racial segregation (as many on the political left contended) or to individual characteristics or decisions (as those on the political right emphasized).

Rather, he describes the pattern as a dynamic ecological effect, the result of a *vicious cycle* of change starting with a disproportionately biased employment specialization of African American men at the time in manufacturing jobs, the disappearance of those particular jobs because of economic recession and globalization, consequent impoverishment and family disintegration (or lack of formation, as unemployed males remained single), and the flight from decaying neighborhoods by middle-class residents (figure 6.3A). Wilson argued that if you run this cycle forward, you will obtain American-style inner-city ghettos. Measure individual characteristic associations and you will conclude that being African American and being a single head of household, among other individual factors, are the "causes" of poverty and violence. But Wilson's framework is fundamentally different. He argued that this sort of vicious cycle, amplifying certain individual characteristics and concentrating them spatially, is an absolutely general mechanism: it magnifies

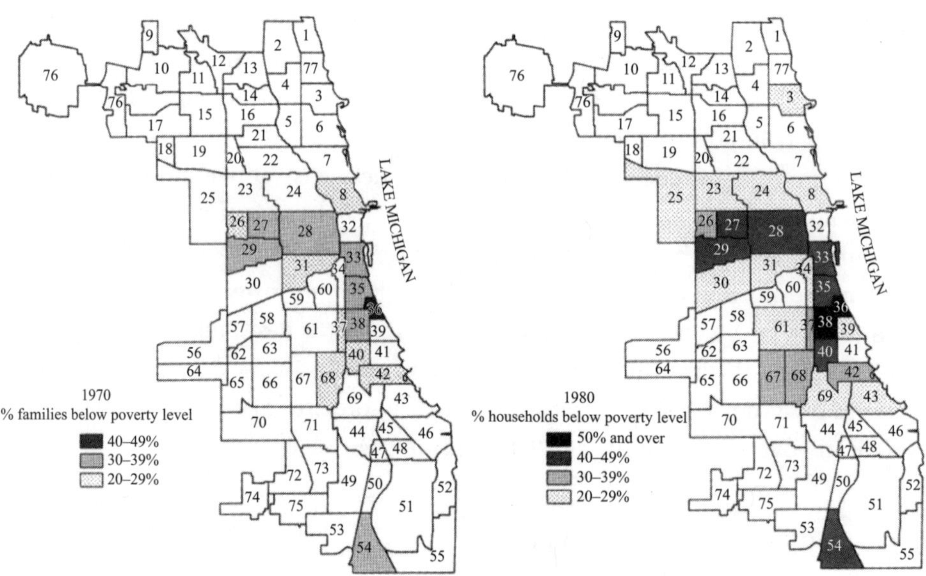

6.1 Percentage of households below poverty level (shades of gray, see legend) in Chicago community areas (numbered in the standard way, for example 32 = Loop, 41 = Hyde Park, 38 = Grand Boulevard) from 1970 to 1980. The map in 1980 mimics present spatial patterns of poverty in the city four decades later. *Source:* Adapted from *Local Community Fact Book: Chicago Metropolitan Area, 1970 and 1980*, edited by the Chicago Fact Book Consortium (Chicago: Chicago Review Press, 1984).

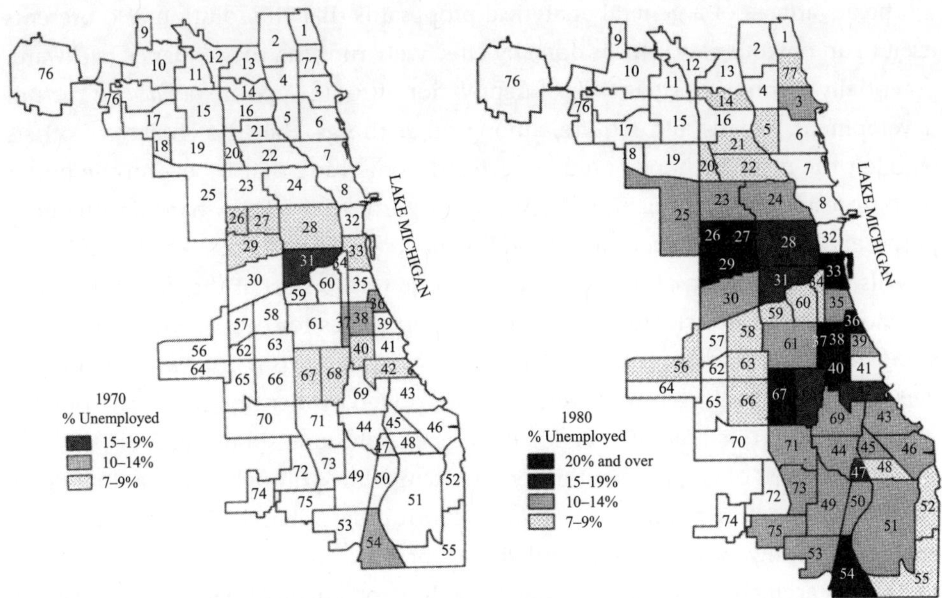

6.2 Unemployment rates in Chicago community areas from 1970 to 1980. Wilson's argument was that loss of employment triggered a vicious cycle of concentrated poverty in specific neighborhoods. To turn the situation around, employment programs for those whose jobs had disappeared was key. *Source*: Adapted from *Local Community Fact Book: Chicago Metropolitan Area, 1970 and 1980*, edited by the Chicago Fact Book Consortium (Chicago: Chicago Review Press, 1984).

a seemingly innocuous bias in the occupational structure by race or ethnicity into a full-fledged pattern of racially place-based concentrated poverty. In Wilson's own words, "the dwindling presence of middle- and working-class households in the *ghetto* makes it more difficult for the remaining residents of these communities to sustain basic formal and informal institutions in the face of high and prolonged joblessness and attendant economic hardships. And as the basic institutions decline, the social organization of inner-city ghetto neighborhoods disintegrates, further depleting the resources and limiting the life-chances of those who remain mired in these blighted areas."[7] Moreover, Wilson describes the condition of the remaining residents as a state of *social isolation*, meaning that their access to contacts with individuals of different classes and racial backgrounds becomes minimal and uncertain. Thus, these communities become deprived not only of income but more fundamentally of the connections that could allow them to make the most of the rich human ecology of their cities. As a consequence of these dynamics, the inner-city ghetto becomes a specialized ecological niche—with its own survival modes and behaviors—isolated from most of the rest of the opportunities of the city. It also becomes increasingly frozen in its ability to obtain resources and promote its own recovery and development.

The advantage of a general analytical proposal is that the solution also presents itself in an obvious way. This is done by effectively running the sequence backward, potentially turning a *vicious cycle* of deprivation into its opposite, a *virtuous cycle* of development. This would require, among other things, that the choices of others who left the neighborhood could be reversed, something that is beyond the power of local residents. Turning vicious cycles into virtuous cycles is hard and requires purposeful effort and a good understanding of system dynamics.

Wilson's own proposal for reversing the cycle was to start at the initial trigger of the vicious cycle and create employment opportunities for people who start out in a state of social isolation. He emphasized, however, that this point was often misunderstood in that such programs were not to be driven by identifying the race or even economic poverty status of individuals. Rather, solutions should address the root causes of the loss of employment in certain occupations through the creation of new employment and/or retraining or other opportunities. That such programs would end up targeting predominantly individuals of a certain race or ethnicity, gender, or age was accidental in the same way that the problems had been accidental, as a result of the extant occupational biases of some racial or ethnic groups as products of past history. By the same token, doing better than just reversing this specific cycle of isolation and poverty requires that biases in employment by race be abolished and that racism in all its forms vanish, so all individuals experience the same opportunities. This remains a major challenge for American cities as this book is being written.

Since Wilson's revival of the concept of neighborhood effects, many sociologists, economists, public health experts, and even political scientists have embraced the subject and searched for spatialized behaviors and patterns that may be systemic and self-reinforcing. Some of the best-known work updates and generalizes empirical findings and proposes new concepts associated with neighborhood effects; the reader is referred to a few excellent recent reviews.[8] One important general concept is the idea of *ecometrics*, proposed by Raudenbush, Sampson, and O'Brien[9] as measures of human ecological effects, especially in neighborhoods. The same authors also propose ways in which new ambient data from cell phones, surveys, and city records may be combined to provide systemic live assessments of the human ecology of different places.[10]

Associated with these ideas is the concept of *collective efficacy*, on which we now focus more specifically. Raudenbush and Sampson describe collective efficacy[11] as a type of informal social control, mediated by the intervention of individual residents, that may stop or mitigate many kinds of antisocial behavior. They propose ways to study collective efficacy in terms of emergent ecological quantities, such as *social cohesion* and *mutual trust*, among neighborhood residents, which they propose to measure via survey questionnaires, for example. This work came to prominence during a debate in the 1990s on the proximate causes of crime in US cities and how best to fight it. Around this time, there were intense debates about the controversial but politically appealing *broken windows* theory,[12] which proposed that stopping minor infractions such as graffiti and minor vandalism, often by tough use of police force and incarceration, would be effective in preventing more serious crimes. Raudenbush and Sampson argued instead that physical disorder is more a symptom than a cause, resulting, like crime, from lack of collective efficacy.[13] In this sense, they argue that the causal pathway from physical disorder to crime is spurious and that instead both disorder and crime are fairly "high bar" outcomes, typically preceded by many minor antisocial behaviors. Their point is the result of the analysis of evidence from the Project on Human Development in Chicago Neighborhoods,[14] a long-term study of the antecedents of antisocial and criminal behavior being conducted among a large group of people in a number of the city's neighborhoods. The contrast between these different perspectives on the causes of poverty and violence, and therefore the choice of interventions, is illustrated in terms of schematic *causal graphs* in figure 6.3. Causal graphs are a formal way to reason about cause-and-effect probabilistic relations (probabilistic models) in complex phenomena.[15] I find them particularly useful in clarifying hypotheses in social theory.

Finally, another fundamental process connected to neighborhood effects is the concept of *cumulative (dis)advantage*.[16] Cumulative (dis)advantage is the result of the virtuous, and more often vicious, cycles that connect spatial concentration with an amplification of positive or negative individual-level outcomes over time. These concepts integrate the effects of neighborhood environments on individuals throughout their life courses. This has the clearest consequences in terms of criminal behavior[17] and health.[18]

This discussion exposes essential questions about "prime mover" effects in socioeconomic processes and especially on interrelated issues of human development, crime, and spatially concentrated poverty in urban neighborhoods. The ecological approach emphasizes a much more sophisticated web of causal structure than individual-level attributes or structural determinism (racism, power), with feedbacks that typically lead to vicious and virtuous cycles of change for both individuals and places.

Disentangling variables that may be prime movers (inputs) for spinning up or down these cycles versus those that are links in amplifying chains is essential for creating systemic effective solutions for *wicked problems*[19] of human development.

Policy Application: Moving to Opportunity and Cumulative Environmental Exposure   The idea of neighborhood effects has remained somewhat unsettled in terms of mechanism but has led to some singular important policy interventions. The most famous of these was Moving to Opportunity (MOT),[20] a US government program in the 1990s.

Moving to Opportunity was a randomized social experiment involving about 4,600 low-income families with children living in public housing in poor neighborhoods, the kind of accumulated disadvantage situation identified by Wilson. Families who chose to enter the program were randomly assigned to one of three groups. The first

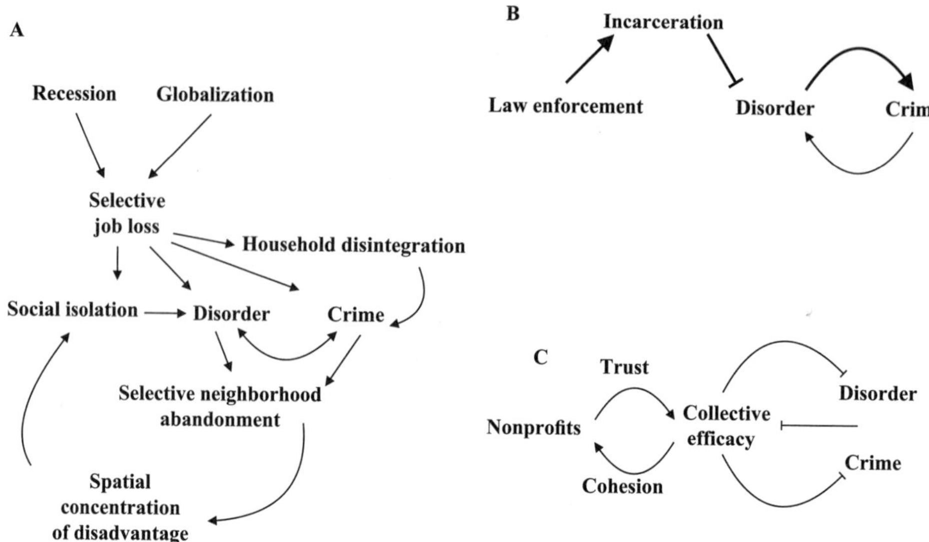

6.3 Schematic causal graphs for hypothesized explanations of spatially concentrated poverty and its connection to crime. Arrows mean positive causal influences, whereas ⊣ means a damping causal relationship. (A) Wilson's view of selective employment loss as concentrating disadvantage. (B) "Broken windows" theories posit that suppressing minor disorders via harsh law enforcement controls more serious crimes. (C) Collective efficacy as the centerpiece of social control, mediated by trust and social cohesion where individuals are willing to intervene, possibly aided by community organizations and nonprofits. Clearly, depending on which theory of crime one adopts, the target variable for causal intervention becomes very different: jobs, disorder suppression via law enforcement, or supporting collective efficacy via the nonprofit sector for (A), (B), and (C), respectively. Note that (B) and (C) may be incompatible if policing erodes trust but compatible if it somehow supports collective efficacy, though likely not via incarceration.

two groups received housing vouchers (to help pay for some of their rent), which could be used only in low-income neighborhoods (group 1) versus anywhere (group 2). Group 1 also received counseling to find rental units and were allowed to use their vouchers anywhere after the first year. The third group was a control and received no vouchers but remained eligible for other social assistance programs. The study was run in five major US cities: Baltimore, Boston, Chicago, Los Angeles, and New York City.[21]

General expectations of the experiment were to demonstrate a broad spectrum of improvements in the conditions of families able to move to lower-poverty neighborhoods relative to the control groups. The program was mandated to specifically evaluate impacts on housing, incomes, and education of the family members involved. The vast majority of program participants were African American and Hispanic single mothers with children. Ethnographic studies revealed some of the motivations for the participants, which were mostly to escape danger and mental and emotional stresses above and beyond "moving to opportunity."[22]

The initial statistical analysis of the outcome of the experiment was disappointing. The most significant, but relatively small, finding was that of better mental health and a feeling of improved well-being among those who moved to lower-poverty neighborhoods.[23] However, there were no significantly positive effects in either educational attainment or economic earnings.[24] In fact, there was an initial dip in employment in the first two years that vanished over time but did not translate into manifestly positive results. The study, which did engage with fundamental questions in the social sciences besides aiming at practical policy,[25] was also criticized for being unrepresentative given those who enrolled and was somewhat naive in terms of exploring the mechanisms by which moving between neighborhoods with different characteristics does or does not affect people's lives, including those of children, over time.[26]

For a few years, the story remained there. However, much more interesting findings were found hidden under the econometric covers, so to speak. It turns out that the initial statistical assessments of the MOT data had pooled together effects on children at different ages, but the length and stage of exposure to neighborhoods with more resources was actually critical, an effect that had been washed out by earlier data treatments. (The moral of the story is that the data won't just speak to you; you have to ask good questions.) In 2015, a group of economists led by Raj Chetty, Nathaniel Hendry, and Lawrence Katz stratified their analysis by the age at which children had moved to the new neighborhood and their length of exposure to the new environment.[27] They found very significant results in terms of later economic effects on children who moved when they were young and no effects, or even negative ones, on children who moved to lower-poverty environments in their late teens (figure 6.4). These insights were also bolstered by the group's main research effort, which uses tax records over about four decades to assess the effects later in life of where in America people grew up.[28] The effects of early moves and longer exposure to less deprived neighborhoods are clear in this much larger dataset of millions of people. Moreover, the consequences are broad, involving higher incomes later in life, higher probability of being married, greater likelihood of attending college, better health, and fewer teenage pregnancies.[29]

The main conclusion of these empirical analyses—made possible by experiments but above all from *big data* on human development—is that people learn from and adapt to their local environments and that such adaptations in childhood often set the course for the rest of their lives. Neighborhood characteristics are critically important during childhood and are cumulative over the life course, being manifested in adult incomes, health, or relationships much later in life. The mechanisms by which these effects accumulate (dis)advantage over the long term and how disorder, crime, mental health,[30] opportunity, income, and the physical characteristics of neighborhoods are interrelated remain to be better understood. Creating more enlightened systemic public policy supporting long-term self-reinforcing dynamics that create positive neighborhood effects for all urban residents is a fundamental problem for human development in cities.

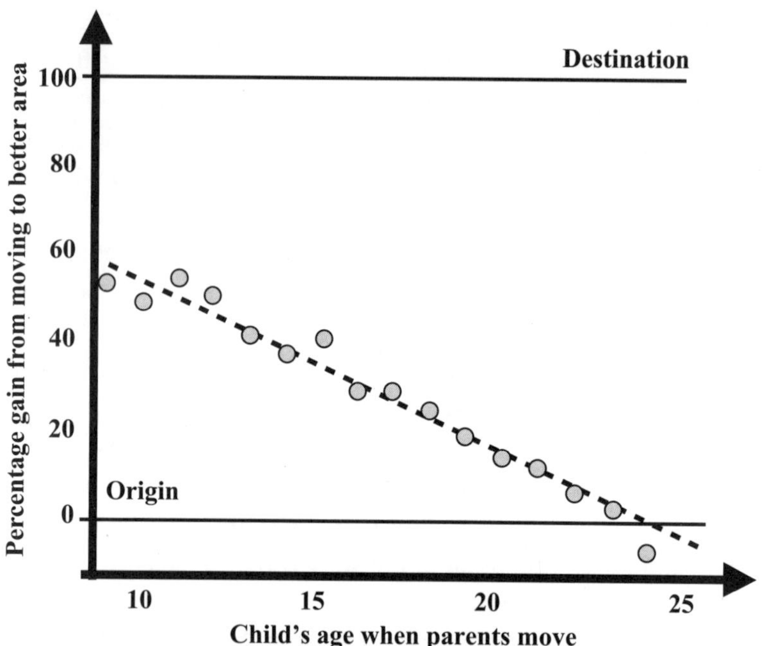

6.4 Cumulative effects on children from exposure to different neighborhood environments.
Source: Adapted from Raj Chetty and Nathaniel Hendren, "The Impacts of Neighborhoods on Intergenerational Mobility II: County-Level Estimates," *Quarterly Journal of Economics* 133, no. 3 (August 1, 2018): 1163–1228, https://doi.org/10.1093/qje/qjy006.

6.1.2 THE SCHELLING MODEL OF NEIGHBORHOOD SEGREGATION

While empirical studies of neighborhood characteristics are essential, there has been a parallel tradition of seeking simple models of residential choice that can account for observed (in a loose sense) segregated neighborhoods, starting from relatively few assumptions. This was typical of early approaches to complex systems, developed under the logic that *simple rules can lead to complex emergent behavior*. The reference mathematical model for these effects is due to economist Thomas Schelling and is referred to as the *Schelling model*.[31]

The Schelling model has several variations in terms of implementation but in its simplest form considers a two-dimensional checkerboard plane, where people of two types, say o and #, are distributed spatially (figure 6.5). The fractions of o and # are assumed fixed, so all that can happen is for individuals to move around. The model's "dynamic" decision rule is that people of one type do not like to be in the minority (below a chosen threshold) among their neighbors. So, for example, a person of type o does not like to be surrounded by #s and will attempt to move if in such a situation. Usually, movements incur no costs as long as there is an empty spot on the board where the individual in question can move to. The model is initialized in some given (random) configuration and iterated until it reaches a late stage where no additional moves are possible or necessary because all agents are satisfied. The typical end state is one with coarse spatial clusters of each type in space, so there are neighborhoods

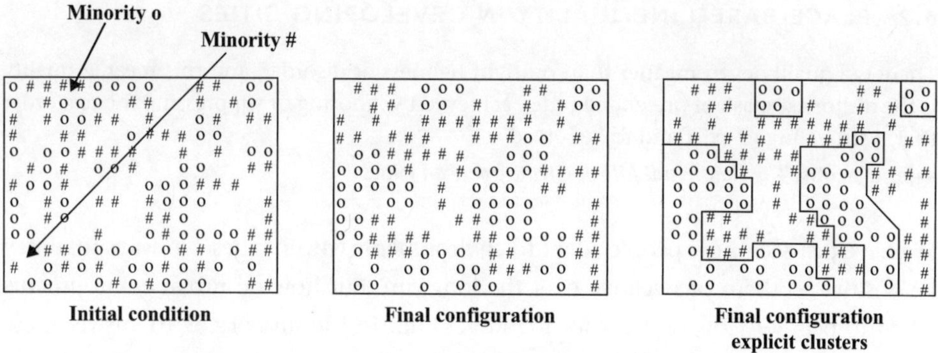

6.5 Schematic illustration of the Schelling model of residential segregation. The model posits that residents of a given type will move to an available empty space if they find themselves a minority type relative to their neighbors. The "minority" threshold may vary, as do many other characteristics of models of this type. The iterated "dynamics" over time tends to produce spatial clusters segregated by type, as identified in the rightmost panel.
Source: Adapted from Thomas C. Schelling, "Dynamic Models of Segregation," *Journal of Mathematical Sociology* 1, no. 2 (July 1971): 143–186, https://doi.org/10.1080/0022250X.1971.9989794.

of all *o*s and other neighborhoods of all #s. The point of the model is to demonstrate that a simple rule—where agents dislike being a type minority—leads to emergent citywide neighborhood segregation (figure 6.5).

The Schelling model has been immensely appealing to computationally oriented social scientists and consequently exists in many variants. At its heart, the Schelling model is intimately connected to models of physical magnets, such as the Ising model in physics, specified under conservation laws that preserve the fraction of types in a population.[32] Many results and generalizations can be co-opted from mappings to the statistical physics literature.[33]

Sociologists have investigated whether simple binary decisions about residence given neighbor types are typical or realistic observed behavior. They have also explored the possible consequences of softening the simple ingredients of the Schelling model. In general, it is now known that residential decisions are more subtle and more random[34] and that the introduction of continuous choice (either because we may be considering continuous types such as income, because choice thresholds vary, or because the types are multidimensional) softens the transition to strong segregation and may indeed destroy it,[35] even under certain relatively mild conditions.[36]

What these models—simple as they are—help us see is that the overall spatial distributions of types within cities can be relatively fluid and very sensitive to simple (binary) preferences for homophily or barriers to integration, such as racist or classist policies. In all these cases, segregated neighborhoods can easily emerge, even from apparently mild local choices, leading to very different lives well into the future. To better appreciate these issues, it is now time to turn to data and to a systematic study of type distributions in real cities.

6.2 PLACE-BASED INEQUALITY IN DEVELOPING CITIES

There is a quality even meaner than outright ugliness or disorder, and this meaner quality is the dishonest mask of pretended order, achieved by ignoring or suppressing the real order that is struggling to exist and to be served.

—Jane Jacobs, *The Death and Life of Great American Cities*

We have just seen how people adapt to environments within cities—in ways that may be positive to them or negative over the long run. But how do urban environments adapt to people? How do they form and get built in the first place? To answer these questions, we will refer to history in chapter 7 and, in this section, to neighborhoods in developing cities. Such cities are still building much of their infrastructure and services, so they are often characterized by neighborhoods in transition—such as informal settlements or slums—with only incipient connections to the rest of the city in terms of the networks of chapter 3. These contexts also paint neighborhood effects, policies, and mechanisms of collective efficacy in a new light that forces us into a broader international perspective relative to studies of US cities and their particular histories.

6.2.1 THE CASE FOR LOCALIZING URBAN SUSTAINABLE DEVELOPMENT

From the point of view of fast-growing cities today, especially in Asia, Africa, and Latin America, there are three fundamental reasons to approach development at the neighborhood scale. This is sometimes referred to as *localizing sustainable development* and, in the context of United Nations' Agenda 2030, of *localizing Sustainable Development Goals (SDGs)*.[37] These three reasons are equity, design, and collective efficacy.

Equity and Distributional Effects   In terms of equity, most inequality in cities is spatially concentrated and takes place between neighborhoods. Measuring any development goals at the national, city, and neighborhood levels therefore has very different consequences. Large-scale averages will hide extremes, especially those associated with cumulative disadvantage. Thus, development policies and other solutions designed to avoid so-called *distributional effects* need to disaggregate populations across space and be concerned with different development patterns and outcomes in different places and for different people. This resonates with Jane Jacobs's recommendation to avoid dealing with averaged behavior.

As the name indicates, the term *distributional effects* relates to quantities beyond the mean. They are studied by analyzing higher statistical moments (such as the variance), inequality indices (such as the Gini coefficient), or by characterizing frequency or probability distributions (such as for income or life expectancy). The discussion of distributional effects has become particularly relevant in the context of policies on the environment and public goods provision and their different effects on distinct segments of the population, especially when stratified by income.[38] A pervasive concern in the literature is whether policies are *regressive*, meaning that they impose a disproportionate burden on poorer populations, such as happens with consumption taxes[39] or flat fees for basic services such as water or power.

The discussion of distributional effects can be characterized in terms of the types of policies attempted, the typology of the population to be served (e.g., income groups), and the level of spatial aggregation in the analysis. Most past studies relied on relatively high levels of spatial aggregation within developed nations or were limited to just a few places.

The study of environmental quality in cities was one of the earliest to emphasize distributional effects related to air quality in the US.[40] It was established that poor air quality disproportionally impacted the poor (and certain other populations at risk), and therefore policies for improving air quality should be more targeted in order to disproportionally improve the lives of those at greater risk.

Similar concerns and more contemporary methods of analysis have been used to foresee or measure the impacts of other sustainable development policies. For example, Bitler and her colleagues[41] analyzed the distributional consequences of specific welfare reforms in Connecticut and found that policy results are more varied and more extensive than when evaluated in terms of means. Similarly, Hammer and his colleagues studied the impacts of social sector policies in Malaysia[42] between 1974 and 1989, particularly investments in education, finding that those policies targeted at universal primary education have had tremendous progressive consequences over the long term, while others had less impact. Thus, the analysis of the heterogeneity of effects of policies provides a finer and often more insightful view of processes and aids policy design and assessment.

A number of recent studies have analyzed distributional effects resulting from the privatization of services in Bolivia[43] and the UK,[44] water-pricing models in São Paulo,[45] environmental and renewable energy policies in Germany,[46] and road congestion charges in the US.[47] Studies of household consumption, as it relates to greenhouse gas emissions, have also been analyzed in terms of their heterogeneity.[48] The overall conclusions from all these studies are that there is strong heterogeneity in patterns of consumption and emissions across households with different socioeconomic status and that policies and assessments that forgo distributional analyses will be unnecessarily blunt and may generate unintended consequences, such as being regressive. Most past analyses of the distributional impacts of specific development policies, however, apply to entire nations at once, without performing a scale-dependent disaggregation or emphasizing diverse urban areas and their constituent neighborhoods.

Urban Design and Accountability The second issue motivating the localization of processes of development has to do with the role of local information in the processes of urban planning and design and whether proposed solutions meet their intended objectives.

The holy grail of architecture and urban design is to be able to work with local information, close to people and their needs.[49] Architects and urbanists often admire vernacular architecture, buildings and neighborhoods created in traditional ways by common builders, because of their organic quality, their human scale, and the rich pattern of functionality and human expression that these processes generate.[50] Everyone's favorite urban settings, whether in Florence, Kyoto, Cairo, or Mexico City, have this organic character, which evolved through the actions of many stakeholders over a long time. This is very hard to do using conventional urban planning, especially in poor neighborhoods, where formal designers often create the dullest, cheapest, ugliest solutions as a result of limited budgets and a remedial attitude toward policy, echoing Jane Jacobs's quotation at the beginning of this section. Such policy interventions almost always produce unlivable environments over the long term and generate poverty traps in the short term, as they fail to be accountable to the development objectives they were meant to meet.

Thus, working at the neighborhood level in ways that are "evolutionary," upgrading and promoting improvements in the built environment whenever and wherever possible, is often a better strategy. It was the preferred approach at the birth of modern planning, as proposed by Patrick Geddes,[51] for example. It requires that architects and planners become coproducers, with communities and local governments, of urban design solutions. It also requires that necessarily incremental interventions create traction in terms of long-term tangible measures of development for the communities involved, while at the same time not being so narrow or technical as to preclude human expression and serendipity. This is very hard to do citywide or nationwide, but it is perfectly possible—even easy—at the neighborhood scale.

Community Organization, Collective Efficacy, and Politics   Politics is often blamed for making the possible impossible, for its glacial pace of decision making, the madness of crowds, and other ailments, but the etymology of *politics* is just "the stuff of cities." Politics is an essential part of city life and indeed a necessary means for human communities to solve problems of collective action. I will refer to this more aspirational sense of the term as *Politics* (with a capital *P*). Urban science should have been called politics—in analogy with physics or economics—but it is probably too late. Here we merely want to point out that neighborhoods are ideal environments that make community organization possible and natural and that consequently can create practical Politics for human sustainable development.

In the US, Saul Alinsky is often considered the "founder of modern community organization." He is also a bridge between the Chicago School of Sociology—having taken courses with Park, Burgess, and others—and the manifestly nonacademic world of neighborhood communities. His work was focused on devising nonviolent but provocative strategies to call attention to the living conditions of people in poor neighborhoods and demand change. His work was concentrated in working-class neighborhoods and especially in black ghettos in Chicago and other American cities.

His book *Rules for Radicals* still reads fresh today; it is full of humor and enlightened advice for those wanting to change the world from the bottom up. His strategy is "evolutionary," playing with existing structures but at the same time attempting to subvert them. In his own words: "As an organizer I start from where the world is, as it is, not as I would like it to be. That we accept the world as it is does not in any sense weaken our desire to change it into what we believe it should be—it is necessary to begin where the world is if we are going to change it to what we think it should be. That means working in the system."[52]

Alinsky's tactics and principles were confrontational and controversial, even among other community organizers, including, famously, a young Barack Obama. But because his approach tends to be confrontational, the qualities of his and other similar approaches sometimes lead to gridlock and stasis, whereby stakeholders become entrenched in mutual opposition and fail to see potential positive outcomes for themselves and their city. Politics as a process freezes and so does development.

In my view, the subsequent reinvention of these ideas and of modern community organization in Asia and Africa addressed some of the shortcomings of these approaches, at least in part. Figure 6.6 distills the principles of another legendary community organizer, Jockin Arputham, who started out organizing informal settlement communities (slums) in Mumbai, India. These principles were written down by Celine D'Cruz, another extraordinary community organizer, who learned much of

Principles of Community Organization according to Jockin Arputham

1. Begin with the poorest and most vulnerable communities to ensure all are included.
2. The greater the vulnerability, the greater the motivation of the community to act and bring change.
3. By organizing communities into networks and federations according to the lands they occupy, it is easy to manage the large numbers of urban poor in the city.
4. When communities organize citywide, they bring together their collective knowledge and resources to address their specific and collective needs.
5. Caring for each other develops capacity to think about each other's problems and solutions.
6. Collective savings and information are essential tools to organize communities and build their collective power.
7. When communities do their homework and organize, they build capacity to find alternative solutions that work for themselves and the city.
8. When communities are prepared with facts and workable solutions, it builds trust and opens the doors for engagement with government.
9. Women are natural organizers. Their instinct to protect their children and families makes them invaluable agents of change.
10. By creating separate and safe spaces for women to organize, young and adult women do not have to compete with the traditional leadership.
11. When members of the community build trust in each other, they can solve big and small problems.
12. Regular community meetings and exchanges open the space for collective learning, reflection, and consolidation.
13. When communities implement projects, they build capacity to influence policy and practice.
14. Everything is workable when communities are organized.

6.6 Principles of community organization at the National Slum Dwellers Federation (India) and Slum Dwellers International.
Source: Described by Jockin Arputham and compiled by Celine D'Cruz.

her trade from Arputham and the many people at the National Slum Dwellers Federation (India) and Slum Dwellers International (SDI). SDI took these ideas, which continued to evolve and mesh with technology and new contexts, to many other nations, especially in Africa. Today, SDI federates community organizations across 33 nations in Asia, Africa, Latin America, and the Caribbean.

Notice, among many other interesting things, the emphasis and innovation on at least three critical issues: first, the explicit strategy of identification of positive outcomes for people, communities, and their cities; second, the networked, multiscale character of the organizations, with citywide (and eventually worldwide with SDI) peer-to-peer connections being critically empowering to local processes in each place; and third, a focus on specific processes (savings), facts, and information, which in time (via SDI) would constitute the largest census-like dataset on slum communities in the world. Data in this context is not a cold technocratic commodity but a means for various self-reinforcing ends. This includes community organization itself, building trust and therefore collective efficacy, but also identifying common problems objectively and "speaking the language" of governments and bureaucracies, while at the same time outdoing them in terms of the quality of the evidence. In this way, information and data become part of the solution to complicated antagonistic stakeholder coordination problems. In other words, data becomes one of the mechanisms of Politics, not a tool of technocratic oppression.

This approach has been so successful that it has spread throughout SDI's international network and, with variations, has been adopted by many other organizations throughout the world. In my own research practice, this approach has allowed us to create collaborations between slum dwellers, researchers, technologists, and others that can produce state-of-the-art surveys, enumerations, maps, and data archives that support processes of human development at the neighborhood level. The key is that data and technology start out as part of existing processes of collective organization and action working to serve community practices and empowering them by making some of the aspects of the work easier and more reliable. The result so far has been the mapping and enumeration of tens of thousands of slum neighborhoods, which in many cases constitute a full self-reported record of all such neighborhoods in given cities (see figure 6.7).

We see that this type of community organization has now achieved a worldwide dimension capable of connecting individual slum dwellers in the poorest urban neighborhoods in Africa or Asia with each other and with research and policy resources anywhere in the world. More fundamentally, this approach represents, in my view, the spontaneous convergence of scientific methods and community organization practices, whereby neighborhood residents working together ask questions, collect evidence, create hypotheses, and propose solutions that are tested and improved systematically in networks involving many places and millions of people. SDI communities often chant the motto that "Knowledge Is Power." This power can

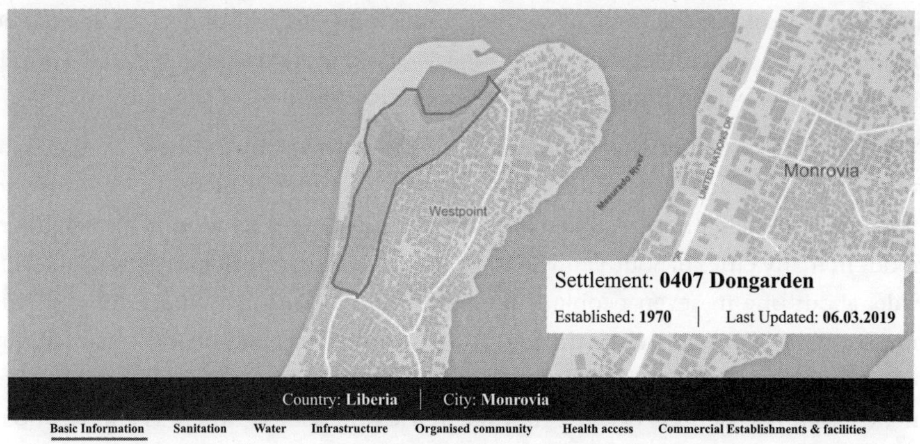

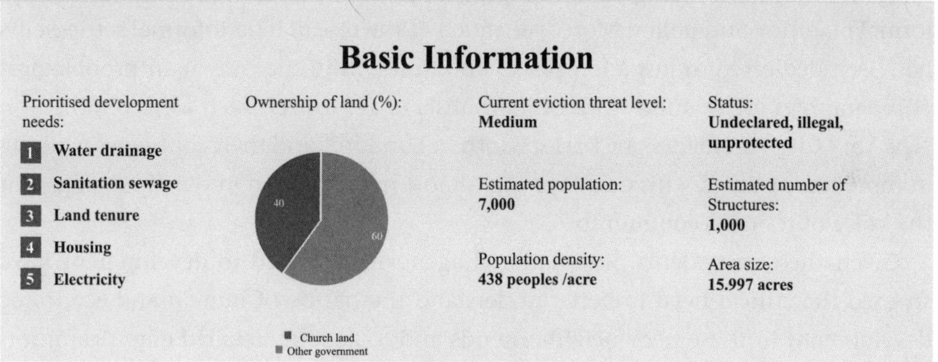

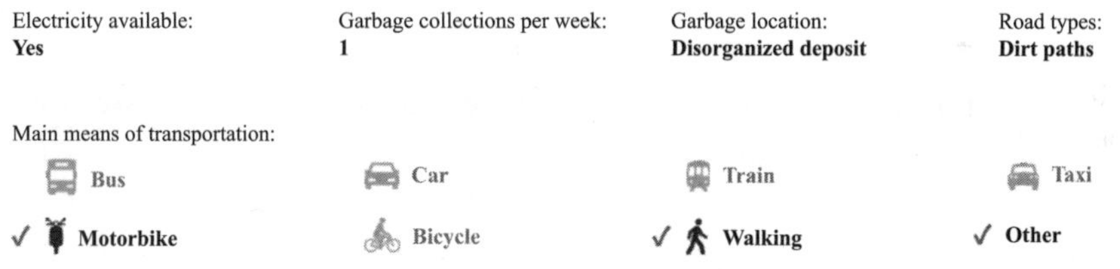

6.7 Settlement profile of Dongarden, an informal settlement in Monrovia, Liberia. Over the last few years, thousands of slums have been mapped and characterized by their own communities throughout the world, raising the prospect of an empirically rich, collaborative, and community driven development process in millions of neighborhoods worldwide.
Source: Slum Dwellers International Know Your City campaign (knowyourcity.info).

change the world in the sense of creating a much deeper, real understanding of the human condition in cities and unleashing faster and more sustainable parallel development processes in millions of neighborhoods worldwide.

The Challenge of Slums: Neighborhood Priorities in Developing Cities To illustrate some of the consequences of this kind of work, consider its impact as a bridge to other kinds of data analysis. Slums constitute a substantial fraction of all neighborhoods in many cities of South and Southeast Asia and in sub-Saharan Africa.[53] Worldwide, about one in seven people is presently estimated to live in a slum, but this number rises to one in two or three in parts of South Asia and Africa.[54] In a famous report in 2003 titled *The Challenge of Slums*, UN-Habitat called these informal settlements "zones of silence," because they felt at the time that so little was known about these communities, at least in terms of the official statistics traditionally used for formal planning and policy. Moreover, much of the research on informal settlements had been dedicated to just a few places and times, as in the case of anthropological ethnographies, or was the work of journalists or reformers, such as Jacob Riis[55] on New York City tenements or Charles Booth in London[56] and their colleagues working in more recent times. This evidence was almost never created in the "first tense," in the voice of resident communities.

Given these precedents, international agencies dedicated to development have stressed the critical need to better understand the nature of human and economic development in these poor neighborhoods and to acquire detailed empirical information on their primary needs and priorities.[57] However, extensive direct information on residents' priorities is still rare.

Recent efforts in this direction by SDI communities (figure 6.7) provide insights on the most important development needs expressed by residents[58] answering the same consistent surveys in many different contexts. Table 6.1 and figure 6.8C show priorities expressed by residents of 677 neighborhoods in 10 nations and 59 cities, mostly in sub-Saharan Africa. These data pertain to large and fast-growing urban areas, such as Lagos, Nairobi, Dar-es-Salaam, Kampala, Blantyre, Freetown, Johannesburg, Cape Town, and Windhoek.

While there is broad agreement among communities on the most important priorities, there are also a number of differences across nations and cities. Overall, water and drainage is the most frequent problem, mentioned 36.9% of the time, followed by issues of housing (21.3%), sanitation and sewage (13.9%), land tenure (13.7%), and electricity (6.2%). These priorities emphasize the dual role of basic services and improved housing in promoting the resilience of communities against both chronic stresses and extreme events,[59] such as flooding. Other issues, related to health, transportation, waste collection, jobs, and education, also come up frequently but are stated as comparatively less critical. Apart from the issue of land tenure, all others deal with daily living challenges and are intimately connected to inclusion in the networks of their cities, specifically through access to improved basic services.

Table 6.1 Self-identified community development priorities from 677 informal settlement profiles in 10 nations and 59 cities

Priorities	Total	Nations							
		South Africa	Tanzania	Kenya	Uganda	Malawi	Namibia	Sierra Leone	Nigeria
All	677	26.90%	26.70%	22.20%	13.10%	4.40%	2.70%	1.60%	1.50%
Water and drainage	36.90%	20.30%	43.50%	33.30%	57.30%	76.70%	11.10%	81.80%	10.00%
Housing	21.30%	44.00%	2.80%	32.00%	5.60%	0%	11.10%	0%	10.00%
Sanitation and sewage	13.90%	8.20%	14.90%	10.70%	27.00%	16.70%	27.80%	0%	0%
Land tenure	13.70%	18.70%	4.40%	21.30%	4.50%	3.33%	33.30%	9.10%	60.00%
Electricity	6.20%	8.20%	8.30%	1.30%	4.50%	0%	16.70%	0%	20.00%
Others	7.80%	0.50%	27.10%	1.30%	1.10%	0%	0%	9.10%	0%

Note: There are 10 nations and 59 cities in the dataset. Four neighborhoods in the Philippines and two in Ghana are not shown but are included in the totals.

These findings resonate with most measures of sustainable development,[60] to which we now turn using extensive census data from two large middle-income nations: Brazil and South Africa.

6.2.2 ACCESS TO SERVICES IN NEIGHBORHOODS OF BRAZIL AND SOUTH AFRICA

Because the priorities expressed by slum dwellers in table 6.1 are mostly about urban services and the condition of homes and buildings, we can sometimes extend the analysis of these deficits of development using systematic data from official sources. As an example, we can analyze patterns of neighborhood development in a range of low- and middle-income cities in Brazil and South Africa, where good official census data allow us to perform a complete comparative assessment of access to services across all neighborhoods. To do this in a synthetic way, let us create a summary index of development, X_i, for neighborhood i, as

$$X_i = \sqrt[4]{X_i^{water}\, X_i^{electricity}\, X_i^{sanitation}\, X_i^{homes}}, \tag{6.1}$$

where X_i^{water} is the fraction of the population in neighborhood i with access to an improved *water* source (such as piped city water). Similarly, the superscripts *electricity*, *sanitation*, and *homes* refer to access to electrical power, improved sanitation, and permanent housing. We can now measure this index across scales, from neighborhoods to cities and nations. We will refer to the components of X_i collectively as *services*. As defined, the index is bounded between $X_i = 0$, when at least one of the services is completely missing, and $X_i = 1$, when there is universal access to all services within area i. The multiplicative character of the index—it is the geometric mean of the various factors—emphasizes that all its components are essential to achieving a desired level of development, much as in a typical production function[61] or the construction of the Human Development Index[62] (figure 1.3). This is also consistent with UN-Habitat's definition of a "slum household" as a household that lacks access to *any* one of these services and with their construction of a composite *secure tenure index.*[63]

The multiplicative character of the index, X, has another distinct advantage: additional dimensions of sustainable development can be easily included in the product without changing the definition as a geometric mean (equation 6.1). Possible extensions of this analysis include other sustainable development goals, such as education or gender equality (goals 4 and 5), or the fraction of the population using clean energy.

Figure 6.8A gives a first impression of the spatial heterogeneity of X_i by showing a map of South Africa, highlighting its metropolitan areas, each consisting of hundreds of neighborhoods (see also figures 6.9–6.11 for more details on South African and Brazilian cities).

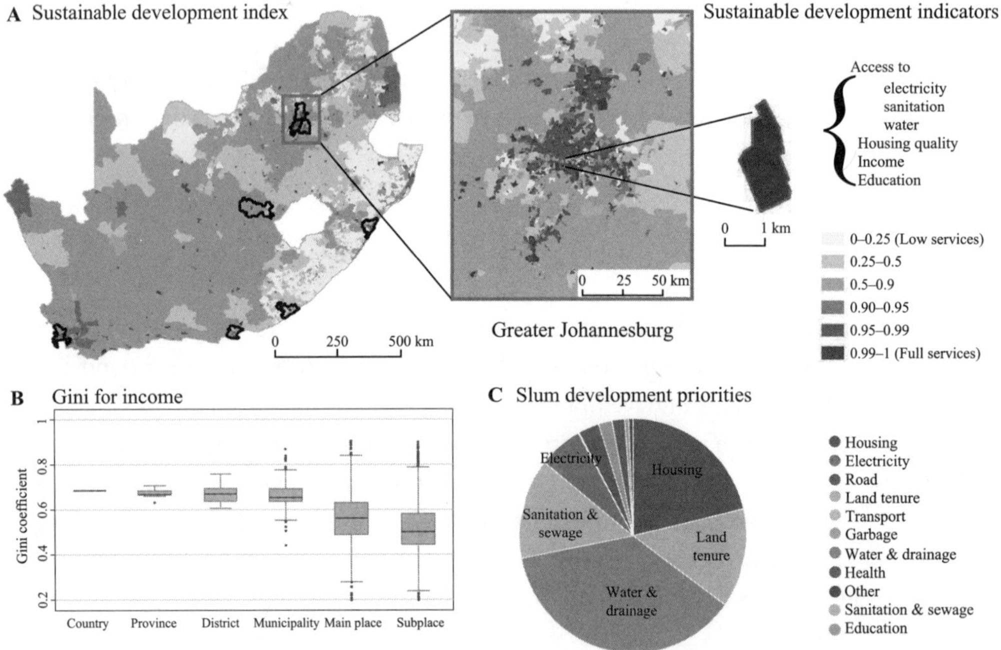

6.8 Heterogeneity and scale of sustainable development in cities. (A) The sustainable development index, X_i, at the subplace level for all of South Africa, the Johannesburg metropolitan area, and a single neighborhood. (B) Values of the Gini coefficient for income across scales for South Africa. The median across all units of analysis within a class is shown by a horizontal black line, with the twenty-fifth to seventy-fifth percentiles (gray box). We see that the highest levels of inequality occur at the city (municipal) level and are smaller within neighborhoods. (C) Development priorities identified by slum residents in the 10 countries of table 6.1.

Source: Adapted from Christa Brelsford et al., "Heterogeneity and Scale of Sustainable Development in Cities," *Proceedings of the National Academy of Sciences* 114, no. 34 (May 1, 2017): 8963–8968, https://doi.org/10.1073/pnas.1606033114.

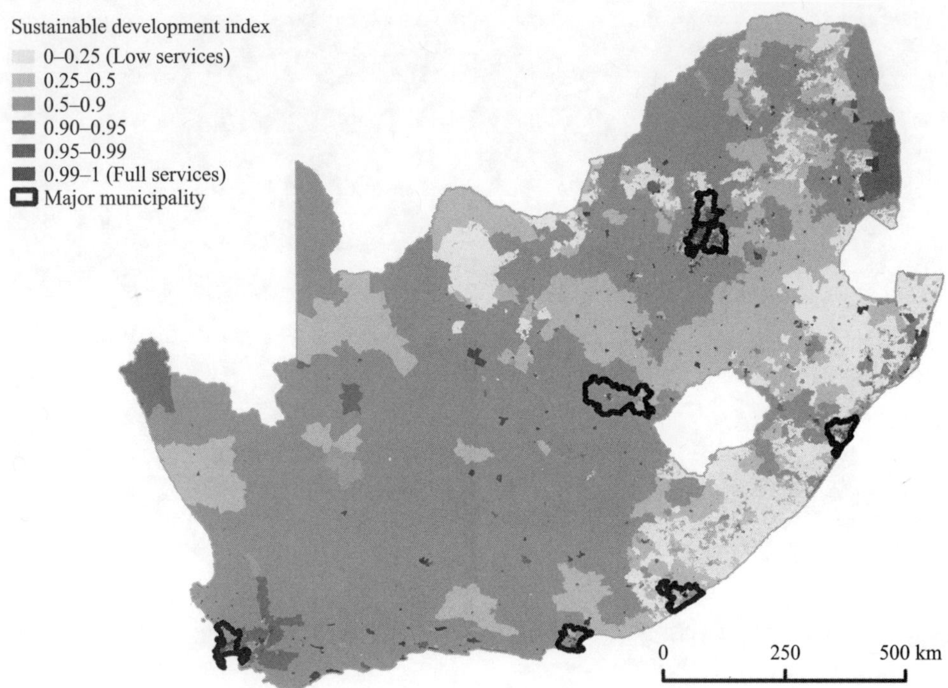

6.9 Map of South Africa showing the nationwide distribution of the sustainable development index. Shades of gray show values of the sustainable development index, *X*, which varies from the total absence of services (white) to universal access (darkest shade). Note that despite their small geographic size, large cities are much more likely than rural areas to have high levels of services (figures 6.10 and 6.11). Note also the positive role played by other small cities relative to the countryside. *Source*: Adapted from Christa Brelsford et al., "Heterogeneity and Scale of Sustainable Development in Cities," *Proceedings of the National Academy of Sciences* 114, no. 34 (May 1, 2017): 8963–8968, https://doi.org/10.1073/pnas.1606033114.

What is most critical about this sort of analysis is that measuring any sustainable development characteristic—such as access to basic services—at different scales results in different levels of heterogeneity expressed by measures of inequality such as the Gini index, which is generally large at the citywide level but smaller within neighborhoods (figure 6.8B). In other words, this means that most inequality in cities is expressed across—not within—neighborhoods, much as we could have expected from the preceding discussion of inequities in US cities.

Figure 6.12A shows total income for the metropolitan areas of South Africa and Brazil versus their population size (see also table 6.2). These units of analysis are analogous to other functional city definitions, such as Metropolitan Statistical Areas (MSAs) in the US and in OECD countries (chapter 2). In Brazil, they typically include many (political) municipalities, whereas in South Africa they are made up of a single large municipality, with the possible exception of Greater Johannesburg (figure 6.10 and table 6.2). Figure 6.12A and table 6.2 show the scaling results for the two nations as well as their combined behavior (after centering the regression

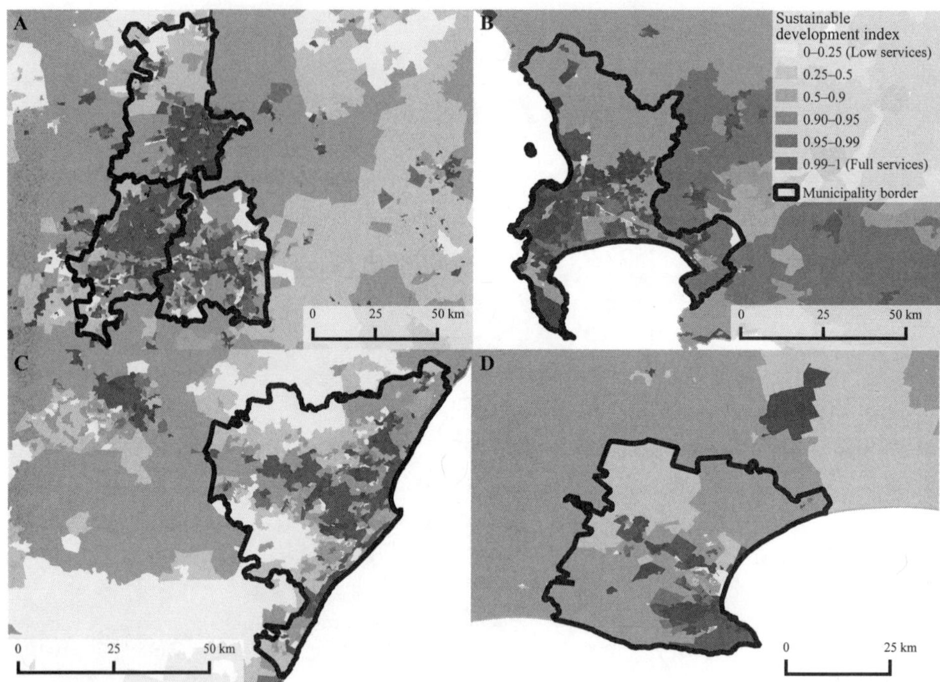

6.10 Sustainable development index distribution in selected South African metropolitan areas. Each panel shows the estimated sustainable development index, X_i, at the subplace level (neighborhood). (A) Johannesburg area, which includes the city of Johannesburg metropolitan area, Ekurhuleni metropolitan area (East Rand), and the city of Tshwane metropolitan area (Pretoria). (B) City of Cape Town metropolitan area. (C) and (D) show the metropolitan areas for eThekwini (Durban) and Nelson Mandela (Port Elizabeth), respectively. With the exception of Cape Town, widespread access to services is generally concentrated within metropolitan areas and in the denser central parts of those cities. *Source*: Adapted from Christa Brelsford et al., "Heterogeneity and Scale of Sustainable Development in Cities," *Proceedings of the National Academy of Sciences* 114, no. 34 (May 1, 2017): 8963–8968, https://doi.org/10.1073/pnas.1606033114.

and pooling the data, following the procedures introduced in chapter 4). The scaling exponent $\beta=1.11$ estimated for Brazil is very similar to that for the US and to the scaling of GDP for Brazilian metropolitan areas.[64] The relatively large number of metropolitan areas in Brazil and their wider size range allows us to establish with higher confidence that this result is consistent with the theory of chapter 3.[65] The smaller number of South African cities shows stronger scaling effects, with a larger $\beta=1.35$ but also a wider confidence interval. The combined dataset (figure 6.12A) shows scaling that is statistically indistinguishable from the simplest theoretical prediction, with $\beta=7/6$,[66] shown as a light gray line.

A consequence of this superlinear scaling behavior is that larger cities have greater incomes per capita and therefore may have greater capacity to dedicate more resources (at least in nominal terms) to services and infrastructure[67] according to the logic that incomes and costs are approximately balanced, developed in chapters 3 and 4. This may happen directly via local taxes or indirectly via higher receipts and

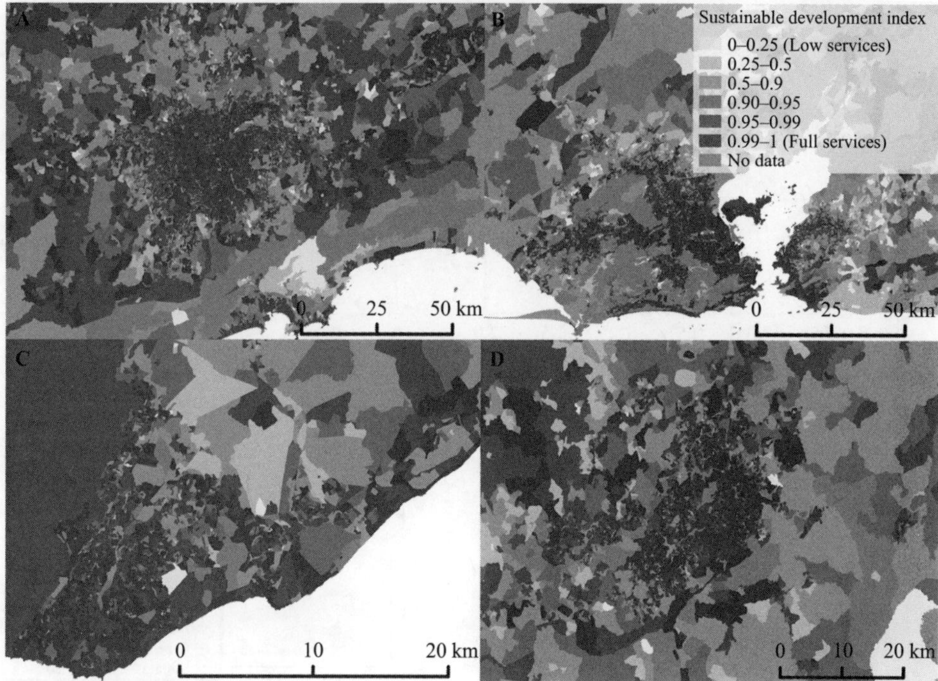

6.11 Sustainable development index distribution in selected Brazilian metropolitan areas. Panels show the estimated sustainable development index, X_i, at the sector level (neighborhood): (A) São Paulo, (B) Rio de Janeiro, (C) Salvador, and (D) Belo Horizonte. We observe that, relative to South African cities, Brazilian metropolitan areas have higher overall levels of services, which is particularly visible for São Paulo, the nation's largest city.

Source: Adapted from Christa Brelsford et al., "Heterogeneity and Scale of Sustainable Development in Cities," *Proceedings of the National Academy of Sciences* 114, no. 34 (2017): 8963–8968, https://doi.org/10.1073/pnas.1606033114.

reinvestments managed at the national level. At any rate, feedback between higher economic productivity and better services and infrastructure in larger cities has historically been the basis for the central role of cities in development.[68] Figure 6.13 shows the average value of X for urban areas of different population sizes in Brazil and South Africa. In general, the level of service access increases with city size, a trend that is especially clear in South Africa. In Brazil, there are also some important regional disparities, with smaller cities showing a wider range of service delivery, which is better in the richer southern area of the country. This trend also occurs in other nations, such as India.[69] Thus, living in larger cities means that, on average, residents obtain faster access to many public services associated with development. However, these averages also hide large neighborhood heterogeneities.

Measures of Spatial Heterogeneity and Inequality   Measures of heterogeneity within metropolitan areas are especially important because at this scale residents share the same labor and real estate markets and thus many of the same opportunities and costs.[70] As a consequence, inequalities within urban areas translate into true relative socioeconomic (dis)advantages.

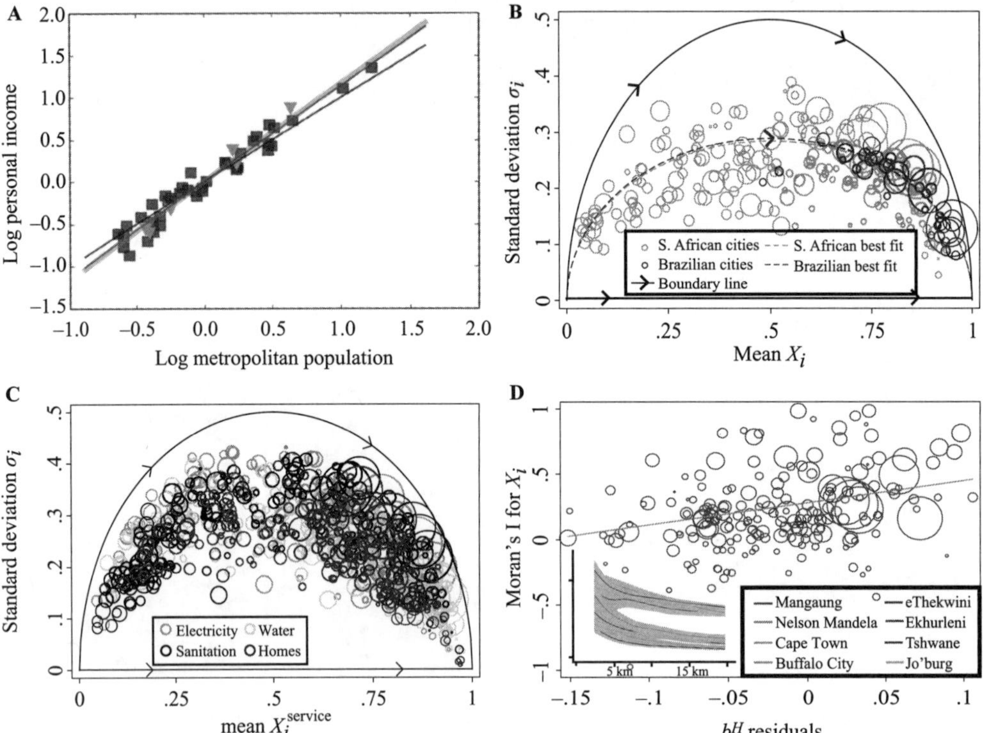

6.12 Agglomeration effects and heterogeneity of sustainable development in Brazilian and South African cities. (A) Scaling of personal income with population for Brazil's (squares) and South Africa's (triangles) metropolitan areas. The thick gray line shows the theoretical slope of 7/6, the mostly overlapping solid line shows the best fit, and the lower line shows linear scaling. The best fit demonstrates that larger cities have, on average, higher resources per capita, which can be invested in sustainable development. (B) Relationship between the standard deviation and the mean of the sustainable development index, X_i, for Brazil's 38 metropolitan areas and 207 South African municipal regions, where the size of the circle is proportional to population. The two black lines bind the area in which (X_i, σ_i) pairs can exist, with the upper curved line showing maximum inequality (Kuznets curve $b^H = 1$) and the horizontal line corresponding to total equality ($b^H = 0$). The dashed lines show the estimated best fit for the mean heterogeneity index b^H, which is close to maximum in both nations. (C) Decomposition of X_i into subcomponents $X_i^{electricity}$, X_i^{water}, $X_i^{sanitation}$, and X_i^{homes} for Brazil's metropolitan regions, which allows us to see the role of larger cities in providing improved services. (D) Positive association between Moran's *I* (distance threshold 5 km) and for South African municipalities, showing that higher spatial clustering is associated with higher inequality of access to services. The inset shows the variation of Moran's *I* with the distance thresholds for South Africa's major metropolitan regions.

Source: Adapted from Christa Brelsford et al., "Heterogeneity and Scale of Sustainable Development in Cities," *Proceedings of the National Academy of Sciences* 114, no. 34 (2017): 8963–8968, https://doi.org/10.1073/pnas.1606033114.

Table 6.2 Superlinear scaling of income and heterogeneity of sustainable development at the neighborhood level

Metropolitan areas	Summary statistics			
	N_c	Estimate	95% CI	Fit
Brazil (metros)				
Income exponent β	39	1.11	[1.03, 1.20]	$R^2 = 0.90$
Heterogeneity index b^H	38	0.58	[0.56, 0.60]	$R^2 = 0.99$
South Africa (metropolitan municipalities)				
Income exponent (metros) β	8	1.35	[1.19, 1.53]	$R^2 = 0.97$
Heterogeneity index (municipalities) b^H	207	0.57	[0.54, 0.60]	$R^2 = 0.96$

Notes: The scaling fit without aggregation of the three municipalities in the Johannesburg area gives $\beta = 1.49$, with 95% CI = [1.17, 1.81], $R^2 = 0.87$. The best fit for the combined dataset after centering is $\beta = 1.14$, with 95% CI = [1.06, 1.23], $R^2 = 0.89$, statistically indistinguishable from the simplest theoretical expectations (light gray) in figure 6.12A. One metropolitan area in Brazil was excluded from b^H's estimate because of data completeness issues.

Measures of heterogeneity may be spatially explicit or may consider only variation within a population. The most commonly used measure is the *Gini coefficient* (figure 6.12B). This is a well-known *nonspatial* measure of heterogeneity. An even simpler measure of variation is the standard deviation and its relation to the mean of any socioeconomic variable. In contrast, *Moran's I* (I_M) is one of the most widely used measures of *spatial* heterogeneity.[71] It accounts for the level of correlation between the values of a given characteristic at two spatial locations within a given physical distance from each other. The Gini coefficient (or the standard deviation) and Moran's *I* are not necessarily correlated, as this depends on the spatial structure of mixing between different people (e.g., with different levels of income). Any resource within a population may be spatially distributed in a manner that is maximally clustered, meaning that Moran's *I* approaches $I_M = 1$, or perfectly anticorrelated (as in a checkerboard pattern), so that Moran's *I* approaches $I_M = -1$, or a random (well-mixed) pattern, when it approaches $I_M = 0$. Schematic illustrations of these situations are given in figure 6.14.

We will now show how these quantities, taken together, characterize the heterogeneity of any socioeconomic indicator in cities. In particular, a sustainable development index like X_i has a number of simple statistical properties. First, from its definition, we see that the variance of X, σ_i^2, must vanish when everyone has services, $X = 1$, or when they are nonexistent, $X = 0$, while it is typically maximum when $X_i = 0.5$. Thus, we can parameterize the standard deviation of X_i as

$$\sigma_i = b_i^H \sqrt{\overline{X}_i (1 - \overline{X}_i)}, \tag{6.2}$$

where the square root corresponds to the standard deviation for a random Bernoulli process. This means that $b^H = 1$ gives the *maximum* possible variance at each value of

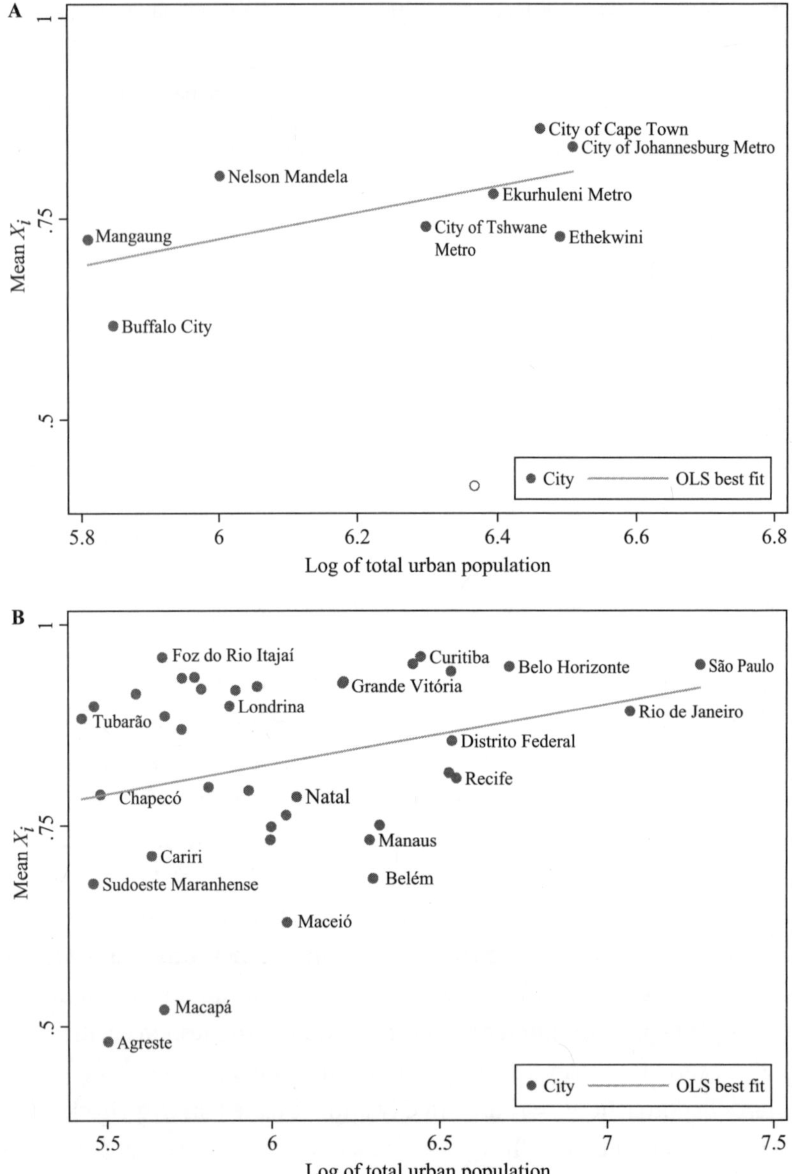

6.13 Mean sustainable development index versus total metropolitan population. (A) South African metropolitan municipalities. The line indicates a significant correlation between city size and improved service provision (slope=0.164, R^2=0.29). (B) Brazilian metropolitan areas. There is a slight correlation (slope=0.075, R^2=0.051), indicating that larger cities tend to provide their residents greater access to services. Importantly, some smaller cities in Brazil's richest regions, such as Curitiba, Tubarão, and Londrina, are performing well in service provision.
Source: Adapted from Christa Brelsford et al., "Heterogeneity and Scale of Sustainable Development in Cities," *Proceedings of the National Academy of Sciences* 114, no. 34 (2017): 8963–8968, https://doi.org/10.1073/pnas.1606033114.

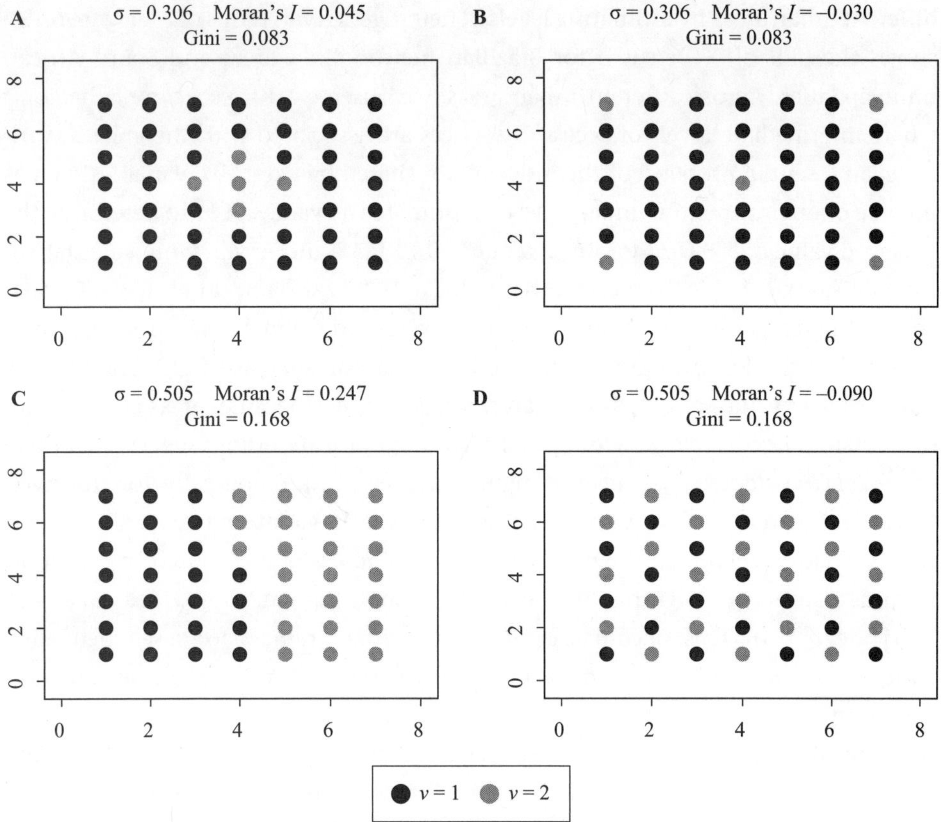

6.14 Illustrations of different relationships between the standard deviation, Gini coefficient, and Moran's *I*. Only Moran's *I* is sensitive to the spatial configuration of different types (black and gray), while the other quantities express how much mixing there is overall. Note that σ and Moran's *I* are unchanged by linear transformations of the quantities of gray and black dots, but the Gini coefficient is not. For example, using the same spatial layout as in panel D, with black = 100 and gray = 101, yields σ = 0.505, Moran's I_M = –0.090, and Gini = 0.002.
Source: Adapted from Christa Brelsford et al., "Heterogeneity and Scale of Sustainable Development in Cities," *Proceedings of the National Academy of Sciences* 114, no. 34 (2017): 8963–8968, https://doi.org/10.1073/pnas.1606033114.

the average of X, $\bar{X}$ (see figures 6.12B and C). It follows from the properties of the standard deviation that $b^H \geq 0$. Consequently, we can characterize two-dimensional *trajectories* in the space of $(\bar{X}_i, \sigma_i)$ as levels of development increase in each unit i and the values of $(\bar{X}_i, \sigma_i) \rightarrow (1, 0)$. Given $\bar{X}_i$, these trajectories are characterized by a single number: the value of b^H as a function of time. There are two special trajectories—of maximum and minimum heterogeneity—characterized by $b^H = 1$ and $b^H = 0$, respectively, indicated in figures 6.12B and C by solid lines. Because of these properties, we can refer to b^H as a (normalized) *heterogeneity index*. Each region's individual trajectory, at any given time, is characterized by a value of b^H such that $0 \leq b^H \leq 1$.

Although data used in figure 6.12 are cross-sectional and consequently do not allow examination of temporal trends or testing of causal relations, we can compare different urban areas by estimating levels of heterogeneity in terms of b^H. Figure 6.12B shows the plot of $\bar{X}$ versus σ for Brazilian metropolitan areas and South African municipalities. Across different urban areas, we observe a *Kuznets curve* behavior,[72] where intermediate levels of access to services are associated with the greatest variance, an essential property of the index X not shared by extensive variables such as income or environmental impact. We can estimate the values of b^H to determine the expected value of $b^H = 0.73$ for Brazil and $b^H = 0.71$ for South Africa, which are statistically indistinguishable from each other (table 6.2). It is also important to realize that levels of heterogeneity in service provision are scale dependent, as we already indicated in figure 6.8C. Adopting smaller units of analysis, such as neighborhoods, one obtains lower values of b^H, while at larger scales, for metropolitan areas and beyond, one obtains larger levels of heterogeneity. These empirical findings suggest that there are *generic trajectories of development* (figures 6.12B and C). Empirically, for any given level of infrastructure access across a city, the observed variation between neighborhoods is closer to the case where infrastructure access is distributed in an all-or-nothing manner ($b^H \to 1$) than where access, though limited, is provided equally to everyone ($b^H \to 0$). This, of course, creates patterns of extreme place-based inequality, which show that while cities almost anywhere can deliver services to some neighborhoods, they provide hardly any to others, creating a developing city parallel to the social isolation and cumulative disadvantage effects with which we started this chapter. This is not inevitable, but it does require that governments see the whole picture and act in ways that are more equitable across social groups and places.

Development trajectories allow us to measure most naturally what happens over time in different places. Comparing the situation in South African cities between 2001 and 2011 (figure 6.15) should give us some hope. We observe a general improvement in public service delivery and housing improvements—and a corresponding drop in inequality across neighborhoods in most cities—as we hypothesized earlier based on cross-sectional data.

Finally, to explicitly take into account the effects of space, we use Moran's I to measure the similarity of conditions between a neighborhood and a number of others nearby, determined by a distance matrix defined over a chosen length scale.[73] This shows clear evidence of strong spatial clustering in access to services. The magnitude of spatial clustering is strongest when the distance threshold is a "walkable" distance, less than a few kilometers, and subsequent decays for larger distances (figure 6.12D inset). This spatial correlation is also higher for socioeconomic quantities—such as income and racial composition[74]—than for X. This suggests that assortative preferences and constraints, which generate strong spatial economic and racial inequalities in US cities,[75] as discussed in section 6.1, are likely also at work in developing urban areas and in the cities of Brazil and South Africa at any rate. This analysis also shows that higher levels of spatial clustering, measured by the magnitude of I_M, are statistically associated with higher levels of heterogeneity (inequality) in access to services, measured via the magnitude of b^H (figure 6.12D).

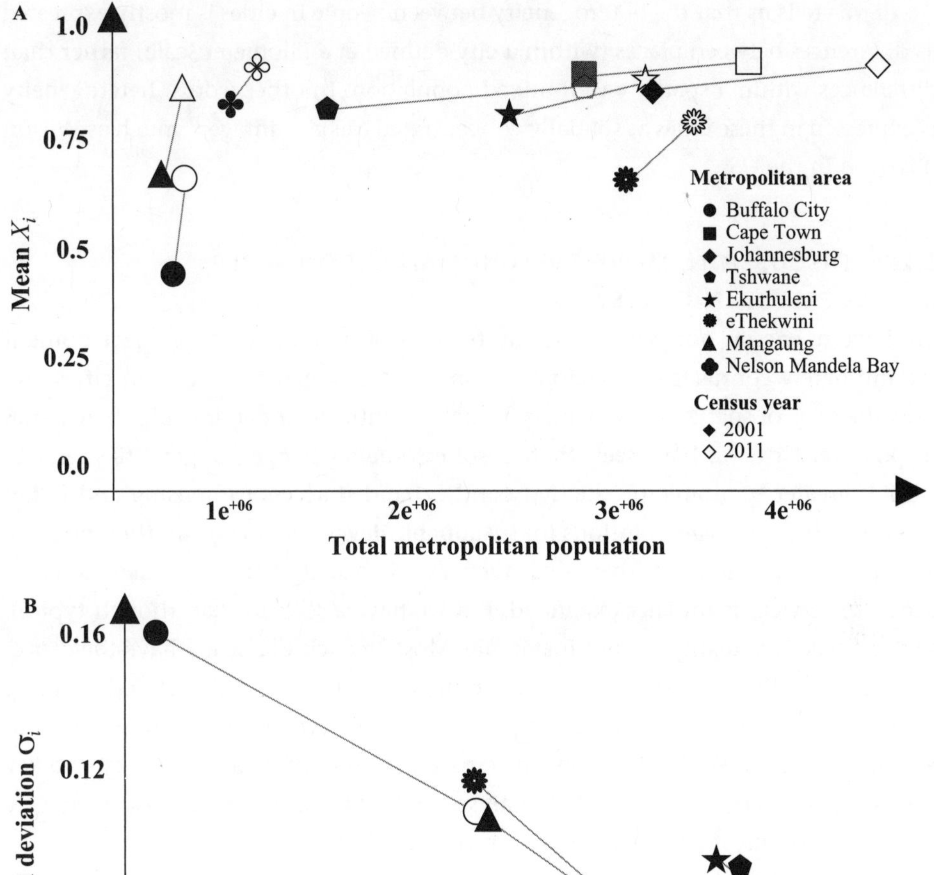

6.15 Development trajectories for the cities of South Africa between 2001 and 2011 (decennial census years). (A) Changes in the sustainable development index are most pronounced in smaller cities. (B) Inequality, expressed as the standard deviation of X_i across city neighborhoods, has dropped, as expected in urban systems at a stage approaching full service delivery.
Source: Adapted from an original analysis by Mollie Gaines and Christa Brelsford.

All this tells us that the heterogeneity between people in cities is mostly expressed as differences between places (within a city defined at a kilometer scale) rather than differences within a spatially well-mixed population. In other words, heterogeneity is expressed in these cities as spatially concentrated (dis)advantage,[76] much as Wilson observed in the US.

6.2.3 DISCUSSION: MORE EVEN HUMAN SUSTAINABLE DEVELOPMENT IN CITIES?

We have now seen how several central features of urban sustainable development are intimately connected to agglomeration and heterogeneity effects in cities and how the scale of spatial units of analysis matters critically for addressing these issues in practice. First, we have seen that, despite some challenges, larger cities tend to exhibit greater economic productivity and expanded access to housing and urban services, which nucleate solutions for sustainable development within their nations. Second, despite these positive consequences, large inequality patterns emerge as access to services is initially expanded. But we have also seen that, though typical, high levels of inequality are not inevitable. Most large cities already have the capacity to provide the highest levels of services to some of their neighborhoods. Scaling up these capabilities, they could, in principle, provide much more even access to all their residents. While the problem transcends issues of data availability, the key theme of this section has been that analyses such as the ones we just discussed were not possible in most developing cities even a decade ago.

This type of analysis is starting to establish a general analytical and conceptual framework for promoting faster and more equitable urban sustainable development everywhere. This is enabled by better information both generated by communities and from a variety of other verifiable data sources, from local collections to official statistics and remote sensing. As we have just seen, emerging results suggest general patterns of change in which social and economic agglomeration at the level of functional urban areas feeds back onto spatial patterns of neighborhood development and vice versa. These in turn are internalized by individuals, especially young people, affecting their outlook, life paths, and socioeconomic opportunities later in life, which dictate to a large extent the vitality and productivity of cities and nations decades out. The dynamic interplay between uneven local improvements in living conditions and the resulting inequality between people and places also tells us that attempts to reduce inequities must cross a tricky intermediate stage, at which inequality is highest and prone to generate disaffection and conflict, before it can start to fall and universal access to services and other opportunities can be established. Continuing to better understand the general nature of these transformations over space and time and how they can be achieved most quickly, effectively, and equitably will remain a critical issue for urban science and practice over the next few decades.

6.3 MEASURING NEIGHBORHOOD STRUCTURE: SPATIAL SELECTION AND INFORMATION

We have so far introduced ideas of neighborhood effects and observed some of their consequences both in the context of a rich nation such as the US and in developing cities, where land uses and services are still being worked out. These examples have demonstrated that patterns of heterogeneity and development are very complex and require sophisticated scale-dependent methods of analysis that can get us closer to the decisions—by necessity or choice—leading to residence in one neighborhood versus another. Like any other patterns in complex systems, spatial distributions of types must be compared at different scales, and this comparison has a very special meaning in terms of *information*.

To see this, we start by asking a simple general question: *If I know your income, can I guess where you live?* This question can also be turned around: *If I know where you live, can I guess your income?* This is, after all, what we mean by *different neighborhoods*. The difference is not just about their location in space but instead tends to focus on the information it provides on residents. We often hear of "White" or "Black" neighborhoods, which presumably tell us about the residents' likely race. Similarly, poor or rich neighborhoods presumably tell us about their residents' income, working-class, artist, or hipster neighborhoods tell us about other aspects of the populations, and so on. It turns out that such wholesale classifications are only very impressionistic; neighborhoods are always mixtures of people and can be more or less biased toward certain types. For example, neighborhoods in the US are often called "Black" when their self-reported African American proportion is greater than 20%–30%! This objectification of neighborhoods by type is simplistic and almost certainly not helpful. It likely forgoes important avenues for change resulting from a neighborhood's detailed composition and mixing of types. To appreciate all these issues more quantitatively, we need to adopt the general language of information.

6.3.1 INFORMATION AND SPATIAL SELECTION

As an illustration of the problem, consider the complex pattern of household income in New York City neighborhoods (figure 6.16A). Figure 6.17 shows the same type of map for a wider swath of New York City and for a few other US metropolitan areas. Neighborhoods here are taken as *block groups*, a standard small area unit defined by the US Census consistently across the entire country. Block groups (BK_GP in figure 6.16) have an average population of 1,500 people, so looking at these maps, we see many small patches in dense parts of cities versus larger ones in less dense regions, such as suburbs.

Looking at patterns of income, we do not observe a simple picture of rich and poor neighborhoods at all. Instead, we see strong heterogeneity at different spatial scales, from adjacent neighborhoods with different average household incomes, such

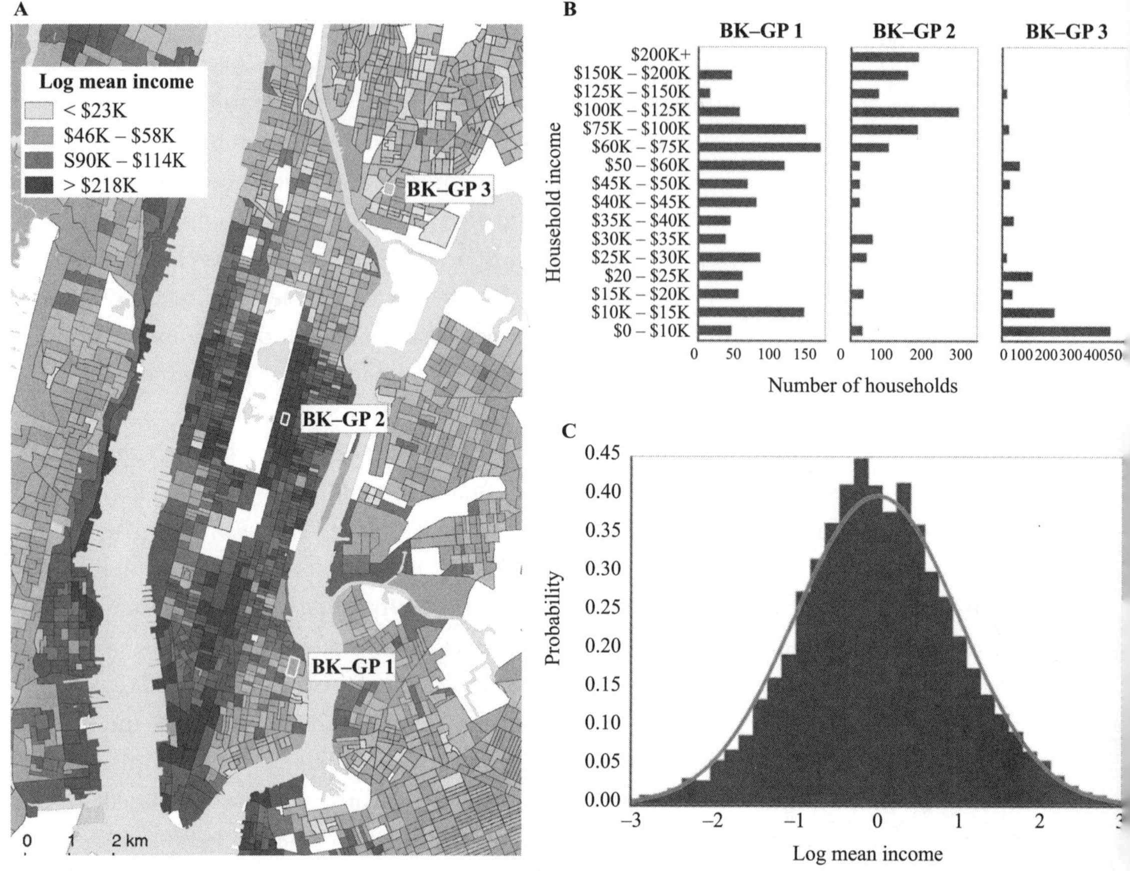

6.16 Heterogeneity of neighborhoods in a section of New York City. (A) Average household income in New York City census block groups. (B). Income distributions in selected neighborhood shown in (A). (C) The citywide distribution of household income is well described by a lognormal distribution (solid line), which is a very good general model for the household income distribution in all US MSAs.

as on the Lower East Side (figure 6.16, BK_GP 1), to larger recognizable patches of wealth and poverty, such as the Upper East Side (the richest part of Manhattan, BK-GP 2 in figure 6.16, by Central Park) or the Bronx (generally rather poor, BK-GP 3 in figure 6.16). Figure 6.16B shows the distribution of incomes in these three example neighborhoods, the first "middle class," the second "rich," and the last "poor."

As we have already seen, this spatial heterogeneity is long lived,[77] persisting for decades or longer, through many economic cycles and substantial demographic turnover. For example, the Lower East Side is still poor after perhaps 400 years of demographic and economic turnover, where it was successively an immigrant enclave for different ethnic groups, including Germans, Italians, Eastern European Jews, Greeks, and many others. Along with its people, its built environment also changed, from a concentrated set of tenements (slums) to predominantly public housing today. Despite all these transformations, it remained poor compared to neighboring parts of the city, perhaps because its function stayed much the same: as a foothold in the city for wave after wave of poor immigrants and other disadvantaged populations.

We see that these patterns are the result not of accidental fluctuations but rather of decades of choice and adaptation by successive waves of different individuals sharing certain traits. In other words, the immensely complicated spatial patterns of types that we observe in cities, even if they start out by chance, are the result of a continuous process of selection, whereby different communities and places may better suit, and in turn be preferred by, different types of people.

This is made clear mathematically because such rich and detailed neighborhood patterns contrast with the simple normal distribution for (the logarithm of) household income across the entire metropolitan area (figure 6.16C). Recall that this quantity is an old friend that we have already encountered in chapter 4, where we

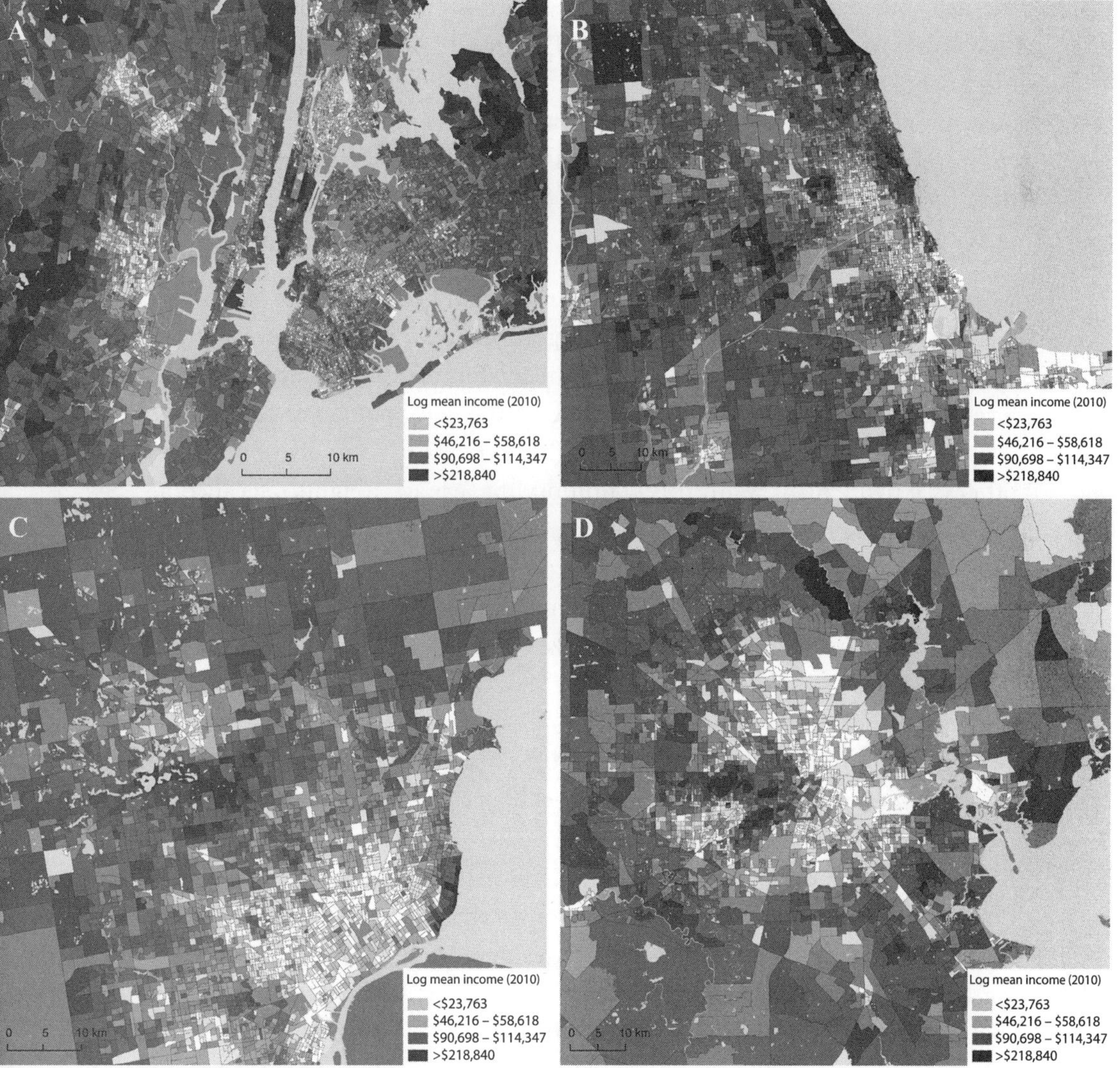

6.17 Patterns of mean income in neighborhoods of various US metropolitan areas. (A) New York City, (B) Chicago, (C) Detroit, and (D) Houston. In all cases, we observe complex patterns, with structure at many different spatial scales.

developed a statistical dynamics of incomes, costs, and investments that gives rise to approximately lognormal distributions of urban indicators, as we now see also here.

This tells us that a seemingly universal statistical regularity—a scaling "law," with well-behaved lognormal statistical deviations—emerges at the citywide scale only as the result of averaging over a more complex pattern of local neighborhood variations. Better still, we can think of the same thing in reverse: Given an integrated labor market in each metropolitan area that produces well-behaved scaling effects, neighborhoods are the result of subsequent biased choices or constraints of place of residence, creating a complicated and manifestly nonuniversal variety of local patterns of income (figure 6.16B).

How then should we try to understand the composition of neighborhoods and the rich phenomenology discussed in the previous sections? This second point of view allows us to focus on the structure of the neighborhood variations by using the macroscopic regularity across the urban area as the reference. Specifically, we can quantify the complexity of the pattern of variations at the neighborhood level by comparing (income) probability distributions at different levels of spatial aggregation. Let us write this explicitly as

$$P(y_i|n_j) = w_{ij}\, P(y_i), \tag{6.3}$$

where $P(y_i|n_j)$ is the distribution (i.e., the normalized frequency) of income y in discrete bins labeled by i (such as those in figure 6.16B) in neighborhood n_j (the different patches in figure 6.16A), and $P(y_i)$ is the income distribution at a more aggregate level (figure 6.16C), which we will take to be the metropolitan area. Equation (6.3) *defines* the weights, $w_{ij} \equiv P(y_i \mid n_j)/P(y_i)$, which transform one distribution into the other (see figure 6.18). With this definition, the average weights over income obey the normalization property $w_j = \sum_i w_{ij} P(y_i) = 1$ for all neighborhoods j.

So far, we have only transferred the complexity of patterns of income to the weights, w_{ij}. However, something fundamental was gained because equation (6.3) is well known and can be readily recognized from two different and very generative points of view. (This is the kind of *trafficking in meaning* that a mathematical correspondence affords.)

First, equation (6.3) is the haploid model of population genetics.[78] In evolutionary game theory, it is also known as the *replicator equation*.[79] In that context, the two distributions are related across time (not space), and the weights w_{ij} measure the *fitness* of a trait (allele) i, expressing its differential propagation into the next generation, over the period indexed by j. The stronger the deviation of w_{ij} away from 1, the stronger the selection for allele i. This corresponds to high fitness if $w_{ij} > 1$, and vice versa if $w_{ij} < 1$. When $w_{ij} = 1$, the dynamics is *neutral*, and there is *no selection* over the specific time period (generation) indexed by j. This interpretation gives a mathematical correspondence between genetic evolutionary dynamics (in time) and neighborhood sorting (in space). The point is *not* that neighborhood choice is like genetic

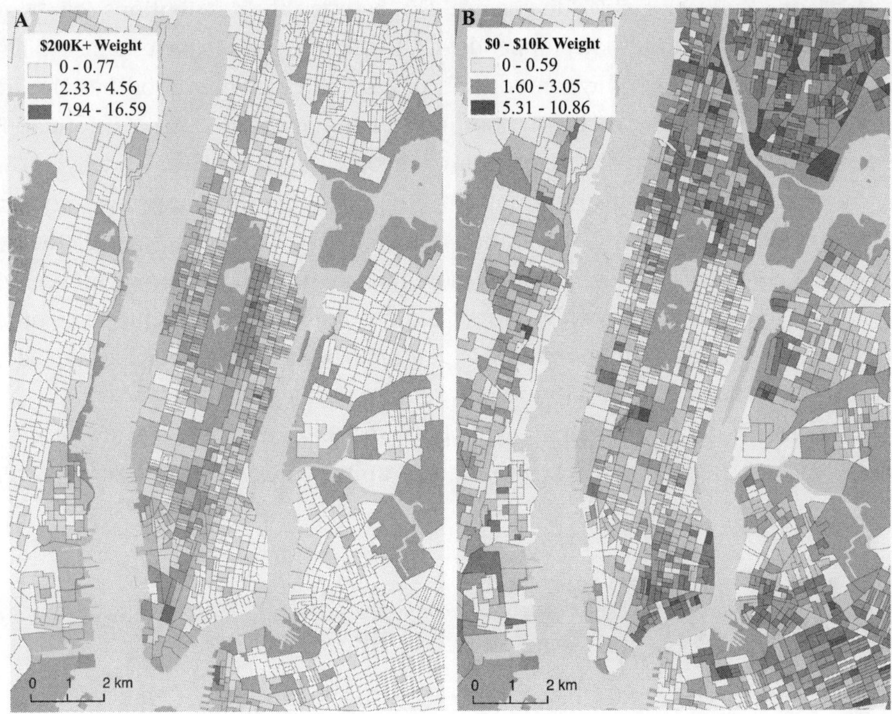

6.18 Neighborhood selection weights, w_{ij}, for the highest (A) and lowest (B) income groups in each block group in central New York City. Note how the likelihood measured by these weights is different in different parts of the city but that there are also some areas of strong overlap, such as in parts of the West Side. Neighborhoods are local ecologies that in many cases support diversity.

evolution but rather that both processes are the result of *selection*, and selection is about information. Information is, in this sense, the opposite of disorder: the structures that develop as the result of people's choices and limitations. A rich pattern of neighborhoods therefore expresses a lot of information.

Second, equation (6.3) is a form of Bayes's relation, which leads to the interpretation of w_{ij} in terms of probability ratios, specifically

$$P(y_i|n_j) = \frac{p(n_j|y_i)}{P(n_j)} P(y_i) \rightarrow w_{ij} = \frac{P(n_j|y_i)}{P(n_j)} = \frac{P(y_i|n_j)}{P(y_i)} = \frac{P(y_i, n_j)}{P(y_i)P(n_j)}. \tag{6.4}$$

Here, $P(n_j \mid y_i)$ is the probability that a person in the city resides in neighborhood n_j given that they have income y_i. $P(n_j)$ is the (income-independent) probability of living in neighborhood n_j, and $P(y_i, n_j)$ is the joint probability. This second perspective leads to another powerful mathematical correspondence between probability theory, inference, and neighborhood structure. In this context, $\log w_{ij}$ in equation (6.4) is the (nonaveraged) Shannon *mutual information*[80] (appendix C) between neighborhood j and the distribution of income, y. To see this, consider the average of $\log w_{ij}$ over income groups:

$$\log w_j = \sum_i P(y_i|n_j) \log \frac{P(y_i|n_j)}{P(y_i)} = D_{KL}[P(y|n_j)\|P(y)]. \tag{6.5}$$

This is the Kullback-Leibler divergence, D_{KL}, between the distributions of income citywide and in neighborhood j (appendix C). In other words, we have some explaining to do in order to get the composition of a specific neighborhood by selecting from the city at large. For each neighborhood j, log w_j is the amount of information needed to describe its statistical pattern of income, given that we start by knowing the aggregate income distribution across the city. From this perspective, atypical neighborhoods with income distributions that are very different from the city as a whole will require a *longer explanation* (more information), whereas neighborhoods that already reflect the citywide pattern require no further description. In other words, atypical neighborhoods require *local theories* of neighborhood effects in addition to an explanation of the citywide distribution of traits (chapter 4).

In this specific sense, the magnitude of log w_j expresses the *strength of neighborhood effects*[81] in each neighborhood j, measured in units of information.[82] Figure 6.19A

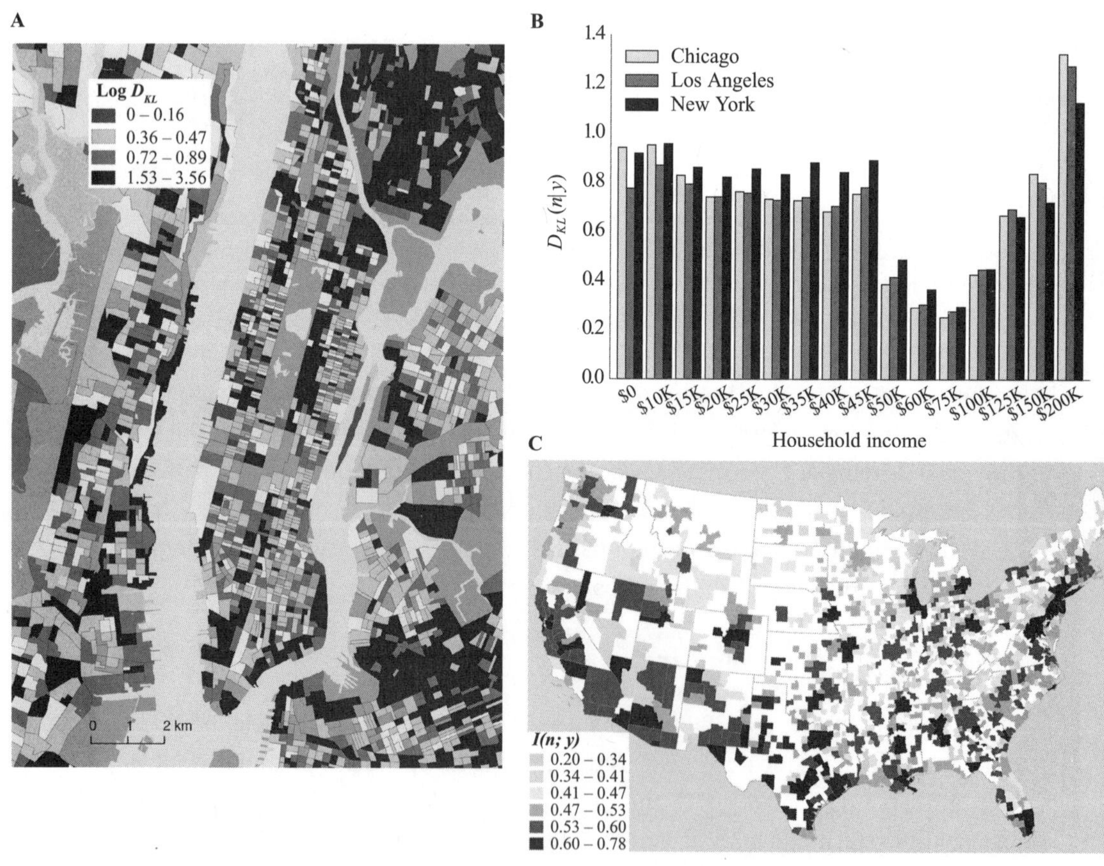

6.19 Strength of neighborhood selection in New York City. (A) Specific strength of selection in each neighborhood, log w_j; see equation (6.5). (B) Strength of neighborhood selection for different income groups, log w_i; see equation (6.6). Note how the richest income group is the most segregated, followed by the poorest. Middle-income groups are the least segregated spatially and provide the most diversity in typical neighborhoods. (C) Strength of neighborhood selection in each metropolitan area in the US, measured by the mutual information between neighborhoods and income structure.

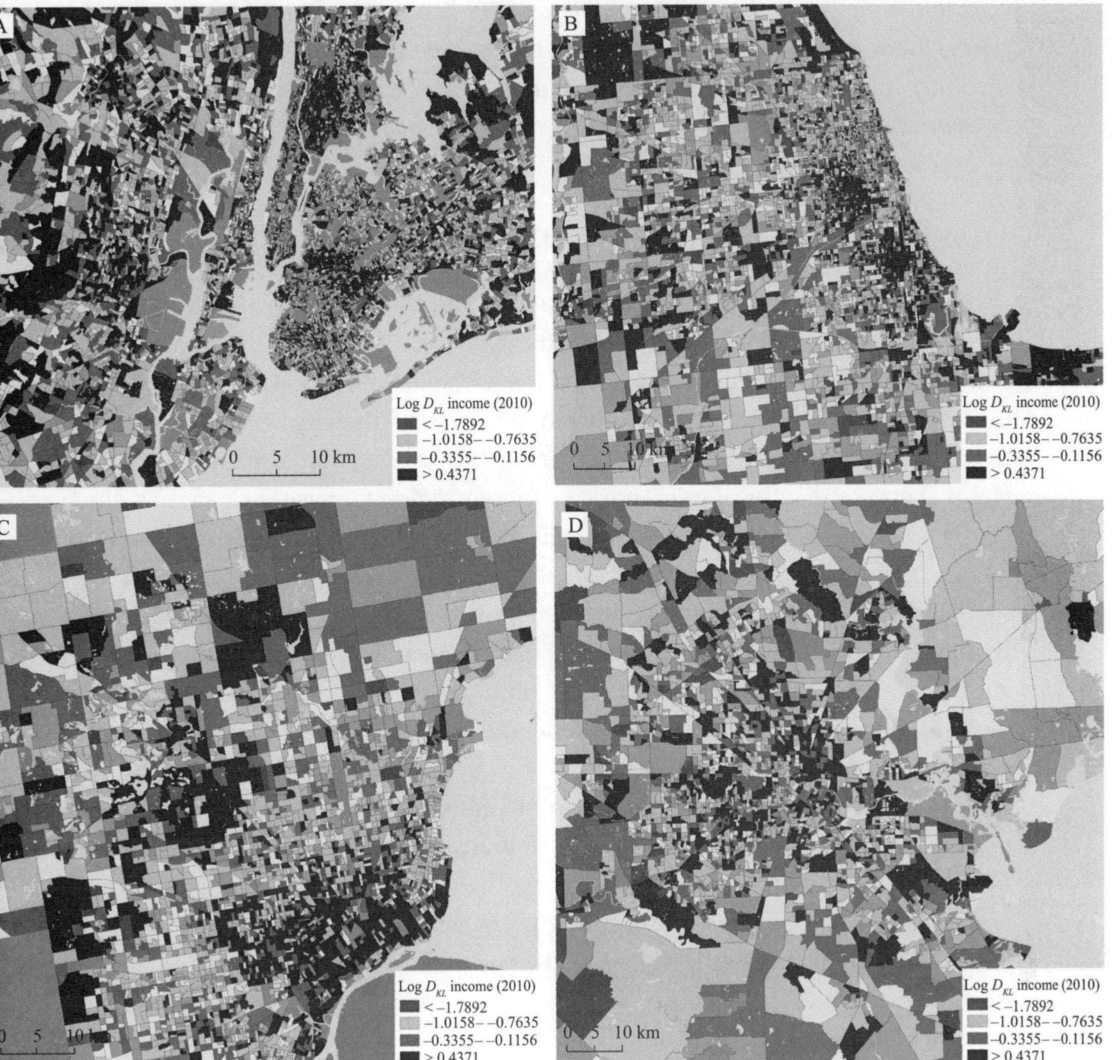

6.20 Strength of selection in each neighborhood of selected cities. (A) New York City, (B) Chicago, (C) Detroit, and (D) Houston. In general, comparison with the maps of figure 6.17 shows that it is the richest and poorest neighborhoods that are associated with more information, thus requiring a more complex and specific theory of change to explain them than for the city at large.

shows the strength of selection by income for each neighborhood across New York City, and figure 6.20 shows this information for a few other large US metropolitan areas. We observe a very mixed pattern of local selection, with many neighborhoods closely reflecting the distribution of income for the city as a whole but also with a significant fraction of others manifesting primarily a very strong local flavor. We can verify that the magnitude of the observed differences could not be the result of a purely random process of sorting by building maps analogous to figures 6.19 and 6.20 using the same corresponding population sizes in the city and neighborhoods but drawing individuals at random from the metropolitan income distribution in each place.

Comparing figures 6.16–6.17 and figures 6.19–6.20 suggests that the most atypical neighborhoods tend to have both the highest and the lowest average household incomes! It turns out that this is a general pattern of selection across all US metropolitan areas. We can easily quantify this effect systematically via the average of log w_{ij} over neighborhoods j, which is

$$\log w_i = \sum_j P(n_j | y_i) \log \frac{P(n_j | y_i)}{P(n_j)} = D_{KL}[P(n|y_i) \| P(n)]. \tag{6.6}$$

This quantity is the average information necessary to explain the distribution of specific income ranges y_i across the city, given that we know its neighborhood structure. In other words, we also have a longer explanation to give if we find that income groups are distributed in less random ways in the city. In the absence of neighborhood selection, this quantity is zero. Thus, its magnitude quantifies the different average strengths of *neighborhood effects for different income levels* in each city. Figure 6.19B shows that neighborhood effects are strongest for the highest (richest) income group, followed by the lowest. Middle-income groups are observed to be spatially the most mixed and thus less determined by specific neighborhoods. This is an interesting finding because it shows that different income groups make different kinds of choices—either by preference or necessity—in terms of their residential location. Thus, any realistic model of residential choice in US cities needs to be an explicit function of income levels.

We can also go back to Wilson's map of Chicago (figures 6.1 and 6.2) and see indeed that the patterns of spatially concentrated poverty in the South and West Sides are identified in this way as requiring their own relatively lengthy explanations. The same is also true of the strong polarization between the poor inner-city parts of Detroit in the southeast part of the city and the rich suburbs in the northwest. Each city presents situations analogous to these (in)famous cases that require their own *specific* explanations and, if one wishes to mitigate neighborhood deprivation, interventions.

These effects of selection specific to each neighborhood and income group are summarized in turn by a single quantity that captures the overall strength of neighborhood selection for each city in units of information, shown in figure 6.19C. This is the total (mutual) information, $I(y;n) = \log w$, between spatial neighborhood structure and income, given as the average of the previous quantities over the remaining variable,

$$\log w = \sum_j P(n_j) D_{KL}[P(y|n_j) \| P(y)] = \sum_i P(y_i) D_{KL}[P(n|y_i) \| P(n)]$$

$$= \sum_{i,j} P(y_i, n_j) \log w_{ij} = I(y; n). \tag{6.7}$$

Again, this means that if every neighborhood was a *statistical microcosm* (a truly random sample) of the city as a whole, then all income groups would be spatially well mixed and there would be no neighborhood effects, leading to $I(y; n) = 0$. Conversely, in cities where every neighborhood has its own unique flavor, not at all like the distribution of traits across the city, there is strong sorting of incomes by neighborhood and $I(y;n)$ will be large. How large depends on the relative amount of information needed to describe the system at the local level (figure 6.17A) versus as a whole (figure 6.17C). Thus, for each city, the mutual information $I(y; n)$ gives a summary measure of how well a coarse-grained pattern describes a complex system observed at a more disaggregated level. In other words, $I(y; n)$ quantifies the average complexity

Table 6.3 Ranking of US metropolitan and micropolitan areas by highest and lowest aggregate neighborhood selection strength

Top 10 US metropolitan areas by $I(y; n)$			Lowest 10 US metropolitan areas by $I(y; n)$		
City	Mutual information	Total population	City	Mutual information	Total population
Dallas, TX	0.697	6,154,265	Mount Vernon, WA	0.378	115,231
New York City, NY	0.689	18,700,715	Hinesville, GA	0.372	76,996
New Orleans, LA	0.685	1,105,020	Palm Coast, FL	0.362	91,806
Reno, NV	0.681	416,860	Wausau, WI	0.357	132,644
College Station, TX	0.680	219,058	Glens Falls, NY	0.328	128,795
Morgantown, WV	0.677	125,691	Dover, DE	0.327	156,918
Memphis, TN	0.671	1,301,248	Coeur d'Alene, ID	0.323	134,851
Midland, TX	0.667	132,103	Mankato, MN	0.319	94,990
Fresno, CA	0.666	908,830	Sheboygan, WI	0.315	115,328
San Antonio, TX	0.665	2,057,782	St. George, UT	0.310	134,033
Top 10 US micropolitan areas by $I(y; n)$			Lowest 10 US micropolitan areas by $I(y; n)$		
City	Mutual information	Total population	City	Mutual information	Total population
Lamesa, TX	0.774	13,853	Sayre, PA	0.260	62,415
Beeville, TX	0.763	31,896	Huntingdon, PA	0.252	45,830
Bay City, TX	0.723	36,647	Cadillac, MI	0.250	47,615
Hobbs, NM	0.710	62,503	Bradford, PA	0.245	43,853
Edwards, CO	0.690	57,832	DeRidder, LA	0.241	35,000
Wauchula, FL	0.680	27,521	Platteville, WI	0.235	50,716
Greenville, MS	0.651	52,455	Menomonie, WI	0.230	43,365
Arcadia, FL	0.649	34,557	Miami, OK	0.229	32,193
Clewiston, FL	0.648	39,030	Natchitoches, LA	0.222	39,274
Clovis, NM	0.645	46,924	Baraboo, WI	0.206	60,957

of any theory of *local* neighborhood effects versus a theory of the same quantity at the metropolitan level, in this case connecting urban neighborhoods with income distribution.

The top and bottom metropolitan areas in the US as ranked by the magnitude of $I(y;n)$ are shown in table 6.3. We see, for example, that Dallas, TX, New York City, and New Orleans, LA, respectively, have the highest $I(y; n)$ and that many cities in Texas show generally strong income segregation by neighborhood. This is particularly interesting because these cities are currently among the fastest growing in the nation (chapter 8), so at least some of the observed income segregation is the result of *recent* residential choices. Smaller cities, especially in parts of the upper Midwest (e.g., Wisconsin) but also in other states, show the lowest neighborhood segregation by income.

6.3.2 INFORMATION, INCOME INEQUALITY, AND THE AGGREGATION PROBLEM

Informational quantities are also well suited for quantifying issues of inequality, not just segregation. An approach similar to the one we developed earlier aimed at characterizing economic *inequality* is commonly used in econometrics.[83] Seeking to adopt the desirable properties of information-theoretic quantities in the characterization of economic inequality, Henri Theil[84] proposed in pioneering work an index, T_I, which is defined analogously to equations (6.5) and (6.6) as

$$T_I(y) = \sum_{i=1}^{N} \frac{y_i}{N\bar{y}} \log \frac{y_i}{\bar{y}} = \sum_i q(y_i) \log \frac{q(y_i)}{P(y_i)} = D_{KL}[q(y)\|P(y)]. \tag{6.8}$$

The Theil index, T_I, compares the income share, $q(y_i) \equiv \frac{y_i}{\bar{y}} P(y_i)$, to the corresponding population share, $P(y_i)$, of a population structured into income bins labeled by i and where $\bar{y}$ is the average income in the total population. The first expression in equation (6.8) is obtained when we take groups, i, as single individuals in a population of size N. The second equality refers to arbitrary finite groups and makes T_I's informational interpretation explicit.

Both T_I and the spatial information-theoretic quantities in equations (6.5)–(6.7) have interesting and important properties under (dis)aggregation, which in fact motivated the original use of T_I for the study of inequality.[85] If we disaggregate the population into a number of groups, n_j, the Theil index can be decomposed into two terms as

$$T_I(y) = T_I(n) + \sum_j P(n_j)T_I(y|n_j). \tag{6.9}$$

Bettencourt, Hand, and Lobo[86] give a detailed derivation. This expression shows how the total inequality in a population with several levels of aggregation can be expressed as the *inequality across groups*, n_j, plus the average *inequality within each group*, weighted by that group's relative size. This feature of group structures is paramount in problems of collective action, which we will address in chapter 9.

The information quantities defined in subsection 6.3.1 have a similar property that extends their definitions to an arbitrary number of (dis)aggregation levels. For example, if we take the groups n_j to be further decomposed into groups m_i, we can define quantities analogous to the ones in the previous subsection and generalized mutual information $I(y; m, n)$, which obeys the multilevel relation

$$I(y; m, n) = I(y; n) + \sum_j P(n_j) I(y; m | n_j), \tag{6.10}$$

which shows that the total information in a pattern is that contained in the first level of disaggregation plus the average information contained in each of its subgroups, and so on. We therefore see that information quantities provide a systematic and recursive way to characterize both inequality and spatial selection in multilevel structured heterogeneous populations.[87] This property is general and open-ended, and is indeed the reason why informational quantities are often judged superior to other mathematical indices for characterizing complex patterns in data, be they secret messages, natural languages, neighborhood structures, or, as we will see in chapter 9, planning decisions that can lead statistically to future growth and human development.

This important property is not shared by other measures of inequality, such as the Gini index. In principle, the property of self-similarity under aggregation can be used to actively discover specific scales, places, and special characteristics (e.g., barriers or connections) at which systems become more strongly sorted.[88] Consequently, this approach applied across scales has the potential to help identify the mechanisms by which inequality and exclusion take place in practice and become entrenched, or indeed how they may be reversed and mitigated.

6.3.3   DISCUSSION: THE PATTERNS OF OUR LIVES

Complex systems—such as cities, ecosystems, or biological organisms—are often recognizable by the presence of *structure with variations*.[89] Such a description is deceptively simple, however, as it glosses over the fact that local structures in a patch of forest or on a street of a great city represent not mere accident but rather a long cumulative history of serendipity and adaptation, typically transcending the elements present at any single time.[90]

The main conceptual obstacle to building theories of cities as complex systems *at different scales* is clearly patent in the distinct approaches to the same problem developed by different disciplines.[91] For example, in order to model macroscopic regularities, physicists emphasize the behavior of averaged quantities over large populations and spatiotemporal scales.[92] This "coarse-graining" approach tells us specifically that, in many known systems, most local details do not contribute to macroscopic behavior.[93] But Jane Jacobs warned us not to do this in the context of cities!

Such "large-size" limits are much less productive for insights in many other important situations, as we have seen in our introduction to neighborhood effects. For example, they are anathema to anthropologists or ethnographers, who study primarily the detailed behavior of people in small groups. Approaching cities from the "bottom up" emphasizes that local variations matter because they contain critical information about how people operate within urban systems.[94] This information should not, in general, be averaged over, as is typically done in physics[95] or in economic models that assume representative agent behavior.[96] If we do so, we will incur great deficits in our understanding of cities. We will also create blunt policies that will suffer from stark *distributional effects*. Thus, this is not only a point of principle but also a necessity for building general theories of change—for example, reflecting patterns of interaction between agents,[97] which in turn feed evolutionary and adaptive dynamics.

It follows from the analysis in this section that proceeding in the direction of coarse graining leads to *information loss* as local states are replaced by averages over larger scales.[98] Conversely, proceeding in the opposite direction ("fine graining"), such as when we insist on the different characteristics of neighborhoods within cities, requires that we specify *more information* as new degrees of freedom on finer scales come into play and take specific values.[99] These general considerations tell us that we can navigate theories of cities as complex systems at different scales by keeping track of their information content.

Selection is a general process by which individuals learn and adapt to their environment by acquiring information.[100] Processes of selection apply generally in many different complex systems and are described by the same mathematical formalism. When applied to spatial sorting, this approach provides a means for studying how local heterogeneities can arise within a context of broader statistical regularities,[101] reconciling macroscopic phenomena, such as scaling, with microscopic behavior—for example, expressed as individual residential choice.

An important dimension of this problem is how spatial sorting patterns form in the first place and change explicitly over time. For example, data that may enable comparisons of income patterns in the same neighborhoods over time[102] through direct and comprehensive access to the choices and movements of households are becoming more available. Several recent studies in this direction in US and Canadian cities—using different methods—suggest that neighborhoods are becoming more segregated by income, a phenomenon known as *neighborhood polarization*.[103] This corresponds to stronger neighborhood effects and suggests that the mutual information between cities' neighborhood structure and income distributions is increasing over time.

A more systematic understanding of spatial population sorting by personal income and other characteristics remains at the root of some of the most challenging problems for urban science and policy, including the causes and consequences of economic inequality,[104] ethnic and racial segregation, disparate access to opportunity,[105] and spatially concentrated (dis)advantage,[106] including issues of crime and violence.[107] Extensions of present models and analytical approaches to more urban systems (other nations) and several other demographic dimensions (e.g., income, race, education, and gender) remain necessary to make urban policy and practice more effective in the face of radically different challenges faced by specific individuals and places.

EPILOGUE: NEIGHBORHOODS, INFORMATION, AND HUMAN SUSTAINABLE DEVELOPMENT

Neighborhoods are deeply embedded in our experience of cities, but, from the point of view of the body of urban theory developed in chapters 2–5, they are seemingly unnecessary. As we just saw, the formation of neighborhoods with specific local characteristics different from their cities, requires *additional information* on the mechanisms of spatial selection—both by choice and by necessity—on the part of different segments of the population.

This spatial selection can cause concentrated (dis)advantage, but it also produces different human ecologies within cities, where people can live different lives, with lower costs or with better services, or with neighbors they trust and support. In all these senses, neighborhood heterogeneities are, among other things, a means for cities to produce environments that may innovate in terms of new ways of living by

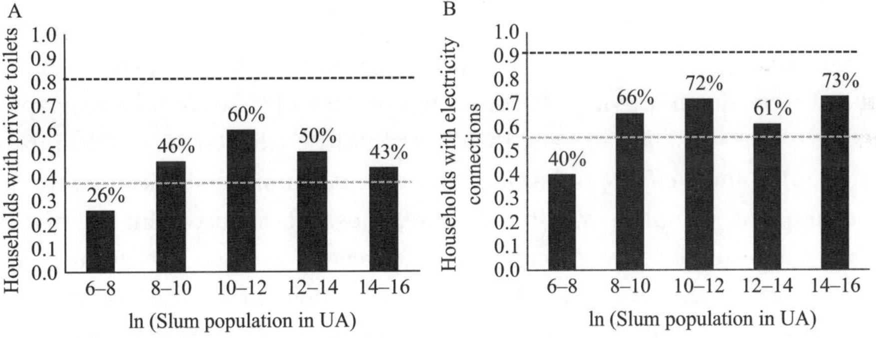

6.21 Comparison of access to services between urban slums and rural areas in Indian urban agglomerations (UAs). (A) Fraction of households with access to private toilets versus ln(slum population in UA). The dashed horizontal lines show the average fraction of rural households with private toilets, 31% (gray), and the average fraction of urban households with private toilets, 81% (black). (B) Fraction of households with access to domestic electricity connections versus ln(slum population in UA). The gray dashed line shows the average fraction of rural households with electricity connections (55%), and the black dashed line shows the average fraction of urban households with electricity connections (93%). Only the UAs with the lowest slum populations appear to have lower service levels (both for toilets and electricity connections) than rural areas. Otherwise, urban slums offer significantly better basic service delivery than in rural areas but worse than in other neighborhoods in their city.
Source: Data from the Office of the Registrar General and Census Commissioner, "Census of India, 2011" (New Delhi: Ministry of Home Affairs, 2011), https://censusindia.gov.in/2011-common /censusdata2011.html.

preserving and creating subcultures, new technologies, new architecture, specialty food or retail, and more. The spatial patterns of neighborhoods within cities also produce gradual ways for individuals to enter the city's fray ("arrival cities"[108]) and indeed ways of falling off its promise and opportunities. Informal settlements in developing cities have, in this sense, an intermediate character between the rural village and the global metropolis (figure 6.21). They are incipient cities not only as physical environments but also as socioeconomic networks.

Decoding the *language of neighborhoods* by identifying their *information content* gives researchers windows into fundamental processes of human development, specifically the ways in which people adapt to various physical and socioeconomic environments, and, as we have seen, in the case of developing cities, how local urban environments adapt to people's needs. In this sense, our touchstone equation of balancing benefits minus costs (chapters 2–4) can take many different forms over space in that reduced costs in the short term (e.g., by living in poorer neighborhoods) may be either a trap or a ladder to the opportunities of an urban environment.

This dynamic, bottom-up view of local neighborhood adaptation and associated theories of human development remains, in my view, in a fledgling state, whether we are discussing crime and poverty in US cities or the upgrading of slums in developing urban areas. Empirically, we have seen that we are in the midst of a space-time resolution revolution that allows us to measure many social, economic, and infrastructural aspects of cities systematically, including people's experience and mobility, neighborhood by neighborhood.[109] This allows us to see that typical imputations of segregation by place of residence can be mitigated by mixing resulting from travel and commuting across the city, especially to places of work and common commercial and recreational activities.[110] This brings us back to issues of time geography[111] (chapter 2), people's life paths and their interactions[112] (chapter 3), and the prospect of measuring these effects, on average and with variations and selection, in much richer and more complete ways in the future. Thus, data are becoming less of a limitation; slums are no longer "zones of silence," even for those officials far away, in national governments or the headquarters of development agencies. What remains fundamentally missing, then, is a richer causal framework of human cognition and development through the life course that is capable of identifying not only "problem neighborhoods" but also the means by which any urban environment, whether initially rich or poor, can be meaningfully improved to generate integrated opportunities anywhere in the world, for everybody. Such a "universal" theory of sustainable human development in neighborhoods would be a major achievement for urban science. The prospects are bright that growing knowledge and the shared experience of change in millions of neighborhoods worldwide over the next few decades will point the way forward.

we start from the beginning and consider some of the drivers—and the barriers—to larger-scale socialization in the simplest human societies.

CHAPTER OUTLINE

This chapter is divided into three sections. Section 7.1 provides a brief summary of the properties of early cities in light of comparative analysis in archeology and anthropology. We develop proxies in the archeological record for quantities characterizing modern cities, which allow us to test hypotheses about the general features of spatially localized human interaction networks in different cultural and historical contexts. Such settings also provide us with unique *experiments in urbanism*, including the independent advent of cities in the New and Old Worlds. Quantitative analysis of these situations helps establish a stronger case for the generality of scaling properties of human settlements. In section 7.2, we push these patterns all the way back to the first camps of mobile hunter-gatherer peoples to discover situations where scaling relations and agglomeration effects become more temporary and contingent and ultimately break down. We develop models of the social and energetic factors at work in such circumstances, which can tell us how a transition to denser, more permanent settlements (and to urbanism more generally) might have occurred historically. In section 7.3, we briefly discuss the phenomenon of economic growth in premodern societies, its connection to scaling effects and urbanization, and its typical magnitude and volatility. We finish the chapter with a general reflection on the trade-offs between costs and benefits of human large-scale socialization and the kinds of functional innovations necessary to sustain and grow this unstable but immensely generative connected state of social interdependence and cooperation.

7.1 CITIES IN HISTORY

We start with a brief overview of what may have been the first cities, before we engage with more detailed archeological evidence from a variety of contexts throughout history.

7.1.1 THE FIRST CITIES

It is still debated which city was the very first. The earliest permanent settlements discovered by archeologists so far were small and relatively simple, even when compared to small towns today. Very early permanent sites, such as Jericho (today in the West Bank), or some of the settlements discovered in modern Turkey, such as Çatalhöyük, seem to have been spatial population agglomerations of farming communities with perhaps a few thousand people at their largest (figure 7.2). These settlements would have more in common with small subsistence agriculture towns today, lacking the many ingredients that result from being part of a larger urban

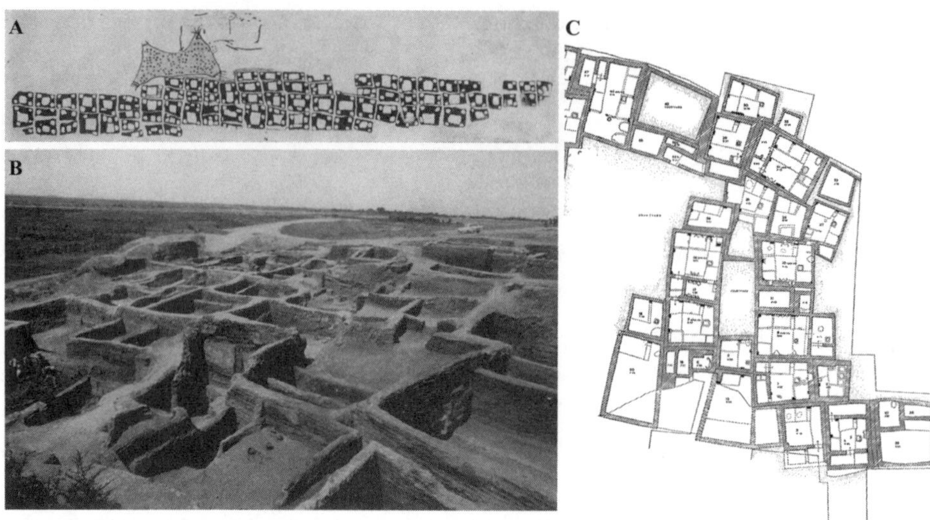

7.2 Early Neolithic settlements of Çatalhöyük. The site was composed exclusively of domestic mud-brick houses and may have housed a population of about 5,000 people, but that fluctuated over the period 7100–5600 BC. The local culture included religious rituals, ritual burials, and art, as well as new technologies of building and tools and, possibly, the first urban map (A). The black and white regular shapes are thought to be houses, against the background of an extinct volcano (Hasan Dag). The interpretation of this wall pattern as a map remains controversial among archeologists, however. (B) Houses were set in dense clusters, as the partial archeological map (C) shows. Sites around Jericho show some settlements that may go back to around 10,000 BC, to the Natufian culture, and are sometimes thought to predate agriculture. Early Jericho was notable for its walls and tower and survived through the ages into modern times.
Source: Images from James Mellaart, "Excavations at Hacılar: Third Preliminary Report, 1959," *Anatolian Studies* 10 (1960): 83–104, https://doi.org/10.2307/3642430.

system, such as access to more sophisticated technology, socioeconomic management practices, and politics.

By the time of the "first cities" in Mesopotamia, many of these ingredients were clearly present. A common position in archeology and geography (chapter 8) is that *true cities* only appeared when they became part of settlement (urban) systems. This argument suffers from the logical fallacy of recursion, of course. The smallest urban system is likely to have had a single "city," perhaps together with other nonpermanently occupied settlements.

Historical studies have often interpreted early cities and urban development as a consequence of the advent of a few general critical functions that sure enough seem to have been present across many of the first settlements.[3] Famously, Lewis Mumford, in his landmark book *The City in History*, proposed three main general functions of early cities: *defense*, *markets*, and *religion*. Other influential writers emphasize the importance of pooling resources together, storage and redistribution,[4] the rise of political systems (the *state*),[5] and of hierarchical (political) societies with more sophisticated bureaucracies and governance as a result of population pressure, a phenomenon anthropologist Robert Carneiro memorably described as generating *quality from quantity*.[6] In this view, political, religious, economic, and other forms of social organization result from the need to manage larger populations[7] because of conquest or natural growth, leading to a segmentation and differentiation of individual and collective functions and perhaps to hierarchical stratification and growing inequality (chapter 5). A complementary tack, connected to ideas of *central place theory* (chapter 8), is the more practical concept that population centers nucleated around shared infrastructure, such as trade routes, waterworks, and canals, which were important for food production and storage in many early settlements and likely required a coordination of labor above and beyond what was possible (or necessary) in smaller and less dense societies. Agricultural surpluses could then be stored and used more strategically, including in ways that supported long-distance trade and the division of labor, creating full-time nonprimary producers, such as administrative classes associated with religion and emergent forms of political organization.[8] All these ideas are likely correct to some extent. However, they leave us with a sense that there are many proximate ways for a city to exist and grow, and thus none of these drivers individually or in subgroups provides us with a general path to early urbanism.

In this chapter, we take these ideas as background but embark on a quantitative comparative exploration of how similar ancient settlements were to modern cities, not so much in terms of their culture, size, or technology but rather in terms of their spatialized costs and benefits, expressed through scaling relations and their specific interpretation in history.

7.1.2   THE MOTHER OF ALL SOCIAL EXPERIMENTS

The best place to begin a comparative study of urbanism in history is surely the mother of all experiments: the independent advent of settled societies and cities in the New World (pre-Columbian Americas) versus their counterparts in the Old World. People came to the New World before there were cities, but by the time Europeans arrived, Native Americans had invented some of the largest and most spectacular cities that ever existed. This is an instance of "convergent evolution," where similar functions are developed despite independent histories. Focusing on the comparison between instances of independent convergent evolution is then the best way to zero in on function rather than form.

Undertaking the comparison between the independent advent of cities in the Old and New Worlds was a brilliant insight by Robert McCormick Adams, then the director of the Oriental Institute (OI) at the University of Chicago. The OI pioneered Middle Eastern archeology, including the scientific studies of the first cities and urban systems, such as Ur and Uruk in Sumer. Adams's comparative work crystallized in 1965 with an invitation to give a famous lecture series in archeology—the Lewis Henry Morgan Lectures at the University of Rochester. Adams's lectures were titled "Evolution of Urban Society: Early Mesopotamia and Pre-Hispanic Mexico." The materials would later be published as a book. An extract from its opening makes its objectives clear:

This volume is concerned with the presentation and analysis of regularities on our two best documented cases of early, independent urban societies. It seeks to provide as systematic a comparison as the data permits of institutional forms and trends of growth that are to be found in both of them.

Emphasizing basic similarities in structure rather than the many acknowledged formal features by which each culture is rendered distinguishable from all others, it seeks to demonstrate that both the societies in question can usefully be regarded as variants of a single processual pattern.[9]

I do not think that these objectives should have been controversial then or are today, but at the time, in the 1960s and the years that followed, archeologists and anthropologists were just beginning to use patterns in data to identify common "regularities" that could cut across time and culture. To some scholars, these patterns felt too deterministic, too oblivious of subjectivity, or too disrespectful of human agency to be relevant. To others, an appeal to extreme cultural relativism and independence left no space for the kind of synthesis Adams was seeking and therefore for cumulative scholarship or even science. These crudely polarized academic disputes are by and large features of the past, but we would do well to keep them in mind today and not fall victim to extreme positions of either overgeneralization or sterile particularism.

We will carry forward in this book the dual preoccupation that quantitative regularities and models actually follow from relatively weak constraints on averaged patterns of daily life where interpretation, choice, and agency are not only abundant but necessary (chapters 3 and 9). The regularities that Adams and others began to identify provide frameworks for human choice and agency to become possible over new and expanded realms beyond more constrained biological adaptations to natural environments.

7.1.3 THE URBAN PACKAGE

Adams's main place of work—the OI at the University of Chicago—has a simple and beautiful exhibition of artifacts from the earliest cities of the Middle East that I encourage you to visit. Within the small space of a few glass exhibition cases, one can cover the first millennia over which cities with modern features appeared. These functional features never again ceased to be part of human societies. These innovations took forms that were at once economic, political, energetic, bureaucratic, and informational; for example:

- Standardized bowls, thought to represent daily wages or rations in grain,
- Mass construction technologies (e.g., mudbricks, masonry, and canals),
- Property records and records of warehousing and economic transactions,
- Written laws, especially regulating conflict and theft, and associated standardized penalties,

- Writing and early reflections on the human condition,
- Accounting and mathematics, including time keeping,
- Political hierarchy and propaganda,
- Copious production of religious and artistic objects.

Of these, the most extraordinary to me is writing, the technology taken by scholars to symbolize the formal beginning of *history*. In the beginning, writing was not really what it is today (figure 7.3). It was mathematics, accounting, and natural language, all wrapped together in the same script. Most of the first documents will disappoint the literary buff and delight the accountant or mathematician: they are the Excel spreadsheets of their time. Data, mathematics, and recorded natural language were thus born together in the same medium, in a beautiful expression of what cities are about. Soon after the advent of this medium, the first voices could be heard speaking to us across history, describing poignant aspects of their lives, such as the pains of being a scribe or the vicissitudes of their love life, in ways that to me feel thoroughly modern.

What I think is important here is not so much that a single innovation produced and sustained these early cities but that a full *urban package* of new technologies— mostly about accounting, communication, regulation of conflict, and social and political life—was there from the beginning. The essence of these innovations remains with us today as we continue to struggle to keep our modern cities efficient, fair, and collaborative places for human sociality.

As we will see, this urban package of technologies was *not* part of some of the simplest human societies prior to cities, which express different quantitative patterns of land use and socialization in both space and time. Art, for example, precedes cities, though it is spectacularly magnified—but sometimes also institutionalized—in urban environments.

7.3 Early evolution of writing. In the first cities of Sumer, counting, record keeping, and a limited verbal script were all part of the same system. In this way, data and written narrative have a common origin. Over time, these media would become more specialized and separate, but both remain essential to the functioning of urban societies.
Source: Courtesy of the Oriental Institute of the University of Chicago.

7.1.4 THE GREAT CITIES OF THE BASIN OF MEXICO

We beheld on that great lake a great multitude of canoes, some coming with supplies of food and others returning loaded with cargoes of merchandise; and we saw that from every house of that great city and of all the other cities that were built in the water it was impossible to pass from house to house, except by drawbridges which were made of wood or in canoes; and we saw in those cities temples and oratories like towers and fortresses and all gleaming white, and it was a wonderful thing to behold. . . .

After having examined and considered all that we had seen we turned to look at the great market place and the crowds of people that were in it, some buying and others selling, so that the murmur and hum of their voices and words that they used could be heard more than a league off. Some of the soldiers among us who had been in many parts of the world, in Constantinople, and all over Italy, and in Rome, said that they had never beheld so large a market place and so full of people, and so well regulated and arranged.

—Bernal Díaz del Castillo, *True Story of the Conquest of New Spain*

We all know the story of the first encounter of Spanish conquistadores with the great Aztec civilization whose capital—Tenochtitlán—described here by Bernal Díaz del Castillo, was one of the greatest cities in the world at that time. The astonishment of these Europeans at the sight of something in many ways grander and more extraordinary than anything they had ever experienced or created is clear from all the chronicles of the time.

We tend to remember this clash of civilizations for the pain and glory of the fight on both sides and the subsequent conquest and cultural, political, and demographic genocide of a rich and complex pre-Hispanic culture at the hands of a crude European empire. But something else about this encounter was arguably more profound and should stay with us through the fog and pain of war and destruction: the realization that great cities, with all dimensions of the urban package of markets, politics, religion, and daily life, were independently invented processes in the Americas and the Old World.

While historians like Adams were pioneers in establishing a qualitative analytical basis for these comparisons, we can now do a much more exacting job by testing ideas of urban scaling and agglomeration, developed earlier in this book. Figure 7.4 shows an artist's rendering of Tenochtitlán as described in the early 1500s, at the time of the Spanish Conquest. The second panel shows that this great city was the capital of a large regional urban system made up of settlements of many sizes. The region benefited from its setting on a lake, which facilitated communication and transport.

These settlements have been extensively and consistently surveyed by archeologists in a way that allows us today to infer both their population and areal extent. This creates a wonderful setting to test scaling patterns of settled area, A, versus population, N. Because population cannot be measured directly in archeological settings (everyone is dead, by definition), it is necessary that we find proxies. This is a subject of much work in archeology.[10] Two solutions, both available in the Basin of Mexico sites, consist of assessing population density via sherd (debris) deposition rates and via room counts in houses (see figure 7.5). The idea is that sherds (durable

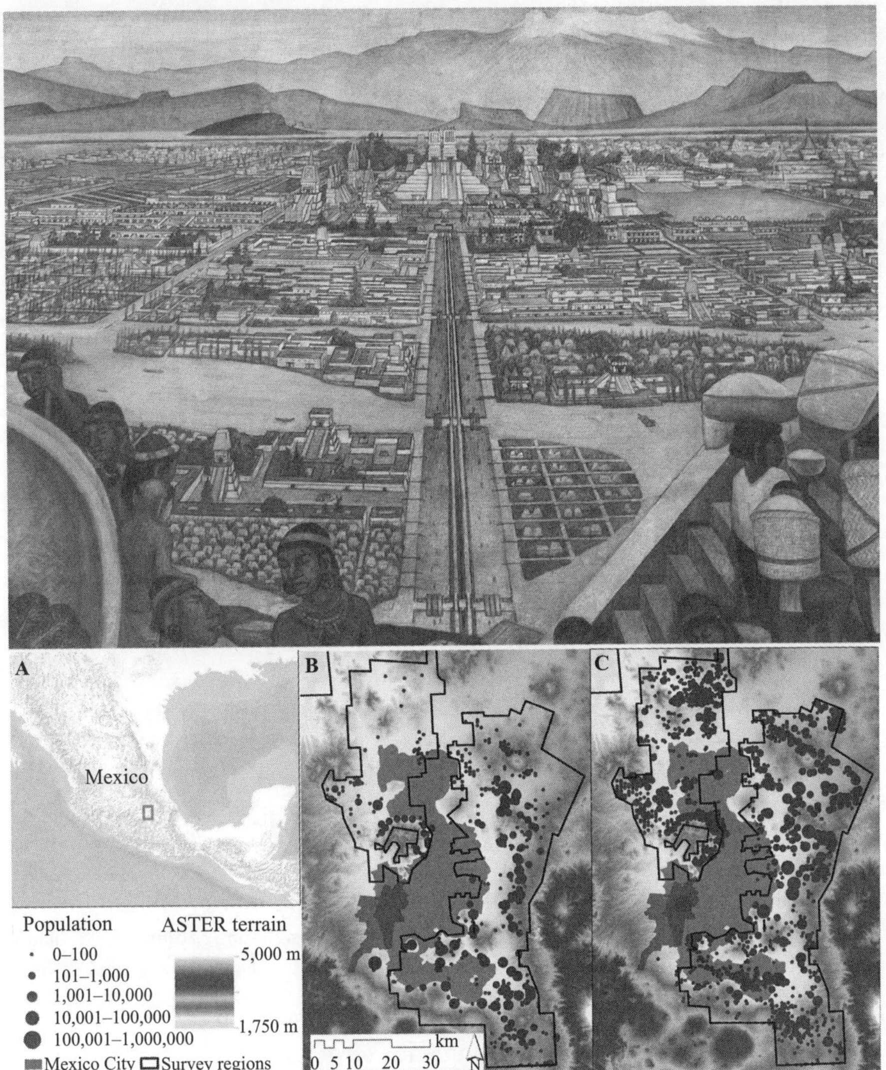

7.4 Diego Rivera's rendering of Tenochtitlán at the time of the Spanish Conquest in the first decades of the sixteenth century and settlement map of the Basin of Mexico. The city was estimated then to have a population of about 200,000 people and to be the capital of an urban system with hundreds of other settlements (lower panels). This urban system had existed for about 2,000 years, through four culturally distinctive periods—Formative, (B) Classic, Toltec, and (C) Aztec—for which detailed archeological surveys exist. The lines show the limits of the surveyed area, and the shaded gray area shows the extent of Mexico City in 1960.

trash) accumulate at a rate proportional to population size and time, while room counts give us a sense of housing capacity, at least at time of maximum occupation.

Because the survey of the Basin of Mexico is complete, mapping all settlements from the smallest site to the largest city, it provides us with a rare possibility to study scaling of the area of settlements across population sizes down to very small villages with no discernible spatial infrastructure. In our development of urban scaling theory (chapter 3), we introduced the simplest model of a town as an *amorphous*

Population density in archeology

Method 1: Sherd densities

> Very Light – A wide scattering of surface debris so that only one or two sherds may be present every few meters; associated with compact rancherias of 2–5 persons/ha.

> Light – A continuous distribution of sherds every 20–30 cm, but with no significant buildup in sherd density beyond that point; associated with scattered villages of 5–10 persons/ha.

> Light-Moderate – Although most of the area contains light surface remains, delimited areas of substantial buildup containing as many as 100–200 sherds per square meter consistently appear; associated with compact low-density villages of 10–25 persons/ha.

> Moderate – A continuous layer of sherds, so that any randomly placed 1-meter square might yield 100 to 200 pieces of pottery; associated with compact high-density villages of 25-50 persons/ha.

> Moderate-Heavy – Over most of the area occupation occurs in moderate densities. However, in a few localized areas a 1-m square might contain 200–400 pieces of pottery; upper range of compact high-density villages of 50–100 persons/ha.

> Heavy – Densities of 200–400 sherds per 1-m square are continuous such that sherds are literally one atop another, so that a randomly placed 1-m square might produce as many as 400–800 pieces of pottery; associated with the upper range of compact high-density villages of 50–100 persons/ha.

Method 2: Room and house counts

> Multiply room occupancy by total number of rooms.

7.5 Methods for independent measurement of population size and spatial area in settlements from the archeological record. Surveys, such as those in the Basin of Mexico, often measure average occupation density over a period of time via amounts of debris deposition. These can also be arranged in time periods to reconstitute site history. Sherd density does not give an absolute estimate of population size, as this may depend on the materials and technologies involved, but its variation (relative density) is hypothesized to track population density variations. In addition, where available, house and room counts allow a more direct estimate of the population, assuming an average number of people per room. Comparing these two methods and identifying whether they converge on the same population estimates gives archeologists a consistency check for estimating settlement populations.

settlement, a spatial concentration of population over space without the need to consider special features of the built environment except its (low) density. We can now test these ideas and observe also if and when larger cities develop networked infrastructure by using the scaling relation

$$A(N) = aN^{\alpha}, \tag{7.1}$$

with $\alpha \simeq \frac{2}{3}$ for (small) amorphous settlements and $\alpha \simeq \frac{5}{6}$ for networked settlements, typical of larger, denser cities (figure 7.6), as we have seen in chapter 3.

Table 7.1 shows a first pass at the analysis, pooling together all types and sizes of settlements in the Basin of Mexico. Using two estimation methods, we see that exponents are clearly sublinear for the four different historical periods, with numerical values roughly compatible but somewhat larger in some cases than predicted by the amorphous settlement model.

This is not bad as a first look at the data, but we have to recognize that smaller (more amorphous) sites make up the vast majority of settlements and may naturally pull the exponents down toward their expected value around $\alpha \simeq \frac{2}{3}$. A second pass

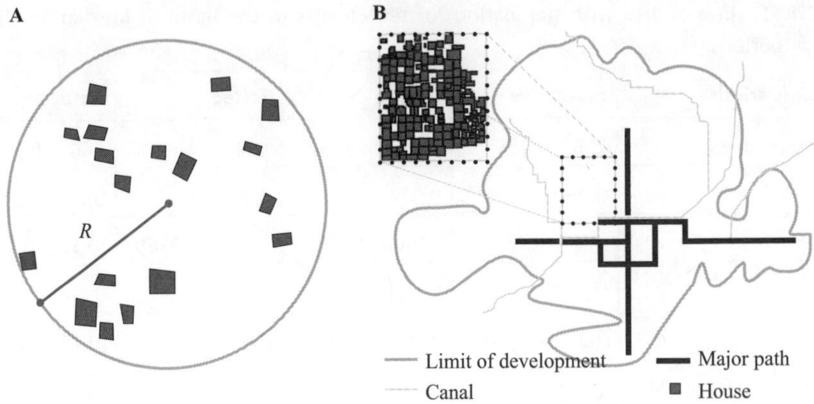

7.6 Amorphous versus networked settlements in the archeological record. (A) The small agricultural town of Capilco (recall figure 3.6) is a good candidate for an amorphous settlement, as it consists basically of a cluster of houses, without a street plan or other networked infrastructure. (B) The classical city of Teotihuacán is the archetype in pre-Hispanic American antiquity of a city with a street plan, broad avenues, and canals, which thread the built space of the city and facilitate movement of people, goods, and information. These two types of settlements are posited to have different scaling exponents, $\alpha \approx \frac{2}{3}$ and $\alpha \approx \frac{5}{6}$, respectively, as observed empirically (tables 7.1 and 7.2).

at the data, where we stratify sites into two classes, large settlements with some spatial organization and all others, is shown in table 7.2.[11] Repeating the parameter estimation in each case, we now find exponents for larger sites compatible with the networked settlement model and urban scaling theory more generally. This result is further reinforced by the parameter estimation of agricultural sites in the same region from the 1960s Census of Mexico, which also shows an exponent compatible with the amorphous settlement model but with a larger baseline area. This smaller population density in modern agricultural towns is possibly the result of improved transportation methods and therefore a smaller c_{T_0}.

Other predictions that follow from the application of settlement scaling theory to the archeological record deal with the superlinearity of rates of socioeconomic products on population size. The societies of the Basin of Mexico, like many other early civilizations, had very different means of measuring wealth than our societies today. They were also much more limited in how they could accumulate it. For example, the Aztecs did not have money in the modern sense and are thought to have used standardized goods, such as cotton blankets and cocoa beans, as proxies.[12] Likewise, measures of innovation or of the division of labor seem consistent in the broadest qualitative terms with narratives of the time but are difficult to measure based on the quantities available to us in the archeological record. Necessarily, measuring these quantities requires the identification of context-appropriate proxies for wealth, innovation, and other quantities.

In the case of the Basin of Mexico, the average amount of construction—both public, measured as monuments, and private, measured by houses—scales superlinearly[13] with population size and also shows the telltale statistical distribution of

Table 7.1 Scaling of area with population for settlements in the Basin of Mexico for distinct historical periods

Variable/periods	Formative	Classic	Toltec	Aztec
Number of sites	230	272	484	546
a (ha)	0.200	0.274	0.196	0.180
95% CI	[0.174–0.277]	[0.206–0.400]	[0.167–0.256]	[0.154–0.230]
α	0.700	0.627	0.708	0.750
95% CI	[0.654–0.740]	[0.544–0.705]	[0.655–0.752]	[0.714–0.785]
Population of largest site	33,850	95,597	22,502	212,500

Table 7.2 Amorphous versus networked settlements in the Basin of Mexico and corresponding estimates of scaling exponents

Group	Amorphous	Networked	1960
Number of sites	1,510	22	181
a (ha)	0.237	0.109	0.445
95% CI	[0.217–0.259]	[0.009–1.303]	[0.250–0.945]
α	0.671	0.853	0.641
95% CI	[0.651–0.691]	[0.598–1.109]	[0.552–0.729]
R^2	0.741	0.709	0.532

Notes: Separating settlements into two sets, one with the vast majority of sites made up of small settlements and the other including all large sites, allows us to test more precisely the estimated values of scaling exponents, which now agree well with theory for the two settlement types. Also interesting is that a result similar to that for amorphous settlements is also obtained from the 1960 Census of Mexico for small agricultural towns in the same area, with a smaller prefactor signaling lower overall population densities. Estimation methods are as in table 7.1.

deviations about this mean, which is reasonably well described by a lognormal distribution (see figure 7.7), as we saw in chapter 4.

Taken together, the evidence constitutes our first indication that urban scaling theory may apply to settlements throughout history. It is particularly noteworthy—following Robert Adams's strategy of comparative analysis between Old and New World cities—that the same general adaptations would have emerged in contemporary cities and, completely independently, in the civilizations of the Basin of Mexico.

A similar strategy was pursued by Ortman and Coffey,[14] to discover patterns of settlement scaling also consistent with theory in Pueblo Indian sites of the American Southwest, and more recently by a number of authors in other pre-Hispanic urban systems, which were part of the Inca Empire in Peru.[15] In this latter example, it is also possible to identify an episodic expansion of living standards around this region's culture integration into the Inca Empire in the form of changes in the scaling prefactors (see section 7.3).

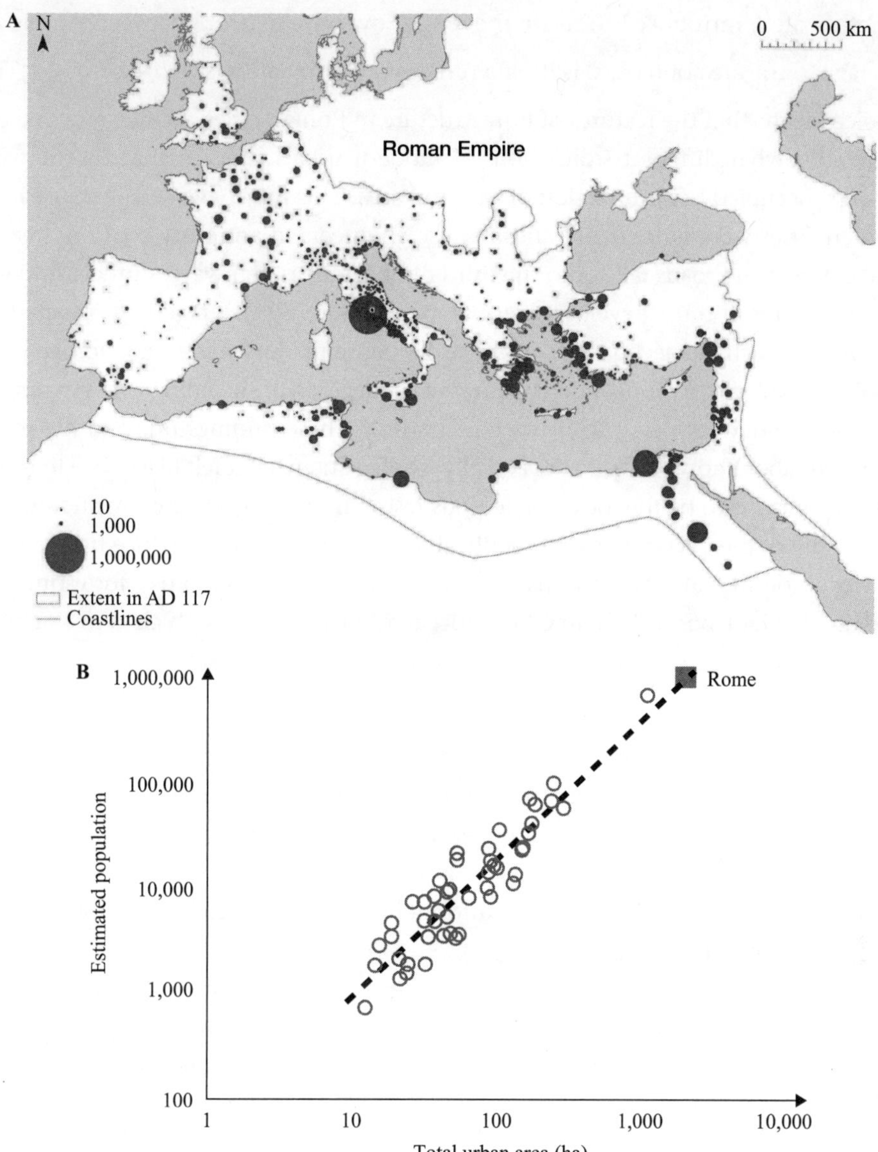

7.8   Estimated population size of Roman cities in the first century AD. The authors compiled the areal extent of all cities on the map and computed estimates of the population from archeological evidence of rooms and houses (lower panel). This allowed them to derive a scaling law with an exponent $\alpha \approx \frac{2}{3}$ (best-fit line). Extrapolating this line predicts the population of Rome from a number of independent estimates at about a million (gray square).

Source: Adapted from J. W. Hanson and S. G. Ortman, "A Systematic Method for Estimating the Populations of Greek and Roman Settlements," *Journal of Roman Archaeology* 30 (2017): 301–324, https://doi.org/10.1017/S1047759400074134.

length scale l, introduced to relate the length over the network between people on average to the area of blocks, is itself a function of population size, $l \sim N^{\delta}, \delta \approx \frac{1}{6}$. This choice means that the features of infrastructure in Roman cities—while networked— were somewhat different from those of modern urban areas in that the network (streets) occupied a fixed fraction of the land area. This may have been because large Roman cities were quite dense and because engineers in antiquity could not easily make streets and roads take onto the third dimension, as highways, tunnels, and via- ducts. The result must have been very crowded and busy streets (energy dissipation $W \sim N^{4/3}$), which is anecdotally confirmed by contemporary narratives. Roman cities also included certain innovations in traffic management, including one-way streets and time-of-day restrictions on wheeled traffic.[24] These findings bring to life many questions about how Roman cities actually worked and what it felt like to live in them, which continue to be the focus of vigorous research on classical cities, including into the nature of their economies and political institutions.[25] Some evidence from epigra- phy on professional organizations known as *collegia* provides a proxy for estimating the division of labor in Roman cities[26] (occupational richness), which is in line with the quantitative expectations discussed in chapter 5.

7.1.6   MEDIEVAL EUROPEAN CITIES

Another set of interesting urban systems deals with medieval European cities, which provide us with a sort of midpoint between cities of the Roman Empire and modern European urban areas. Figure 7.9 shows a number of cities circa AD 1300 for which both population estimates and area information could be constructed by Cesaretti and his collaborators.[27]

The now familiar estimation of the area-population scaling relation generates exponent and prefactor estimates in line with theory and with other historical and modern cases (see figure 7.10). The estimates of sublinear exponents for these data, organized in terms of national units, typically fall in intermediate ranges between an amorphous settlement and the networked city prediction. However, cities at this time were fairly small. Considering the urban systems with the largest ranges of population and areas sizes, such as France and Belgium taken together, displays exponents arguably approaching the expectations of the networked city model and consistent with it statistically.

7.1.7   SUPERLINEAR SCALING OF TOWN ECONOMIES
IN TUDOR ENGLAND

The sublinear results for the area-population scaling relationship can be supple- mented by some data indicating corresponding superlinear effects in economic pro- ductivity. There is, at present, no bona fide comprehensive measure of the economies

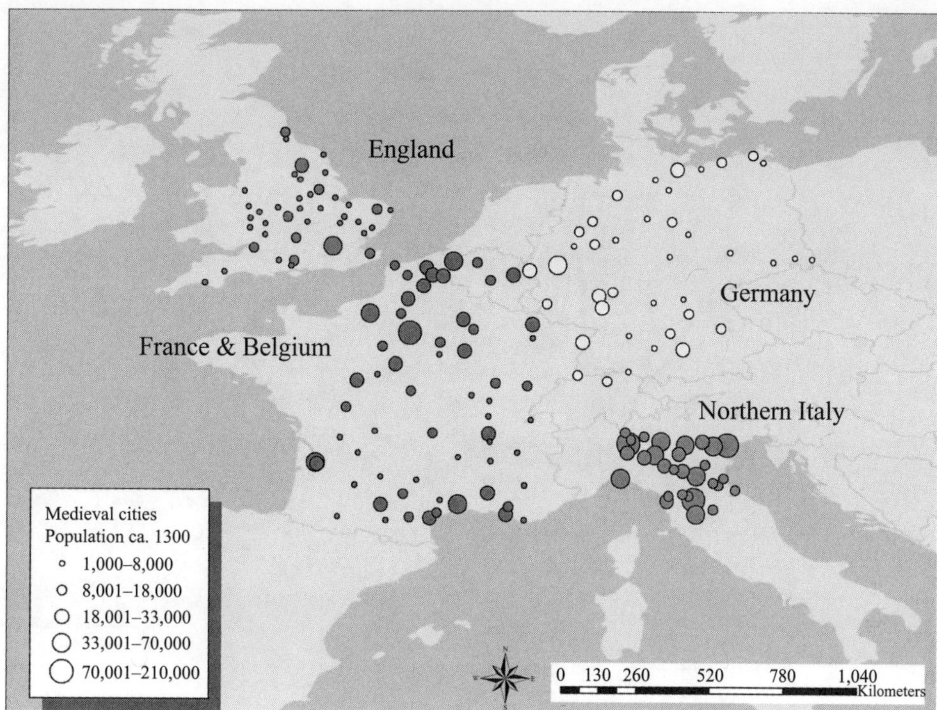

7.9   Medieval cities of France, Belgium, Germany, England, and northern Italy. Circles indicate population sizes, while names and different tones suggest integrated urban systems. The population area relationships for these cities reveal scaling results that are sublinear and that are roughly in agreement with urban scaling theory (see figure 7.11 and table 7.4).

of medieval European cities. Nevertheless, as we have shown throughout this chapter, there are historical episodes for which specific data can provide illuminating proxies.

The *Lay Subsidies of 1524 and 1525* provide a rare window of opportunity to test the presence of increasing returns to population scale among the provincial towns of Tudor England. The Lay Subsidies were taxes levied by the Crown on certain forms of private wealth in England. Conveniently, they include both taxpayer counts and tax receipts for a large sample of towns that is well aligned with the urban functional units of the time.

Numerous small towns and a few larger ones (including Southwark, Newcastle, Chester, Durham, Kendal, and Rye) were either not included in the 1524 and 1525 subsidies or lack surviving records of taxpayer counts. Thus, the data analyzed are a sample, but the coverage rate increases as one goes up the urban size hierarchy. As a demographic metric, taxpayer counts have been taken to be proportional to town populations. Indeed, the 1524 and 1525 taxpayer figures are the most frequently used data for estimating town populations for this period.[28]

As an economic measure, historians have traditionally treated the 1524 and 1525 tax receipts as being proportional to household wealth. Consequently, these data

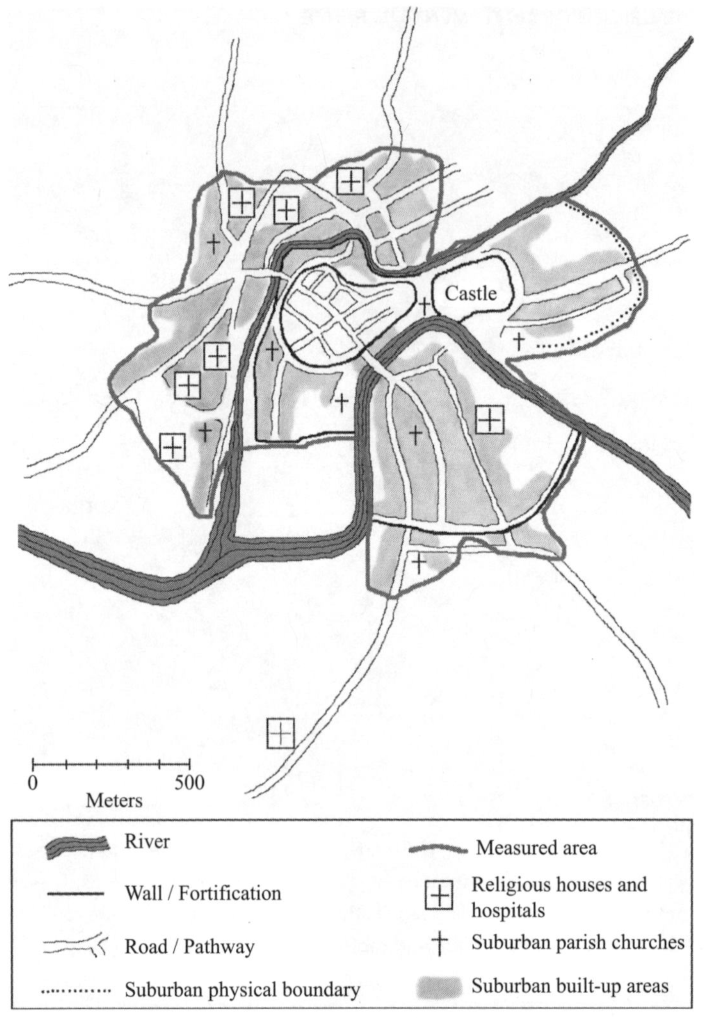

Dependent variable	N_c	Exponent (95% CI)	Prefactor (95% CI)	R^2
France and Belgium	63	0.790 (0.665–0.914)	0.05 (0.02–0.16)	0.84
England	40	0.730 (0.604–0.856)	0.12 (0.04–0.36)	0.79
Germany	40	0.754 (0.616–0.891)	0.09 (0.03–0.31)	0.77
Northern Italy	30	0.720 (0.566–0.874)	0.11 (0.02–0.51)	0.71
All cities	173	0.714 (0.662–0.766)	0.12 (0.07–0.19)	0.81

7.10 Measuring the area of medieval European cities from maps. A map of Bristol, England, illustrates measuring the built extent of cities and towns. The table shows estimated parameters for the area and the population scaling relationship, with exponents in the range $\frac{2}{3} \leq \alpha \leq \frac{5}{6}$, as roughly expected from theory. Also compare the baseline densities of medieval cities and observe that they vary from nation to nation. Compared to other historical cases, medieval cities were quite dense, roughly in line with the larger networked settlements in the Basin of Mexico (table 7.2) and potentially denser than most small Roman cities but not Rome itself, which was much larger (table 7.3).

Table 7.4 Scaling analysis of error-type subsets in the 1524 and 1525 Lay Subsidies. Loglinear ordinary least squares regression of log tax on log taxpayer count

Subset of cities and towns	N_c	R^2	β	95% CI	log Y_0	95% CI
All cases	93	0.676	1.270	[1.10, 1.44]	0.051	[0.02, 0.14]
Without municipal/rural error subset	68	0.677	1.255	[1.07, 1.44]	0.056	[0.02, 0.17]
Without problem error subset	77	0.719	1.229	[1.05, 1.41]	0.065	[0.02, 0.18]
Excluding both error subsets	55	0.739	1.284	[1.09, 1.48]	0.047	[0.01, 0.15]

have been used to evaluate the distribution of private wealth across space,[29] among towns,[30] and within towns.[31] However, the 1524 and 1525 returns are in fact a better proxy for economic income than for wealth. They included movable goods, coins, rents, and credit, but excluded all fixed capital. Because before the eighteenth century[32] the vast majority of capital consisted of land and housing, the data provide an especially useful metric of economic *activity*.

The results of the standard scaling regression for the Lay Subsidies, equation (3.1), are shown in table 7.4, including several sensitivity tests where the dataset was reduced to subsets for which the authors had greater confidence. The estimated exponents in these various situations are clearly superlinear, a little larger in fact than the simplest predictions from urban scaling theory but compatible with them within statistical uncertainty.

As with any partial dataset, there are some caveats to these results. For example, the number of people *not* explicitly counted by the taxes is a potential source of systematic error. This is either the result of exemption because of poverty or because their demographic category was not liable to taxation. To estimate the actual total population, historians always multiply the taxpayer counts by constant "modifiers" derived from other available demographic data.[33] The use of constant multipliers assumes that the proportion of uncounted persons does not covary with town population size.

However, some scholars have suggested that larger towns may have had greater proportions of taxpayers exempted because of higher poverty rates.[34] If so, then the undercounting of their population may overestimate the scaling exponent, analogous with the undercounted populations of Chinese prefectural cities in chapter 4.

7.1.8 DISCUSSION: ECONOMIES OF SCALE AND INCREASING RETURNS FOR CITIES IN HISTORY

We have now gotten a glimpse of a recent but fast-growing body of literature quantifying scaling properties of historic human settlements over many historical periods and different geographies. In this way, the agenda of comparative analysis started by Adams and others—motivated by the hypothesis of common processes shared by all human settlements—has in recent years been rendered much more systematic and quantitative. This is in part the result of using settlement scaling analysis and its associated theory. This framework allows us to connect spatial and material aspects of settlements available in the archeological record to social and economic network processes and their products, including a society's collective capacity to produce private and public goods and its associated division of labor and knowledge.

The discussion of this section was meant to be illustrative; it is far from complete. Table 7.5 provides a summary that includes additional quantities, studies, and cultures.

As this book is being written, more studies of a greater variety of societies are rapidly becoming possible following the path of comparative analysis outlined here. This raises the hope for a more integrated, quantitative, and generative understanding of settlement systems throughout history. Particularly interesting are cases that have been classified by Fletcher[35] as "low-density urbanism," specifically the Maya[36] of Central America and the Khmer of Angkor Wat,[37] both civilizations of tropical forest environments. Settlement sites for these cultures are presently the focus of great attention and of a number of surveys using new technologies such as LiDAR.[38] This type of convergence between remote sensing surveying and landscape archeology allows mapping of much more extensive areas at greater spatial resolution, and the results are quite spectacular. These methods are particularly useful in tropical regions where vegetation tends to obscure features of the built environment.

Improved surveys under way, digitization of data from previous studies, and a more functional delineation of settlements and "urban systems" may therefore open many data-rich possibilities for more quantitative comparative research of cities in history. Several methodological challenges in urban science may in fact be easier to tackle in historical settings than in contemporary metropolitan areas and, in any case, benefit from a comparative historical perspective where greater variation is at work.[39]

7.2 HUNTER-GATHERER SOCIETIES AND THE ORIGINS OF SETTLEMENTS

In our path back toward simpler human societies, we have now reached the last stage: the consideration of human societies that do not have "technologies" like agriculture or permanent settlements. The relevance of these considerations is that they provide us with a picture of what kinds of innovations must occur with settlement and the difficulties inherent to acquiring and maintaining them. Above all, consideration of the interplay between hunter-gatherer ways of life and their uses of space opens up a new window into the origins of the balancing act involved in living in cities and some measure of their dynamical nature and underlying instabilities.

The place to start is the full appreciation of how recent cities are in human history. This is fully revealed only by contemplating the entire history of our species. Figure 7.1 shows the spread of modern humans across the earth, with numbers indicating times to reach diverse parts of the world from an inferred common origin

Table 7.5 Summary of archeological and historical settlement scaling studies

Culture/period	Variable	N_c	Exponent	95% CI/SE	R^2	Reference
Ancestral Pueblo villages Southwest Colorado, US, AD 1060–1280	Settled area	278	0.662	0.513–0.812	0.216	Ortman and Coffey
Ancestral Pueblo villages Southwest Colorado, US, AD 1060–1280	Total house area	130	1.167	1.044–1.289	0.735	Ortman and Coffey
Ancestral Mandan/Hidatsa villages North Dakota, US, AD 1200–1886	Settled area	35	0.643	0.483–0.802	0.654	Ortman and Coffey
Ancestral Mandan/Hidatsa villages North Dakota, US, AD 1200–1886	Mean house area	17	0.163	0.038–0.287	0.305	Ortman and Coffey
Farming/administrative settlements Central Andes, Peru, AD 1000–1532	Settled area	57	0.696	0.065	0.679	Ortman et al. (2016)
Herding settlements Central Andes, Peru, AD 1000–1532	Settled Area	39	0.655	0.158	0.318	Ortman et al. (2016)
Wanka settlements Central Andes, Peru, AD 1000–1532	Domestic structure size	91	0.139	0.037	0.135	Ortman et al. (2016)
Amorphous settlements (pop. <5,000) Basin of Mexico, Mexico, AD 1150–1520	Settled area	1,510	0.671	0.651–0.691	0.741	Ortman et al. (2014)
Networked settlements (pop. >5,000) Basin of Mexico, Mexico, AD 1150–1520	Built area	22	0.853	0.598–1.109	0.709	Ortman et al. (2014)
Pre-Hispanic settlements Basin of Mexico, Mexico, AD 1150–1520	Civic mound volume	48	1.177	1.028–1.327	0.852	Ortman et al. (2015)
Pre-Hispanic settlements Basin of Mexico, Mexico, AD 1150–1520	Mean domestic area	80	0.190	0.083–0.298	0.863	Ortman et al. (2015)
Medieval European cities and towns 1300	Settled area	173	0.714	0.026	0.810	Cesaretti et al.
Ancient Greek and Roman cities 100 BCE–AD 300	Settled area	53	0.654	0.587–0.721	0.877	Hanson and Ortman
Imperial Roman cities	Association diversity	210	0.657	0.614–0.797	0.660	Hanson, Ortman, and Lobo
Northwest coast villages Alaska and British Columbia, AD 19th century	Settled area	50	0.741	0.101	0.410	Lobo et al. (2019)
Rosario Valley Mexico (Maya), AD 700–950	Public works volume	41	1.184	0.988–1.380	0.850	Ortman et al. (2020)
Santa Valley Peru, 1000 BCE–AD 1532	Public works volume	110	1.161	0.983–1.338	0.810	Ortman et al. (2016)

in Africa. With the exception of the spread into remote islands, including Pacific islands, Iceland, and Madagascar, humans reached all other parts of the world (except Antarctica) well before they developed cities. During this long formative period, lasting over 200,000 years, hunting and gathering suitably adapted to different natural environments was the only way of life. This way of life was, in this sense, remarkably stable, exhibiting very slow rates of material and technological change.

7.2.1 FEATURES OF HUNTER-GATHERER SOCIETIES

Many excellent anthropological accounts of hunting and gathering cultures exist in the literature; see, for example, the overview by Kelly.[40] For the purposes of the current discussion, we will simplify many of the characteristics of diverse cultures and focus on a few of their key functional features. First, while most hunter-gatherers are *mobile*, meaning they have no permanent settlements, a few cultures are *settled*, thanks to especially rich patches of natural resources. Archetypal examples are Pacific Northwest Native American cultures, such as the Haida (figure 7.11), who live primarily off salmon.

Mobile hunter-gatherers will be the main focus of the analysis that follows. Their societies and modes of resource extraction from the environment cannot typically sustain large, concentrated populations without incurring resource flow deficits (meaning that energetically $y - c < 0$). For these and other reasons, mobile hunter-gatherer groups are often characterized by recurrent temporal patterns of social fusion and fission. Sometimes, many families can come together in camps, while

7.11 Hunter-gatherer societies may be sedentary or mobile. Some Native American cultures of the Pacific Northwest, such as the Haida (A), live in villages controlling rich salmon runs. Most hunter-gatherer cultures, however, are mobile, such as the San of southern Africa (B), meaning they have no permanent settlement and make several moves a year, often principally motivated by the abundance of natural resources. Mobile hunter-gatherers typically experience periods of group fusion and fission, living in camps sometimes made up of a large number of families, while at other times kin-based family groups disperse over the land.
Source: Courtesy of Library and Archives Canada under the reproduction reference number PA-037756 and under the MIKAN ID number 3368507, Der Bildbestand der Deutschen Kolonialgesellschaft in der Stadt- und Universitätsbibliothek Frankfurt am Main.

at other times they disperse into single-family units. Mobile hunter-gatherers are often described as egalitarian societies, in that there is little scope for rank or private property. For example, the result of a successful hunt is expected to be shared with the rest of the camp. These societies typically have limited means of conflict resolution. When disputes occur, some individuals or families may simply walk away from others. Camp structures are simple and impermanent, and thus again there is little scope for privacy or protection except that afforded by physical distancing. Food storage is also very limited in contrast to agricultural societies or sedentary peoples like the Haida. As a result of these general conditions, when larger hunter-gatherer groups come together in seasonal camps, there are socially accepted uses of space, which can help minimize conflict and preserve some privacy. Physical distancing, in particular, is often adopted and is typically organized by kin distance (figure 7.12). This is therefore a situation in which actual or perceived biological relations organize much of human social life, unlike in modern cities.

We will build simple models of social interactions over space and time that capture some of the most elemental characteristics of these hunter-gatherer societies. In particular, we will focus on four important characteristics of these societies: (1) the need for food and other resources obtained from foraging, and the tension this

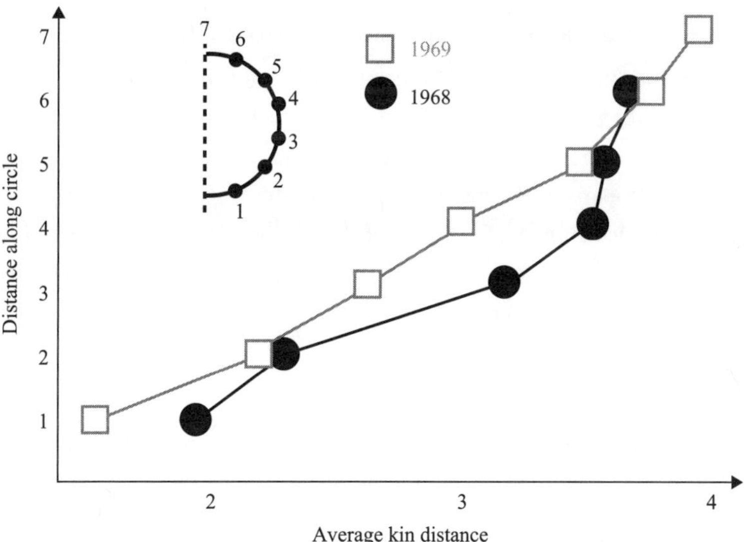

7.12 Kinship distance is strongly associated with physical distance in Dobe dry season camps over a two-year period (1968–1969). The plot shows the average kinship distance versus radial distance between huts (inset). This arrangement contributes to making camps less and less dense with population size, since larger populations must accommodate more distant kin. The effect is attributed to significant scalar stress between extended family groups.
Source: Adapted from Todd Matthew Whitelaw, "The Social Organisation of Space in Hunter-Gatherer Communities: Some Implications for Social Inference in Archeology," PhD thesis, University of Cambridge, 1989, https://doi.org/10.17863/CAM.19734.

requirement poses to (2) the attractive forces for larger-scale socialization. We will see that this naturally generates a pattern of temporal group fusion and fission in these societies under specific circumstances. This tension, moreover, needs to account for the (3) particular kind of conflict that can arise in hunter-gatherer camps and be reflected in the (4) kinship versus physical distancing expressed in camping arrangements. We will see that these conditions predict interesting general scaling patterns for these societies and lead to a curious predicament related to the land uses adopted by mobile hunter-gatherer societies versus those of settled (urbanizing) societies.

7.2.2 HUNTER-GATHERER CAMPS: THE RING MODEL

We can obtain a first simple model—with some real-world applicability—by considering the spatial configurations of some of the camps of the San, depicted in figure 7.13.

According to empirical observations, the ring model, in which families arrange themselves along the perimeter of an area, is a good general representation of San camps, especially larger ones. In an interesting twist, the ring model developed by Wiessner[41] shares a common origin with urban scaling theory, as they were both inspired by Nordbeck's analysis of Swedish settlements (which, recall, found an exponent $\alpha \simeq \frac{2}{3}$ for the area-population scaling relation). Upon measurement of her !Kung San camp data, however, Wiessner found a very different value for the same exponent, more like $\alpha \simeq 1.96$, curiously close to $\alpha = 2$.

To see how this exponent arises, consider the simplest area: a disk circumscribed by a circle. Then, the area is $A = \pi R^2$ and the perimeter is $P_R = 2\pi R$, where R is the radius as usual. The ring model places families not at the center but along the perimeter; let's say at distance l_F from each other. Then we can write $P_R = l_F N_F = 2\pi R$, where N_F is the number of families. It follows that

$$R = \frac{l_F}{2\pi} N_F \rightarrow A(N) = \frac{l_F^2}{4\pi} N_F^2 = \frac{l_F^2}{4\pi n_F^2} N^2. \tag{7.2}$$

With population size $N = n_F N_F$, where n_F is the average family size, this is the exponent estimated by Wiessner.[42] This exponent is clearly very superlinear! This is *completely different* from the area-population scaling relationships we encountered for cities and other permanent settlements. Contrary to such settlements, hunter-gatherer camps following the ring model get less and less dense with their population size. Their population density is inversely proportional to size, since $n_A = \frac{N}{A} = \frac{4\pi n_F^2}{l_F^2} \frac{1}{N}$. This looks more like a snapshot of a population *explosion* than a population *implosion*, the term used by Lewis Mumford[43] to describe the first cities.

It is easy to generalize this simple model to any area-perimeter relationship and obtain the same scaling exponent, even if some factors in the intercept change. Are all hunter-gatherer camps like those of the !Kung San?

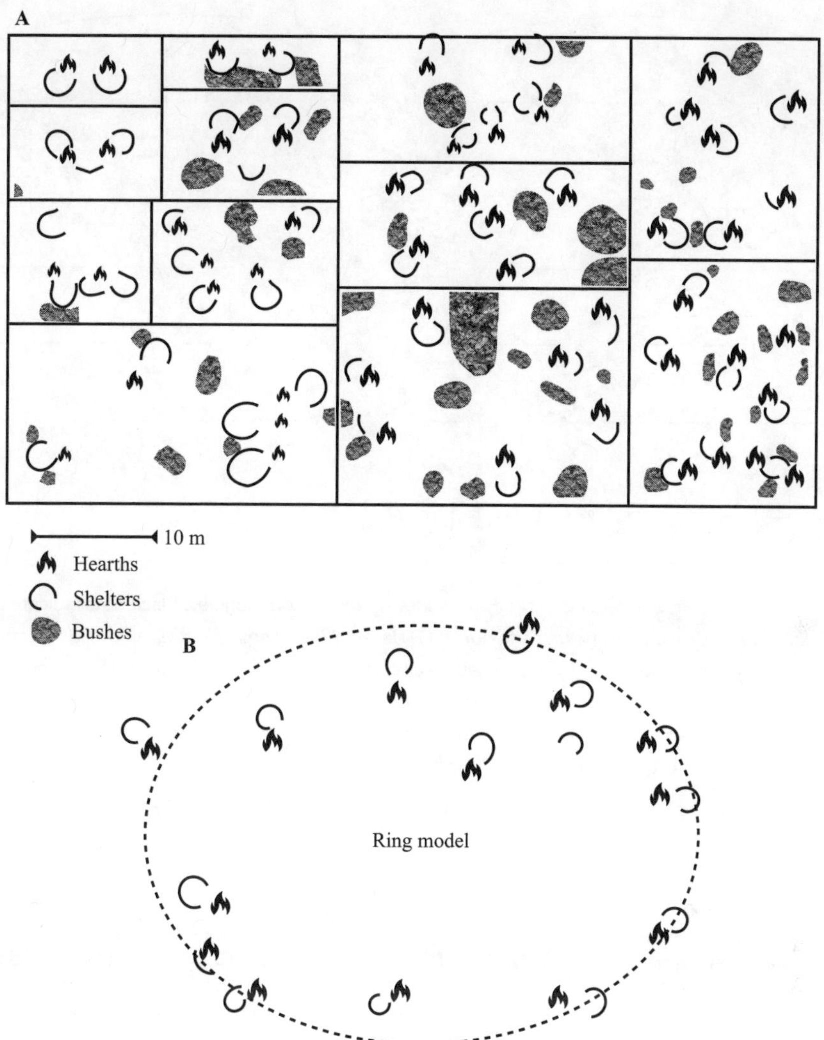

7.13 Smaller and (A) larger camps of the San of Southern Africa. Large camps were interpreted by Wiessner and later by Yellen to follow the "ring model." According to this model, each family's site is arranged roughly along the perimeter of a (quasi-)circular area, like pearls on a necklace. This arrangement naturally leads to (B) the superlinear scaling of camp area with population size.

Source: Adapted from Todd Matthew Whitelaw, "The Social Organisation of Space in Hunter-Gatherer Communities: Some Implications for Social Inference in Archeology," PhD thesis, University of Cambridge, 1989, https://doi.org/10.17863/CAM.19734.

7.2.3 AREA-POPULATION SCALING RELATIONS ACROSS ETHNOGRAPHIC HUNTER-GATHERERS

There is a large body of empirical evidence characterizing many hunter-gatherer cultures in various geographic and climatic regions of the world. Figure 7.14 summarizes a large dataset of camps compiled by Whitelaw,[44] which will be the basis for the analysis shown here.

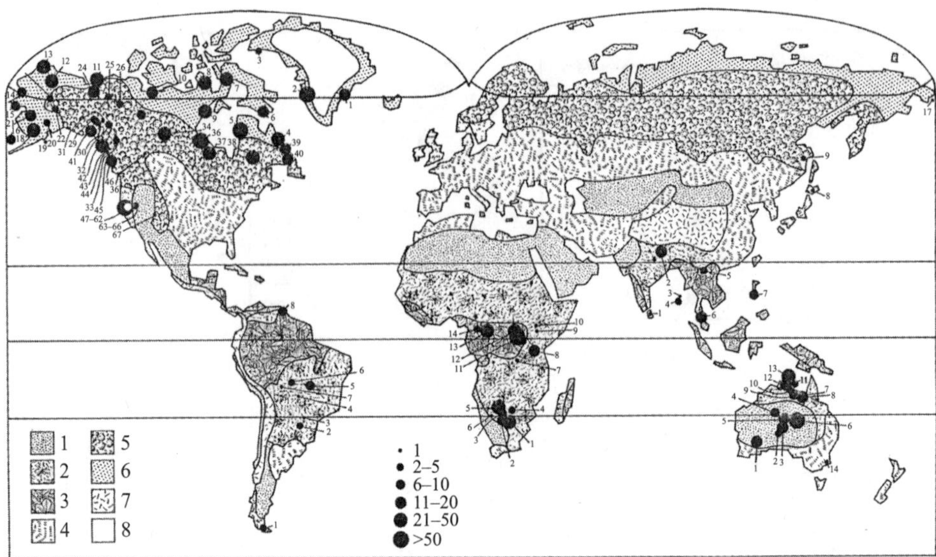

7.14   Worldwide compilation of ethnographic hunter-gatherer communities. Black dots indicate sample size. Environmental zones are shown as textures: (1) desert, (2) savanna, (3) tropical forest, (4) temperate grassland and forest, (5) subarctic boreal forest, (6) arctic tundra, (7) mountain zone, (8) Greenland ice cap. *Source*: Adapted from Todd Matthew Whitelaw, "The Social Organisation of Space in Hunter-Gatherer Communities: Some Implications for Social Inference in Archeology," PhD thesis, University of Cambridge, 1989, https://doi.org/10.17863/CAM.19734.

Table 7.6   Measured area-population size exponent for hunter-gatherer camps across cultures and geographies

Hunter-gatherer camps	N_c	R^2	α	95% CI	a (m^2)	STE
All observations	1,209	0.68	1.698	[1.631, 1.766]	16.78	0.132
Controlling for ecological type	1,209	0.78	1.533	[1.471, 1.596]	70.15	0.124
Controlling for regional group	1,209	0.76	1.503	[1.437, 1.572]	90.16	0.132
Controlling for cultural type	1,209	0.89	1.631	[1.571, 1.694]	29.92	0.121

Note: In general, exponents are superlinear but smaller than the ring model's prediction.

Standard analysis of this dataset, which includes over 1,200 observations (table 7.5) shows that scaling exponents are *always superlinear* for the area-population relation of mobile hunter-gatherer camps. On the whole, however, measured exponents differ from the value derived for the ring model, $\alpha=2$. In general, exponents are closer to about $\alpha \simeq 1.5$, and vary somewhat with culture and geography, which can be controlled for to some extent by using standard econometric methods, as in table 7.6.

To understand how these scaling exponents can all be superlinear but also depend on other factors, we need to turn our attention to a few additional quantitative aspects of hunter-gatherer camps. The key is to understand the superlinear nature of social conflict, which is known in this context through the concept of *scalar stress*.

7.2.4 SCALAR STRESS

Some of the literature in anthropology and organizational science focuses not so much on the advantages of large-scale human socialization, which we have been stressing in previous chapters, but on the stress of human interactions between strangers, even in small groups. This has a parallel in the idea of *diseconomies of scale* in urban economics from chapter 2, but here this is more explicitly associated with social conflict rather than congestion or pollution. This issue is very relevant to hunter-gatherer camps and often gets discussed under the theme of *scalar stress*, a concept developed by Johnson; see figure 7.15.

Scalar stress is the result of *negative network effects*, where conflict increases faster than group size or the capacity for making good group decisions degrades in a similar way.

In the context of hunter-gatherer camps, Johnson emphasized conflict as a source of fission (centrifugal forces) and assumed, without much reference to spatial organization, that social links involved in conflict have the potential to increase as the square of the group size, following Metcalfe's law. He attempted to fit this result with observations of the increase in conflict rates with group size, with mixed results, but was able to hypothesize convincingly, based on the same evidence, that it is conflict between extended families (clans) that tends to lead to most stress and group fission. We should then expect scalar stress to be a major factor in hunter-gatherer camps and that its magnitude should be measured in terms of interactions between different family groups. In this sense, it is exacerbated by close proximity to nonkin but mitigated by greater distance from them. These features certainly seem to affect the spatial organization of hunter-gatherer camps, which we would like to include in any model.

7.2.5 FORAGING AREA DENSIFICATION

One more quantitative property of hunter-gatherer societies is potentially important in setting the nature of land use in these societies, this time at large spatial scales and low densities. We have just seen how close physical proximity in camps increases scalar stress (e.g., in the form of interpersonal conflict, especially between different extended family groups), but this happens because hunter-gatherers do have reasons to come together in larger groups in the first place: to socialize, find mates, tell stories, and try to have a good time. Thus, there must be a centripetal force lurking, which may be most visible when these societies are at their lowest densities.

Data of this type remain controversial, but there are some indications that over entire foraging areas these societies are actually *denser* the larger their population size, as shown by Hamilton and collaborators.[45] Scaling exponents of this type are rather noisy but suggest values that are manifestly sublinear, $1 > \alpha \geq \frac{2}{3}$ (table 7.7).

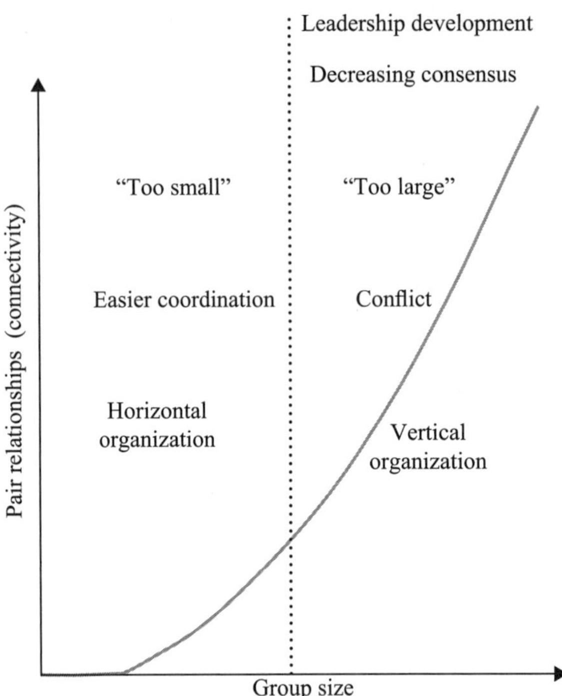

7.15 Concept of scalar stress. Scalar stress emphasizes the difficulty of conflict resolution and collective decision making as the number of social contacts increases superlinearly with group size. Johnson assumes that this increase follows Metcalfe's law, so pair relationships increase quadratically with group size.

Source: Adapted from Gregory A. Johnson, "Organizational Structure and Scalar Stress," in *Theory and Explanation in Archaeology*, edited by Colin Renfrew, Michael Rowlands, and Barbara A. Segraves-Whallon, 389–421 (Cambridge, MA: Academic Press, 1982).

Table 7.7 Scaling of home range foraging area with population for several hunter-gatherer types

Hunter-gatherer foraging areas	α	95% CI	a (km^2)	STE	R^2
All observations	0.70	[0.57, 0.84]	84.77	0.47	0.24
Hunters	0.90	[0.71, 1.10]	86.48	0.66	0.52
Gatherers	0.64	[0.44, 0.84]	100.48	0.66	0.22
Aquatic foragers	0.78	[0.56, 1.00]	25.53	0.79	0.31
Terrestrial foragers	0.79	[0.63, 0.96]	64.72	0.56	0.29

7.2.6 A SCALING MODEL FOR HUNTER-GATHERER CAMPS

We would now like to put the ingredients and findings discussed so far into a common framework so that we may appreciate how hunter-gatherer societies may or may not have a connection to more permanent settlements and their associated social networks and uses of space.

Let us first consider the stock of energy, E_{HG}, and of social products (one could think of this as social capital or culture), I_{HG}, for a typical individual in a hunter-gatherer society. We can write the dynamics expressing the accumulation and decay of these quantities as

$$\frac{dE_{HG}}{dt} = \gamma_{E_{HG}} = \gamma_0 - G_E \frac{N}{A}, \; \frac{dI_{HG}}{dt} = \gamma_{I_{HG}} = G \frac{N}{A} - \gamma_C. \tag{7.3}$$

This allows us to focus on the two rates, which we can write as

$$\gamma_{E_{HG}} = G_E \left(n_E - \frac{N}{A} \right), \; \gamma_{I_{HG}} = G \left(\frac{N}{A} - n_I \right), \tag{7.4}$$

where the two critical spatial population densities, $n_E = \frac{\gamma_0}{G_E}, n_I = \frac{\gamma_C}{G}$, set the thresholds for net positive energy and social products to be accumulated, respectively. You can see where this is going: staying net positive in terms of energy is a must for survival but requires population densities $n_A = \frac{N}{A} < n_E$, which in turn depends on how productive the environment per unit time and unit area, γ_0, is and on the average rate of consumption of other humans, G_E. Accumulating social products, such as culture and technology, on the other hand, requires a high population density, $n_A > n_I = \frac{\gamma_C}{G}$, which in turn depends on the cost of realizing social connections, γ_C, divided by the productivity per connection, our old friend the social productivity of interactions, G. This is analogous to the cost-benefit analysis of socioeconomic network links we discussed in chapter 5.

It is the tension between satisfying these two objectives—staying fed and being social—in an environment with relatively low energy productivity that encapsulates the dilemma of spatial organization for hunter-gatherers. Technology and social institutions play critical roles in these parameters; for example, by making the environment more or less productive (affecting γ_0) or decreasing conflict or movement costs (affecting γ_C). We will now deal with some aspects of scalar stress and spatial distancing of kin in terms of these parameters.

Figure 7.16 shows a schematic representation of the spatial and temporal configurations predicted by this kind of model, so foraging human societies can produce both necessary energy and socialization over extended periods of time.

We see that in environments with low energy productivity per unit area and more costly socialization, $n_E < n_I$, so in order to be gathering energy, populations must be in situations where their social products decay (are forgotten). To replenish culture, populations can come together for short periods of time, using accumulated energy.

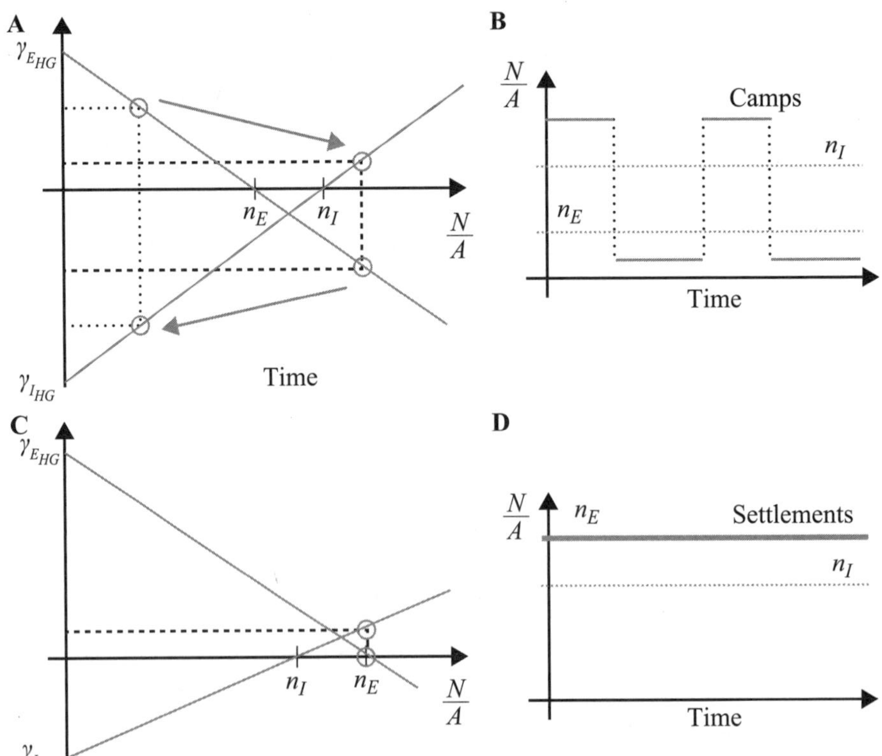

7.16 Rates of energy harvesting and social production as functions of population density and their consequences for social arrangements over space and time. (A) A situation of low environmental productivity per unit area and low social productivity does not allow a population density at which both energy sufficiency and socioeconomic production are positive. As a result (B), the population alternates between states of low density (energy sufficiency) and higher density (social production). When energy productivity is sufficiently high and/or social costs are low (C), both social production and subsistence are possible in a place, at higher densities (D), possibly leading to a settlement.

But doing so consumes more energy than can be produced, and they must soon split apart again. Consequently, to have both, populations must alternate in time between low-density periods of energy sufficiency but socialization deficits and high-density periods with more socialization but energy deficits. However, when both the environment and socialization are sufficiently productive, the population can sustain a state of high spatial density and settlements may nucleate, as in the case of the Haida.

In addition to the fusion-fission dynamics of mobile hunter-gatherer societies, we can also account for potential densification effects over foraging areas and with the superlinear scaling of camp area and the spatially detailed structuring by kin caused by scalar stress. As we saw in previous subsections, these phenomena involve the cost of socialization, γ_C, which we now think of as depending on population size as well as area (distance). We can write it as

$$\gamma_C = c_{T_0} R + c_{ss} \frac{\ell_{ss}}{R}, \tag{7.5}$$

where R is the characteristic distance (radius) of the territory occupied by the human population (camp or foraging area), $A \sim R^2$. As before, the first term is the cost of movement, while the second term is a parameterization of scalar stress cost, which increases at smaller distances and eventually vanishes in a very dilute population. The variable ℓ_{ss} is the distance at which scalar stress effects become strong; c_{ss} accounts for its cost per unit time and unit area.

With this parameterization, we now write the boundary condition for the social rate, $\gamma_{I_{HG}} = 0$, as

$$G \frac{N}{R^2} - \epsilon R - c_{ss} \frac{\ell_{ss}}{R} = 0 \rightarrow R^3 + R_*^2 R - \frac{G}{c_{T_0}} N = 0. \tag{7.6}$$

The critical radius, $R_* = \sqrt{\frac{c_{ss}}{c_{T_0}} \ell_{ss}}$, sets the scale at which scalar stress costs dominate versus when standard movement costs are the most important, specifically when

$$R \ll R_* : R \simeq \frac{G}{c_{T_0} R_*^2} N \rightarrow A(N) = A_0 N^2, \tag{7.7}$$

$$R \gg R_* : R^3 \simeq \frac{G}{c_{T_0}} N \rightarrow A(N) = A_0' N^{\frac{2}{3}}. \tag{7.8}$$

Thus, we can have densification on very large scales (foraging areas) and decreases in density on small scales (camps), as the full solution of equation (7.6) demonstrates (figure 7.17).

Finally, we can include the effects of kinship, via a parameterization of the length scale, ℓ_{ss}. Let us first consider the dependence of kinship, $kin(N)$, on group size, N. Because households have a typical average size, n_F, and kinship is given by the number of branches along a genealogical tree, it follows that $kin(N) = kin_0 N^{-1/n_F}$. Hamilton et al.[46] give these numbers as $n_F \simeq 4$. Now, we expect physical distance to be inversely related to kinship, as in figure 7.12; the simplest assumption is

$$\ell_{ss}(N) \sim \frac{1}{kin(N)} = \frac{1}{kin_0} N^{\frac{1}{4}}.$$

This has an effect in camps when $R \ll R_* = \sqrt{\frac{c_{ss}}{c_{T_0}}} \ell_{ss}(N) \sim N^{\frac{1}{2n_F}}$, leading to the scaling of camp area as

$$A(N) = A_0 N^{2-\frac{2}{n_F}} \simeq A_0 N^{1.5}. \tag{7.9}$$

This is closer to the scaling exponent observed for most camps (table 7.5). This calculation also emphasizes that scaling exponents are less universal than in other situations and should depend on how well mobile hunter-gatherer societies handle scalar stress across kin-related individuals and on their overall balance of social benefits, costs, and energetics. Nevertheless, we can now see how the possibility of a

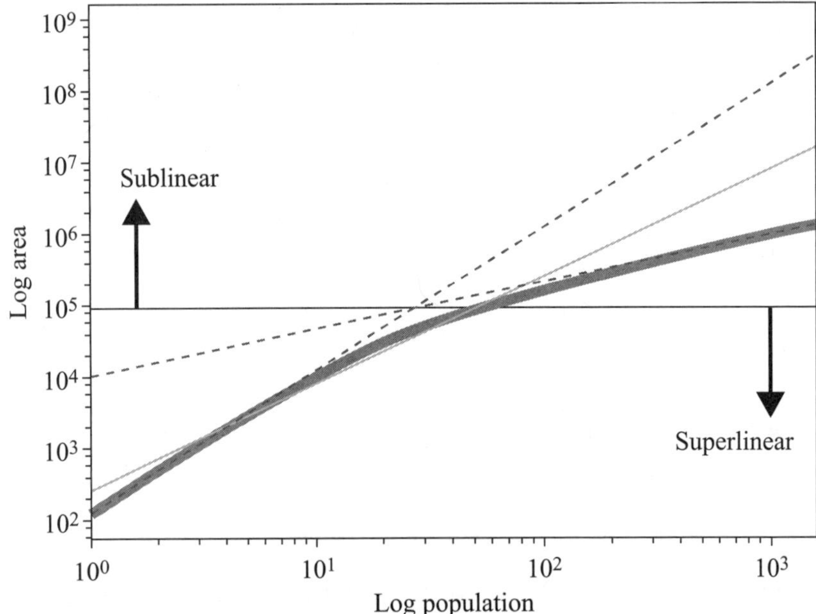

7.17 Full solution (thick gray line) of the area-population scaling relation with scalar stress. For small areas, the solution scales superlinearly with population (camps), while for large areas it becomes sublinear, in agreement with balancing the typical movement costs against benefits of the population density in terms of beneficial interactions. The two dashed lines show the ring model solution ($\alpha = 2$) and the foraging area solution ($\alpha = 2/3$), which is analogous to amorphous settlement scaling. The thin gray line shows scaling of area with population with an exponent $\alpha = 1.5$, similar to the best fit values in table 7.6.

population implosion into permanent settlements and eventually cities may already be latent in the dynamics of hunter-gatherer societies. For these to be manifested, however, requires critical innovations in both energy management and conflict resolution, so that effectively $R_* \to 0$.

7.3 THE PUZZLE OF LOW ECONOMIC GROWTH IN HISTORICAL URBAN SYSTEMS

The observation of increasing returns to scale in economic activity for cities in history poses a puzzle related to the absence of strong economic growth in these societies. If these societies shared most of the same mechanisms of socialization and organization of space as in modern urbanizing societies, why did they not sustain higher rates of economic expansion?

Many historical studies in economic history have shed light on this puzzle by mapping the circumstances associated with sustained economic growth *after* the Industrial Revolution.[47] They call our attention to macroeconomic factors such as the availability of energy on an unlimited scale (thanks to fossil fuels), new political and economic institutions, and the advent of modern science. The study of socio-economic development in the past also highlights the role of urbanization in economic change,[48] as have historical experiences of urbanization "without economic growth."[49] As useful as these case studies and historical examinations are, comparative analyses that can help us make sense of different outcomes have been hampered partly by a perceived lack of common empirical evidence across eras and geographies.

From what we have learned so far about cities, there are a number of ingredients that may be useful for framing urbanization's role in economic growth across time: (1) sustained economic growth is a system-level property (chapter 4), with the same average growth rates characterizing all cities; (2) higher growth rate volatilities σ reduce rates of economic growth; (3) very small rates of economic growth, below 1%, are not perceptible over a human lifetime (recall that a 1% growth rate entails a doubling every 70 years); and (4) the accumulation of material wealth resulting from low levels of growth is very vulnerable to exogenous shocks (such as disease, theft, or changes in climate). As a consequence, growth "in the beginning" will almost certainly go unnoticed and remain accidental.

The first point may not be obvious, as we often think of rich and poor settlements, even within the same nation or polity. It is, however, generally true that the type of sustained and fast economic growth observed in modern urban systems is a system-level property (so information, ideas, resources, and individuals can flow among settlements), with all cities experiencing about the same annual rate of growth (figure 4.1). In chapter 8, we will provide a general theoretical argument for why this is so. The happy consequence of this observation is that studying systemic economic growth may require only a number of local assessments, which should agree in magnitude whether they were measured in small towns or in larger cities. This also means that *golden ages* often associated with large cities, such as classical Athens or Rome, whether triggered by technological innovation or by conquest and theft, may not be sustainable unless they induce economic growth across their settlement systems.[50] This means, for example, that in the presence of systemic economic growth, we should see the living experience of primary producers in small settlements change so they can enjoy some of the products of large cities and vice versa, in a virtuous cycle of exchange and shared development. We know that prior to the Industrial Revolution, such periods, if they existed at all, were not associated with large growth rates, and change was typically more localized in space and time.

The second and third properties of economic growth follow from its character as a stochastic (fluctuating) process. We saw in chapter 4 that the actual growth rate is $\gamma = \bar{\eta} - \dfrac{\sigma^2}{2}$, which is the geometric mean of fluctuating growth rates in time. Thus, higher volatility, σ, renders any small growth rate zero or even negative (figure 4.17). This means that, in earlier societies, innovations to reduce instability in the economy were likely more important than those creating a positive average growth rate.

The final argument we wish to emphasize here is that the economic growth rate for any preindustrial economy over any extended time period (say decades) was likely very small. Figure 7.18 shows lead flux, a signal for the quantities of metals mined, as a proxy for economic activity.[51] We see a very noisy signal, but if we focus on the time of the height of the Roman Empire—between 150 BC and AD 150, the best of times in Western classical antiquity—we can estimate $\bar{\eta} \simeq 0.17\%$, certainly lower than 0.3% a year. This translates, at the most, into a timescale for the economy to double of 240 years! This timescale is too long to be felt by anyone over their own lifetime. Thus, even if slow economic growth was present in preindustrial societies, it was likely too slow to become apparent, likely precluding the advent of intentional institutions that could sustain it. The perception would then be of an effectively static society, where any positive economic expansion would soon be reversed by negative shocks.

In conclusion, processes of human development and economic growth recognizable to us today were probably at work throughout history and almost certainly in most urban societies. However, even during the best of times, premodern rates of change may have been too local, too volatile, and too short lived to be acted on and sustained intentionally over the long term. Certainly, there were energetic and material barriers to growth, but coal and petroleum were known in preindustrial times and could have been mined and transported on a much larger scale then.[52] As a consequence,

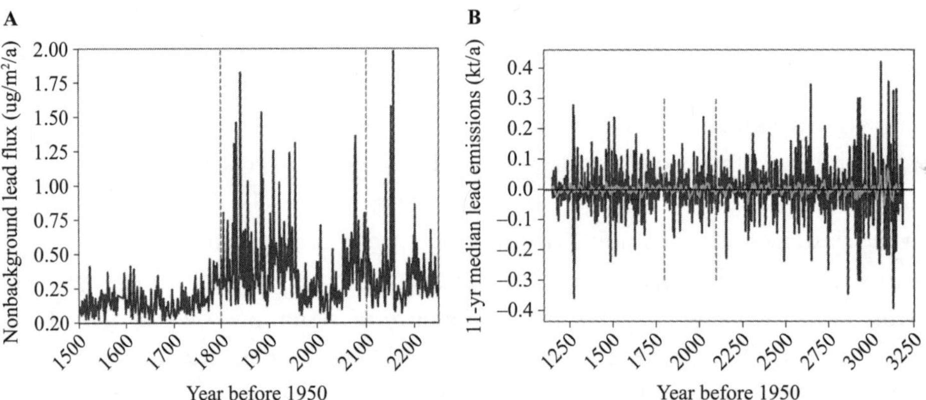

7.18 Economic growth and its historical volatility, measured by lead emissions. (A) Estimated emissions over a long period. (B) Corresponding growth rate in emissions. Vertical lines delimit the period between 150 BC and AD 150, associated with the rise of the Roman Empire. For this period, the effective growth rate is very small because of high volatility. The annual average growth rate is about $\bar{\eta} = 0.17\%$/year.

Source: Created by the author with data from Joseph R. McConnell, Andrew I. Wilson, Andreas Stohl, Monica M. Arienzo, Nathan J. Chellman, Sabine Eckhardt, Elisabeth M. Thompson, A. Mark Pollard, and Jørgen Peder Steffensen, "Lead Pollution Recorded in Greenland Ice Indicates European Emissions Tracked Plagues, Wars, and Imperial Expansion during Antiquity," *Proceedings of the National Academy of Sciences* 115, no. 22 (May 29, 2018): 5726–5731, https://doi.org/10.1073/pnas.1721818115.

transformations in living conditions, technology, and institutions associated with human development were primarily the result of scaling and agglomeration effects as larger cities arose over some periods of time. Civilizations that produced these cities—from China to the Aztecs and from Babylon to Greece and Rome—have left profound (informational) legacies, which are at the heart of how we live today: in how we talk, count, write, tell time, plan space, or organize our modern legal and political systems.

Deeper searches for some of the telltale signs of these historical episodes, especially in the systemic change of living conditions across settlement sizes, may give us precious new insights into the actual time-dependent variability of human development and on the human experience in cities during long periods of very slow growth and even decay.

EPILOGUE: LESSONS FROM HISTORY

If a metropolite would "get ahead" he usually must become "aggressive," but aggressiveness on the part of one person or of a group is often an invasion of the status of other persons or groups. Hence social-distance reactions are kept in turmoil. To the extent that a city is composed of aggressive persons, eager to succeed, social-distance attitudes will be kept active despite the fact that physical distances have been largely overcome.

—E. S. Bogardus, *Social Distance in the City*

We have seen how relatively simple processes dealing with an average picture of social interactions in cities and their spatialized benefits and costs allow us to make many observable predictions about the properties of contemporary cities. In this chapter, we have seen how the same strategy allows us to extend these predictions to cities in history all the way back to the smallest and least permanent human camps and settlements.

We discussed a tradition in archeology and anthropology fostering comparative approaches to make sense of different cultures and time periods, including spectacular cases involving the independent advent of urbanism in the Old and New Worlds. From this perspective, we were able to address some of the concerns of postprocessualist scholars, who object that stressing common patterns across cultures, space, and time leads to intolerable reductions of human culture and the human condition to a number of deterministic simple processes. By contrast, we have seen that general quantitative statements about human settlements are the result of very general statistical constraints—on the nature of social networks, the costs of energy, and of using space—that leave ample space for choice, human agency, and subjectivity at an individual scale and for culture at the collective level.

This is also the appropriate place to discuss research in anthropology and evolutionary theory on human social cooperation and cultural change.[53] Cooperation toward a common goal is a human universal, which is at the root of why social relations can lead to *positive sum games* and thus generate collective material and cultural expansion. However, evolutionary scientists and anthropologists have shown that cooperation is unstable, exposing both parties in a relationship to cheating and defection, which in the short term benefits only the villain. In this sense, cooperation requires trust, and trust requires arrangements between individuals (e.g., mediated by kinship and its social extensions) and is itself a product of culture. Expanding cooperation to nonkin involves shared morals and ethics as well as the formal development of law and punishment, often associated with organized religion and Politics. We have seen how the formalization of these social and political institutions arose with the first cities, and identified the difficulties their absence poses for human societies, especially those without permanent settlements. This suggests a feedback loop between cultural evolution, the scale of a society, and the material outputs of cooperative agreements. The models developed in this chapter suggest a *discontinuous transition* (a "tipping point") between permanent denser settlements, where all this becomes sustainable, and mobile hunter-gatherer ways of life, where large-scale sociality and cooperation is only episodic and remains very volatile and ultimately unstable.

From this perspective, permanent settlements can become cultural self-constructed niches, where interdependence between humans and a set of technologies and rules of conduct become common to all and a condition of entry and success in larger-scale human societies. Only with the advent of cities have humans been able to transcend kinship as the main channel for trust and social organization, and only then did it become possible to create large-scale social systems with deep divisions of knowledge and labor, which together can generate virtuous cycles of material improvement, innovation, cultural expansion, and population growth.

These processes leave a quantitative trace in the form of nonlinear scaling relations manifesting both economies of scale and increasing returns in socioeconomic production. Although more research is necessary, we can already see here that these effects are a common—perhaps universal—feature of cities throughout history and a necessary condition for the advent and growth of permanent settlements!

8

URBAN SYSTEMS, DEMOGRAPHY, AND THE LAWS OF GEOGRAPHY

There are no relationships between type of city distribution and either relative economic development or the degree of urbanization of countries, although urbanization and economic growth are highly associated. It appears that there is a scale from primate to lognormal distributions which is somehow tied to the number and complexity of forces affecting the urban structure of countries, such that when few strong forces obtain primacy results, and when many forces act in many ways with none predominant, a lognormal city size distribution is found.

—Brian J. L. Berry, "City Size Distributions and Economic Development"

So far, we have dealt with cities without much consideration of their specific *external* influences arising from exchanges with other places: urban, rural, and international. On reflection, given that cities are open systems, it may seem surprising that we could say so much about the general processes that create and sustain them and make general predictions about their properties without considering how cities depend on each other. Elucidating why will be the main goal for this chapter.

This will require that we continue to articulate urban processes across scales, now connecting city size and scaling to the relative dynamics of cities in national urban systems. Cities, of course, do not really have their own dynamics; they depend on decisions made by people, corporations, governments, and others. The aggregate statistics of all their decisions will therefore emerge as key and provide another connection to the uses of information in urban science.

The interdependencies and relative statistics of cities have been the subject of many empirical studies—especially in economic geography and demography. These fields have started the quantitative characterization of cities not so much in terms of their internal organization and associated network processes, as we have done so far, but rather in terms of the distributions (finite frequencies) of city characteristics, taking urban systems (nations) as sets (*ensembles*). Methodologically, such approaches deal with relatively small ensembles (tens or hundreds of cities) by necessity. In practice, this means that statistical interpretations must be carried out with care, in the absence of simplifications characteristic of infinite limits in conventional statistics.

The systematic quantitative study of aggregate quantities across cities goes back almost a century. Its synthesis, in the second half of the twentieth century, is known as the *quantitative revolution* in geography,[1] a brief golden age during which researchers uncovered a number of famous empirical regularities that we will refer to as the "laws of geography." These include *Zipf's law* for the distribution of relative city sizes, the *gravity law* of flows between cities, *Gibrat's law* of proportional city growth, and a number of other related observations and statistical regularities characterizing spatial influence, migration, or the spatial and functional characteristics of cities of different sizes.

Historically, these quantitative regularities—and the very macroscopic perspective they assume—have been the most common entry point to the quantitative modeling of cities and thus provided some of the early foundations for urban science. However, as the quotation at the beginning of the chapter suggests, many of the fundamental properties of urban systems have remained only partially understood or explained. They have also remained fairly disconnected from approaches in other urban disciplines, which primarily engage with cities at smaller internal scales or involve quantities such as economic growth, a situation that is clearly untenable.

To deal with these issues, in this chapter we will analyze the properties of urban systems through the lens of the *interaction flows* between cities. We will show that these dynamics can be very general but also that they present—in special regimes—a number of constraints that result in the collective organization of an interacting set of cities. We will see that a number of fundamental results in formal demography play a role analogous to limit theorems in more conventional statistics, guaranteeing certain general structural outcomes for the dynamics of a network of interacting cities. These emergent collective dynamics will explain why cities can continue to grow exponentially—in terms of their population sizes, economies, and other quantities—while many of their *relative* properties are preserved, creating the structural signatures of *integrated urban systems*.

CHAPTER OUTLINE

In chapter 4, we started to derive the importance of exponential stochastic growth in defining the statistical properties of cities. We will now deal specifically with *demographic* growth, by which city populations increase (or decrease) over time. We will show when a set of cities operates as an *integrated urban system* and what quantitative properties follow for their relative sizes.

This chapter is structured in three main sections. Section 8.1 is a general overview of several empirical regularities that emerge at the level of urban systems, which we will call the "laws of geography." These include Tobler's two laws, Zipf's law for the relative size distribution of cities, Gibrat's law of proportional growth, the gravity law of migration, and a few others. These laws are manifested empirically only in approximate forms, so models and theory consistent with all other known urban processes that can also explain their emergence and deviations become especially important in urban science.

To do this, section 8.2 takes a step back to define the demographic dynamics of a general population in a system of cities. This will provide us with a firm stepping-stone, to which we will return whenever necessary. In particular, we will show that ideas of *urban hierarchy*, the gravity law, and Gibrat's law are all intimately connected with each other and have Zipf's law as a corollary, but only in specific simplifying circumstances. We will also discuss some of the actual demographic properties of cities, illustrated by the US system of micropolitan and metropolitan areas. Section 8.3 discusses the connection between the demographic transition by which human population growth slows down urbanization at the national level. The chapter concludes with an epilogue discussing issues of choice, demography, and the structure of urban systems.

8.1   THE LAWS OF GEOGRAPHY

In the nineteenth and twentieth centuries, geography went through several waves of qualitative and quantitative emphasis. In the decades that followed World War II, there was a period of particular focus and excitement toward the systematization of various statistical patterns in geography, often known as the *quantitative revolution*.[2] Brian J. L. Berry, whose opening quotation will orient us throughout the chapter, was one of its protagonists, along with other geographers at the University of Washington, Iowa, Chicago, and a few other places.

This historical period was marked by the advent of much better data about cities and regions and saw geographers, especially in the US, France, and Britain, use these data in new and more ambitious ways, aspiring to the standards of generality and mathematical rigor of the natural sciences.[3] As a consequence, many of urban geography's results from this period became expressed in terms of "laws." Some of these laws are actually very qualitative and approximate and will not be developed much in this chapter, except for some commentary. Others are more quantitative and will be tested and rederived. The quantitative revolution came to a head in the mid-1970s with the establishment of a number of remarkable results. It was followed by a fairly abrupt pause (and "counterrevolution"), which would bring mainstream geography away from seeking general patterns and toward an emphasis on context, history, critical theory, and qualitative methods. This period is sometimes known as the *cultural turn*.[4] The tension between these two approaches remains unresolved today and is at the root of both the present enthusiasm and derision for big data and mathematics in the social sciences.

Whatever one's stance on these matters, I find that the statements of these laws and the context in which they arise useful in framing the general nature of urban systems. Thus, we start the chapter by describing them as a prelude for the models of formal demography to be analyzed in section 8.2.

8.1.1 CENTRAL PLACE THEORY AND URBAN HIERARCHY

The framework of *central place theory* and *urban hierarchy* provides the most general setting for discussing other regularities in the geography and economics of urban systems. Central place theory was developed in the early twentieth century by geographers, mostly working in Germany,[5] and by Christaller[6] in particular. It emerged from the observation of the distribution of settlement sizes—from small agricultural towns to large cities—in southwest Germany, France, and Switzerland, and the relative placement of these population centers (see figure 8.1).

From these observations, Christaller hypothesized a series of simple general principles by which he proposed any urban system should be organized. First, he assumed the initial ingredients for an idealized urban system: (1) an evenly distributed

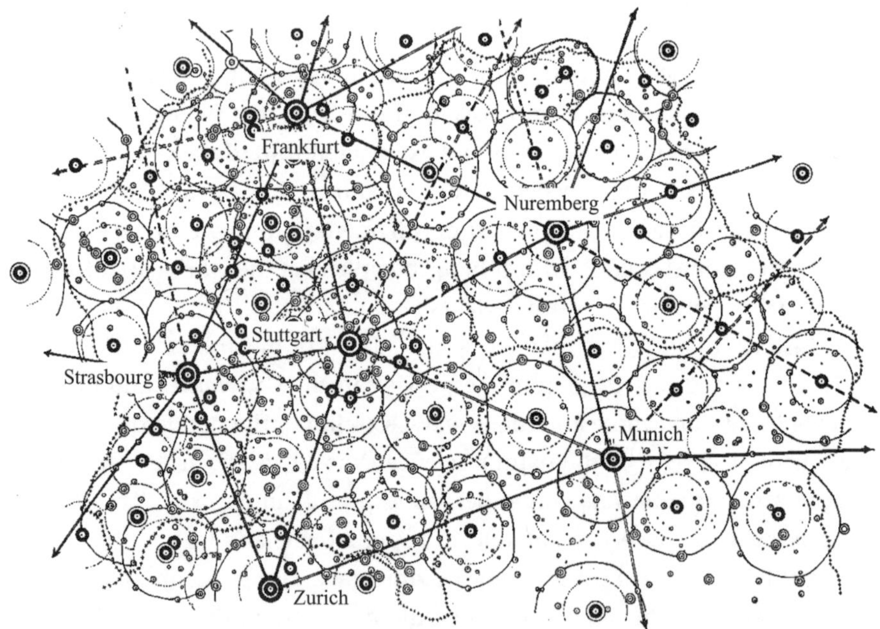

8.1 Distribution of human settlements and their population sizes in southwest Germany. Larger cities, such as Zurich, Munich, Stuttgart, and Frankfurt, are represented by larger symbols, while smaller cities are shown as small dots. Christaller posited a hierarchical occupation of space, with larger cities occupying larger territories, separated by larger distances. This leads to a series of interlocking hexagonal lattices associated with cities of different—discrete—size classes, with lattice size (vertex of hexagon) growing with population.
Source: Adapted from Walter Christaller, *Central Places in Southern Germany* (Englewood Cliffs, NJ: Prentice-Hall, 1966).

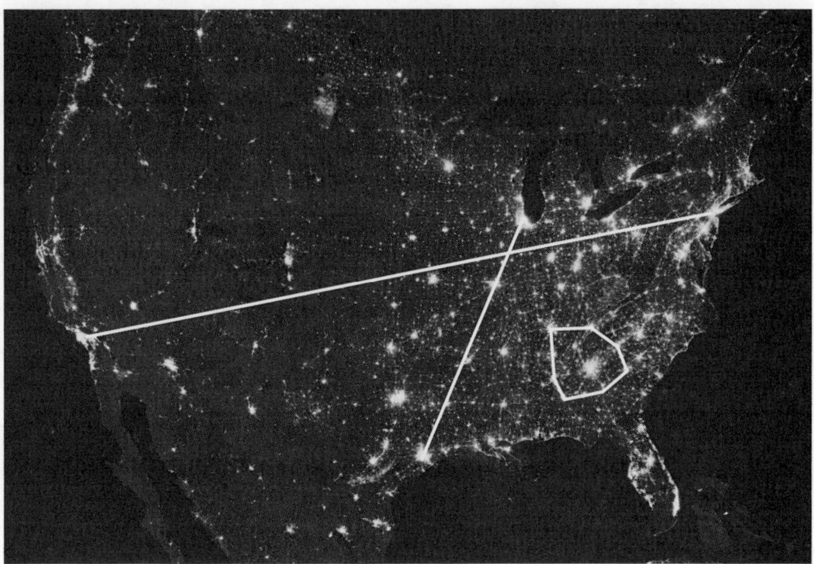

8.3 Spatial distribution of city sizes can be appreciated via night lights over North America. While cities (white spots) clearly are not distributed following hexagonal lattices, some of the gross assumptions of central place theory hold approximately. For example, the largest US metropolitan areas span the entire east–west (New York City to Los Angeles) and north–south (Chicago–Houston) directions of the country (straight white lines), being about as far as possible from each other. The settlement system is very different in the east and west, with very different population densities, which distort any pattern of regular spatial infilling. Moreover, careful attention reveals lines of organization associated with rivers, railways, and highways. In the east, one can attempt to map settlements forming a very roughly hexagonal tiling of the territory, such as around Atlanta (lines forming a lattice cell), but such patterns are clearly only very approximate.
Source: Background image courtesy of NASA Earth Observatory/NOAA NGDC.

established a general methodology to measure business frequencies in towns and cities (figure 8.4). They found patterns in Washington State that were generally in agreement with the hypotheses of specialization and higher-order functions of central place theory and its early extensions. This work was able to carefully spatialize, quantify, and systematize patterns of location and urbanization that had previously been essentially anecdotal and/or hypothetical.

Much subsequent work continued the spirit of the quantitative revolution and its pursuit of more general and predictive theories of urban systems. Economic geography and regional science pioneered by Walter Isard[11] and others around the same time would continue the analysis of economic patterns over space and the pursuit of regional models based on spatial equilibria. This tradition would culminate with so-called *new economic geography*, which followed from the extensions and applications of the core-periphery model of chapter 2. This approach continues today with more elaborate models and better data.

The mainstream of geography would in turn also continue to explore and develop methods for quantifying and analyzing socioeconomic patterns over space. This led

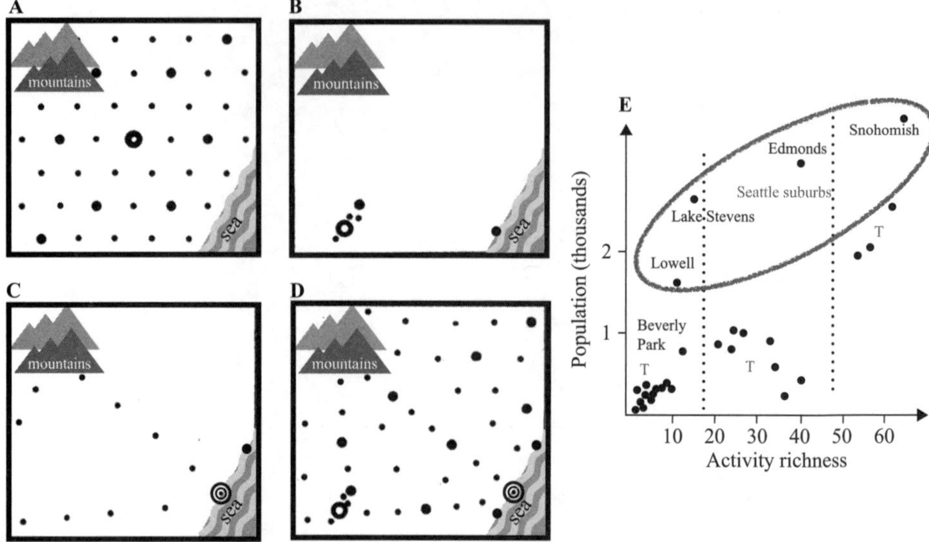

8.4 Generalized spatial organization of a settlement system. (A) Central place theory provides a model for the hierarchical, hexagonal tiling of land by an urban hierarchy starting with agricultural settlements, associated with city size. (B) There are also specialized-function settlements such as those associated with mining and specific resources. Industrial cities have often been associated with coal or mineral deposits nearby, for example. (C) Transport centers and routes also organize towns and cities spatially. (D) The full spatial pattern of any urban system is the result of different effects creating a more complicated settlement pattern than hypothesized by central place theory. For these reasons, the specific spatial pattern of central place theory has become associated primarily with relatively homogeneous agricultural landscapes, with other factors becoming important or dominant in urban systems with a different nature. Panel (E) shows the positive correlation between the number of distinct business activities (richness) and population in Washington State by Berry and Garrison, supporting the idea of urban hierarchy.
Source: Adapted from Chauncy D. Harris and Edward L. Ullman, "The Nature of Cities," *Annals of the American Academy of Political and Social Science* 242, no. 1 (November 1945): 7–17, https://doi.org /10.1177/000271624524200103.

to much interest in methods of spatial correlation and clustering,[12] spatial econometrics,[13] network theory for commodity flows, migration, and other spatialized exchanges. The convergence of these mathematical methodologies with emerging computing led in turn to geospatial information systems (GIS),[14] which became a body of methods and theory that today enables all mapping and software analysis, including in your phone or car. During this later period, the development of methods and data has gained more and more prominence. Theory, while being elaborated all along, remained "qualitatively quantitative," describing patterns in data but typically not capable of making systematic falsifiable predictions.[15]

8.1.2 TOBLER'S TWO LAWS

Waldo Tobler was a fellow student of Garrison's at the University of Washington, alongside Berry. He was to become known for many important contributions to quantitative geography and especially for his approach to mapping, which antici-pated and inspired many uses of GIS. In a set of lectures in the 1970s, he formulated two general statements to characterize urban systems, which are still a reference point for empirical work today:

Tobler's first law: Everything is related to everything else, but near things are more related than distant things.

Tobler's second law: The phenomenon external to an area of interest affects what goes on inside.

These two statements are, of course, rather obvious and purely qualitative. How-ever, they do distill many facts known to geographers, at least approximately. I see their role as being not so much explanatory but necessary. The first law is a gen-eralization of the *gravity law*, which is more specific and will be discussed next. Tobler's second law is interesting because it poses a conundrum to some of the earlier approaches in this book, which modeled cities as self-consistent complex systems (chapters 2–4). Specifically, it asks us to deal with phenomena *external* to the city as shapers of their *internal* dynamics.

This is problematic from the point of view of building any theory because it seem-ingly opens up each city to being arbitrarily driven by complex dynamics outside its control. We will see that there is a beautiful solution to this conundrum in the form of the dynamical emergence of the urban system, which respects cities' internal organization but simultaneously entangles their growth together self-consistently. To see this, we must now understand how urban systems are put together and, in due course, how they may fall apart.

8.1.3 THE GRAVITY LAW

We can only speak of urban *systems* when a set of cities becomes interconnected by sufficiently strong flows of people, goods, and information. The gravity law is an empirically motivated simple mathematical model for such flows. As such, it is one of the oldest and most important empirical regularities in geography. It has been used as a model not only for flows between cities but also those between other places, from nations to neighborhoods. The gravity law models the *current* or *flow*, J_{ij} (e.g., number of people per year), between two places, i and j, with populations N_i and N_j separated by distance d_{ij}, as

$$J_{ij} = G_M \frac{N_i N_j}{d_{ij}^{\alpha_g}}. \tag{8.1}$$

Here, G_M is a constant setting the magnitude of the migration flow, meaning that it does not depend on the sizes of the two populations or on the distance between them. Like G in the scaling law for socioeconomic products, we can think of G_M as set-ting the "productivity" of contacts toward producing migration. G_M typically depends on *time*, as it has dimensions of a temporal rate. The term *gravity* speaks to the mathematical form of equation (8.1), which resembles Newton's law for the gravitational force between two masses (N_i, N_j) in three spatial dimensions. This is, of course, different than two populations in two dimensions, so the analogy is only skin-deep.

The gravity law of geography has a curious and somewhat checkered history. In the 1940s, several researchers started to analyze emerging data for several flows between places. The two main characters were not geographers at all: linguist George Kingsley Zipf and physicist John Q. Stewart. Stewart was initially motivated by his curiosity about the geographic footprint of the students coming to study in four universities: Harvard, Princeton, Vassar, and Yale.[16] Being a physicist, he thought of the spatial pattern for each university as its *attractive potential* (an idea keenly adopted by Tobler). Plotting these data, he found a strikingly simple pattern: *The number of undergraduates or alumni of a given college who reside in a given area is directly proportional to the total population of that area and inversely proportional to the distance from the college.*[17] Later, Stewart, Zipf, and others[18] continued to find that the magnitude of many different flows between places was often reasonably well described by the product of the population size of the two places and a decaying power-law function of distance. Many variations followed with different functions (usually power laws) of distance and of the size of places, but a rough general pattern persisted.

The gravity law has since been a main fixture of flow modeling—empirically or by assumption—in thousands of papers, for example in cities, between cities, in archeology, and in trade flows. While the general form of equation (8.1) is often a rough description of data, many of its features have been questioned and extended, especially in terms of different functions of distance. For these reasons, my take-home message is that the specific form of the distance dependence of the flow is not universal, varies through time, and depends on different definitions of spatial units and distinct quantities. The population size dependence of equation (8.1) also seems to vary somewhat but is more conserved. Some authors have proposed more general forms, with extra exponents for each population (different from unity).[19] For these reasons, developing theory-based specific parametric models for flows between cities remains an open question, and there may not be a simple universal form like equation (8.1) in all circumstances. We will see some of these situations and justify them both empirically and starting from theory.

Many attempts have also been made to explain the gravity law using more fundamental theory, so far without definite or unambiguous success, in my view. Three approaches deserve some discussion: maximum-entropy estimation of flows, the radiation model, and a variant of urban scaling theory.

Maximum-Entropy Model of Flows The maximum-entropy (*MaxEnt*) approach in geography followed from a more general interest during the quantitative revolution on quantifying information, migration, and choice.[20] Alan Wilson,[21] in particular, developed ideas of statistical physics to derive most probable statistical models for geographic flows and other associated quantities. The procedure has the virtue of being clear mathematically and general. The same approach has been applied to other complex systems, such as in ecology,[22] following the formulation of maximum-entropy probability estimation in statistical physics by Jaynes.[23] All remarkable equilibrium statistical distributions in physics, such as the Maxwell-Boltzmann distribution for the velocities in a gas, are MaxEnt distributions derived from averaging individual agent dynamics under appropriate constraints, such as fixed average energy per degree of freedom. This is because the state of equilibrium is the state of maximum entropy given such constraints. We will make use of some of these ideas in forms that are appropriate for cities.

To appreciate how the MaxEnt approach generates a derivation of the gravity law, consider Wilson's simplest model[24] for a single agent traveling between two zones, i and j. Let's define the number of trips between these two zones as

$$T_{ij} = A_i^T B_j^T O_i^T D_j^T \phi_T(c_{ij}), \text{ with } A_i^T = \left[\sum_j B_j^T D_j^T \phi_T(c_{ij}) \right]^{-1}, B_j^T = \left[\sum_i A_i^T O_i^T \phi_T(c_{ij}) \right]^{-1}, \quad (8.2)$$

where O_i^T is the total number of trips with an origin at i, and D_j^T is analogously the total number of trips that end at destination j. The critical unknown in this approach is the function $\phi_T(c_{ij})$, which expresses the dependence of the trips on costs, $c_{ij} > 0$, which are rather general here and can represent distance, time, monetary expenditures, or some combination thereof. In addition, the construction of the flows must be constrained in terms of three additional equations, $\sum_j T_{ij} = O_i$, $\sum_i T_{ij} = D_j^T$, and $\sum_{ij} T_{ij} c_{ij} = C_T$, where C_T is the total cost expended on all trips, across all possibilities. Wilson determines the most likely form of $\phi_T(c_{ij})$ by maximizing the entropy[25] of the frequency, $P_{ij} = \dfrac{T_{ij}}{T}$, where $T = \sum_{ij} T_{ij}$, subject to these constraints. This corresponds to solving a constrained optimization problem,

$$\max\left[H[P_{ij}] - \lambda_0 \left(\sum_{ij} T_{ij} c_{ij} - C_T \right) - \lambda_1 \left(\sum_j T_{ij} - O_i^T \right) - \lambda_2 \left(\sum_i T_{ij} - D_i^T \right) \right], \quad (8.3)$$

where λ_0, λ_1, and λ_2 are Lagrange multipliers.

Taking derivatives and setting them to zero, one obtains the maximum-entropy solution $\phi_T(c_{ij}) = e^{-\lambda_0 c_{ij}}$. The actual value of the exponent λ_0 is a function of C_T or can be measured directly by the probability of trips. Thus, the MaxEnt procedure can derive features of the gravity law, given appropriate constraints. More elaborate models of this kind are discussed in the original literature.[26]

The maximum-entropy approach highlights a remarkable property of human mobility. In simple physical systems, we typically think of the cost of movement as proportional to distance, as there is an amount of work that needs to be done against dissipative forces that is set by how far one moves. However, to obtain a power-law dependence on distance in the gravity law consistent with such an argument, we need to assume in maximum-entropy models that the cost of travel is proportional to the *logarithm of distance*! This gives us a strong hint that the MaxEnt procedure is missing something important about the nature of cities, which can be included in translating costs to distance but requires additional insights.

The Radiation Model Another much more recent but compelling proposal for modeling mobility flows is the so-called *radiation model*.[27] It is also based on simple ideas from physics for particles emitted by a source and the expectation that they will be found at a sink some distance away. The expression for the expected (average) flow between zones i and j is

$$T_{ij} = O_i^T P_{ij} = O_i^T \frac{N_i N_j}{(N_i + N_{ij})(N_i + N_j + N_{ij})},$$ (8.4)

where O_i^T is the number of trips starting at region i, N_{ij} is the total population of a circle centered at i, with a radius extended to just touch j, excluding the source and destination populations, and P_{ij} is the probability of a single emission absorption at locations i and j. Equation (8.4) is the expectation value of a multinomial distribution in the space of origin-destination pairs i, j. The essential ingredient is the probability for a trip between the two places, P_{ij}.

The radiation model hinges on the calculation of this probability. To do so, Simini et al.[28] assumed the following situation: Consider a statistical quantity z_b, called *absorbance*, with an associated probability $P(z_b)$, common to all zones and the entire population. The absorbance is intended to model the benefits of a potential employment opportunity, which may be a combination of economic and social factors. The idea is that z_b characterizes the employment quality of a person so the higher z_b, the smaller the likelihood that it will be absorbed (i.e., find a job there). Then, by extension, each location j has a certain probability of absorbing each of these workers by matching the worker's own z_b with the z_b in that region. The region's z_b is obtained as the maximum value over N_j independent draws from $P(z_b)$. The worker is "absorbed" by the closest location to their residence whose absorbance is greater than his own.

From these modeling assumptions, one can calculate the form of equation (8.4) as the decomposition of the probabilities

$$P_{ij} = \int_0^{+\infty} dz_b \, P_{N_i}(z_b) P_{N_{ij}}(<z_b) P_{N_j}(>z_b),$$ (8.5)

where $P_{N_i}(z_b)$ is the probability that the maximum from $P(z_b)$ after N_i trials is z_b; $P_{N_{ij}}(<z_b)$ is the probability that the agent is not absorbed in between (i.e., that N_{ij} random numbers are lower than z_b); and $P_{N_j}(>z_b)$ is the probability of absorption: that N_j random numbers are all larger than z_b. Because all these random number draws from $P(z_b)$ are *assumed* to be statistically independent, they have the simple form

$$P_{N_i}(z_b) = \frac{dP_{N_i}(<z_b)}{dz_b} = N_i P(<z_b)^{N_i - 1} \frac{dP(<z_b)}{dz_b}, \; P_{N_{ij}}(<z_b) = P(<z_b)^{N_{ij}},$$

$$P_{N_j}(>z_b) = 1 - P(<z_b)^{N_j},$$

leading to

$$P_{ij} = N_i \int_0^{+\infty} dz_b \, \frac{dP(<z_b)}{dz_b} \left[P(<z_b)^{N_i + N_{ij} - 1} - P(<z_b)^{N_i + N_j + N_{ij} - 1} \right]$$

$$= N_i \left(\frac{1}{N_i + N_{ij}} - \frac{1}{N_i + N_j + N_{ij}} \right),$$

$$(8.6)$$

which is equation (8.4). What is most remarkable about the radiation model is that it does not depend on the statistical model for the absorbances, $P(z_b)$, or on many other possible complications. We see that a simple probabilistic matching of origin-destination jobs and population leads to a very simple prediction in terms of population fractions.

How does this model connect to the original gravity law or its MaxEnt derivation? Clearly, all models agree on the fact that flows between regions are proportional to the product of the two populations. The distance dependence, however, is a function of the spatial distribution of population. For the simplest case of a population distribution with uniform spatial density, n_A, we get $N_{ij} = n_A \pi d_{ij}^2$. Then, the radiation model predicts that

$$T_{ij} = T_i \frac{N_i N_j}{(N_i + n_A \pi d_{ij}^2)(N_i + N_j + n_A \pi d_{ij}^2)} \xrightarrow{\text{large } d_{ij}} T_i \frac{N_i N_j}{d_{ij}^4}. \qquad (8.7)$$

For large regions $\left(\text{when } d_i = \sqrt{\frac{N_i}{\pi n_A}} \ll d_{ij} = \sqrt{\frac{N_{ij}}{\pi n_A}} \right)$, the gravity law exponent is predicted to be $\alpha_g \simeq 4$. Whether this is a good or bad description of data is an empirical question[29] along with the more fundamental question of what exactly the value of α_g should be.[30] In any case, we see that the radiation model gives us a generalized version of the gravity law and a more particular prediction for its distance exponent, which is found to be large compared to many empirical observations.

Urban Scaling Theory   Urban scaling theory gives us another, perhaps more direct, route to obtaining the mathematical form of the gravity law, equation (8.1). The necessary additional assumption is that, like other socioeconomic outputs, migration flows are also the result of (and proportional to) rates of socioeconomic interactions. The twist here is simply that the interactions that become relevant are now *between the populations of the two separate places* (origin and destination cities) connected by the flow. To see this, recall that we wrote the average rate of interactions over some time t as given by counting the coincidence points between all the space-time life paths of the two populations. We can compute this in practice by focusing on the *worldsheet* of someone in city i as $\int_{x_i(0)}^{x_i(t)} a_0 \, dx_i(t') = \int_0^t a_0 v_i(t') \, dt'$, where $x_i(t)$ is the agent's trajectory over space—its life path—and $v_i(t) = \frac{dx_i(t)}{dt}$ is the agent's velocity. The expected number of interactions with individuals of city j is then given by their coincidence in space and time with our agent, which we write as

$$k_{ij} = \int_0^t a_0 \, \Gamma[x_j(t') - x_i(t')] \, dx_i(t') \simeq \frac{a_0 \ell \, N_j}{A_{ij}},$$ just as in chapter 3, but where A_{ij} is now the total area relevant to the interactions between people of the two cities. The expected value of the full set of interactions (per city, not per person) is then

$$K_{ij} \simeq a_0 \ell \frac{N_i N_j}{A_{ij}}. \tag{8.8}$$

Finally, we need to assume that the number of people moving is a fraction of these interactions. We can model this by introducing a probability per person of leaving city i, P_i^{out}, and a corresponding probability of going to city j, $P_{i,j}^{out,in}$. The factor associated with the interaction area may be written dimensionally in terms of the distance between places as $A_{ij} = a_g d_{ij}^{\alpha_g}$, where a_g is a scaling prefactor. This association suggests an exponent $\alpha_g = 2$. However, the area A_{ij} will not necessarily have a regular fractal dimension ($D = 2$). In such cases, there will be a fractal (noninteger) correction to the exponent, just as we have seen—for other reasons—for the built area of cities in chapter 3. For example, it may be much more natural to consider a line (or, at any rate, a thin area) between the two urban centers far away, which would result in $\alpha_g \approx 1$. In general, we would expect that this fractal dimension may be a (slow) function of distance itself and of the type of movement (migration of people versus movement of commodities, etc.), infrastructure, and transportation modes. With these definitions in hand, we get equation (8.1), with $G_{M;i,j} = P_{i,j}^{out,in} a_0 \ell / a_g$, where if the probabilities of leaving and arriving are independent of the particular cities given their distance (which they usually are not), a simpler expression, $G_M = P^{in} P^{out} a_0 l / a_g$, results.

The most obvious shortfall of the gravity law is that it is *symmetric* in $i \leftrightarrow j$, so it predicts the *same flow* in both directions. This obviously fails to account for why some places are more attractive than others, which would be encoded here in $P_{i,j}^{out,in}$. This symmetry (or indifference) of preferences will become consequential later as a necessary condition for the emergence of Zipf's law for the relative size abundance of cities.

8.1.4 GIBRAT'S LAW

Gibrat's law[31]—also known as the *law of proportional growth*—states that the average growth rates of different cities are the *same* in an urban system. This means in particular that the growth rate of cities is statistically independent of their population size. This is a remarkable statement in light of the scaling results of previous chapters, which could be taken to suggest that larger cities could grow faster by reinvesting their superlinear productivity effects. Whenever this is possible, growth rates would accelerate and lead to quantities going to infinity in a finite amount of time (this is called a *finite-time singularity*), and faster and faster innovations would be necessary to forestall such a catastrophe.[32] However, we already saw empirically in chapter 4 that this expectation is not borne out by data, because both incomes and costs are superlinear with the same exponent, which means that real incomes are approximately independent of city size. This also means that growth rates for cities are small, stochastic quantities, typically with no clear discernible scale dependence.

In practice and in light of such results, Gibrat's law is meant as a statistical extension of the growth rate size independence, which as we will see is important in terms of stating that neither the *average* growth rate nor its *variance* (squared volatility) are functions of city size within an urban system. As we have already seen in the context of US metropolitan areas (figure 8.5), this is an assumption that holds approximately true when tested against data. This subject has itself been much debated in the literature, and the observations of deviations may be dependent on the timescale and the type of statistical analysis used.

The origins of Gibrat's law have remained a puzzle. In my opinion, it has never been well explained theoretically in general terms; we will provide a new and, I believe, more fundamental argument later in this chapter. Like the advent of the gravity law, Gibrat's law is justified primarily by data. Gibrat first posited this "law" after observing the growth behavior of *businesses*, not cities. Nevertheless, as we have already seen, Gibrat's law also applies, at least approximately, for cities within a nation, such as the US. Quantitatively, the most important aspect of Gibrat's law is that it provides a

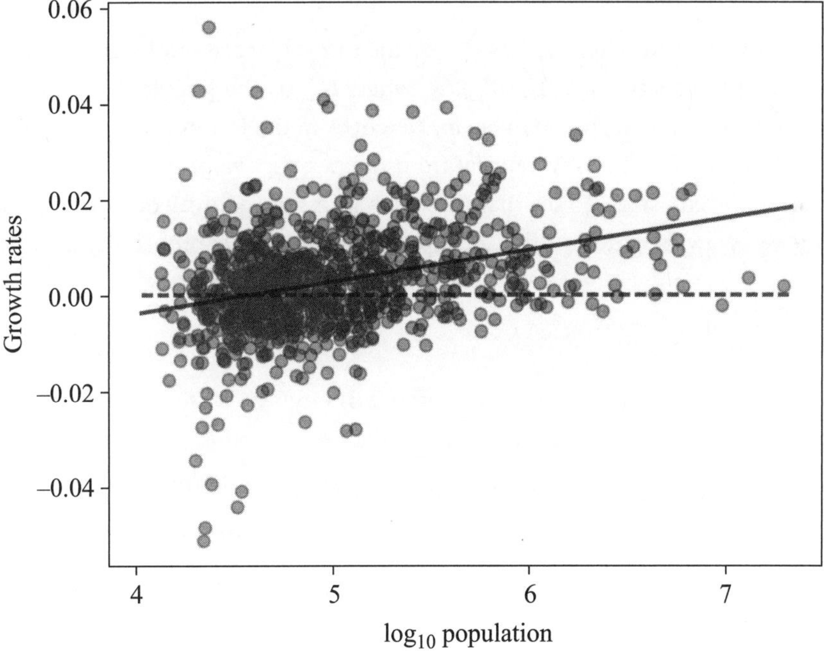

8.5 Growth rates for Metropolitan and Micropolitan Statistical Areas in the US from Census 2010 data (N_c=933). The mean growth rate across cities in this sample is 0.00282, with variance 0.00012. The dashed line shows a zero growth rate for reference, while the solid line shows the best fit with city size, $\gamma_{N_i} = -0.03050 + 0.00667\log_{10} N$, with 95% confidence interval for the slope of 95% CI=[0.00543, 0.00792] and [−0.03676, −0.02424] for the intercept. This slight average increase in growth rates with city size is clearly caused by medium and large metropolitan areas but not the system's largest cities (New York, Los Angeles, Chicago), which at present show overall growth rates close to zero.

critical modeling assumption to derive Zipf's law as a result of multiplicative random growth of cities.[33]

8.1.5 ZIPF'S LAW FOR THE RELATIVE CITY SIZE DISTRIBUTION

Zipf's rank-size rule is arguably the most famous law of urban geography. It is often used to argue that cities are complex systems because they do not obey simpler size statistics, such as exponentials or Gaussian distributions, which are typical of *simple* physical systems, or of problems of disorganized complexity, in Jane Jacobs's terminology. We will see later that this is overstating the case: there is not much complexity in Zipf's law at all; its emergence is contingent on a number of strong simplifications.

Like the gravity law, Zipf's law was first observed empirically. In its strictest form, it says that the city size probability distribution takes the form

$$P_z(N) = \frac{P_{z_0}}{N^{1+z}},$$

(8.9)

with $z=1$ being Zipf's specific exponent and $P_{z_0} = 1/\int dN \frac{1}{N^{1+z}}$ a normalization constant ensuring that the probability adds up to unity.

The Rank-Size Rule Sometimes Zipf's law is stated, equivalently to equation (8.9), in terms of the so-called *rank-size rule*, which says that the *rank* of a city within its urban system (*rank*=1 for the largest, *rank*=2 for the second largest, and so on) is inversely proportional to its size, *rank* $(N) = N_{max}/N$, where N_{max} is the population of the largest city in the urban system (Tokyo in Japan, New York in the US, São Paulo in Brazil, etc.). This form has a more intuitive appeal from the perspective of the urban system as a *hierarchy* set by city sizes. To see that these two forms are equivalent, consider that we can use Zipf's law to write first the corresponding cumulative probability distribution

$$P_z(n>N) = P_{z_0} \int\limits_N^{N_{max}} \frac{1}{N'^{1+z}} dN' \propto \frac{P_{z_0}}{N^z}.$$

The cumulative distribution is monotonic in city size N, so it is proportional to the rank of a city of that size, *rank* (N): Thus, $P_z(n>N) \propto rank$ (N). Consequently, we can change variables (as we did in chapter 5) and conclude that $rank(N) \propto \frac{1}{N^z}$. The missing multiplicative constant can be determined by setting $rank(N_{max})=1$, which implies

$$rank(N) = \left(\frac{N_{max}}{N}\right)^z,$$

(8.10)

which is the usual form of the famous *rank-size rule* (see figure 8.6): *a city's rank is inversely proportional to its size* ($z=1$).

Similar power laws related to the frequency of other items, such as words (recall that Zipf was a linguist) or income, in many complex systems often obey similar rank-size distributions. As a consequence, there have been a truly remarkable number

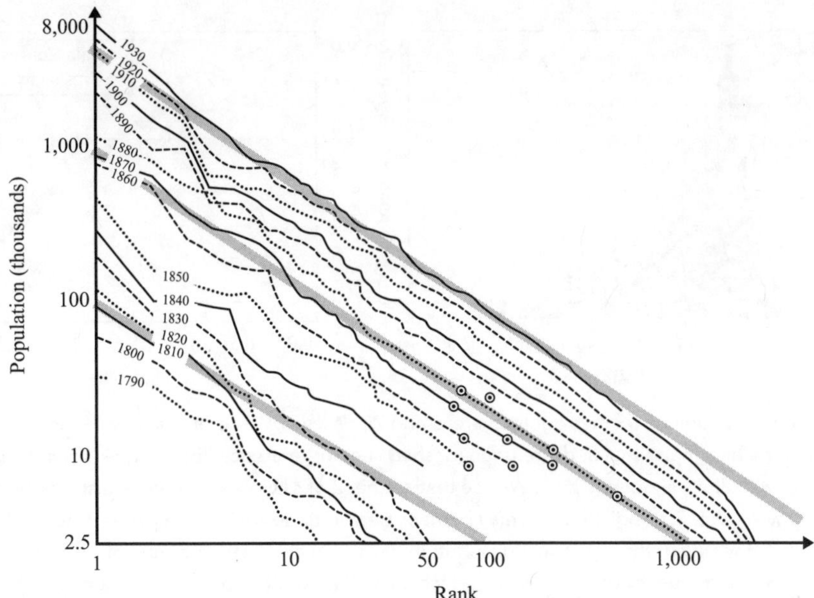

8.6 Zipf's illustration of the rank-size rule for US cities between 1790 and 1930. Thick gray lines show the rank-size rule (equation (8.10)) with $z = 1$, making it clear that, even in the original, Zipf's law is an approximate description of the city size distribution, with some visible systematic deviations in terms of smaller city sizes and slopes.

of attempts at explaining the origin of Zipf's law in many different contexts. Zipf himself tried to develop an explanation based on what he called the *principle of least effort*,[34] but it is widely accepted that his mathematical argument was flawed. Most of the better existing explanations are mechanistic, in the sense of deriving Zipf's law from the long time limit of some plausible stochastic process. We will go over the most relevant such arguments pertaining to the city size distribution at the end of the section 8.2 to see that Zipf's law is the simplest long-term outcome of a stochastic demographic growth process, analogous to what a uniform distribution is for simple diffusion. Zipf's law is often a pretty poor description of the size distribution of cities (see figure 8.7), but how good or how poor remains a little in the eye of the beholder, see for example figure 8.7.

In any case, as a result of common discrepancies to data, there have been a large number of proposals for generalized power-law, lognormal, and other related functions to fit empirical city size distributions.[35] We will have a lot to say about this at the end of the section 8.2.

We close this introduction with a short summary of some empirical difficulties and theoretical considerations. In a debate typical of the difficulties of trying to decide the merit of Zipf's law for cities purely on statistical grounds, Eeckhout,[36] based on the analysis of administrative (political, not functional) cities, argued that the distribution is in fact lognormal. In a reply, Levy[37] used a number of cuts of the same

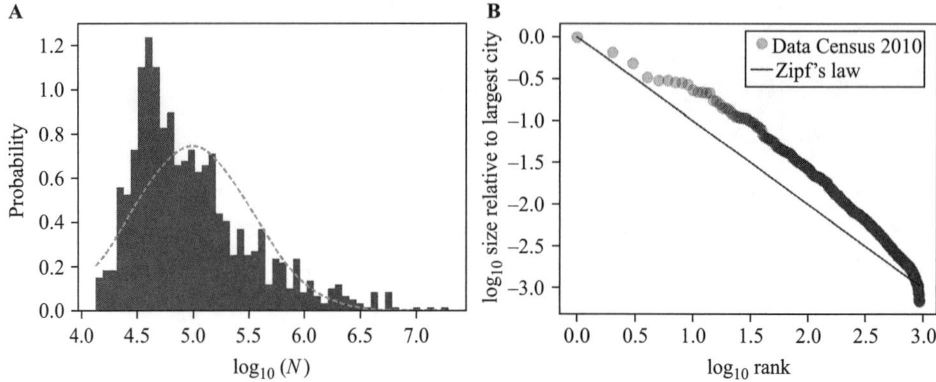

8.7 Size distribution of US metropolitan areas and Zipf's law. (A) The probability distribution histogram and the best lognormal fit distribution (dashed line) for reference. (B) The rank-size rule and the exact line, with Zipf's exponent, $z=1$. We see that neither Zipf's law or a lognormal distribution fits the data very well, while Zipf's distribution may perhaps be said to do well for the largest three to four cities. On the other hand, the lognormal distribution has the qualitatively correct feature of accounting for a drop in the frequency of small places, which Zipf's law fails to capture, as we see in terms of the decay in size at large ranks. This appears as a small effect in the range of the rank-size plot in (B) but involves a very large number of small cities.

data, as well as standard statistical tests, to discuss the nature of a lognormal versus power-law form of the distribution, especially for large cities; see also Saichev, Malevergne, and Sornette[38] for a longer and more detailed discussion.

Another issue with Zipf's law is what definition of the urban area to adopt. While we have argued in previous chapters that cities, as spatial integrated networks, are best captured by metropolitan definitions, a number of authors in quantitative geography have searched for spatial definitions that would yield Zipf's law as the gold standard.[39] Such approaches use percolation models to merge (or split) nearby spatial clusters of population or built spaces and do tend to find Zipf's law for such units, at least for the largest cities.[40]

In terms of explanations for the emergence of Zipf's law, the agreed starting point is that it arises from multiplicative random growth processes.[41] The problem with such an explanation is that two additional key assumptions are necessary. The first is that Gibrat's law applies, enforcing the same growth rate statistics (the same mean and volatility) for all cities in an urban system. The second is that even in these circumstances one typically obtains a lognormal distribution of city sizes. To obtain Zipf's law, one needs special *boundary conditions* on city growth and decay dynamics to stop the city distribution from leaking into increasingly smaller places.[42] Both these conditions are critical and meaningful: Why should all cities in a system grow at the same average rate and with the same volatility? Over what timescale? What may enforce such extraordinary conditions? What, if anything, stops small places from losing population?

8.2.1   THE DEMOGRAPHY OF URBAN SYSTEMS

Let us begin with simple accounting of births, deaths, and migration. For a set of cities labeled by $i = 1, 2, \ldots, N_c$, with population sizes $N_1(t), N_2(t), \ldots, N_{N_c}(t)$, we can write the general population dynamics as

$$N_i(t + dt) = N_i(t) + dt\left[Births_i - Deaths_i + M_i^R + M_i^F + \sum_{j=1, j \neq 1}^{N_c} (J_{ji} - J_{ij}) \right]. \tag{8.11}$$

This just says that the population of a city i increases because, over the time period dt, there were so many $Births_i$, M_i^R immigrants from rural areas, M_i^F foreign immigrants, and $\sum_{j=1,\, j \neq i}^{N_c} J_{ji}$ migrants from other cities j in the urban system. Similarly, the population of the same city decreases because there are so many $Deaths_i$ over the same period and because $\sum_{j=1,\, j \neq i}^{N_c} J_{ij}$ people left for other cities. Note also that migration from rural areas or foreign countries can be negative, meaning that on balance people leave the city for these regions. This is rare in present-day high-income urban systems and against a backdrop of urbanization (chapter 1) but could be a factor in other settings. We can, in principle, modify equation (8.11) to include explicit flows between our city and a list of rural places or foreign cities, but data of this kind are not typically available, so in practice we must deal with such flows in the aggregate.

It is useful to write all these quantities as *per capita rates*, so equation (8.11) becomes

$$N_i(t + dt) = N_i(t) + dt\left[(1 + v_i)N_i(t) + \sum_{j=1, j \neq 1}^{N_c} J_{ji} - J_{ij} \right] \tag{8.12}$$

with $v_i \equiv \dfrac{Births_i - Deaths_i}{N_i} + m_i^R + m_i^F$, which is the city's *vital rate*, where there are only births and deaths. Here, $m_i^R = \dfrac{M_i^R}{N_i}$, $m_i^F = \dfrac{M_i^F}{N_i}$. We have written this equation in discrete form in time, $N_i(t+dt) = N_i(t) + dt(\ldots)$, instead of the time derivative, $\dfrac{dN_i(t)}{dt}$, because data are typically measured in relatively long time intervals, such as years. To keep the notation simple, we will work in units in which $dt = 1$. Thus, all rates are taken as the average over this interval; say, for example, v_i is the vital rate per person *per year* in city i.

Although city sizes are often the focus of our attention, we will show that the structure of an urban system is best captured by the population *structure vector*, n_i, whose components are defined as the population fractions in each city i, $n_i(t) = \dfrac{N_i(t)}{N_T(t)}$, with the total population given by $N_T(t) = \sum_{i=1}^{N_c} N_i(t)$.

We now need a useful parameterization of the intercity migration flows, J_{ij}. As we noted earlier, the gravity law is symmetric: the number of people moving from any city, i, to another, j, equals the number of people moving in the opposite direction, so using it at face value produces the counterfactual result of no net migration flow in or out of *any* city.

8.2.2 MATRIX POPULATION MODELS

To make progress, in the absence of assuming the gravity law for migration, we can introduce another well-developed tradition in demography and population biology and write the urban system dynamics in the form of a *matrix population model*.[46] To do this, we write each migration flow as $J_{ij}=m_{ij}\,N_i$, where m_{ij} is the probability per unit time for a person in city i to move to city j. This allows us to write the dynamics as a matrix equation,

$$N_i(t+1) = \sum_{j=1}^{N_c} e_{ij}N_j(t),\tag{8.13}$$

where the matrix e_{ij}—which is sometimes called the *environment*—follows from the dynamics of births, deaths, and migration as

$$e_{ij} = (1+v_i - m_i^{out})1_{ij} + m_{ji},\tag{8.14}$$

with the "delta function" $1_{ij}=1$ when $i=j$ and zero otherwise. The quantity $m_i^{out} = \sum_{j=1,\,j\neq i}^{N_c} m_{ij} <1$ is the probability that a person leaves city i for any other city in the urban system. Note that generally the matrix is a function of time, $e_{ij}(t)$, if the parameters in it are time dependent, as will always happen to some extent. The linearity of equation (8.13) is the result of the *assumption* that these parameters are not functions of city sizes, which we will revisit.

General Solution The point of writing the equation for the demographic dynamics of cities in matrix form is that it has a formal solution for the population vector $N(t) = (N_1(t),\ldots,N_i(t),\ldots,N_{N_c}(t))$ (for simplicity, vectors and matrices without explicit indices will be written in bold) as

$$N(t) = e(t)\,e(t-1)\ldots e(1)\,N(0).\tag{8.15}$$

This means that we can write the solution for all city sizes if we know the matrix e at each time t. The product of the matrices at each time is just another matrix. When

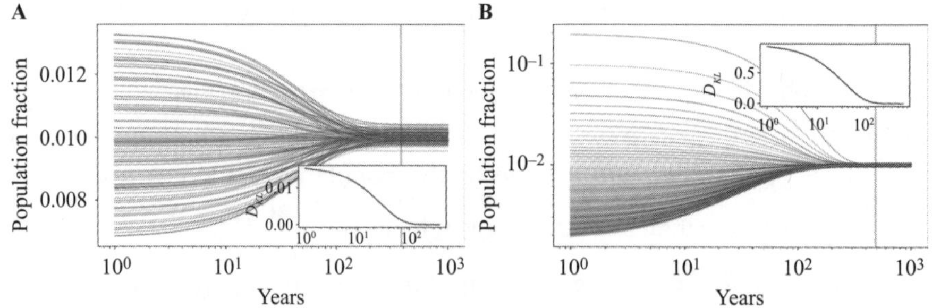

8.9 Simulated demographic trajectories for given fixed environments. (A) The final population distribution is independent of the initial distribution and defined by the projection matrix, **e**. Both simulations have the same environment but different initial population distribution: the initial distribution (A) is random with uniform probability, (B) Zipf's law. Insets depict the distance (in terms of the Kullback-Leibler divergence, D_{KL}) between the dynamical population distribution and that given by the leading eigenvector of the projection matrix. The vertical lines mark the characteristic time to converge to this limit, which is of the order of hundreds of years.

the product matrix is well behaved, we can guarantee the existence of a distribution of city sizes with certain properties. This is easy to check numerically (see figure 8.9), but, at a more fundamental level, it is also the subject of so-called *ergodic theorems of formal demography*, to which we now turn.

8.2.3   ERGODIC THEOREMS AND LONG-TERM SYSTEM DYNAMICS

Ergodic theorems are appealing because they promise liberation from history. Initial conditions are usually regarded as more accidental than interesting; we want explanations of the present in terms of the *mechanisms* governing population dynamics in the present and hopefully recent past.

—Hal Caswell, *Matrix Population Models*

So far, we have done a fair amount of mathematical setup. We are now ready to get to the science; that is, to understand some of the general consequences of the urban system's demographic dynamics. Echoing Caswell's quotation at the beginning of this subsection, the main idea in modeling urban systems has been that the initial state of the population—the sizes of cities today—is less important than the system's demographic dynamics, at least given sufficient time. *If* this is indeed the case, then the structure of the urban system—the relative distribution of city sizes—is ultimately set by the properties of the matrix e in equations (8.13) and (8.14). This generalizes the concept of *ergodicity* in statistical physics to growing populations in complex systems. In statistical mechanics, the system dynamics is ergodic when over the long term it explores all available state space (variables take all possible values) subject to energy conservation and other constraints. Ergodicity is a property of temporal averages as the dynamics blur single states into probabilities reflecting where the system spends time. In population dynamics, ergodicity is different: it means simply independence from initial conditions in situations where the system may be growing (or decaying) exponentially. In statistical mechanics, ergodicity is associated with the approach to a state of maximum entropy (thermal equilibrium). In population dynamics, the long-term state of the system may instead be a structured population, as the matrix e typically implements *selection*, manifested as some cities growing faster than others. It follows that when the matrix e has "less structure" (a statement that we will later make precise), the resulting city size distribution will be more random, in fact closer to expectations from statistical physics. Then—and only then—can we ignore most socioeconomic factors.

In this respect, there are two limiting situations: one in which e has structure and some cities or regions are manifestly preferred to others, as signaled by converging migration, and the other, where the dynamics is random and migration is nondirectional. Under additional, specific conditions, this random growth dynamics results in Zipf's law, a characteristic that has led many authors to emphasize random demographic growth as the norm.[47] We will show that this is generally not true.[48] Working on a larger frame where the dynamics has both structure and randomness is essential when discussing change in real urban systems.

Ergodic Properties of Population Dynamics   A remarkable set of results in population dynamics is known as the *ergodic theorems*.[49] Appendix D introduces these four theorems as described by Caswell.[50] In general, ergodic theorems guarantee certain properties of the structure vector solution for long-term dynamics, given specific conditions on the environment. There are several ergodic theorems of varying complexity, applying to deterministic and noisy (stochastic) dynamics (figure 8.10).

Static Environment and the Strong Ergodic Theorem   The simplest ergodic theorem applies to situations when the matrix e is independent of time and *primitive*. A matrix e is primitive if it is nonnegative (all its entries $e_{ij} \geq 0$) and its n-power (the matrix multiplied by itself n times) is a positive matrix (all its elements are greater than zero). This is a little abstract, but its usefulness will soon become apparent. There is a more intuitive way to state what being a primitive matrix means in terms of the directed graph associated with the migration flows in e (figure 8.11).

A primitive matrix is an irreducible matrix with period 1, meaning that its directed graph is strongly connected and the lengths of the closed paths that we get from following its arrows are not multiples of each other. In other words, the maximum common denominator between these numbers is 1. This is best illustrated and discussed in the caption of figure 8.11, but it is clearly a feature of a set of cities exchanging migrants with finite probability. Interestingly enough, this is *not* a feature of cities that only inject or receive migrants into the urban system (as may be the case for cities outside the nation). Such cities are *not* part of the urban system, by the same argument!

Evolution matrix e_{ij}
Ergodic theorems

		deterministic	stochastic
Mixing	**weak**	independent cities	independent cities statistical distribution
	strong	urban system asymptotic Gibrat's hierarchy as centrality	urban system asymptotic Zipf's law

8.10   Demographic evolution, ergodic theorems, and the emergence of the urban system (see also appendix D). There are four distinct regimes for the long-term behavior of demographic growth in a set of cities, depending on the nature of the evolution (properties of the matrix **e**) and the strength of intercity mixing. Under strong mixing, an urban system emerges, regardless of the details of **e**, as long as the matrix is primitive. If the matrix **e** is deterministic, the asymptotic dynamics is set by its dominant eigenvector, which gives a hierarchy of cities based on their eigenvalue centrality. If the evolution is stochastic, however, the city size distribution approaches a different distribution, sometimes close to Zipf's law, depending on boundary conditions. If mixing is weak (migration rates are smaller than vital rates), no urban system emerges and each city remains essentially independent of others. This is typically the case for the relationship between cities across national borders.

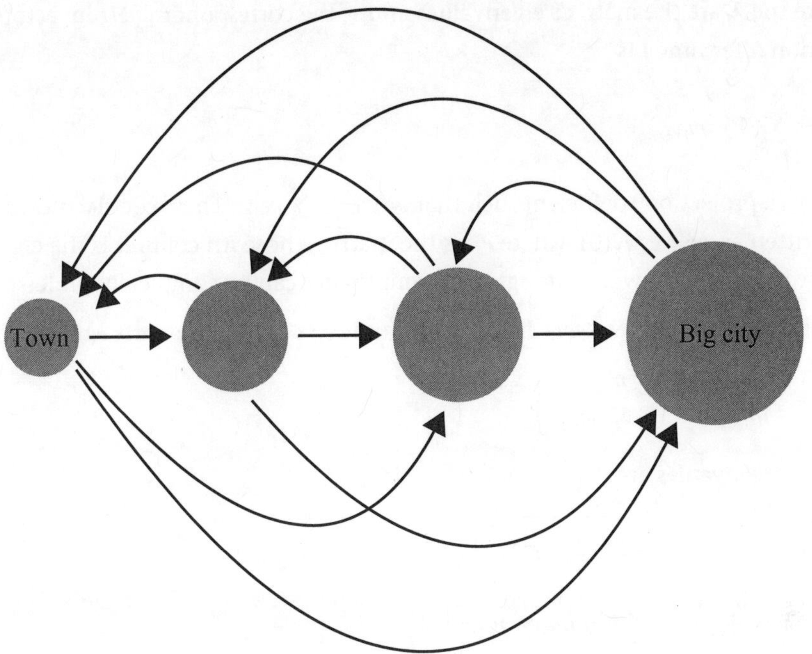

8.11 Schematic directed graph representing migration flows between cities in an urban system. Here the urban system consists of only four cities of various sizes (gray circles, with size denoting population), while the arrows show migration flows between pairs of places. In general, there is a positive probability of migration between any two places. This means that the graph is strongly connected (each node can be reached from any other node by following the arrows), which implies that the matrix e is irreducible. In addition, the arrows form loops, whereby we can return to the same node after a certain number of steps. If the graph is fully connected, there are loops of lengths 2, 3, 4, and so on up to the matrix dimension N_c. These numbers' largest common denominator is 1. These two conditions guarantee that the matrix e is primitive. We see that these properties are natural—even inevitable—for an urban system with strong migration flows.

If the environment e is primitive, then only its structure matters. The *strong ergodic theorem* is based on a set of famous results in linear algebra known as the Perron-Frobenius theorem.[51] For a primitive matrix, the theorem applies and guarantees a set of simple properties for the eigenvalues and eigenvectors of e. Specifically, we are guaranteed that the largest eigenvalue is positive and simple (unique), $\lambda_0 > Re(\lambda_1) \geq Re(\lambda_1) \geq \ldots$, and that its corresponding eigenvector is also positive, $v = (v_{01}, v_{02}, v_{0j}, \ldots)$, with $v_{oj} > 0$, for all components j. This allows us to write the solution for the sizes of cities over time by solving the demographic dynamics *exactly*. Specifically,

$$N(t) = (e)^t N(0). \tag{8.16}$$

We can then write the solution explicitly in terms of the eigenvalues and eigenvectors of e. To see this, let us write the eigenproblem of e as

$$ev = \lambda_i v_i, \tag{8.17}$$

where the λ_i are the matrix's eigenvalues and v_i the corresponding eigenvectors. The solution after time t is

$$N(t) = \sum_{i=1}^{N_c} (\lambda_i)^t \, pr_i v_i,$$

(8.18)

with pr_i a projection coefficient such that $N(0) = \sum_{i=1}^{N_c} pr_i \, v_i$. These coefficients can also be written as $pr = e^{-1}N(0)$, where e^{-1} is the matrix whose ith column is the eigenvector v_i. It is useful to work through an example that can be completely understood.

Example: The Two-City System   In the case of only two cities, the matrix e takes the form

$$e = \begin{bmatrix} 1 + v_1 - m_{12} & m_{21} \\ m_{12} & 1 + v_2 - m_{21} \end{bmatrix}.$$

The eigenvalues are

$$\lambda_\pm = 1 + \bar{v} - \frac{\bar{m}}{2} \pm \sqrt{\left(\frac{v_1 - v_2}{2}\right)^2 + \bar{m}^2 - \frac{1}{2}(v_1 - v_2)(m_{12} - m_{21})},$$

where $\bar{v} = \dfrac{v_1 + v_2}{2}$ and $\bar{m} = m_{12} + m_{21}$.

In the simplifying limit where $v_1 \to v_2$, we get

$$\lambda_0 = 1 + \bar{v} > \lambda_1 = 1 + \bar{v} - \bar{m},$$

with eigenvectors

$$v_0 = \left(\frac{m_{21}}{m_{12}}, 1\right) \text{ and } v_1 = (-1, 1).$$

The projection coefficients in turn are

$$pr_0 = \frac{m_{12}}{\bar{m}}(N_1(0) + N_2(0)) = \frac{m_{12}N_T(0)}{m_{12} + m_{21}}, \quad pr_1 = \frac{m_{21}N_2(0) - m_{12}N_1(0)}{\bar{m}}.$$

Clearly, the leading eigenvalue sets the persistent time evolution, with the second decaying exponentially relative to the first. The decay of secondary eigenvalues is proportional to $(\lambda_1/\lambda_0)^t = e^{-\ln\frac{\lambda_0}{\lambda_1}t}$, so the decay rate is $\ln\dfrac{\lambda_0}{\lambda_1} \approx \bar{m}/(1 + \bar{v})$. We see explicitly that the magnitude of the mixing rate $\bar{m}$ is critical for the emergence of the urban system. In the limit where $\bar{m} \to 0$, there is no mixing and cities grow separately at their own rate, not as an urban system. For very small mixing parameters, the urban system may take a long time to emerge: a 1% mixing via migration per year translates into a hundred-year decay rate!

We can complement this example with solutions of the demographic dynamics given any matrix e. Figure 8.12 and table 8.1 show the result of projecting forward in time the present vital and migration rates in the US urban system compiled for Census 2010.

Power, Influence, and the Emergence of Urban Hierarchy   Sociologists measure *power and influence* in terms of the structural positions of agents (nodes) in complex networks.[52] Within any complex network of actors, the largest eigenvector is a measure

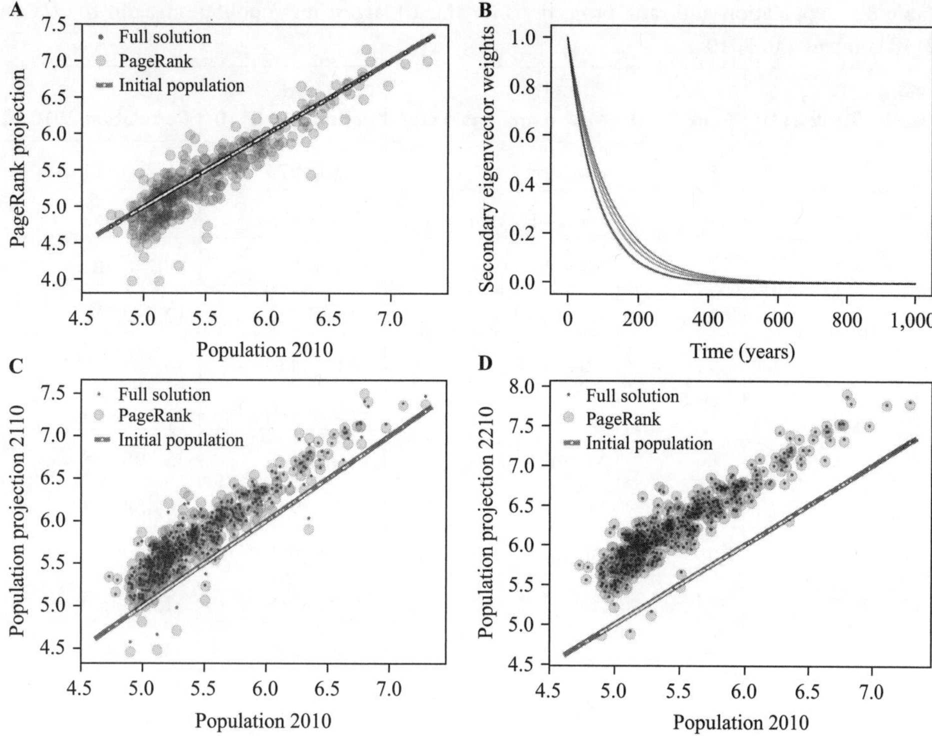

8.12 Demographic time evolution of city sizes for US Metropolitan Statistical Areas (MSAs) according to equation (8.12). (A) Initial leading eigenvalue projection (PageRank, points) versus the initial population. Cities with high PageRank will grow faster than others in the urban system and vice versa. The solid line shows the correlation between the PageRank and the initial population size (slope 0.99, 95% CI [0.95, 1.07], $R^2 = 0.66$). The ranks for the top cities are shown in table 8.1. (B) shows the relative decay of the secondary eigenvalues $\left(\dfrac{\lambda_i}{\lambda_0}\right)^t$ for $i = 1, 2, 3, 4$. Using US Census 2010 data, we see that it takes centuries for the effect of all leading eigenvectors to disappear, a timescale in which we expect the matrix e not to be constant in time. (C) and (D) show the corresponding solutions as a function of the original population in 2110 and 2210, respectively. We see that, as time goes by, the exact solution approaches the PageRank (coincidence of darker small dots with larger gray circles) and all city sizes continue to grow at a single growth rate dictated by $\gamma_N = \ln \lambda_0$. The initial solution is shown as the black line.

of the *centrality* of that actor within a network. This is a particular form of centrality, different from others, such as betweenness or highest degree.[53] Cities with larger dominant eigenvectors are said to have higher rank and may have more power and influence in the urban system. This measure had been used for decades by geographers[54] and sociologists[55] before it was rediscovered more recently by Google founders Larry Page and Sergey Brin,[56] who used it to rank the power and influence of a web page (*PageRank*).

Using recent data for demographic quantities in US metropolitan areas, we observe that the highest-centrality cities at present are Houston and Dallas, followed by New York City and Los Angeles (see table 8.1). As a consequence, we can project the population growth of the US urban system forward in time and predict

Table 8.1 Population and rank projections for the 10 largest metropolitan areas in the US in 2110 compared to 2010

Page Rank	Rank 2110	Rank 2010	MSA name (main city)	Projected population 2110	Population 2010
1	2	5	Houston	26,107,974	6,260,171
2	4	4	Dallas–Ft. Worth	22,415,885	6,741,942
3	1	1	New York City	30,160,729	19,748,581
4	3	2	Los Angeles	24,658,051	12,999,512
5	8	9	Atlanta	13,995,430	5,468,366
6	6	7	Washington, DC	14,250,130	5,872,661
7	5	8	Miami	14,631,123	5,798,818
8	9	12	Phoenix	12,692,948	4,352,661
9	7	3	Chicago	14,099,901	9,420,194
10	15	35	Austin	9,327,568	1,865,084
11	12	15	Seattle	10,648,859	3,570,470
12	10	11	San Francisco	11,164,725	4,478,883

the future size and rank of every city, if e remains fixed. Extrapolation of present demographics would lead to dramatic shifts in the US urban hierarchy, with Houston and Dallas eventually predicted to become the largest cities in the nation. Other metropolitan areas are also predicted to get much larger, with New York City topping 30 million people by 2110 and many other cities more than quadrupling their present population by then. Many cities in the South and West are expected to rise through the ranks, including Austin, Atlanta, Phoenix, and Seattle. Traditionally dominant cities, such as Chicago (rank 3), Philadelphia (rank 6), Boston (rank 10), and Detroit (rank 14), are predicted to experience significant relative declines. Cities in Puerto Rico are hit the hardest and decline the most in relative population. However, other cities, in the industrial Midwest and in Alaska, are also expected to become smaller, while many small places in Texas, Utah, and Colorado are predicted to grow. This process is very slow and even in a century, we should expect to see an urban system hierarchy similar to what we have today (see also figure 8.9).

Dynamical Environments: General Statements from Ergodic Theorems Continuing to generalize the possible classes of demographic dynamics, we now ask what happens when the matrix $e(t)$ is time dependent. There are some additional results for the city size distribution given by the remaining three ergodic theorems.

First, the so-called *weak ergodic theorem* (see appendix D) guarantees that for some dynamical sequence of environments, $e(t_0)$, $e(t_1)$, . . . , $e(t_n)$, . . . , the difference between two initial structure vectors, $n \neq n'$, decays to zero in time. This means that there is typically still an asymptotic relative city size distribution that is a function of environments and independent of initial conditions.

When the environment is stochastic but otherwise time independent (stationary), the *strong stochastic ergodic theorem* states that the structure vector becomes a random variable whose probability distribution converges to a fixed stationary distribution, regardless of initial conditions. This is the sense in which most derivations of Zipf's law apply, as we will also see later. For stochastic environments, only probability distributions of structure vectors under environmental noise averaging can be predicted.

Finally, in situations where the environment is time dependent *and stochastic,* the weak stochastic ergodic theorem tells us that the difference between the probability distributions for the structure vectors resulting from any two initial populations exposed to independent sample paths decays to zero. Again, in cases where the environment is explicitly dynamic, besides being stochastic in a stationary sense, we cannot say much about the distribution of city sizes, only that the importance of initial conditions vanishes for long times.

We see that, regardless of specific circumstances, this set of ergodic theorems allows us to make some general fundamental statements. The most important is the generality of circumstances in which an urban system may become independent of its initial conditions and in this specific sense, as emphasized by Caswell, of its past history. But this does not mean that the state of the system is independent of the history of environments e at all. In fact, it is the shared historic sequence of environments that determines the convergence of population structure vectors to a common state over long times. The most general consequences of these results are still to be explored in the context of the evolution of urban systems.

8.2.4 ANALYTICAL MEAN-FIELD SOLUTION AND THE SIGNIFICANCE OF THE GRAVITY LAW

To make sense of a large number of different possible dynamical regimes, it is desirable to get a little more intuition of general solutions analytically. This will also allow us to better understand further assumptions necessary to derive some of the laws of geography and specifically the gravity law and Zipf's law. To see this, we write the total migration currents J_{ij} in equation (8.12) as

$$J_{ij} = \left(\frac{j_{ij}^S + j_{ij}^A}{2} \right) \frac{N_i N_j}{N_T} \rightarrow m_{ij} = \left(\frac{j_{ij}^S + j_{ij}^A}{2} \right) \frac{N_j}{N_T}. \tag{8.19}$$

Here the matrix j_{ij}^S is symmetric (i.e., $j_{ij}^S = j_{ji}^S$) and j_{ij}^A is antisymmetric ($j_{ij}^A = - j_{ji}^A$). This means we can write the reverse matrix element as $J_{ji} = \left(\frac{j_{ij}^S - j_{ij}^A}{2} \right) \frac{N_i N_j}{N_T}$, which defines the *relative flow asymmetry,* $\Delta_{J^{ij}} = \frac{J_{ij} - J_{ji}}{J_{ij} + J_{ji}} = \frac{j_{ij}^A}{j_{ij}^S}$.

As we stressed already, the gravity law model is symmetric with $j_{ij}^A = 0$, and $j_{ij}^S = G_M N_T \phi_T(d_{ij})$, where $\phi_T(d_{ij})$ is a decreasing function of the distance, d_{ij}, between the two cities, just as in the MaxEnt problem. The antisymmetric part of the migration current, however, is *the only part that contributes to relative demographic change* in the system of cities. This is because if the migration currents were symmetric, there would be no *net* population flow between any two cities. We can see this by rewriting the dynamical equation as

$$N_i(t) = (1 + \gamma_{N_i})N_i(t-1) \rightarrow \gamma_{N_i} = v_i - \sum_{j=1}^{N_c} j_{ij}^A \frac{N_j}{N_T}. \tag{8.20}$$

Because $n_j \equiv \dfrac{N_j}{N_T}$ is a fraction of the total population in city j, we can treat the last term as an *average over destination cities* and write it as $j_i^A = \sum_j j_{ij}^A n_j$. This quantity is the *net* migration rate (per capita and per unit time) *out of city i*. (For cities receiving net migration, this quantity is negative.) Thus, the interpretation of the quantity j_{ij}^A as the fraction of net migration out of city i attributable to city j is also clear. This quantity is similar to a contact rate in an epidemic model between a susceptible population (to emigrate) and an infectious fraction of a population, which promotes the change of state, justifying the interpretation of the gravity law in terms of social interactions as in subsection 8.1.3. Because of these properties, it also follows that $j^A = \sum_j j_i^A \dfrac{N_i}{N_T} = 0$, which is a consequence of the conservation of total people migrating. This means that the average of j_i^A over cities (the ensemble average) is always zero by construction. This quantity alternates signs among cities in the system: in each time period, some must be net recipients, while others must be net exporters of people.

Now we can glimpse some of the properties of a long-term solution. First, consider the rate of growth for the total population, γ_N,

$$N_T(t) = (1 + \gamma_N)N_T(t-1) \rightarrow \gamma_N = \sum_j \gamma_j n_j = \bar{v}. \tag{8.21}$$

Note that the contribution from the currents vanishes because of the antisymmetry of j_{ij}^A. We can now write the time evolution of the structure vector, $n_i = \dfrac{N_i}{N_T}$, as

$$n_i(t) = (1 + \epsilon_i)\, n_i\,(t-1), \tag{8.22}$$

with the "fluctuations" $\epsilon_i = v_i - \bar{v} - j_i^A$, which is very simple and has a direct correspondence with stochastic growth processes (recall chapter 4). This is because equation (8.22) is a discrete version of the geometric random model, $\dfrac{dn_i}{dt} = \epsilon_i n_i$, with $\bar{\eta}_{n_i} = 0$. When all cities grow at the *same* rate (Gibrat's law), $\gamma_{N_i} - \gamma_N = \epsilon_i \rightarrow 0$, the fluctuations in growth rates in each city are zero on average, so that $j_i^A \rightarrow v_i - \bar{v}$. This leads to the expectation that cities with larger vital rates experience more net emigration and those with smaller vital rates experience less. Figure 8.13 shows that there is indeed evidence for some (weak) correlation in this direction. It will also give us a basis to justify deriving Zipf's distribution, following an argument pioneered by Gabaix,[57] by assuming that cities grow following geometric random growth (chapter 4) under some additional critical constraints.

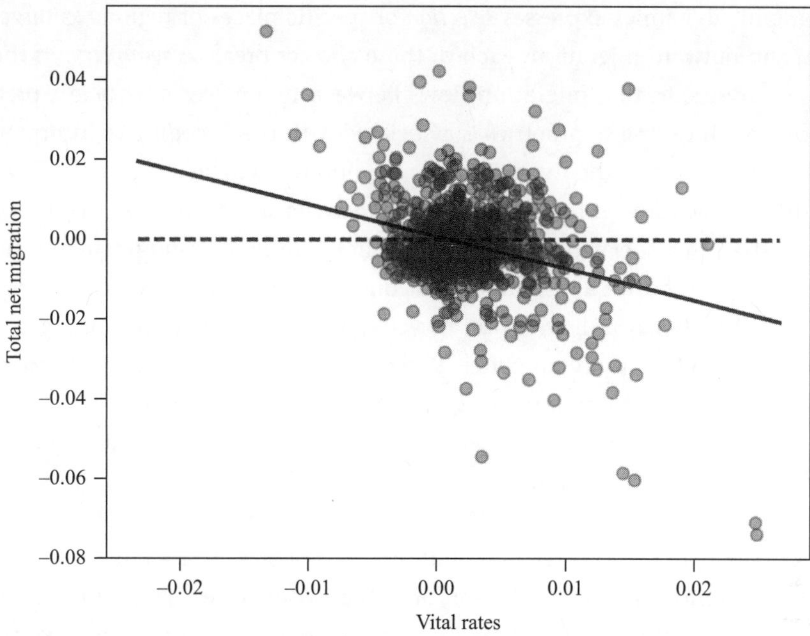

8.13 Anticorrelation between total net migration (domestic plus foreign) and vital rates for US metropolitan and micropolitan areas. The solid line shows the best-fit correlation line, $j_i^A(v_i) = 0.00 - 0.80 v_i$, with 95% confidence interval for the slope of $[-0.97, -0.64]$ and (low) $R^2 = 0.09$. The dashed line shows the no correlation line for reference.

Note that this assumption can be violated from one time period to the next as long as the time-averaged growth rate fluctuations over the long term are zero. This is then a *mean-field solution* in the sense that all cities share the same *average* growth rate.

The gravity law now comes into focus as an *approximate* regularity of population flows on average, both over time and across places. To the extent that the net migration flow between cities, j_{ij}^A, vanishes, the flows are characterized only by their symmetric piece. The irony is that a *nonzero net flow* (and therefore some violation of the gravity law) is critical for the achievement of both these limits and for the formation of an integrated dynamics of cities. The following sections make some of these statements more precise (see also figures 8.14–8.15).

Noise and Structure   The general logic of any population dynamics—common to all complex systems—is that it is the result of structured and random components. Structured parts involve some explicit *preference* or *selection* for some states over others. For example, over the last few years in the US, most cities in Texas and the Southwest have been net recipients of internal migration, while most cities in the Midwest have been net losers. Other historical examples have been preferences for the largest city in the urban system in nations such as the UK, France, or Japan, the great northern migration in the US in the twentieth century, or the western expansion of the US urban system, especially in the nineteenth century. Thus, the structured part of the demographic dynamics expresses *selection* of specific places or regions as targets for inward and outward migration. Each of these choices breaks a *symmetry*, in the language of physics, in that migration flows between two places now take a preferred net direction: Breaking symmetries is associated with the encoding of information.

The random part of the dynamics has the opposite character. It is an equalizing force that, statistically, enforces the most *disordered* state of the system, compatible with constraints associated with the dynamics. Familiar examples in physics are thermal forces that drive a system toward equilibrium; for example, characterized by the Maxwell-Boltzmann distribution of velocities for the molecules of a gas or the uniform spread of milk in your coffee. Random dynamics drive systems to *maximum disorder* (technically, maximum entropy, or MaxEnt), which is typically a state with the least amount of selection or net choice, or equivalently with maximum symmetry. We will make these statements more precise as we develop the corresponding mathematics, but we will see that Zipf's law for the distribution of city sizes is one of these maximally disordered distributions, analogous, in a strange but rigorous way, to the homogeneous distribution of milk in your coffee. This will also help us interpret the meaning of deviations from Zipf's law in terms of the relative sizes of cities. We begin with the character of the structured dynamics and then introduce randomness to explore its consequences.

8.2.5 NOISE-DRIVEN RELATIVE CITY SIZE DISTRIBUTION

We now assume that the variable ϵ_i is statistical, with zero mean and variance (volatility) σ_n^2. The stochastic dynamics[58] of n_i is now

$$dn_i = \sigma_n\, n_i\, d\Theta_W\,(t). \tag{8.23}$$

This is a very simple equation, so we can easily derive its associated probability distribution. We will suppress the i subscripts for simplicity and treat the structure vector as a positive continuous stochastic variable. As in chapter 4, we can use Itō's lemma to produce an equation for the probability distribution of the structure vector, n,

$$\frac{d}{dt}P[n,t\,|n',t'] = \frac{d^2}{dn^2}\sigma_n^2 n^2 P[n,t\,|n',t'] = \frac{dJ_n}{dn}. \tag{8.24}$$

The last equality defines a probability current

$$J_n = \frac{d}{dn}\sigma_n^2 n^2 P[n,t\,|n',t'], \tag{8.25}$$

which drives the distribution of relative city sizes.

Zipf's Law as a Stationary Solution   The derivation of Zipf's law now follows from asking for the stationary solution for the probability equation, $P_0[n]$. Because this is a second-order equation, there are *two* solutions. The more familiar one derives from asking that the current vanish; that is,

$$J_n(t) = \frac{d}{dn}\sigma_n^2 n^2 P_0[n] = 0, \rightarrow \sigma_n^2 n^2 P_0[n] = const \rightarrow P_0[n] = \frac{P_0}{\sigma_n^2 n^2}, \tag{8.26}$$

with $P_0 = 1/\int dn \frac{1}{\sigma_n^2 n^2}$. If σ_n^2 is independent of relative city size (Gibrat's law!), we can now convert from n back to N and—voilà!—get Zipf's law, $P_0[N] = P_z[N] = \frac{P_{z0}}{N^2}$. If σ_N^2 has a dependence on scale, such as $\sigma_N^2 \sim N^{\alpha_s} \rightarrow P_0[N] \sim \frac{1}{N^{2+\alpha_s}}$, the stationary distribution will deviate from Zipf's law correspondingly.

The other stationary solution corresponds to a constant current $J_n(t) = J_n$, which leads to

$$P_0[n] = \frac{P_0'}{\sigma_n^2 n}, \tag{8.27}$$

with $P_0' = 1/\int dn \frac{1}{\sigma_n^2 n}$. This solution applies when there is a constant flow of people, J_n, up or down the urban hierarchy. This can happen, for example, if there is a cascade of immigrants from large cities to smaller and smaller towns, as may have happened during the decline and fall of the Roman Empire, or it may apply to situations where the flow is in the opposite direction, when migrants from rural areas come to larger towns and cities, as may be the case in some developing nations today.

Full Dynamical Solution Because the equation for the probability is so simple, it is fully solvable dynamically. These solutions will help us better characterize the approach to the stationary limiting forms and whether it can happen in practice. A full treatment of the problem is given in appendix E.

It is easy to show that, apart from the stationary solutions, there is another general solution, of the form

$$P[n, t \mid n_0, t_0] = \sqrt{\frac{1}{\pi\,\sigma_n^2(t - t_0)}}\, e^{-\frac{\left(\ln\frac{n}{n_0} + \frac{\sigma_n^2}{2}(t - t_0)\right)^2}{2\,\sigma_n^2(t - t_0)}}\, d\ln n, \tag{8.28}$$

which is a lognormal distribution for n, with a time-dependent mean (for $\ln n$), $\bar{\eta} = \ln n_0 - \frac{\sigma_n^2}{2}(t - t_0)$, and time-dependent log-variance, $\sigma_n^2(t - t_0)$. This solution is analogous to simple diffusion, the spreading of one concentrated substance into a given volume, with initial solution at time $t = 0$, $P[n, 0 \mid n_0, 0] = \delta(n - n_0)$, but for multiplicative random growth dynamics. This immediately tells us that the lognormal solution, so often advocated to fit the distribution of city sizes,[59] is also quite suspect, as it is dynamical and will continue to spread out, its mean becomes more and more peaked around zero over time, and it derives from an initial condition with a single city of a given size.

Alternatively, starting from any actual distribution of cities, its probability distribution will generally be a mixture of the static and time-dependent solutions (see appendix E) in a way that respects any initial starting point as well as boundary conditions. On a very long timescale, such that $t \gg t_0 + \frac{1}{\sigma_n^2}$ the time-dependent components of this solution vanish and, under appropriate boundary conditions, the stationary (Zipfian) distribution emerges as the distribution of city sizes. Until then, when observed on shorter timescales, the distribution of city sizes will be a mixture of these solutions. We saw in chapter 4 that the average volatility of the growth rates of metropolitan areas in the US is of order $\sigma_n^2 \sim 0.001$, implying a timescale $t_z \gg 1,000$ years. This compares with the gap (the ratio of the first two eigenvalues of e), which we have seen is of order $t_e = 1/\left|\ln\dfrac{\lambda_1}{\lambda_0}\right| \sim 114$ years. Both times are very long, but the diffusional timescale for Zipf's law is almost an order of magnitude longer. If this estimate is even close to being right, it means that the diffusional dynamics of the relative sizes of cities plays a relatively unimportant role in the US urban system. Depending on these numbers, we may of course find different scenarios.

Under these circumstances, what should we expect? If the dynamics of cities retain the properties necessary for the approximations and assumptions of subsection 8.2.5 to hold, then sufficiently old urban systems (or those with the strongest migration flows) may show a city size distribution that follows Zipf's law (figure 8.15). In most cases, however, various events and shocks on natural timescales of years to decades may perturb the urban system away from these simplest scenarios, and city sizes may have to be derived from a dynamical model with fuller demographics (figure 8.16). Nevertheless, Zipf's law stands as a singular limiting reference point for the demographic dynamics of an urban system, so it is worth pointing out some of its remarkable properties (figure 8.14) as well as demystifying their meaning.

Properties of Zipf's Distribution: Neutrality, Coherence, and Screening In population biology and complex systems, the term *neutral* refers to the important situation where there is a dynamical equilibrium (or steady state) where all entities grow at the same rate. (Economists refer to a similar situation as a *balanced growth path*.) The term has its origins in evolutionary theory, where *neutral* refers to the *absence of selection*, meaning that all population types have the same fitness (the same relative growth rate). In our context, this means that people, on average, have *no net preference* for larger or smaller cities when they migrate.

Thus, we see immediately that Zipf's city size distribution is a *neutral* law, given Gibrat's condition and, more specifically, the symmetry of the gravity law. But we can say a little more about its meaning and the significance of its deviations. As we have seen, Zipf's law is associated with a vanishing net probability current between cities of different sizes. Explicitly, this current, expressed in term of the original variables, is

$$J_N[P(N)] = \frac{d}{dN}\frac{\sigma_N^2}{2}N^2P(N) \simeq \frac{\sigma_N^2}{2}[(N+1)^2P(N+1) - N^2P(N)]. \tag{8.29}$$

Substituting $P(N) \sim 1/N^2$ into J_N shows that the current vanishes if cities are distributed according to Zipf's law. If we naively substituted a uniform probability, $P(N) \sim const$, independent of city size, we would see instead that there is a net current

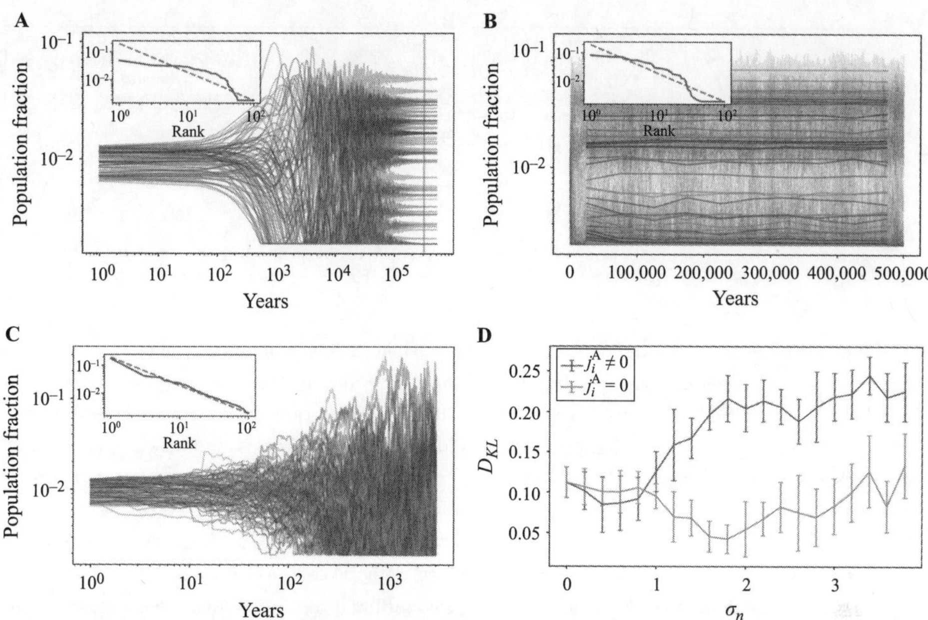

8.14 Necessary conditions for Zipf's law to emerge from the demographic dynamics in a system of cities. Relative to the arbitrary structure of the projection matrix **e** (see figure 8.8), we need to establish a number of symmetries. (A) Migration flows are expressed in terms of gravity law parameterization, with some antisymmetric structure, $j_{ij}^A \neq 0$.(The inset shows the resulting distribution versus Zipf's law as a dashed straight line.) (B) Multiplicative stochastic noise is added to migration currents, showing a similar city size distribution but with fluctuations. (C) The gravity law is made statistically symmetric, $j_{ij}^A = 0$, while random fluctuations are preserved. This now shows the convergence to Zipf's law (inset). (D) The average symmetry of fluctuations becomes a necessary condition when fluctuations are large. Whereas in the nonsymmetric case the population distribution might sometimes approximate Zipf's law by chance (dark gray), the symmetry condition decreases the distance from Zipf's law (light gray), measured as the magnitude of the KL-divergence between the relative city size distribution and Zipf's law.

down the size hierarchy, $J_N[const] = \dfrac{\sigma_N^2}{2}(2N + 1)const$. Thus, to keep the distribution of city sizes stationary, there have to be many more smaller cities than larger ones; the distribution must be far from uniform.

The property of neutrality for Zipf's law is highly suspect in light of the disaggregated features of actual migration flows. A brief overview will be given in section 8.3, where we will see that cities of different sizes express different selection effects (i.e., they are not neutral), with young and educated people tending to flock to larger cities, while others are more likely to move down the urban hierarchy. However, Zipf's law, Gibrat's law, and the gravity law, as used here, only apply to the total number of people across all socioeconomic types, which is much better conserved over sufficiently long times.

In an interesting recent paper, Cristelli, Batty, and Pietronero[60] made the point that "there is more than a power law in Zipf," emphasizing that the distribution of city sizes must obey certain *global* properties, which they describe as *coherence* and *screening*. These concepts are illustrated by the fact that most subsamples of city

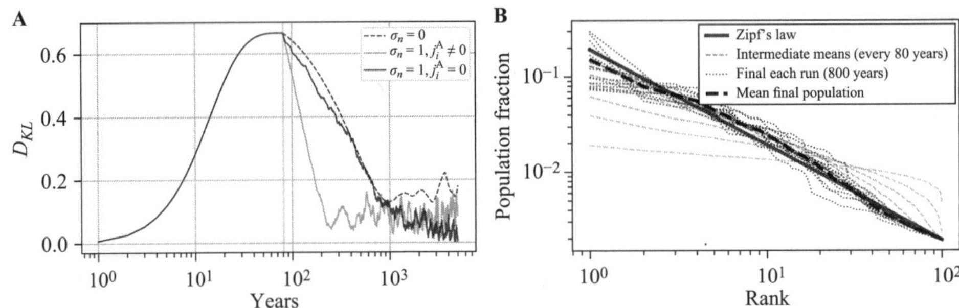

8.15 Zipf's law becomes independent of population dynamics, given specific dynamical symmetries. (A) Starting with an initial Zipf size distribution, the simulation runs in a stationary ergodic setting until the stable state corresponding to the leading eigenvector of **e**. Subsequently, this system is evolved only under gravity law migration dynamics: the light gray line includes fluctuations, and darker gray indicates the symmetry of these fluctuations. As visible, the successively more symmetric conditions improve the approximation of the system to Zipf's limit, measured as a vanishing KL-divergence. (B) The thick solid line shows the average over 10 simulation runs, and the dashed lines show the intermediate steps. The initial population distribution is set as Zipf's law. The figure depicts how the population first diverges from a Zipfian distribution until the stable state of the ergodic setting is reached. When the necessary conditions are added to the dynamics, the population distribution approaches a Zipfian distribution again.

populations (say a random subsample of cities, or the lower half of the distribution) do not follow Zipf's law (they show "lack of *coherence*") and that cities of similar sizes *screen* each other in terms of their growth dynamics: if one grows faster or disappears, the others will have to compensate for the change. In particular, they show that the largest city in the ensemble plays a critical role in the sense that it cannot be replicated or removed without severely distorting Zipf's law.

These interesting properties can be understood from the results in this section, where we see Zipf's law not as a static structural property but as the dynamical result of keeping $J_N[P(N)] = 0$.

The properties of coherence follow from the fact that most operations that remove or add cities change the current J_N away from zero and induce a systemic dynamical response involving many other cities that smoothens such perturbation (see appendix E). Note that J_N only applies to the *probability* of a city of a certain relative size, not to specific cities, so if some grow more, others could grow less and still enforce the statistical conservation law. This kind of screening corresponds to an interesting geometric equipartition property: the total number of people in any percentage population size range of cities $(N, \lambda N)$, $\lambda > 1$, is constant. This is because

$$\int_{N}^{\lambda N} dN'\, N' P_z(N') = P_{z_0} \ln \frac{\lambda N}{N} = P_{z_0} \ln \lambda = const.$$

This result shows again that Zipf's law is a kind of uniform distribution but in a geometric sense of proportion. Perturbations that leave Zipf's law unchanged and do not beget a dynamical demographic response must affect the same percentage of the population across all percentage (logarithmic) partitions, which means affecting

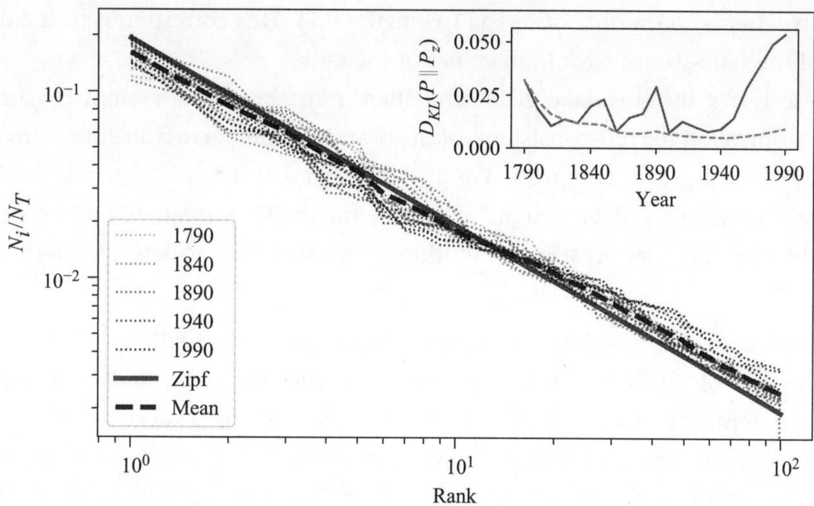

8.16 Historical dynamics of the rank-size distribution for the largest 100 cities in the US between 1790 and 1990. The panel shows the population structures at all available times (dashed lines) and the average distribution over all distributions (dashed). The inset depicts the $D_{KL}(P\|P_z)$ of the population structure for all available years, and the average over all structure vectors up the specific year (dashed) relative to Zipf's law. The average steadily decreases as more years are added. After an initial phase, the average is always closer to Zipf's law than the city-size distribution in any single year. In recent decades, deviations from Zipf's law have become stronger and, for the first time in US history, the average has started to deviate from Zipf's law.

a different number of cities in each logarithmic size bin. This means that screening is larger in size ranges with a smaller number of cities and less relevant in those with many cities. Because the largest city is unique and, for small enough λ, stands alone in its own group, removing it, or at any rate perturbing it strongly, sets the entire distribution into disarray.

Finally, the vanishing of the current translates into a *boundary condition* that is especially sensitive at both ends of the distribution, as was observed by Gabaix[61] and many other authors since.[62] The vanishing of the current between two size classes, n, n', can be written as

$$P(n') = \left(\frac{n}{n'}\right)^2 P(n),\tag{8.30}$$

where the variation $dn = n - n' > 0$. For $n = 1$ (the largest city), we get $P(n') = \left(\frac{1}{n'}\right)^2 P(1)$ and therefore that the probability of all size classes is pegged in magnitude to the probability of the largest city. At the other extreme, for the smallest cities, we need to consider a minimum nonvanishing relative city size, n_m. We then get $P(n') = \left(\frac{n_m}{n'}\right)^2 P(n_m)$, meaning that to stabilize the distribution in Zipf's form we need to have a "shadow" group of cities with $n' < n_m$ that enforce an appropriate nonzero $P(n_m)$. Without it, the distribution will not be Zipf's for small cities, and in fact we may see that the distribution of city sizes accumulates increasingly more probability at this end, which is roughly what is commonly observed (see figure 8.7). This corresponds to the down-turn of the rank-size rule for high values of the rank.

These issues should make clear why there must be global system dynamics—manifesting observed self-consistent *coherence* and *screening* across all cities—involved in preserving Zipf's distribution. We also see that Zipf's law is not the "ultimate expression of an integrated system": there are many other integrated urban systems with different population size distributions, corresponding to less symmetric environments e.

Maximum Entropy In addition to neutrality and related to it, another interesting property of Zipf's law is that it is a *maximum-entropy distribution* (MaxEnt).[63] Maximum-entropy distributions play an important role because they are statistical attractors, in the sense of long time averages, if the dynamics of a system are disordering. For the purposes of illustrating this property of Zipf's law, consider first a more general Pareto (power-law) distribution, written as

$$P(n) = z \frac{n_m^z}{n^{1+z}},$$ (8.31)

where, as earlier, Zipf's law means $z = 1$, and n_m is a characteristic minimum size of the city ($n \geq n_m$). It follows that the corresponding Shannon entropy is

$$H(n) = -\int dx \, P(n) \log P(n) = E(\log P(n)) = \left(1 + \frac{1}{z}\right) \log \frac{n_m}{z},$$ (8.32)

which is maximal for the smallest exponent, z. For a distribution that can still be normalized to unity and at fixed n_m, this implies $z \to 1$, obtaining Zipf's specific exponent. This turns out to be equivalent to maximizing the entropy of $P(n)$ under the constraint that the average logarithm of n is given. The average of $\log P(n)$ is both the entropy itself and the temporal average of the growth rate.

Information in the Deviations from Zipf's Law We will finish our tour of the properties of Zipf's law by making sense of deviations in the city size distribution away from it. We started the chapter with the general concept that the evolution of the urban system—as in any complex system—is the result of both selection (actual preferences) and randomness. We have now seen that Zipf's law is the maximum randomness distribution for exponential growth processes subject to constraints, analogous to a uniform distribution of a liquid in a volume. Let us now measure selection. To do this, let us return to the equation for the time evolution of the structure vector n and write it in the form

$$P'(n) = \hat{O}_n P(n),$$ (8.33)

where $\hat{O}_n$ is an operator on the previous probability density, meaning that it may contain derivatives or integrals. We have seen that, for probability densities not too far from Zipf's, we can write

$$\hat{O}_n = \gamma_n + \frac{d^2}{dn^2} \sigma_n^2 n^2, \text{ with } \gamma_n = v_n - \bar{v} + j_n^A,$$ (8.34)

where the first term contains any nonrandom size-dependent components of the growth rate and the second term arises from random multiplicative growth around them. Then, if we start with Zipf's distribution $P(n) = P_z(n)$, the second term gives zero and we obtain

$$P'(n) = \gamma_n P_z(n), \tag{8.35}$$

which expresses which relative city size classes grow faster or slower (note that $\sum_n \gamma_n P(n) = 1$). As a selection effect, this is completely analogous to a process of learning (i.e., of generating information), which optimally obeys a Bayes relation, as we showed in chapter 6.

It follows that, by definition,

$$\gamma_n = \frac{P'(n)}{P_z(n)}. \tag{8.36}$$

The average of the logarithm of this quantity is then

$$\sum_n P'(n) \log \gamma_n = \sum_n P'(n) \log \frac{P'(n)}{P_z(n)} = D_{KL}(P' \| P_z), \tag{8.37}$$

which is the relative entropy (or Kullback-Leibler divergence,[64] appendix C). Recall that this is a semipositive quantity, $D_{KL}(P' \| P_z) \geq 0$, that measures the additional information in $P'(n)$ from the environment e compared to assuming that the distribution of city sizes is neutral (i.e., Zipf). In turn, the unaveraged quantity $\log \gamma_n = \log \frac{P'(n)}{P_z(n)}$, is sometimes known as the *surprise* of state n, as it measures the deviation (positive or negative) of the actual frequency compared to the standard expectation.

Thus, deviations in the city size distribution can be given a meaning in terms of an amount of information that results from the presence of net choice or *selection* (figure 8.17). The analysis of section 8.2 deals only with city size classes, but the idea can be generalized to more disaggregated reference distributions beyond Zipf's law.

8.2.6 EMPIRICAL PROPERTIES OF DEMOGRAPHIC QUANTITIES IN THE US URBAN SYSTEM

We have spent most of this chapter making sense of the status of several rather idealized urban system regularities and discussing models and theories that derive them. In closing this discussion, it is interesting to visit some empirical quantities related to vital rates and migration. These will illustrate how simple patterns in the form of the "laws of geography" sometimes arise because of population and temporal averaging. Assessing these quantities directly will also help us appreciate more complex real situations and even make sense of some of the deviations from Gibrat's law and Zipf's law identified earlier in this chapter.

These illustrations will deal only with the US urban system, though the same analysis can be performed elsewhere, subject to data availability. Figure 8.18 shows four basic quantities for US micropolitan and metropolitan urban areas (all urban areas with populations above about 10,000 people). We see that, for example, birth

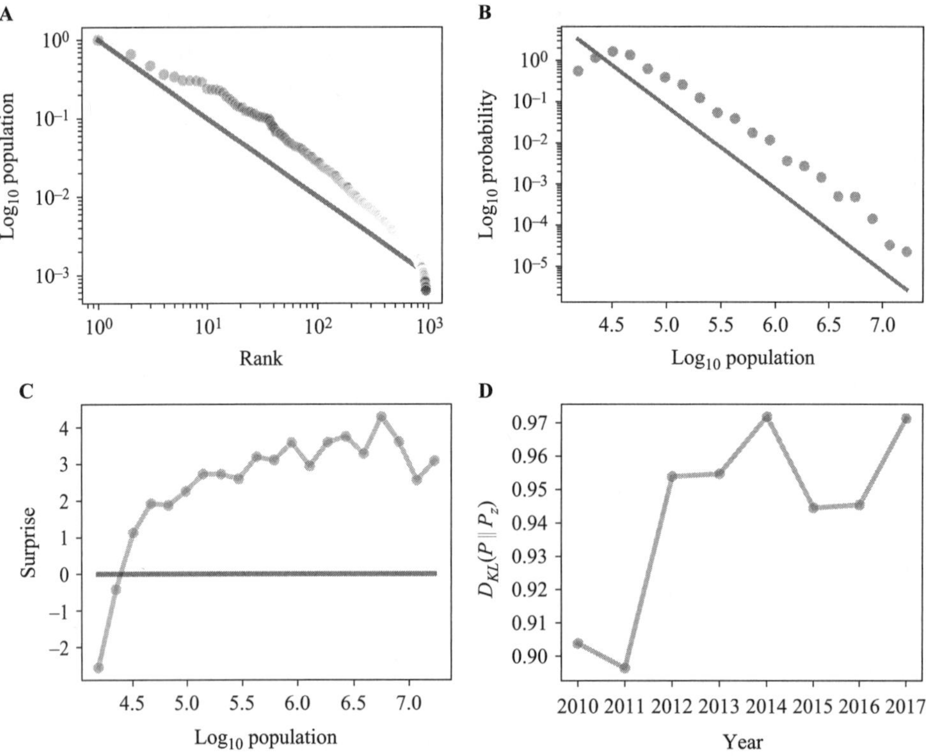

8.17 Deviations from Zipf's law interpreted as information. (A) Rank-size rule for US Micropolitan and Metropolitan Statistical Areas in 2017 (straight line is Zipf's law). Most large and medium cities are too large compared to New York City, the largest urban area in the system, while at some point we also observe a deficit of small cities (below the line). (B) The probability density function (straight line again is Zipf's law). Although the data may approximate a power law (linear in logarithmic axes), we see again a deficit of small cities and an excess of midsized ones (note that the points represent logarithmic bins, which average over many urban areas of similar sizes). (C) The *surprise* of each size class relative to Zipf's law. We see a negative surprise for small cities and larger for others, especially medium to large cities of a few million people. (D) The average surprise, the distance between the actual city size probability distribution and Zipf's law over time. There is no tendency for the distribution to converge to Zipf's law over this time interval (i.e., for the Kullback-Leibler divergence to vanish), but see also figure 8.16 for much longer timescales but fewer cities.

rates scale slightly superlinearly with city size, while death rates have the opposite tendency. This means that vital rates, birth rates minus death rates, also increase slightly superlinearly with city size. This is partly because larger cities have slightly younger populations, as they attract young adults, while retirees often leave for places in Florida and other states where death rates become correspondingly higher. There are also a number of other curious regional patterns, with some postindustrial cities showing an aging population, college towns a young population, and several cities in states such as Utah, Kansas, and North Dakota showing especially large outflows of internal migrants, paired with higher birth rates.

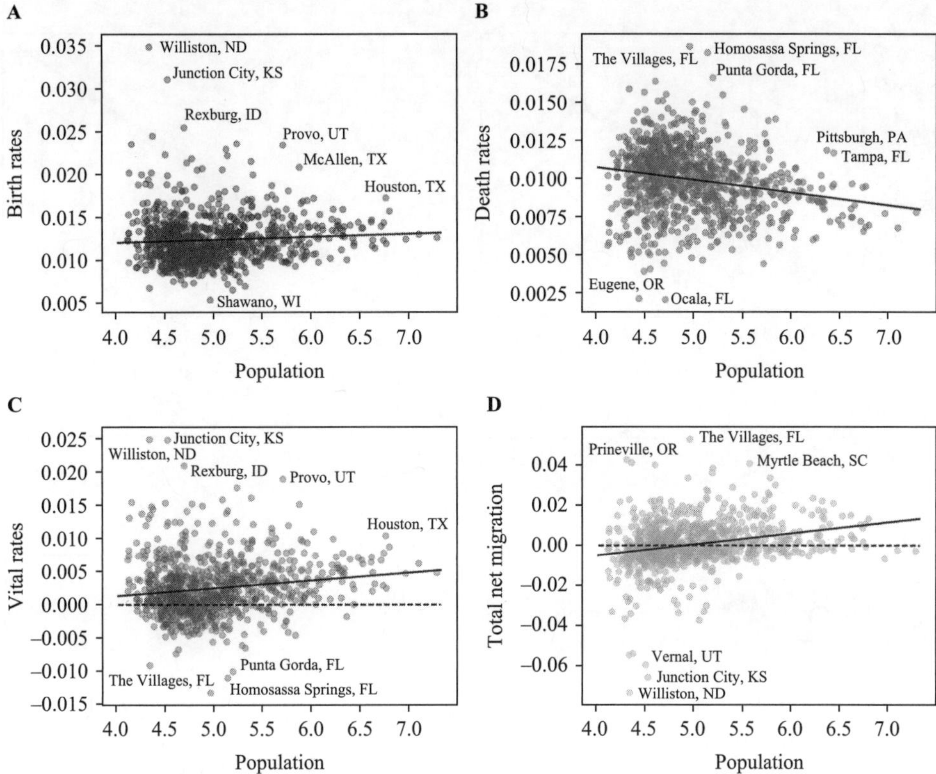

8.18 Vital and migration rates for US metropolitan areas. (A) The birth rate for each metropolitan and micropolitan area. This number is just slightly above 1% for most cities. (Some exceptions are identified by their city name.) Birth rates increase slightly with city size (black solid line, Births$(N)/N = 0.0107 + 0.0003 \log_{10} N$)), but the effect is very small and very noisy. (B) The death rates for US metropolitan and micropolitan areas. Death rates tend to be somewhat smaller than birth rates and decrease slightly with city size (solid line, Deaths$(N)/N = 0.0141 - 0.0008 \log_{10} N$); some cities with exceptionally high and low numbers are indicated by name. Cities with large death rates have an aging population and are often retirement communities. (C) The vital rates for the same cities (black solid line, $v(N) = -0.0034 + 0.0012 \log_{10} N$). The fit, though not very good, predicts that cities, on average, will have a positive vital rate only above the critical population size, $N_* \simeq 680$ people. (D) Total rate of migration (domestic + foreign) into the same cities (black solid line, $-0.0271 + 0.0550 \log_{10} N$). In both cases, vital rates and net migration increase slightly with population size (solid lines), with the dashed line showing zero population growth rates for reference. Many small cities with high birth rates experience outward migration flows; similarly, many of the cities with high death rates experience high inward migration, primarily from other cities in the urban system.

Figure 8.19 confirms and expands some of these demographic patterns, showing the slightly superlinear growth in total births with city size and the corresponding sublinear behavior of total deaths. In addition, we see in figure 8.19C the strongly superlinear behavior of foreign-born populations, emphasizing that large cities are disproportionately the arrival places (and *habitats*) for foreigners in the US. Figure 8.19D shows the same quantity as figure 8.18D but now limited to only internal

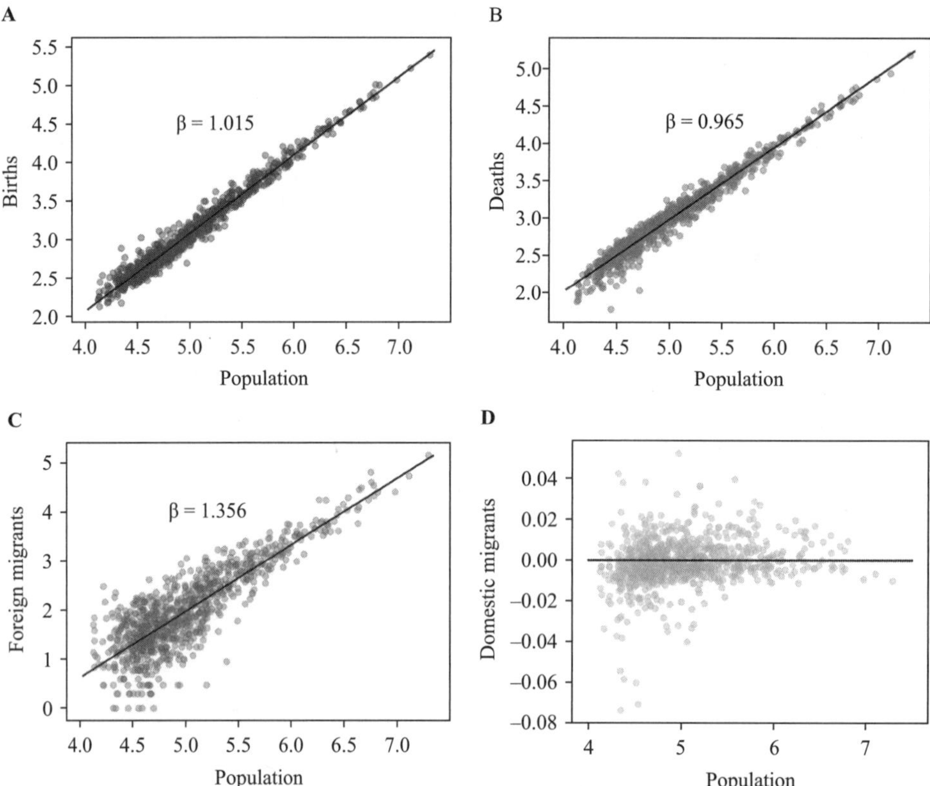

8.19 Scaling of total births, deaths, and foreign and domestic migration in US MSAs. In terms of their scaling, both births (A) and deaths (B) are approximately proportional to population in each city. However, we observe a small but very consistent effect for births to be slightly superlinear ($\beta = 1.015$, 95% CI=[1.004, 1.026]) and deaths slightly sublinear ($\beta = 0.965$, 95% CI=[0.925, 0.953]). This is consistent with the disproportionate presence of young and working-age populations in larger cities and of retired and aging populations in smaller places. (C) The scaling of foreign net migration into US metropolitan areas, displaying a strongly superlinear effect with an exponent much larger than unity ($\beta = 1.356$, 95% CI=[1.301, 1.411]). This means that foreign populations come to the US disproportionally through its largest cities. Conversely, domestic net migration (D) tends to be approximately independent of city size, with the three largest cities in the urban system (New York, Los Angeles, Chicago) losing US-born population. Large cities in the US at present continue to grow thanks to both slightly positive vital rates and foreign migration.

migration between cities, which excludes people arriving in and leaving the US. It is important to note that many of the largest cities, including the *big three*—New York, Los Angeles, and Chicago—presently show a net *outflow* of domestic migrants so their net population growth is entirely dependent on a combination of net foreign arrivals and positive vital rates. Incoming foreign populations are increasingly critical contributors to continued growth in large US metropolitan areas.

Besides characterizing vital rates, migration data disaggregated by type shed light on typical decisions made by individuals and households. The US has good internal migration data dating back to the end of World War II, giving us a long temporal window on a variety of interesting issues.

Despite spectacular development in transportation and communications, and the associated democratization of automobile and air transportation, the postwar period has been characterized by what William Frey refers to as "the Great American Migration Slowdown."[65] Over this period, rates of migration in the US have halved, from about one in five people moving every year to a total rate now closer to one in ten. More than half these moves are relatively local (within a state) and are associated with residential instability typical of poorer and less educated populations. In this respect, a reduction of total migration rates is, at least in part, likely a good thing as it may signal a decrease in residential instability.

As Ravenstein had observed, migration is more characteristic of younger populations. For the US, the peak migratory age is just over 25 (figure 8.20). This type of *age migration probability curve* is characteristic of many other nations and is presumably connected to the life changes involved in becoming an independent adult, including forming a new household, higher education and training, and new employment.

Long-distance migration is more characteristic of more educated populations, especially those with college or postgraduate degrees. At the same time, migration is also more characteristic of renters (rather than homeowners), the unemployed, and the unmarried or divorced. All these features are correlated with younger populations.

An especially interesting demographic group is the small segment of the population that is *young, single, and college educated*.[66] Their movement is a good indicator of the vitality of an urban area. Such people tend to migrate to larger cities, with some

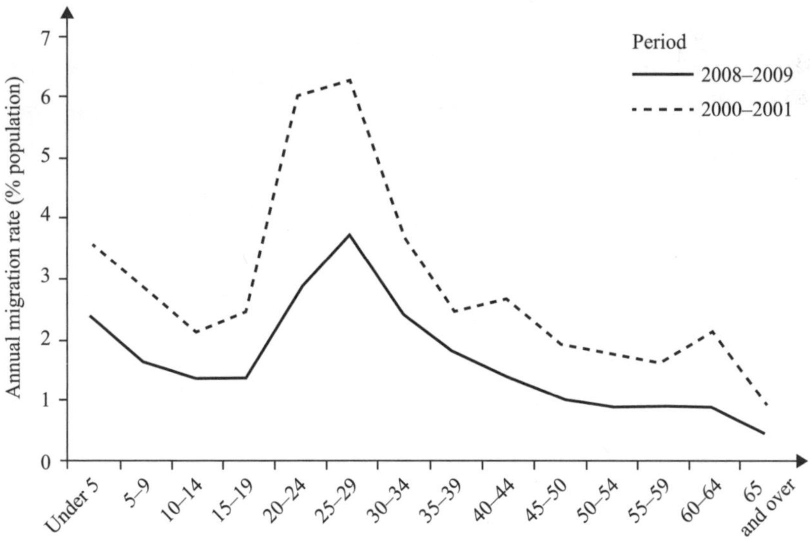

8.20 Age of interstate migration for the US over two periods, 2000–2001 and 2008–2009, the latter coincident with the Great Recession. Note how the two curves are similar in shape but also show a significant difference in amplitude. Data for other nations typically display similar curves, with a peak of propensity to migrate in early adulthood.
Source: Adapted from William H. Frey, *The Great American Migration Slowdown* (Washington, DC: Brookings Institution, 2009).

Table 8.2 Migration rates of the general population and the young, single, and college educated for the 20 largest metropolitan areas in the US

Metropolitan Statistical Area	2000 Population (in thousands)	Young, single, and college-educated net migration rate				Total population net migration rate			
		1965 to 1970	1975 to 1980	1985 to 1990	1995 to 2000	1965 to 1970	1975 to 1980	1985 to 990	1995 to 2000
New York–Northern New Jersey–Long Island, NY–NJ–PA	18,323	143.7	16.9	17.7	56.3	17.7	–66.4	–63.9	–48.4
Los Angeles–Long Beach–Santa Ana, CA	12,366	283.6	146.6	126.8	104.0	57.1	–48.0	–59.6	–54.7
Chicago–Naperville–Joliet, IL–IN–WI	9,098	145.8	26.0	88.2	73.7	27.4	–53.9	–37.0	–37.6
Philadelphia–Camden–Wilmington, PA–NJ–DE–MD	5,687	120.3	–44.8	30.7	–12.6	63.4	–31.6	–5.4	–14.9
Dallas–Fort Worth–Arlington, TX	5,162	333.2	277.0	169.4	238.7	157.7	59.8	8.8	33.3
Miami–Fort Lauderdale–Miami Beach, FL	5,008	438.4	321.5	277.3	90.4	359.4	170.2	110.1	–7.5
Washington–Arlington–Alexandria, DC–VA–MD–WV	4,796	568.1	181.5	224.5	124.6	144.9	–34.8	16.5	–13.5
Houston–Baytown–Sugar Land, TX	4,715	471.0	463.7	60.3	138.7	137.9	85.7	–40.6	–2.4
Detroit–Warren–Livonia, MI	4,453	151.7	0.6	23.7	66.8	31.9	–53.4	–36.1	–29.2
Boston–Cambridge–Quincy, MA–NH	4,391	78.3	–9.6	45.3	34.6	41.4	–32.0	–27.7	–15.6
Atlanta–Sandy Springs–Marietta, GA	4,248	512.2	236.1	303.4	281.7	136.9	38.8	82.8	70.0
San Francisco–Oakland–Fremont, CA	4,124	362.0	161.3	158.0	250.6	65.0	–37.1	–30.6	–25.5
Riverside–San Bernardino–Ontario, CA	3,255	220.3	113.7	273.5	–20.8	143.3	163.1	231.6	27.6
Phoenix–Mesa–Scottsdale, AZ	3,252	260.0	208.7	108.4	250.5	189.6	136.8	77.7	93.6

Seattle–Tacoma–Bellevue, WA	3,044	294.9	256.6	249.5	206.5	175.9	60.3	67.7	10.4
Minneapolis–St. Paul–Bloomington, MN–WI	2,969	176.2	107.8	122.5	123.5	76.6	–7.0	20.6	12.9
San Diego–Carlsbad–San Marcos, CA	2,814	334.1	109.0	140.4	99.5	205.4	74.6	61.5	–2.4
St. Louis, MO–IL	2,699	132.4	5.5	46.1	7.7	62.1	–33.8	–14.6	–17.2
Baltimore–Towson, MD	2,553	104.2	51.8	145.6	38.7	67.0	–11.6	13.8	–6.6
Pittsburgh, PA	2,431	–16.0	–74.4	–109.4	–129.3	1.6	–36.4	–38.9	–25.8

Notes: Rates are per 1,000 people aged 25–39 for the young, single, and college educated and out of 1,000 age 5 and older for the general population. For 1995–2000, the net migration rate for the young, single, and college educated is based on an approximated 1995 population so characterized in 2000. This approximated population is the sum of people who reported living in the area in both 1995 and 2000 and those who reported living in that area in 1995 but lived elsewhere in 2000. The net migration rate is the net migration from1995–2000 divided by the approximated 1995 population and then multiplied by 1,000. A similar approach is used for earlier periods and for the total population.

Source: Adapted from Justyna Goworowska, "Historical Migration of the Young, Single, and College Educated: 1965 to 2000." US Census Working Paper Number POP-WP094 (Washington, DC: US Census Bureau, April 2012).

telling exceptions, as shown in table 8.2. For example, we can see how urban areas such as Pittsburgh, Philadelphia, and Riverside, California, have lost this segment of the population, but especially how in Pittsburgh these losses were above general population losses. On the brighter side, we also see how cities such as Los Angeles, Atlanta, and Dallas have become younger, more single, and more college educated as this segment of the population grew faster than their general population. These types of churn and selection are very interesting because they allow what may seem like a neutral replacement of population (Gibrat's law) to actually lead to the accumulation of certain types (e.g., connected to age, race, or education). We will develop an analytical formalism to deal with this type of selection in chapter 9 in order to explain the association between higher GDP per capita and urbanization.

Ravenstein's laws of migration, along with other laws of geography, are not totally vindicated by this rich and mixed evidence. As we can see, there are many important decisions throughout a person's life course that play different roles in influencing moves between places and potentially contribute to their different growth rates. Analyzing only the statistics of city sizes and other laws of geography gives us only a very aggregate synthesis of these effects, integrated over the entire history of the urban system. The main lesson is that the most interesting observables are dynamical, the result of choices of where to have children, go to school, build a network of friends and colleagues, and grow old and die. For most people today, these choices unfold throughout their lifetimes but are also associated with a wide range of experiences offered by different places across the urban system, such as whether to pursue an advanced education or stay close to family. It is the understanding of the aggregate of these choices that roots the laws of geography in consequential socioeconomic phenomena, both in terms of each person's experience and the future of cities and nations. Such understanding requires that we be able to deal with demographic dynamics at many different scales, both in terms of disaggregating populations by type and in finer intervals of time. Dynamical demographic models of structured populations give us a general way to do this, bridging detailed quantitative dynamics with aggregate systemic statistics.

8.3 URBANIZATION AND THE DEMOGRAPHIC TRANSITION

All premodern societies (chapter 7) showed low rates of urbanization, certainly below 30% and in most cases below 10%–15%, defined as the fraction of people living in cities not dedicated to subsistence production.[67] Why were these numbers so low compared to those of modern nations?

The general answer is twofold.[68] The first reason for low urbanization rates in premodern societies is tied to resource flow limitations and, in particular, the difficulty of obtaining surpluses and transporting food and energy to cities.[69] The second reason is purely demographic:[70] there is substantial evidence that premodern cities were unhealthy environments, characterized by high mortality and low birth rates,[71] so net immigration from rural areas was necessary to avoid urban decay. The high mortality mostly resulted from contagious diseases associated with crowding and the lack of developed sanitation, modern medicine, or even decent nutrition. The issue of the change from a demographic regime with high birth and mortality rates to one of low mortality and subsequently low birth rates is one of the most important phenomena in demography and is known as the *demographic transition*.[72] The connection to urbanization should be clear: a decrease in mortality together with net migration of rural populations to cities produces fast urban growth.

Here we want to investigate the mechanics of how urbanization and the demographic transition (figure 8.21) are connected, based on purely demographic models. To get at the essence of the issue, we can use a particularly simplified model with two states, which we will call N_R and N_U, a rural and an urban population, respectively. Each population has its own birth and death rates and associated vital rates, v_R and v_U. There are also migration currents between the two populations: $J_{RU} = j_{RU} \dfrac{N_R N_U}{N_T}, J_{UR} = j_{UR} \dfrac{N_R N_U}{N_T}$. We will be interested in the situation, observed in most historical instances, where $v_U < v_R$, so that there must be a compensating net population flow from rural to urban areas for cities to persist, $\Delta j = j_{RU} - j_{UR} > 0$. The dynamical equations for the two populations are then

$$\frac{d}{dt}N_R = (v_R - \Delta ju)N_R; \; \frac{d}{dt}N_U = (v_U + \Delta j(1-u))N_U, \tag{8.38}$$

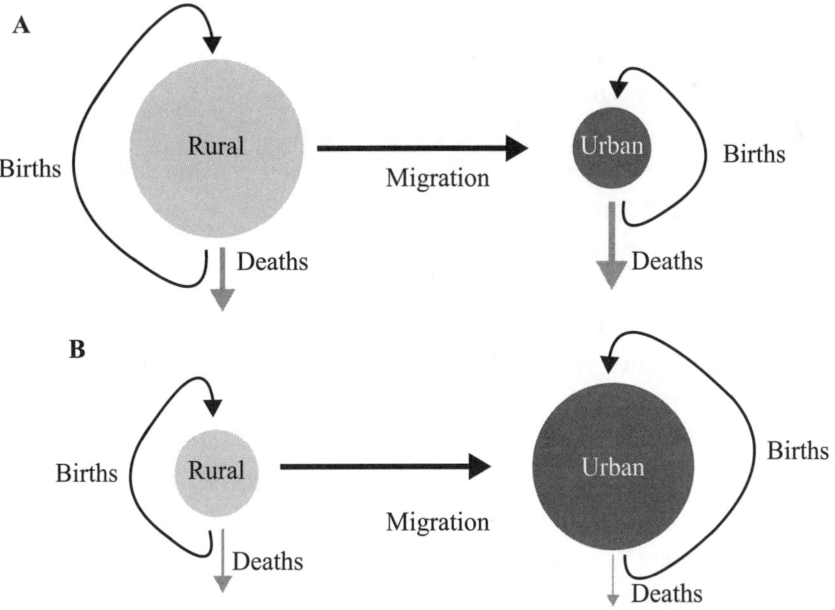

8.21 Demographic transition and urbanization. (A) The situation where the rural population is larger than the urban population (low urbanization rate) despite substantial migration to cities, because of high urban mortality rates. (B) The reverse situation (high urbanization rate) with similar migration rates but very low mortality, especially in cities. In this situation, the urbanization rate will continue to increase.

where $u = \dfrac{N_U}{N_T} = 1 - \dfrac{N_R}{N_T}$ is the urbanization rate and $N_T = N_U + N_R$ is the total population. From this equation, it follows that the two effective growth rates for the rural and urban populations are

$$v_R' = v_R - \Delta j\, u; \; v_U' = v_U + \Delta j\,(1 - u). \tag{8.39}$$

The condition that there is increasing urbanization over time means that the growth rate of the urban population is larger than the rural population, $v_R' > v_U'$. When these two rates are equal, $v = v_R' = v_U'$, we get $u = \dfrac{v_R - v}{\Delta j}$. For an almost static total population growth rate, as observed historically, $v \simeq 0$, so an urbanization rate of, say, 20% requires that $\Delta j \geq 5 v_R$, which is a strong migration current from rural to urban areas, especially when compared to the difference between births and deaths in both populations, which is small.

We can get a bit more intuition on the dynamics of u by writing the dynamical equation for the total population, $\dfrac{d}{dt} N_T = \bar{v} N_T$, with $\bar{v} = v_U u + v_R (1 - u)$. It follows from this last relation that we can write the urbanization rate as

$$u = 1 - \frac{\bar{v} - v_U}{v_R - v_U}. \tag{8.40}$$

We can also use these expressions to derive the equation of motion for the urbanization rate itself,

$$\frac{d}{dt} u = (v_U' - \bar{v})u, \tag{8.41}$$

which just says that the growth rate of urbanization is simply the difference between that for cities and the systemwide population growth rate.

If the two effective rates are the same, then u is a constant in time and so is $\bar{v} = v_R' = v_U'$. We can immediately see that the urbanization rate vanishes, $u \to 0$, when $\bar{v} \to v_R$, and that it goes to unity, $u \to 1$, as $\bar{v} \to v_U$.

We can also see that when $v_U < v_U^* = v_R - \Delta j$, cities grow more slowly than rural areas, as the urban system disappears (*ruralization*, or an urban "explosion") into a landscape of subsistence production. In the converse regime, when $v_U > v_U^*$, the system urbanizes and an increasingly larger fraction of its population will live in cities. Note that the boundary case, where the urbanization rate is constant, is independent of the urban growth rate and the level of urbanization. It only depends on the rural vital rates and probability of migrating to the city. Thus, urbanization can occur even when $v_U < 0$, provided there is a strong current from rural areas to cities.

In summary, we have seen how a human population can experience fast urbanization caused by shifts in its vital rates and, in particular, from a decrease in urban mortality, even if migration rates remain constant. This urban implosion—to use Lewis Mumford's famous expression[73]—can be caused by innovations endogenous to cities, for example improved urban services and infrastructure such as clean(er) water, sanitation, better access to food, or conflict resolution. Any of these improvements in urban life would contribute to the fast growth of cities to the extent that they reduced mortality due to infectious diseases and violence, for example. Many of these innovations are of course accessible to cities throughout the world today, promoting current trends in global urbanization, especially in Asia and Africa (chapter 1). Once in the city, a growing number of people must develop social and economic activities that can support them, so the demographic argument is not independent of economic development, technology, infrastructure, and institutions, as we saw in previous chapters.

Demographers have vigorously debated which of these two processes—urbanization or the demographic transition—drives the other.[74] The arguments in this section suggest that these two general processes should not be considered independent. In my view, it is simpler and more compelling that they can form virtuous cycles of growth (or vicious cycles of decay) given even slight changes in the balance of several variables. Thus, fast urbanization is a complex, broad phenomenon, associated with changes at many scales across entire urban systems in both large cities and rural areas.

EPILOGUE: CHOICE, DEMOGRAPHY, AND THE STRUCTURE OF URBAN SYSTEMS

Some of the oldest and most revered empirical regularities about cities are known as a set of "laws of geography." Though there has been extensive work—empirical and theoretical—about these regularities, there has not been, in my view, a systemic understanding of their origins or their interdependence, or a clear interpretation of the observed variations away from their simplest forms.

In this chapter, we have tried to show how the laws of geography arise naturally—sometimes inevitably—from the basic *demographic dynamics* of births, deaths, and migration in a system of cities. Most critically, it is the interdependence of cities' demographic changes via migration that makes a set of cities a *system*.

We have seen that because the structure of migration flows within nations is a strongly connected graph, where every city is connected with all others with finite probability, this condition is sufficient to create a hierarchical urban system and eventually equalize growth rates across its cities. The timescale for the temporal convergence to this collective state hinges on the strength of migration flows between cities: for strong flows, cities quickly come to "grow as one," whereas if migration rates vanish, each city acts independently and no urban system can exist at all. This simple fact also clarifies why cities across national borders—especially when international migration rates are low—are almost certainly *not* part of the same urban system. They can become integrated if migration restrictions are removed, as in the case of the European Union, or they can also become part of an international economic (but not demographic) system of cities if there are reciprocal flows of capital, goods, and services.

These ergodic results, together with fast and volatile vital and migration rates, create the conditions for the emergence of simple general features in the properties of cities, but only under substantial averaging and specific constraints. The gravity law, Gibrat's law, and eventually Zipf's law can then emerge as average regularities over time and sets of cities. We have seen how Zipf's law is typically associated with very long—often unrealistically long—timescales and peculiar boundary conditions, especially for the smallest settlements. In this sense, Zipf's law is likely to remain an interesting but rather imperfect regularity in any actual urban system over the short run. It is more likely to apply to larger cities and may often assume more lognormal forms or different exponents as conditions affecting the growth of (smaller) cities violate some of its necessary conditions.

We have also seen that Zipf's law is a *neutral* law in the sense that it corresponds to the most general (maximum-entropy) distribution compatible with random geometric growth under the constraints of common growth rate statistics across all cities and a vanishing population size current. In this sense, Zipf's law is not really a special sign of complexity or systemic integration. The main feature that distinguishes it from the simplest of statistical distributions (such as a Maxwell-Boltzmann distribution for gas velocities or a uniform spatial distribution for particles in a box) is that the underlying dynamics of population is geometric, not arithmetic. Conversely, we have seen how deviations from Zipf's distribution, and consequently also from Gibrat's law and the gravity law, signal preferences for certain cities over some periods of time. As in any other complex system, such preferences have *meaning*, as broken symmetries that are naturally measured as *information*. The role of these choices, and the imperative of information as the engine for growth and change in human societies, is the subject of chapter 9.

9

GROWTH, INFORMATION, AND THE EMERGENCE OF INSTITUTIONS

The city is a body and a mind—a physical structure as well as a repository of ideas and information. Knowledge and creativity are resources. If the physical (and financial) parts are functional, then the flow of ideas, creativity and information are facilitated.

The city is a fountain that never stops: it generates its energy from the human interactions that take place in it.

—David Byrne, "If the 1% Stifles New York's Creative Talent, I'm Out of Here"

We are now ready to tackle the last big conceptual issue addressed in this book: the origins of growth and change in cities and urban systems. In particular, we want to elucidate where rates of economic growth come from and create a mechanistic framework to calculate them. This will demand that we understand how people learn and pool resources and information together to create organizations and institutions that can seize new possibilities. Such an endeavor is one of the most difficult and fragile dynamics in any human society, underlying collective-action problems ranging from fair governance, to issues of power and inequality, to the organization of economic production and the management of common resources, including the earth's biosphere and climate. By necessity rather than by virtue, urban environments are especially propitious for the emergence of new knowledge and organizations capable of tackling this type of challenge. Thus, cities tend to be at the leading edge of knowledge and models of collective governance, more apt at addressing the most pressing problems of any society. Let us find out why.

CHAPTER OUTLINE

This chapter consists of three main sections. Section 9.1 deals with current models of economic growth, their appeal for a better understanding of the role of *knowledge* in human societies, and their struggles formalizing this quantity and disaggregating it across levels of socioeconomic organization. In section 9.2, we revisit the evidence at the national level on the association between levels of urbanization and GDP per capita in order to understand its mechanics across scales, with an emphasis on cities. In section 9.3, we formalize how economic agents—people and organizations—invest their resources in uncertain environments to derive a quantitative theory of how information sets economic growth rates. This analysis will allow us to establish a set of methods for understanding the origins of economic and social change grounded in the everyday decisions of individual agents. It will also provide a new perspective on the trade-offs involved in creating and sustaining every collective social or political organization and the role of cities as social environments that promote the pooling of resources and information. An epilogue on cities as a socially "constructed niche" concludes the chapter.

9.1 MODELS OF ENDOGENOUS ECONOMIC GROWTH

Economic growth is a subject of universal interest in both research and practice. While everybody talks about it—especially in politics—being able to predict or indeed determine future economic growth rates (beyond a year or two) remains beyond the scope of present theory or practice. Empirical approaches to monitoring investments, employment, trade, and other factors produce a lot of evidence that allows short-term forecasts and nudges, such as monetary policy. However, many fundamental questions cannot be answered in this "data-driven" way. Such questions include knowing the necessary ingredients for sustained economic growth over long periods of time, the determinants of the value of an economy's growth rate and volatility, and the capacity for anticipating periods of economic contraction (recessions) and possibly the means for avoiding them. The Great Recession of 2008 was seen by many as a major test of present economic models and theory, exposing their inadequacies for prediction both in terms of looming events and as a body of knowledge capable of proposing effective policies for systemic recovery beyond relatively superficial asset bubbles.[1] To appreciate these facts and some of their connections to economic expansion in cities requires diving into some of the models used to discuss the phenomenon of economic growth.

Economic growth theory is a fundamental subfield of economics. It is particularly interesting not only because it deals with the origin of prosperity in modern economies[2] but also because it requires new conceptual ingredients not contained in the standard general equilibrium theory of microeconomics.

This is because, by definition, growth requires temporal change, but microeconomic theory—which describes a system of consumers and producers in interaction—makes assumptions of equilibrium to derive its main results. Situations where open-ended growth becomes possible appear as instabilities in such models and are often associated with issues of *increasing returns to scale* (which, as we have seen throughout the book, cities realize almost by definition) and *path dependence* of innovation and economic change.[3] In contrast, global equilibrium models must stabilize interactions, so they typically assume decreasing returns to scale (measured in terms of both labor and capital) at the firm level but also at the system level, be that a city or a nation. Thus, the challenge to economic theory posed by cities and economic growth is not just technical or empirical; it is existential. This is, of course, a sweet spot for scientific innovation.

9.1.1 EXOGENOUS GROWTH THEORY

To solve the conundrum of introducing (exponential) growth in models built for equilibrium, at first economists tried to fit the sources of growth into existing variables. The great empirical breakthrough came in the late 1950s from Robert Solow,[4] who asked how well the simplest and most traditional model of the economy—the Cobb-Douglas production function of chapters 2 and 3—could explain the economic growth of the US. The exercise is so simple that it is worth reproducing here; it will also set us up for later developments. The idea is that the total income (GDP) of a given unit, $Y(t, L_P, K_P)$, is given by the Cobb-Douglas form

$$Y(t, L_P, K_P) = A_P(t) L_P^{\alpha_Y}(t) K_P^{1-\alpha_Y}(t),$$

where the multiplicative factor $A_p(t)$ is known as the *total factor productivity* (TFP), which is independent of labor, L_p, and capital, K_p, by construction. The exponents α_Y and $(1 - \alpha_Y)$ are—as we saw earlier—the fractions of income attributable to labor and capital, respectively. This means that $\alpha_Y = \dfrac{Y}{L_P}$ and $1 - \alpha_Y = \dfrac{Y}{K_P}$. Empirically, the fraction of income from labor wages $\alpha_Y \simeq 0.6 - 0.7$ for the US since 1950, with a slight decrease since the year 2000. The fact that these two factors add up to 1 means that there are *constant returns to scale*; that is, income cannot increase faster than proportionally to labor or capital (this is an assumption violated by cities). Solow reasoned that whenever we can measure Y, L_P, and K_P as functions of time, we can test whether A_P is a constant. As usual, this is easier to do in logarithmic variables, as we have done for other quantities (the TFP is similar to the scaling prefactors we saw in chapters 3 and 4):

$$\ln A_P(t) = \ln Y(t) - \alpha_Y \ln L_P(t) - (1 - \alpha_Y) \ln K_P. \tag{9.1}$$

Here, growth rates are the time derivatives of the logarithmic quantities; for example, recall that the growth rate of GDP is $\gamma_Y = \dfrac{d}{dt} \ln Y(t, L_P, K_P)$. Solow found that TFP's growth rate has been nonzero for as long as he could measure it, so he concluded that something other than increases in labor or capital must be creating economic growth.[5] More recently, other authors have found that A_P grew at a rate of about 1% per year for many leading national economies for most of the twentieth century.[6] The challenge is to find what drives this growth. It has to be something that is not subject to decreasing returns to scale, something that could be linked to clear societal change. *Technology* was thought to be such a thing, and then, more abstractly, *knowledge* and *ideas* quickly gained momentum.[7] However, none of these quantities are measurable in unambiguous ways, so their effects have remained hard to pin down.

9.1.2 KNOWLEDGE AND ECONOMIC GROWTH

The quest to find observable causes of economic growth led in the late 1980s to the next breakthrough, known as *endogenous growth theory*. This work, led by Paul Romer and others, made a number of important conceptual observations. Specifically, it posited that (1) *new money comes from new ideas*, or more formally that the growth of knowledge in an economy is the driver of TFP's growth, (2) that knowledge, unlike labor or capital, is a *nonrival* quantity, meaning that it does not get expended as it is used (think about the calculus) and may indeed improve with practice. This also means that the same knowledge can be used by different people and industries, so to a large extent knowledge is *nonexcludable*: you cannot really stop people from using an idea once they have it. Finally, (3) knowledge is created (*endogenously*) by people and organizations and therefore requires previous knowledge as well as labor and capital. Therefore, it should be possible to produce a theory of economic growth as a dynamical system where all these quantities—knowledge, labor, and capital—are interdependent and endogenous, instead of given as external outputs.

These ideas are clearly on the right track and must be part of any solution. Romer won the Nobel Prize in Economics in 2018 for his contributions. The remaining big problem has been how to implement a predictive model in terms of observable variables. As you might imagine, there are actually many models starting with Romer's, most based on systems of differential equations that endogenize economic growth. Charles Jones has shown that most of these models are related to each other, starting with relatively simple early assumptions and adding extensions in order to address some early counterfactuals. In this section, we will follow his synthesis[8] and refer the interested reader to these and other reviews for greater detail and substance.[9]

Endogenizing Ideas: First Attempts We start with the earliest models, by Romer,[10] Grossman and Helpman,[11] and Aghion and Howitt.[12] The central concept of these models is to identify the role of the *stock of ideas* in a society, A_P, as a *nonrival* input to production (GDP), Y, which can be written in terms of a (simpler) production function as

$$Y = A_P^{\sigma_A} L_P, \tag{9.2}$$

where we have omitted capital from the production function earlier. The idea is that capital is not where the action is for economic growth (think about it!). This expression has constant returns to scale (exponent 1) in labor, L_P, the rival "good," and increasing returns to scale for the product, characterized by the exponent $\sigma_A > 0$. To make the model dynamical, it is assumed that the growth rate of ideas is proportional to the population dedicated to creating productive concepts (or "research"), which we call L_A,

$$\frac{d}{dt}\ln A_P \equiv \gamma_A = \delta_A L_A, \tag{9.3}$$

and that $L_A = f_A L_P$. Here, $0 < f_A < 1$ is the fraction of labor dedicated to research. Finally, it will be useful to write the growth rate of labor (which is approximately proportional to population) as $\frac{dL_P/dt}{L_P} = \gamma_L \to L_P(t) = L_P(0)e^{\gamma_L t}$. It follows that the growth rate of the output per worker is given by

$$\gamma_y \equiv \frac{dY/dt}{Y} - \frac{dL_P/dt}{L_P} = \sigma_A \delta_A f_A L_P(t) = \sigma_A \delta_A f_A L_P(0)e^{\gamma_L t}. \tag{9.4}$$

This shows a *scale effect* (not scaling!) on the growth rate, in that it is proportional to labor, which is itself growing exponentially in time. This is clearly not acceptable, because it is way too fast. The other factors are also interesting. For example, increases in research intensity, f_A, result in proportionally larger growth rates.

Addressing the Scale-Effect Problem   The next wave of models essentially tried to fix the *scale effect* on the growth rates by introducing a modification to the equation for the growth rate in the stock of ideas as

$$\frac{dA_P}{dt} = \delta_A L_A A_P^{\phi_A}, \tag{9.5}$$

where the exponent $\phi_A \leq 1$. (The first-generation models are recovered in the limit $\phi_A \to 1$.) The functional freedom introduced by ϕ_A means that more diverse dynamical behaviors are possible. From equation (9.2), we derive immediately that $\gamma_y = \sigma_A \gamma_A$. From equation (9.5), assuming a constant growth rate ansatz for A_P such that $A_P(t) = A_P(0)e^{\gamma_A t}$, we obtain

$$\gamma_A = \delta_A L_A A_P^{\phi_A - 1} = \delta_A f_A L_P(t) A_P^{\phi_A - 1} = \delta_A f_A L_P(0) A_P^{\phi_A - 1}(0)e^{[\gamma_L + \gamma_A(\phi_A - 1)]t}.$$

This shows that, in general, the growth rate of knowledge still grows exponentially in time. To avoid this, and specifically for γ_A to be a constant in time, requires that the growth rate in the previous expression vanish, which implies

$$\gamma_A = \frac{\gamma_L}{1 - \phi_A} = \delta_A f_A L_P(0) A_P^{\phi_A - 1}(0). \tag{9.6}$$

We see that the expressions for the growth rate of income per capita and ideas no longer depend on labor, $L_P(t)$, but are instead proportional to its growth rate, γ_L. This is perhaps better but is still counterfactual: economic growth is not typically proportional to population growth, even if there is some correlation. Moreover, it is extremely *fine-tuned*, meaning that any deviation from these parameter values sends the trajectories crashing or exploding again.

Including More Typical Microeconomic Assumptions   To fix the dependence of the growth rate for output on both population scale and growth rate, another set of subsequent models made a few extra assumptions, based on standard microeconomic theory. The idea is to describe economic production (output=income) in terms of a number of different products adding up to a total n_p and using a production function with constant elasticity of substitution (CES), like the one in the core-periphery model of chapter 2. Then, we can express total consumption, C, as earlier, as

$$C = \left(\sum_{i=1}^{n_p} Y_i^{\frac{1}{i_s}} \right)^{i_s}, \tag{9.7}$$

with $i_s > 1$ related to the elasticity of substitution between products $i_s = \dfrac{\sigma_S}{\sigma_S - 1}$. One can then assume that the production of each product Y_i is of the form in equation (9.1) and that these are all the same, $Y_i = Y$. Then we obtain that $C = Y n_p^{i_s}$ and that the consumption per capita $c = \dfrac{C}{L_P}$ has a growth rate γ_c,

$$\gamma_c = i_s \gamma_{n_p} + \gamma_y = i_s \gamma_{n_p} + \sigma_A \gamma_A. \tag{9.8}$$

To calculate this rate explicitly, we need to specify the dependence of n_p on L_P. These authors assume a form like $n_p \sim L_P^{\beta_p}$, which then gives $\gamma_{n_p} = \beta_p \gamma_L$. Moreover, the growth rate of ideas per good is now $\gamma_A = \delta_A f_A L_P^{1-\beta_p}$, so we can write the consumption growth rate as

$$\gamma_c = i_s \gamma_{n_p} + \sigma_A \gamma_A = \sigma_A \delta_A f_A L_P^{1-\beta_p} + i_s \beta_p \gamma_L. \tag{9.9}$$

We see that for the special case where $\beta_p = 1$, the growth rate is now independent of scale, L_P. Moreover, even though it still depends on the growth rate of labor, it is no longer simply proportional to it and consequently does not vanish as a population stops growing. As before, changes in research intensity also contribute to a higher base growth rate, even though the scale dependence is absent.

This is perhaps better, but the price to pay, of course, besides the various modeling assumptions, is again the extreme fine-tuning necessary, specifically the condition that $\beta_p = 1$, away from which all familiar problems reappear. This value of β_p corresponds to a special situation in which the number of researchers per sector (product) is constant and, though acceptable as a modeling assumption, it is clearly totally counterfactual in that there is no *high-* or *low-tech* sectors in the economy. Jones has also shown that generalizing to the case where $\phi_A \neq 1$, one derives an expression where scale effects also take place as a function of the magnitude of the stock of ideas:

$$\gamma_c = \sigma_A \delta_A f_A \frac{L_P^{1-\beta_p}}{A_P^{1-\phi_A}} + i_s \beta \gamma_L \tag{9.10}$$

Romer-Jones Model   The technical difficulties of the models discussed so far led to a more fundamental reevaluation of assumptions and a search for factors that may help reframe the problem. No great model exists at the moment that takes into account people's actual knowledge in a sufficiently rich fashion and that can be compared with data without gross disagreements, most of them already illustrated by the preceding discussion.

In a more recent paper, Jones and Romer[13] review the state of the art in endogenous growth theory and propose a simple model that is slightly different from the one discussed earlier. The idea is to deal with the historic conundrum of why fast economic growth rates per capita are a modern phenomenon (see also section 7.3), while during most of history population growth absorbed most productivity gains. It is interesting to discuss Jones and Romer's model here because of its simplicity. They assume that output (GDP) follows the production function

$$Y(t) = A_P(t) X_P^{\alpha_Y}(t) L_P(t)^{1-\alpha_Y},\tag{9.11}$$

where, as earlier, A_P contains "ideas," L_P accounts for labor, and X_P is another rival input to production, such as land. To simplify matters, they assume that $X_P(t)=X_P$ is independent of time. Additionally, they assume that *ideas grow proportionally to population*, meaning that, on average, each worker produces n_I ideas per unit time and these are never forgotten: $\dfrac{d}{dt} A_P(t) = n_I L_P(t)$. To close the dynamical system, Jones and Romer make the simplifying assumption that—during the Malthusian regime where resource gains are fully used to grow the population—the income per capita remains constant, $\dfrac{Y(t)}{L_P(t)} = \bar{y} = A_P X_P^{\alpha_Y} L_P^{-\alpha_Y}$, tied to subsistence-level incomes. Then, it follows that the dynamical equation for A_P becomes

$$\frac{d}{dt} A_P(t) = a_A A_P^{1/\alpha_Y}, \text{ with } a_A = \frac{n_I X_P}{\bar{y}^{\frac{1}{\alpha_Y}}}.\tag{9.12}$$

With a_A constant, this leads to the solution

$$A_P(t) = \frac{1}{\left[A_P(0)^{\frac{\alpha_Y-1}{\alpha_Y}} - \frac{1-\alpha_Y}{\alpha_Y} a_A t \right]^{\frac{\alpha_Y}{1-\alpha_Y}}}.\tag{9.13}$$

This solution clearly blows up to infinity in the *finite* time $t = \dfrac{\alpha_Y}{a_A(1-\alpha_Y)} A_P(0)^{\frac{\alpha_Y-1}{\alpha_Y}}$, which generally is quite short. Because they are positive powers of A_P, total income and labor also blow up in a similar way. This is consistent with historical evidence by Kremer,[14] who shows that modeling GDP over historical times suggests faster than exponential growth. Jones and Romer clearly do not intend that this model be used at face value to describe data, but they do make the essential point that the coupling between population size, ideas, and economic output can create a positive feedback, or virtuous cycle, phenomenon that can lead to accelerating economic growth in some circumstances. Creating the modern logic of economic growth per capita then requires decoupling demographic expansion from greater resource availability, something that happens when a demographic transition kicks in. This addresses the economic transformations in cities that must accompany urbanization happening in tandem with a demographic transition, introduced in section 8.3.

9.1.3 PRODUCT SPACES, MISALLOCATION, AND INSTITUTIONS

We have seen how an expansion in knowledge is important for creating the conditions for economic growth but also how difficult—and unnatural—it is to try to model these effects using simple differential equations over aggregate variables, without a richer statistical theory.

This is a good place to look back at some of the ideas that we have already associated with economic development in urban systems. First, in structural terms, we know that richer societies also possess deeper divisions of labor and knowledge and manifest more functions—such as those proxied by professional occupations and business types. We have seen how these types are distributed among cities of different sizes in urban systems (chapters 5 and 8). We emphasized the singular role of the largest cities in sustaining the greatest functional diversity within nations and also in incubating new types. This "economic complexity" has also been measured at the national level. Hidalgo and Hausmann[15] have used a database of international trade to make the empirical case that richer nations also have more diverse "product spaces."[16] In addition, they analyzed the network of co-occurring products at the national level to propose patterns of economic development (which product arises after which other set of products) for nations that are *not at the frontier* of economic development, which they showed is quite predictive of future development patterns. This is very similar to the subject of chapter 5 and also partially explains the link between urbanization and economic development in a much richer structural way.

Second, another set of important ideas in the recent literature in economics deals with the subjects of so-called *misallocation* and *institutions*. We have already seen how economists conceive of allocations of labor and capital to activities that produce output (GDP). It follows that different allocations will typically produce different outputs and different growth trajectories. This gets us closer to statistical ideas linking individual knowledge to aggregate growth, which we will develop later in this chapter. In the economics literature, *misallocation* has come to be connected to many things, including professional opportunities (talent allocation) afforded to people of different genders, races, and ethnicities;[17] allocations of labor, capital, and credit to different industries;[18] and regulation; among others.[19] It is a common argument that people in poorer nations *misallocate* their assets, in the sense that many people are not given a chance to acquire and use advanced skills and knowledge, for example.[20] To me, the term *misallocation* conveys the wrong meaning here, as we are really thinking of processes of human development, not asset placement. In section 9.3 we will show, using a different formalism, that there is a way to think about the allocation of resources in uncertain environments in an optimal way in order to generate the maximum (economic) growth rate, with implications for processes of learning and the development of organizations.

Finally, economists have used analyses of historical events to advocate for the fact that *institutions* matter for economic development.[21] Institutions again mean many different (noneconomic) things, which include law and governance, property rights, trust, corruption, culture, and ethics, for example.[22] Historical "experiments" that illustrate the importance of developing different institutions include the separation of the two Koreas in 1953, the separation and reunification of East and West Germany, and the US-Mexico border, among others. In each of these cases, regions sharing an initially common culture diverged and adopted different institutions, especially in terms of political and economic systems, leading to clearly divergent economic outcomes. These examples might suggest the beneficial role of freer markets, more open societies, and better governance in spurring economic growth. However, history is hard to read unambiguously, and any observer today would have to conclude that many fast-growing Asian nations may have better institutions than, say, Western Europe or North America. It might follow that one could then argue that greater government intervention in political and economic life are institutional factors that encourage fast and steady economic growth.[23] Such statements seem to me to contradict each other, at least to some extent, illustrating the difficulties of historic approaches and any argument that ties the "quality" of a culture or its political institutions to aggregate economic growth. Teasing out what functional elements and processes various institutions actually enable or disable is key.[24] This requires translating broad environmental variables into calculations for economic growth rates and volatilities, which is a program that remains largely to be developed. Doing so requires a statistical approach to modeling growth across scales, as we started to do in chapter 4 and will now continue in the sections that follow.

The discussion of models of endogenous economic growth presented here was quite limited. It does not do full justice to a vital and fascinating field of economics. However, the essential difficulties of the approach are made clear through these examples. In summary, current models of endogenous economic growth are likely correct in emphasizing the importance of creating new knowledge, especially for economic growth in high-income urbanized nations (at the "frontier"), but struggle with capturing mathematically, even in the most basic ways, how information can drive growth. The root of these difficulties is the simplistic treatment of ideas, their creation, and the way they are used as inputs (how they are "allocated") to economic production. To do better, we need to look elsewhere, at places in science where a statistical approach to information, growth, and strategic behavior go hand in hand.

9.2 ECONOMIC GROWTH AND URBANIZATION: THE NATIONAL EVIDENCE REVISITED

Before we embark on a different approach to calculating endogenous growth rates, we must first make sense of one of the most salient facts about cities and urbanization, with which we started this book (in figure 1.3). Exactly how is urbanization associated with higher GDP per capita at the national level?

9.2.1 THE RELATIONSHIP BETWEEN URBANIZATION AND REAL GDP PER CAPITA

Figure 9.1 elaborates on figure 1.2 to show one of the most commonly observed associations between a nation's urbanization rate, u, measured in percent, and the corresponding GDP per capita, y, measured in comparable terms (consumption adjusted) using a benchmark in US dollars in a given year; see, for example, Duranton[25] for a recent discussion. We clearly see a striking pattern, though noisy, showing that higher levels of urbanization are associated on average with higher levels of per capita GDP. Note that we are plotting $\log_{10} y\,(u)$, which shows an approximate straight-line relationship to u; this will be consequential later.

Statistically, we see that the relationship is very noisy but, on average over nations and time, fairly consistent. The best fit (solid line) has the form

$$\log_{10} y\,(u) = \log_{10} y\,(u=0) + a_y\, u, \tag{9.14}$$

where the slope, a_y, is a constant in u. This corresponds to a relation $y(u) = y(u=0)10^{a_y u} = y(u=0)e^{a'_y u}$, with $a'_y = a_y \ln 10$. The relationship in figure 9.1 is also observed in a number of more disaggregated ways. First, it is found cross-sectionally over nations for any single year (figure 9.2). The slope, $a_y \approx 0.02$, varies somewhat with dataset and time but remains quantitatively consistent and thus can be considered a target for prediction. This corresponds to an increase in per capita GDP of about $a'_y = a_y \times \ln 10 \approx 4\% - 5\%$, on average, with each percent increase in urbanization a number that Duranton singles out as being particularly difficult to explain based on standard economic considerations and econometric estimation.[26]

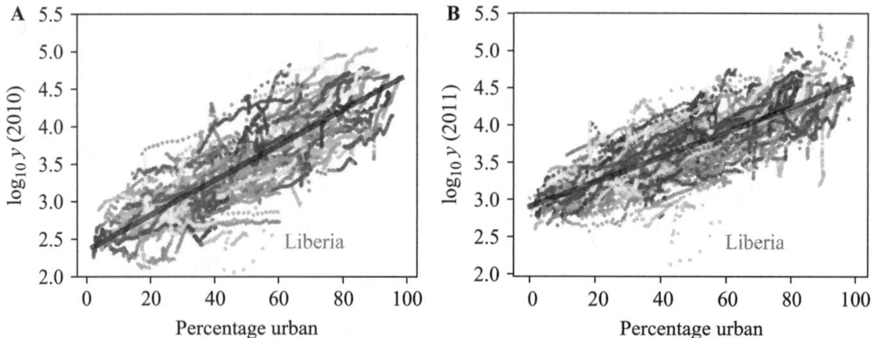

9.1 Variation of national GDP per capita with urbanization rate. (A) Data from the World Bank Country Indicators Database for the years 1960–2016 normalized to 2010 US dollars. (B) Data available from Our World in Data, which extends the dataset of (A) in time and normalizes the values to 2011 US dollars. The thick gray line shows a best fit for the data taken together, with a slope $a_y = 0.0233$ (95% CI [0.0230, 0.0237]), intercept 2.35 (95% CI [2.33, 2.37]), and $R^2 = 0.51$ for (A) and slope of $a_y = 0.0167$ (95% CI [0.0164, 0.0169]), intercept 2.90 (95% CI [2.89, 2.92]), and $R^2 = 0.45$ for (B). Using the numbers for (A), this says that rural societies start out with a GDP per capita of about \$235 and increase this number by a factor of approximately 1.054 ($a'_y = 5.4\%$) with each percentage point increase in urbanization rate ($a'_y = 3.8\%$, panel B), reaching a per capita GDP of about \$50,000 when fully urbanized. This is a substantially averaged result, as single-nation trajectories (shaded) can deviate strongly over time.

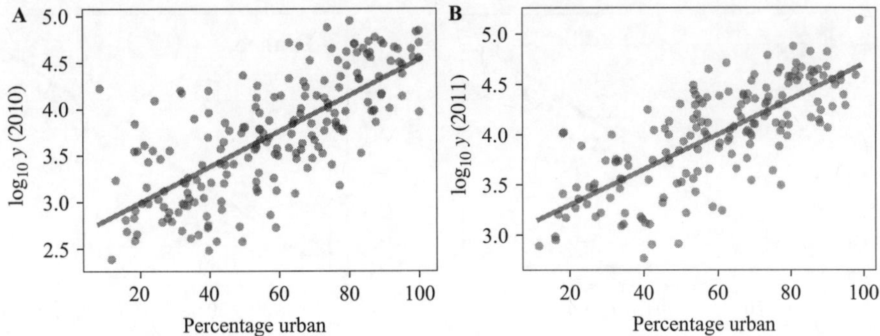

9.2 Cross-sectional variation of national GDP per capita with urbanization rate. (A) Cross section for year 2014 (World Bank data) and best fit (black line) with a slope of $a_y = 0.0192$ (95% CI [0.0166, 0.0219]), intercept 2.61 (95% CI [2.44, 2.77], $a'_y = 4.4\%$), and $R^2 = 0.28$. For (B) the best-fit parameters are 0.0176 (95% CI [0.0151, 0.0201]), intercept 2.95 (95% CI [2.79, 3.10]), and $R^2 = 0.31$, resulting in an estimate of $a'_y = 4.1\%$.

Finally, the same relationship is also observed for the trajectory of each nation over time (figure 9.3). Here, there are some clear exceptions, most flagrantly Liberia, as noted in figure 9.1. Nevertheless, most nations with enough range in urbanization rates and income per capita show trajectories in these two variables that are broadly consistent with equation (9.14), though sometimes with some temporary kinks and jumps. The central question that we must address is the origin of equation (9.14) and the associated prediction of its parameters, $\log_{10} y(u=0)$, and especially the slope, a_y.

The main challenge arises from the fact that the parameters in these fits are functions of time. By plotting them versus only the urbanization rate, u, we conflate two issues: (1) the direct effects of urbanization and (2) the temporal growth across a set of heterogeneous places within each nation (starting with the distinction between urban and rural). To unpack the relationship (9.14) in terms of actual growth processes, we need to consider the time trajectories for the urbanization rate and income separately.

9.2.2   NATIONAL URBANIZATION TRAJECTORIES IN TIME

A number of temporal processes are at work in generating these patterns. On the one hand, there is a dynamical pattern of urbanization, which is different in terms of speed and scope in distinct nations. On the other hand, as urban systems form, rural and urban income growth rates tend to vary according to different trajectories in different nations. Let us now see that, when these two effects are taken together, they allow us to create a simple model of the association between economic growth and urbanization that is empirically consistent with data.

Figure 9.4 shows examples of the variation of the urbanization rate over time for a number of different nations. In the first few cases, for the US, Britain, and France, we observe relatively slow urbanization, taking place on the timescale of about a century. In the other cases, we see faster urbanization, especially for nations in Asia, including the well-known cases of Japan and South Korea.

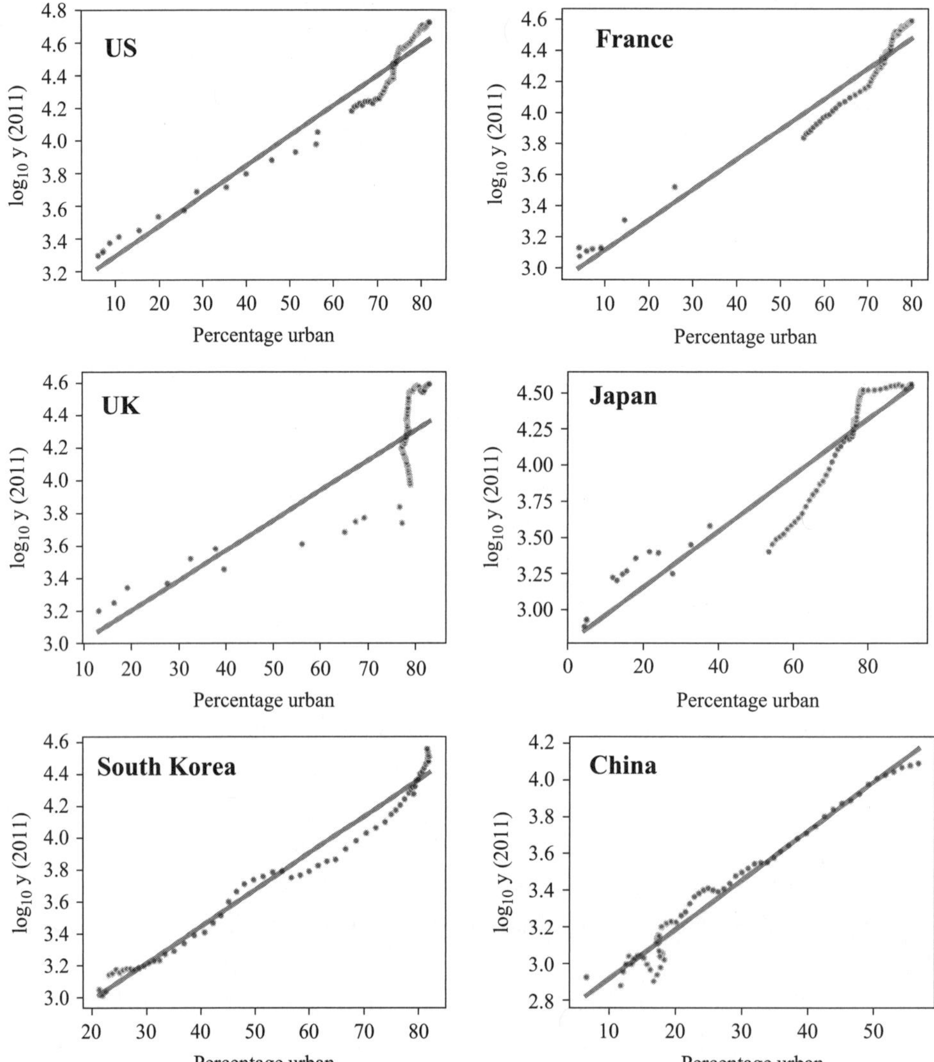

9.3 Association between the urbanization rate and per capita GDP (real dollars) for select nations over time. We observe that each nation's trajectory (points) differs at some times from a simple straight line but that each one on average over time follows a relationship similar to what is observed cross-sectionally. The estimated parameters, 95% confidence intervals, and goodness of fit are as follows: US (a_y=0.0184, 95% CI [0.0175, 0.0194], $\log_{10} y(u=0)$=3.1085, 95% CI [3.0404, 3.1765], R^2=0.8953); UK (a_y=0.0184, 95% CI [0.0155, 0.0214], $\log_{10} y(0)$=2.8353, 95% CI [2.6139, 3.0568], R^2=0.4440); France (a_y=0.0195, 95% CI [0.0184, 0.0205], $\log_{10} y(u=0)$=2.9197, 95% CI [2.8495, 2.9899], R^2=0.9042); Japan (a_y=0.0194, 95% CI [0.0177, 0.0211], $\log_{10} y(0)$=2.7689, 95% CI [2.6474, 2.8904], R^2=0.7469); South Korea (a_y=0.0230, 95% CI [0.0221, 0.0239], $\log_{10} y(u=0)$=2.5262, 95% CI [2.4734, 2.5792], R^2=0.9560); China (a_y=0.0268, 95% CI [0.0256, 0.0280], $\log_{10} y(u=0)$=2.6484, 95% CI [2.6133, 2.6835], R^2=0.9390). This translates into doubling rates a'_y = 4.2%, 4.2%, 4.5%, 4.4%, 5.3%, and 6.2%, respectively.

In all cases, the time evolution of the urbanization rate is well described by a logistic curve of the form

$$u(t) = \frac{u_M}{1 + e^{-s_u(t-t_0)}},$$ (9.15)

where $u_M \simeq 1$ (or 100%) is the maximum urbanization rate, s_u measures the (unsaturated) temporal rate ("speed") of urbanization, and t_0 is a timescale marking the start date of the process. This is necessary because, as we have seen, nations have remained nonurban for most of their history.

We can appreciate where this type of urbanization trajectory comes from by starting with a few elementary considerations. Consider a nation, and define its urban and rural populations by N_U and N_S (S is for subsistence), respectively. Then the urbanization rate is given by $u = \dfrac{N_U}{N_U + N_S}$. Now define the temporal growth rates for these two subpopulations as $\eta_U = \dfrac{d}{dt} \ln N_U$ and $\eta_S = \dfrac{d}{dt} \ln N_S$. It follows after some algebra that the dynamical equation for the growth of the urbanization rate is

$$\frac{du}{dt} = (\gamma_U - \gamma_S)\, u(1 - u),$$ (9.16)

which is the logistic differential equation with solution (9.15) for $s_u = \gamma_U - \gamma_S$ and $u_M = 1$. Note for future reference that the fastest speed of urbanization, $v_u = \dfrac{du}{dt}$, given by this equation is $v_u^{max} = \dfrac{s_u}{4}$, at the midpoint of the urbanization trajectory, $u = 0.5$. We therefore see that a nation will urbanize as long as the growth rate of its urban population is greater than that of its rural population. This growth rate is given in terms of v_u, but this rate is typically much slower in the beginning stages of urbanization and eventually vanishes again as nations become fully urbanized. It follows that s_u^{-1} is the characteristic time over which urbanization takes place in each nation. The lesson from figure 9.4 is that urbanization can proceed in terms of similar temporal shapes but at a very different pace in different nations, with s_u^{-1} ranging from a few decades for the US, the UK, France, and Spain to less than 20 years for Japan and just 8 years for South Korea. Thus, the economic "miracles" of these Asian nations are associated with especially fast urbanization (remember figure 1.3). The consequence of this relation holding for many different nations is that there is a tight mapping between time and the urbanization rate of any nation. This allows us to trade the time coordinates for urbanization rates, since

$$t - t_0 = \frac{1}{s_u} \ln \frac{u}{u_M - u}.$$ (9.17)

This relation is a slowly varying function of u except at the extremes, where the logarithm diverges. This is the case for nearly fully urbanized nations but also for nations with very low urbanization, which will tend to also show very slow economic growth.

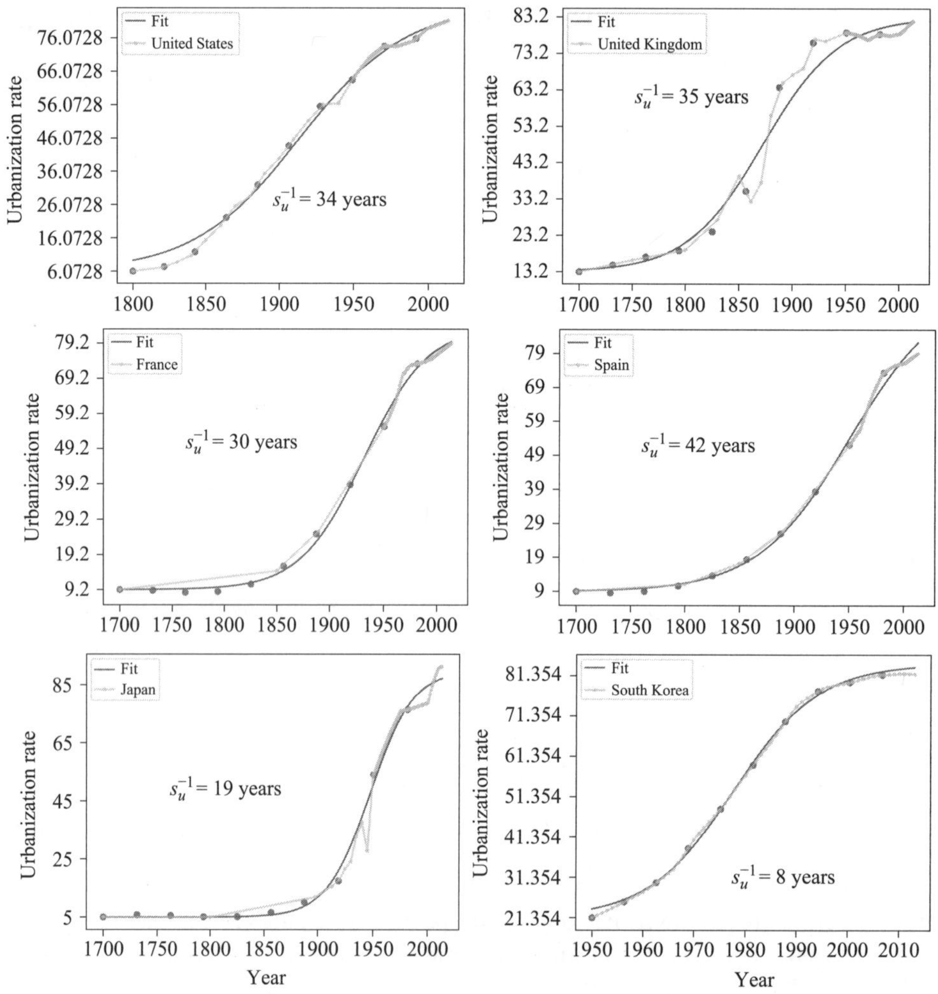

9.4 Urbanization trajectories for select nations, showing different speeds, measured by s_u. Nations that are still urbanizing lead to more uncertain fits, but, for example, Brazil has been slow, on a scale comparable to European nations, while China has been fast, with a characteristic time between those of Japan and South Korea. The fit lines show equation (9.15), with parameters estimated in each case.

9.2.3 NATIONAL TRAJECTORIES FOR PER CAPITA ECONOMIC GROWTH

We now relate equation (9.14) to rates of economic growth in cities versus rural areas. First, note that $\log_{10} y$ is an averaged quantity in the sense of both time and population. It is (up to a change in the base of the logarithm) the time integral of the average national income growth rate: $\log_{10} y(t) = \dfrac{1}{\ln 10} \displaystyle\int^{t} dt' \dfrac{d}{dt'} \ln y(t')$. Defining the average national growth rate as $\gamma_y \equiv \dfrac{1}{t - t_0} \displaystyle\int_{t_0}^{t} dt' \dfrac{d}{dt'} \ln y(t')$ leads to $\ln y\,(t) \sim \gamma_y\,(t - t_0)$.

So, to obtain an expression like equation (9.14), we need to express *both* the growth rate, γ_y, and time, t, in terms of the urbanization rate.

Second, because this is such an aggregated quantity, it is far from capturing direct effects of where and who leads processes of economic growth. To get to these issues, we need to unpack this quantity and decompose each nation in terms of its urban and nonurban components. More ambitiously, we would like to develop an analytical framework that goes further and achieves the decomposition of aggregated growth rates—without additional assumptions, such as specific production functions[27]— into those associated with actual economic agents, including governments, cities, firms, and people. We will show next that this decomposition of growth processes can be achieved rigorously using the mathematical formalism of population dynamics in ecology and evolution in the form of the *Price equation*.

9.2.4   SPEED BOOST TO NATIONAL INCOME GROWTH FROM URBANIZATION

What may we expect from the most general considerations for the behavior of the growth rate of income per capita as a nation urbanizes? Let us frame our expectations by the two most extreme situations. For a *rural nation* focused primarily on *subsistence production*, we expect the growth rate of GDP per capita, γ_S, to be perhaps nonzero but very small (chapters 5 and 7). It is wider economic exchange between households and between firms for nonbasic goods that creates substantial GDP; such dynamics become necessary in cities,[28] as we have seen throughout the book.

On the other hand, for a *fully urbanized* nation, we expect the growth rate for income on average to be nonzero and larger, $\gamma_U > \gamma_S$. These growth rates will depend on the nation's variable capacity to learn and the value of its knowledge, as well as some of its natural endowments and institutions.[29] We can now think of the process of urbanization as a *selection effect* taking agents from a state of a low growth rate (subsistence) to a higher one (urban economic interdependence), thus increasing overall production and incomes (and corresponding costs).[30]

Let us now derive this effect mathematically. At the national level, there is an urbanized fraction of the population, $u(t)$, and a subsistence-based population, $1 - u(t)$. These populations have different economic growth rates, $\gamma_U > 0$ and $\gamma_S \approx 0$, respectively, as well as levels of income. These numbers are generally time dependent and subject to fluctuations (volatilities, as we emphasized in chapter 4). The national-level growth rate is a *mixture* of these two populations and their growth rates. Moving population to a state of a higher growth rate (urbanization) provides a temporary acceleration in national growth rates. To see this, let us write $\ln y(t)$ as the average over the fraction of the population that is urban versus subsistence,

$$\ln y' \equiv \ln y(t + \Delta t) = \sum_{i=U,S} n_i(t + \Delta t) \ln y_i(t + 1); \quad \ln y = \sum_{i=U,S} n_i(t) \ln y_i(t), \qquad (9.18)$$

where $n_{U,S}(t) = (u(t), 1 - u(t))$, the urbanized and nonurbanized (subsistence) fractions of the population. It follows that the change over one time unit, Δt, is

$$\frac{\Delta \ln y}{\Delta t} = \frac{\ln y' - \ln y}{\Delta t} = \frac{1}{\Delta t} \sum_{i=U,S} n_i(t+1)\ln y_i(t+1) - n_i(t)\ln y_i(t)$$

$$= \sum_{i=U,S} \frac{\Delta n_i}{\Delta t}\ln y_i(t) + n_i(t)\frac{\Delta \ln y_i}{\Delta t}. \tag{9.19}$$

This is the familiar Price equation.[31] It is the fundamental relation expressing how changes in any population average are the result of the combined effect of a variation in frequencies of types (*selection* or *sorting*; first term) and changes in the quantities themselves over time (*transmission* or *endogenous growth*; second term). The second term is an average over subtypes (here urban or subsistence). This average can be written in terms of its own Price equation, further disaggregating the quantity of interest; for example, in terms of the sets of cities that make up urban areas and regions that make up rural areas (see subsection 9.2.5). We can then proceed to describe organizations within each place, such as firms, and then go down yet another level to the individuals who make up each organization. At each level, we pick up a covariance term that associates differential growth rates at that scale with types of groups. In this way, we can create a microscopic picture of economic growth (or any other population-averaged quantity) and understand in principle, given appropriate data, which levels and types of organizations contribute most to generating the aggregate effect. This approach therefore allows us a quantitative window into the relative importance of various collectives ("institutions" writ large) at different levels of social, economic, and political organization.[32]

Let us see how this works at the first level of selection between urban and non-urban aggregate populations in each nation. Selection here means a choice between two broad states: urban or subsistence. Note that $\frac{\Delta(1-u)}{\Delta t} = -\frac{\Delta u}{\Delta t}$, which leads to

$$\frac{\Delta \ln y}{\Delta t} = \frac{\Delta \ln y_S}{\Delta t} + u\left[\frac{\Delta \ln y_U}{\Delta t} - \frac{\Delta \ln y_S}{\Delta t}\right] + \frac{\Delta u}{\Delta t}[\ln y_U - \ln y_S]. \tag{9.20}$$

With $v_u = \frac{\Delta u}{\Delta t}$, one obtains

$$\frac{\Delta \ln y}{\Delta t} = \gamma_S + u[\gamma_U - \gamma_S] + v_u \ln \frac{y_U}{y_S}. \tag{9.21}$$

The last term can be further simplified as $\ln \frac{y_U}{y_S} = \ln \frac{y_U(t_0)}{y_S(t_0)} + [\gamma_U - \gamma_S](t - t_0)$, which leads to a general fit for the dependence of $\frac{\Delta \ln y}{\Delta t}$ on the urbanization rate and its speed of change as

$$\frac{\Delta \ln y}{\Delta t}(t) = a_0 v_u(t) + a_1[u(t) + v_u(t)(t - t_0)] + a_2, \tag{9.22}$$

with $a_0 = \ln \frac{y_U(t_0)}{y_S(t_0)}$, $a_1 = \gamma_U - \gamma_S$, $a_2 = \gamma_S \approx 0$, so $\gamma_U = a_1 + a_2 \approx a_1$. We see that, to the extent that $a_0, a_1 > 0$, as may be expected generally, the growth rate for national income will receive a boost from higher urbanization rates *and* higher speeds of urbanization. These effects will be higher the larger the urban income and growth rates are relative to the same subsistence quantities. They will also typically be highest at intermediate levels of urbanization, where the speed of urbanization v_u is largest, as predicted by the logistic curves (9.15) and figure 9.4.

This is what is empirically observed. Figure 9.5A shows the average instantaneous growth rate across nations against urbanization rate. We see that the growth rate is highest at intermediate urbanization rates, around 50%. For mostly rural nations, the growth rate of per capita income is lowest, while it takes an intermediate positive value for almost entirely urban nations.

Finally, we can return to the relationship in figure 9.1. It is clear that equation (9.20) is a total derivative, which using equation (9.17) can be integrated to give

$$
\begin{aligned}
\ln y(t) &= \ln y_0 + u(t)\ln\frac{y_U(t)}{y_S(t)} + \ln y_S(t) \\
&= \ln y_0 + \ln y_S(t_0) + u(t)\ln\frac{y_U(t_0)}{y_S(t_0)} + \frac{1}{s_u}[u(t)(\gamma_U - \gamma_S) + \gamma_S]\ln\frac{u(t)}{u_M - u(t)},
\end{aligned}
\tag{9.23}
$$

where $\ln y_0$ is an integration constant set by the initial value of $\ln y(t_0)$. We can now use our disaggregated model of economic growth to understand the parameters of equation (9.14). We see that the slope is

$$
\begin{aligned}
a_y(u) &= \ln\frac{y_U(t_0)}{y_S(t_0)} + \frac{(\gamma_U - \gamma_S)}{s_u}\ln\frac{u}{u_M - u} + \frac{1}{s_u}[u(\gamma_U - \gamma_S) + \gamma_S]\frac{u_M}{u(u_M - u)} \\
&= a_0 + \frac{a_1}{s_u}\ln\frac{u}{u_M - u} + \frac{1}{s_u}[ua_1 + a_2]\frac{u_M}{u(u_M - u)}.
\end{aligned}
\tag{9.24}
$$

The intercept requires specifying $u(t_0)$, $v_u(t_0)$. In the simplest case, where $u(t_0)=v_u(t_0)=0$, $\log_{10} y(u=0)=\log_{10} y_S(t_0)$, so the initial value of income in equation (9.14) corresponds to its subsistence level in the absence of urbanization, which may indeed be very low, on the order of $1 per day. This number is considered by the World Bank to be well below the threshold of extreme poverty.[33]

In terms of the magnitude of the slope a_y in equation (9.24), the first (constant) term, a_0, generally dominates, but there are expected corrections to a simple linear relationship between the urbanization rate and per capita GDP, because of the last two nonlinear terms in u (see figure 9.5). The nonlinear corrections are typically only significant when urbanization vanishes, $u \to 0$, or nears completion, $u \to u_M$. This is shown by the solid lines (for different values of s_u^{-1}) in figure 9.5B.

We now understand that the origins of the slope in the association between per capita GDP and the urbanization rate are set primarily by the difference in urban and rural (subsistence) levels of GDP per capita *early on*, at the beginning of the process of urbanization; this contributes 3.2% of the $a_y=3.8\%$ slope in figure 9.1B, for example. This initial seed, which characterizes a very small urban population (perhaps just a few percent; preindustrial societies typically have $u<15\%$),[34] nevertheless introduces

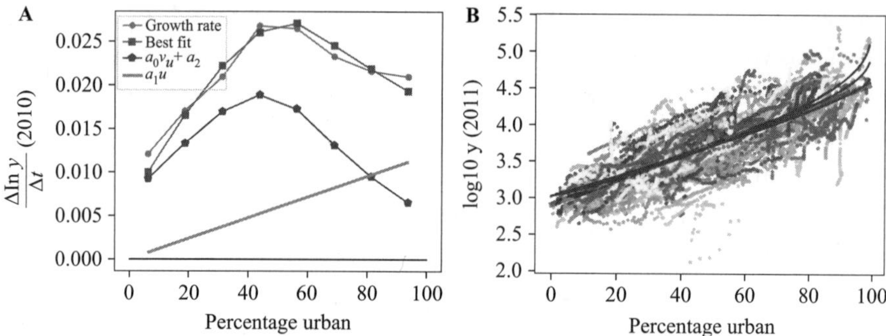

9.5 National GDP per capita and its growth rate versus urbanization. (A) Instantaneous growth rate of GDP per capita (in real 2011 dollars) versus levels of urbanization. The average across nations (circles) shows that the highest growth rates, around 2.7% per year, occur at intermediate levels of urbanization, 40%–60%, when the speed of urbanization is highest (see figure 9.2 and the text). The best fit is obtained with $\gamma_S = 0$ and $\ln \frac{y_U}{y_S}(0) = 3.2$ (3.2% in a'_y) and $\gamma_U = 1.2\%$ per year. Another good fit, letting the subsistence growth rate be nonzero, translates into $\gamma_U = 1.4\%$ per year, $\gamma_S = 0.3\%$ per year, $\ln \frac{y_U}{y_S}(0) = 2.6$. (Confidence intervals on this second fit tell us that the estimate of γ_S is consistent with zero.). The other lines show the time derivative of the urbanization rate and its value, demonstrating that neither of these variables by themselves describes the growth rate of income well. (B) Prediction (solid lines) for the slope of figure 9.1 (equation 9.14) from equation (9.23) and the parameters of figure 9.5A. Different lines correspond to different choices of $s_u^{-1} = 10, 20, 30$ years (bottom to top). Clearly, these are average lines, which do not account for the variations in initial values and shocks along the way peculiar to each nation.

the possibility of subsequent sorting if this differential can be maintained as cities grow relative to rural populations. Such a differential is of course the result of general network effects leading to superlinear scaling of GDP with city size (chapter 3), which we have shown to be very general, including throughout history (chapters 3 and 7).

When measured as an annual rate, as is commonly done, this dependence of the slope of equation (9.24) on u introduces a "speed boost" proportional to the temporal rate of urbanization, v_u. The magnitude of this effect will vary with the speed of urbanization (and the magnitude of endogenous rates), from a fraction of a percent on average to a few percent for rapidly urbanizing nations, such as the "Asian miracles" illustrated in figure 9.4. What may be surprising is that the endogenous growth rates of urban (and subsistence) economies play only a secondary role in this association. Thus, an initial difference between urban and rural incomes at times when most of the population still is not urban is likely a necessary condition for igniting a full-fledged process of systemic economic growth and urbanization. Nations that urbanize very quickly, such as Japan, South Korea, and now China, may be strong beneficiaries of the *speed boost effect* in their GDP growth but will later struggle to maintain high growth rates as the continued sorting of their population into cities ceases to be an option.

9.2.5 LEVELS OF SELECTION: GROWTH-LEVEL DISAGGREGATION AND INSTITUTIONS

We have just emphasized in passing that the Price equation provides us with an exact and systematic procedure for decomposing the contributions to *national* aggregate economic growth from successively lower levels of organization. This is important because it is widely expected that economic growth will ultimately be generated by the decisions of economic *agents*, namely firms and individuals (or households). This decomposition corresponds to the simultaneous consideration of *multiple levels of selection* in the usual language of evolutionary population dynamics.[35] It naturally includes issues related to *institutions*, in the sense that individuals can choose to participate in (or be excluded from) distinct firms, places, and other collective spaces, bringing a different perspective to issues of (mis)allocation emphasized in economics. The problem of collective behavior and levels of organization and selection is a major theme in evolutionary population dynamics that is treated in the context of a multilevel Price equation.[36]

To do this formally, let us write per capita income more abstractly in terms of a series of labels for urban and rural places (including different urban and rural areas), firms, and individuals, respectively, as y_{ijkl}. To keep this structure simple, we are assuming that this decomposition is hierarchical so each individual works for a single firm (including the self-employed) or is retired in a specific place that is either urban or not. (There are clear exceptions to this; for example, individuals deriving income from capital gains arising in several firms and places.) Associated with these labels is a frequency distribution for each type, P_{ijkl}, normalized as usual, in the sense that $1 = \Sigma_{i,j,k,l} P_{ijkl}$. The marginal frequencies also follow $P_{ijk} = \Sigma_l P_{ijkl}$, $P_{ij} = \Sigma_{k,l} P_{ijkl}$, $P_i = \Sigma_{j,k,l} P_{ijkl}$, as usual. The frequencies $P_U = u$ and $P_S = 1 - u$ correspond to those in the previous sections. The final ingredient is the *change in these frequencies* over time, which corresponds to agents' decisions as to where to live and work. We will write this change in the usual notation of evolutionary population dynamics (recall neighborhood selection in chapter 6) as

$$P'_{ijkl} \equiv P_{ijkl}(t+1) = \frac{w_{ijkl}}{w} P_{ijkl}(t). \tag{9.25}$$

This relationship applies at each level of analysis so that, for example, $P'_i = \frac{w_i}{w} P_i$. The speed of urbanization is $v_u \Delta t = P'_U - P_U = \left(\frac{w_U}{w} - 1 \right) u$, or $w_U = w(1 + v_u \Delta t)$; $w_S = w$ $(1 - v_u \Delta t)$. This shows that the w's account for *differential population growth rates across population types*; in evolutionary dynamics, this is known as the type's *fitness*. These quantities are simply the growth rates for each type relative to the average over all types at the same level: they should not be taken to mean an organism's fitness in the sense of biological evolution.

The selection coefficients inherit the normalization of the frequencies since

$$1 = \sum_{i,j,k,l} P'_{ijkl} \rightarrow w = \sum_{i,j,k,l} w_{ijkl} P_{ijkl}.$$

In general, there is a relationship between the relative growth rates, w, of each group (e.g., urbanization, relative place performance, firm market share, individual wealth) and levels of income, $\ln y$, for each.

We can now write the decomposition of the income growth rate. At the first level of decomposition, as we have seen, we have

$$\Delta \ln y = \mathrm{covar}_i\left(\frac{w_i}{w}, \ln y_i\right) + E_i\left[\frac{w_i}{w}\Delta \ln y_i\right], \tag{9.26}$$

where $E_i[\ldots]$ is the expectation value over the population indexed by i, and similarly for the $\mathrm{covar}_i[w_i y_i]$, as the covariance between w and y. We can then write the Price equation for $\Delta \ln y_i$ as

$$\Delta \ln y_i = \mathrm{covar}_j\left(\frac{w_{ij}}{w_i}, \ln y_{ij}\right) + E_j\left[\frac{w_{ij}}{w_i}\Delta \ln y_{ij}\right], \tag{9.27}$$

and so on. By unpacking all four levels, we get

$$\Delta \ln y = \mathrm{covar}_i\left(\frac{w_i}{w}, \ln y_i\right) + E_i\left[\mathrm{covar}_j\left(\frac{w_{ij}}{w}, \ln y_{ij}\right)\right] + E_{ij}\left[\mathrm{covar}_k\left(\frac{w_{ijk}}{w}, \ln y_{ijk}\right)\right]$$
$$+ E_{ijk}\left[\mathrm{covar}_l\left(\frac{w_{ijkl}}{w}, \ln y_{ijkl}\right)\right] + E_{ijkl}\left[\frac{w_{ijkl}}{w}\Delta \ln y_{ijlk}\right]. \tag{9.28}$$

The various covariance terms express *selection* (or perhaps better in our context, *sorting*) at each level, specifically whether places, firms, or individuals with higher income per capita, $\ln y$, become more frequent, or those with lower income less frequent, in the population over time because of covarying higher or lower w. This may happen because of migration between rural and urban places (first term), but it may happen more specifically because people choose between places to live (different cities, second term), as we saw in chapter 8. These choices, in turn, may result from employment mobility between firms (third term). The last term accounts for the endogenous processes of growth directly as they accrue to individuals in their own context (city and firm). These rates are measurable quantities given personal income data and corporate accounting.[37]

We can write this equation as a temporal growth rate for the national economy as

$$\gamma_y(t) = \mathrm{covar}_i\left(\frac{w_i}{w}, \ln y_i\right) + E_i\left[\mathrm{covar}_j\left(\frac{w_{ij}}{w}, \ln y_{ij}\right)\right] + E_{ij}\left[\mathrm{covar}_k\left(\frac{w_{ijk}}{w}, \ln y_{ijk}\right)\right]$$
$$+ E_{ijk}\left[\mathrm{covar}_l\left(\frac{w_{ijkl}}{w}, \ln y_{ijkl}\right)\right] + E_{ijkl}\left[\frac{w_{ijkl}}{w}\gamma_{ijlk}\right], \tag{9.29}$$

where $\gamma_y(t) = \dfrac{\Delta \ln y}{\Delta t}$ is the growth rate of the national income per capita and $\gamma_{ijlk}(t) = \dfrac{\Delta \ln y_{ijlk}}{\Delta t}$ is that for each individual given their specific context. The changes in frequencies are evaluated over the same time period as the growth rates, Δt, typically a year. This expression gives an exact form of growth accounting that differs from what is typically assumed in economic theory,[38] such as equation (9.1), which makes additional assumptions about the form of production functions. Expression (9.29) shows explicitly how aggregate growth is the result of both a *multilevel selection* process based on choices of location and employment and a fundamental endogenous process affecting each economic agent in their own context, based on their knowledge, agency, and information, as well as their socioeconomic environment.

This multilevel Price equation provides an *exact calculus* for how income per capita will increase. What is missing from the expression of these preferences (in the specification of w) is input from perspectives that include the cost-benefit analysis for relevant agents, including not just incomes but also costs and other characteristics of their living and working environments (see chapter 3). The singular question the Price equation asks of these other variables is whether they are positively or negatively correlated, thus driving selection for higher or lower levels of aggregate income in the corresponding nation.

As an example of the specification of w, consider a correlation model between fitness and income,

$$\frac{w_i - w}{w} = a_w \ln y_i + \epsilon_i, \tag{9.30}$$

where a_w is a regression coefficient and ϵ_i is a noise term that averages to zero across population types. This leads to

$$\text{covar}_i\left(\frac{w_i}{w}, \ln y_i\right) = a_w \, \text{var}(\ln y), \tag{9.31}$$

where $\text{var}(\ln y) \geq 0$ is the variance over the population types that results from any difference in income across types. If the correlation is positive, $a_w > 0$, as during urbanization, then selection *always* produces economic growth. For preferred organizations in this sense—nations, cities, or firms—with incomes higher than average, the challenge is to harness these opportunities to continue to spur their own growth and, as if "led by an invisible hand," that of the aggregate system.

9.2.6 DISCUSSION: GROWTH AND MULTILEVEL SELECTION

The analysis of national economic growth and its relationship to levels of urbanization led us down the path of disaggregating processes of choice across successively lower levels of socioeconomic organization. We are now left with two important questions: (1) how do levels of organization interact to produce benefits and costs for various agents, and (2) how do we *compute endogenous growth rates* for each agent in its own context? The second question is the subject of section 9.3. Let us now discuss the first before returning to it at the end of this chapter.

It is common to encounter conflicts between socioeconomic organizations at different levels. For example, firms often complain of regulations or taxes imposed by local or national governments, which, they argue, slow down their innovation, profits, and growth. Workers, in turn, often struggle with the wages they collect from their employers, which, in their view, curtail their personal development and well-being. These dilemmas lie at the heart of the most fundamental questions about political organization and economic production and have led to such classic works as the debates between Aristotle and Plato on politics, Marx's critique of capitalism, Lefebvre's analysis of power structures in cities,[39] and, of course, much of the current debate on economic policy.

In terms of practical decisions, it is the rich ecology of agents and organizations that sets the self-consistent framework for the cost-benefit trade-offs experienced by mobile agents such as households and firms, who must choose, within their own constraints, where to locate and whom to interact with. For policymakers, and specifically for national and local governments, the choice is more about how to affect these costs and benefits via their actions, including levels of taxation for different groups and entities and the creation of public goods such as a safe environment, reliable urban services, health care, and a pool of knowledge via sponsored education, research, and migration support, for example.

I find it illuminating to illustrate these dilemmas in light of the classic calculus of altruism and selection in evolutionary theory.[40] Consider the simplest case of two levels of selection that you can think of as workers and firms or firms and cities.[41] Let us simply define a fitness rate, w_{ij}, where the indices refer to individuals and groups, respectively, as

$$\frac{w_{ij}}{w} = -c_C(N_i - 1)\ln y_{ij} + b_C\, n_{ij}(N_i - 1)\ln y_i. \tag{9.32}$$

The first term expresses the cost, c_C, of supporting a link with all other individuals, $N_i - 1$, in group i, whereas the second term describes benefits, b_C, of that interaction in units of the average pooled resources of the group, $\ln y_i = \Sigma_j \ln y_{ij} P(j|i)$ (with $P(j|i)$, the assignment of individual j in group i), accruing to each individual j in group i, determined by a *distributional allocation*, n_{ij}. Using the preceding arguments for two levels of selection and ignoring the last term, which takes endogenous growth into account, we obtain (neglecting covariation between group size, allocation, and resources, covar $(n_{ij}, \ln y_{ij}) = 0$)

$$\gamma(t) = \mathrm{covar}_i\!\left(\frac{w_i}{w}, \ln y_i\right) + E_i\!\left[\mathrm{covar}_j\!\left(\frac{w_{ij}}{w}, \ln y_{ij}\right)\right] \tag{9.33}$$
$$= (N-1)E_i[\sigma^2{}_{\ln y_i}][(b_C\bar{n} - c_C)r_y - c_C],$$

where $r_y = \dfrac{\sigma^2{}_{\ln y}}{E_i[\sigma^2{}_{\ln y_i}]}$ is known as the *coefficient of relatedness*, which measures the dispersion of income across groups (inequality, in the numerator) versus that within groups, on average in the denominator. In this expression, N is the average group size and $\bar{n} \sim 1$ is the average fraction of log resources accruing to a person.

The coefficient r_y measures the strength of selection between groups versus that within them. The condition for a positive growth rate in the aggregate is that

$$\text{Benefits } r_y > \text{Costs,} \tag{9.34}$$

with (net) $\text{Benefits} = b_C \bar{n} - c_C$ and $\text{Costs} = c_C$, which is known as *Hamilton's rule* in the context of evolutionary theory.[42] This shows that for groups to form and spread in the population, the essential benefits b_C of being in a group must be large enough compared to the associated costs, while it also helps (and requires!) that the distribution of benefits within each group is equitable. For these happy and fair groups, growth is possible and will be fastest. The fundamental reasons why collectives can be more productive than the same number of individuals will become clearer from the properties of information, in section 9.3.

Note that this reasoning asks for the highest average growth rate, thus benefiting everybody in a population, which in turn requires group participation and within-group collaboration, not competition. Models where within-group competition is suppressed at additional cost,[43] such as, presumably, in most social organizations, have in fact been shown to be more robust when relatedness is low, making a case that such institutional arrangements are necessary in large and diverse social collectives, such as cities. This is another way of stating the case in favor of collective efficacy (see chapter 6). Nevertheless, in this picture, group success is facilitated by higher relatedness in terms of similarity of resource distribution within groups and thus is promoted by groups with less inequality within than across the population at large. We have seen that this was a characteristic of neighborhoods, but this approach asks the same question of firms and cities, as they compete with like organizations to attract people. This reasoning also exposes a potential pathology leading to growing inequality within organizations, often blamed for the current growth in income inequality in the US and other nations. The mechanism described here requires that group participants be able to exercise choice between organizations; if labor markets present a uniform picture of (unequal) collective income distribution across organizations and places, then this choice is moot. The present analysis and associated body of literature then suggest that individuals would be more encouraged to "free ride" their organizations than to contribute actively to their success.[44]

In this view, the emergence of collective organizations is, as economists often remind us, the ultimate result of self-interest. However, it is a fundamental mistake to take this self-interest narrowly ("selfishness" at a single level of selection), as agents' net benefits are actually the result of environments where people cooperate for better results that can only be achieved through collective action. Thus, narrow selfishness tends to beget more narrow selfishness, lack of cooperation, and low incomes. On the other hand, enlightened self-interest helps create and sustain large successful collectives, where knowledge and resources can be pooled together for the common good of mutual cooperators, likely leading to more sophisticated and valuable production as well as greater fairness. This situation is always a balancing act. It is an unstable state that requires an initial leap of faith via collective self-organization before tangible joint benefits are felt. We will see how some of these insights are fleshed out in section 9.3.

9.3 STATISTICAL MECHANICS OF GROWTH AND INFORMATION

We have now seen how a very aggregated approach to the role of ideas in production and consumption leads to a number of counterfactual predictions about economic growth. We have also seen that we can disaggregate these patterns in a systematic way and that such a procedure leads to one remaining puzzle: How to compute endogenous growth rates for individuals and organizations?

The main inadequacy of the economic models discussed earlier is the lack of a principled engagement with the concept of knowledge or information. We already started to develop the concept of information as a statistical quantity in chapters 4, 5, and 6 and saw some of its implications for urban systems in chapter 8. What was left out previously was to devise the means to compute growth rates from a more fundamental perspective. Some of the necessary framework was developed at an important interdisciplinary juncture between information theory,[45] financial mathematics,[46] and evolutionary theory.[47] Here we will take these original insights and formalizations and go a little further toward a more statistical theory of (economic) growth, with cities as the backdrop.

Information is measured in *bits*. This sounds very technological, but the key for us here is the recognition that information, expressed in these formal terms, measures *units of choice*. For example, when you play the *game of 20 questions*, you are trying to identify the target object by asking a sequence of questions that you think are most informative. Each yes/no question reveals a bit of information and a choice you made. It is a fascinating fact about the world that you can identify *anything* or *anybody* in the world in 20 questions or less (20 bits).

This is also true of any other choices, not just guessing things. In the complex environments of cities, people must make choices between alternatives all the time, and these choices structure their behavior and shape their worldlines and associated events, as in chapter 3. As we saw in that context, such choices have consequences for the social interactions that people will experience and the cost-benefit trade-offs associated with them. It follows that answering specific questions will prove better suited to acquiring resources, broadly understood, and, as these are reinvested repeatedly over cycles (days, years), will thereby lead to a larger average growth rate. With these ideas in mind, we now return to individual behavior.

There will be three main ingredients necessary for setting up a statistical theory of growth. The first two have to do with the probabilities of various events in the world and the payoffs from predicting them correctly. The third ingredient deals with the allocation of the agent's resources to various alternative stochastic events, given the specific information available to them. Let us deal with each of these issues separately in order to disentangle their distinct contributions. We will see that all these quantities have a meaning in terms of probabilities and that their relationships can therefore be studied in terms of information theory.

9.3.1 EVENT PROBABILITIES AND PAYOFFS

To set up the mathematical framework, consider a partition of the world available to agents in terms of events and their outcomes. Consider a discrete space, e_1, e_2, . . . , e_i, . . . , $e_E \in e$, where e is a general *environment*, external to our agents, and each e_i is a distinct type of event that they can experience. (Note that here e is not a matrix, but we have used the same symbol for a similar general idea in chapter 8.) Each of these variables is stochastic and codes for different outcomes over time. Some are states of the physical environment, such as sunshine or rain, and others may be properties of the socioeconomic environment, such as a trade or business opportunity. There are a very large number of these events that an agent can in principle experience; for example, associated with all other people and places in a large city. The subset actually experienced over some time period will depend on the life path each individual takes, so, realistically, not all types of environmental states will be available to all people. Economic or racial segregation, for example, will limit peoples' social horizons and thus their experienced events and associated opportunities.

To proceed and establish the connection to information, we will assume that agents will seek to maximize their average resource growth rate over many cycles of choice (e.g., days).[48] This is equivalent to the maximization of a *logarithmic utility* but different from the behavior that would follow from other forms of utility optimized over the short term, as is often done in microeconomics. There is a growing body of literature in experimental economics[49] and on financial portfolio theory[50] that help us justify this choice, but it has also been pointed out in the economics literature that an agent may prefer to maximize a short-term goal, which in some circumstances will lead to different behavior.[51] If it does, it would be an instance of "misallocation," as discussed in subsection 9.1.3, at least from the point of view of maximizing lifetime aggregated consequences.

Let us now develop a simple scenario sufficient to motivate the introduction of individualized information for each agent. Consider the case in which the agent's resources are apportioned to different environmental stochastic events, e_i, in terms of a fraction $f_r(e_i)$, $\sum_{i=1}^{e} f_r(e_i) = 1$, and that predicting the outcome correctly at each time provides a proportional payoff $o(e_i)$. Thus, at each step, if the environment happens to return state e_i, the agent's resources grow according to

$$r \rightarrow r' = o\,(e_i)\, f_r\,(e_i) r,$$

with the expectation that the payoff is large enough that $o(e_i) f_a(e_i) \geq 1$; otherwise, such an event type is not worthy of consideration and maybe should be avoided. Note that the agent will also need to dedicate time and resources to other activities that support this investment: being productive at work requires rest, food, shelter, family care, basic services, leisure time, and other things. These "costs" are always necessary regardless of the particular investment choice. In a scenario with choices, they are in effect directed toward alternative productive opportunities, $o(e_i) > 1$, through the differential allocation of the agent's time and effort. A certain amount of time, t, the most important quantity in this respect, is equivalent to resources through the cost of time in terms of wages, $y_W\, t = r$.[52]

The general idea is that in cities there are large sets of events that are, in principle, worth dedicating time and effort to. Then, after n_c cycles, the agent's resources will be $r_{n_C} = \prod_{j=1}^{n_C} o(e^j) f_r(e^j) r_0$, where e^j is the event type that occurred at cycle j. The average growth rate of resources over a time, t_c, in which n_c allocations were made, is then

$$\bar{\eta}_r = \lim_{n_C \to \infty} \frac{v_r}{n_C} \ln \frac{r_{n_C}}{r_0} = v_r \sum_{i=1}^{e} P(e_i) \ln o(e_i) f_r(e_i), \tag{9.35}$$

where we assumed that event types occur according to their underlying probability, $P(e_i)$, under the condition that the law of large numbers applies. (We are assuming implicitly that this probability is effectively stationary, at least over long time intervals, t_C.) The quantity $v_r = \dfrac{n_C}{t_c}$ is the average temporal rate at which choice allocations occur and returns are obtained. This quantity may vary over time, reflecting ebbs and flows of optimism and economic opportunity. For example, during recessions, agents may slow down their resource allocation rate because environmental opportunities may be more scarce or uncertain. For simplicity, we will work in units where v_r is constant. Nevertheless, there are interesting phenomena that require consideration of the variation of v_r over time.

We now see that the realm of choice for agents is defined by the allocation function $f_r(e_i)$. In general, people can allocate their resources in any way that suits them. However, there is a special allocation that *maximizes the average growth rate*. To determine what that is, we need to solve a constrained optimization problem because the allocations must add up to unity. This results in $f_r(e_i) = P(e_i)$, which is a strategy that in gambling is known as *proportional betting*.[53] It is interesting that this result is independent of the payoff. The maximum rate then becomes

$$\bar{\eta}_r = \overline{\ln o} - H(e), \tag{9.36}$$

where $\overline{\ln o} = \sum_{i=1}^{e} P(e_i) \ln o(e_i)$ and $H(e) = -\sum_{i=1}^{e} P(e_i) \ln P(e_i) \geq 0$ is the Shannon entropy of the environment! We see that for the growth rate to be positive, the average rewards, $\overline{\ln o}$, must be large enough. This means that there must be a "free lunch" in the environment, a source of net resource flows (free energy or cash). This situation may appear strange at first if we stay within the context of zero-sum games or fixed budget allocations as in microeconomics, but that is not so unusual. For example, farmers get a free lunch from the sun, and many forms of public support may be considered free lunches in cities, injecting money into the system. On the other hand, a less predictable environment (larger $H(e)$) hurts the agent proportionally. This is also interesting because it tells us that agents will do better in more controlled environments (with higher payoffs) and should, in this sense, try to avoid the full complexity and extent of choices in the city. This is a different sense in which specialization may be better: having a finite social horizon is a good thing, as long as it has positive opportunities.

We can now explore the meaning of this maximum growth rate: it is related to the contention that markets (and bookies!) are *perfect*! In gambling,[54] the payoffs $o(e_i)$ are given by an aggregator, such as a bookie or "the house," which has access to the resource allocation choices of many agents. Prediction markets work in a similar way: prices provide estimates of the participants' average beliefs.[55] The "market" estimate is $o(e_i) = 1/P_m(e_i)$, where $P_m(e_i)$ is the frequency of events estimated by the aggregator. Then, the average growth rate can be written as

$$\bar{\eta}_r = \sum_{i=1}^{e} P(e_i) \ln \frac{f_r(e_i)}{P(e_i)} \frac{P(e_i)}{P_m(e_i)} = D_{KL}(P\|P_m) - D_{KL}(P\|f_r), \tag{9.37}$$

where D_{KL} is again the Kullback-Leibler divergence (see appendix C) between the two probability estimates, a quantity that we already encountered in the context of neighborhood selection and deviations from Zipf's law. Recall that this is a positive quantity that measures how different two distributions are, vanishing when they coincide. In our situation here, this means that agents can benefit from the aggregator's wrong estimates, but they also pay a price for their ignorance of the real event probabilities. If *markets are perfect* estimators of these probabilities (they never are, but they could be good), the best someone can do is to also perfectly estimate the event probabilities. Then, their maximum growth rate would be zero! This simply reflects that the agent has no particular insight relative to the crowd and is, in the sense of information, *redundant*.[56] We conclude that unless there are free lunches, positive growth requires an information advantage over others. This is the ratcheting of ideas that keeps things interesting.

9.3.2 INDIVIDUAL INFORMATION

To understand this point better, we need to construct a slightly more elaborate picture of the growth rates by accounting for information *specific* to particular agents. It is well known in gambling and financial markets that if an agent has *inside knowledge* of the states of the environment, they can generate higher returns on their resources.[57] Let us call the information-bearing variables available to the agent *signals*, $s = s_1, s_2, \ldots, s_s$. Signals may be obtained from observing the environment or from the agent's past experience, education, or research (as in knowledge). They can also be obtained from other well-informed agents. It is interesting to think of examples that utilize these different sources of information, but the distinction will not be critical for our argument.

Let us suppose that at each time of resource allocation, the agent can consult these private signals. Then, the agent should apportion resources conditional on its knowledge, s. This makes the estimation of the growth rate become instead

$$\bar{\eta}_r = \sum_{i,j=1} P(e_i, s_j) \ln o(e_i) f_r(e_i | s_j). \tag{9.38}$$

Maximizing this rate gives the allocation choice, $f_r(e_i|s_j) = P(e_i|s_j)$. For *any payoff structure*, $o(e_i)$, the gain in average rate from using the signal (versus ignoring it) is

$$\Delta\bar{\eta}_r = I(e, s) = \sum_{i,j} P(e_i, s_j) \ln \frac{P(e_i, s_j)}{P(e_i)P(s_j)} , \tag{9.39}$$

which is another old friend: the *mutual information* $I(e, s)$ between the states of the environment and the signal. If there is no "free lunch" (fair odds), then $\bar{\eta}_r = I(e, s)$. We now see how information (or knowledge or ideas) is connected to the growth rate when agents make the best possible allocation of their resources (no misallocation). This means that the maximum growth rate is set by the personal information that the agent has about opportunities in its environment. This helps us understand *why good information is local and scarce*[58] and explains why there is an incentive to obtain it in the first place.

9.3.3   LEARNING

We have just seen that the better private information an agent has on the states of the environment, the higher its growth rate can be. Under these circumstances, it pays to learn.

In order to do so, the agent must have an internal model of the probability of the signal given the state of the environment, $P(s_j \mid e_i)$. This means that the agent has a model of what the signal would look like (statistically) if the environment were in a particular state. This model can be used in turn to *learn*, via Bayesian inference, the probability of the environment given the signal:

$$f_r(e_i|s_j) = \frac{P(s_j|e_i)}{P(s_j)} f_r(e_i). \tag{9.40}$$

This means that, over repeated cycles, the agent will observe joint states of the signal and environment, which allow it to improve its estimate of the conditional distribution toward its real probability, $f_r(e_i|s_j) \rightarrow P(e_i|s_j)$. In this way, the agent's life path is a source of income as well as evidence, which can drive the accumulation of *both* resources and information. For example, a naive agent may need to dedicate their time primarily to learning (*exploration*), while for longer times, when their knowledge of opportunities in the environment is better and more unique, they may primarily want to reap the fruits of this learning (*exploitation*). The preceding arguments indicate that, for long time horizons, investing in learning is fundamental because it leads to an improvement in the exponential growth of the agent's resources. To the extent that learning is imperfect, the growth rate will be diminished by a factor of $D_{KL}[P(e|s) \| f_r(e|s)]$, so the best learners can generate the highest returns over the long run.

9.3.4 THE AGGREGATION OF INFORMATION: REDUNDANCY AND SYNERGY

We have now derived the connection between the growth rate of resources for agents in a stochastic environment and knowledge of its opportunities. We would like to understand how this individual behavior translates to observed growth rates in the population.

To do this, we need to know how information aggregates in populations across scales. The critical point is that information does not follow the familiar rules of conserved quantities, such as energy or time, which just add up. Instead, information can be *redundant* or *synergistic*,[59] as we started to see in chapter 5. Redundant information means that several agents have the same knowledge. In other words, the second agent's knowledge is the same as the first agent's. This is typical of subsistence societies, where primary modes of production are replicated over the land. As a result, the total information in such a society is not much larger than that of a single household and does not scale up with total population size.[60] Such subsistence societies show very low rates of economic growth but on the upside can be very stable ($\gamma_s \simeq 0$). Recall from chapter 7 that this was characteristic of hunter-gatherer societies, a mode of living that dominated the history of our species.

Conversely, information can be *synergistic*, meaning that different agents have different knowledge of the environment, which, when taken together, leads to *greater information than the sum of the parts*. This occurs in interdependent "ecologies" and is typical of the deep divisions of labor and knowledge characteristic of cities, as we saw in chapter 5. The familiar parable of the *blind men and the elephant* is related to the property of information synergy: each man has only a limited but accurate perception of some of the features that make up an elephant. Based on this partial information, they make wrong (and comical) guesses of what they are perceiving. Putting the pieces together as a group, however, will tell them that it is an elephant.

In the case of synergy, information will scale up with the addition of every agent's knowledge, because each has some unique piece of the larger puzzle. Let us express these insights mathematically. The joint information for a set of variables (signals), $\{s_i\} = s_1, s_2, \ldots, s_N$, on some environmental state of the world, e, can be written as[61]

$$I(e;\{s_i\}) = H[e] - H[e|\{s_i\}] = -\sum_{i=1}^{N} \frac{\Delta H[e]}{\Delta s_i} - \sum_{i>j=1}^{N} \frac{\Delta^2 H[e]}{\Delta s_i \Delta s_j} - \cdots \frac{\Delta^N H[e]}{\Delta s_1 \ldots \Delta s_N}, \tag{9.41}$$

where the variations of the Shannon entropy $H[e]$ relative to the agent's knowledge are given by a chain rule of conditioning as

$$\frac{\Delta H[e]}{\Delta s_i} = H[e] - H[e|s_i] = I(e, s_i),$$

$$\frac{\Delta H[e]}{\Delta s_i \Delta s_j} = \frac{\Delta}{\Delta s_j}\left[\frac{\Delta H[e]}{\Delta s_i}\right] = H[e|\{s_i, s_j\}] - H[e|s_i] - H[e|s_j] + H[e] = I[e, s_i|s_j] - I(e|s_i), \quad (9.42)$$

and so on. There are a number of equivalent ways to write these relations by conditioning different sets of variables on others.[62] We can write the simplest example for a pair of agents, for which the joint information is given by

$$I(e;\{s_1, s_2\}) = I(e; s_1) + I(e; s_2) - R_I(e; s_1, s_2), \quad R_I(e; s_1, s_2) = I(s_1; s_2) - I(s_1; s_2|e). \quad (9.43)$$

The quantity $R_I(e; s_1, s_2)$ is known as the *coefficient of redundancy*; it can be positive, negative, or zero, corresponding to three different situations. When positive, the total information is less than the sum of the independent mutual information on our target problem, e, meaning that they contain some joint information $I(s_1; s_2) > I(s_1; s_2|e)$. When $R_I = 0$, the two agents have statistically independent information, and while they do not share common knowledge, there is also no incentive to aggregate their information in any specific way. The last case, $R_I < 0$, is known as *synergy* and corresponds to when the two agents have a priori separate information that becomes especially meaningful in determining e, since $I(s_1; s_2|e) > I(s_1, s_2)$. This means that the information known to the two agents is complementary in answering the questions posed by our environmental statistical opportunity. This reasoning generalizes to any number of variables representing larger groups and gives a compelling framework for calculating the scope of collective "intelligence" and, in the present context, the growth rate of collective resources.[63]

Consequently, maximizing the growth rate of a collective of learning agents leads to the maximization of their joint information on any given problem, which in turn requires *maximum synergy*. This means arranging agents in a relative organizational configuration where their individual information, expressed in their coordinated choices and actions, has minimal overlap (there is strong division of labor and knowledge) but at the same time is combined together so as to be most informative given a specific collective goal. This is the way extremely complex products and services can be created, be they airplanes or the daily edition of a newspaper.

9.3.5 CITIES AS ENGINES OF SYNERGY?

What then happens in cities—redundancy or synergy? Necessarily, there will be a bit of both. An argument for the value of the total information in the city can be given as follows. First, consider different professions as instantiations of different productive knowledge. In US cities and according to the theory of chapter 5, the total number of different professions scales with city size approximately as $D_S(N) = D_{S_0} N^v$, $v \approx 1 - \delta = 5/6$. This is a measure of specialization because it implies that the number of different tasks per person is declining with city size as $\frac{D_S(N)}{N} = D_{S_0} N^{-\delta}$, which is observed in occupational data (chapter 5). If these agents have a fixed total "productive" time, t_T, allocated to all tasks, they will therefore spend more time per task by a factor of about $t_T(N) = t_0 N^{\delta}$. This implies a proportionately larger number of learning opportunities for getting better at the specific task. Thus, we may estimate that the average information per individual will scale as $I(e; s) = D_{s_0} N^{-\delta} t_0 N^{\delta} = D_{s_0} t_0$, independent of city size. That is, even though in larger cities there are more professions, each with different specialized knowledge, there are fewer per capita. This is compensated for by greater depth of "learning by doing,"[64] gaining more information on the processes involved. As a consequence, in an urban system, the overall growth rate of income can be independent of city size (recall Gibrat's law, now for economic growth), even though it will depend on how many people can participate in the collective learning process at the national level.

9.3.6 DISCUSSION: INFORMATION, PUBLIC GOODS, AND THE EMERGENCE OF INSTITUTIONS

We have now seen how important it is for humans to be able to collaborate by pooling resources and knowledge in order to generate higher incomes and growth. The institutions that promote these dynamics—besides cities—are themselves the product of processes that promote these net advantages of large-scale human sociality. These institutions have many distinct purposes, ranging from conflict resolution, to the provision of basic services, to the management of common resources.

Here we should recognize a body of work on the emergence of social and economic institutions, and the work of Elinor Ostrom in particular (see table 9.1). Ostrom's seminal research unified many instances of fieldwork and case studies, which she used to identify and synthesize a number of factors that influence—positively and negatively—the emergence of organizations for the sustainable management of common resources. It is interesting to analyze these various factors in light of our discussion of economic growth. Ostrom found that common resource collapse tends to be associated with very large, highly valuable, open-access systems, where the resource harvesters are diverse, do not communicate, and fail to develop rules and norms for common management. Ostrom singled out a number of factors that are especially important (table 9.1) and emphasized that "simple blueprints do not work" for creating institutions managing resources sustainably. They must instead emerge out of context-appropriate collective action.

A full discussion of how urban environments solve collective-action and management problems is beyond the scope of this section. However, we reflect on how cities have found solutions to typical challenges of common resource management posed by the *size of the resource system*, its *productivity*, its *number of users*, or the *lack*

Table 9.1 Ostrom's key variables for the emergence of collective institutions

Key variables	Effect	Reason
Size of resource system	Negative	More difficult self-organization
Productivity of system	Mixed	Moderate scarcity triggers organization
Resource mobility	Negative	Higher costs of monitoring
Number of users	Negative/positive	High transaction costs/network effects
Leadership	Positive	Know-how, respect, mobilizing capacity
Norms and social capital	Positive	Shared morals, ethics, trust
Knowledge of resource dynamics	Positive	Appropriate timescales and actions
Importance to users	Positive	Benefits and incentives of cooperation
Free collective-choice rules	Positive	Lower transaction costs, better contextual fit

Note: Although most of these factors have been extrapolated from case studies of natural resource management—forests and fisheries—it is interesting to discuss them in light of mechanisms of collective organization and growth in cities and urban systems.

Sources: Elinor Ostrom, "A General Framework for Analyzing Sustainability of Social-Ecological Systems," *Science* 325, no. 5939 (July 24, 2009): 419–422, https://doi.org/10.1126/science .1172133; Elinor Ostrom, "Crossing the Great Divide: Coproduction, Synergy, and Development," *World Development* 24, no. 6 (June 1996): 1073–1087, https://doi.org/10.1016/0305 -750X(96)00023-X.

of knowledge of the resource dynamics. Indeed, urban scaling illustrates how network effects can be brought to bear on some of these issues, often also requiring supportive transformations of new institutions (public works departments, metropolitan authorities, police departments) and infrastructure (metro systems, public parks, and other amenities) and a dedicated effort regarding education and research. The emergence of *leadership* is ubiquitous in urban environments in neighborhoods, politics, and firms, as is the emergence of *local norms* and diverse forms of *social capital*, from collective efficacy to urban subcultures (chapter 6). Urban environments also typically allow a larger diversity of organizations, which contributes to a larger scope and experimentation with *collective-choice rules*. Indeed, the local urban environments where many of these processes are lacking have been identified as places of concentrated disadvantage in the context of the study of neighborhood effects (chapter 6). Other issues, such as the *mobility of resources* and indeed the *number and diversity of users*, pose perennial challenges to processes of human development and sustainable growth not only in cities but in their interaction with more remote environments, their societies, and ecosystems. It is interesting that at present many leading cities all over the world are working to incorporate some of these remote consequences of how they operate and consume resources into their sustainability and resiliency plans.

A final point, not emphasized so much by Ostrom, is the role of *knowledge as a public good*. As with any other public good, knowledge requires effort and collective action so it can be preserved and expanded. Romer[65] emphasizes that the nonrival character of knowledge creates disincentives for private economic actors—individuals and firms—to produce it. This is because the total value that knowledge creates will be captured not only by its creators but also by society at large. It therefore requires social investment and support for its creation and for the redistribution of its benefits.

EPILOGUE: OUR CONSTRUCTED NICHE

We have come full circle now, to the key idea that growth and change are the result of new productive information, specifically good information on the allocation of resources to events with high (and, whenever possible, open-ended) returns. Seizing "free lunches" is critical; channeling local and scarce information into productive collective arrangements is the name of the game. Building environments where all this is possible—and indeed *par for the course*—is the key to fulfilling humans' collective potential as learners and creative agents.

We have seen how traditional economic models struggle to implement these general ideas in the absence of a formal treatment of information and of the explicit consideration of different levels of cooperation and selection. Adopting a framework of statistical population dynamics and treating strategic human choices about environmental possibilities in terms of trade-offs and information fills this gap and allows us to study the origins of growth and change across different scales.

Much of this calculus of growth depends on the consequences of alternative choices of where to live, where to work, whom to collaborate with, and whom to avoid. Because these choices are framed by existing social organizations—including cities— they are *path dependent*, amplifying seed ideas and organizations to loom much larger in the future but not necessarily always pursuing the absolute best scenarios, which must be discovered through learning. Because the production and strategic application of knowledge and resources must involve large networks of diverse people and organizations, the emergent dynamics of growth and change are naturally subject to synergy, superlinear effects, and associated increasing returns to scale. Creating and sustaining cities as large social reactors becomes key.

The structure of these choices presupposes two important facts: (1) the importance of cities as the environments that can seed and nurture new ideas and organizations, and (2) the ability of people and organizations to access opportunities and make choices while having an incentive to learn and acquire new information. Each human life is a complex assembly of potentially precious information, playing out through the structure of our life paths and our socioeconomic relations.

The subject of cities as environments associated with valuable and local information, innovation, and higher incomes has been amply covered in this book. The issue of choice and learning is, of course, at the heart of a much more fundamental understanding of processes of human development, which at present remains inadequate.

The evidence and theory discussed throughout this book suggest that endogenous rates of economic growth in frontier urban systems are low, on the order of 1%–3% a year. This translates into a doubling every generation. Studies of mobility and migration of adults seem to partially reinforce this association, in that people's economic potential seems to form early in life.[66] Thus, sustaining economic growth requires providing the largest number of people with the best access to knowledge in the largest number of places and endowing them from early on in their life paths with environments where opportunities and collaboration are natural, safe, and likely to be profitable. Most cities have plenty of ground for improvement in each of these matters.

These standards are relative to other places and to the past, but we have seen that cities have played and continue to play the major role in creating the complex adaptive systems where large-scale sociality is possible and where collective-action problems are (eventually, painfully) worked out via interacting networks of people and institutions of many kinds.

In this sense, cities are a kind of social technology—a means to a higher end. They are the social reactors where creative but limited creatures such as ourselves can interact intensely to take advantage of their numbers in terms of highly textured, interdependent, and diverse arrangements of effort and knowledge. Evolutionary biologists refer to "constructed niches" as external environments built by organisms to benefit their kind and their descendants,[67] channeling evolutionary forces over time to their own benefit. I believe that cities are our constructed master niche: the primary environments where an open-ended, sustainable future for our kind and for life on earth may be imagined and constructed. They may just allow us to survive the ever-greater crises of our unstable and inventive history by the skin of our teeth, one dream of bright lights and one hustle at a time, billions and billions of times.

10

WHAT ARE CITIES FOR?
THE CHALLENGES AHEAD

The chief function of the city is to convert power into form, energy into culture, dead matter into the living symbols of art, biological reproduction into social creativity.
—Lewis Mumford, *The City in History*

10.1   WHAT ARE CITIES FOR?

We have come a long way from classical models of cities to a more statistical and detailed perspective of how urban environments work empirically in many different contexts and across diverse scales. We have seen how many urban processes can be understood theoretically and also be measured across levels of organization. We showed how cities likely arose in history and identified and measured many of their properties that have persisted over time and space. We have seen how development and change can occur naturally in urban environments and at the same time express stark inequalities among people and between neighborhoods, in part because of spatial sorting and selection. We have also shown how drivers of fundamental change, such as demographic and economic growth, are general properties of urban systems but not so much of single cities, and rely specifically on large-scale exchanges of material goods, energy, and information between cities of all sizes, each deriving certain advantages and costs. This kind of systemic dynamics across settlements of all sizes requires a level of integration and coordination that has become common only recently. This is the era in which we live today, when urbanization has become widespread and where processes of exponential change in time, including economic growth, can be sustained over the long run, provided individuals can invest their time and effort creatively and act collectively in their common interest. Bringing all this together into a coherent theory shows that there is a general logic about cities as processes.

We can now reflect on Jane Jacobs's three pieces of advice on how best to study cities, described at the beginning of this book. We have indeed focused on urban *processes* such as social interactions, mobility over space and time, active cost-benefit management, learning, and investment of resources and information toward collective production and exchange. Elaborating these general processes in ever-larger networks, we have found new routes for understanding cities as (approximate) spatial equilibria, for deriving their structural complexity in terms of professions and neighborhoods, for understanding the first cities and their "urban package" of technologies and institutions, and for demystifying the microscopic foundations of learning and strategic investment underpinning economic growth.

We used *deductive reasoning* to derive general properties of cities, such as scaling relations and the laws of geography, as averages of processes over populations and time. We have seen that such "laws" describe the system as a whole but, like any average, do not actually apply to any specific individual or even to any particular city. This is an important point that often leads to confusion and that I hope this book clarifies.

Finally, the most difficult piece of advice from Jane Jacobs was that we should seek *unaveraged clues*. This point only makes sense in the light of *information* and related measures of structural diversity: average too much and all the sources of novelty, innovation, and future solutions in cities blur away. Creating ways of thinking that allow us to identify and measure—not just appreciate—the uniqueness of individuals and places, and how their ideas and inventions may be the basis for future systemic solutions, is key for understanding how cities can indeed be engines of innovation and prosperity. Ultimately, we achieved this by being able to unpack general averages in terms of finer and finer constituent processes through a hierarchical statistical approach to urban dynamics. This allowed us to connect individual behavior over the short term to whole urban areas and even urban systems over the long term, sliding the scale and sharpening the focus as needed. This methodology allowed us to derive that information does not aggregate across collectives as other conserved quantities do; it can remain local and scarce, yet generative and powerful, as it is integrated into synergetic arrangements in social collectives.

Along the way, a number of general themes have emerged and recurred. Let us bring them together to reflect on the ultimate function of cities in human societies.

First, even though we have often used the analytical device of thinking of cities as spatial equilibria, we have found that, at a more fundamental level, living in cities is always a dynamical balancing act, constantly matching costs to benefits that sometimes are best conceived as energetic and at other times economic. This *balancing act* requires agency and is implemented in diverse ways by individuals, households, firms, and governments, each in their own realm. Understanding how each of these agents balances the costs and benefits of urban environments creates an important meeting point for ideas of feedback control and homeostasis, scaling, and stochastic growth and statistics, which together allow us to think of cities in a rich and nuanced way across scales, from microscopic individual choices to the "laws of geography."

In managing these costs and benefits, the *connectivity* of agents is everything. Living in the city is a condition of deep interdependence with other people and the organizations they form for economic production and exchange, civics, politics, services, education, and more. Making good choices in terms of the present and the future becomes essential for living well. This is always a work in progress, involving discovery and some struggle in dense and rich environments replete with socioeconomic opportunities but also characterized by barriers and finite social horizons. These features of social networks in cities have many general implications, which include the fluidity of social life in large cities and their associated capacity to produce change but simultaneously the impossibility for general optimization.[1] Complex systems are not perfect systems; the point is that they can keep improving indefinitely.

The issue of *connectivity* is especially poignant in light of inequality, segregation, poverty, and other challenges of human development. Being disconnected in the city—in terms of transportation, housing, services, civil rights, and information—is especially disabling because subsistence production and the independence it affords is not an option. The condition of poverty is more fundamentally a state of disconnection than of low monetary income, as the capabilities approach to human development makes clear.[2] Deficits of connectivity can be temporary or more permanent. All great cities absorb a staggering number of poor migrants, echoing the book's opening quotation. Cities excel—relative to other social environments—at opening up pathways for their human development and eventual prosperity, but too often cities also exclude some people, passively or actively, taking actions that create ghettos, forgo integration, create barriers to learning and entrepreneurship, and close opportunities for development. There are elements of this tragic dynamics in every city I know. These are situations where cities become less than what they are meant to be, with consequences not only for the populations excluded but also—because of network effects—for the prosperity and future possibilities of the entire population.

This brings us to the last and most recurring theme: *information*. Information in cities is both structural and the driver of temporal change. We have seen how the diversity of cities, measured as professions, business types, and neighborhood composition, should be described as information in the sense that the patterns manifested by actual cities are different from more random situations with the same average ingredients, entailing agency and choice. In this sense, the balances and connectivity of cities are subtly interwoven, encoding nonrandom patterns of structural (economic) complexity that express strong synergies between the diverse skills and knowledge of different people and their organizations.[3] We have seen how paying the high costs of increasing connectivity in urban environments only makes sense in light of the productivity gains that emerge from these deep divisions and articulations of knowledge and action. This state of heterogeneity, density, diversity, interdependence, and complementarity is then the condition that allows human societies to embed ever more information and to generate greater socioeconomic collective capacity, which is at the root of progress toward human well-being and prosperity.

This is ultimately what cities are for. Lewis Mumford expresses it best in the quotation that began this chapter. Large cities have very little to offer the rest of the world that is material. What they do offer is indeed *form, culture, living symbols, art,* and *social creativity,* among other primarily *informational* things. That these pieces of information become the most valuable things of all, the ones that are most difficult to create, and the most enduring throughout history is a tribute to the complex nature and the fundamental importance of cities. We just do not know how to create them in any other way.

10.2 CHALLENGES AHEAD

Provided that some groups on earth continue either muddling or revolutionizing themselves into periods of economic development, we can be absolutely sure of a few things about future cities.

The cities will not be smaller, simpler or more specialized as cities of today. Rather, they will be more intricate, comprehensive, diversified and larger than today's and will have even more complicated jumbles of old and new things as ours do.

—Jane Jacobs, *The Economy of Cities*

The test and value of any body of scientific knowledge hinges on the success of its application in real situations. Urban science is predicated on the creation of general knowledge that can apply to our existing cities but that should also provide guidance and frame solutions to *entirely new situations* far from present or past experience.

To that end, let us finish by discussing what, in my view, are the greatest challenges ahead not only for urban science but also for our rapidly urbanizing planet. This choice of challenges is dictated by planetary trends that are hard to reverse, including human demography, universal human rights to development and economic growth in low-income communities, the right to the city, the imperatives of development that is more sustainable, and the prospect for the complete substitution of our current energy technology systems to achieve decarbonization goals and control climate change.

10.2.1 GIGACITIES

Based on standard demographic trends, it is projected that in the next few decades we will reach the historical peak of human population worldwide. As part of these trends, the largest cities that will ever exist will come into being. By the end of this century, each of the world's 10 largest cities will likely have a population exceeding 50 million people, possibly reaching as much as 70 or 80 million; I like to call them *gigacities*. This would be twice as large as the largest city that ever existed: contemporary Tokyo, with a population of about 40 million in its metropolitan area.

Table 10.1 Population projections for the world's 10 largest cities

Rank	City	Projected population in 2025	City	Projected population in 2050	City	Projected population in 2075	City	Projected population in 2100
1	Tokyo	36.40	Mumbai	42.40	Kinshasa	58.42	Lagos	88.30
2	Mumbai	26.39	Delhi	36.16	Mumbai	57.86	Kinshasa	83.53
3	Delhi	22.50	Dhaka	35.19	Lagos	57.20	Dar-es-Salaam	73.68
4	Dhaka	22.02	Kinshasa	35.00	Delhi	49.34	Mumbai	67.24
5	São Paulo	21.43	Kolkata	33.04	Kolkata	45.09	Delhi	57.33
6	Mexico City	21.01	Lagos	32.63	Karachi	43.37	Khartoum	56.59
7	New York	20.63	Tokyo	32.62	Dhaka	42.45	Niamey	56.15
8	Kolkata	20.56	Karachi	31.70	Dar-es-Salaam	37.49	Dhaka	54.25
9	Shanghai	19.41	New York	24.77	Cairo	33.00	Kolkata	52.40
10	Karachi	19.10	Mexico City	24.33	Manila	32.75	Kabul	50.30

Note: Numbers for projected populations are given in millions. Note how all top 10 cities are expected to have populations exceeding 50 million people by the end of this century. All the world's largest cities will be in Asia and Africa, with none in Europe and only a few in the Americas.

Source: Daniel Hoornweg and Kevin Pope, "Population Predictions for the World's Largest Cities in the 21st Century," *Environment and Urbanization 29*, no. 1 (April 1, 2017): 195–216, https://doi.org/10.1177/0956247816663557.

Needless to say, we do not know how to create or manage cities that are this large, especially because these urban areas will be part of still urbanizing systems in Africa and in Asia (see table 10.1). At present, these urban areas have immense infrastructure deficits and suffer from weak public and civic institutions. Cities such as Lagos, Nigeria, projected to become the world's largest by the end of the century, or Mumbai, India, projected to peak just before Lagos, are examples of some of the world's most challenged urban areas today, with more than 50% of their populations living in slums. Instead, we would like to imagine a future where the fast-growing cities of today's low-income nations can build their own steady path to development and become the beacons of urbanism for the twenty-first century, much as Tokyo and New York City were for the twentieth and London and Paris for the nineteenth.

What will it take? If the problem of fast-developing cities is "too many people," then "too many people" must also be the solution. These people must work together to invent new ways to be interdependent, connected to each other along many productive dimensions, and learn new forms of information to manifest the increasing returns to scale and the capacity for human development and economic growth that is latent in each city and that is especially explosive in cities that are so large. Doing so will require political courage and vision to enable the agency of much more people. Knowledge of how cities work will no doubt frame solutions but will not determine what these cities will be. The reader can nevertheless go ahead and use some of what was learned in this book to project the land area, volume of infrastructure, level of congestion, and size of the economy that these cities will achieve by using urban scaling. Can you imagine how fast and exciting life in Lagos will be in 2100? (Well, at least you can calculate it.)

To frame a possible vision for these urban futures, it is not too hard to imagine Tokyo as it exists today (figure 1.1) and "double it" (with some nonlinear scaling) to produce a future Lagos or Mumbai. The challenge of these gigacities is not primarily technical or financial but rather a problem of innovation, cultural change, and Politics, which must emerge to solve collective-action problems that are appropriate to new cultures and contexts but must also operate at an unprecedented scale in human history. Failure is not an option; success will be incredibly exciting!

10.2.2 SLUMS: HUMAN DEVELOPMENT IN A MILLION NEIGHBORHOODS

Slums and informal settlements are one of the starkest expressions of urban poverty anywhere. We saw in chapter 6 that there are about 1 billion people worldwide living in around 1 million informal and underserviced neighborhoods. While slums occur primarily in fast-growing low- and middle-income nations, there are informal settlements in most urban areas, including homeless encampments in American and European cities and overcrowded quarters in many developed Asian cities. A rule of thumb is that about 20% of the population in each city cannot afford market housing. In cities where housing provision is especially under pressure—because of barriers to development, land scarcity, high construction costs, or speculation—this fraction is easily higher.

This problem is best grasped by a term used by urbanist John F. C. Turner,[4] who referred to "housing as a verb," meaning that housing is not only shelter but also a necessary condition for obtaining basic services, for having an address, for privacy and safety, and for access to emergency services and most forms of civic support. Systematically creating these and other essential bases for human development in a million poor neighborhoods requires that we engage with an incremental path of improvements that gradually better connects people, provides them with incentives and bridges for developing their human capital and socioeconomic participation, and subjects all agents in the city to a cost-benefit logic where positive-sum gains between advantaged and disadvantaged populations become the norm. If the goal of eradicating poverty worldwide in the next decade is to become a reality, we have to imagine running the evolutionary and ecological processes discussed in this book, which create cities as networks, forward at a much higher speed and in more equitable ways.

This is now possible from a perspective of integrating technology, information, and community organization, but achieving a worldwide collaboration for human development in neighborhoods, cocreating formal knowledge and practical solutions, remains a challenge.

10.2.3 SHRINKING CITIES

The counterpoint to the gigacities of South Asia and Africa and to the proliferation of slums is the prospect for population declines in most other parts of the world. This phenomenon is already common in Europe, high-income Asian nations, and the Americas, but it will intensify and become more typical of more places in the decades ahead. Nations in eastern and southern Europe, Japan, and regions such as northeast China and the midwestern US are "poster children" for the challenges of cities facing population and economic contraction. It is especially important to learn how to deal with shrinking cities in these contexts, because the present examples of postindustrial transitions have been particularly painful and, arguably, waste so much human potential and infrastructure.

A relatively simple solution would be to allow worldwide population migration between places with strong population growth and those experiencing population decline. However, current resistance to much smaller immigration flows into high-income nations signals that such solutions may be politically unacceptable. In the absence of substantial foreign migration, current policy approaches have been singularly inadequate for reversing the fates of shrinking cities—big and small.

The most common denominator for shrinking cities is manufacturing specialization that became irrelevant or ceased to be competitive, especially in the face of globalization. Other common examples of decline, often in smaller towns, deal with the demise of mining and other primary industries. Most of these cities are hard to revive in terms of reversing population losses through migration and reinstating sustained economic growth. Postindustrial cities that eventually stopped shrinking did so partly against a backdrop of large national investment, profound economic restructuring, and by starting to capture population from existing local sources of churn, such as universities and colleges. Even then, urban areas such as Buffalo, Detroit, Pittsburgh, and many other postindustrial cities are substantially smaller today than they were a half century ago.

Over the next few decades, with sharper demographic stabilization and declines becoming the norm, these challenges will become much harder to tackle and much more widespread. Present trends in nations already losing population on the whole, such as Japan or nations in eastern and southern Europe, show that decline is not equally distributed along the urban hierarchy and that the largest cities (Tokyo, Moscow, Milan) may actually fare better (and continue to grow) even as many smaller urban and rural areas shrink. If such trends persist, we may end up with an even more urbanized world not only because of the growth of larger cities but also because of the faster decline of rural towns and smaller cities.

The main difficulty of maintaining balances in terms of costs and benefits between large cities and smaller towns along an urban hierarchy is twofold. On the side of benefits, the best and most critical public goods and services—such as advanced health care and education—are typically only available in larger urban areas. This means that, with greater choice, both younger and older populations may prefer to live in well-connected larger cities than in more isolated small towns. On the side of costs, the lag between material infrastructure and population change that when cities grow quickly plays out so tragically in the form of slums also plays a detrimental role when cities shrink. This is manifested through a legacy of aging infrastructure and associated maintenance costs that can hardly be paid for under the network effects that a smaller population can sustain. The compounding of increased relative costs and decreasing relative benefits can then entangle shrinking cities in a vicious cycle of growing debt and decay, creating situations where people and businesses choose to emigrate to places with better demographic and economic prospects.

Urban science, and specifically the mathematical models of cities developed in this book, allows us to foresee and predict these systemic dynamics and identify situations where, in principle, vicious cycles can be managed and even reversed. How this type of understanding will play out in urban systems where *most cities are shrinking* remains a huge challenge for the decades to come.

10.2.4 DECARBONIZATION OF ENERGY SYSTEMS

The advent of large cities with more than about a million people came about only with the massive adoption of fossil fuels as the primary source of energy supply in modern human societies. As we now know, the use of fossil fuels on such a large scale tips the chemical composition of the earth's atmosphere, specifically disrupting the global carbon cycle and promoting the capture of solar energy in the atmosphere and the oceans. The associated greenhouse effects cause climate change, ocean acidification, polar cap melting, seawater rise, and biodiversity loss. These compounding challenges are creating a planetary crisis that threatens life on earth and human aspirations for global sustained development.

The solution to this crisis is also abundantly clear: decouple human energy generation and use from the carbon cycle through the direct capture of renewable energy from the sun via solar panels and wind turbines. Because of very fast technological change, these transformations are now becoming not only possible but also tangible and economically attractive. A global transformation of our energy systems may be achievable in as little as a couple of decades, perhaps in just enough time to avert the worst consequences of climate change.

For cities, replacing the current dominant systems of fossil fuel energy generation, distribution, and use is a bit akin to a heart transplant. We must know a lot about the energy systems of cities and all their social, economic, and health consequences so that performing this substitution does not kill the patient.

Thinking about this transition from the perspective of any large city suggests some of the contours of the challenges ahead as well as the solutions. First, cities are not created to save energy; they are environments displaying some of the largest power densities on earth (energy per unit time and per unit area). For example, a typical block in Manhattan consumes energy at a rate of 1,000 kWh per square meter per year. In physical units, this is a power density of over 100 W/m^2. Given current technology limitations, this is a larger energy flow than we can get from the sun in the same location, which implies that large cities will continue to have to import a substantial fraction of their power as we transition to renewables (figure 10.1).

Second, because cities have such high power usage, there are many opportunities for efficiency gains. We already saw in chapter 3 that the shape and materials of buildings influence power usage considerably. Mobility and transportation were one of our main focuses in terms of theory, and in this sector there is scope for vast efficiency improvements through electrification.[5]

Renewable energy generation has also made inroads into mainstream energy systems, because it is becoming exponentially cheaper. For example, the price of energy generated by solar panels has decreased by a factor of about seven (from $350 to $50 per megawatt-hour) since 2012 and is now cheaper than energy generated by fossil fuels in many sunny locations, though storage still needs to improve substantially and various subsidies (especially to fossil fuels) and technological and financial "lock in" make the picture more complicated.

If we bravely extrapolate these trends into the future, what would cities be like if energy became essentially free and green? Returning to our recurring themes, this

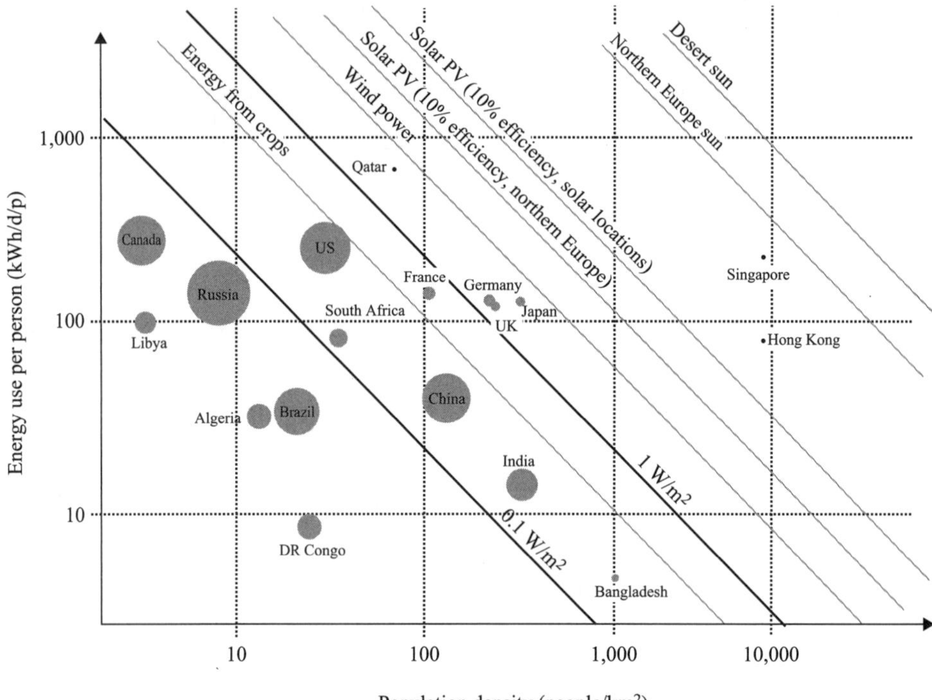

10.1 Power density consumption per capita versus the population density of select nations, including several city-states. Notice how at present the density of solar energy production is typically lower than the power consumption density in large cities, implying that a fraction of their power must be imported from suburban and rural areas.
Source: Adapted from David J. C. MacKay, www.withouthotair.com.

would make every process in the city cheaper, allowing new savings and reinvestment opportunities that can generate new knowledge and substantial growth! Second, it should allow us to recycle almost everything, making the economy much more *circular*,[6] which because of basic thermodynamic considerations can only be done at the expense of more energy. Third, it is critical to foresee where and how vast amounts of new renewable energy will be produced. There is a tangible prospect in many urban areas that each building in low-density suburbs could supply the central business district. Then, the cycle of energy production and consumption could be internalized at the level of many metropolitan areas. If these trends were compounded with more circular food production and material flows within urban areas, then the impact of urbanized human activity could be contained in the relatively small regions circumscribed by cities. These trends may be beneficial to natural environments, raising the potential for limiting human ecological footprints and allowing the rewilding of many current land uses. But they will also throw urban systems completely off balance, making larger cities more self-sufficient and removing some of the current economic rationale for smaller cities and towns to exist as population centers specializing in primary production and manufacturing.

10.2.5 GLOBAL SUSTAINABLE DEVELOPMENT GOALS

All the major challenges just discussed come together in one grand goal of creating processes of global development that are fair, environmentally sustainable, and open-ended. This is ultimately the practical objective of urban science,[7] the holy grail of interdisciplinary knowledge where the humanities, social sciences, ecology and evolution, the physical sciences, and engineering must converge to create something new. At this point in our discussion, I hope to have convinced the reader that such an objective is not so far-fetched and that in fact it may be conceived as an extrapolation of the processes identified and analyzed in this book.

There is currently a set of internationally agreed goals and a policy framework[8] to achieve global sustainable development over the next few decades, with critical progress needed by 2030. Cities all around the world are taking the lead, often by setting more ambitious goals of their own. For example, 30 of the largest cities in the world have just announced that they have reached "peak carbon."[9] Surely many challenges remain, especially those connected with the sustainability of the world's new gigacities and their kindred urban areas in rapidly developing parts of the world, but if you can make it *there*—in New York City, London, Paris, Tokyo, or Shanghai—you can make it anywhere.

Even as we contemplate the political turmoil, congestion, pollution, and sometimes the conflict in our cities, we should remember that these challenges also are part of a more urban world. When cities are allowed to work, each of these challenges can be brought to the surface and tackled, mitigated, and sometimes eliminated. Solutions require courage, optimism, and collaboration and arise from new knowledge and new forms of action. Creating a world that is more just, more sustainable, and that continues to nurture and promote the human imagination and well-being isn't easy, but that is what cities are for; what they are capable of. We just do not know how to do it in any other way.

APPENDIX A: BACKGROUND DERIVATIONS FOR THE CORE-PERIPHERY MODEL

Here we provide some additional rationale and derivations supporting the mathematical calculations of the core-periphery model.

A.1 ELASTICITY OF SUBSTITUTION

Functions of the form of equation (2.4) are part of a family of utility functions known as *constant elasticity of substitution* functions, introduced in a famous paper by Ken Arrow and his collaborators[1] to characterize how the consumption of one good may be replaced by another.

We have mentioned without proof that the parameter σ_s measures the elasticity of substitution. We now provide the standard derivation here for completeness.

The elasticity of substitution for two products, i and j, is defined mathematically by the double logarithmic derivative

$$\sigma_S = \frac{d \ln \dfrac{q_i}{q_j}}{d \ln \dfrac{dU}{dq_j} \bigg/ \dfrac{dU}{dq_i}}. \tag{A.1}$$

The derivatives of the utility relative to the quantity of good i consumed q_i, $\dfrac{dU}{dq_i}$, are known in economics jargon as *marginal utilities* (marginal = derivative of). The quantity $\dfrac{dU}{dq_j} \bigg/ \dfrac{dU}{dq_i}$ is known as the marginal rate of substitution of i by j. It measures the ratio of the change in utility from consuming one product versus another. Starting with equation (2.6), the calculation is straightforward but tedious. The best strategy is to write the marginal utilities in terms of logarithmic derivatives:

$$\frac{dU}{dq_i} = \frac{q_i}{U} \frac{d \ln U}{d \ln q_i} \rightarrow \frac{\dfrac{dU}{dq_j}}{\dfrac{dU}{dq_i}} = \left(\frac{q_i}{q_j} \right)^{\left(1 - \frac{\sigma_S - 1}{\sigma_S} \right)}. \tag{A.2}$$

Substituting back into the equation for the elasticity of substitution (A.1), we get

$$\sigma_S = \frac{d \ln \dfrac{q_i}{q_j}}{d \ln \left(\dfrac{q_i}{q_j} \right)^{\frac{1}{\sigma_S}}}, \tag{A.3}$$

which is the desired result.

A.2 THE RELATION BETWEEN PRICES AND CONSUMPTION

Prices, p, for goods, q, can be obtained from utility functions by taking derivatives, as these are *conjugate variables* in the sense that $p = \dfrac{dU}{dq}$. Using the specific form of utility function

$$c_M = \left[\sum_{i=1}^{n_M} q_i^{(\sigma_S - 1)/\sigma_S} \right]^{\sigma_S/(\sigma_S - 1)} \tag{A.4}$$

gives

$$p_i = c_M^{\frac{1}{\sigma_S}} q_i^{-\frac{1}{\sigma_S}} \rightarrow q_i = p_i^{-\sigma_S} c_M \sim p_i^{-\sigma_S}. \tag{A.5}$$

This also implies that $\dfrac{q_i}{q_j} = \left(\dfrac{p_i}{p_j} \right)^{-\sigma_S}$. Substituting this expression for q_i in c_M and bringing out the terms in j that are not summed over gives

$$q_i = \frac{p_i^{-\sigma_S}}{\left[\sum_{j=1}^{n_M} p_j^{1-\sigma_S} \right]^{\sigma_S/(\sigma_S - 1)}} c_M. \tag{A.6}$$

Using this expression in the total expenditure on products,

$$\sum_{i=1}^{n_M} q_i p_i = \left[\sum_{i=1}^{n_M} p_i^{1-\sigma_S} \right]^{\frac{1}{\sigma_S - 1}} c_M, \tag{A.7}$$

suggests that we define the price index as

$$\bar{p} = \left[\sum_{i=1}^{n_M} p_i^{1-\sigma_S} \right]^{\frac{1}{1-\sigma_S}}, \tag{A.8}$$

since it normalizes expenditures in units of utility. When we consider two regions with transportation costs associated with travel between them, there will be two components to the sum inside the brackets, involving *home market* products and imported products subject to transportation costs. Expressing prices in terms of wages, for convenience, leads to region-specific cost indices,

$$\bar{p}_1 = \left[f_1 y_{w_1}^{1-\sigma_S} + (1 - f_1) \left(\frac{y_{w_2}}{\tau} \right)^{1-\sigma_S} \right]^{1/(1-\sigma_S)},$$

$$\bar{p}_2 = \left[f_1 \left(\frac{y_{w_1}}{\tau} \right)^{1-\sigma_S} + (1 - f_1) y_{w_2}^{1-\sigma_S} \right]^{1/(1-\sigma_S)}, \tag{A.9}$$

which show that a region with few workers that imports most of its products has a high "cost of living" and a lower real wage.

A.3   FIRMS' BEHAVIOR AND THE RELATION BETWEEN PRICES AND WAGES

It is assumed that firms produce products such that the corresponding labor input is $l_b = F_b + cq_M$. This means that there are some fixed labor inputs, F_b, and then a component that is proportional to the quantity of product.

Then the profits, π_M, of a manufacturing firm, taking only labor costs of production into account, are

$$\pi_M = pq - l_b y_w = pq - (F_b + cq)y_w. \tag{A.10}$$

Maximizing these costs leads to the price,

$$\frac{d\pi_M}{dq} = \frac{dp}{dq}q + p + cy_w = 0. \tag{A.11}$$

Recalling that $p \propto q^{-1/\sigma_S}$, $\dfrac{dp}{dq} = -\dfrac{1}{\sigma_S}\dfrac{p}{q}$, which implies the price

$$p = \frac{c}{1 - 1/\sigma_S} y_w. \tag{A.12}$$

This shows that the coordination of firm plus consumer behavior makes prices proportional to wages. We can also use the fact that profits are zero in a market with free entry (firms are assumed to develop until profit is driven to zero) to say that the firm's output is

$$q = \frac{F_b}{c}(\sigma_S - 1). \tag{A.13}$$

The associated labor input is $l_b = F_b\,\sigma_S$. Note how both production and labor inputs are independent of prices. As a consequence, considering our two zones in the core-periphery model, we can say that $\dfrac{p_1}{p_2} = \dfrac{y_{w_1}}{y_{w_2}}$ but also note that both production and labor inputs are the same across the two regions, since $q_1 = q_2 = \dfrac{F_b}{c}(\sigma_S - 1)$ and $l_{b1} = l_{b2} = F_b\,\sigma_S$. This means that the output per firm is the same in each region. Given that each firm produces a different good, this also implies that the total labor in each region is proportional to the number of firms and products, implying that $\dfrac{N_{M1}}{N_{M2}} = \dfrac{n_{M1}}{n_{M2}}$.

A.4   SYSTEM OF EQUATIONS AND NUMERICAL SOLUTION

The solution to the core-periphery model with two regions can be found by solving the two coupled nonlinear equations,

$$y_{w_1} = [y_1\,\bar{p}_1^{\sigma_S-1} + y_2\,\bar{p}_2^{\sigma_S-1}\tau^{\sigma_S-1}]^{\frac{1}{\sigma_S}}, \; y_{w_2} = [y_1\,\bar{p}_1^{\sigma_S-1}\tau^{\sigma_S-1} + y_2\,\bar{p}_2^{\sigma_S-1}]^{\frac{1}{\sigma_S}}, \tag{A.14}$$

with y_i, $\bar{p}_i$ functions of the nominal wages in the two regions and of the model parameters, as

$$y_1 = n_{MF}\,f_1 y_{w_1} + \frac{1 - n_{MF}}{2}, \; y_2 = n_{MF}(1 - f_1)y_{w_2} + \frac{1 - n_{MF}}{2},$$

$$\bar{p}_1 = \left[f_1 y_{w_1}^{1-\sigma_S} + (1 - f_1)\left(\frac{y_{w_2}}{\tau}\right)^{1-\sigma_S} \right]^{\frac{1}{1-\sigma_S}}, \tag{A.15}$$

$$\bar{p}_2 = \left[f_1\left(\frac{y_{w_1}}{\tau}\right)^{1-\sigma_S} + (1 - f_1)y_{w_2}^{1-\sigma_S} \right]^{\frac{1}{1-\sigma_S}}.$$

With the solutions for y_{w_1}, y_{w_2} in hand, we can then evaluate the real wages

$$y_{\omega_1} = y_{w_1}\,\bar{p}_1^{-n_{MF}}, \; y_{\omega_2} = y_{w_2}\,\bar{p}_2^{-n_{MF}}, \tag{A.16}$$

and plot their difference as a function of model parameters f_1, σ_S, n_{MF}, $T = 1/\tau$.

APPENDIX B: URBAN ECONOMICS MODELS

We have seen how the structure of urban economics models can be set by five distinct kinds of relations:

1. The utility function, $U(c, a_f)$, for the consumption of goods, c, and housing, a_f;
2. A production function, $A_H(a_l, K_p)$, for housing developers;
3. The budget condition, $y = p_f\, a_f + c_{T_0}R + c$, which is applied to every household;
4. The boundary condition at the edge of the city, $p_l(R_{max}, y, c_{T_0}, U) = p_{lr}$;
5. Sum rules on population and area: $2\pi \int_0^{R_{max}} dR\, R n_A(R) = N$; $A = \pi R_{max}^2$.

The general strategy is straightforward and mechanical, but tedious. To derive the properties of cities, the utility function will be maximized for housing floor area, a_f. The utility is a growing function of consumption and housing area, but its shape is *assumed* to be concave from below, meaning that its second derivatives related to consumption and housing are negative. The budget condition's main use here is to eliminate consumption of goods, c, from the utility function through the substitution $c = y - p_f\, a_f - c_{T_0}R$. The developers' production function and assumption of zero profits relate consumed housing and prices to the prices of land and capital. The boundary condition and population sum rules allow us to trade variables, introducing the effects of population size and agricultural land rents into the calculation.

We now want to derive how the area of the city (or equivalently its radius, R_{max}) depends on the other given (exogenous) variables, N, p_{l_r}, y, and c_{T_0}. The main difficulty is that the utility maximum in the *closed city* situation varies and contributes to other variations of interest. In the open city case, we instead assume demographic equilibrium (net zero migration between cities), which means that all cities are characterized by the *same level of utility*, U, but that their populations may vary in response to the other exogenous variables. Thus, for the *open city* model, the exogenous variables are U, p_{l_r}, y, and c_{T_0}.

B.1 CLOSED CITY

Let us now consider the situation of a closed city where population is given but utility varies. To see the implications of these assumptions requires taking two preparatory steps.

First, recall that the variation of land rents with various parameters was computed in equation (2.28) and is $\dfrac{dp_l}{d\phi_e} = a_H \dfrac{dp_f}{d\phi_e}$, with exogenous parameters $\phi_e = R, c_{T_0}, y, U$, which with the variations of p_f derived in the main text give explicitly

$$\frac{dp_l}{dR} = -a_H \frac{c_{T_0}}{a_f} < 0, \quad \frac{dp_l}{dy} = \frac{a_H}{a_f} > 0, \quad \frac{dp_l}{dc_{T_0}} = -a_H \frac{R}{a_f} < 0, \quad \frac{dp_l}{dU} = -a_H \frac{1}{a_f \frac{dU}{dc}} < 0. \tag{B.1}$$

Now recall that the population density in this model is simply $n_A = \frac{a_H}{a_f} = -\frac{1}{c_{T_0}} \frac{dp_l}{dR}$. This allows us to integrate the population sum rule

$$N = 2\pi \int_0^{R_{max}} dR \, R \, n_A(R) = -\frac{2\pi}{c_{T_0}} \int_0^{R_{max}} dR \, R \frac{dp_l}{dR} = \frac{2\pi}{c_{T_0}} \left(\int_0^{R_{max}} dR \, p_l - R_{max} \, p_{l_r} \right), \tag{B.2}$$

where we also used the area sum rule implicitly. This constraint can now be differentiated to show the dependencies of various quantities on exogenous quantities. Let us take them as $\phi_e = N, \, p_{l_r}, \, y, \, c_{T_0}$. This results in

$$\int_0^{R_{max}} dR \left[\frac{dp_l}{d\phi_e} + \frac{dp_l}{dU} \frac{dU}{d\phi_e} \right] = \frac{1}{\pi} \left(c_{T_0} \frac{dN}{d\phi_e} + N \frac{dc_{T_0}}{d\phi_e} \right) + \frac{dp_{l_r}}{d\phi_e} R_{max}. \tag{B.3}$$

Because the utility is a global variable in the city, independent of distance to the central business district, R, we can take it out of the integral and rearrange terms to get

$$\frac{dU}{d\phi_e} = \frac{\frac{1}{\pi} \left(c_{T_0} \frac{dN}{d\phi_e} + N \frac{dc_{T_0}}{d\phi_e} \right) + \frac{dp_{l_r}}{d\phi_e} R_{max} - \int_0^{R_{max}} dR \frac{dp_l}{d\phi_e}}{\int_0^{R_{max}} dR \frac{dp_l}{dU}}. \tag{B.4}$$

The denominator is negative as a consequence of the relationships derived earlier for the variations of land rents. This shows, for example, that

$$\frac{dU}{dN} = \frac{c_{T_0}}{\pi} \frac{1}{\int_0^{R_{max}} dR \frac{dp_l}{dU}} < 0, \tag{B.5}$$

so, in this model, more people leads to less happiness (utility). The signs of the other variations follow from analogous analyses. Noting that exogenous variables are independent of each other so their relative derivatives are zero, and that $\frac{dp_l}{dp_{l_r}} = \frac{dp_l}{dN} = 0$, gives the various signs

$$\frac{dU}{dN} < 0, \quad \frac{dU}{dp_{l_r}} < 0, \quad \frac{dU}{dy} > 0, \quad \frac{dU}{dc_{T_0}} < 0. \tag{B.6}$$

In general, this is as expected. For a fixed income, increasing population, land prices at the boundary, and transportation costs reduce people's budgets for consuming goods and land and make them less happy. Increasing income, everything else being equal, has the reverse effect.

We now have the necessary relations to compute the variations of R_{max} with the exogenous set of variables (and consequently the variations of the area of the city). To do this, we take derivatives of the boundary condition at the edge of the city to obtain

$$\frac{dp_l}{dR} \frac{dR}{d\phi_e} + \frac{dp_l}{dU} \frac{dU}{d\phi_e} + \frac{dp_l}{d\phi_e} = \frac{dp_{l_r}}{d\phi_e}, \tag{B.7}$$

which shows how the variations of the utility contribute. This allows us to write

$$\left. \frac{dR}{d\phi_e} \right|_{R=R_{max}} = \frac{\frac{dp_{l_r}}{d\phi_e} - \frac{dp_l}{dU} \frac{dU}{d\phi_e} - \frac{dp_l}{d\phi_e}}{\frac{dp_l}{dR}} = -\frac{a_f}{c_{T_0} a_H} \left. \left(\frac{dp_{l_r}}{d\phi_e} - \frac{dp_l}{dU} \frac{dU}{d\phi_e} - \frac{dp_l}{d\phi_e} \right) \right|_{R=R_{max}}. \tag{B.8}$$

For example, to find out the dependence on the population size, we take $\phi_e = N$ to get

$$\frac{dR_{max}}{dN} = -\frac{a_f}{c_{T_0} a_H}\left(\frac{dp_{l_r}}{dN} - \frac{dp_l}{dU}\frac{dU}{dN} - \frac{dp_l}{dN}\right)\Bigg|_{R=R_{max}}. \tag{B.9}$$

Now note that $\dfrac{dp_{l_r}}{dN} = \dfrac{dp_l}{dN}\Big|_{R=R_{max}} = 0$, so we obtain $\tag{B.10}$

$$\frac{dR_{max}}{dN} = \frac{a_f}{c_{T_0} a_H}\left(\frac{dp_l}{dU}\frac{dU}{dN}\right)\Bigg|_{R=R_{max}} = -\frac{1}{\pi\dfrac{dU}{dc}\displaystyle\int_0^{R_{max}} dR\,\dfrac{dp_l}{dU}} > 0. \tag{B.11}$$

Thus, the radius of the city, and therefore its total land area, increases with the city's population size. The specific manner in which this happens is "nonuniversal" in the sense that it depends on the choice of the specific utility function. We will see that we often find that the total area of the city varies with the population size as a power law: $A = A_0 N^\alpha \to R_{max} \sim N^{\alpha/2}$. This would then result in a relationship where

$$\frac{dR_{max}}{dN} = \frac{\alpha}{2}\frac{N}{R_{max}} = -\frac{1}{\pi\dfrac{dU}{dc}\displaystyle\int_0^{R_{max}} dR\,\dfrac{dp_l}{dU}}. \tag{B.12}$$

Taken at face value, this would provide a constraint on the space of utility functions that are empirically appropriate. We can also take similar steps to obtain the dependence of the spatial extent of the city on the other exogenous parameters. This leads to the signs

$$\frac{dR_{max}}{dp_{l_r}} < 0, \quad \frac{dR_{max}}{dy} > 0, \quad \frac{dR_{max}}{c_{T_0}} < 0, \tag{B.13}$$

which are all intuitive, since the city will be spatially smaller if it can afford less land, because it is more expensive or because transportation is. When incomes are higher, more land can be afforded and the city can sprawl.

B.2 OPEN CITY

The calculation here is analogous but simpler, because we can now drop the variations of the utility. For the radius of the city, we obtain

$$\frac{dR}{d\phi_e}\Bigg|_{R=R_{max}} = \frac{\dfrac{dp_{l_r}}{d\phi_e} - \dfrac{dp_l}{d\phi_e}}{\dfrac{dp_l}{dR}} = -\frac{a_f}{c_{T_0} a_H}\left(\frac{dp_{l_r}}{d\phi_e} - \frac{dp_l}{d\phi_e}\right)\Bigg|_{R=R_{max}}. \tag{B.14}$$

Thus,

$$\frac{dR_{max}}{dp_{l_r}} = -\frac{a_f}{c_{T_0} a_H} < 0, \quad \frac{dR_{max}}{dN} = \frac{a_f}{c_{T_0} a_H}\frac{dp_l}{dN} = 0,$$

$$\frac{dR_{max}}{dy} = \frac{a_f}{c_{T_0} a_H}\frac{dp_l}{dy} = \frac{1}{c_{T_0}} > 0, \quad \frac{dR_{max}}{dc_{T_0}} = \frac{a_f}{c_{T_0} a_H}\frac{dp_l}{dc_{T_0}} = -\frac{R_{max}}{c_{T_0}} < 0, \tag{B.15}$$

where all expressions are evaluated at the city boundary. See the main text for a discussion of the meaning of these results. It is actually possible to solve for R_{max}: integrating each equation gives

$$R_{max} = -\frac{a_f}{c_{T_0} a_H} p_{l_r} + c_0(y, c_{T_0}, N), \quad R_{max} = c_0'(y, c_{T_0}, p_{l_r}),$$

$$R_{max} = \frac{y}{c_{T_0}} + c_0''(c_{T_0}, N, p_{l_r}), \quad R_{max} = \frac{c(y, N, p_{l_r}, c_{T_0} = 0)}{c_{T_0}}. \tag{B.16}$$

where the various c_0's are constants of integration on the focal variable. Reconciling all the constants of integration to obtain a single unique form gives

$$R_{max} = \frac{\left(y - \dfrac{p_{lr}a_f}{a_H}\right)}{c_{T_0}}. \tag{B.17}$$

This is just a refinement of the straightforward Alonso model result where we account for the price of land and square footage consumed at the city boundary because $\dfrac{a_f}{a_H}(R_{max}) = \dfrac{1}{n_A(R_{max})}$, so the second term in parentheses is the mean per capita cost of housing at $R = R_{max}$.

APPENDIX C: INFORMATION THEORY AND LEARNING

Throughout the book we made use of quantities that measure *information*. Here we provide a brief summary of their properties. The reader interested in learning more about the subject is referred to excellent textbooks, such those by Cover and Thomas,[1] and MacKay.[2] Information theory appears in many different contexts in the study of cities, including in the measure of *searchability* (chapter 3), *diversity* (chapter 5), *neighborhood effects* (chapter 6), migration preferences (chapter 8), and *learning* and investing in opportunities that can generate wealth (chapter 9).

Any measure of information starts out from a probability distribution, $P(y_i)$, over a space of alternative choices or possibilities, labeled by i. We have seen that the space of y_i could be many things, from spatial routes, to population types, to allocational choices of residence and resources. This probability is normalized in the sense that $\sum_i P(y_i) = 1$. For a single stochastic variable, the central quantity of information theory is the Shannon entropy

$$H(y) = -\sum_i P(y_i) \log P(y_i) = \langle \log 1/P(y_i) \rangle \geq 0. \tag{C.1}$$

This quantity is the average of $1/P(y_i)$, which is sometimes known as the *surprise*. The entropy measures the overall uncertainty (or diversity) in the state of the variable y_i. It is usually measured in *bits* (using logarithmic base 2). Bits are units of alternative (yes/no) choice.

If the state of y_i is known with certainty, for example $P(y_0) = 1$, then $H(y) = 0$. Conversely, the entropy is maximal for the widest possible distribution of states, which, without further constraints, is the uniform distribution, $P(y_i) = 1/N$, for all i, which results in $H(y) = \sum_{i=1}^{N} \frac{1}{N} \log N = \log N$. The Shannon entropy is the only function that obeys these properties and allows for multilevel recursion of probabilities under conditioning[3] of the type we explored in chapters 6 and 9, for example using groups of groups. This was the reason it was singled out by Shannon to describe complex signals.[4]

But the Shannon entropy is often considered less fundamental because it suffers from a problem of normalization, if we count the types in y_i more finely, we will typically generate higher values of $H(y)$. This is a problem with most measures of diversity over taxonomies as we saw in chapter 5. In this sense, any measure of information is always relative to some standard distribution.

This issue is addressed through the introduction of the *relative entropy* (or *Kullback-Leibler divergence*) D_{KL} and the mutual information, I, which both emerge as we compare two (or more) distributions.

The Kullback-Leibler divergence (KL-divergence) is given by

$$D_{KL}[P\|P'] = \sum_i P(y_i) \log \frac{P(y_i)}{P'(y_i)} \geq 0,$$ (C.2)

where $P'(y_i)$, $P(y_i)$ are two different distributions over the states of possibilities, y_i. It vanishes when these two distributions coincide and is positive otherwise, becoming larger if the two distributions are more different from each other. The KL-divergence is very versatile and is the main tool in information theory to express the magnitude of the difference between any two distributions.

Finally, the mutual information, or simply *information* is given by

$$I(x; y) = \sum_{i,j} P(x_i, y_j) \log \frac{P(x_i, y_j)}{P(x_i)P(y_j)} = D_{KL}[P(x, y)\|P(x)P(y)] \geq 0.$$ (C.3)

This measures how statistically dependent two variables x_i, y_j are, in the sense of how well one can predict the other. The information vanishes if the two variables are statistically independent, meaning that $P(x_i, y_j) = P(x_i)P(y_j)$, in which case they have nothing to say about each other. A non-zero information is a stronger condition than the existence of a correlation between the same two variables, because it involves the entire distribution and not just its second moment (covariance).

There are a number of interesting and important relations for conditional distributions, typical of learning processes following from Bayes theorem

$$P(y_j|x_i) = \frac{P(x_i|y_j)}{P(x_i)} P(y_j) = \frac{w_{ij}}{w_i} P(y_j),$$ (C.4)

which is the optimal way to update our knowledge of the distribution of y given new data, x.

Specifically, we can write the *selection coefficient*, or *fitness*, as

$$\log \frac{w_{ij}}{w_j} = \log \frac{P(x_i|y_j)}{P(x_i)} = \log \frac{P(y_j|x_i)}{P(y_j)} = \log \frac{P(x_i, y_j)}{P(x_i)P(y_j)},$$ (C.5)

which shows that

$$D_{KL}[P(x_i|y_j)\|P(x_i)] = \sum_i P(x_i|y_j) \log \frac{P(x_i|y_j)}{P(x_i)};$$ (C.6)

$$D_{KL}[P(y|x_i)\|P(y)] = \Sigma_j\, P(y_j|x_i) \log \frac{P(y_j|x_i)}{P(y_j)};$$ (C.7)

and

$$I(x; y) = \sum_{i,j} P(x_i, y_j) \log \frac{P(x_i, y_j)}{P(x_i)P(y_j)} = \sum_i P(x_i) D_{KL}[P(y|x_i)\|P(y)]$$
$$= \sum_j P(y_j) D_{KL}[P(x|y_j)\|P(x)].$$ (C.8)

These quantities express the strength of *sorting* or *selection* and measure the quality of our predictive information on environmental states in terms of units of information, measured in bits.

APPENDIX D: OVERVIEW OF THE ERGODIC THEOREMS OF DEMOGRAPHY

The ergodic theorems of demography express the asymptotic trend over time for the population dynamics to become independent of initial conditions. These theorems hinge on writing the demographic dynamics in the form of equations (8.12–8.14) and on the properties of the matrix e, known as the *environment*. Closely following Caswell,[1] the four ergodic theorems can be described as follows:

1. *Strong ergodic theorem* In a constant environment e in time, any initial population vector converges to a fixed, stable structure given by the leading eigenvector of e. This is guaranteed to exist if e is a strongly connected, primitive graph, as we expect for migration flows between cities, where any city should be reachable from any other in a finite number of intermediate steps. The leading eigenvector is the PageRank of the urban system, and the convergence to this vector is given by the ratio of secondary eigenvalues to the dominant one.
2. *Weak ergodic theorem* If two initial populations are exposed to the same sequence of environments e, which is now dynamical, the difference between their structure vectors (relative population sizes) decays to zero.
3. *Strong stochastic ergodic theorem* In a homogeneous (i.e., time-independent) stochastic environment, the structure vector is a random variable whose probability distribution converges to a fixed, stationary distribution, regardless of initial conditions.
4. *Weak stochastic ergodic theorem* In an inhomogeneous stochastic environment e, the difference between the probability distributions for the structure vector resulting from any two initial populations exposed to independent sample paths of the stochastic environment decays to zero.

In each of these cases, the theorems require restrictions on the environmental sequences of matrices $e(t)$. In the deterministic strong ergodic theorem, the matrix must be *primitive*. In the ergodic theorems for variable environments, the set of matrices must meet conditions that guarantee that sufficiently long sequences (the product of many instantaneous matrices) become positive matrices. The caveat to these results is that the environmental matrices generally depend on the structure vectors, n, making the problem nonlinear. In the cases explored in this book we have shown that these nonlinearities are not particularly important and that their role vanishes close to the asymptotic states, where n is varying little. Nevertheless, making such observations more rigorous remains, to the best of my knowledge, an open problem. Numerical solutions also provide alternative approaches in complex cases.

APPENDIX E: GENERAL PROBABILITY SOLUTION FOR GEOMETRIC RANDOM GROWTH

The Fokker-Planck equation for geometric random growth is

$$\frac{dP}{dt} = \frac{\sigma_n^2}{2} \frac{d^2}{dn^2} n^2 P,$$ (E.1)

where $P = P[n, t|n_0, t_0]$ is the conditional probability of observing the state n of the random variable at time t given that we started with state n_0 at time t_0.

This equation has some similarities with the heat (or diffusion) equation in physics. It can be solved exactly in a similar way using an elaboration of familiar methods. First, it is useful to change variables so as to eliminate the nonlinear term in n^2.

Let us introduce $y = \ln \dfrac{n}{n_0}, \tau = \dfrac{\sigma_n^2}{2}(t - t_0)$ and change variables to find

$$\frac{dP}{d\tau} = P'' + 3P' + P,$$ (E.2)

where the prime symbol denotes a derivative with respect to y. The equation is now linear. We can proceed in two ways. One is to turn the equation into the well-known *heat equation* via the factorization

$$P = e^{-\frac{3}{2}y - \frac{1}{4}\tau} g(y, \tau) \rightarrow \frac{dg}{d\tau} = g'',$$ (E.3)

and solve the equation for g by standard methods. Another is to solve directly for $P[y, \tau]$ via a Fourier transform in y, so

$$P[y, \tau] = \int dk\, e^{iky} P[k, \tau],$$ (E.4)

where k is the Fourier variable (not connectivity), which leads to

$$\frac{dP[k, \tau]}{d\tau} = (-k^2 + 3ik + 2)P[k, \tau].$$ (E.5)

This equation can now be solved via a separation of variables, $P[k, \tau] = f(k)T(\tau)$, leading to the eigenvalue problem

$$\frac{dT}{d\tau} = -wT; \; (-k^2 + 3ik + 2)f(k) = -wf(k).$$ (E.6)

The values of k that solve equation (E.6) are

$$k = \frac{3}{2}i \pm \frac{1}{2}i\sqrt{1+4w}.$$ (E.7)

In particular, there are two *stationary solutions* ($w=0$), with $k=2i$, i. Substituting this solution in (E.4) we see that the first of these solutions corresponds to $P \sim e^{-2y} \sim \dfrac{1}{n^2}$, which, of course, is Zipf's distribution. The other solution corresponds to the existence of a static probability current up or down the urban hierarchy, as discussed in equation (8.27) in the main text. This solution would be relevant if there were a systematic flow of people up or down the urban hierarchy, which may happen in some circumstances; for example, if strong foreign migration enters larger cities and subsequently spreads to progressively smaller towns (figure 8.14).

E.1   LOGNORMAL SOLUTION FOR SPECIAL INITIAL AND BOUNDARY CONDITIONS

As we have seen, the general solution for the probability can be written as

$$P[y, \tau] = \int dk \, P[k, 0] e^{iky - (k^2 - 3ik - 2)\tau},$$ (E.8)

with $P[k, 0] = T(0)f(k)$. A particularly important solution is for the initial probability to be a delta function, $P[y, 0] = \delta(y)$, which corresponds to the case where $N(t=0) = N_T$. Then, $P[k, 0] = 1$, and the solution for all times is

$$P[y, \tau] = \int dk \, e^{iky - (k^2 - 3ik - 2)\tau} = \frac{e^{-y}}{\sqrt{2\pi\tau}} e^{-\frac{(y+\tau)^2}{4\tau}}.$$ (E.9)

[Exercise: Obtain this solution by completing the square in k, performing the Gaussian integral, and absorbing the factors of τ back into the exponent by again completing the new square.]

Returning to our original variables transforms this solution into a more familiar form,

$$P[n, t \mid n_0, t_o] = \frac{n_0}{n} \frac{1}{\sqrt{\pi\sigma_n^2(t - t_0)}} e^{-\frac{\left(\ln\frac{n}{n_0} + \frac{\sigma_n^2}{2}(t-t_0)\right)^2}{2\sigma_n^2 (t-t_0)}},$$ (E.10)

which is the lognormal solution to geometric Brownian motion. Note, however, that this solution is *not to be expected in general* unless we start out with the entire population in a single city of a given initial size.

E.2   FULL SOLUTION AND CONVERGENCE TO ZIPF'S DISTRIBUTION

Let us now reflect on how the lognormal solution is unnatural for our case of urban demographic growth. It requires that we start with the entire population in a single city. It also requires that we impose no limitations on how big or small cities can be. This implies that when we look at any subset of city size ranges, we would be constantly losing population to both larger and smaller cities outside the initial range. This happens eventually regardless of the range chosen, and consequently the distribution will never be stationary.

In order to fix this issue and obtain a stationary distribution at long times, we must therefore solve for geometric random growth under *additional constraints*. To see this explicitly, consider the full dynamical solution, which can be written in terms of the y variables as

$$P[y, \tau] = P_1 e^{-2y} + P_2 e^{-y} + \int dk \, a_k e^{iky - (k^2 - 3ik - 2)\tau}.$$ (E.11)

We now need the following additional conditions:

- The integration constant $P_2 \to 0$ when we set the probability current to zero, which in terms of y reads as $J(y) = e^{-2y} \dfrac{d}{dy} \sigma_n^2 e^{2y} P[y, \tau].$

- The constant P_1 can now be fixed by normalizing Zipf's distribution as a probability:
$P_1 \int_{n_m}^{n_M} dx \frac{1}{n^2} = 1 \rightarrow P_1 = \frac{n_M n_m}{n_M - n_m}$. Thus, P_1 is sensitive to the maximum and minimum values of n.

- We can now set boundary conditions on the time-varying solutions, which are now $g(y, \tau) = P[y, \tau] - P_1 e^{-2y}$ and can be taken to be homogeneous at the boundaries in y. We need their integral over the range of city sizes to be zero in order to preserve the probability normalization. For example, we can ask that these solutions be real and vanish at the boundaries so $g(y = y_m, \tau) = g(y = y_M, \tau) = 0$. This leads to

$$g[y, \tau] = \sum_n a_n \sqrt{\frac{2}{y_M - y_m}} \sin k_n[(y - y_m) - 3\tau] e^{-(k_n^2 - 2)\tau}, \tag{E.12}$$

with $k_j = \dfrac{2\pi}{y_M - y_m} j;\ j = 1, 2, 3, \ldots$.

The coefficients a_n are determined via the initial condition, $g[y, 0]$, in the usual way, since the sine functions are an orthonormal basis under integration over the domain of y:

$$a_n = \sqrt{\frac{2}{y_M - y_m}} \int_{y_m}^{y_M} dy\, g[y, 0] \sin k_n(y - y_m). \tag{E.13}$$

Even though these functions will now obey boundary conditions, the temporal structure is similar to the lognormal, and the decay of the initial amplitudes occurs on a timescale set by τ, $t - t_0 = \dfrac{1}{2\sigma_n^2}$, which can be very long for small volatility, σ_n.

NOTES

1 WHY CITIES? WHAT IS URBAN SCIENCE?

1. UN-Habitat, *World Cities Report 2016*.

2. Bettencourt and West, "A Unified Theory of Urban Living"; Solecki, Seto, and Marcotullio, "It's Time for an Urbanization Science"; Batty, *The New Science of Cities*; Acuto, Parnell, and Seto, "Building a Global Urban Science."

3. Park, Burgess, and McKenzie, *The City*; Wirth, "Urbanism as a Way of Life."

4. Ramaswami et al., "Sustainable Urban Systems Report."

5. Bettencourt and West, "A Unified Theory of Urban Living"; Batty, *The New Science of Cities*.

6. Solecki, Seto, and Marcotullio, "It's Time for an Urbanization Science"; Acuto, Parnell, and Seto, "Building a Global Urban Science"; Ramaswami et al., "Sustainable Urban Systems Report."

7. Ramaswami et al., "Sustainable Urban Systems Report."

8. Bettencourt, "Designing for Complexity."

9. UN-Habitat, *The Challenge of Slums*.

10. Rittel and Webber, "Dilemmas in a General Theory of Planning."

11. Park, Burgess, and McKenzie, *The City*.

12. Geddes, *Cities in Evolution*.

13. Raudenbush and Sampson, "Ecometrics."

14. Raudenbush and Sampson, "Ecometrics"; Sampson, *Great American City*.

15. Mumford, *The City in History*.

16. Alexander, *Notes on the Synthesis of Form*; Alexander, Ishikawa, and Silverstein, *A Pattern Language*.

17. Whyte, *The Social Life of Small Urban Spaces*.

18. Jacobs, *The Death and Life of Great American Cities*.

19. Lynch, *Good City Form*.

20. Castells, *The Informational City*.

21. Turner, *Housing by People*.

22. Batty, *The New Science of Cities*.

23. Batty, *The New Science of Cities*; Bettencourt, "Designing for Complexity"; Batty, *Cities and Complexity*; Allen, *Cities and Regions as Self-Organizing Systems*.

24. United Nations, *Sustainable Development Goals*.

25. Jacobs, *The Death and Life of Great American Cities*.

26. Shannon and Weaver, *The Mathematical Theory of Communication*.

27. Jacobs, *The Death and Life of Great American Cities*.

28. Bettencourt, "The Kind of Problem a City Is."

29. Durkheim, *The Division of Labour in Society*, 39, 60, 108.

30. Geddes, *Cities in Evolution*; Park, Burgess, and McKenzie, *The City*; Jacobs, *The Nature of Economies*.

31. Jacobs, *The Death and Life of Great American Cities*; Bettencourt, "The Kind of Problem a City Is."

32. Bettencourt and West, "A Unified Theory of Urban Living"; Batty, *Cities and Complexity*.

33. Glaeser and Gottlieb, "The Wealth of Cities."

34. Ramaswami et al., "Sustainable Urban Systems Report."

2   CLASSICAL MODELS OF CITIES AND URBAN FUNCTIONAL DEFINITIONS

1. Jacobs, *The Death and Life of Great American Cities*.

2. Wirth, "Urbanism as a Way of Life."

3. Fujita, *Urban Economic Theory*.

4. Samuelson, *Foundations of Economic Analysis*.

5. Krugman, "Increasing Returns and Economic Geography."

6. The reader should certainly consider modern (industrialized) agriculture, which relies on intensification and thus is subject to some economies of scale.

7. Mumford, *The City in History*.

8. Arthur, *Increasing Returns and Path Dependence in the Economy*; Arthur, "Complexity and the Economy."

9. In the jargon of economics, these are also known as *backward* and *forward linkages*. This means that one can have self-reinforcing dynamic instabilities that are naturally sensitive to initial conditions and are thus path dependent.

10. Utilities are vaguely defined in practice and can mean many different things, such as consumer satisfaction or "happiness." In economic modeling, they are a mathematical device for specifying putative consumer choices. They are typically rising but concave functions of consumption, whether that refers to goods or housing.

11. Taking $c = \dfrac{U}{U_0}$ to be the individual total consumption, this result follows from considering the fixed fractions $\dfrac{c_M}{c} = n_{MF}$ and $\dfrac{c_F}{c} = 1 - n_{MF}$, so they add up to 1.

12. Samuelson, "The Transfer Problem and Transport Costs, II: Analysis of Effects of Trade Impediments."

13. This concept will play an important role in models of the system of cities and migration. We will see that despite the fact that nominal wages are higher on average in larger cities, real wages are approximately constant across city sizes.

14. Fujita, Krugman, and Venables, *The Spatial Economy*; Fujita and Thisse, *Economics of Agglomeration*.

15. Krugman, "Increasing Returns and Economic Geography."

16. Venables, "Equilibrium Locations of Vertically Linked Industries."

17. Baldwin, "Agglomeration and Endogenous Capital."

18. Fujita and Thisse, *Economics of Agglomeration*.

19. Baldwin et al., *Economic Geography and Public Policy*; Gaspar, "A Prospective Review on New Economic Geography."

20. Fujita and Thisse, *Economics of Agglomeration*; Gaspar, "A Prospective Review on New Economic Geography."

21. Park, Burgess, and McKenzie, *The City*.

22. Remarkably, at the very end of Burgess's paper in *The City*, and what feels to me as almost an afterthought, he spends a couple of paragraphs discussing data on letters and phone calls exchanged in various American cities as they grew. These data clearly demonstrate that social contacts increase faster than population in cities and to the best of my knowledge provides the first direct empirical evidence for urban *network effects*.

23. Marshall, *Principles of Economics*.

24. Smith, *The Wealth of Nations*, 24.

25. Griliches, "The Search for R&D Spillovers"; Acs, Audretsch, and Feldman, "R & D Spillovers and Recipient Firm Size"; Anselin, Varga, and Acs, "Local Geographic Spillovers between University Research and High Technology Innovations"; Feldman, "The New Economics of Innovation, Spillovers and Agglomeration."

26. Ellison, Glaeser, and Kerr, "What Causes Industry Agglomeration?"

27. Griliches, "The Search for R&D Spillovers"; Aharonson, Baum, and Feldman, "Desperately Seeking Spillovers?"

28. Marchio and Parilla, "Export Monitor 2018."

29. Alonso, *Location and Land Use*.

30. Mumford, *The City in History*.

31. Jacobs, *The Death and Life of Great American Cities*.

32. Alexander, *Notes on the Synthesis of Form*.

33. Mills, "An Aggregative Model of Resource Allocation in a Metropolitan Area"; Mills and Hamilton, *Urban Economics*.

34. Muth, *Cities and Housing*.

35. Wheaton, "On the Optimal Distribution of Income among Cities."

36. O'Sullivan, *Urban Economics*; Glaeser, *Cities, Agglomeration, and Spatial Equilibrium*; Brueckner, *Lectures on Urban Economics*.

37. Brueckner, "The Structure of Urban Equilibria."

38. Brueckner, "The Structure of Urban Equilibria."

39. Brueckner, "The Structure of Urban Equilibria."

40. Angel et al., "The Dimensions of Global Urban Expansion."

41. Angel et al., "Atlas of Urban Expansion."

42. Angel et al., "The Dimensions of Global Urban Expansion."

43. Wheaton, "On the Optimal Distribution of Income among Cities."

44. Angel et al., "The Dimensions of Global Urban Expansion."

45. Glaeser, *Cities, Agglomeration, and Spatial Equilibrium*.

46. Brueckner, Thisse, and Zenou, "Why Is Central Paris Rich and Downtown Detroit Poor?"

47. O'Sullivan, *Urban Economics*; Glaeser, *Cities, Agglomeration, and Spatial Equilibrium*; Brueckner, *Lectures on Urban Economics*; McCann, *Modern Urban and Regional Economics*.

48. Becker, "Crime and Punishment"; Glaeser and Sacerdote, "Why Is There More Crime in Cities?"

49. Fujita, Krugman, and Venables, *The Spatial Economy*; Glaeser, "A World of Cities."

50. Hägerstrand, "What about People in Regional Science?"; Pred, "The Choreography of Existence."

51. Pred, "The Choreography of Existence."

52. Hägerstrand, "What about People in Regional Science?"

53. Hägerstrand, "What about People in Regional Science?"

54. Pred, "The Choreography of Existence"; Thrift and Pred, "Time-Geography."

55. Ewing and Cervero, "Travel and the Built Environment."

56. Jaffe, "Why Commute Times Don't Change Much Even as a City Grows"; Zahavi and Talvitie, "Regularities in Travel Time and Money Expenditures"; Baylis, "Zahavi."

57. Marchetti, "Anthropological Invariants in Travel Behavior."

58. Lobo et al., "Settlement Scaling Theory."

59. Berry, Goheen, and Goldstein, *Metropolitan Area Definition*.

60. Angel et al., "The Dimensions of Global Urban Expansion."

61. Dijkstra, Poelman, and Veneri, "The EU-OECD Definition of a Functional Urban Area."

62. Florida, "Just How Urban Is the World?"

63. Lobo et al., "Settlement Scaling Theory."

3   COMPLEX NETWORKS AND URBAN SCALING

1. Bettencourt and Lobo, "Quantitative Methods for the Comparative Analysis of Cities in History."

2. Barenblatt, *Scaling, Self-Similarity, and Intermediate Asymptotics*; Barenblatt, *Scaling*.

3. Goldenfeld, *Lectures on Phase Transitions and the Renormalization Group*.

4. Kardar, *Statistical Physics of Particles*.

5. Kardar, *Statistical Physics of Particles*.

6. Kennedy, Pincetl, and Bunje, "The Study of Urban Metabolism and Its Applications to Urban Planning and Design."

7. Bettencourt and Brelsford, "Industrial Ecology."

8. West, "A General Model for the Origin of Allometric Scaling Laws in Biology"; West, "The Fourth Dimension of Life"; Rodríguez-Iturbe et al., "Fractal Structures as Least Energy Patterns"; Banavar et al., "Topology of the Fittest Transportation Network."

9. Nordbeck, "Urban Allometric Growth"; Coffey, "Allometric Growth in Urban and Regional Social-Economic Systems"; Dutton, "Foreword: Size and Shape in the Growth of Human Communities"; Newling, "Urban Growth and Spatial Structure."

10. Bettencourt, "The Origins of Scaling in Cities."

11. Thompson and Bonner, *On Growth and Form*.

12. Sveikauskas, "The Productivity of Cities."

13. Bettencourt et al., "Growth, Innovation, Scaling, and the Pace of Life in Cities"; Bettencourt, Lobo, and Strumsky, "Invention in the City"; Pumain et al., "An Evolutionary Theory for Interpreting Urban Scaling Laws."

14. Bettencourt et al., "Growth, Innovation, Scaling, and the Pace of Life in Cities."

15. Wirth, "Urbanism as a Way of Life."

16. Barabási and Pósfai, *Network Science*; Jackson, *Social and Economic Networks*.

17. Tobler, "Satellite Confirmation of Settlement Size Coefficient."

18. Nordbeck, "Urban Allometric Growth."

19. Samaniego and Moses, "Cities as Organisms"; Barthélemy, "Spatial Networks."

20. Samaniego and Moses, "Cities as Organisms"; Barthélemy, "Spatial Networks."

21. Angel et al., "The Dimensions of Global Urban Expansion."

22. Simmel and Levine, *On Individuality and Social Forms*; Park et al., *The City*; Wirth, "Urbanism as a Way of Life"; Milgram, "The Experience of Living in Cities."

23. Schläpfer et al., "The Scaling of Human Interactions with City Size."

24. Jacobs, *The Death and Life of Great American Cities*; Jacobs, *The Economy of Cities*.

25. Wang et al., "Linked Activity Spaces"; Schertz et al., "Neighborhood Street Activity and Greenspace Usage Uniquely Contribute to Predicting Crime."

26. Marshall, *Principles of Economics*; Fujita, Krugman, and Venables, *The Spatial Economy*.

27. Nordbeck, "Urban Allometric Growth"; Samaniego and Moses, "Cities as Organisms."

28. Downs, "The Law of Peak-Hour Expressway Congestion"; Duranton and Turner, "The Fundamental Law of Road Congestion."

29. West, "The Fourth Dimension of Life"; Rodríguez-Iturbe and Rinaldo, *Fractal River Basins*.

30. Nordbeck, "Urban Allometric Growth."

31. Rosenthal and Strange, "Evidence on the Nature and Sources of Agglomeration Economies"; Puga, "The Magnitude and Causes of Agglomeration Economies"; Black and Henderson, "A Theory of Urban Growth"; Glaeser, *Cities, Agglomeration, and Spatial Equilibrium*.

32. Bettencourt et al., "Growth, Innovation, Scaling, and the Pace of Life in Cities."

33. Arbesman, Kleinberg, and Strogatz, "Superlinear Scaling for Innovation in Cities."

34. Pan et al., "Urban Characteristics Attributable to Density-Driven Tie Formation."

35. Bettencourt, Lobo, and Youn, "The Hypothesis of Urban Scaling."

36. Pumain et al., "An Evolutionary Theory for Interpreting Urban Scaling Laws."

37. Gomez-Lievano, Patterson-Lomba, and Hausmann, "Explaining the Prevalence, Scaling and Variance of Urban Phenomena."

38. Yang, Papachristos, and Abrams, "Modeling the Origin of Urban-Output Scaling Laws."

39. Sassen, *The Global City*.

40. Pumain et al., "An Evolutionary Theory for Interpreting Urban Scaling Laws"; Jacobs, *Cities and the Wealth of Nations*.

41. Schläpfer et al., "The Scaling of Human Interactions with City Size."

42. Andris and Bettencourt, "Development, Information and Social Connectivity in Côte d'Ivoire."

43. Schläpfer et al., "The Scaling of Human Interactions with City Size."

44. Clauset, Shalizi, and Newman, "Power-Law Distributions in Empirical Data."

45. Schläpfer et al., "The Scaling of Human Interactions with City Size"; Gibrat, *Les inégalités économiques*; Gabaix, "Zipf's Law for Cities."

46. Simon, "On a Class of Skew Distribution Functions"; Price, "A General Theory of Bibliometric and Other Cumulative Advantage Processes"; Barabási, "Emergence of Scaling in Random Networks."

47. Gibrat, *Les inégalités économiques*; Gabaix, "Zipf's Law for Cities"; Montroll and Shlesinger, "On 1/f Noise and Other Distributions with Long Tails."

48. Durkheim and Lukes, *The Division of Labor in Society*; Simmel and Levine, *On Individuality and Social Forms*.

49. Anderson and May, *Infectious Diseases of Humans*.

50. Schläpfer et al., "The Scaling of Human Interactions with City Size"; Dalziel et al., "Urbanization and Humidity Shape the Intensity of Influenza Epidemics in U.S. Cities"; Chowell, Nishiura, and Bettencourt, "Comparative Estimation of the Reproduction Number for Pandemic Influenza from Daily Case Notification Data."

51. Bettencourt, Lobo, and Strumsky, "Invention in the City"; Feldman and Audretsch, "Innovation in Cities"; Acs, "Innovation and the Growth of Cities"; Dalziel et al., "Urbanization and Humidity Shape the Intensity of Influenza Epidemics in U.S. Cities."

52. Anderson and May, *Infectious Diseases of Humans*; Bettencourt et al., "The Power of a Good Idea."

53. Anderson and May, *Infectious Diseases of Humans*.

54. Schläpfer et al., "The Scaling of Human Interactions with City Size"; Zhong et al., "Revealing Centrality in the Spatial Structure of Cities from Human Activity Patterns"; Wang et al., "Linked Activity Spaces."

55. Fischer, *To Dwell among Friends*.

56. Wellman and Berkowitz, *Social Structures*; Carrasco et al., "Collecting Social Network Data to Study Social Activity-Travel Behavior"; Carrasco et al., "Agency in Social Activity Interactions."

57. Sampson, *Great American City*.

58. Sampson, *Great American City*; Chetty et al., "The Fading American Dream"; Sampson and Laub, *Crime in the Making*; Sampson and Laub, "Crime and Deviance over the Life Course"; Sharkey and Faber, "Where, When, Why, and for Whom Do Residential Contexts Matter?"

59. Eagle, Macy, and Claxton, "Network Diversity and Economic Development."

60. Hausmann and Hidalgo, "The Network Structure of Economic Output."

61. Hidalgo and Hausmann, "The Building Blocks of Economic Complexity."

62. Bonacich, "Power and Centrality"; Berry and Garrison, "Recent Developments of Central Place Theory."

63. Milgram, "The Experience of Living in Cities."

64. Simmel and Levine, *On Individuality and Social Forms*; Park, Burgess, and McKenzie, *The City*; Wirth, "Urbanism as a Way of Life."

65. Fischer, "The Subcultural Theory of Urbanism."

66. Fischer, "The Subcultural Theory of Urbanism."

67. Park, Burgess, and McKenzie, *The City*.

68. Bettencourt, Samaniego, and Youn, "Professional Diversity and the Productivity of Cities"; Wirth, "Urbanism as a Way of Life"; Feldman and Audretsch, "Innovation in Cities."

69. Rosvall et al., "Searchability of Networks."

70. Rosvall et al., "Searchability of Networks."

71. Rosvall et al., "Searchability of Networks."

72. Watts and Strogatz, "Collective Dynamics of 'Small-World' Networks."

73. Angel et al., "The Dimensions of Global Urban Expansion"; Seto et al., "A Meta-analysis of Global Urban Land Expansion."

74. Zünd and Bettencourt, "Growth and Development in Prefecture-Level Cities in China."

75. Batty and Longley, *Fractal Cities*; Benguigui et al., "When and Where Is a City Fractal?"; Batty, *Cities and Complexity*.

76. Thomas, Frankhauser, and Keersmaecker, "Fractal Dimension versus Density of Built-Up Surfaces in the Periphery of Brussels."

77. Batty and Longley, *Fractal Cities*; Thomas, Frankhauser, and Keersmaecker, "Fractal Dimension versus Density of Built-Up Surfaces in the Periphery of Brussels."

78. Barenblatt, *Scaling*.

79. Thomas, Frankhauser, and Keersmaecker, "Fractal Dimension versus Density of Built-Up Surfaces in the Periphery of Brussels."

80. Thomas, Frankhauser, and Keersmaecker, "Fractal Dimension versus Density of Built-Up Surfaces in the Periphery of Brussels."

81. Shen, "Fractal Dimension and Fractal Growth of Urbanized Areas."

82. Molinero and Thurner, "How the Geometry of Cities Explains Urban Scaling Laws and Determines Their Exponents."

83. Bettencourt and Lobo, "Urban Scaling in Europe"; Arcaute et al., "Constructing Cities, Deconstructing Scaling Laws."

84. Schläpfer, Lee, and Bettencourt, "Urban Skylines."

85. Barthélemy, *The Structure and Dynamics of Cities*.

86. Bettencourt, "The Origins of Scaling in Cities."

87. Brelsford et al., "Toward Cities without Slums."

88. UN-Habitat, *The Challenge of Slums*.

89. King and Roberts, "Manhattan's Population Density, Past and Present."

90. Lemoy and Caruso, "Evidence for the Homothetic Scaling of Urban Forms."

91. Lemoy and Caruso, "Evidence for the Homothetic Scaling of Urban Forms."

92. Schläpfer, Lee, and Bettencourt, "Urban Skylines."

93. Lobo et al., "Urban Scaling and the Production Function for Cities."

94. Levine, *A Geography of Time*.

95. Becker, "A Theory of the Allocation of Time."

96. UN-Habitat, *The Challenge of Slums*.

97. Brelsford et al., "Toward Cities without Slums."

98. Brelsford et al., "Toward Cities without Slums."

99. Brelsford et al., "Toward Cities without Slums"; Brelsford, Martin, and Bettencourt, "Optimal Reblocking as a Practical Tool for Neighborhood Development."

100. Alexander, *The Timeless Way of Building*.

101. Bettencourt, "The Kind of Problem a City Is."

102. Hayek, "The Use of Knowledge in Society"; Bettencourt, "The Uses of Big Data in Cities."

103. Bettencourt, "The Uses of Big Data in Cities."

104. Glaeser, *Triumph of the City*.

105. Laland, Matthews, and Feldman, "An Introduction to Niche Construction Theory."

106. Henrich, *The Secret of Our Success*.

4 THE STATISTICS OF URBAN QUANTITIES

1. Alonso, *Location and Land Use*; O'Sullivan, *Urban Economics*; Fujita, *Urban Economic Theory*; Glaeser, *Cities, Agglomeration, and Spatial Equilibrium*.

2. Bettencourt, "The Origins of Scaling in Cities"; Ortman et al., "The Pre-history of Urban Scaling."

3. Alonso, *Location and Land Use*; Glaeser, *Cities, Agglomeration, and Spatial Equilibrium*; Bettencourt, "The Origins of Scaling in Cities"; Fujita, Krugman, and Venables, *The Spatial Economy*; Anas, Arnott, and Small, "Urban Spatial Structure."

4. Bettencourt, "The Origins of Scaling in Cities."

5. Fischer, "The Subcultural Theory of Urbanism"; Bettencourt, Samaniego, and Youn, "Professional Diversity and the Productivity of Cities"; Youn et al., "Scaling and Universality in Urban Economic Diversification"; Feldman and Audretsch, "Innovation in Cities."

6. Jacobs, *Cities and the Wealth of Nations*; Sampson, *Great American City*; Lee et al., "Neighborhood Income Composition by Household Race and Income, 1990–2009."

7. Sampson, *Great American City*; Bruch, "How Population Structure Shapes Neighborhood Segregation"; Intrator, Tannen, and Massey, "Segregation by Race and Income in the United States 1970–2010"; Reardon and Bischoff, "Income Inequality and Income Segregation."

8. Chetty et al., "The Fading American Dream"; Chen, Myles, and Picot, "Why Have Poorer Neighbourhoods Stagnated Economically while the Richer Have Flourished?"

9. Sampson, *Great American City*; Chetty et al., "The Fading American Dream"; Krivo et al., "Social Isolation of Disadvantage and Advantage."

10. Sampson, *Great American City*; Solari, "Affluent Neighborhood Persistence and Change in U.S. Cities."

11. Hannon, "Poverty, Delinquency, and Educational Attainment"; O'Rand, "The Precious and the Precocious"; Shuey and Willson, "Cumulative Disadvantage and Black-White Disparities in Life-Course Health Trajectories."

12. Acs, "Innovation and the Growth of Cities"; Bettencourt et al., "Growth, Innovation, Scaling, and the Pace of Life in Cities"; Briggs et al., "Inclusive Economic Growth in America's Cities."

13. Barro and Sala-i-Martin, *Economic Growth*.

14. Bettencourt and Lobo, "Urban Scaling in Europe."

15. Bettencourt et al., "Urban Scaling and Its Deviations."

16. Bettencourt et al., "Urban Scaling and Its Deviations."

17. Alves et al., "Distance to the Scaling Law"; Alves et al., "Scale-Adjusted Metrics for Predicting the Evolution of Urban Indicators and Quantifying the Performance of Cities."

18. Sahasranaman and Bettencourt, "Urban Geography and Scaling of Contemporary Indian Cities."

19. Sahasranaman and Bettencourt, "Urban Geography and Scaling of Contemporary Indian Cities"; Sahasranaman and Bettencourt, "Economic Geography and the Scaling of Urban and Regional Income in India."

20. Zünd and Bettencourt, "Growth and Urban Development in Prefecture-Level China."

21. Zünd and Bettencourt, "Growth and Urban Development in Prefecture-Level China."

22. Alonso, *Location and Land Use*; Glaeser, *Cities, Agglomeration, and Spatial Equilibrium*; Bettencourt, "The Origins of Scaling in Cities."

23. Åström and Murray, *Feedback Systems*.

24. Åström and Murray, *Feedback Systems*.

25. Zinn-Justin, *Phase Transitions and Renormalization Group*.

26. Peters and Adamou, "Insurance Makes Wealth Grow Faster."

27. Ma, *Statistical Mechanics*; Caswell, *Matrix Population Models*.

28. Caswell, *Matrix Population Models*; Cohen, "Ergodic Theorems in Demography."

29. Ma, *Statistical Mechanics*.

30. Goldenfeld, *Lectures on Phase Transitions and the Renormalization Group*.

31. Arcaute et al., "Constructing Cities, Deconstructing Scaling Laws"; Leitão et al., "Is This Scaling Nonlinear?"; Barthélemy, *The Structure and Dynamics of Cities*.

32. Bettencourt et al., "Urban Scaling and Its Deviations"; Alves et al., "Distance to the Scaling Law"; Gomez-Lievano, Youn, and Bettencourt, "The Statistics of Urban Scaling and Their Connection to Zipf's Law."

33. Bettencourt et al., "Urban Scaling and Its Deviations"; Gomez-Lievano, Youn, and Bettencourt, "The Statistics of Urban Scaling and Their Connection to Zipf's Law"; Gomez-Lievano, Patterson-Lomba, and Hausmann, "Explaining the Prevalence, Scaling and Variance of Urban Phenomena."

34. Bettencourt et al., "Urban Scaling and Its Deviations."

35. Arthur, *Increasing Returns and Path Dependence in the Economy*; Johnson, *Non-equilibrium Social Science and Policy*; Depersin and Barthélemy, "From Global Scaling to the Dynamics of Individual Cities."

5 DIVERSITY AND THE PRODUCTIVITY OF CITIES

1. Darwin, *The Descent of Man*, 752.

2. Johnson and Munshi-South, "Evolution of Life in Urban Environments."

3. Durkheim and Lukes, *The Division of Labor in Society*.

4. Simmel and Levine, *On Individuality and Social Forms*.

5. Park, Burgess, and McKenzie, *The City*; Wirth, "Urbanism as a Way of Life"; Zorbaugh and Chudacoff, *The Gold Coast and the Slum*; DuBois, Anderson, and Eaton, *The Philadelphia Negro*.

6. Wirth, "Urbanism as a Way of Life."

7. Wirth, "Urbanism as a Way of Life."

8. Wirth, "Urbanism as a Way of Life."

9. Simmel and Levine, *On Individuality and Social Forms*.

10. Durkheim and Lukes, *The Division of Labor in Society*; Simmel and Levine, *On Individuality and Social Forms*.

11. Fischer, "Toward a Subcultural Theory of Urbanism"; Fischer, "The Subcultural Theory of Urbanism."

12. Durkheim and Lukes, *The Division of Labor in Society*.

13. Hayek, "The Use of Knowledge in Society."

14. Polanyi, *The Great Transformation: The Political and Economic Origins of Our Time*.

15. Jacobs, *The Death and Life of Great American Cities*.

16. Jacobs, *The Economy of Cities*; Jacobs, *Cities and the Wealth of Nations*.

17. Jacobs, *Cities and the Wealth of Nations*, 11.

18. Hayek, "The Use of Knowledge in Society."

19. Arthur, *The Nature of Technology*.

20. Cover and Thomas, "Information Theory and Statistics"; Jaynes, "Information Theory and Statistical Mechanics."

21. Frank, "Mutual Policing and Repression of Competition in the Evolution of Cooperative Groups."

22. Walls, "National Establishment Time-Series Database."

23. Darwin and Mayr, *On the Origin of Species*.

24. Bettencourt, Samaniego, and Youn, "Professional Diversity and the Productivity of Cities."

25. Christaller, *Central Places in Southern Germany*; Haggett, Cliff, and Frey, *Locational Analysis in Human Geography*; Batty, "Hierarchy in Cities and City Systems."

26. Hidalgo and Hausmann, "The Building Blocks of Economic Complexity"; Hausmann and Hidalgo, "The Network Structure of Economic Output."

27. Hong et al., "A Common Trajectory Recapitulated by Urban Economies."

28. Bettencourt, Samaniego, and Youn, "Professional Diversity and the Productivity of Cities."

29. Arrow, "The Economic Implications of Learning by Doing."

30. Ericsson, *The Cambridge Handbook of Expertise and Expert Performance*; Nagy et al., "Statistical Basis for Predicting Technological Progress."

31. Simon, "The Architecture of Complexity."

32. Arthur, *The Nature of Technology*; Simon, "The Architecture of Complexity"; Feldman, "Knowledge Complementarity and Innovation."

33. Kelly, *The Lifeways of Hunter-Gatherers*.

34. Bettencourt, Samaniego, and Youn, "Professional Diversity and the Productivity of Cities"; Bettencourt, "The Origins of Scaling in Cities"; Youn et al., "Scaling and Universality in Urban Economic Diversification."

35. Kline and Boyd, "Population Size Predicts Technological Complexity in Oceania."

36. Henrich, *The Secret of Our Success*; Collard et al., "Population Size and Cultural Evolution in Nonindustrial Food-Producing Societies"; Collard et al., "What Drives the Evolution of Hunter–Gatherer Subsistence Technology?"; Kolodny, Creanza, and Feldman, "Evolution in Leaps."

37. Bettencourt, "The Origins of Scaling in Cities."

38. Carneiro, "The Transition from Quantity to Quality."

39. Bettencourt, "Impact of Changing Technology on the Evolution of Complex Informational Networks."

40. Kirsch, "The Incredible Shrinking World?"; Kolko, "The Death of Cities? The Death of Distance?"; Glaeser, *Triumph of the City*.

41. Kirsch, "The Incredible Shrinking World?"; Kolko, "The Death of Cities? The Death of Distance?"; Glaeser, *Triumph of the City*; Tranos and Nijkamp, "The Death of Distance Revisited."

42. Kolko, "The Death of Cities? The Death of Distance?"; Sinai and Waldfogel, "Geography and the Internet."

43. Mumford, *The City in History*.

44. Kolko, "The Death of Cities? The Death of Distance?"; Sinai and Waldfogel, "Geography and the Internet"; Tranos and Nijkamp, "The Death of Distance Revisited."

45. Zhu, "Are Telecommuting and Personal Travel Complements or Substitutes?"

46. Zhu, "Are Telecommuting and Personal Travel Complements or Substitutes?"

47. Simon, "The Architecture of Complexity"; Chang, "Infrastructure Resilience to Disasters."

6   NEIGHBORHOODS AND HUMAN DEVELOPMENT

1. Smith, "The Archaeological Study of Neighborhoods and Districts in Ancient Cities."

2. Park, Burgess, and McKenzie, *The City*, 63–64.

3. Zimbardo, *The Lucifer Effect*.

4. O'Brien, *The Urban Commons*.

5. Wilson, *The Truly Disadvantaged*.

6. Riis, *How the Other Half Lives*; Morgan and Sinclair, *Charles Booth's London Poverty Maps*.

7. Wilson, "A Response to Critics of the Truly Disadvantaged."

8. Small and Newman, "Urban Poverty after *The Truly Disadvantaged*"; Sampson, "Neighbourhood Effects and Beyond"; Ioannides and Loury, "Job Information Networks, Neighborhood Effects, and Inequality."

9. Raudenbush and Sampson, "Ecometrics"; O'Brien, Sampson, and Winship, "Ecometrics in the Age of Big Data."

10. O'Brien, Sampson, and Winship, "Ecometrics in the Age of Big Data"; O'Brien, *The Urban Commons*.

11. Sampson and Raudenbush, "Systematic Social Observation of Public Spaces"; Morenoff, Sampson, and Raudenbush, "Neighborhood Inequality, Collective Efficacy, and the Spatial Dynamics of Urban Violence."

12. Wilson and Kelling, "Broken Windows."

13. O'Brien, Sampson, and Winship, "Ecometrics in the Age of Big Data"; Sampson, *Great American City*.

14. Sampson, *Great American City*.

15. Pearl, *Causality*; Morgan and Winship, *Counterfactuals and Causal Inference*.

16. Sampson, *Great American City*; Hannon, "Poverty, Delinquency, and Educational Attainment"; Shuey and Willson, "Cumulative Disadvantage and Black-White Disparities in Life-Course Health Trajectories."

17. Elliott et al., "The Effects of Neighborhood Disadvantage on Adolescent Development"; Hipp, "A Dynamic View of Neighborhoods"; Sampson and Laub, *Crime in the Making*.

18. Shuey and Willson, "Cumulative Disadvantage and Black-White Disparities in Life-Course Health Trajectories."

19. Rittel and Webber, "Dilemmas in a General Theory of Planning."

20. Sanbonmatsu et al. "Moving to Opportunity for Fair Housing Demonstration Program—Final Impacts Evaluation."

21. Briggs et al., "Inclusive Economic Growth in America?"

22. Briggs, Popkin, and Goering, *Moving to Opportunity*.

23. Ludwig et al., "Neighborhood Effects on the Long-Term Well-Being of Low-Income Adults"; Sampson, "Moving and the Neighborhood Glass Ceiling."

24. Ludwig et al., "Long-Term Neighborhood Effects on Low-Income Families."

25. Sampson, "Moving and the Neighborhood Glass Ceiling."

26. Briggs, Popkin, and Goering, *Moving to Opportunity*; Sampson, "Moving and the Neighborhood Glass Ceiling"; Sampson, "Moving to Inequality."

27. Chetty, Hendren, and Katz, "The Effects of Exposure to Better Neighborhoods on Children."

28. Chetty et al., "The Fading American Dream"; Chetty and Hendren, "The Impacts of Neighborhoods on Intergenerational Mobility I: Childhood Exposure Effects"; Chetty and Hendren, "The Impacts of Neighborhoods on Intergenerational Mobility II: County-Level Estimates."

29. Chetty, Hendren, and Katz, "The Effects of Exposure to Better Neighborhoods on Children"; Chetty and Hendren, "The Impacts of Neighborhoods on Intergenerational Mobility I: Childhood Exposure Effects"; Chetty and Hendren, "The Impacts of Neighborhoods on Intergenerational Mobility II: County-Level Estimates"; Chetty et al., "Childhood Environment and Gender Gaps in Adulthood."

30. Sharkey, "The Acute Effect of Local Homicides on Children's Cognitive Performance"; Sharkey et al., "The Effect of Local Violence on Children's Attention and Impulse Control."

31. Schelling, *Micromotives and Macrobehavior*.

32. Stauffer and Solomon, "Ising, Schelling and Self-Organising Segregation."

33. Stauffer and Solomon, "Ising, Schelling and Self-Organising Segregation"; Vinkovic and Kirman, "A Physical Analogue of the Schelling Model"; Clark and Fossett, "Understanding the Social Context of the Schelling Segregation Model."

34. Bruch and Mare, "Neighborhood Choice and Neighborhood Change."

35. Bruch, "How Population Structure Shapes Neighborhood Segregation."

36. Sahasranaman and Jensen, "Dynamics of Transformation from Segregation to Mixed Wealth Cities"; Sahasranaman and Jensen, "Ethnicity and Wealth."

37. United Nations, "17 Goals to Transform Our World."

38. Gianessi, Peskin, and Wolff, "The Distributional Effects of Uniform Air Pollution Policy in the United States"; Richardson, "A Note on the Distributional Effects of Road Pricing"; Layard, "The Distributional Effects of Congestion Taxes."

39. Gianessi, Peskin, and Wolff, "The Distributional Effects of Uniform Air Pollution Policy in the United States"; Parry, "Are Emissions Permits Regressive?"; Johnstone and Serret, *The Distributional Effects of Environmental Policy*; Price and Hancock, "Distributional Effects of Liberalising UK Residential Utility Markets"; Metcalf and Weisbach, "The Design of a Carbon Tax," *Harvard Environmental Law Review* 33 (2009): 499; Büchs, Bardsley, and Duwe, "Who Bears the Brunt? Distributional Effects of Climate Change Mitigation Policies."

40. Gianessi, Peskin, and Wolff, "The Distributional Effects of Uniform Air Pollution Policy in the United States"; Sharma et al., "Indoor Air Quality and Acute Lower Respiratory Infection in Indian Urban Slums"; Brunekreef and Holgate, "Air Pollution and Health"; Pope et al., "Particulate Air Pollution as a Predictor of Mortality in a Prospective Study of U.S. Adults."

41. Bitler, Gelbach, and Hoynes, "What Mean Impacts Miss."

42. Hammer et al., "Distributional Effects of Social Sector Expenditures in Malaysia, 1974–1989."

43. Barja and Urquiola, "Capitalization, Regulation and the Poor."

44. Price and Hancock, "Distributional Effects of Liberalising UK Residential Utility Markets."

45. Ruijs, Zimmermann, and van den Berg, "Demand and Distributional Effects of Water Pricing Policies."

46. Neuhoff et al., "Distributional Effects of Energy Transition"; Schlör, Fischer, and Hake, "Sustainable Development, Justice and the Atkinson Index."

47. Layard, "The Distributional Effects of Congestion Taxes"; Richardson, "A Note on the Distributional Effects of Road Pricing."

48. Weber and Matthews, "Quantifying the Global and Distributional Aspects of American Household Carbon Footprint."

49. Alexander, *Notes on the Synthesis of Form*.

50. Jacobs, *The Death and Life of Great American Cities*; Alexander, *The Timeless Way of Building*.

51. Geddes, *Cities in Evolution*.

52. Alinsky, *Rules for Radicals*, xix.

53. UN-Habitat, *The Challenge of Slums*.

54. UN-Habitat, *State of the World's Cities 2012/2013, Prosperity of Cities*; UN-Habitat, *The Challenge of Slums*.

55. Riis, *How the Other Half Lives*.

56. Morgan and Sinclair, *Charles Booth's London Poverty Maps*.

57. UN-Habitat, *The Challenge of Slums*; UN-Habitat, *State of the World's Cities 2012/2013, Prosperity of Cities*.

58. Patel, Baptist, and D'Cruz, "Knowledge Is Power—Informal Communities Assert Their Right to the City through SDI and Community-Led Enumerations"; Mitlin and Satterthwaite, *Urban Poverty in the Global South*.

59. Mitlin and Satterthwaite, *Urban Poverty in the Global South*; Satterthwaite, "Missing the Millennium Development Goal Targets for Water and Sanitation in Urban Areas."

60. UN-Habitat, *The Challenge of Slums*; Satterthwaite, "Missing the Millennium Development Goal Targets for Water and Sanitation in Urban Areas."

61. Lobo et al., "Urban Scaling and the Production Function for Cities."

62. United Nations Development Programme, "Human Development Report 2013."

63. UN-Habitat, *The Challenge of Slums*.

64. Bettencourt, "The Origins of Scaling in Cities."

65. Bettencourt, "The Origins of Scaling in Cities."

66. Bettencourt, "The Origins of Scaling in Cities."

67. Hoch, "Income and City Size"; Henderson, *Urban Development*; Bettencourt et al., "Growth, Innovation, Scaling, and the Pace of Life in Cities"; Bettencourt, "The Origins of Scaling in Cities."

68. Mumford, *The City in History*.

69. Vishwanath et al., "Urbanization beyond Municipal Boundaries: Nurturing Metropolitan Economies and Connecting Peri-urban Areas in India."

70. Bettencourt, "The Origins of Scaling in Cities"; Glaeser, Scheinkman, and Shleifer, "Economic Growth in a Cross-Section of Cities."

71. Anselin, *Spatial Econometrics*.

72. Kuznets, "Economic Growth and Income Inequality."

73. Brelsford et al., "Heterogeneity and Scale of Sustainable Development in Cities."

74. Brelsford et al., "Heterogeneity and Scale of Sustainable Development in Cities."

75. Sampson, *Great American City*; Reardon and Bischoff, "Income Inequality and Income Segregation."

76. Sampson, *Great American City*; Reardon and Bischoff, "Income Inequality and Income Segregation."

77. Sampson, *Great American City*.

78. Frank, "Natural Selection. III. Selection versus Transmission and the Levels of Selection."

79. Page and Nowak, "Unifying Evolutionary Dynamics."

80. Cover, *Elements of Information Theory*; Theil, *Economics and Information Theory*.

81. Sampson, *Great American City*; Ludwig et al., "Neighborhood Effects on the Long-Term Well-Being of Low-Income Adults"; Intrator, Tannen, and Massey, "Segregation by Race and Income in the United States 1970–2010"; Reardon and Bischoff, "Income Inequality and Income Segregation."

82. Cover, *Elements of Information Theory*; Frank, "Natural Selection. V. How to Read the Fundamental Equations of Evolutionary Change in Terms of Information Theory"; Theil, *Economics and Information Theory*.

83. Theil, *Economics and Information Theory*; Roberto, "The Divergence Index."

84. Theil, *Economics and Information Theory*.

85. Theil, *Economics and Information Theory*; Roberto, "The Divergence Index."

86. Bettencourt, Hand, and Lobo, "Spatial Selection and the Statistics of Neighborhoods."

87. Roberto, "The Divergence Index."

88. Owens, "Neighborhoods on the Rise"; Ludwig et al., "Neighborhood Effects on the Long-Term Well-Being of Low-Income Adults"; Roberto and Hwang, "Barriers to Integration."

89. Goldenfeld and Kadanoff, "Simple Lessons from Complexity."

90. Darwin and Mayr, *On the Origin of Species*; Mumford, *The City in History*; Jacobs, *The Death and Life of Great American Cities*.

91. Anderson, "More Is Different."

92. Landau et al., *Statistical Physics, Part 1*; Kadanoff, *Statistical Physics*; Ma, *Statistical Mechanics*.

93. Goldenfeld, *Lectures on Phase Transitions and the Renormalization Group*; Zinn-Justin, *Phase Transitions and Renormalization Group*.

94. Schelling, *Micromotives and Macrobehavior*; Bruch and Mare, "Neighborhood Choice and Neighborhood Change"; Smith, "The Archaeological Study of Neighborhoods and Districts in Ancient Cities."

95. Zinn-Justin, *Phase Transitions and Renormalization Group*; Goldenfeld, *Lectures on Phase Transitions and the Renormalization Group*; Kadanoff, *Statistical Physics*.

96. Glaeser, *Cities, Agglomeration, and Spatial Equilibrium*.

97. Jackson, *Social and Economic Networks*; Sampson, *Great American City*.

98. Kadanoff, *Statistical Physics*.

99. Elad and Feuer, "Restoration of a Single Superresolution Image from Several Blurred, Noisy, and Undersampled Measured Images"; Yang et al., "Image Super-resolution via Sparse Representation."

100. Frank, "Natural Selection. V. How to Read the Fundamental Equations of Evolutionary Change in Terms of Information Theory"; Page and Nowak, "Unifying Evolutionary Dynamics"; Nelson and Winter, *An Evolutionary Theory of Economic Change*; Smith and Krueger, *The Wealth of Nations*.

101. Goldenfeld and Kadanoff, "Simple Lessons from Complexity."

102. Browning, Cagney, and Boettner, "Neighborhood, Place, and the Life Course"; South et al., "Neighborhood Attainment over the Adult Life Course"; Chetty et al., "The Fading American Dream"; Hipp, "A Dynamic View of Neighborhoods."

103. Reardon and Bischoff, "Income Inequality and Income Segregation"; Chen, Myles, and Picot, "Why Have Poorer Neighbourhoods Stagnated Economically while the Richer Have Flourished?"

104. Chen, Myles, and Picot, "Why Have Poorer Neighbourhoods Stagnated Economically while the Richer Have Flourished?"; Krivo et al., "Social Isolation of Disadvantage and Advantage"; Firebaugh and Farrell, "Still Large, but Narrowing: The Sizable Decline in Racial Neighborhood Inequality in Metropolitan America, 1980–2010."

105. Lens, "Measuring the Geography of Opportunity"; Chetty et al., "The Fading American Dream."

106. Krivo et al., "Social Isolation of Disadvantage and Advantage"; Elliott et al., "The Effects of Neighborhood Disadvantage on Adolescent Development"; Wilson, "Studying Inner-City Social Dislocations."

107. Wilson, "Studying Inner-City Social Dislocations"; Wilson, *When Work Disappears*; Sampson, *Great American City*; Intrator, Tannen, and Massey, "Segregation by Race and Income in the United States 1970–2010"; Besbris et al., "Effect of Neighborhood Stigma on Economic Transactions."

108. Saunders, *Arrival City*.

109. Wang et al., "Urban Mobility and Neighborhood Isolation in America's 50 Largest Cities"; Manduca and Sampson, "Punishing and Toxic Neighborhood Environments Independently Predict the Intergenerational Social Mobility of Black and White Children."

110. Sahasranaman and Jensen, "Dynamics of Transformation from Segregation to Mixed Wealth Cities"; Farber et al., "Measuring Segregation Using Patterns of Daily Travel Behavior"; Le Roux, Vallée, and Commenges, "Social Segregation around the Clock in the Paris Region (France)."

111. Pred, "The Choreography of Existence"; An et al., "Space–Time Analysis."

112. Bettencourt, "The Origins of Scaling in Cities"; An et al., "Space–Time Analysis."

7 CITIES AND THE ORIGINS OF SETTLEMENTS IN HISTORY

1. Richerson and Boyd, *Not by Genes Alone*; Henrich, *The Secret of Our Success*.

2. Wirth, "Urbanism as a Way of Life."

3. Manzanilla, *Emergence and Change in Early Urban Societies*.

4. Manzanilla, *Emergence and Change in Early Urban Societies*.

5. Carneiro, "The Circumscription Theory."

6. Carneiro, "The Transition from Quantity to Quality."

7. Carneiro, "The Circumscription Theory"; Carneiro, "A Theory of the Origin of the State."

8. Manzanilla, *Emergence and Change in Early Urban Societies*.

9. Adams, *The Evolution of Urban Society*.

10. Kintigh et al., "Grand Challenges for Archaeology"; Ortman et al., "The Pre-history of Urban Scaling"; Ortman et al., "Settlement Scaling and Increasing Returns in an Ancient Society."

11. Ortman et al., "The Pre-history of Urban Scaling."

12. Smith, *The Aztecs*.

13. Ortman et al., "Settlement Scaling and Increasing Returns in an Ancient Society."

14. Ortman and Coffey, "Settlement Scaling in Middle-Range Societies."

15. Ortman et al., "Settlement Scaling and Economic Change in the Central Andes."

16. Hanson, *An Urban Geography of the Roman World, 100 BC to AD 300*.

17. Ober, *The Rise and Fall of Classical Greece*.

18. Hanson, *An Urban Geography of the Roman World, 100 BC to AD 300*.

19. Scheidel, Morris, and Saller, *The Cambridge Economic History of the Greco-Roman World*; Jongman, Jacobs, and Goldewijk, "Health and Wealth in the Roman Empire."

20. Hanson, *An Urban Geography of the Roman World, 100 BC to AD 300*.

21. Hanson and Ortman, "A Systematic Method for Estimating the Populations of Greek and Roman Settlements."

22. Hanson et al., "Urban Form, Infrastructure and Spatial Organisation in the Roman Empire."

23. Hanson et al., "Urban Form, Infrastructure and Spatial Organisation in the Roman Empire."

24. Hanson et al., "Urban Form, Infrastructure and Spatial Organisation in the Roman Empire."

25. Scheidel, Morris, and Saller, *The Cambridge Economic History of the Greco-Roman World*; Bresson and Rendall, *The Making of the Ancient Greek Economy*; Ober, *The Rise and Fall of Classical Greece*.

26. Hanson, Ortman, and Lobo, "Urbanism and the Division of Labour in the Roman Empire."

27. Cesaretti et al., "Population-Area Relationship in Medieval European Cities."

28. Dyer, "'Urban Decline' in England, 1377–1525"; Goose and Hinde, "Estimating Local Population Sizes at Fixed Points in Time: Part II—Specific Sources"; Rigby, "Urban Population in Late Medieval England"; Dyer, *Decline and Growth in English Towns 1400–1640*; Dyer, "How Urbanized Was Medieval England?"

29. Schofield, "The Geographical Distribution of Wealth in England, 1334–1649"; Darby et al., "The Changing Geographical Distribution of Wealth in England"; Sheail, "The Regional Distribution of Wealth in England as Indicated in the 1524/5 Lay Subsidy Returns."

30. Dyer, *Decline and Growth in English Towns 1400–1640*; Britnell, "The Economy of British Towns 1300–1540"; Bridbury, *Economic Growth*; Sheail, "The Regional Distribution of Wealth in England as Indicated in the 1524/5 Lay Subsidy Returns."

31. Cornwall, *Wealth and Society in Early Sixteenth Century England*; Hoskins, *The Age of Plunder*.

32. Piketty, *Capital in the 21st Century*; Piketty and Zucman, "Capital Is Back."

33. Cesaretti et al., "Increasing Returns to Scale in the Towns of Early Tudor England."

34. Cornwall, "The People of Rutland in 1522"; Rigby, "Urban Population in Late Medieval England."

35. Fletcher, "Low-Density, Agrarian-Based Urbanism."

36. Canuto et al., "Ancient Lowland Maya Complexity as Revealed by Airborne Laser Scanning of Northern Guatemala."

37. Evans et al., "Uncovering Archaeological Landscapes at Angkor Using Lidar."

38. Chase et al., "Geospatial Revolution and Remote Sensing LiDAR in Mesoamerican Archaeology"; Evans et al., "Uncovering Archaeological Landscapes at Angkor Using Lidar"; Canuto et al., "Ancient Lowland Maya Complexity as Revealed by Airborne Laser Scanning of Northern Guatemala."

39. Lobo et al., "Settlement Scaling Theory."

40. Kelly, *The Lifeways of Hunter-Gatherers*.

41. Wiessner, "A Functional Estimator of Population from Floor Area"; Yellen, *Archaeological Approaches to the Present*.

42. Wiessner, "A Functional Estimator of Population from Floor Area."

43. Mumford, *The City in History*.

44. Whitelaw, "The Social Organisation of Space in Hunter-Gatherer Communities."

45. Hamilton et al., "Nonlinear Scaling of Space Use in Human Hunter-Gatherers."

46. Hamilton et al., "Nonlinear Scaling of Space Use in Human Hunter-Gatherers."

47. Wrigley, *Energy and the English Industrial Revolution*.

48. Ober, *The Rise and Fall of Classical Greece*; Algaze, *Ancient Mesopotamia at the Dawn of Civilization*; Cowgill, *Ancient Teotihuacan*; Harper, *The Fate of Rome*.

49. Jedwab and Vollrath, "Urbanization without Growth in Historical Perspective."

50. Ober, *The Rise and Fall of Classical Greece*.

51. Delile et al., "Lead in Ancient Rome's City Waters."

52. Ober, *The Rise and Fall of Classical Greece*; Kander, Malanima, and Warde, *Power to the People*; Manning, *The Open Sea*.

53. Richerson and Boyd, *Not by Genes Alone*; Henrich, *The Secret of Our Success*.

8 URBAN SYSTEMS, DEMOGRAPHY, AND THE LAWS OF GEOGRAPHY

1. Berry, "Geography's Quantitative Revolution."

2. Bunge, *Theoretical Geography*; Burton, "The Quantitative Revolution and Theoretical Geography."

3. Bunge, *Theoretical Geography*.

4. Barnes, "Retheorizing Economic Geography."

5. Lösch, Woglom, and Stolper, *The Economics of Location*; Christaller, *Central Places in Southern Germany*; Isard, *Location and Space-Economy*.

6. Christaller, *Central Places in Southern Germany*.

7. Harris and Ullman, "The Nature of Cities."

8. Park, Burgess, and McKenzie, *The City*.

9. Lösch, Woglom, and Stolper, *The Economics of Location*; Isard, *Location and Space-Economy*.

10. Berry and Parr, *Market Centers and Retail Location*; Berry, "Internal Structure of the City"; Berry and Garrison, "A Note on Central Place Theory and the Range of a Good."

11. Isard, *Location and Space-Economy*.

12. Anselin, "Local Indicators of Spatial Association-LISA."

13. Anselin, *Spatial Econometrics*.

14. DiBiase, "The 50th Anniversary of GIS | ArcNews"; Goodchild, "Twenty Years of Progress."

15. Berry and Garrison, "Alternate Explanations of Urban Rank-Size Relationships."

16. Stewart, "The 'Gravitation,' or Geographical Drawing Power, of a College"; Stewart, "An Inverse Distance Variation for Certain Social Influences."

17. Stewart, "An Inverse Distance Variation for Certain Social Influences."

18. Zipf, *Human Behavior and the Principle of Least Effort*; Zipf, "On Dr. Miller's Contribution to the P1 P2/D Hypothesis"; Zipf, "The P1 P2/D Hypothesis"; Warntz, "The Topology of a Socio-economic Terrain and Spatial Flows"; Fotheringham and Webber, "Spatial Structure and the Parameters of Spatial Interaction Models."

19. Park, Lee, and Kim, "Generalized Gravity Model for Human Migration."

20. Curry, "The Random Spatial Economy"; Curry, "Central Places in the Random Space Economy"; Olsson, "Central Place Systems, Spatial Interaction, and Stochastic Processes"; Berry and Schwind, "Information and Entropy in Migrant Flows."

21. Wilson, *Entropy in Urban and Regional Modelling*.

22. Harte, *Maximum Entropy and Ecology*.

23. Jaynes, "Information Theory and Statistical Mechanics"; Jaynes, "Information Theory and Statistical Mechanics. II."

24. Wilson, *Entropy in Urban and Regional Modelling*.

25. Actually, Wilson originally computed the total number of configurations of all trips, Ω_H, but the two procedures are equivalent because $H = \log \Omega_H$, as is well known in statistical physics.

26. Wilson, *Entropy in Urban and Regional Modelling*.

27. Simini et al., "A Universal Model for Mobility and Migration Patterns."

28. Simini et al., "A Universal Model for Mobility and Migration Patterns."

29. Simini et al., "A Universal Model for Mobility and Migration Patterns"; Masucci et al., "Gravity versus Radiation Models."

30. Buch, Kleinert, and Toubal, "The Distance Puzzle."

31. Gibrat, *Les inégalités économiques*; Sutton, "Gibrat's Legacy."

32. Bettencourt et al., "Growth, Innovation, Scaling, and the Pace of Life in Cities."

33. Gabaix, "Zipf's Law for Cities: An Explanation."

34. Zipf, *Human Behavior and the Principle of Least Effort*.

35. Saichev, Malevergne, and Sornette, *Theory of Zipf's Law and Beyond*; Ioannides and Overman, "Zipf's Law for Cities."

36. Eeckhout, "Gibrat's Law for (All) Cities."

37. Levy, "Gibrat's Law for (All) Cities: Comment"; Eeckhout, "Gibrat's Law for (All) Cities: Reply."

38. Saichev, Malevergne, and Sornette, *Theory of Zipf's Law and Beyond*.

39. Rozenfeld et al., "The Area and Population of Cities"; Makse, Havlin, and Stanley, "Modelling Urban Growth Patterns."

40. Rozenfeld et al., "The Area and Population of Cities"; Makse, Havlin, and Stanley, "Modelling Urban Growth Patterns"; Swerts and Pumain, "A Statistical Approach to Territorial Cohesion."

41. Saichev, Malevergne, and Sornette, *Theory of Zipf's Law and Beyond*; Krugman, *The Self-Organizing Economy*; Gabaix, "Zipf's Law for Cities."

42. Gabaix, "Zipf's Law for Cities"; Levy and Solomon, "Power Laws Are Logarithmic Boltzmann Laws."

43. In addition to reading the original, E. G. Ravenstein, "The Laws of Migration," I highly recommend a talk given by Waldo Tobler toward the end of his life, on migration, change, and Ravenstein's work and its context. Tobler was always really interested in visualizations and maps, and you can find some, together with his review of a number of historical facts, at https://www.geog.ucsb.edu/~tobler/presentations/Maps-&-models-talk.pdf.

44. Ravenstein states that he is writing this paper motivated by a statement by "Dr. William Farr, to the effect that migration appeared to go on without any definite law."

45. White, *Chains of Opportunity*.

46. Caswell, *Matrix Population Models*.

47. Gibrat, *Les inégalités économiques*; Saichev, Malevergne, and Sornette, *Theory of Zipf's Law and Beyond*; Gabaix, "Zipf's Law for Cities."

48. Ioannides and Overman, "Zipf's Law for Cities."

49. Cohen, "Ergodic Theorems in Demography."

50. Caswell, *Matrix Population Models*.

51. Caswell, *Matrix Population Models*.

52. Bonacich, "Power and Centrality."

53. Barabási and Pósfai, *Network Science*.

54. Gould, "On the Geographical Interpretation of Eigenvalues."

55. Bonacich, "Power and Centrality."

56. To me, this and other examples make the case that the present tech industry should not be seen primarily in terms of its methods (computers and the internet) but rather in terms of its objectives, which are in the realm of applied social sciences or indeed social engineering. I made the case for a deeper engagement of academic social science with the possibilities opening up via these technologies in Bettencourt, "Make It Bigger! Science for the Age of Digital Social Technologies."

57. Gabaix, "Zipf's Law for Cities."

58. This is sometimes known as the *stage structure* in demographic models with life tables, where agents progress between them as they age or develop.

59. Berry and Garrison, "Alternate Explanations of Urban Rank-Size Relationships"; Eeckhout, "Gibrat's Law for (All) Cities."

60. Cristelli, Batty, and Pietronero, "There Is More than a Power Law in Zipf."

61. Gabaix, "Zipf's Law for Cities."

62. Saichev, Malevergne, and Sornette, *Theory of Zipf's Law and Beyond*.

63. Visser, "Zipf's Law, Power Laws and Maximum Entropy."

64. Cover and Thomas, "Information Theory and Statistics."

65. Frey, *The Great American Migration Slowdown*.

66. Goworowska, "Historical Migration of the Young, Single, and College Educated."

67. Woods, "Urbanisation in Europe and China during the Second Millennium"; Bairoch, *Cities and Economic Development*; De Vries, *European Urbanisation: 1500–1800*.

68. Dyson, "The Role of the Demographic Transition in the Process of Urbanization"; Bocquier and Costa, "Which Transition Comes First?"

69. Kander, Malanima, and Warde, *Power to the People*.

70. Dyson, "The Role of the Demographic Transition in the Process of Urbanization"; Mumford, *The City in History*.

71. Jongman, Jacobs, and Klein Goldewijk, "Health and Wealth in the Roman Empire"; Rawcliffe, *Urban Bodies*.

72. Dyson, "The Role of the Demographic Transition in the Process of Urbanization"; Coale, "Demographic Transition"; Preston, "Urban Growth in Developing Countries."

73. Mumford, *The City in History*.

74. Dyson, "The Role of the Demographic Transition in the Process of Urbanization"; Bocquier and Costa, "Which Transition Comes First?"; Preston, "Urban Growth in Developing Countries."

9 GROWTH, INFORMATION, AND THE EMERGENCE OF INSTITUTIONS

1. Appelbaum, *The Economists' Hour*.

2. Famously, Nobel Prize–winning economist Robert Lucas stated that understanding economic growth was important because "once you start thinking about this problem, you cannot think of anything else." See Lucas, "On the Mechanics of Economic Development."

3. Arthur, *Increasing Returns and Path Dependence in the Economy*; Arthur, "Complexity and the Economy"; Romer, "Increasing Returns and Long-Run Growth."

4. Barro and Sala-i-Martin, *Economic Growth*.

5. Solow, "Technical Change and the Aggregate Production Function."

6. Breton, "World Total Factor Productivity Growth and the Steady-State Rate in the 20th Century."

7. Barro and Sala-i-Martin, *Economic Growth*; Acemoglu, *Introduction to Modern Economic Growth*; Jones, "Growth and Ideas."

8. Jones, "Growth and Ideas"; Jones, "Growth: With or without Scale Effects?"

9. Barro and Sala-i-Martin, *Economic Growth*; Acemoglu, *Introduction to Modern Economic Growth*; Romer, *Advanced Macroeconomics*.

10. Romer, "Increasing Returns and Long-Run Growth"; Romer, "Endogenous Technological Change."

11. Grossman and Helpman, "Endogenous Innovation in the Theory of Growth."

12. Aghion and Howitt, "A Model of Growth through Creative Destruction."

13. Jones and Romer, "The New Kaldor Facts."

14. Kremer, "Population Growth and Technological Change: One Million B.C. to 1990."

15. Hidalgo and Hausmann, "The Building Blocks of Economic Complexity"; Hausmann and Hidalgo, "The Network Structure of Economic Output."

16. Hidalgo et al., "The Product Space Conditions the Development of Nations."

17. Hsieh et al., "The Allocation of Talent and U.S. Economic Growth."

18. Hsieh and Klenow, "Misallocation and Manufacturing TFP in China and India."

19. Jones, "Growth and Ideas."

20. Banerjee and Duflo, "Growth Theory through the Lens of Development Economics."

21. Acemoglu, *Introduction to Modern Economic Growth*; Olson, "Distinguished Lecture on Economics in Government: Big Bills Left on the Sidewalk."

22. Jones and Romer, "The New Kaldor Facts"; Acemoglu, Johnson, and Robinson, "Institutions as the Fundamental Cause of Long-Run Growth"; Bresson and Rendall, *The Making of the Ancient Greek Economy*; North, *Transaction Costs, Institutions, and Economic Performance*.

23. Glaeser et al., "Do Institutions Cause Growth?"

24. North, *Transaction Costs, Institutions, and Economic Performance*; North, "Institutions, Transaction Costs and Economic Growth."

25. Duranton, "The Urbanization and Development Puzzle."

26. Duranton, "The Urbanization and Development Puzzle."

27. Barro and Sala-i-Martin, *Economic Growth*; Hsieh and Klenow, "Misallocation and Manufacturing TFP in China and India."

28. Jacobs, *The Economy of Cities*; Lucas, "On the Mechanics of Economic Development."

29. Jones and Romer, "The New Kaldor Facts"; Jones, "Growth and Ideas"; Acemoglu, Johnson, and Robinson, "Institutions as the Fundamental Cause of Long-Run Growth."

30. Glaeser, *Cities, Agglomeration, and Spatial Equilibrium*; Bettencourt, "The Origins of Scaling in Cities"; Lucas, "On the Mechanics of Economic Development"; Alonso, *Location and Land Use*.

31. Price, "Selection and Covariance"; Andersen, "Population Thinking, Price's Equation and the Analysis of Economic Evolution."

32. Jones and Romer, "The New Kaldor Facts"; Acemoglu, Johnson, and Robinson, "Institutions as the Fundamental Cause of Long-Run Growth"; North, "Institutions, Transaction Costs and Economic Growth."

33. World Bank, "Extreme Poverty Income Definition."

34. Bairoch, *Cities and Economic Development*; De Vries, *European Urbanisation: 1500–1800*.

35. Okasha, *Evolution and the Levels of Selection*.

36. Price, "Selection and Covariance"; Frank, "Natural Selection. VII. History and Interpretation of Kin Selection Theory"; Frank, *Foundations of Social Evolution*.

37. Chetty et al., "The Fading American Dream."

38. Barro and Sala-i-Martin, *Economic Growth*.

39. Lefebvre and Nicholson-Smith, *The Production of Space*.

40. Price, "Selection and Covariance"; Frank, *Foundations of Social Evolution*.

41. If the reader is an academic, I would recommend trying this reasoning on faculty in universities, which takes out the purely economic realm.

42. Frank, *Foundations of Social Evolution*.

43. Frank, "Mutual Policing and Repression of Competition in the Evolution of Cooperative Groups."

44. Frank, *Foundations of Social Evolution*.

45. Cover and Thomas, "Information Theory and Statistics."

46. Cover and Thomas, "Information Theory and Statistics"; Kelly, "A New Interpretation of Information Rate."

47. Frank, "Natural Selection. V. How to Read the Fundamental Equations of Evolutionary Change in Terms of Information Theory"; Rice, *Evolutionary Theory*.

48. Cover and Thomas, "Information Theory and Statistics"; Kelly, "A New Interpretation of Information Rate."

49. Meder et al., "Ergodicity-Breaking Reveals Time Optimal Economic Behavior in Humans"; Bombardini and Trebbi, "Risk Aversion and Expected Utility Theory."

50. Ingersoll, *Theory of Financial Decision Making*.

51. Samuelson, "The 'Fallacy' of Maximizing the Geometric Mean in Long Sequences of Investing or Gambling."

52. Becker, "A Theory of the Allocation of Time."

53. Cover and Thomas, "Information Theory and Statistics."

54. Cover and Thomas, "Information Theory and Statistics"; Kelly, "A New Interpretation of Information Rate."

55. Wolfers and Zitzewitz, "Interpreting Prediction Market Prices as Probabilities."

56. Bettencourt, "The Rules of Information Aggregation and Emergence of Collective Intelligent Behavior."

57. Cover and Thomas, "Information Theory and Statistics"; Kelly, "A New Interpretation of Information Rate."

58. Hayek, "The Use of Knowledge in Society."

59. Bettencourt, "The Rules of Information Aggregation and Emergence of Collective Intelligent Behavior."

60. Bettencourt, "Impact of Changing Technology on the Evolution of Complex Informational Networks."

61. Bettencourt, "The Rules of Information Aggregation and Emergence of Collective Intelligent Behavior."

62. Bettencourt et al., "Functional Structure of Cortical Neuronal Networks Grown *in Vitro*."

63. Bettencourt, "The Rules of Information Aggregation and Emergence of Collective Intelligent Behavior."

64. Arrow, "The Economic Implications of Learning by Doing."

65. Romer, "Endogenous Technological Change."

66. Chetty et al., "The Fading American Dream"; Chetty, Hendren, and Katz, "The Effects of Exposure to Better Neighborhoods on Children."

67. Laland, Matthews, and Feldman, "An Introduction to Niche Construction Theory."

10   WHAT ARE CITIES FOR? THE CHALLENGES AHEAD

1. Bettencourt, "The Uses of Big Data in Cities."

2. Sen, *Development as Freedom*; Sen, *Commodities and Capabilities*.

3. Smith and Krueger, *The Wealth of Nations*; Hidalgo and Hausmann, "The Building Blocks of Economic Complexity."

4. Turner, *Housing by People*.

5. Romero Lankao et al., "Urban Electrification."

6. World Economic Forum, "The Circular Economy Could Save Life on Earth—Starting with Cities."

7. Waldrop, "The Quest for the Sustainable City."

8. United Nations, *Sustainable Development Goals*.

9. Poon, "Carbon Emissions Are Already Falling in 30 Cities."

APPENDIX A

1. Arrow et al., "Capital-Labor Substitution and Economic Efficiency."

APPENDIX C

1. Cover and Thomas, "Information Theory and Statistics."

2. MacKay, *Information Theory, Inference, and Learning Algorithms*.

3. Shannon and Weaver, *The Mathematical Theory of Communication*.

4. Shannon and Weaver, *The Mathematical Theory of Communication*.

APPENDIX D

1. Caswell, *Matrix Population Models*.

BIBLIOGRAPHY

Acemoglu, Daron. *Introduction to Modern Economic Growth*. Princeton, NJ: Princeton University Press, 2009.

Acemoglu, Daron, Simon Johnson, and James Robinson. "Institutions as the Fundamental Cause of Long-Run Growth." In *Handbook of Economic Growth*, Vol. 1, edited by Philippe Aghion and Steven N. Durlauf, 385–472. Amsterdam: Elsevier, 2005. https://doi.org/10.1016/S1574-0684(05)01006-3.

Acs, Zoltan J. "Innovation and the Growth of Cities." In *Urban Dynamics and Growth: Advances in Urban Economics*, 635–658. Contributions to Economic Analysis 266. Amsterdam: Elsevier, 2004. http://www.sciencedirect.com/science/article/pii/S0573855504660202.

Acs, Zoltan J., David B. Audretsch, and Maryann P. Feldman. "R & D Spillovers and Recipient Firm Size." *Review of Economics and Statistics* 76, no. 2 (1994): 336–340. https://doi.org/10.2307/2109888.

Acuto, Michele, Susan Parnell, and Karen C. Seto. "Building a Global Urban Science." *Nature Sustainability* 1, no. 1 (January 2018): 2–4. https://doi.org/10.1038/s41893-017-0013-9.

Adams, Robert McCormick. *The Evolution of Urban Society: Early Mesopotamia and Prehispanic Mexico*. New Brunswick, NJ: Aldine Transaction, 2005. Originally published in 1964.

Aghion, Philippe, and Peter Howitt. "A Model of Growth through Creative Destruction." *Econometrica* 60, no. 2 (1992): 323–351. https://doi.org/10.2307/2951599.

Aharonson, Barak S., Joel A. C. Baum, and Maryann P. Feldman. "Desperately Seeking Spillovers? Increasing Returns, Industrial Organization and the Location of New Entrants in Geographic and Technological Space." *Industrial and Corporate Change* 16, no. 1 (February 1, 2007): 89–130. https://doi.org/10.1093/icc/dtl034.

Alexander, Christopher. "A City Is Not a Tree." *Architectural Forum* 122, no. 1 (1965): 58–62. http://www.patternlanguage.com/archive/cityisnotatree.html.

Alexander, Christopher. *Notes on the Synthesis of Form*. Cambridge, MA: Harvard University Press, 1964.

Alexander, Christopher. *The Timeless Way of Building*. Center for Environmental Structure Series 1. New York: Oxford University Press, 1979.

Alexander, Christopher, Sara Ishikawa, and Murray Silverstein. *A Pattern Language: Towns, Buildings, Construction*. New York: Oxford University Press, 1977.

Algaze, Guillermo. *Ancient Mesopotamia at the Dawn of Civilization: The Evolution of an Urban Landscape*. Chicago: University of Chicago Press, 2008.

Alinsky, Saul David. *Rules for Radicals: A Practical Primer for Realistic Radicals*. New York: Vintage Books, 1989.

Allen, Peter M. *Cities and Regions as Self-Organizing Systems: Models of Complexity*. Environmental Problems and Social Dynamics 1. Luxembourg: Gordon and Breach, 1997.

Alonso, William. *Location and Land Use: Toward a General Theory of Land Rent*. Cambridge, MA: Harvard University Press, 1977. Originally published in 1964.

Alves, Luiz G. A., Renio S. Mendes, Ervin K. Lenzi, and Haroldo V. Ribeiro. "Scale-Adjusted Metrics for Predicting the Evolution of Urban Indicators and Quantifying the Performance of Cities." *PLoS One* 10, no. 9 (September 10, 2015): e0134862. https://doi.org/10.1371/journal.pone.0134862.

Alves, Luiz G. A., Haroldo V. Ribeiro, Ervin K. Lenzi, and Renio S. Mendes. "Distance to the Scaling Law: A Useful Approach for Unveiling Relationships between Crime and Urban Metrics." *PLoS One* 8, no. 8 (August 5, 2013): e69580. https://doi.org/10.1371/journal.pone.0069580.

An, Li, Ming-Hsiang Tsou, Stephen E. S. Crook, Yongwan Chun, Brian Spitzberg, J. Mark Gawron, and Dipak K. Gupta. "Space–Time Analysis: Concepts, Quantitative Methods, and Future Directions." *Annals of the Association of American Geographers* 105, no. 5 (September 3, 2015): 891–914. https://doi.org/10.1080/00045608.2015.1064510.

Anas, Alex, Richard Arnott, and Kenneth A. Small. "Urban Spatial Structure." *Journal of Economic Literature* 36, no. 3 (1998): 1426–1464.

Andersen, Esben Sloth. "Population Thinking, Price's Equation and the Analysis of Economic Evolution." *Evolutionary and Institutional Economics Review* 1, no. 1 (November 2004): 127–148. https://doi.org/10.14441/eier.1.127.

Anderson, P. W. "More Is Different." *Science* 177, no. 4047 (August 4, 1972): 393–396. https://doi.org/10.1126/science.177.4047.393.

Anderson, Roy M., and Robert M. May. *Infectious Diseases of Humans: Dynamics and Control*. Oxford: Oxford University Press, 2010.

Andris, Clio, and Luís Bettencourt. "Development, Information and Social Connectivity in Côte d'Ivoire." *Infrastructure Complexity* 1, no. 1 (2014): 1–18. https://doi.org/10.1186/s40551-014-0001-4.

Angel, Shlomo, et al. "Atlas of Urban Expansion." Accessed September 20, 2019. http://www.atlasofurbanexpansion.org/.

Angel, Shlomo, Jason Parent, Daniel L. Civco, Alexander Blei, and David Potere. "The Dimensions of Global Urban Expansion: Estimates and Projections for All Countries, 2000–2050." *Progress in Planning* 75, no. 2 (February 2011): 53–107. https://doi.org/10.1016/j.progress.2011.04.001.

Anselin, Luc. "Local Indicators of Spatial Association—LISA." *Geographical Analysis* 27, no. 2 (1995): 93–115.

Anselin, Luc. *Spatial Econometrics: Methods and Models*. Studies in Operational Regional Science 4. Dordrecht: Springer Netherlands, 2013. http://link.springer.com/10.1007/978-94-015-7799-1.

Anselin, Luc, Attila Varga, and Zoltan Acs. "Local Geographic Spillovers between University Research and High Technology Innovations." *Journal of Urban Economics* 42, no. 3 (November 1997): 422–448. https://doi.org/10.1006/juec.1997.2032.

Appelbaum, Binyamin. *The Economists' Hour: False Prophets, Free Markets, and the Fracture of Society.* New York: Little, Brown, 2019.

Arbesman, Samuel, Jon M. Kleinberg, and Steven H. Strogatz. "Superlinear Scaling for Innovation in Cities." *Physical Review E* 79, no. 1 (January 30, 2009): 016115. https://doi.org/10.1103/PhysRevE.79.016115.

Arcaute, Elsa, Erez Hatna, Peter Ferguson, Hyejin Youn, Anders Johansson, and Michael Batty. "Constructing Cities, Deconstructing Scaling Laws." *Journal of the Royal Society Interface* 12, no. 102 (November 19, 2014): 20140745. https://doi.org/10.1098/rsif.2014.0745.

Arrow, Kenneth J. "The Economic Implications of Learning by Doing." In *Readings in the Theory of Growth*, edited by F. H. Hahn, 131–149. London: Palgrave Macmillan UK, 1971. http://link.springer.com/10.1007/978-1-349-15430-2_11.

Arrow, Kenneth J., Hollis B. Chenery, Bagicha Singh Minhas, and Robert M. Solow. "Capital-Labor Substitution and Economic Efficiency." *Review of Economics and Statistics* 43, no. 3 (1961): 225–250. https://doi.org/10.2307/1927286.

Arthur, W. Brian. "Complexity and the Economy." *Science* 284, no. 5411 (April 2, 1999): 107–109. https://doi.org/10.1126/science.284.5411.107.

Arthur, W. Brian. *Increasing Returns and Path Dependence in the Economy.* Economics, Cognition, and Society. Ann Arbor: University of Michigan Press, 1994.

Arthur, W. Brian. *The Nature of Technology: What It Is and How It Evolves.* New York: Free Press, 2011.

Åström, Karl J., and Richard M Murray. *Feedback Systems: An Introduction for Scientists and Engineers.* Princeton, NJ: Princeton University Press, 2008. http://www.cds.caltech.edu/~murray/amwiki.

Ausubel, Jesse H., Cesare Marchetti, and Perrin S. Meyer. "Toward Green Mobility: The Evolution of Transport." *European Review* 6, no. 2 (May 1998): 137–156. https://doi.org/10.1017/S1062798700003185.

Bairoch, Paul. *Cities and Economic Development: From the Dawn of History to the Present.* Translated by Christopher Braider. Chicago: University of Chicago Press, 1991.

Baldwin, Richard E. "Agglomeration and Endogenous Capital." *European Economic Review* 43, no. 2 (February 1999): 253–280. https://doi.org/10.1016/S0014-2921(98)00067-1.

Baldwin, Richard E., Rikard Forslid, Philippe J. Martin, Gianmarco I. P. Ottaviano, and Frédéric Robert-Nicoud, eds. *Economic Geography and Public Policy.* Princeton, NJ: Princeton University Press, 2003.

Banavar, Jayanth R., Francesca Colaiori, Alessandro Flammini, Amos Maritan, and Andrea Rinaldo. "Topology of the Fittest Transportation Network." *Physical Review Letters* 84, no. 20 (2000): 4745–4748. http://dx.doi.org/10.1103/PhysRevLett.84.4745.

Banerjee, Abhijit V., and Esther Duflo. "Growth Theory through the Lens of Development Economics." In *Handbook of Economic Growth*, Vol. 1, edited by Philippe Aghion and Steven N. Durlauf, 473–552. Amsterdam: Elsevier, 2005. https://doi.org/10.1016/S1574-0684(05)01007-5.

Barabási, A. "Emergence of Scaling in Random Networks." *Science* 286, no. 5439 (October 15, 1999): 509–512. https://doi.org/10.1126/science.286.5439.509.

Barabási, Albert-László, and Márton Pósfai. *Network Science.* Cambridge: Cambridge University Press, 2016.

Barenblatt, G. I. *Scaling, Self-Similarity, and Intermediate Asymptotics.* Cambridge Texts in Applied Mathematics 14. Cambridge: Cambridge University Press, 1996.

Barenblatt, Grigory Isaakovich. *Scaling*. Cambridge: Cambridge University Press, 2003.

Barja, Gover, and Miguel Urquiola. "Capitalization, Regulation and the Poor: Access to Basic Services in Bolivia." WIDER Discussion Papers. World Institute for Development Economics (UNU-WIDER), 2001. http://www.econstor.eu/handle/10419/52808.

Barnes, Trevor J. "Retheorizing Economic Geography: From the Quantitative Revolution to the 'Cultural Turn.'" In *Theory and Methods: Critical Essays in Human Geography*, edited by Chris Philo. London: Routledge, 2008. https://doi.org/10.4324/9781315236285-4.

Barro, Robert J., and Xavier I. Sala-i-Martin. *Economic Growth*. 2nd ed. Cambridge, MA: MIT Press, 2003.

Barthélemy, Marc. "Spatial Networks." *Physics Reports* 499, nos. 1–3 (February 2011): 1–101. https://doi.org/10.1016/j.physrep.2010.11.002.

Barthélemy, Marc. *The Structure and Dynamics of Cities: Urban Data Analysis and Theoretical Modeling*. Cambridge: Cambridge University Press, 2016.

Batty, Michael. *Cities and Complexity: Understanding Cities with Cellular Automata, Agent-Based Models, and Fractals*. Cambridge, MA: MIT Press, 2007.

Batty, Michael. "Hierarchy in Cities and City Systems." In *Hierarchy in Natural and Social Sciences*, edited by Denise Pumain, 143–168. Methodos Series 3. Dordrecht: Springer Netherlands, 2006. http://dx.doi.org/10.1007/1-4020-4127-6_7.

Batty, Michael. *The New Science of Cities*. Cambridge, MA: MIT Press, 2017.

Batty, Michael. "The Size, Scale and Shape of Cities." *Science* 319, no. 5864 (2008): 769–771. https://doi.org/ 10.1126/science.1151419.

Batty, Michael. "A Theory of City Size." *Science* 340, no. 6139 (2013): 1418–1419 https://doi.org/10.1126/science.1239870.

Batty, Michael, and Paul Longley. *Fractal Cities: A Geometry of Form and Function*. London: Academic Press, 1994.

Baylis, David. "Zahavi." *Transport Reviews* 4, no. 1 (January 1984): 115–116. https://doi.org/10.1080/01441648408716548.

Becker, Gary S. "Crime and Punishment: An Economic Approach." *Journal of Political Economy* 76, no. 2 (March 1968): 169–217. https://doi.org/10.1086/259394.

Becker, Gary S. "A Theory of the Allocation of Time." *Economic Journal* 75, no. 299 (1965): 493–517.

Benguigui, Lucien, Daniel Czamanski, Maria Marinov, and Yuval Portugali. "When and Where Is a City Fractal?" *Environment and Planning B: Planning and Design* 27, no. 4 (2000): 507–519. https://doi.org/10.1068/b2617.

Berry, Brian J. L. "City Size Distributions and Economic Development." *Ekistics* 13, no. 76 (February 1962): 90–97. http://www.jstor.org/stable/43613634.

Berry, Brian J. L. "Geography's Quantitative Revolution: Initial Conditions, 1954–1960. A Personal Memoir." In *Urban Geography in America, 1950–2000*. New York: Taylor & Francis Group, 2005. https://www.taylorfrancis.com/books/e/9781134728589/chapters/10.4324%2F9781315880952-14.

Berry, Brian J. L. "Internal Structure of the City." *Law and Contemporary Problems* 30, no. 1 (1965): 111–119. https://doi.org/10.2307/1190688.

Berry, Brian J. L., and William L. Garrison. "Alternate Explanations of Urban Rank-Size Relationships." *Annals of the Association of American Geographers* 48, no. 1 (March 1958): 83–90. https://doi.org/10.1111/j.1467-8306.1958.tb01559.x.

Berry, Brian J. L., and William L. Garrison. "A Note on Central Place Theory and the Range of a Good." *Economic Geography* 34, no. 4 (October 1, 1958): 304–311. https://doi.org/10.2307/142348.

Berry, Brian J. L., and William L. Garrison. "Recent Developments of Central Place Theory." *Papers in Regional Science* 4, no. 1 (January 1, 1958): 107–120. https://doi.org/10.1111/j.1435-5597.1958.tb01625.x.

Berry, Brian J. L., and Paul J. Schwind. "Information and Entropy in Migrant Flows." *Geographical Analysis* 1, no. 1 (1969): 5–14. https://doi.org/10.1111/j.1538-4632.1969.tb00601.x.

Berry, Brian Joe Lobley, Peter G. Goheen, and Harold Goldstein. *Metropolitan Area Definition: A Re-evaluation of Concept and Statistical Practice*. Washington, DC: U.S. Bureau of the Census, 1969. https://www.google.com/books/edition/Metropolitan_Area_Definition/IanWuQEACAAJ?hl=en.

Berry, Brian Joe Lobley, and John B. Parr. *Market Centers and Retail Location*. Englewood Cliffs, NJ: Prentice-Hall, 1988. http://agris.fao.org/agris-search/search.do?recordID=US201300652479.

Besbris, Max, Jacob William Faber, Peter Rich, and Patrick Sharkey. "Effect of Neighborhood Stigma on Economic Transactions." *Proceedings of the National Academy of Sciences* 112, no. 16 (April 21, 2015): 4994–4998. https://doi.org/10.1073/pnas.1414139112.

Bettencourt, L. M. A. "Impact of Changing Technology on the Evolution of Complex Informational Networks." *Proceedings of the IEEE* 102, no. 12 (December 2014): 1878–1891. https://doi.org/10.1109/JPROC.2014.2367132.

Bettencourt, L. M. A. "The Kind of Problem a City Is." In *Decoding the City: Urbanism in the Age of Big Data*, edited by Dietmar Offenhuber and Carlo Ratti, 168–179. Basel: Birkhauser, 2014.

Bettencourt, L. M. A. "Make It Bigger! Science for the Age of Digital Social Technologies." *Items* (blog). Accessed August 9, 2019. https://items.ssrc.org/parameters/make-it-bigger-science-for-the-age-of-digital-social-technologies/.

Bettencourt, L. M. A., Joe Hand, and José Lobo. "Spatial Selection and the Statistics of Neighborhoods." Santa Fe Institute. Accessed October 20, 2015. http://www.santafe.edu/research/working-papers/abstract/f59612222e160f34073a70d0eab490e7/.

Bettencourt, Luís, and Geoffrey West. "A Unified Theory of Urban Living." *Nature* 467, no. 7318 (October 21, 2010): 912–913. https://doi.org/10.1038/467912a.

Bettencourt, Luís, Vicky Chuqiao Yang, José Lobo, Chris Kempes, Diego Rybski, and Marcus Hamilton. "The Interpretation of Urban Scaling Analysis in Time." *Journal of the Royal Society Interface* 17, no. 163 (2020): 20190846. http://doi.org/10.1098/rsif.2019.0846.

Bettencourt, Luís M. A. "Designing for Complexity: The Challenge to Spatial Design from Sustainable Human Development in Cities." *Technology|Architecture +Design* 3, no. 1 (January 2, 2019): 24–32. https://doi.org/10.1080/24751448.2019.1571793.

Bettencourt, Luís M. A. "The Origins of Scaling in Cities." *Science* 340, no. 6139 (June 21, 2013): 1438–1441. https://doi.org/10.1126/science.1235823.

Bettencourt, Luís M. A. "The Rules of Information Aggregation and Emergence of Collective Intelligent Behavior." *Topics in Cognitive Science* 1, no. 4 (October 2009): 598–620. https://doi.org/10.1111/j.1756-8765.2009.01047.x.

Bettencourt, Luís M. A. "Towards a Statistical Mechanics of Cities." *Comptes rendus physique* 20, no. 4 (May–June 2019): 308–318. https://doi.org/10.1016/j.crhy.2019.05.007.

Bettencourt, Luís M. A. "Urban Growth and the Emergent Statistics of Cities." *Science Advances* 6, no. 34 (August 19, 2020): eaat8812. https://doi.org/10.1126/sciadv.aat8812.

Bettencourt, Luís M. A. "The Uses of Big Data in Cities." *Big Data* 2, no. 1 (March 2014): 12–22. https://doi.org/10.1089/big.2013.0042.

Bettencourt, Luís M. A., and Christa Brelsford. "Industrial Ecology: The View from Complex Systems." *Journal of Industrial Ecology* 19, no. 2 (April 2015): 195–197. https://doi.org/10.1111/jiec.12243.

Bettencourt, Luís M. A., Ariel Cintrón-Arias, David I. Kaiser, and Carlos Castillo-Chávez. "The Power of a Good Idea: Quantitative Modeling of the Spread of Ideas from Epidemiological Models." *Physica A: Statistical Mechanics and Its Applications* 364 (May 2006): 513–536. https://doi.org/10.1016/j.physa.2005.08.083.

Bettencourt, Luís M. A., and José Lobo. "Quantitative Methods for the Comparative Analysis of Cities in History." *Frontiers in Digital Humanities* 6 (November 1, 2019). https://doi.org/10.3389/fdigh.2019.00017.

Bettencourt, Luís M. A., and José Lobo. "Urban Scaling in Europe." *Journal of the Royal Society Interface* 13, no. 116 (March 1, 2016): 20160005. https://doi.org/10.1098/rsif.2016.0005.

Bettencourt, Luís M. A., José Lobo, Dirk Helbing, Christian Kühnert, and Geoffrey B. West. "Growth, Innovation, Scaling, and the Pace of Life in Cities." *Proceedings of the National Academy of Sciences* 104, no. 17 (April 24, 2007): 7301–7306. https://doi.org/10.1073/pnas.0610172104.

Bettencourt, Luís M. A., José Lobo, and Deborah Strumsky. "Invention in the City: Increasing Returns to Patenting as a Scaling Function of Metropolitan Size." *Research Policy* 36, no. 1 (February 2007): 107–120. https://doi.org/10.1016/j.respol.2006.09.026.

Bettencourt, Luís M. A., José Lobo, Deborah Strumsky, and Geoffrey B. West. "Urban Scaling and Its Deviations: Revealing the Structure of Wealth, Innovation and Crime across Cities." *PLoS One* 5, no. 11 (November 10, 2010): e13541. https://doi.org/10.1371/journal.pone.0013541.

Bettencourt, Luís M. A., José Lobo, and Hyejin Youn. "The Hypothesis of Urban Scaling: Formalization, Implications and Challenges." *ArXiv:1301.5919 [Nlin, Physics.so-ph]*, January 24, 2013. http://arxiv.org/abs/1301.5919.

Bettencourt, Luís M. A., Horacio Samaniego, and Hyejin Youn. "Professional Diversity and the Productivity of Cities." *Scientific Reports* 4 (June 23, 2014). https://doi.org/10.1038/srep05393.

Bettencourt, Luís M. A., Greg J. Stephens, Michael I. Ham, and Guenter W. Gross. "Functional Structure of Cortical Neuronal Networks Grown *in Vitro*." *Physical Review E* 75, no. 2 (February 23, 2007). https://doi.org/10.1103/PhysRevE.75.021915.

Bettencourt, Luís M. A., and Daniel Zünd. "Demography and the Emergence of Universal Patterns in Urban Systems." *Nature Communications* 11 (2020). https://doi.org/10.1038/s41467-020-18205-1.

Bitler, Marianne, Jonah Gelbach, and Hilary Hoynes. "What Mean Impacts Miss: Distributional Effects of Welfare Reform Experiments." NBER Working Paper 10121. Cambridge, MA: National Bureau of Economic Research, November 2003. http://www.nber.org/papers/w10121.

Black, Duncan, and Vernon Henderson. "A Theory of Urban Growth." *Journal of Political Economy* 107, no. 2 (April 1999): 252–284. https://doi.org/10.1086/250060.

Bocquier, Philippe, and Rafael Costa. "Which Transition Comes First? Urban and Demographic Transitions in Belgium and Sweden." *Demographic Research* 33 (December 17, 2015): 1297–1332. https://doi.org/10.4054/DemRes.2015.33.48.

Bogardus, Emory S. "Social Distance in the City." *Proceedings and Publications of the American Sociological Society* 20 (1926): 40–46. https://brocku.ca/MeadProject/Bogardus/Bogardus_1926.html8.

Bombardini, Matilde, and Francesco Trebbi. "Risk Aversion and Expected Utility Theory: An Experiment with Large and Small Stakes." *Journal of the European Economic Association* 10, no. 6 (2012): 1348–1399. https://doi.org/10.1111/j.1542-4774.2012.01086.x.

Bonacich, Phillip. "Power and Centrality: A Family of Measures." *American Journal of Sociology* 92, no. 5 (March 1987): 1170–1182. https://doi.org/10.1086/228631.

Brelsford, Christa, José Lobo, Joe Hand, and Luís M. A. Bettencourt. "Heterogeneity and Scale of Sustainable Development in Cities." *Proceedings of the National Academy of Sciences* 114, no. 34 (May 1, 2017): 8963–8968. https://doi.org/10.1073/pnas.1606033114.

Brelsford, Christa, Taylor Martin, and Luís M. A. Bettencourt. "Optimal Reblocking as a Practical Tool for Neighborhood Development." *Environment and Planning B: Urban Analytics and City Science* 46, no. 2 (June 12, 2017): 303–321. https://doi.org/10.1177/2399808317712715.

Brelsford, Christa, Taylor Martin, Joe Hand, and Luís M. A. Bettencourt. "Toward Cities without Slums: Topology and the Spatial Evolution of Neighborhoods." *Science Advances* 4, no. 8 (August 2018): eaar4644. https://doi.org/10.1126/sciadv.aar4644.

Bresson, Alain, and Steven Rendall. *The Making of the Ancient Greek Economy: Institutions, Markets, and Growth in the City-States*. Princeton, NJ: Princeton University Press, 2016.

Breton, Theodore R. "World Total Factor Productivity Growth and the Steady-State Rate in the 20th Century." *Economics Letters* 119, no. 3 (June 2013): 340–343. https://doi.org/10.1016/j.econlet.2013.03.013.

Bridbury, Anthony Randolph. *Economic Growth: England in the Later Middle Ages*. London: George Allen & Unwin, 1962.

Briggs, Xavier de Souza, Rolf Pendall, and Victor Rubin. "Inclusive Economic Growth in America's Cities: What's the Playbook and the Score?" SSRN Scholarly Paper. Rochester, NY: Social Science Research Network, June 22, 2015. https://papers.ssrn.com/abstract=2621876.

Briggs, Xavier de Souza, Susan J. Popkin, and John M. Goering. *Moving to Opportunity: The Story of an American Experiment to Fight Ghetto Poverty*. New York: Oxford University Press, 2010.

Britnell, Richard H. "The Economy of British Towns, 1300–1540." In *The Cambridge Urban History of Britain, Volume I: 600–1540*, 313–334. Cambridge: Cambridge University Press, 2000.

Browning, Christopher R., Kathleen A. Cagney, and Bethany Boettner. "Neighborhood, Place, and the Life Course." In *Handbook of the Life Course*, edited by Michael J. Shanahan, Jeylan T. Mortimer, and Monica Kirkpatrick Johnson, 597–620. Handbooks of Sociology and Social Research. Cham, Switzerland: Springer International Publishing, 2016. https://doi.org/10.1007/978-3-319-20880-0_26.

Bruch, Elizabeth E. "How Population Structure Shapes Neighborhood Segregation." *American Journal of Sociology* 119, no. 5 (March 1, 2014): 1221–1278. https://doi.org/10.1086/675411.

Bruch, Elizabeth E., and Robert D. Mare. "Neighborhood Choice and Neighborhood Change." *American Journal of Sociology* 112, no. 3 (2006): 667–709. https://doi.org/10.1086/507856.

Brueckner, Jan K. *Lectures on Urban Economics*. Cambridge, MA: MIT Press, 2011.

Brueckner, Jan K. "The Structure of Urban Equilibria: A Unified Treatment of the Muth-Mills Model." In *Handbook of Regional and Urban Economics*, Vol. 2, *Urban Economics*, edited by Edwin S. Mills, 821–845. Amsterdam: Elsevier, 1987. https://doi.org/10.1016/S1574-0080(87)80006-8.

Brueckner, Jan K., Jacques-François Thisse, and Yves Zenou. "Why Is Central Paris Rich and Downtown Detroit Poor?" *European Economic Review* 43, no. 1 (January 1999): 91–107. https://doi .org/10.1016/S0014-2921(98)00019-1.

Brunekreef, Bert, and Stephen T. Holgate. "Air Pollution and Health." *The Lancet* 360, no. 9341 (October 2002): 1233–1242. https://doi.org/10.1016/S0140-6736(02)11274-8.

Buch, Claudia M., Jörn Kleinert, and Farid Toubal. "The Distance Puzzle: On the Interpretation of the Distance Coefficient in Gravity Equations." *Economics Letters* 83, no. 3 (June 2004): 293–298. https://doi.org/10.1016/j.econlet.2003.10.022.

Büchs, Milena, Nicholas Bardsley, and Sebastian Duwe. "Who Bears the Brunt? Distributional Effects of Climate Change Mitigation Policies." *Critical Social Policy* (February 16, 2011): 285–307. https://doi.org/10.1177/0261018310396036.

Bunge, William. *Theoretical Geography*. Lund: Gleerup, 1966.

Burton, Ian. "The Quantitative Revolution and Theoretical Geography." *The Canadian Geographer/Le géographe canadien* 7, no. 4 (December 1, 1963): 151–162. https://doi.org/10.1111/j.1541-0064.1963 .tb00796.x.

Byrne, David. "If the 1% Stifles New York's Creative Talent, I'm Out of Here." *Guardian*, October 7, 2013. https://www.theguardian.com/commentisfree/2013/oct/07/new-york-1percent-stifles-creative -talent.

Canuto, Marcello A., Francisco Estrada-Belli, Thomas G. Garrison, Stephen D. Houston, Mary Jane Acuña, Milan Kováč, Damien Marken, Philippe Nondédéo, Luke Auld-Thomas, Cyril Castanet, David Chatelain, Carlos R. Chiriboga, Tomáš Drápela, Tibor Lieskovský, Alexandre Tokovinine, Antolín Velasquez, Juan C. Fernández-Díaz, and Ramesh Shrestha. "Ancient Lowland Maya Complexity as Revealed by Airborne Laser Scanning of Northern Guatemala." *Science* 361, no. 6409 (September 28, 2018): eaau0137. https://doi.org/10.1126/science.aau0137.

Carneiro, R. L. "A Theory of the Origin of the State: Traditional Theories of State Origins Are Considered and Rejected in Favor of a New Ecological Hypothesis." *Science* 169, no. 3947 (August 21, 1970): 733–738. https://doi.org/10.1126/science.169.3947.733.

Carneiro, R. L. "The Transition from Quantity to Quality: A Neglected Causal Mechanism in Accounting for Social Evolution." *Proceedings of the National Academy of Sciences* 97, no. 23 (November 7, 2000): 12926–12931. https://doi.org/10.1073/pnas.240462397.

Carneiro, Robert L. "The Circumscription Theory: Challenge and Response." *American Behavioral Scientist* 31, no. 4 (March 1988): 497–511. https://doi.org/10.1177/000276488031004010.

Carrasco, Juan Antonio, Bernie Hogan, Barry Wellman, and Eric J. Miller. "Agency in Social Activity Interactions: The Role of Social Networks in Time and Space." *Tijdschrift voor economische en sociale geografie* 99, no. 5 (December 2008): 562–583. https://doi.org/10.1111/j.1467-9663.2008.0 0492.x.

Carrasco, Juan Antonio, Bernie Hogan, Barry Wellman, and Eric J Miller. "Collecting Social Network Data to Study Social Activity–Travel Behavior: An Egocentric Approach." *Environment and Planning B: Planning and Design* 35, no. 6 (December 2008): 961–980. https://doi.org/10.1068/b3317t.

Carter, Richard. *Breakthrough: The Saga of Jonas Salk*. New York: Trident Press, 1966.

Castells, Manuel. *The Informational City: Information Technology, Economic Restructuring, and the Urban-Regional Process*. Oxford: Blackwell, 1999.

Castillo, Bernal Díaz del. *True Story of the Conquest of New Spain*. Indianapolis, IN: Hackett Publishing Company, 2012. Originally published in 1632.

Caswell, Hal. *Matrix Population Models: Construction, Analysis, and Interpretation*. 2nd ed. Sunderland, MA: Sinauer Associates, 2001.

Cesaretti, Rudolf, José Lobo, Luís M. A. Bettencourt, Scott Ortman, and Michael Smith. "Population-Area Relationship in Medieval European Cities." *PLoS ONE* 11, no. 10 (October 5, 2016): e0162678. https://doi.org/10.1371/journal.pone.0162678.

Cesaretti, Rudolf, José Lobo, Luís M. A. Bettencourt, and Michael E. Smith. "Increasing Returns to Scale in the Towns of Early Tudor England." *Historical Methods: A Journal of Quantitative and Interdisciplinary History* 53, no. 3 (2020): 147–165. https://doi.org/10.1080/01615440.2020.1722775.

Chang, Stephanie. "Infrastructure Resilience to Disasters." *National Academy of Engineering* 39, no. 4 (December 2009). http://www.nae.edu/Publications/TheBridge/Archives/17281/17548.aspx.

Chase, A. F., D. Z. Chase, C. T. Fisher, S. J. Leisz, and J. F. Weishampel. "Geospatial Revolution and Remote Sensing LiDAR in Mesoamerican Archaeology." *Proceedings of the National Academy of Sciences* 109, no. 32 (August 7, 2012): 12916–12921. https://doi.org/10.1073/pnas.1205198109.

Chen, Wen-Hao, John Myles, and Garnett Picot. "Why Have Poorer Neighbourhoods Stagnated Economically while the Richer Have Flourished? Neighbourhood Income Inequality in Canadian Cities." *Urban Studies* 49, no. 4 (March 1, 2012): 877–896. https://doi.org/10.1177/0042098011408142.

Chen, Yanguang. "Characterizing Growth and Form of Fractal Cities with Allometric Scaling Exponents." *Discrete Dynamics in Nature and Society* 2010 (2010): 1–22. https://doi.org/10.1155/2010/194715.

Chetty, Raj, David Grusky, Maximilian Hell, Nathaniel Hendren, Robert Manduca, and Jimmy Narang. "The Fading American Dream: Trends in Absolute Income Mobility since 1940." *Science* 356, no. 6336 (April 28, 2017): 398–406. https://doi.org/10.1126/science.aal4617.

Chetty, Raj, and Nathaniel Hendren. "The Impacts of Neighborhoods on Intergenerational Mobility I: Childhood Exposure Effects." *Quarterly Journal of Economics* 133, no. 3 (August 1, 2018): 1107–1162. https://doi.org/10.1093/qje/qjy007.

Chetty, Raj, and Nathaniel Hendren. "The Impacts of Neighborhoods on Intergenerational Mobility II: County-Level Estimates." *Quarterly Journal of Economics* 133, no. 3 (August 1, 2018): 1163–1228. https://doi.org/10.1093/qje/qjy006.

Chetty, Raj, Nathaniel Hendren, and Lawrence F. Katz. "The Effects of Exposure to Better Neighborhoods on Children: New Evidence from the Moving to Opportunity Experiment." *American Economic Review* 106, no. 4 (April 2016): 855–902. https://doi.org/10.1257/aer.20150572.

Chetty, Raj, Nathaniel Hendren, Frina Lin, Jeremy Majerovitz, and Benjamin Scuderi. "Childhood Environment and Gender Gaps in Adulthood." *American Economic Review* 106, no. 5 (May 2016): 282–288. https://doi.org/10.1257/aer.p20161073.

Chicago Fact Book Consortium, ed. *Local Community Fact Book: Chicago Metropolitan Area, 1970 and 1980*. Chicago: Chicago Review Press, 1984.

Chowell, Gerardo, Hiroshi Nishiura, and Luís M. A. Bettencourt. "Comparative Estimation of the Reproduction Number for Pandemic Influenza from Daily Case Notification Data." *Journal of the Royal Society Interface* 4, no. 12 (February 22, 2007): 155–166. https://doi.org/10.1098/rsif.2006.0161.

Christaller, Walter. *Central Places in Southern Germany.* Englewood Cliffs, NJ: Prentice-Hall, 1966.

Clark, W. A. V., and M. Fossett. "Understanding the Social Context of the Schelling Segregation Model." *Proceedings of the National Academy of Sciences* 105, no. 11 (March 18, 2008): 4109–4114. https://doi.org/10.1073/pnas.0708155105.

Clauset, Aaron, Cosma Rohilla Shalizi, and M. E. J. Newman. "Power-Law Distributions in Empirical Data." *SIAM Review* 51, no. 4 (November 4, 2009): 661–703. https://doi.org/10.1137/070710111.

Coale, Ansley J. "Demographic Transition." In *Social Economics*, 16–23. London: Palgrave Macmillan, 1989. https://doi.org/10.1007/978-1-349-19806-1_4.

Coffey, William J. "Allometric Growth in Urban and Regional Social-Economic Systems." *Canadian Journal of Regional Science* 11, no. 1 (1979): 49–65.

Cohen, Joel E. "Ergodic Theorems in Demography." *Bulletin of the American Mathematical Society*, n.s., 1, no. 2 (March 1979): 275–295.

Collard, Mark, Briggs Buchanan, Jesse Morin, and Andre Costopoulos. "What Drives the Evolution of Hunter-Gatherer Subsistence Technology? A Reanalysis of the Risk Hypothesis with Data from the Pacific Northwest." *Philosophical Transactions of the Royal Society B: Biological Sciences* 366, no. 1567 (April 12, 2011): 1129–1138. https://doi.org/10.1098/rstb.2010.0366.

Collard, Mark, April Ruttle, Briggs Buchanan, and Michael J. O'Brien. "Population Size and Cultural Evolution in Nonindustrial Food-Producing Societies." *PLoS One* 8, no. 9 (September 12, 2013): e72628. https://doi.org/10.1371/journal.pone.0072628.

Cornwall, Julian. "The People of Rutland in 1522." *Transactions of the Leicestershire Archaeological and Historical Society* 37 (1962): 7–28.

Cornwall, Julian. *Wealth and Society in Early Sixteenth Century England.* London: Routledge, 1988.

Cover, T. M. *Elements of Information Theory.* Wiley Series in Telecommunications. New York: Wiley, 1991.

Cover, Thomas M., and Joy A. Thomas. "Information Theory and Statistics." In *Elements of Information Theory*, 347–408. Hoboken, NJ: Wiley, 2005. http://onlinelibrary.wiley.com/doi/10.1002/047174882X.ch11/summary.

Cowgill, George L. *Ancient Teotihuacan: Early Urbanism in Central Mexico.* Case Studies in Early Societies. New York: Cambridge University Press, 2015.

Cristelli, Matthieu, Michael Batty, and Luciano Pietronero. "There Is More than a Power Law in Zipf." *Scientific Reports* 2, no. 1 (December 2012): 812. https://doi.org/10.1038/srep00812.

Curry, Leslie. "Central Places in the Random Space Economy." *Journal of Regional Science* 7 (1967): 217–238.

Curry, Leslie. "The Random Spatial Economy: An Exploration in Settlement Theory." *Annals of the Association of American Geographers* 54, no. 1 (March 1964): 138–146. https://doi.org/10.1111/j.1467-8306.1964.tb00479.x.

Dalziel, Benjamin D., Stephen Kissler, Julia R. Gog, Cecile Viboud, Ottar N. Bjørnstad, C. Jessica E. Metcalf, and Bryan T. Grenfell. "Urbanization and Humidity Shape the Intensity of Influenza Epidemics in U.S. Cities." *Science* 362, no. 6410 (October 5, 2018): 75–79. https://doi.org/10.1126/science.aat6030.

Darby, H. C., R. E. Glasscock, J. Sheail, and G. R. Versey. "The Changing Geographical Distribution of Wealth in England: 1086–1334–1525." *Journal of Historical Geography* 5, no. 3 (1979): 247–262. https://doi.org/10.1016/0305-7488(79)90071-9.

Darwin, Charles. *The Descent of Man and Selection in Relation to Sex*. New York: P. F. Collier and Sons, 1901.

Darwin, Charles, and Ernst Mayr. *On the Origin of Species*. Facsimile of the 1st ed. Cambridge, MA: Harvard University Press, 2003. Originally published in 1859.

Delile, H., J. Blichert-Toft, J.-P. Goiran, S. Keay, and F. Albarede. "Lead in Ancient Rome's City Waters." *Proceedings of the National Academy of Sciences* 111, no. 18 (May 6, 2014): 6594–6599. https://doi.org/10.1073/pnas.1400097111.

Depersin, Jules, and Marc Barthélemy. "From Global Scaling to the Dynamics of Individual Cities." *Proceedings of the National Academy of Sciences* 115, no. 10 (March 6, 2018): 2317–2322. https://doi.org/10.1073/pnas.1718690115.

de Vries, Jan. *European Urbanisation: 1500–1800*. London: Routledge, 2013.

DiBiase, David. "The 50th Anniversary of GIS | ArcNews." ESRI (blog). Accessed February 16, 2020. https://www.esri.com/news/arcnews/fall12articles/the-fiftieth-anniversary-of-gis.html.

Dijkstra, Lewis, Hugo Poelman, and Paolo Veneri. "The EU-OECD Definition of a Functional Urban Area." OECD Regional Development Working Papers, No. 2019/11. Paris: Organisation for Economic Co-operation and Development, 2019. https://doi.org/10.1787/d58cb34d-en.

Downs, A. "The Law of Peak-Hour Expressway Congestion." *Traffic Quarterly* 16, no. 3 (July 1962). https://trid.trb.org/view/694596.

DuBois, W. E. B., Elijah Anderson, and Isabel Eaton. *The Philadelphia Negro: A Social Study*. Philadelphia: University of Pennsylvania Press, 1996.

Duranton, Gilles. "The Urbanization and Development Puzzle." In *The Buzz in Cities: New Economic Thinking*, edited by Shahid Yusuf. New York: Institute for New Economic Thinking, 2014.

Duranton, Gilles, and Matthew A. Turner. "The Fundamental Law of Road Congestion: Evidence from US Cities." *American Economic Review* 101, no. 6 (October 2011): 2616–2652. https://doi.org/10.1257/aer.101.6.2616.

Durkheim, Émile, and Steven Lukes. *The Division of Labor in Society*. New York: Free Press, 2014. Originally published in 1893.

Dutton, Geoffrey. "Foreword: Size and Shape in the Growth of Human Communities." *Ekistics* 36, no. 215 (1973): 241–243.

Dyer, Alan. *Decline and Growth in English Towns 1400–1640*. Cambridge: Cambridge University Press, 1995.

Dyer, Alan. "'Urban Decline' in England, 1377–1525." In *Towns in Decline, AD 100–1600*, edited by Terry R. Slater, 266–288. Aldershot, UK: Ashgate, 2000.

Dyer, Christopher. "How Urbanized Was Medieval England?" In *Peasants and Townsmen in Medieval Europe: Studia in Honorem Adriaan Verhulst*, edited by J.-M. Duvosquel and E. Thoen, 169–183. Ghent, Belgium: Snoeck-Ducaju & Zoon, 1995.

Dyson, Tim. "The Role of the Demographic Transition in the Process of Urbanization." *Population and Development Review* 37 (2011): 34–54. https://doi.org/10.1111/j.1728-4457.2011.00377.x.

Eagle, N., M. Macy, and R. Claxton. "Network Diversity and Economic Development." *Science* 328, no. 5981 (May 21, 2010): 1029–1031. https://doi.org/10.1126/science.1186605.

Eeckhout, Jan. "Gibrat's Law for (All) Cities." *American Economic Review* 94, no. 5 (November 2004): 1429–1451. https://doi.org/10.1257/0002828043052303.

Eeckhout, Jan. "Gibrat's Law for (All) Cities: Reply." *American Economic Review* 99, no. 4 (August 2009): 1676–1683. https://doi.org/10.1257/aer.99.4.1676.

Elad, M., and A. Feuer. "Restoration of a Single Superresolution Image from Several Blurred, Noisy, and Undersampled Measured Images." *IEEE Transactions on Image Processing* 6, no. 12 (December 1997): 1646–1658. https://doi.org/10.1109/83.650118.

Elliott, D. S., W. J. Wilson, D. Huizinga, R. J. Sampson, A. Elliott, and B. Rankin. "The Effects of Neighborhood Disadvantage on Adolescent Development." *Journal of Research in Crime and Delinquency* 33, no. 4 (November 1, 1996): 389–426. https://doi.org/10.1177/0022427896033004002.

Ellison, Glenn, Edward L. Glaeser, and William R. Kerr. "What Causes Industry Agglomeration? Evidence from Coagglomeration Patterns." *American Economic Review* 100, no. 3 (June 2010): 1195–1213. https://doi.org/10.1257/aer.100.3.1195.

Ericsson, K. Anders, ed. *The Cambridge Handbook of Expertise and Expert Performance.* Cambridge: Cambridge University Press, 2006.

Evans, D. H., R. J. Fletcher, C. Pottier, J.-B. Chevance, D. Soutif, B. S. Tan, S. Im, D. Ea, T. Tin, S. Kim, C. Cromarty, S. De Greef, K. Hanus, P. Bâty, R. Kuszinger, I. Shimoda, and G. Boornazian. "Uncovering Archaeological Landscapes at Angkor Using Lidar." *Proceedings of the National Academy of Sciences* 110, no. 31 (July 30, 2013): 12595–12600. https://doi.org/10.1073/pnas.1306539110.

Ewing, Reid, and Robert Cervero. "Travel and the Built Environment: A Synthesis." *Transportation Research Record: Journal of the Transportation Research Board* 1780 (January 1, 2001): 87–114. https://doi.org/10.3141/1780-10.

Farber, Steven, Morton O'Kelly, Harvey J. Miller, and Tijs Neutens. "Measuring Segregation Using Patterns of Daily Travel Behavior: A Social Interaction Based Model of Exposure." *Journal of Transport Geography* 49 (December 2015): 26–38. https://doi.org/10.1016/j.jtrangeo.2015.10.009.

Feldman, Maryann P. "Knowledge Complementarity and Innovation." *Small Business Economics* 6, no. 5 (October 1994): 363–372. https://doi.org/10.1007/BF01065139.

Feldman, Maryann P. "The New Economics of Innovation, Spillovers and Agglomeration: A Review of Empirical Studies." *Economics of Innovation and New Technology* 8, nos. 1–2 (January 1, 1999): 5–25. https://doi.org/10.1080/10438599900000002.

Feldman, Maryann P., and David B. Audretsch. "Innovation in Cities: Science-Based Diversity, Specialization and Localized Competition." *European Economic Review* 43, no. 2 (February 15, 1999): 409–429. https://doi.org/10.1016/S0014-2921(98)00047-6.

Firebaugh, Glenn, and Chad R. Farrell. "Still Large, but Narrowing: The Sizable Decline in Racial Neighborhood Inequality in Metropolitan America, 1980–2010." *Demography* 53, no. 1 (February 1, 2016): 139–164. https://doi.org/10.1007/s13524-015-0447-5.

Fischer, Claude S. *To Dwell among Friends: Personal Networks in Town and City.* Chicago: University of Chicago Press, 1982.

Fischer, Claude S. "The Subcultural Theory of Urbanism: A Twentieth-Year Assessment." *American Journal of Sociology* 101, no. 3 (1995): 543–577. https://doi.org/10.1086/230753.

Fischer, Claude S. "Toward a Subcultural Theory of Urbanism." *American Journal of Sociology* 80, no. 6 (May 1975): 1319–1341. https://doi.org/10.1086/225993.

Fletcher, Roland. "Low-Density, Agrarian-Based Urbanism." In *The Comparative Archaeology of Complex Societies,* edited by Michael E. Smith, 285–320. Cambridge: Cambridge University Press, 2011. https://doi.org/10.1017/CBO9781139022712.013.

Florida, Richard. "Just How Urban Is the World? The Great Debate." Bloomberg CityLab, December 6, 2018. https://www.citylab.com/life/2018/12/global-urbanization-un-majority-city-measure/577090/.

Fotheringham, A. Stewart, and M. J. Webber. "Spatial Structure and the Parameters of Spatial Interaction Models." *Geographical Analysis* 12, no. 1 (January 1, 1980): 33–46. https://doi.org/10.1111/j.1538-4632.1980.tb00016.x.

Foucault, Michel. "Of Other Spaces: Utopias and Heterotopias." *Architecture/Mouvement/Continuité* (October 1984). https://web.mit.edu/allanmc/www/foucault1.pdf.

Frank, S. A. "Natural Selection. III. Selection versus Transmission and the Levels of Selection." *Journal of Evolutionary Biology* 25, no. 2 (February 2012): 227–243. https://doi.org/10.1111/j.1420-9101.2011.02431.x.

Frank, S. A. "Natural Selection. V. How to Read the Fundamental Equations of Evolutionary Change in Terms of Information Theory." *Journal of Evolutionary Biology* 25, no. 12 (December 2012): 2377–2396. https://doi.org/10.1111/jeb.12010.

Frank, S. A. "Natural Selection. VII. History and Interpretation of Kin Selection Theory." *Journal of Evolutionary Biology* 26, no. 6 (June 2013): 1151–1184. https://doi.org/10.1111/jeb.12131.

Frank, Steven A. *Foundations of Social Evolution.* Monographs in Behavior and Ecology. Princeton, NJ: Princeton University Press, 1998.

Frank, Steven A. "Mutual Policing and Repression of Competition in the Evolution of Cooperative Groups." *Nature* 377, no. 6549 (October 1995): 520–522. https://doi.org/10.1038/377520a0.

Frey, William H. *The Great American Migration Slowdown.* Washington, DC: Brookings Institution, 2009. https://www.brookings.edu/wp-content/uploads/2016/07/1209_migration_frey-1.pdf.

Fujita, Masahisa. *Urban Economic Theory: Land Use and City Size.* Cambridge: Cambridge University Press, 1990.

Fujita, Masahisa, Paul Krugman, and Anthony J. Venables. *The Spatial Economy: Cities, Regions, and International Trade.* Cambridge, MA: MIT Press, 2001.

Fujita, Masahisa, and Jacques-François Thisse. *Economics of Agglomeration: Cities, Industrial Location, and Globalization.* 2nd ed. Cambridge: Cambridge University Press, 2013.

Gabaix, X. "Zipf's Law for Cities: An Explanation." *Quarterly Journal of Economics* 114, no. 3 (August 1, 1999): 739–767. https://doi.org/10.1162/003355399556133.

Gaspar, José M. "A Prospective Review on New Economic Geography." *Annals of Regional Science* 61, no. 2 (September 2018): 237–272. https://doi.org/10.1007/s00168-018-0866-5.

Geddes, Patrick. *Cities in Evolution: An Introduction to the Town Planning Movement and to the Study of Civics.* London: Williams and Norgate, 1915.

Gianessi, Leonard P., Henry M. Peskin, and Edward Wolff. "The Distributional Effects of Uniform Air Pollution Policy in the United States." *Quarterly Journal of Economics* 93, no. 2 (1979): 281–301. https://doi.org/10.2307/1883195.

Gibrat, Robert. *Les inégalités économiques; applications: aux inégalités des richesses, à la concentration des entreprises, aux populations des villes, aux statistiques des familles, etc., d'une loi nouvelle, la loi de l'effect proportionnel.* Paris: Recueil Sirey, 1931.

Glaeser, Edward L. *Cities, Agglomeration, and Spatial Equilibrium.* Lindahl Lectures. Oxford: Oxford University Press, 2008.

Glaeser, Edward L. "A World of Cities: The Causes and Consequences of Urbanization in Poorer Countries." *Journal of the European Economic Association* 12, no. 5 (October 1, 2014): 1154–1199. https://doi.org/10.1111/jeea.12100.

Glaeser, Edward L., and Joshua D. Gottlieb. "The Wealth of Cities: Agglomeration Economies and Spatial Equilibrium in the United States." *Journal of Economic Literature* 47, no. 4 (December 2009): 983–1028. https://doi.org/10.1257/jel.47.4.983.

Glaeser, Edward L., Rafael La Porta, Florencio Lopez-de-Silanes, and Andrei Shleifer. "Do Institutions Cause Growth?" *Journal of Economic Growth* 9, no. 3 (September 1, 2004): 271–303. https://doi.org/10.1023/B:JOEG.0000038933.16398.ed.

Glaeser, Edward L., and Bruce Sacerdote. "Why Is There More Crime in Cities?" *Journal of Political Economy* 107, no. S6 (December 1999): S225–258. https://doi.org/10.1086/250109.

Glaeser, Edward L., José A. Scheinkman, and Andrei Shleifer. "Economic Growth in a Cross-Section of Cities." *Journal of Monetary Economics* 36, no. 1 (August 1995): 117–143. https://doi.org/10.1016/0304-3932(95)01206-2.

Glaeser, Edward Ludwig. *Triumph of the City: How Our Greatest Invention Makes Us Richer, Smarter, Greener, Healthier, and Happier.* New York: Penguin Books, 2012.

Gleick, James. *Chaos: Making a New Science.* New York: Viking Press, 1987.

Goldenfeld, Nigel. *Lectures on Phase Transitions and the Renormalization Group.* Frontiers in Physics 85. Reading, MA: Addison-Wesley, 1992.

Goldenfeld, Nigel, and Leo P. Kadanoff. "Simple Lessons from Complexity." *Science* 284, no. 5411 (April 2, 1999): 87–89. https://doi.org/10.1126/science.284.5411.87.

Gomez-Lievano, Andres, Oscar Patterson-Lomba, and Ricardo Hausmann. "Explaining the Prevalence, Scaling and Variance of Urban Phenomena." *Nature Human Behaviour* 1, no. 1 (December 22, 2016): 0012. https://doi.org/10.1038/s41562-016-0012.

Gomez-Lievano, Andres, HyeJin Youn, and Luís M. A. Bettencourt. "The Statistics of Urban Scaling and Their Connection to Zipf's Law." *PLoS One* 7, no. 7 (July 18, 2012): e40393. https://doi.org/10.1371/journal.pone.0040393.

Goodchild, Michael F. "Twenty Years of Progress: GIScience in 2010." *Journal of Spatial Information Science*, no. 1 (July 27, 2010): 3–20. https://doi.org/10.5311/JOSIS.2010.1.2.

Goose, Nigel, and Andrew Hinde. "Estimating Local Population Sizes at Fixed Points in Time: Part II—Specific Sources." *Local Population Studies*, no. 78 (2007): 74–88.

Gould, P. R. "On the Geographical Interpretation of Eigenvalues." *Transactions of the Institute of British Geographers*, no. 42 (1967): 53–86. https://doi.org/10.2307/621372.

Goworowska, Justyna, and Todd K. Gardner. "Historical Migration of the Young, Single, and College Educated: 1965 to 2000." US Census Working Paper Number POP-WP094. Washington, DC: U.S. Census Bureau, April 2012. https://www.census.gov/library/working-papers/2012/demo/POP-twps0094.html.

Griliches, Zvi. "The Search for R&D Spillovers." *Scandinavian Journal of Economics* 94 (1992): S29–47. https://doi.org/10.2307/3440244–

Grossman, Gene M., and Elhanan Helpman. "Endogenous Innovation in the Theory of Growth." *Journal of Economic Perspectives* 8, no. 1 (1994): 23–44. https://doi.org/10.1257/jep.8.1.23.

Hägerstrand, Torsten. "What about People in Regional Science?" *Papers of the Regional Science Association* 24, no. 1 (December 1970): 6–21. https://doi.org/10.1007/BF01936872.

Haggett, Peter, A. D. Cliff, and Allan E. Frey. *Locational Analysis in Human Geography*. 2nd ed. London: Arnold, 1977.

Hamilton, M. J., B. T. Milne, R. S. Walker, and J. H. Brown. "Nonlinear Scaling of Space Use in Human Hunter-Gatherers." *Proceedings of the National Academy of Sciences* 104, no. 11 (March 13, 2007): 4765–4769. https://doi.org/10.1073/pnas.0611197104.

Hammer, Jeffrey S., Ijaz Nabi, and James A. Cercone. "Distributional Effects of Social Sector Expenditures in Malaysia, 1974–89." In *Public Spending and the Poor: Theory and Evidence*, edited by Dominique van de Walle and Kimberly Nead. Baltimore, MD: Johns Hopkins University Press, 1995.

Hannon, Lance. "Poverty, Delinquency, and Educational Attainment: Cumulative Disadvantage or Disadvantage Saturation?" *Sociological Inquiry* 73, no. 4 (November 1, 2003): 575–594. https://doi.org/10.1111/1475-682X.00072.

Hanson, J. W. *An Urban Geography of the Roman World, 100 BC to AD 300*. Oxford: Archaeopress Publishing, 2016.

Hanson, J. W., and S. G. Ortman. "A Systematic Method for Estimating the Populations of Greek and Roman Settlements." *Journal of Roman Archaeology* 30 (2017): 301–324. https://doi.org/10.1017/S1047759400074134.

Hanson, J. W., S. G. Ortman, and J. Lobo. "Urbanism and the Division of Labour in the Roman Empire." *Journal of the Royal Society Interface* 14, no. 136 (November 30, 2017): 20170367. https://doi.org/10.1098/rsif.2017.0367.

Hanson, John W., Scott G. Ortman, Luís M. A. Bettencourt, and Liam C. Mazur. "Urban Form, Infrastructure and Spatial Organisation in the Roman Empire." *Antiquity* 93, no. 369 (June 2019): 702–718. https://doi.org/10.15184/aqy.2018.192.

Harper, Kyle. *The Fate of Rome: Climate, Disease, and the End of an Empire*. Princeton, NJ: Princeton University Press, 2018. https://doi.org/10.1515/9781400888917.

Harris, Chauncy D., and Edward L. Ullman. "The Nature of Cities." *Annals of the American Academy of Political and Social Science* 242, no. 1 (November 1945): 7–17. https://doi.org/10.1177/000271624524200103.

Harte, John. *Maximum Entropy and Ecology: A Theory of Abundance, Distribution, and Energetics*. Oxford Series in Ecology and Evolution. Oxford: Oxford University Press, 2011.

Hausmann, Ricardo, and César A. Hidalgo. "The Network Structure of Economic Output." *Journal of Economic Growth* 16, no. 4 (December 2011): 309–342. https://doi.org/10.1007/s10887-011-9071-4.

Hayek, F. A. "The Use of Knowledge in Society." *American Economic Review* 35, no. 4 (1945): 519–530. https://doi.org/10.1142/9789812701275_0025.

Henderson, John Vernon. *Urban Development: Theory, Fact, and Illusion*. New York: Oxford University Press, 1991.

Henrich, Joseph Patrick. *The Secret of Our Success: How Culture Is Driving Human Evolution, Domesticating Our Species, and Making Us Smarter*. Princeton, NJ: Princeton University Press, 2016.

Hesiod. *Works and Days*. Translated by M. L. West. Oxford: Oxford University Press, 1996.

Hidalgo, C. A., and R. Hausmann. "The Building Blocks of Economic Complexity." *Proceedings of the National Academy of Sciences* 106, no. 26 (June 30, 2009): 10570–10575. https://doi.org/10.1073/pnas.0900943106.

Hidalgo, C. A., B. Klinger, A.-L. Barabási, and R. Hausmann. "The Product Space Conditions the Development of Nations." *Science* 317, no. 5837 (July 27, 2007): 482–487. https://doi.org/10.1126/science.1144581.

Hipp, John R. "A Dynamic View of Neighborhoods: The Reciprocal Relationship between Crime and Neighborhood Structural Characteristics." *Social Problems* 57, no. 2 (2010): 205–230. https://doi.org/10.1525/sp.2010.57.2.205.

Hoch, Irving. "Income and City Size." *Urban Studies* 9, no. 3 (October 1, 1972): 299–328. https://doi.org/10.1080/00420987220080451.

Hong, Inho, Morgan R. Frank, Iyad Rahwan, Woo-Sung Jung, and Hyejin Youn. "The Universal Pathway to Innovative Urban Economies." *Science Advances* 6, no. 34 (August 21, 2020): eaba4934. https://doi.org/ 10.1126/sciadv.aba4934.

Hoornweg, Daniel, and Kevin Pope. "Population Predictions for the World's Largest Cities in the 21st Century." *Environment and Urbanization* 29, no. 1 (April 1, 2017): 195–216. https://doi.org/10.1177/0956247816663557.

Hoskins, William George. *The Age of Plunder: King Henry's England 1500–1547.* London: Longman, 1976.

Hsieh, Chang-Tai, Erik Hurst, Charles I. Jones, and Peter J. Klenow. "The Allocation of Talent and U.S. Economic Growth." *Econometrica* 87, no. 5 (2019): 1439–1474. https://doi.org/10.3982/ECTA11427.

Hsieh, Chang-Tai, and Peter J. Klenow. "Misallocation and Manufacturing TFP in China and India." *Quarterly Journal of Economics* 124, no. 4 (November 1, 2009): 1403–1448. https://doi.org/10.1162/qjec.2009.124.4.1403.

Ingersoll, Jonathan E. *Theory of Financial Decision Making.* Rowman and Littlefield Studies in Financial Economics. Totowa, NJ: Rowman and Littlefield, 1987.

Intrator, Jake, Jonathan Tannen, and Douglas S. Massey. "Segregation by Race and Income in the United States 1970–2010." *Social Science Research* 60 (November 2016): 45–60. https://doi.org/10.1016/j.ssresearch.2016.08.003.

Ioannides, Yannis M., and Linda Datcher Loury. "Job Information Networks, Neighborhood Effects, and Inequality." *Journal of Economic Literature* 42, no. 4 (November 2004): 1056–1093. https://doi.org/10.1257/0022051043004595.

Ioannides, Yannis M., and Henry G. Overman. "Zipf's Law for Cities: An Empirical Examination." *Regional Science and Urban Economics* 33, no. 2 (March 2003): 127–137. https://doi.org/10.1016/S0166-0462(02)00006-6.

Isard, Walter. *Location and Space-Economy: A General Theory Relating to Industrial Location, Market Areas, Land Use, Trade, and Urban Structure.* Regional Science Studies Series 1. Cambridge, MA: MIT Press, 1972.

Jackson, Matthew O. *Social and Economic Networks.* Princeton, NJ: Princeton University Press, 2008.

Jacobs, Jane. *Cities and the Wealth of Nations: Principles of Economic Life.* New York: Vintage Books, 1985.

Jacobs, Jane. *The Death and Life of Great American Cities.* New York: Vintage Books, 1992; 50th anniversary ed., New York: Modern Library, 2011.

Jacobs, Jane. *The Economy of Cities.* New York: Vintage Books, 1970.

Jacobs, Jane. *The Nature of Economies.* New York: Vintage Books, 2001.

Jaffe, Eric. "Why Commute Times Don't Change Much Even as a City Grows." Bloomberg City-Lab, June 20, 2014. http://www.citylab.com/commute/2014/06/why-commute-times-dont-change-much-even-as-a-city-grows/373051/.

Jaynes, E. T. "Information Theory and Statistical Mechanics." *Physical Review* 106, no. 4 (May 15, 1957): 620–630. https://doi.org/10.1103/PhysRev.106.620.

Jaynes, E. T. "Information Theory and Statistical Mechanics. II." *Physical Review* 108, no. 2 (October 15, 1957): 171–190. https://doi.org/10.1103/PhysRev.108.171.

Jedwab, Remi, and Dietrich Vollrath. "Urbanization without Growth in Historical Perspective." *Explorations in Economic History* 58 (October 2015): 1–21. https://doi.org/10.1016/j.eeh.2015.09.002.

Johnson, Gregory A. "Organizational Structure and Scalar Stress." In *Theory and Explanation in Archaeology*, edited by Colin Renfrew, Michael Rowlands, and Barbara A. Segraves-Whallon. Cambridge, MA: Academic Press, 1982.

Johnson, Jeffrey. *Non-equilibrium Social Science and Policy: Introduction and Essays on New and Changing Paradigms in Socio-economic Thinking*. New York: Springer, 2016.

Johnson, Marc T. J., and Jason Munshi-South. "Evolution of Life in Urban Environments." *Science* 358, no. 6363 (November 3, 2017): eaam8327. https://doi.org/10.1126/science.aam8327.

Johnstone, Nick, and Ysé Serret, eds. *The Distributional Effects of Environmental Policy*. Cheltenham, UK: Edward Elgar, 2006.

Jones, Charles I. "Growth and Ideas." In *Handbook of Economic Growth*, Vol. 1, edited by Philippe Aghion and Steven N. Durlauf, 1063–1111. Amsterdam: Elsevier, 2005. http://www.sciencedirect.com/science/article/pii/S1574068405010166.

Jones, Charles I. "Growth: With or without Scale Effects?" *American Economic Review* 89, no. 2 (1999): 139–144. https://doi.org/10.1257/aer.89.2.139.

Jones, Charles I., and Paul M. Romer. "The New Kaldor Facts: Ideas, Institutions, Population, and Human Capital." *American Economic Journal: Macroeconomics* 2, no. 1 (2010): 224–245. https://doi.org/10.1257/mac.2.1.224.

Jongman, Willem M., Jan P. A. M. Jacobs, and Geertje M. Klein Goldewijk. "Health and Wealth in the Roman Empire." *Economics and Human Biology* 34 (August 2019): 138–150. https://doi.org/10.1016/j.ehb.2019.01.005.

Kadanoff, Leo P. *Statistical Physics: Statics, Dynamics and Renormalization*. Singapore: World Scientific, 2000.

Kander, Astrid, Paolo Malanima, and Paul Warde. *Power to the People: Energy in Europe over the Last Five Centuries*. Princeton Economic History of the Western World. Princeton, NJ: Princeton University Press, 2015.

Kardar, Mehran. *Statistical Physics of Particles*. Cambridge: Cambridge University Press, 2007.

Kelly, J. L. "A New Interpretation of Information Rate." *IRE Transactions on Information Theory* 2, no. 3 (September 1956): 185–189. https://doi.org/10.1109/TIT.1956.1056803.

Kelly, Robert L. *The Lifeways of Hunter-Gatherers: The Foraging Spectrum*. 2nd ed. Cambridge: Cambridge University Press, 2013.

Kennedy, C., S. Pincetl, and P. Bunje. "The Study of Urban Metabolism and Its Applications to Urban Planning and Design." *Environmental Pollution* 159, nos. 8–9 (August 2011): 1965–1973. https://doi.org/10.1016/j.envpol.2010.10.022.

King, Ritchie S., and Graham Roberts. "Manhattan's Population Density, Past and Present." *New York Times*, March 1, 2012. https://archive.nytimes.com/www.nytimes.com/interactive/2012/03/01/realestate/manhattans-population-density-past-and-present.html.

Kintigh, Keith W., Jeffrey H. Altschul, Mary C. Beaudry, Robert D. Drennan, Ann P. Kinzig, Timothy A. Kohler, W. Fredrick Limp, Herbert D. G. Maschner, William K. Michener, Timothy R. Pauketat, Peter Peregrine, Jeremy A. Sabloff, Tony J. Wilkinson, Henry T. Wright, and Melinda A. Zeder. "Grand Challenges for Archaeology." *Proceedings of the National Academy of Sciences* 111, no. 3 (January 21, 2014): 879–880. https://doi.org/10.1073/pnas.1324000111.

Kirsch, Scott. "The Incredible Shrinking World? Technology and the Production of Space." *Environment and Planning D: Society and Space* 13, no. 5 (October 1995): 529–555. https://doi.org /10.1068/d130529.

Kline, M. A., and R. Boyd. "Population Size Predicts Technological Complexity in Oceania." *Proceedings of the Royal Society B: Biological Sciences* 277, no. 1693 (August 22, 2010): 2559–2564. https://doi.org/10.1098/rspb.2010.0452.

Kolko, Jed. "The Death of Cities? The Death of Distance? Evidence from the Geography of Commercial Internet Usage." Paper presented at the Telecommunications Policy Research Conference. Newcastle upon Tyne, 1999.

Kolodny, Oren, Nicole Creanza, and Marcus W. Feldman. "Evolution in Leaps: The Punctuated Accumulation and Loss of Cultural Innovations." *Proceedings of the National Academy of Sciences* 112, no. 49 (December 8, 2015): E6762–E6769. https://doi.org/10.1073/pnas.1520492112.

Kremer, M. "Population Growth and Technological Change: One Million B.C. to 1990." *Quarterly Journal of Economics* 108, no. 3 (August 1, 1993): 681–716. https://doi.org/10.2307/2118405.

Krivo, Lauren J., Heather M. Washington, Ruth D. Peterson, Christopher R. Browning, Catherine A. Calder, and Mei-Po Kwan. "Social Isolation of Disadvantage and Advantage: The Reproduction of Inequality in Urban Space." *Social Forces* 92, no. 1 (2013): 141–164. https://doi.org /10.1093/sf/sot043.

Krugman, Paul. "Increasing Returns and Economic Geography." *Journal of Political Economy* 99, no. 3 (June 1, 1991): 483–499. https://doi.org/10.1086/261763.

Krugman, Paul. *The Self-Organizing Economy*. Cambridge, MA: Blackwell, 1995.

Kuznets, Simon. "Economic Growth and Income Inequality." *American Economic Review* 45, no. 1 (1955): 1–28. https://www.jstor.org/stable/1811581.

Laland, Kevin, Blake Matthews, and Marcus W. Feldman. "An Introduction to Niche Construction Theory." *Evolutionary Ecology* 30, no. 2 (April 2016): 191–202. https://doi.org/10.1007 /s10682-016-9821-z.

Landau, Lev Davydovič, Evgenii Mikhailovič Lifšic, and Lev Petrovič Pitaevskij. *Statistical Physics, Part 1*. 3rd ed. Course of Theoretical Physics 5. Amsterdam: Elsevier, 2008.

Layard, Richard. "The Distributional Effects of Congestion Taxes." *Economica* 44, no. 175 (1977): 297–304. https://doi.org/10.2307/2553654.

Lee, Barrett A., Glenn Firebaugh, John Iceland, Stephen A. Matthews, Sean F. Reardon, Lindsay Fox, and Joseph Townsend. "Neighborhood Income Composition by Household Race and Income, 1990–2009." *Annals of the American Academy of Political and Social Science* 660, no. 1 (July 1, 2015): 78–97. https://doi.org/10.1177/0002716215576104.

Lefebvre, Henri, and Donald Nicholson-Smith. *The Production of Space*. Malden, MA: Blackwell, 2011.

Leitão, J. C., J. M. Miotto, M. Gerlach, and E. G. Altmann. "Is This Scaling Nonlinear?" *Royal Society Open Science* 3, no. 7 (July 2016): 150649. https://doi.org/10.1098/rsos.150649.

Lemoy, Rémi, and Geoffrey Caruso. "Evidence for the Homothetic Scaling of Urban Forms." *Environment and Planning B: Urban Analytics and City Science* (November 19, 2018): 870–888. https://doi.org/10.1177/2399808318810532.

Lens, Michael C. "Measuring the Geography of Opportunity." *Progress in Human Geography* 41, no. 1 (February 1, 2017): 3–25. https://doi.org/10.1177/0309132515618104.

Le Roux, Guillaume, Julie Vallée, and Hadrien Commenges. "Social Segregation around the Clock in the Paris Region (France)." *Journal of Transport Geography* 59 (February 2017): 134–145. https://doi.org/10.1016/j.jtrangeo.2017.02.003.

Levine, Robert. *A Geography of Time: The Temporal Misadventures of a Social Psychologist, or How Every Culture Keeps Time Just a Little Bit Differently*. New York: Basic Books, 1998.

Levy, Moshe. "Gibrat's Law for (All) Cities: Comment." *American Economic Review* 99, no. 4 (August 2009): 1672–1675. https://doi.org/10.1257/aer.99.4.1672.

Levy, Moshe, and Sorin Solomon. "Power Laws Are Logarithmic Boltzmann Laws." *International Journal of Modern Physics C* 7, no. 4 (August 1996): 595–601. https://doi.org/10.1142/S0129183196000491.

Lobo, José, Luís M. A. Bettencourt, Michael E. Smith, and Scott Ortman. "Settlement Scaling Theory: Bridging the Study of Ancient and Contemporary Urban Systems." *Urban Studies* 57, no. 4 (October 17, 2019): 731–747. https://doi.org/10.1177/0042098019873796.

Lobo, José, Luís M. A. Bettencourt, Deborah Strumsky, and Geoffrey B. West. "Urban Scaling and the Production Function for Cities." *PLoS One* 8, no. 3 (March 27, 2013): e58407. https://doi.org/10.1371/journal.pone.0058407.

Lösch, August, William H. Woglom, and Wolfgang F. Stolper. *The Economics of Location*. New Haven, CT: Yale University Press, 1978.

Lucas, Robert E. "On the Mechanics of Economic Development." *Journal of Monetary Economics* 22, no. 1 (July 1988): 3–42. https://doi.org/10.1016/0304-3932(88)90168-7.

Ludwig, J., G. J. Duncan, L. A. Gennetian, L. F. Katz, R. C. Kessler, J. R. Kling, and L. Sanbonmatsu. "Neighborhood Effects on the Long-Term Well-Being of Low-Income Adults." *Science* 337, no. 6101 (September 21, 2012): 1505–1510. https://doi.org/10.1126/science.1224648.

Ludwig, Jens, Greg J. Duncan, Lisa A. Gennetian, Lawrence F. Katz, Ronald C. Kessler, Jeffrey R. Kling, and Lisa Sanbonmatsu. "Long-Term Neighborhood Effects on Low-Income Families: Evidence from Moving to Opportunity." *American Economic Review* 103, no. 3 (May 2013): 226–231. https://doi.org/10.1257/aer.103.3.226.

Lynch, Kevin. *Good City Form*. Cambridge, MA: MIT Press, 1984.

Ma, Shang-Keng. *Statistical Mechanics*. Singapore: World Scientific, 1985.

MacKay, David J. C. *Information Theory, Inference, and Learning Algorithms*. Cambridge: Cambridge University Press, 2003.

Makse, Hernán A., Shlomo Havlin, and H. Eugene Stanley. "Modelling Urban Growth Patterns." *Nature* 377, no. 6550 (October 1995): 608–612. https://doi.org/10.1038/377608a0.

Manduca, Robert, and Robert J. Sampson. "Punishing and Toxic Neighborhood Environments Independently Predict the Intergenerational Social Mobility of Black and White Children." *Proceedings of the National Academy of Sciences* 116, no. 16 (April 16, 2019): 7772–7777. https://doi.org/10.1073/pnas.1820464116.

Manning, Joseph Gilbert. *The Open Sea: The Economic Life of the Ancient Mediterranean World from the Iron Age to the Rise of Rome.* Princeton, NJ: Princeton University Press, 2018.

Manzanilla, Linda, ed. *Emergence and Change in Early Urban Societies.* Fundamental Issues in Archaeology. New York: Plenum Press, 1997.

Marchetti, C. "Anthropological Invariants in Travel Behavior." *Technological Forecasting and Social Change* 47, no. 1 (September 1994): 75–88. https://doi.org/10.1016/0040-1625(94)90041-8.

Marchio, Nicholas, and Joseph Parilla. "Export Monitor 2018." *Brookings Report*, April 24, 2018. https://www.brookings.edu/research/export-monitor-2018/.

Marshall, Alfred. *Principles of Economics.* London: Macmillan, 1890.

Masucci, A. Paolo, Joan Serras, Anders Johansson, and Michael Batty. "Gravity versus Radiation Models: On the Importance of Scale and Heterogeneity in Commuting Flows." *Physical Review E* 88, no. 2 (August 22, 2013). https://doi.org/10.1103/PhysRevE.88.022812.

McCann, Philip. *Modern Urban and Regional Economics.* 2nd ed. Oxford: Oxford University Press, 2013.

McConnell, Joseph R., Andrew I. Wilson, Andreas Stohl, Monica M. Arienzo, Nathan J. Chellman, Sabine Eckhardt, Elisabeth M. Thompson, A. Mark Pollard, and Jørgen Peder Steffensen. "Lead Pollution Recorded in Greenland Ice Indicates European Emissions Tracked Plagues, Wars, and Imperial Expansion during Antiquity." *Proceedings of the National Academy of Sciences* 115, no. 22 (May 29, 2018): 5726–5731. https://doi.org/10.1073/pnas.1721818115.

Meder, David, Finn Rabe, Tobias Morville, Kristoffer H. Madsen, Magnus T. Koudahl, Ray J. Dolan, Hartwig R. Siebner, and Oliver J. Hulme. "Ergodicity-Breaking Reveals Time Optimal Economic Behavior in Humans." *ArXiv:1906.04652 [Econ, q-Fin]*, June 19, 2019. http://arxiv.org/abs/1906.04652.

Mellaart, James. "Excavations at Hacılar: Third Preliminary Report, 1959." *Anatolian Studies* 10 (1960): 83–104. https://doi.org/10.2307/3642430.

Metcalf, Gilbert E., and David Weisbach. "The Design of a Carbon Tax." *Harvard Environmental Law Review* 33 (2009): 499–556.

Metspalu, Mait, Toomas Kivisild, Ene Metspalu, Jüri Parik, Georgi Hudjashov, Katrin Kaldma, Piia Serk, Monika Karmin, Doron M. Behar, M. Thomas P Gilbert, Phillip Endicott, Sarabjit Mastana, Surinder S. Papiha, Karl Skorecki, Antonio Torroni, and Richard Villems. "Most of the Extant MtDNA Boundaries in South and Southwest Asia Were Likely Shaped during the Initial Settlement of Eurasia by Anatomically Modern Humans." *BMC Genetics* 5 (2004): 26. https://doi.org/10.1186/1471-2156-5-26.

Milgram, S. "The Experience of Living in Cities." *Science* 167, no. 3924 (March 13, 1970): 1461–1468. https://doi.org/10.1126/science.167.3924.1461.

Miller, Harvey J. "Tobler's First Law and Spatial Analysis." *Annals of the Association of American Geographers* 94, no. 2 (2004): 284–289. https://doi.org/10.1111/j.1467-8306.2004.09402005.x.

Mills, Edwin S. "An Aggregative Model of Resource Allocation in a Metropolitan Area." *American Economic Review* 57, no. 2 (1967): 197–210. https://www.jstor.org/stable/1821621.

Mills, Edwin S., and Bruce W. Hamilton. *Urban Economics.* 5th ed. HarperCollins Series in Economics. New York: HarperCollins, 1994.

Mitlin, Diana, and David Satterthwaite. *Urban Poverty in the Global South: Scale and Nature.* London: Routledge, 2013.

Molinero, Carlos, and Stefan Thurner. "How the Geometry of Cities Explains Urban Scaling Laws." *Journal of the Royal Society: Interface* 18, no. 176 (March 17, 2021). https://royalsocietypub lishing.org/doi/10.1098/rsif.2020.0705.

Montroll, Elliott W., and Michael F. Shlesinger. "On 1/f Noise and Other Distributions with Long Tails." *Proceedings of the National Academy of Sciences* 79, no. 10 (May 1, 1982): 3380–3383. https://doi.org/10.1073/pnas.79.10.3380.

Morenoff, Jeffrey D., Robert J. Sampson, and Stephen W. Raudenbush. "Neighborhood Inequality, Collective Efficacy, and the Spatial Dynamics of Urban Violence." *Criminology* 39, no. 3 (2001): 517–558. https://doi.org/10.1111/j.1745-9125.2001.tb00932.x.

Morgan, Mary S., and Ian Sinclair. *Charles Booth's London Poverty Maps.* London: Thames and Hudson, 2019.

Morgan, Stephen L., and Christopher Winship. *Counterfactuals and Causal Inference: Methods and Principles for Social Research.* 2nd ed. Analytical Methods for Social Research. New York: Cambridge University Press, 2015.

Mumford, Lewis. *The City in History: Its Origins, Its Transformations, and Its Prospects.* New York: Harcourt Brace Jovanovich, 1961.

Muth, Richard F. *Cities and Housing: The Spatial Pattern of Urban Residential Land Use.* Chicago: University of Chicago Press, 1971.

Nagy, Béla, J. Doyne Farmer, Quan M. Bui, and Jessika E. Trancik. "Statistical Basis for Predicting Technological Progress." *PLoS One* 8, no. 2 (February 28, 2013): e52669. https://doi.org/10.1371/journal.pone.0052669.

Nelson, Richard R., and Sidney G. Winter. *An Evolutionary Theory of Economic Change.* Cambridge, MA: Harvard University Press, 2009.

Neuhoff, Karsten, Stefan Bach, Jochen Diekmann, Martin Beznoska, and Tarik El-Laboudy. "Distributional Effects of Energy Transition: Impacts of Renewable Electricity Support in Germany." *Economics of Energy and Environmental Policy* 2, no. 1 (2013): 41–54. https://ideas.repec.org/a/aen/eeepjl/2_1_a03.html.

Newling, Bruce E. "Urban Growth and Spatial Structure: Mathematical Models and Empirical Evidence." *Geographical Review* 56, no. 2 (April 1966): 213–225. https://doi.org/10.2307/212879.

Nordbeck, Stig. "Urban Allometric Growth." *Geografiska Annaler, Series B: Human Geography* 53, no. 1 (1971): 54–67. https://doi.org/10.2307/490887.

North, Douglass C. "Institutions, Transaction Costs and Economic Growth." *Economic Inquiry* 25, no. 3 (1987): 419–428. https://doi.org/10.1111/j.1465-7295.1987.tb00750.x.

North, Douglass C. *Transaction Costs, Institutions, and Economic Performance.* Occasional Papers/International Center for Economic Growth 30. San Francisco: ICS Press, 1992.

Ober, Josiah. *The Rise and Fall of Classical Greece.* Princeton, NJ: Princeton University Press, 2016.

O'Brien, Daniel, Robert J. Sampson, and Christopher Winship. "Ecometrics in the Age of Big Data: Measuring and Assessing 'Broken Windows' Using Large-Scale Administrative Records." *Sociological Methodology* 45 (2015): 101–147. https://doi.org/10.1177/0081175015576601.

O'Brien, Daniel T. *The Urban Commons: How Data and Technology Can Rebuild Our Communities.* Cambridge, MA: Harvard University Press, 2018.

Office of the Registrar General and Census Commissioner. "Census of India, 2011." New Delhi: Ministry of Home Affairs, 2011. https://censusindia.gov.in/2011-common/censusdata2011.html.

Okasha, Samir. *Evolution and the Levels of Selection.* Illustrated ed. New York: Oxford University Press, 2009.

Olson, Mancur. "Distinguished Lecture on Economics in Government: Big Bills Left on the Sidewalk: Why Some Nations Are Rich, and Others Poor." *Journal of Economic Perspectives* 10, no. 2 (June 1996): 3–24. https://doi.org/10.1257/jep.10.2.3.

Olsson, Gunnar. "Central Place Systems, Spatial Interaction, and Stochastic Processes." *Papers in Regional Science* 18, no. 1 (1967): 13–45. https://doi.org/10.1111/j.1435-5597.1967.tb01352.x.

O'Rand, Angela M. "The Precious and the Precocious: Understanding Cumulative Disadvantage and Cumulative Advantage over the Life Course." *The Gerontologist* 36, no. 2 (April 1, 1996): 230–238. https://doi.org/10.1093/geront/36.2.230.

Organisation for Economic Co-operation and Development (OECD), ed. *Redefining "Urban": A New Way to Measure Metropolitan Areas.* Paris: OECD, 2012. https://doi.org/10.1787/9789264174108-en.

Ortman, S. G., A. H. F. Cabaniss, J. O. Sturm, and L. M. A. Bettencourt. "Settlement Scaling and Increasing Returns in an Ancient Society." *Science Advances* 1, no. 1 (February 1, 2015): e1400066. https://doi.org/10.1126/sciadv.1400066.

Ortman, Scott G., Andrew H. F. Cabaniss, Jennie O. Sturm, and Luís M. A. Bettencourt. "The Prehistory of Urban Scaling." *PLoS One* 9, no. 2 (February 12, 2014): e87902. https://doi.org/10.1371/journal.pone.0087902.

Ortman, Scott G., and Grant D. Coffey. "Settlement Scaling in Middle-Range Societies." *American Antiquity* 82, no. 4 (October 2017): 662–682. https://doi.org/10.1017/aaq.2017.42.

Ortman, Scott G., Kaitlyn E. Davis, José Lobo, Michael E. Smith, Luís M. A. Bettencourt, and Aaron Trumbo. "Settlement Scaling and Economic Change in the Central Andes." *Journal of Archaeological Science* 73 (September 2016): 94–106. https://doi.org/10.1016/j.jas.2016.07.012.

Ortman, Scott G., Michael E. Smith, José Lobo, and Luís M. A. Bettencourt. "Why Archaeology Is Necessary for a Theory of Urbanization." *Journal of Urban Archaeology* 1 (2020): 151–167. https://doi.org/10.1484/J.JUA.5.120914.

Ostrom, Elinor. "Crossing the Great Divide: Coproduction, Synergy, and Development." *World Development* 24, no. 6 (June 1996): 1073–1087. https://doi.org/10.1016/0305-750X(96)00023-X.

Ostrom, Elinor. "A General Framework for Analyzing Sustainability of Social-Ecological Systems." *Science* 325, no. 5939 (July 24, 2009): 419–422. https://doi.org/10.1126/science.1172133. .

O'Sullivan, Arthur. *Urban Economics.* 8th ed. New York: McGraw-Hill/Irwin, 2012.

Owens, Ann. "Neighborhoods on the Rise: A Typology of Neighborhoods Experiencing Socioeconomic Ascent." *City and Community* 11, no. 4 (December 1, 2012): 345–369. https://doi.org/10.1111/j.1540-6040.2012.01412.x.

Page, Karen M., and Martin A. Nowak. "Unifying Evolutionary Dynamics." *Journal of Theoretical Biology* 219, no. 1 (November 2002): 93–98. https://doi.org/10.1006/jtbi.2002.3112.

Pan, Wei, Gourab Ghoshal, Coco Krumme, Manuel Cebrian, and Alex Pentland. "Urban Characteristics Attributable to Density-Driven Tie Formation." *Nature Communications* 4 (June 4, 2013). https://doi.org/10.1038/ncomms2961.

Park, H. J., S. H. Lee, and B. J. Kim, "Generalized Gravity Model for Human Migration." *New Journal of Physics* 20 (September 18, 2018): 093018. https://iopscience.iop.org/article/10.1088/1367-2630/aade6b.

Park, Robert Ezra, Ernest Watson Burgess, Roderick D. McKenzie, and Morris Janowitz. *The City: Suggestions for Investigation of Human Behavior in the Urban Environment*. Heritage of Sociology. Chicago: University of Chicago Press, 2010. Originally published in 1925.

Parry, Ian W. H. "Are Emissions Permits Regressive?" *Journal of Environmental Economics and Management* 47, no. 2 (March 2004): 364–387. https://doi.org/10.1016/j.jeem.2003.07.001.

Patel, Sheela, Carrie Baptist, and Celine D'Cruz. "Knowledge Is Power—Informal Communities Assert Their Right to the City through SDI and Community-Led Enumerations." *Environment and Urbanization* 24, no. 1 (April 1, 2012): 13–26. https://doi.org/10.1177/0956247812438366.

Pearl, Judea. *Causality: Models, Reasoning, and Inference*. 2nd ed. New York: Cambridge University Press, 2013.

Peters, Ole, and Alexander Adamou. "Insurance Makes Wealth Grow Faster." *ArXiv:1507.04655 [q-Fin]*, July 16, 2015. http://arxiv.org/abs/1507.04655.

Piketty, Thomas. *Capital in the 21st Century*. Cambridge, MA: Belknap, 2014.

Piketty, Thomas, and Gabriel Zucman. "Capital Is Back: Wealth-Income Ratios in Rich Countries 1700–2010." *Quarterly Journal of Economics* 129, no. 3 (2014): 1255–1310. https://doi.org/10.1093/qje/qju018.

Polanyi, Karl. *The Great Transformation: The Political and Economic Origins of Our Time*. New York: Farrar and Rinehart, 1944.

Poon, Linda. "Carbon Emissions Are Already Falling in 30 Cities." Bloomberg CityLab, October 9, 2019. https://www.bloomberg.com/news/articles/2019-10-09/c40-the-cities-where-emissions-are-dropping.

Pope, C. Arden, Michael J. Thun, Mohan M. Namboodiri, Douglas W. Dockery, John S. Evans, Frank E. Speizer, and Clark W. Heath. "Particulate Air Pollution as a Predictor of Mortality in a Prospective Study of U.S. Adults." *American Journal of Respiratory and Critical Care Medicine* 151, no. 3, pt. 1 (March 1995): 669–674. https://doi.org/10.1164/ajrccm/151.3_Pt_1.669.

Pred, Allan. "The Choreography of Existence: Comments on Hägerstrand's Time-Geography and Its Usefulness." *Economic Geography* 53, no. 2 (April 1, 1977): 207–221. https://doi.org/10.2307/142726.

Preston, Samuel H. "Urban Growth in Developing Countries: A Demographic Reappraisal." *Population and Development Review* 5, no. 2 (1979): 195–215. https://doi.org/10.2307/1971823.

Price, Catherine Waddams, and Ruth Hancock. "Distributional Effects of Liberalising UK Residential Utility Markets." *Fiscal Studies* 19, no. 3 (1998): 295–319.

Price, Derek De Solla. "A General Theory of Bibliometric and Other Cumulative Advantage Processes." *Journal of the American Society for Information Science* 27, no. 5 (September 1976): 292–306. https://doi.org/10.1002/asi.4630270505.

Price, George R. "Selection and Covariance." *Nature* 227, no. 5257 (August 1, 1970): 520–521. https://doi.org/10.1038/227520a0.

Puga, Diego. "The Magnitude and Causes of Agglomeration Economies." *Journal of Regional Science* 50, no. 1 (February 2010): 203–219. https://doi.org/10.1111/j.1467-9787.2009.00657.x.

Pumain, Denise, Fabien Paulus, Céline Vacchiani-Marcuzzo, and José Lobo. "An Evolutionary Theory for Interpreting Urban Scaling Laws." *Cybergeo: European Journal of Geography* (July 5, 2006). https://doi.org/10.4000/cybergeo.2519.

Ramaswami, Anu, Luís M. A. Bettencourt, Andres Clarens, Sajal Das, Garrett Fitzgerald, Elena Irwin, Diane Pataki, Karen Seto, and Paul Waddell. *Sustainable Urban Systems Report.* Alexandria, VA: National Science Foundation, 2018. https://www.nsf.gov/ere/ereweb/ac-ere/sustainable-urban-systems.pdf.

Raudenbush, Stephen W., and Robert J. Sampson. "Ecometrics: Toward a Science of Assessing Ecological Settings, with Application to the Systematic Social Observation of Neighborhoods." *Sociological Methodology* 29, no. 1 (1999): 1–41. https://doi.org/10.1111/0081-1750.00059.

Ravenstein, E. G. "The Laws of Migration." *Journal of the Statistical Society of London* 48, no. 2 (1885): 167–235. https://doi.org/10.2307/2979181.

Rawcliffe, Carole. *Urban Bodies: Communal Health in Late Medieval English Towns and Cities.* Woodbridge, UK: Boydell and Brewer, 2013.

Reardon, Sean F., and Kendra Bischoff. "Income Inequality and Income Segregation." *American Journal of Sociology* 116, no. 4 (2011): 1092–1153. https://doi.org/10.1086/657114.

Rice, Sean H. *Evolutionary Theory: Mathematical and Conceptual Foundations.* Sunderland, MA: Sinauer Associates, 2004.

Richardson, Harry W. "A Note on the Distributional Effects of Road Pricing." *Journal of Transport Economics and Policy* 8, no. 1 (1974): 82–85. https://www.jstor.org/stable/20052404.

Richerson, Peter J., and Robert Boyd. *Not by Genes Alone: How Culture Transformed Human Evolution.* Chicago: University of Chicago Press, 2008.

Rigby, Stephen H. "Urban Population in Late Medieval England: The Evidence of the Lay Subsidies." *Economic History Review* 63, no. 2 (2010): 393–417. https://doi.org/10.1111/j.1468-0289.2009.00489.x.

Riis, Jacob, and Hasia R. Diners, eds. *How the Other Half Lives: Authoritative Text, Contexts, and Criticism.* New York: Norton, 2010.

Rittel, Horst W. J., and Melvin M. Webber. "Dilemmas in a General Theory of Planning." *Policy Sciences* 4, no. 2 (June 1973): 155–169. https://doi.org/10.1007/BF01405730.

Roberto, Elizabeth. "The Divergence Index: A Decomposable Measure of Segregation and Inequality." *ArXiv:1508.01167 [Physics, Stat]*, August 5, 2015. http://arxiv.org/abs/1508.01167.

Roberto, Elizabeth, and Jackelyn Hwang. "Barriers to Integration: Institutionalized Boundaries and the Spatial Structure of Residential Segregation." *ArXiv:1509.02574 [Physics, Stat]*, September 8, 2015. http://arxiv.org/abs/1509.02574.

Rodríguez-Iturbe, Ignacio, and Andrea Rinaldo. *Fractal River Basins: Chance and Self-Organization.* Cambridge: Cambridge University Press, 2001.

Rodríguez-Iturbe, Ignacio, Andrea Rinaldo, Riccardo Rigon, Rafael L. Bras, Ede Ijjasz-Vasquez, and Alessandro Marani. "Fractal Structures as Least Energy Patterns: The Case of River Networks." *Geophysical Research Letters* 19, no. 9 (May 4, 1992): 889–892. https://doi.org/10.1029/92GL00938.

Romer, David. *Advanced Macroeconomics.* 2nd ed. Boston: McGraw-Hill, 2001.

Romer, Paul M. "Endogenous Technological Change." *Journal of Political Economy* 98, no. 5 (1990): S71–S102. https://doi.org/10.1086/261725.

Romer, Paul M. "Increasing Returns and Long-Run Growth." *Journal of Political Economy* 94, no. 5 (October 1986): 1002–1037. https://doi.org/10.1086/261420.

Romero Lankao, Patricia, Alana Wilson, Joshua Sperling, Clark Miller, Daniel Zimny-Schmitt, Luís Bettencourt, Eric Wood, Stan Young, Matteo Muratori, Doug Arent, Mark O'Malley, Benjamin Sovacool, Marilyn Brown, Frank Southworth, Morgan Bazilian, Chris Gearhart, Anni Beukes, and Daniel Zünd. "Urban Electrification: Knowledge Pathway toward an Integrated Research and Development Agenda." SSRN Scholarly Paper. Rochester, NY: Social Science Research Network, August 20, 2019. https://papers.ssrn.com/abstract=3440283.

Rosenthal, Stuart S., and William C. Strange. "Evidence on the Nature and Sources of Agglomeration Economies." In *Handbook of Regional and Urban Economics,* Vol. 4: *Cities and Geography,* edited by J. Vernon Henderson and Jacques-François Thisse, 2119–2171. Amsterdam: Elsevier, 2004. http://www.sciencedirect.com/science/article/pii/S1574008004800063.

Rosvall, M., A. Grönlund, P. Minnhagen, and K. Sneppen. "Searchability of Networks." *Physical Review E* 72, no. 4 (October 17, 2005). https://doi.org/10.1103/PhysRevE.72.046117.

Rozenfeld, Hernán D., Diego Rybski, Xavier Gabaix, and Hernán A. Makse. "The Area and Population of Cities: New Insights from a Different Perspective on Cities." *American Economic Review* 101, no. 5 (August 2011): 2205–2225. https://doi.org/10.1257/aer.101.5.2205.

Ruijs, A., A. Zimmermann, and M. van den Berg. "Demand and Distributional Effects of Water Pricing Policies." *Ecological Economics* 66, nos. 2–3 (June 2008): 506–516. https://doi.org/10.1016/j.ecolecon.2007.10.015.

Sahasranaman, Anand, and Luís M. A. Bettencourt. "Economic Geography and the Scaling of Urban and Regional Income in India." *Environment and Planning B: Urban Analytics and City Science* (October 9, 2019): 239980831987946. https://doi.org/10.1177/2399808319879463.

Sahasranaman, Anand, and Luís M. A. Bettencourt. "Urban Geography and Scaling of Contemporary Indian Cities." *Journal of the Royal Society Interface* 16, no. 152 (March 29, 2019): 20180758. https://doi.org/10.1098/rsif.2018.0758.

Sahasranaman, Anand, and Henrik Jeldtoft Jensen. "Dynamics of Transformation from Segregation to Mixed Wealth Cities." *PLoS One* 11, no. 11 (November 18, 2016): e0166960. https://doi.org/10.1371/journal.pone.0166960.

Sahasranaman, Anand, and Henrik Jeldtoft Jensen. "Ethnicity and Wealth: The Dynamics of Dual Segregation." *PLoS One* 13, no. 10 (October 10, 2018): e0204307. https://doi.org/10.1371/journal.pone.0204307.

Saichev, A. I., Yannick Malevergne, and Didier Sornette. *Theory of Zipf's Law and Beyond.* Lecture Notes in Economics and Mathematical Systems 632. Berlin: Springer, 2010.

Samaniego, Horacio, and Melanie E. Moses. "Cities as Organisms: Allometric Scaling of Urban Road Networks." *Journal of Transport and Land Use* 1, no. 1 (July 15, 2008): 21–39. https://doi.org/10.5198/jtlu.v1i1.29.

Sampson, R. J. "Moving and the Neighborhood Glass Ceiling." *Science* 337, no. 6101 (September 21, 2012): 1464–1465. https://doi.org/10.1126/science.1227881.

Sampson, Robert J. *Great American City: Chicago and the Enduring Neighborhood Effect.* Chicago: University of Chicago Press, 2012.

Sampson, Robert J. "Moving to Inequality: Neighborhood Effects and Experiments Meet Social Structure." *American Journal of Sociology* 114, no. 1 (July 1, 2008): 189–231. https://doi.org/10.1086/589843.

Sampson, Robert J. "Neighbourhood Effects and Beyond: Explaining the Paradoxes of Inequality in the Changing American Metropolis." *Urban Studies* 56, no. 1 (January 2019): 3–32. https://doi.org/10.1177/0042098018795363.

Sampson, Robert J., and John H. Laub. "Crime and Deviance over the Life Course: The Salience of Adult Social Bonds." *American Sociological Review* 55, no. 5 (1990): 609–627. https://doi.org/10.2307/2095859.

Sampson, Robert J., and John H. Laub. *Crime in the Making: Pathways and Turning Points through Life*. Cambridge, MA: Harvard University Press, 1995.

Sampson, Robert J., and Stephen W. Raudenbush. "Systematic Social Observation of Public Spaces: A New Look at Disorder in Urban Neighborhoods." *American Journal of Sociology* 105, no. 3 (November 1999): 603–651. https://doi.org/10.1086/210356.

Samuelson, Paul A. "The 'Fallacy' of Maximizing the Geometric Mean in Long Sequences of Investing or Gambling." *Proceedings of the National Academy of Sciences* 68, no. 10 (October 1, 1971): 2493–2496. https://doi.org/10.1073/pnas.68.10.2493.

Samuelson, Paul A. *Foundations of Economic Analysis*. Enlarged ed. Harvard Economic Studies 80. Cambridge, MA: Harvard University Press, 1983.

Samuelson, Paul A. "The Transfer Problem and Transport Costs, II: Analysis of Effects of Trade Impediments." *Economic Journal* 64, no. 254 (1954): 264–289. https://doi.org/10.2307/2226834.

Sanbonmatsu, Lisa Katz, Lawrence F. Ludwig, Jens Gennetian, Lisa A. Duncan, Greg J. Kessler, Ronald C. Adam, Emma McDade, Thomas W. Lindau, and Stacy Tessler. "Moving to Opportunity for Fair Housing Demonstration Program—Final Impacts Evaluation." Washington, DC: U.S. Department of Housing and Urban Development, 2011. https://www.huduser.gov/portal/publications/pubasst/MTOFHD.html.

Sassen, Saskia. *The Global City: New York, London, Tokyo*. 2nd ed. Princeton, NJ: Princeton University Press, 2001.

Satterthwaite, David. "Missing the Millennium Development Goal Targets for Water and Sanitation in Urban Areas." *Environment and Urbanization* (March 1, 2016): 99–118. https://doi.org/10.1177/0956247816628435.

Saunders, Doug. *Arrival City: How the Largest Migration in History Is Reshaping Our World*. New York: Vintage Books, 2012.

Scheidel, Walter, Ian Morris, and Richard P. Saller, eds. *The Cambridge Economic History of the Greco-Roman World*. Cambridge: Cambridge University Press, 2013.

Schelling, Thomas C. *Micromotives and Macrobehavior*. New York: Norton, 2006.

Schertz, Kathryn E., James Saxon, Carlos Cardenas-Iniguez, Luís M. A. Bettencourt, and Marc Berman. "Neighborhood Street Activity and Greenspace Usage Uniquely Contribute to Predicting Crime." SSRN Scholarly Paper. Rochester, NY: Social Science Research Network, October 21, 2019. https://papers.ssrn.com/abstract=3473331.

Schläpfer, M., L. M. A. Bettencourt, S. Grauwin, M. Raschke, R. Claxton, Z. Smoreda, G. B. West, and C. Ratti. "The Scaling of Human Interactions with City Size." *Journal of the Royal Society Interface* 11, no. 98 (July 2, 2014): 20130789. https://doi.org/10.1098/rsif.2013.0789.

Schläpfer, Markus, Joey Lee, and Luís M. A. Bettencourt. "Urban Skylines: Building Heights and Shapes as Measures of City Size." *ArXiv:1512.00946 [Physics]*, December 2, 2015. http://arxiv.org/abs/1512.00946.

Schlör, Holger, Wolfgang Fischer, and Jürgen-Friedrich Hake. "Sustainable Development, Justice and the Atkinson Index: Measuring the Distributional Effects of the German Energy Transition." *Applied Energy* 112 (December 2013): 1493–1499. https://doi.org/10.1016/j.apenergy.2013.04.020.

Schofield, Roger. "The Geographical Distribution of Wealth in England, 1334–1649." *Economic History Review* 18, no. 3 (1965): 483–510.

Sen, Amartya. *Commodities and Capabilities*. New Delhi: Oxford University Press, 2008.

Sen, Amartya. *Development as Freedom*. Oxford: Oxford University Press, 2001.

Seto, Karen C., Michail Fragkias, Burak Güneralp, and Michael K. Reilly. "A Meta-analysis of Global Urban Land Expansion." *PLoS One* 6, no. 8 (August 18, 2011): e23777. https://doi.org /10.1371/journal.pone.0023777.

Shannon, Claude E., and Warren Weaver. *The Mathematical Theory of Communication*. Urbana: University of Illinois Press, 1975.

Sharkey, Patrick. "The Acute Effect of Local Homicides on Children's Cognitive Performance." *Proceedings of the National Academy of Sciences* 107, no. 26 (June 29, 2010): 11733–11738. https://doi.org /10.1073/pnas.1000690107.

Sharkey, Patrick, and Jacob W. Faber. "Where, When, Why, and for Whom Do Residential Contexts Matter? Moving Away from the Dichotomous Understanding of Neighborhood Effects." *Annual Review of Sociology* 40 (July 30, 2014): 559–579. https://doi.org/10.1146/annurev-soc-071913-043350.

Sharkey, Patrick T., Nicole Tirado-Strayer, Andrew V. Papachristos, and C. Cybele Raver. "The Effect of Local Violence on Children's Attention and Impulse Control." *American Journal of Public Health* 102, no. 12 (December 2012): 2287–2293. https://doi.org/10.2105/AJPH.2012.300789.

Sharma, S., G. R. Sethi, A. Rohtagi, A. Chaudhary, R. Shankar, J. S. Bapna, V. Joshi, and D. G. Sapir. "Indoor Air Quality and Acute Lower Respiratory Infection in Indian Urban Slums." *Environmental Health Perspectives* 106, no. 5 (May 1998): 291–297. https://doi.org/10.1289/ehp.98106291.

Sheail, John. "The Regional Distribution of Wealth in England as Indicated in the 1524/5 Lay Subsidy Returns." University of London, 1968.

Shen, Guoqiang. "Fractal Dimension and Fractal Growth of Urbanized Areas." *International Journal of Geographical Information Science* 16, no. 5 (July 2002): 419–437. https://doi.org/10.1080 /13658810210137013.

Shuey, Kim M., and Andrea E. Willson. "Cumulative Disadvantage and Black-White Disparities in Life-Course Health Trajectories." *Research on Aging* 30, no. 2 (March 1, 2008): 200–225. https://doi .org/10.1177/0164027507311151.

Simini, Filippo, Marta C. González, Amos Maritan, and Albert-László Barabási. "A Universal Model for Mobility and Migration Patterns." *Nature* 484, no. 7392 (April 5, 2012): 96–100. https://doi .org/10.1038/nature10856.

Simmel, Georg, and Donald N. Levine. *On Individuality and Social Forms: Selected Writings*. Heritage of Sociology. Chicago: University of Chicago Press, 2010. Originally published 1971.

Simon, Herbert A. "The Architecture of Complexity." *Proceedings of the American Philosophical Society* 106, no. 6 (1962): 467–482.

Simon, Herbert A. "On a Class of Skew Distribution Functions." *Biometrika* 42, nos. 3–4 (1955): 425–440. https://doi.org/10.1093/biomet/42.3-4.425.

Sinai, Todd, and Joel Waldfogel. "Geography and the Internet: Is the Internet a Substitute or a Complement for Cities?" *Journal of Urban Economics* 56, no. 1 (July 2004): 1–24. https://doi.org /10.1016/j.jue.2004.04.001.

Small, Mario Luis, and Katherine Newman. "Urban Poverty after *The Truly Disadvantaged*: The Rediscovery of the Family, the Neighborhood, and Culture." *Annual Review of Sociology* 27 (August 2001): 23–45. https://doi.org/10.1146/annurev.soc.27.1.23.

Smith, Adam, and Alan B. Krueger. *The Wealth of Nations*. New York: Bantam Classics, 2003. Originally published in 1776.

Smith, Michael E. "The Archaeological Study of Neighborhoods and Districts in Ancient Cities." *Journal of Anthropological Archaeology* 29, no. 2 (June 2010): 137–154. https://doi.org/10.1016/j.jaa.2010.01.001.

Smith, Michael E. *The Aztecs*. 3rd ed. The Peoples of America. Malden, MA: Wiley-Blackwell, 2011.

Solari, Claudia D. "Affluent Neighborhood Persistence and Change in U.S. Cities." *City and Community* 11, no. 4 (December 1, 2012): 370–388. https://doi.org/10.1111/j.1540-6040.2012.01422.x.

Solecki, William, Karen C. Seto, and Peter J. Marcotullio. "It's Time for an Urbanization Science." *Environment: Science and Policy for Sustainable Development* 55, no. 1 (January 1, 2013): 12–17. https://doi.org/10.1080/00139157.2013.748387.

Solow, Robert. "Technical Change and the Aggregate Production Function." *Review of Economics and Statistics* 39, no. 3 (August 1957): 312–320. https://doi.org/10.2307/1926047.

South, Scott J., Ying Huang, Amy Spring, and Kyle Crowder. "Neighborhood Attainment over the Adult Life Course." *American Sociological Review* 81, no. 6 (December 1, 2016): 1276–1304. https://doi.org/10.1177/0003122416673029.

Stauffer, D., and S. Solomon. "Ising, Schelling and Self-Organising Segregation." *European Physical Journal B* 57, no. 4 (June 2007): 473–479. https://doi.org/10.1140/epjb/e2007-00181-8.

Stewart, John Q. "The 'Gravitation,' or Geographical Drawing Power, of a College." *Bulletin of the American Association of University Professors (1915–1955)* 27, no. 1 (1941): 70–75. https://doi.org/10.2307/40219181.

Stewart, John Q. "An Inverse Distance Variation for Certain Social Influences." *Science* 93, no. 2404 (1941): 89–90. https://doi.org/10.1126/science.93.2404.89.

Sutton, John. "Gibrat's Legacy." *Journal of Economic Literature* 35, no. 1 (1997): 40–59. https://www.jstor.org/stable/2729692.

Sveikauskas, Leo. "The Productivity of Cities." *Quarterly Journal of Economics* 89, no. 3 (1975): 393–413. https://doi.org/10.2307/1885259.

Swerts, Elfie, and Denise Pumain. "A Statistical Approach to Territorial Cohesion: The Indian City System." *L'espace géographique* 42, no. 1 (October 8, 2013): 75–90. https://www.jstor.org/stable/26213671.

Theil, Henri. *Economics and Information Theory*. Amsterdam: North-Holland, 1967.

Thomas, Isabelle, Pierre Frankhauser, and Marie-Laurence De Keersmaecker. "Fractal Dimension versus Density of Built-Up Surfaces in the Periphery of Brussels." *Papers in Regional Science* 86, no. 2 (2007): 287–308. https://doi.org/10.1111/j.1435-5957.2007.00122.x.

Thompson, D'Arcy Wentworth, and John Tyler Bonner. *On Growth and Form*. Abridged ed. Cambridge: Cambridge University Press, 1992.

Thrift, Nigel, and Allan Pred. "Time-Geography: A New Beginning." *Progress in Geography* 5, no. 2 (June 1981): 277–286. https://doi.org/10.1177/030913258100500209.

Tobler, Waldo. "Linear Pycnophylactic Reallocation: Comment on a Paper by D. Martin." *International Journal of Geographical Information Science* 13, no. 1 (January 1, 1999): 85–90. https://doi.org/10.1080/136588199241472.

Tobler, Waldo R. "Satellite Confirmation of Settlement Size Coefficient." USGS Numbered Series. Open-File Report. Reston, VA: U.S. Geological Survey, 1968. http://pubs.er.usgs.gov/publication/ofr69285.

Tobler, W. R. "A Computer Movie Simulating Urban Growth in the Detroit Region." *Economic Geography* 46 (1970): 234–240. https://doi.org/10.2307/143141.

Tranos, Emmanouil, and Peter Nijkamp. "The Death of Distance Revisited: Cyber-Place, Physical and Relational Proximities." *Journal of Regional Science* 53, no. 5 (2013): 855–873. https://doi.org/10.1111/jors.12021.

Turner, John F. C. *Housing by People: Towards Autonomy in Building Environments*. New York: Pantheon Books, 1977.

Tutu, Desmond. "Who We Are: Human Uniqueness and the African Spirit of Ubuntu." 2013 Templeton Prize Laureate Address. April 3, 2013. YouTube video, 3:26. https://www.youtube.com/watch?v=0wZtfqZ271w&feature=youtu.be.

UN-Habitat. *The Challenge of Slums: Global Report on Human Settlements*. Nairobi: UN-Habitat, 2003. http://mirror.unhabitat.org/pmss/listItemDetails.aspx?publicationID=1156.

UN-Habitat. *State of the World's Cities 2012/2013, Prosperity of Cities*. Nairobi: UN-Habitat, 2012. http://mirror.unhabitat.org/pmss/listItemDetails.aspx?publicationID=3387.

UN-Habitat. *World Cities Report 2016: Urbanization and Development—Emerging Futures*. Nairobi: UN-Habitat, 2016. https://doi.org/10.18356/d201a997-en.

United Nations. *Sustainable Development Goals*. New York: United Nations, 2015. http://sustainabledevelopment.un.org.

United Nations Development Programme. *Human Development Report 2013*. New York: United Nations Development Programme, 2013. http://hdr.undp.org/en/2013-report.

Venables, Anthony J. "Equilibrium Locations of Vertically Linked Industries." *International Economic Review* 37, no. 2 (May 1996): 341–359. https://doi.org/10.2307/2527327.

Vinkovic, D., and A. Kirman. "A Physical Analogue of the Schelling Model." *Proceedings of the National Academy of Sciences* 103, no. 51 (December 19, 2006): 19261–19265. https://doi.org/10.1073/pnas.0609371103.

Vishwanath, Tara, Somik V. Lall, David Dowall, Nancy Lozano-Gracia, Siddharth Sharma, and Hyoung Gun Wang. "Urbanization beyond Municipal Boundaries: Nurturing Metropolitan Economies and Connecting Peri-urban Areas in India." Directions in Development, Countries, and Regions. Washington, DC: World Bank Group, 2013. http://documents.worldbank.org/curated/en/373731468268485378/Urbanization-beyond-municipal-boundaries-nurturing-metropolitan-economies-and-connecting-peri-urban-areas-in-India.

Visser, Matt. "Zipf's Law, Power Laws and Maximum Entropy." *New Journal of Physics* 15, no. 4 (April 16, 2013): 043021. https://doi.org/10.1088/1367-2630/15/4/043021.

Waldrop, M. Mitchell. "The Quest for the Sustainable City." *Proceedings of the National Academy of Sciences* 116, no. 35 (August 27, 2019): 17134–17138. https://doi.org/10.1073/pnas.1912802116.

Walls, Donald W. "National Establishment Time-Series Database: Data Overview." *SSRN Electronic Journal* (November 2, 2007). https://doi.org/10.2139/ssrn.1022962.

Wang, Qi, Nolan Edward Phillips, Mario L. Small, and Robert J. Sampson. "Urban Mobility and Neighborhood Isolation in America's 50 Largest Cities." *Proceedings of the National Academy of Sciences* 115, no. 30 (July 24, 2018): 7735–7740. https://doi.org/10.1073/pnas.1802537115.

Wang, Yaoli, Chaogui Kang, Luís M. A. Bettencourt, Yu Liu, and Clio Andris. "Linked Activity Spaces: Embedding Social Networks in Urban Space." In *Computational Approaches for Urban*

Environments, edited by Marco Helbich, Jamal Jokar Arsanjani, and Michael Leitner, 313–336. Cham, Switzerland: Springer International Publishing, 2015. http://link.springer.com/10.1007 /978-3-319-11469-9_13.

Warntz, William. "The Topology of a Socio-economic Terrain and Spatial Flows." *Papers of the Regional Science Association* 17, no. 1 (December 1966): 47–61. https://doi.org/10.1007/BF01982509.

Watts, Duncan J., and Steven H. Strogatz. "Collective Dynamics of 'Small-World' Networks." *Nature* 393, no. 6684 (June 4, 1998): 440–442. https://doi.org/10.1038/30918.

Weber, Christopher L., and H. Scott Matthews. "Quantifying the Global and Distributional Aspects of American Household Carbon Footprint." *Ecological Economics* 66, nos. 2–3 (June 15, 2008): 379–391. https://doi.org/10.1016/j.ecolecon.2007.09.021.

Wellman, Barry, and Stephen D. Berkowitz, eds. *Social Structures: A Network Approach*. Structural Analysis in the Social Sciences 2. Cambridge: Cambridge University Press, 1988.

West, G. B., James H. Brown, and Brian J. Enquist. "The Fourth Dimension of Life: Fractal Geometry and Allometric Scaling of Organisms." *Science* 284, no. 5420 (June 4, 1999): 1677–1679. https://doi.org/10.1126/science.284.5420.1677.

West, G. B., James H. Brown, and Brian J. Enquist. "A General Model for the Origin of Allometric Scaling Laws in Biology." *Science* 276, no. 5309 (April 4, 1997): 122–126. https://doi.org/10.1126 /science.276.5309.122.

Wheaton, William C. "On the Optimal Distribution of Income among Cities." *Journal of Urban Economics* 3, no. 1 (January 1, 1976): 31–44. https://doi.org/10.1016/0094-1190(76)90056-5.

White, Harrison C. *Chains of Opportunity*. Cambridge, MA: Harvard University Press, 1970.

Whitelaw, Todd Matthew. "The Social Organisation of Space in Hunter-Gatherer Communities: Some Implications for Social Inference in Archeology." PhD thesis, University of Cambridge, 1989. https://doi.org/10.17863/CAM.19734.

Whyte, William Hollingsworth. *The Social Life of Small Urban Spaces*. New York: Project for Public Spaces, 2010.

Wiessner, Polly. "A Functional Estimator of Population from Floor Area." *American Antiquity* 39, no. 2 (1974): 343–350. https://doi.org/10.2307/279593.

Wilson, A. G. *Entropy in Urban and Regional Modelling*. London: Routledge, 2013. Originally published in 1970.

Wilson, George L., and James Q. Kelling. "Broken Windows." *The Atlantic*, March 1, 1982. https:// www.theatlantic.com/magazine/archive/1982/03/broken-windows/304465/.

Wilson, William J. "Studying Inner-City Social Dislocations: The Challenge of Public Agenda Research: 1990 Presidential Address." *American Sociological Review* 56, no. 1 (1991): 1–14. https://doi .org/10.2307/2095669.

Wilson, William J. *The Truly Disadvantaged: The Inner City, the Underclass, and Public Policy*. Chicago: University of Chicago Press, 2006.

Wilson, William J. *When Work Disappears: The World of the New Urban Poor*. New York: Knopf Doubleday, 2011.

Wilson, William Julius. "A Response to Critics of the Truly Disadvantaged." *Journal of Sociology and Social Welfare* 16, no. 4 (1989): 133–148.

Wirth, Louis. "Urbanism as a Way of Life." *American Journal of Sociology* 44, no. 1 (1938): 1–24. https://doi.org/10.1086/217913.

Wolfers, Justin, and Eric Zitzewitz. "Interpreting Prediction Market Prices as Probabilities." SSRN Scholarly Paper. Rochester, NY: Social Science Research Network, April 1, 2006. https://papers .ssrn.com/abstract=898597.

Woods, Robert. "Urbanisation in Europe and China during the Second Millennium: A Review of Urbanism and Demography." *International Journal of Population Geography* 9, no. 3 (May 1, 2003): 215–227. https://doi.org/10.1002/ijpg.279.

World Bank. "Extreme Poverty Income Definition." World Bank. Accessed February 20, 2020. https://www.worldbank.org/en/topic/poverty/overview.

World Economic Forum. "The Circular Economy Could Save Life on Earth—Starting with Cities." World Economic Forum, March 2018. https://www.weforum.org/agenda/2018/03/circular-economy -in-cities/.

Wrigley, E. A. *Energy and the English Industrial Revolution.* Cambridge: Cambridge University Press, 2010.

Xenophon. *Cyropaedia.* Accessed December 17, 2020. https://en.wikipedia.org/wiki/Division_of _labour#Xenophon.

Yang, Jianchao, John Wright, Thomas S. Huang, and Yi Ma. "Image Super-resolution via Sparse Representation." *IEEE Transactions on Image Processing* 19, no. 11 (November 2010): 2861–2873. https://doi.org/10.1109/TIP.2010.2050625.

Yang, V. Chuqiao, Andrew V. Papachristos, and Daniel M. Abrams. "Modeling the Origin of Urban-Output Scaling Laws." *Physical Review E* 100, no. 3 (September 16, 2019). https://doi.org /10.1103/PhysRevE.100.032306.

Yellen, John E. *Archaeological Approaches to the Present: Models for Reconstructing the Past.* Studies in Archeology. New York: Academic Press, 1977.

Youn, Hyejin, Luís M. A. Bettencourt, José Lobo, Deborah Strumsky, Horacio Samaniego, and Geoffrey B. West. "Scaling and Universality in Urban Economic Diversification." *Journal of the Royal Society Interface* 13, no. 114 (January 2016): 20150937. https://doi.org/10.1098/rsif.2015.0937.

Zahavi, Y., M. J. Beckmann, and T. F. Golob. *The UMOT/Urban Interactions.* Washington, DC: U.S. Department of Transportation, Research and Special Programs Administration, Systems Analysis Division, 1981. https://trid.trb.org/view/206233.

Zahavi, Yacov, and Antti Talvitie. "Regularities in Travel Time and Money Expenditures." *Transportation Research Record*, 750 (1980): 13–19. https://trid.trb.org/view/160276.

Zhong, Chen, Markus Schläpfer, Stefan Müller Arisona, Michael Batty, Carlo Ratti, and Gerhard Schmitt. "Revealing Centrality in the Spatial Structure of Cities from Human Activity Patterns." *Urban Studies* 54, no. 2 (February 2017): 437–455. https://doi.org/10.1177/0042098015601599.

Zhu, Pengyu. "Are Telecommuting and Personal Travel Complements or Substitutes?" *Annals of Regional Science* 48, no. 2 (April 1, 2012): 619–639. https://doi.org/10.1007/s00168-011-0460-6.

Zimbardo, Philip G. *The Lucifer Effect: Understanding How Good People Turn Evil.* New York: Random House, 2008.

Zinn-Justin, Jean. *Phase Transitions and Renormalization Group.* Oxford Graduate Texts. Oxford: Oxford University Press, 2007.

Zipf, George Kingsley. *Human Behavior and the Principle of Least Effort: An Introduction to Human Ecology.* Mansfield Centre, CT: Martino Publishing, 2012.

Zipf, George Kingsley. "On Dr. Miller's Contribution to the P_1P_2/D Hypothesis." *American Journal of Psychology* 60, no. 2 (1947): 284–287. https://doi.org/10.2307/1417879.

Zipf, George Kingsley. "The P1 P2/D Hypothesis: On the Intercity Movement of Persons." *American Sociological Review* 11, no. 6 (1946): 677–686. https://doi.org/10.2307/2087063.

Zorbaugh, Harvey Warren, and Howard P. Chudacoff. *The Gold Coast and the Slum: A Sociological Study of Chicago's Near North Side.* Chicago: University of Chicago Press, 1983.

Zünd, Daniel, and Luís M. A. Bettencourt. "Growth and Development in Prefecture-Level Cities in China." *PLoS One* 14, no. 9 (September 3, 2019): e0221017. https://doi.org/10.1371/journal.pone.0221017.